*Study Guide for*

# THE AMERICAN PROMISE

## A HISTORY OF THE UNITED STATES

**Volume I: To 1877**

Second Edition

# *Study Guide for*

# THE AMERICAN PROMISE

## A HISTORY OF THE UNITED STATES

**Volume I: To 1877**

Second Edition

RACHEL STANDISH
Foothill College

**BEDFORD / ST. MARTIN'S**
Boston ♦ New York

Manufactured in the United States of America.

4 3 2 1 0
f e d b c a

*For information, contact:* Bedford/St. Martin's, 75 Arlington Street, Boston, MA 02116
617-399-4000
www.bedfordstmartins.com

ISBN 0–312–39562–0

# CONTENTS

# PREFACE

Like many students, you might enter the U.S. history survey thinking of history as a dry, complicated catalog of names, dates, and places. *The American Promise*, Second Edition, together with this Study Guide will help you understand the main events, ideas, and themes of the American past as well as gain a sense of their relevance to your own experience. To guide your learning of the what, how, and why presented in the textbook, the Study Guide—which has been developed with the assistance of the author team—focuses on three levels of information: individual facts, thematic and chronological development, and major concepts. It will help you master important facts by highlighting details within the context of larger themes and chronology; then it will help you analyze these facts to develop a strong understanding of historical ideas and interpretation.

## Content and Organization

With these goals in mind, the Study Guide divides the exercises for each chapter into a Chapter Overview and a Chapter Review. By reading the Chapter Overview before you read the corresponding chapter in *The American Promise*, you will introduce yourself to important events and individuals in the narrative; by reading the Overview after you read the text, you will better retain and connect information in and among chapters.

Chapter Reviews allow you to test your memory and comprehension of key facts as well as your understanding of larger themes and chronology. Analytical exercises guide your understanding of the text coverage and help you develop the important skills of critical thinking and historical investigation.

Most questions or answers provide the name and/or page numbers of the text section on which the question is based, allowing you to refer easily to the relevant discussion and to assess comprehension of the material covered. (An answer key at the end of each chapter of the Study Guide includes answers for all exercises.)

### *Chapter Overview*

Each Chapter Overview offers the following materials to help you master the information presented in the chapter.

- A **Chapter Summary** follows the chapter section by section, introducing themes that inform the narrative.
- A **Chronology Activity** includes expanded versions of the entries in the chronology at the end of each text chapter. Descriptions of significant events and developments give you the chronological building blocks to tie together material over a series of chapters, as well as reinforce your grasp of the causal relationships of historical change. Ten multiple-choice questions reinforce chronology and connections among events. (Answers are provided in the answer key.)

- **Defining Terms** explains both specific names and general terms to help you develop a clear understanding of individual historical references and broader ideas and developments. A matching exercise asks you to pair names and terms with examples and definitions, to help you remember this important information. (Answers appear in the answer key.)

### *Chapter Review*

The following exercises make up each Chapter Review, giving you an opportunity to assess what you have learned as well as to increase your skills of historical analysis and interpretation.

- **Multiple-Choice** questions allow you to determine how well you have mastered the material after working through the chapter. The questions extend beyond who and what to explore issues of how and why. (Answers are provided in the answer key.)
- **Short-Answer** questions focus on the main issues covered in the chapter. The paragraph responses required of each question help you prepare for essay exams. (Model answers appear in the answer key.)
- **A Building Historical Skills** section shows you how to analyze sources, from maps and illustrations to primary documents and secondary essays, and guides historical thinking and analytical writing.
- **Map Questions,** based on a map or other graphic in the chapter, ask you to identify basic information as well as connect that information to chapter content. (Model answers appear in the answer key.)
- **Illustration Questions,** based on a picture reproduced in the chapter, help you study visual evidence, think about chapter themes, and increase your interpretive skills. (Model answers appear in the answer key.)
- **Analyzing Sources** questions, based on the Documenting the American Promise, Promise of Technology, or Historical Question feature in the chapter, provide guidance and practice for historical reading and analysis. (Model answers are provided in the answer key.)

## Introducing Students to History

Two essays at the beginning of the Study Guide, "What Is History?" and "Why Study History?," introduce you to the discipline of history and what historians do. Written by Timothy R. Mahoney, University of Nebraska–Lincoln, these clear and interesting essays provide references you can turn to again and again as you read *The American Promise,* work on exercises, and advance your study of history.

"What Is History?" describes history as stories that take place at different times and in different places, thus showing that history consists of not just one but of many forms of experience. The essay notes that all historians study human activity; then discusses the four major themes of human activity—economic, social, political, and cultural.

"Why Study History?" explains how the stories that make up history are similar to the stories we use to describe our own experience: both aim to create meaningful narratives to help people understand their lives and the world around them. Further, the essay makes clear how the intellectual methods and skills developed through the study of history will be useful to you regardless of your major, because the ability to articulate complicated ideas in a simple, straightforward way is a powerful skill.

## Online Study Guide for *The American Promise,* Second Edition

A new Online Study Guide for *The American Promise* takes advantage of the Internet to offer structured and easily accessed help for each chapter and innovative multimedia exercises. Crafted to provide instant feedback and assessment, exercises include content reviews with short-answer questions that you can compare to model answers, content summaries with multiple-choice questions, a terms activity, timeline and map workshops, an analyzing sources activity, and a visual activity. All exercises are designed to help you master content as well as develop skills of analysis. Visit **www.bedfordstmartins.com/tap** to learn more about this unique online study guide.

# WHAT IS HISTORY?

History is the story of the human past. Like all stories, whether told orally or written down, history is full of characters acting their parts within story lines in a wide range of settings. Given the vast diversity and range of human life over thousands of years since people have been recording their experiences, the varieties of history are almost infinite. Generally, however, histories vary according to four characteristics: time frame, setting, subjects, and themes.

The present is considered contemporary time. People record contemporary time by living through it. We mark the passing of time by our physical and mental development and by our living each day as part of a story line of experiences. We create a meaningful story line by placing each experience in the context of our memories of past experiences. Historians consider past time from a broader perspective than we have on contemporary time. Some historians do examine the past over very short periods, telling the story of human activity over the course of a few months, days, even hours or minutes. But the pastness of that time fixes it in place, allowing a perspective that no one has on the present. Most historians take advantage of historical perspective to examine events or processes that occurred over longer periods, ranging from years to decades or generations. Still other histories follow patterns of human activity across centuries or millennia. By creating stories that encompass long passages of time, historians place human activity in a new perspective, giving it meaning that couldn't be appreciated by the people who lived through it.

Historians do more, however, than understand events within the context of the passage of time. They also examine and understand past events within a specific setting. Indeed, understanding events and developments within their specific time and place is what fundamentally defines the study of history. But the scope of the places historians study is as varied as the time frames they tackle. Some histories examine the activities of people in very precise places—a town or city, a village, a section of a town, a neighborhood, a house, or, in the most specific cases, a single room. But most analyze regions, nations, continents, and even the world, placing the events of specific places, including our own, in a broader perspective. Similarly, the subjects historians consider can be as diverse as the places they inhabit. Traditionally, historians have studied the people who make up a state, a region, a nation, groups of nations, a civilization, a culture, or even humankind as a whole in the world. But historians also study people as individuals, as well as families, small groups, and large groups based on occupational, social, ethnic, racial, or gender identity.

Thematically, all histories focus on human activity within at least one of the four major themes or aspects of human life: economic, social, political, or cultural activity. Economic activity involves all human actions and behaviors directed toward or motivated by the human impulse to physically survive and maintain oneself. How people have done this, what returns or gains they made from it, and how they have employed those gains to alter their standard of living are all encompassed within economic activity. Social history focuses on the ways in which people have organized themselves in relation to one another to facilitate their chances of survival and maintenance. History written from a social perspective tells stories of how individuals, groups, or a mass of people in a past time and place went about the business of living their lives and influencing the lives of others. How people grew up, socially interacted with others, formed families, had and reared children, and assumed adult roles in families are central concerns. How people formed small and large social groups based on family ties, occupational status, level of wealth, cultural values, or ethnic, racial, or gender identity and employed these points of reference to achieve the social goals of survival, protection, socialization, and reproduction are questions at the center of most social history.

Such social agendas usually involve some effort to influence or interact with political activity and government. Thus political history studies the negotiation, competition, and struggle among people of various families, clans, groups, classes, parties or sections, and countries for power and control. Traditionally, political history has examined how leaders, politicians, and government officials acquired power and formulated both domestic and foreign policies. It also studies the various ways in which leaders implemented policy, executed laws, and exerted control through leadership over their own people. From another perspective, political history studies how people interacted with government. Sometimes people were removed from government, had little say in its operations, and did not try to exert any influence over it. At other times, people affected government by gaining a voice in choosing leaders, organizing groups, parties, or institutions to influence or change the nature or focus of government policy, or exerting personal influence to affect government. How people and social groups acted politically to influence or respond to their own government's policies or the policies of another country is a central theme of political history. War is the broadest, most violent activity in the national or international realm of politics.

Finally, cultural histories tell stories of how people in past times and places, as they pursued and acted on their various economic, social, and political goals, interpreted their activities in oral, artistic, material, spiritual, or intellectual ways to themselves and to others. Stories of people in the past formulating a theory of the cosmos, founding or reinvigorating or reforming a religious theology or practice, expressing themselves in a certain language, celebrating an event or entertaining themselves or others in a particular behavioral or material way, presenting the human body—male or female—in a specific way and clothed in a specific style, producing art or literature in a certain style with certain subjects and themes, or building, designing, or decorating homes, public buildings, and places of work in certain ways are all stories of people acting and behaving culturally. Indeed, the capacity to express culture seems to be what primarily defines people as human beings and distinguishes them from more advanced species of animal life.

History, therefore, is as varied and diverse as the endless range of possible varieties of time frames, setting themes, and subjects about which one could write in studying people who lived in the past. One of the most powerful aspects of history is trying to discern some of the common patterns and themes in the infinite variety of stories within the human experience. By identifying patterns in history, we fit the many pieces into a comprehensive story or narrative that has relevance to us and thus gives meaning to our own lives. However various and diverse, all these stories are part of the broad canvas, or story of the human past, that is history.

Timothy R. Mahoney

# WHY STUDY HISTORY?

One can, and many people do, live without any exposure to formal history. The dictum that those who do not understand the past are doomed to repeat it is generally true; but at the same time many people live perfectly satisfying lives without giving much thought to or studying history. Nevertheless, all people, by the act of living in an economy, a society, a political system, and a culture in the world, interact with and derive meaning from systems that people in the past helped to establish or construct. All people are, therefore, implicitly historians.

People choose to study history formally, then, because it connects their lives to the lives of other human beings who lived in the past and thus enhances and gives life meaning. History is a fundamental human endeavor that defines one's humanity. In going about everyday activity, every person constructs a story line to plot his or her life. Asking someone who he is is the same as asking him where he has been, what he has done and experienced, where he is going, and what he wants to do. The basic questions we all face — "What do you want to be?" or "What do you do?" — are inextricably bound up with "Who are you?" The answers to all of these questions lie in how well we have formulated the narrative of our lives. Happiness in life could be defined as successfully acting as the protagonist of the plot one has written and directed oneself. This general process of personal development is analogous to the practice of history. As individuals pursue their own lives, so, too, on a larger scale across time and space, do families, clans, groups, classes, and nations.

The study of history has practical value, too. As written by historians, history sharpens one's intellectual and analytic skills. History is a distinctive discipline. It makes use of intellectual methods that are employed across a wide variety of disciplines and uses them in distinctive ways that are shaped by the particular nature of history. By understanding the differences between the methods, assumptions, subjects, and practice of history and those of other disciplines, one sharpens one's intellectual and analytic skills in important, even essential, ways. The subject and methods of history make an understanding of some history, therefore, a foundation for any education, whether its major focus is the liberal arts, the sciences, or professional, technical, or vocational training.

Historians use such rational scientific methods as the study of statistics and data, but their ultimate goal is to tell stories that have a plot. The way they organize the information they gather into that plot is really an interpretation or a theory about how or why something happened the way it did. Many facts seem undisputed — the Boston Tea Party happened on December 16, 1773; South Carolina seceded from the Union on December 20, 1860 — but the significance of those facts, or even the full story of what happened, is less evident than one might think. To understand and explain the past, the historian must develop a thesis, test that thesis, and then defend it, employing the evidence that he or she has gathered.

The type of evidence available to historians is what makes history distinctive. Historians have access only to the evidence that has physically survived over time. Historians of the recent past may have far more evidence than any one person could ever absorb, but even this is not a complete picture. Sometimes new evidence becomes available when it is found by contemporary historians, as when documents, letters, or papers previously believed to have been lost come to light. But in most cases historians find and use new evidence by developing new methods of analysis, asking new questions, or pursuing new story lines that give new relevance to evidence that was previously ignored. Often, historians have evidence, such as diaries, journals, personal letters, or secret documents, that contemporaries living through the events did not have or even know existed. Or they may have no more than fragments of evidence, such as a single statement or a partial list, that do more to obscure than to clarify an understanding of the event in question. Most of the time, historians have an intriguing mix of material that no contemporary would have had, combined with a loss of much material that contemporaries took for granted. Out of this surviving database, historians must develop a theory and try, as best they can, to demonstrate it. Added to these concerns is the fact that most historical evidence is circumstantial, rather than the direct testimony of witnesses. Often, historians try to construct a story with little more than a scrap of evidence placing an individual or a group in a time and place but not addressing the specific questions the historian seeks to answer. Historians must be creative in searching documents in ways that will help to answer their questions. Given the uniqueness of the database (which is in some ways analogous to memories about events in our past, on which we have broader perspective now but find hard to re-create in total), no historian will ever achieve the finality of the scientist. No historical thesis can be indisputably "proved" because in any human activity there is room for interpretation in telling the story. Many historical theses would fail to convince most trial juries beyond a reasonable doubt. Interpretations of a historical event can vary as widely as the range of views it is possible to have about current events or people living today. History thus uses the scientific method, but within a broader interpretive framework often supported by evidence that is not definitive. Every time one tries to understand the past, therefore, one acquires insight into the uncertainty, biases, and fluidity of any knowledge.

While the fluidity of history sometimes makes it more like a detective story or a fictional novel than an experiment in a laboratory, the practice of history as written adds to that fluidity. Historians generally try to present their theses in the colloquial, nontechnical language in which people speak and read in everyday life. As a rule, they present their stories in narrative form, though often with an analytic thematic framework running beneath the prose. The fact that history tries to fuse an understanding of different areas of activity into a general narrative adds to its intellectual power. History is the art of understanding social, economic, political, and cultural activity and then connecting these elements and trying to explain how they interacted to shape the general course of human events. The ability to articulate complicated ideas in a simple, straightforward way is a powerful skill that we can develop by studying history. Acquiring the skill to rationally examine much of the complex real world around us, develop a thesis about it, and argue the evidence to sustain a thesis is, indeed, one of the primary goals of a college education. History adds to that skill an ability to recognize human complexity within the context of its time and place. While putting a powerful intellectual tool in our hands, history also cultivates and satisfies our deepest human impulses.

Timothy R. Mahoney

# ANCIENT AMERICA,
## BEFORE 1492

## Chapter Overview

### *Chapter Summary*

***Introduction*** This chapter begins with the discovery of fossilized bones in Folsom, New Mexico, in the early twentieth century, an archaeological discovery that proved humans had inhabited America for more than ten thousand years, at a time when most experts assumed that humans had been around for only three or four thousand years. The Folsom discovery sparked other major finds that have allowed archaeologists to understand who ancient Americans were, where they came from, and some basic features of their history prior to Columbus's landing in 1492.

***Archaeology and History, pp. P2–P5*** Both archaeologists and historians study the past but use different methods to obtain information. Archaeologists employ physical artifacts to understand human life in the lengthy era known as prehistory, the era before writing was invented, while historians focus on the period in which writing began to be employed. Writing is a relatively recent invention; without written records, it is impossible to lift people out of anonymity, to know about their individual daily lives, thoughts, and emotions. Archaeologists have to use artifacts to fill in the gaps in our knowledge.

***The First Americans, pp. P5–P7*** The American landmass originally was part of a large landmass called Pangaea and so was connected to Europe, Asia, and Africa. Then, about 150 million years ago, Pangaea was slowly broken up by geological forces, and the American landmass became separated from the other continents by large oceans. Thus, while the first human beings emerged in Africa approximately 1.5 million years ago and spread to Asia and Europe, for much of that time, the Western Hemisphere remained uninhabited by people.

**ASIAN ORIGINS** Two factors—climate and human adaptation—made possible the movement of people into the Americas. The world was a much colder place 75,000 years ago, when a great ice age, known as the Wisconsin glaciation, spread over vast expanses of land. This process created Beringia, a massive land bridge across the Bering Strait that connected Asian Siberia with American Alaska. Across this frozen pathway humans, who over time had adapted to the frigid environment of northeastern Siberia, were able to enter the Western Hemisphere. These early migrants are called Paleo-Indians; physical and linguistic evidence confirms that they were almost certainly of Asian descent.

**PALEO-INDIAN HUNTERS** The first arrivals to the Western Hemisphere were nomadic hunters who used stone-tipped spears to pursue large mammals. As ice began to recede and corridors opened through the Rocky Mountains, Paleo-Indians went further south. Archaeologists' discovery of the spearhead they used, known as a Clovis point, at sites throughout North and Central America indicates that Paleo-Indians shared a common ancestry and way of life. Around 11,000 years ago, the Paleo-Indian culture began to diversify significantly as men and women adapted to their different environments and sought new ways of acquiring food in response to the extinction of the big-game animals they had hunted.

***Archaic Hunters and Gatherers, pp. P7–P12*** The term *Archaic* is used to describe the many different hunting and gathering cultures that descended from Paleo-Indians. The Archaic period is the several thousand years in the history of ancient America that followed the Paleo-Indian mammoth hunters and preceded agricultural development. Like their Paleo-Indian ancestors, Archaic Indians hunted with spears but also killed smaller game with traps, nets, and hooks. Also, most Archaic peoples used a variety of stone tools to prepare food from wild plants. Most Archaic Indians were nomadic hunter-gatherers whose migration patterns followed the availability of wild plants and animals.

**GREAT PLAINS BISON HUNTERS** Archaic hunters concentrated on bison, which grazed in huge herds on the plains east of the Rockies. Like their predecessors, these Archaic tribes were nomads who moved constantly to stay near their prey. Until the sixteenth century, the Great Plains inhabitants hunted on foot, killing the bison by hurling their spears or by stampeding the animals over cliffs. By A.D. 500, most Great Plains hunters were using bows and arrows rather than spears, which made it easier for hunters to kill their prey.

**GREAT BASIN CULTURES** The Archaic peoples of the Great Basin—the region between the Rockies and the Sierra Nevada Mountains—inhabited a region of great environmental diversity, from lake shores to arid climates. These zones of habitation changed continually depending on the amount of rainfall they received. To adapt to their changeable environments, Great Basin Indians lived off plants, roots, and seeds such as piñon nuts; small game such as rabbits, rodents, and snakes; and, in some areas, waterfowl and fish. Still, despite the variety of foodstuffs available, Great Basin cultures relied on plants as their most important source of food.

**PACIFIC COAST CULTURES** An abundant natural environment made the California region the most densely populated in all of ancient North America. About 5,000 years ago the Chumash culture emerged near Santa Barbara. Plentiful food allowed the Chumash to establish relatively permanent villages, although there was frequent conflict over food resources between villages. Another culture emerged along the Pacific Northwest coast. These Archaic peoples established large and permanent villages and harvested the bounty of the oceans and rivers, drying their catch to last throughout the year. With time free from the task of food gathering, people of the Northwest cultures became skilled woodworkers, carving canoes (used for both fishing and warfare) and totems that honored the family and displayed wealth.

**EASTERN WOODLAND CULTURES** The forested environment east of the Mississippi River contained numerous Archaic cultures that adapted in a variety of ways to local conditions. Despite this variety, certain fundamental similarities were shared among all Woodland cultures. Deer, for example, was the most important food source for nearly all Woodland hunters. Woodland peoples were also gatherers of edible plants, seeds, and nuts. Around 4000 B.C. Woodland peoples began to establish permanent settlements, and around 2000 B.C. some groups began to cultivate plants for food and use ceramic pottery. The most impressive Archaic Woodland site was Poverty Point in Louisiana with its huge, mysterious earthworks built sometime between 1700 B.C. and 700 B.C.

***Agricultural Settlements and Chiefdoms, pp. P12–P17*** Most Archaic peoples used agriculture as a supplement to hunting and gathering, but peoples in the Southwest came to rely on farming and to build permanent settlements. Beginning around 500 B.C., the Archaic Woodland cultures around the Mississippi River built burial mounds that reflect the existence of a new social and political hierarchy known as a *chiefdom.*

**SOUTHWESTERN CULTURES** To provide themselves with more predictable food sources in their dry environments, Southwestern peoples used irrigation to develop a more sedentary and agriculturally oriented culture. Corn was introduced around 1500 B.C. and became the basic staple crop of the southwestern peoples, forcing them to stop migrating to tend the plants. In southern New Mexico, the Mogollon (A.D. 200–900) and later the Hohokam (A.D. 500) cultures reflected this settled agrarian orientation. North of the Mogollon and Hohokam cultures, the Anasazi and their descendants built extensive pueblos and cliff dwellings, some with hundreds of units that housed whole settlements.

**BURIAL MOUNDS AND CHIEFDOMS** The Adena were Woodlands hunter-gatherers who lived in what is now Ohio between about 500 B.C. and 100 B.C. The burial mounds often contained a wide array of grave goods, including weapons, tools, ritual items, and jewelry. Around 100 B.C., Adena culture evolved into the more complex Hopewell culture. The Hopewell people built larger mounds and filled them with even richer grave goods. Objects found in these mounds suggest that the Hopewell cultures traded with areas as far away as Florida and Wyoming. About A.D. 800, another mound-building culture, the Mississippian, flourished. At Cahokia, Illinois, and other sites, the Mississippian peoples, who worshiped a sun god, built enormous flat-topped earthen mounds containing jewelry, pottery, weapons, and agricultural implements, as well as many sacrificial victims. By 1500, on the eve of European contact, Cahokia and other Mississippian cultures had declined.

***Native Americans in 1492, pp. P17–P19*** Three major groups of tribes inhabited the vast Eastern Woodland region. The Algonquian peoples lived along the Atlantic seaboard from Virginia through Maine, in the Great Lakes region, and in much of the upper Midwest. Coastal Algonquians hunted, fished, and grew corn and other crops, while inland and northern Algonquians did not farm. The Iroquoian tribes, located primarily in Pennsylvania and upstate New York, successfully cultivated corn and other crops, which allowed them to build permanent settlements. Iroquoian societies were matriarchal, with women the overseers of the household and kinship network and also the owners of all property, including land, children, and inheritance. Five Iroquoian tribes—the Seneca, Onondaga, Mohawk, Oneida, and Cayuga—formed a confederation, the League of Five Nations, for purposes of war and diplomacy. The Muskogean peoples, which included the Creek, Choctaw, Chickasaw, and Natchez tribes, were spread throughout the Southeast, south of the Ohio River and east of the Mississippi. This region offered the Muskogean Indians abundant food, both from agriculture and hunting and gathering. Like their Mississippian ancestors, the Muskogean worshipped the sun. West of the Mississippi River were the Great Plains Indians, many of whom had migrated from the Eastern Woodlands because of pressure from Iroquoian and Algonquian tribes. Most of these tribes, including the Teton Sioux, Blackfeet, and Comanche, became dependent on the buffalo for their existence. The Great Basin and Pacific Northwest coast peoples continued to follow earlier subsistence practices. In the Southwest, the descendants of the Anasazi, Hohokam, and Mogollon peoples continued to live in settled agricultural communities. Around A.D. 1300, warlike Athapascan peoples invaded the area, attacking the pueblo Indians. By the time of Columbus's arrival, the Native American population of North America was about 4 million. Indian cultures all depended on hunting and gathering for their food sources, and many engaged in agriculture. All of them used bows and arrows for hunting and warfare, and though they did not use writing, they expressed themselves in a variety of other ways, such as by weaving patterns in baskets and textiles, dancing, and making music. They also engaged in elaborate burial rituals and religious rites.

***The Mexica: A Meso-American Culture, pp. P19–P23*** The ancient peoples of Central and South America were far more numerous than their North American brethren. The Mexica, or Aztec, civilization of Mexico was the most impressive and most powerful of all Native American societies at the time of European contact. In the late fourteenth century, the warrior society of the Mexica consolidated its rule over much of central and southern Mexico. The Mexica empire was fundamentally a military and political system for collecting tribute in the form of goods from conquered peoples. The Mexica also practiced human sacrifice on an unprecedented scale, dedicating victims to their war god, Huitzilopochtli. But depending on military conquest and constant payment was ultimately the empire's downfall. Instead of treating conquered peoples as citizens of Mexica society, the Mexica instead treated them as subjects whose sole function was to provide tribute; thus the Mexica failed to inculcate their subjects with a feeling of allegiance to a larger, legitimate polity. The antipathy these conquered peoples felt toward the Mexica would later help the Spanish conquer the Aztec empire.

***Conclusion: The Legacy of Ancient America*** Until the arrival of Europeans, ancient Americans shaped New World history. Though much about their existence remains a mystery, the artifacts and monuments they left behind give us an idea of what their lives were like. They succeeded in establishing a continuity of human habitation in the hemisphere. They survived and established cultures through their resourceful adaptation to the New World's continually changing environments.

***Chronology Activity*** Read the annotated chronology, and answer the multiple-choice questions.

c. 80,000–10,000 B.C. Wisconsin glaciation exposes Beringia, a land bridge between Siberia and Alaska. When humans mastered the ability to sew clothing out of animal skins, they made it possible to inhabit very cold regions like Siberia. Thus, when the land bridge was exposed, humans were able to take advantage of it, pursuing game across it until they finally trickled into the Western Hemisphere.

c. 13,000–10,000 B.C. First humans arrive in North America. North and South America had begun to drift away from the enormous Pangaea continent beginning about 240 million years ago and remained separated from the other continents by large oceans. When human beings evolved in Africa, they spread into Asia and Europe but were unable to reach the Americas. As a result, the Western Hemisphere remained uninhabited for 95 percent of human existence.

c. 9500–9000 B.C. Paleo-Indians in North and Central America use Clovis points to hunt big game. A Clovis point is a distinctively shaped spearhead. The discovery of Clovis points throughout the Americas demonstrates that Paleo-Indians descended from common ancestors and also that they specialized in hunting very large mammals.

| | |
|---|---|
| c. 9000 B.C. | Mammoths and many other big-game prey of Paleo-Indians become extinct. The extinction of large mammals was a result of the end of the Wisconsin glacial period. As the climate become warmer and sea levels rose, large mammals had difficulty adapting to the warmer climate; overhunting may also have contributed to their extinction. The change forced Paleo-Indians to make important adjustments to their way of life, focusing attention on smaller animals and foraging. Peoples' adaptations to different environmental conditions led to a great deal of diversity. |
| c. 8000–1000 B.C. | Archaic hunter-gatherer cultures dominate ancient America. These peoples hunted with spears but also took smaller game with traps, nets, and hooks. They also used stone tools to prepare food from wild plants, which played a large part in their diet. Archaic peoples did not establish permanent villages, although they did return to particularly abundant hunting and foraging grounds on a yearly basis. |
| c. 5000 B.C. | Corn cultivation begins in Central and South America. Corn became the signature crop of Central and South America and the North American Southwest, encouraging the creation of permanent settlements. |
| c. 2000 B.C. | Some Eastern Woodland people grow gourds and pumpkins and begin making pottery. The cultivation of food and creation of heavy, hard-to-transport ceramic pots indicate that the Woodland people modified their hunter-gatherer lifestyles. They used cultivated crops to alter the quantity, variety, and predictability of their food sources, but they did not fundamentally alter their way of life to tend to their fields. |
| c. 1700–700 B.C. | Poverty Point culture flourishes in Louisiana. Poverty Point was perhaps the most spectacular Archaic Woodland site, featuring enormous earthworks consisting of six concentric half-circles more than half a mile in diameter. At least a thousand people lived near the earthworks and almost a hundred villages clustered nearby. The labor and organization required to build such a structure suggests that important ceremonies were conducted on the site. |
| c. 1500 B.C. | Southwestern cultures begin corn cultivation. The Southwestern cultures were the first in North America to rely on agriculture and built permanent settlements. This was largely the result of corn cultivation, since it demanded the development of complex irrigation systems and careful attention, neither of which was compatible with migratory habits. |
| | Bows and arrows appear among Arctic peoples. Bows and arrows spread into North and South America. They made it easier for hunters to strike an animal from a distance and to shoot repeatedly. |
| | Stone pipes for tobacco smoking appear in Eastern Woodland. Tobacco was an import from South America, which became quite common in the eastern part of North America. |
| c. 500 B.C. | Eastern Woodland cultures start to build burial mounds. The elaborate earthworks they constructed suggest the existence of social and political hierarchies called *chiefdoms*. Although the chiefdoms did not replace the hunter-gatherer lifestyle entirely, they marked an important innovation in the Archaic way of life. |
| c. 500–100 B.C. | Adena culture develops in Ohio. The Adena constructed large burial mounds that they filled with a variety of goods, including spear points, stone pipes, and decorative and ritualistic items. The mounds were often built up over many years. |
| c. 300 B.C. | Some Eastern Woodland peoples begin to cultivate corn. Although corn was the most important plant food in Mexico and the Southwest, it did not become established among the Woodland cultures for thousands of years. |
| c. 100 B.C.–A.D. 400 | Hopewell culture emerges in Ohio and Mississippi Valleys. The Hopewell culture evolved from the Adena culture but was even more elaborate. The goods found in Hopewell burial mounds indicate that a trade network ranging from Wyoming to Florida existed among Native Americans. |
| c. A.D. 200–900 | Mogollon culture emerges in New Mexico. The Mogollon were among the first Southwestern peoples to construct small farming settlements. They usually lived in small clusters of pit houses, with a couple of special kivas, or ceremonial rooms. |
| c. A.D. 500 | Bows and arrows appear in North America south of Arctic. Although the new weapons were employed by North American hunters, they did not necessarily alter age-old techniques of hunting that had developed since the Folsom era. |

Pacific Northwest cultures denote wealth and status with elaborate wood carvings. The peoples of the Pacific Northwest were able to live on an abundance of fish and marine life. This gave them the time to nurture their woodworking skills, which they used both to create practical items like large canoes and also to symbolize their family lineage and status in elaborately carved totems.

C. A.D. 500–1400 Hohokam culture develops in Arizona. The Hohokam peoples appear to have emigrated from Mexico, and their culture was strongly influenced by those of Central America. They made extensive use of irrigation to plant and harvest twice a year. The comparatively high crop yields allowed the Hohokam to expand their population and seek out new land.

C. A.D. 800–1500 Mississippian culture flourishes in Southeast. The Mississippian culture was a mound-building civilization. It included the settlement of Cahokia in Illinois, which was likely the largest settlement in North America with 30,000 inhabitants. Cahokia was ruled by chiefs, who seem to have exercised great authority and commanded unswerving obedience.

C. A.D. 1000–1150 Anasazi peoples build cliff dwellings at Mesa Verde, Colorado, and pueblos at Chaco Canyon, New Mexico. The early Anasazi built pit houses on mesa tops; it is not clear why they decided to move to cliff dwellings. The structures were often enormous, with enough rooms to house the entire population of a settlement. By A.D. 1200 they had been abandoned, perhaps because of conflict exacerbated by a long drought.

Mimbres culture thrives in New Mexico. The Mimbres were descendents of the Mogollon peoples. They produced spectacular pottery with designs that portrayed human and animal forms.

C. A.D. 1325–1500 Mexica conquer neighboring peoples and establish Mexican empire. The Mexica were a fierce and warlike group, with a powerful warrior and priestly elite and a commitment to warfare. Their territory stretched from coast to coast across central Mexico and encompassed as many as 25 million people. However, the Mexica's ruthless demands for tribute meant that subjected peoples did not see them as legitimate leaders. This created discontent that Europeans were able to capitalize on to defeat the empire.

A.D. 1492 Columbus arrives, beginning European conquest of New World. When Columbus landed in the Western Hemisphere, he found peoples who did not have many of the things common in European life, including wheels, sailing ships, large domesticated animals, and sophisticated metallurgy. However, the native peoples of the Americas had developed adaptations to the local environment, making these items irrelevant.

## *Chronology Questions* Choose the letter of the best answer.

1. What is the correct order for the following events?
   1. Wisconsin glaciation exposes land bridge.
   2. Bows and arrows appear in North America south of Arctic.
   3. Archaic hunter-gatherer cultures dominate ancient America.
   4. Paleo-Indians use Clovis points to hunt big game.
   
   a. 3, 2, 1, 4
   b. 1, 4, 3, 2
   c. 1, 2, 4, 3
   d. 1, 3, 4, 2

2. Poverty Point culture flourished in Louisiana from
   a. 80,000 B.C. to 10,000 B.C.
   b. 9500 B.C. to 9000 B.C.
   c. 1700 B.C. to 700 B.C
   d. A.D. 200 to A.D. 900.

3. The first humans arrived in North America around
   a. 13,000 B.C. to 10,000 B.C.
   b. 8000 B.C. to 1000 B.C.
   c. 2000 B.C.
   d. 500 B.C.

4. The Anasazi peoples began building cliff dwellings and pueblos around the time that
   a. the Hohokam culture developed in Arizona.
   b. corn cultivation began in the Southwest.
   c. Columbus arrived in the New World.
   d. the Hopewell culture emerged in the Mississippi Valley.

5. What is the correct order for the following events?
   1. Some Eastern Woodland peoples begin to cultivate corn.
   2. Corn cultivation begins in Central and South America.
   3. Mammoths and other big-game prey of Paleo-Indians become extinct.
   4. Southwestern cultures begin corn cultivation.
   a. 1, 2, 4, 3
   b. 1, 4, 3, 2
   c. 2, 1, 4, 3
   d. 3, 2, 4, 1

6. The Mississippian culture flourished in the Southeast around
   a. 2500 B.C. to 2000 B.C.
   b. 100 B.C. to A.D. 400.
   c. A.D. 800 to A.D. 1500.
   d. A.D. 1400 to A.D. 1600.

7. Evidence for the existence of chiefdoms can be found from about 500 B.C. in
   a. the growing of gourds and pumpkins by the Eastern Woodland peoples.
   b. burial mounds erected by Eastern Woodland cultures.
   c. the Mogollon culture that emerged in New Mexico.
   d. the Hohokam culture that developed in Arizona.

8. The Hopewell culture emerged in the Ohio and Mississippi valleys around
   a. 9000 B.C.
   b. 5000 B.C.
   c. 100 B.C. to A.D. 400.
   d. A.D. 500 to A.D. 1400.

9. Which one of the following did not occur around 1500 B.C.?
   a. Bows and arrows appear among Arctic peoples.
   b. Stone pipes for tobacco smoking appear in Eastern Woodland areas.
   c. Southwestern cultures begin corn cultivation.
   d. Adena culture develops in Ohio.

10. What is the correct order for the following events?
    1. Mexica conquer neighboring peoples and establish Mexican empire.
    2. Mississippian culture flourishes in the Southeast.
    3. Anasazi peoples build cliff dwellings and pueblos.
    4. Columbus arrives, beginning European conquest of the New World.
    a. 2, 3, 1, 4
    b. 3, 1, 2, 4
    c. 1, 2, 4, 3
    d. 4, 2, 1, 3

***Defining Terms*** Match each term with the correct definition.

✓ Athapascans
✓ Muskogean
✓ Mexica
✓ Huitzilopochtli
✓ Chumash
✓ Cahokia
✓ Algonquian
✓ Paleo-Indians
✓ Anasazi
✓ Wisconsin glaciation
✓ Great Basin
✓ continental drift
✓ Archaic
✓ Folsom hunters
✓ Clovis points
✓ Iroquoian tribes
✓ Pangaea
✓ prehistory
✓ corn
✓ burial mounds
chiefdoms
✓ League of Five Nations
tribute
✓ totem
✓ writing
✓ archaeologists
✓ *Homo sapiens*
✓ historians

1. People who study physical artifacts like bones, stones, pots, baskets, textiles, graves, and buildings to obtain information about the activities and ideas of the humans who created them. archaeologists
2. People who study written documents such as journals, laws, speeches, court records, newspapers, and censuses to obtain information about the past. historians
3. A system of symbols that records spoken language and that originated among ancient peoples in China, Egypt, and Central America about 8,000 years ago. writing
4. The modern human who has existed for approximately 300,000 years. Homo sapiens
5. The long era of human existence before the invention of writing. Although ancient peoples had a rich individual and collective history, they did not leave written records that historians can use to recreate their lives. Prehistory
6. The gigantic continent from which North and South America became detached over 200 million years ago. Pangaea

7. The geologic process that has pushed apart the continents to approximately their present positions and isolated the Western Hemisphere during the early spread of human habitation that began in Africa and spread to Europe and Asia. continental drift

8. A global cold spell that lasted from about 80,000 years ago to about 10,000 years ago. This cold spell exposed Beringia, the land bridge that connected Asian Siberia and Western Alaska, and so allowed humans to migrate into the Western Hemisphere. wisconsin glaciation

9. The first Asian migrants to the Americas. Their descendants for the next few millennia spread throughout the Americas, surviving by hunting large mammals. Their adaptation to many natural environments led to a wide variety of cultures in the Americas. Paleo-Indians

10. Distinctively shaped spearheads used by Paleo-Indians. The discovery of these throughout North and Central America in sites dated between 11,500 and 11,000 years ago provides evidence that Paleo-Indians shared a common ancestry and nomadic way of life. Clovis Points

11. Various hunting and gathering cultures that descended from Paleo-Indians. The term also refers to the period of time when these cultures dominated ancient America, roughly from 8000 B.C. to between 2000 and 1000 B.C. Archaic

12. Great Plains nomads who followed and hunted the enormous herds of bison that roamed the area east of the Rocky Mountains. The name refers to their use of flint projectile points that were used at least 10,000 years ago. Folsom hunters

13. The region between the Rocky Mountains and the Sierra Nevada that was environmentally diverse and hosted a large number of different Indian cultures. Great Basin

14. A California culture that centered around modern-day Santa Barbara and that emerged about 5,000 years ago. This group lived in relatively permanent communities but still engaged in violent conflicts over food resources. This group was typical of the California cultures in their hunter-gatherer lifestyle and reliance on acorns for food. chumash

15. Elaborately carved images of animals, supernatural beings, or ancestors. They were constructed by Northwest peoples to honor the lineage of the family clan and to display wealth and status. Time to develop sophisticated woodworking skills existed in this culture due to the abundance of fish and marine life. totems

16. The crop that caused southwestern peoples to settle into permanent villages. Southwesterners turned to agriculture because their erratic food supply depended on irregular rainfall. The cultivation of this crop required that they restrict their migratory habits to tend it. Corn

17. A culture that began to flourish in southern Utah and Colorado and northern Arizona and New Mexico during the first century A.D. Anasazi

18. Elaborate graves that shelter bodies and also various goods, including spear points, stone pipes, and jewelry. They indicate the existence of chiefdoms, social and political hierarchies among Archaic peoples. burial mounds

19. Social and political hierarchies that existed among Archaic peoples. Chiefs could command the authority and obedience of sizeable groups of people. Chiefdoms

20. The largest Mississippian site, located in Illinois across the Mississippi River from St. Louis, Missouri. This settlement covered five square miles and encompassed as many as 30,000 inhabitants, making it the largest settlement in North America. As at other Mississippian sites, the people here evidently worshipped a sun god and created enormous mounds for ceremonial purposes and burial. cahokia

21. The Native Americans who inhabited the Atlantic seaboard, the Great Lakes region, and much of the upper Midwest. Coastal people of this group cultivated corn and other crops, while those inland and in the north focused on hunting and gathering. Algonquian

22. The Native Americans who lived in Pennsylvania, upstate New York, and the hilly upland regions of the Carolinas and Georgia. They clustered in permanent farming settlements and had a matriarchal society that assigned all property to women. Iroquoian tribes

23. An Iroquoian confederation of the Seneca, Onondaga, Mohawk, Oneida, and Cayuga tribes. The group was formed for the purposes of war and diplomacy and remained powerful through the eighteenth century. League of five nations

24. The peoples spread throughout the Southeast, south of the Ohio River and east of the Mississippi. They were the descendants of the Mississippian culture and followed some of their practices, including sun worship and the building of temple mounds. Muskogean

25. Skillful warriors who invaded the Southwest around A.D. 1300. They preyed on the sedentary pueblo Indians. Athapascans

26. The founders of an enormous empire that stretched from coast to coast across central Mexico. Historians know more about this group than any other Native American people of the time, since they left written sources and massive monuments, and their Spanish conquerers left relevant records as well. Mexica

27. A Mexican god of war who was the main deity of the Mexica and indicative of the Mexica's central values. Huitzilopochtli

28. The goods the Mexica collected from subject peoples. The Mexica took everything from basic food products to candidates for human sacrifice. This redistributed to the Mexica as much as a third of the goods produced by conquered tribes. tribute

## Chapter Review

***Multiple-Choice*** Choose the letter of the best answer.

1. Archaeologists and historians
   a. have nothing in common.
   b. do precisely the same thing.
   c. use different methods to obtain information about the past.
   d. employ the same evidence to prove their arguments.

2. Archaeologists study the past by concentrating on
   a. written records.
   b. physical artifacts.
   c. oral accounts.
   d. biological changes.

3. Historians base their interpretation of the past largely on
   a. physical artifacts.
   b. written records.
   c. geologic records.
   d. creative guesswork.

4. The boundary between humans studied by archaeologists and historians is denoted by
   a. the development of architecture.
   b. the use of fire.
   c. the invention of writing.
   d. the use of verbal language.

5. The development use of writing has occurred within the last
   a. 8,000 years.
   b. 16,000 years.
   c. 32,000 years.
   d. 64,000 years.

6. The ancient Americans who inhabited North America in 1492 possessed
   a. no culture whatsoever.
   b. a sophisticated system of writing.
   c. many forms of symbolic representation.
   d. no oral traditions.

7. The era before the invention of writing is known as
   a. oral history.
   b. antihistory.
   c. nonhistory.
   d. prehistory.

8. The term *prehistory* is used because
   a. it applies to a period in which nothing happened.
   b. there were no people during that period.
   c. without written documents it is difficult to know precisely what happened.
   d. the written records have been lost.

9. Archaeologists try to learn about the lives of people who left artifacts by
   a. examining the natural environment that existed when the artifacts were used.
   b. taking them out of context.
   c. making guesses.
   d. comparing them to modern objects.

10. Ancient humans are anonymous because they
    a. left no records at all.
    b. were all alike.
    c. left no written sources and many of their artifacts have rotted away.
    d. did not have any history.

11. Given the absence of written sources, ancient human beings are
    a. entirely mysterious.
    b. anonymous.
    c. still extremely well understood.
    d. completely unknown.

12. The authors' use of the term *prologue* reflects
    a. the unimportance of ancient American cultures.
    b. the lack of variety among ancient American peoples.
    c. the impossibility of understanding anything about ancient American cultures.
    d. historians' present-mindedness.

13. _____ tend to focus on physical objects created by humans to interpret the past.
    a. Anthropologists
    b. Historians
    c. Archaeologists
    d. Geologists

14. Historians generally use _____ to learn about the past.
    a. artifacts
    b. oral records
    c. writings
    d. the natural environment

15. A system of symbols that records spoken language first originated among ancient peoples in _____ about 8,000 years ago.
    a. China, Egypt, and southern Africa
    b. China, southern Africa, and Australia
    c. southern Africa, Egypt, and Central America
    d. China, Egypt, and Central America

16. Writing was developed in the most recent _____ percent of the 300,000 years that modern human beings have existed.
    a. .2
    b. 3
    c. 20
    d. 40

17. The long era before the invention of _____ is often labeled *prehistory*.
    a. language
    b. the wheel
    c. writing
    d. weapons

18. Much of what we would like to know about the history of ancient peoples is _____.
    a. unknown
    b. already known
    c. dependent on excavations of cave paintings
    d. dependent on the translation of written sources

19. Archaeologists examine both objects and the _____ that existed when the artifacts were made.
    a. written documents
    b. oral communications
    c. natural environment
    d. music

20. One problem with using artifacts to understand human history is that so many of them have _____.
    a. rotted away
    b. been hidden
    c. been stolen
    d. been misunderstood

21. Ancient Americans created societies and cultures that _____.
    a. are entirely lost to modern archaeologists
    b. were unsophisticated
    c. were largely similar
    d. were complex and diverse

22. Because ancient Americans did not use _____, it is impossible to identify individuals or know what they thought about themselves or one another.
    a. permanent building materials
    b. music
    c. written language
    d. art

23. Human beings did not live in the Western Hemisphere for a very long time after they evolved because
    a. the climate was poor.
    b. its landmasses had become detached from those of the Eastern Hemisphere before humans evolved.
    c. large predators frightened them away.
    d. food was scarce.

24. *Homo sapiens* evolved in and migrated out of
    a. Africa.
    b. Asia.
    c. Europe.
    d. South America.

25. Humans were able to become permanent residents of cold regions after they
    a. mastered the principles of insulation.
    b. discovered they could grow food even in the cold.
    c. learned how to sew animal skins into warm clothing.
    d. got used to the weather.

26. The land bridge connecting Siberia to Alaska was exposed from 80,000 years ago to about 10,000 years ago as a result of
    a. a drought.
    b. an earthquake.
    c. the Wisconsin glaciation.
    d. human engineering.

27. Ancient humans migrated to the Western Hemisphere by means of Beringia,
    a. the land bridge between Siberia and Alaska.
    b. the North American continent.
    c. eastern Asia.
    d. ancient Africa.

28. Available evidence suggests that Paleo-Indians were almost certainly
    a. from Africa.
    b. from Asia.
    c. people who came across the North Atlantic from Europe.
    d. original Australian inhabitants.

29. Most archaeologists believe that Paleo-Indians migrated into North America by going along
    a. its eastern coast.
    b. the Mississippi River.
    c. Central America.
    d. the eastern side of the Canadian Rockies.

30. The Paleo-Indian population grew because of the
   a. warm climate in North America.
   b. absence of predators.
   c. ample food supply.
   d. abundance of timber to construct shelter.

31. Findings of Clovis points—distinctively shaped spearheads—demonstrates that early humans
   a. had wildly divergent cultures.
   b. shared a common ancestry and similar way of life.
   c. hunted small game.
   d. were warlike and vicious.

32. For the first 4,000 years, Paleo-Indians depended on
   a. fishing.
   b. hunting big mammals.
   c. hunting small mammals.
   d. agriculture.

33. Paleo-Indians confronted a major crisis approximately 11,000 years ago, when
   a. North America flooded.
   b. their food plants became extinct.
   c. the big-game animals they hunted became extinct.
   d. Beringia was submerged again and they were trapped.

34. After the end of the Wisconsin glacial period, Paleo-Indian culture
   a. remained static.
   b. became more uniform.
   c. disappeared.
   d. became more diverse.

35. Human beings existed for about 1.5 million years before they arrived in the _____.
   a. Western Hemisphere
   b. Eastern Hemisphere
   c. African subcontinent
   d. Asian mainland

36. The process of _____ isolated the Western Hemisphere from the other continents.
   a. continental drift
   b. glaciation
   c. migration
   d. rising sea levels

37. Human beings evolved in _____ about 1.5 million years ago.
   a. Europe
   b. Asia
   c. South America
   d. Africa

38. The first human beings to reach the Western Hemisphere had to _____.
   a. build boats
   b. learn to plant food
   c. develop language
   d. adapt to a frigid environment

39. A cold spell called the Wisconsin glaciation caused _____ and made it possible for humans to cross the Bering Strait.
   a. the sea level to drop
   b. the sea to freeze over completely
   c. Beringia to rise several hundred feet off the sea floor
   d. a narrow bridge of ice to develop

40. It is most likely that the first human migrants to North America were from _____.
   a. Siberia
   b. Polynesia
   c. Europe
   d. Japan

41. Ample _____ permitted Paleo-Indian populations in North and South America to grow.
   a. rain
   b. sunshine
   c. food
   d. shelter

42. The discovery of _____ provided powerful evidence that Paleo-Indians shared a common ancestry and way of life.
   a. stone knives
   b. pottery shards
   c. textile remnants
   d. Clovis points

43. When the big-game animals they hunted became extinct, Paleo-Indians responded by _____.
    a. focusing on smaller animals and foraging
    b. finding new big-game animals
    c. returning to Siberia
    d. practicing conservation measures

44. The huge variety of Native American cultures that existed in 1492 arose from _____.
    a. adaptations to local environments
    b. warfare
    c. varied ancestry
    d. isolation

45. The term *Archaic* is used by archaeologists to describe
    a. the cultures that descended from the Paleo-Indians.
    b. Paleo-Indian culture.
    c. anything older than 9,000 years.
    d. the period after European contact.

46. Archaic peoples differed from their Paleo-Indian ancestors in that they
    a. hunted with spears.
    b. practiced agriculture.
    c. used stone tools to prepare food from wild plants.
    d. were vegetarians.

47. The Folsom hunters of the Great Plains
    a. settled in permanent villages.
    b. were nomads.
    c. used horses to hunt.
    d. were farmers for much of each year.

48. By about A.D. 500 on the Great Plains, bows and arrows had
    a. greatly altered the age-old bison-hunting techniques.
    b. were replaced by guns.
    c. had largely replaced spears.
    d. were entirely replaced by spears.

49. The zones where Archaic peoples settled in the Great Basin changed constantly, depending on
    a. religious concerns.
    b. the availability of bison.
    c. the size of the population.
    d. the amount of rainfall.

50. The most important source of food for Great Basin peoples was
    a. plants.
    b. small game.
    c. fish.
    d. large game.

51. The most densely settled area in all of ancient North America was
    a. the Great Plains.
    b. the Northeast.
    c. California.
    d. western Canada.

52. The Chumash people in California were able to establish
    a. peaceful relations with their neighbors.
    b. a prosperous economy based on fishing.
    c. a written culture.
    d. relatively permanent villages.

53. About 5,000 years ago, peoples in the Pacific Northwest began to develop
    a. a culture based on gathering acorns.
    b. sophisticated woodworking skills.
    c. a hunter-gatherer lifestyle.
    d. a culture based on bear hunting.

54. Nearly all Woodland hunters concentrated on
    a. hunting bison.
    b. hunting rabbits and squirrels.
    c. a vegetarian diet.
    d. hunting deer.

55. Around 2000 B.C., Woodland culture was changed by the introduction of
    a. pottery and bows and arrows.
    b. bows and arrows and agriculture.
    c. pottery and agriculture.
    d. agriculture and horses.

56. Ancient Americans at Poverty Point constructed
   a. wooden houses.
   b. an enormous earthworks.
   c. a large temple.
   d. large canoes.

57. The hunting and gathering cultures that descended from Paleo-Indians are known by archaeologists as _____.
   a. post-Clovian
   b. Beringian
   c. Archaic
   d. post-Paleo

58. Most Archaic Indians _____.
   a. established permanent villages
   b. returned to the same fertile areas from year to year
   c. wandered aimlessly
   d. migrated in search of better weather conditions

59. The hunters of the Great Plains stalked bison _____.
   a. individually
   b. on foot
   c. on horses
   d. in huge groups

60. The Archaic peoples who lived in the Great Basin between _____ inhabited a region of environmental diversity.
   a. the Rocky Mountains and the Sierra Nevada
   b. the Mississippi River and the Rocky Mountains
   c. the Rocky Mountains and the Pacific Coast
   d. the Mississippi River and the Sierra Nevada

61. Great Basin peoples were able to adapt to environmental challenges and maintain a hunter-gatherer way of life by _____.
   a. diversifying their food sources
   b. migrating to favorable locations
   c. diversifying their food sources and migrating to favorable locations
   d. relying on hunting and staying in one place

62. _____ was the most densely settled area in ancient North America.
   a. The Great Basin
   b. The Mississippi River Valley
   c. Canada
   d. California

63. The peoples of the Northwest were able to develop _____ because of their abundant and stable sources of marine food.
   a. enormous burial mounds
   b. elaborate hunting rituals
   c. pueblo architecture
   d. sophisticated woodworking skills

64. The peoples of the Woodland culture relied on _____ for food, clothing, weapons, needles, and other tools.
   a. bison
   b. fish
   c. deer
   d. plants

65. Around 2000 B.C., Woodland cultures began to incorporate _____ into their basic hunter-gatherer lifestyles.
   a. acorn-gathering
   b. agriculture and pottery
   c. intertribal warfare
   d. new religious practices

66. The use of _____ indicates that a culture has a more permanent settlement.
   a. ceramic pots
   b. baskets
   c. cloth bags
   d. iron pans

67. Permanent agricultural settlements in North America first emerged in the
   a. Woodland region.
   b. Great Basin.
   c. Pacific Northwest.
   d. Southwest.

68. Southwestern peoples probably developed agriculture because
   a. the climate was dry.
   b. the game animals they hunted became extinct.
   c. they were tired of moving.
   d. there was plenty of rain in the area.

69. The introduction of corn encouraged southwestern hunter-gatherers to
   a. restrict their migratory habits.
   b. stop hunting entirely.
   c. quit gathering wild food.
   d. travel constantly in search of fresh land.

70. The Mogollon culture was marked by its
   a. spectacular pottery.
   b. pueblos.
   c. nomadic hunting.
   d. pit houses.

71. The Hohokam peoples enjoyed
   a. plenty of rainfall.
   b. access to lumber.
   c. comparatively high crop yields.
   d. access to fresh-water lakes and rivers.

72. Beginning around A.D. 1000, the Anasazi moved from pit houses on mesa tops to
   a. large earthworks.
   b. California.
   c. river valleys with more water.
   d. multistory cliff dwellings.

73. Anasazi culture disappeared as a result of
   a. warfare.
   b. a long drought.
   c. an outbreak of disease.
   d. an earthquake.

74. The burial mounds constructed by Woodland cultures suggest
   a. the Asian origins of American native peoples.
   b. an extreme fear of the dead.
   c. profound religious beliefs.
   d. the existence of a social and political hierarchy.

75. According to limited archaeological evidence from Hopewell grave mounds, the most important members of Hopewell groups may have been
   a. male hunters.
   b. young women.
   c. small children.
   d. elderly men.

76. The Mississippian cultures that flourished from about A.D. 800 to about A.D. 1500 were
   a. pueblo cultures.
   b. nomadic cultures.
   c. mound-building cultures.
   d. pit-house cultures.

77. The Mississippian site of Cahokia was
   a. the largest settlement in North America.
   b. the poorest settlement in North America.
   c. extremely agriculturally sophisticated.
   d. the first to use irrigation systems.

78. Cahokia burial mounds demonstrate
   a. the simplicity of the culture.
   b. an elaborate theology.
   c. the power chiefs wielded.
   d. the custom of burying all tribe members.

79. Agriculture _____ hunter-gatherer subsistence strategies among Eastern Woodland peoples and other Archaic cultures.
   a. replaced
   b. was superior to
   c. did not influence
   d. supplemented

80. Later innovations in the Archaic way of life were _____.
   a. hunting and gathering
   b. spears
   c. agricultural settlements and chiefdoms
   d. bison hunting

81. The problems created by _____ probably caused southwestern peoples to adopt agriculture.
   a. living in a dry climate
   b. a lack of wild-plant food
   c. constant warfare
   d. few game animals

82. Around 1500 B.C., peoples in the Southwest altered their hunting and gathering society by starting to _____.
   a. hunt for deer
   b. cultivate corn
   c. weave cotton into textiles
   d. worship the sun

83. The Mogollon culture that emerged in southern New Mexico between A.D. 200 and 900 was characterized by _____.
   a. cliff dwellings
   b. small farming settlements and pit houses
   c. elaborate kivas
   d. large cedar houses

84. Hohokam culture was strongly influenced by _____.
   a. the Mogollon culture
   b. Mexico
   c. the Navajo culture
   d. the Woodlands culture

85. It is likely that a _____ caused the disappearance of the Anasazi culture.
   a. destructive fire
   b. major power struggle
   c. massive earthquake
   d. fifty-year drought

86. The burial mounds of the Mississippi River area suggest the existence of _____, social and political hierarchies.
   a. matriarchies
   b. pueblos
   c. chiefdoms
   d. kingdoms

87. Grave sites indicate that the Hopewell peoples participated in a _____ ranging from Wyoming to Florida.
   a. trade network
   b. religious revival
   c. common ritual
   d. family system

88. In the southeastern floodplains, the mound-building _____ culture emerged about A.D. 800 and lasted until about A.D. 1500.
   a. Acoma
   b. Mississippian
   c. Cahokian
   d. Adena

89. The Algonquian tribes who lived along the Atlantic coast differed from the inland and northern tribes, such as the Abenaki, Penobscot, and Chippewa, because they
   a. fished.
   b. hunted.
   c. grew crops.
   d. gathered wild rice.

90. The Iroquoian tribes of Pennsylvania and upstate New York lived in
   a. temporary campsites.
   b. earthworks.
   c. permanent settlements.
   d. pit houses.

91. Iroquoian societies were unusual because they were
   a. hierarchical.
   b. lacking in any leadership structure.
   c. patriarchal.
   d. matriarchal.

92. The League of Five Nations was a confederacy
   a. of Algonquian tribes.
   b. between the Algonquian and the Iroquois.
   c. headed by women.
   d. of Iroquois tribes.

93. The Muskogean peoples were the descendants of the
   a. Mississippian culture.
   b. Anasazi.
   c. Hopewell culture.
   d. Woodland culture.

94. The Muskogean peoples lived in an environment that provided
    a. food from both agriculture and hunting and gathering.
    b. a very limited food supply.
    c. mostly vegetable food.
    d. mostly animal food.

95. Between A.D. 1300 and 1500, many of the tribes on the Great Plains had
    a. moved west in search of bison.
    b. moved east to hunt bison.
    c. become part of the Iroquois and Algonquian tribes.
    d. been forced out of the East by Iroquian and Algonquian tribes.

96. By 1492, the Great Plains tribes
    a. were all hunters.
    b. were all agricultural.
    c. were very poor.
    d. included both hunters and farmers.

97. The Athapascan tribes of the Southwest
    a. grew large quantities of corn.
    b. constructed huge burial mounds.
    c. moved onto the Great Plains.
    d. preyed on pueblo Indians.

98. By the time Columbus arrived in the Western Hemisphere, the estimated population of North America was about
    a. one million.
    b. four million.
    c. ten million.
    d. fifteen million.

99. Prior to European contact, Native Americans left records of themselves
    a. by writing on rocks in caves.
    b. in drawings, weavings, and dancing.
    c. by writing on bark that has since decayed.
    d. by burying writings in elaborate earthwork mounds.

100. The culture of ancient Americans included
    a. sailing ships.
    b. domesticated animals.
    c. different adaptations to the natural environment.
    d. sophisticated metallurgy.

101. Among the Eastern Woodland people, the Algonquian tribes _____.
    a. hunted, farmed, or foraged, depending on local conditions
    b. were remarkably similar
    c. all depended on growing corn and squash
    d. invented the canoe at about the same time

102. The Iroquois tribes stood out from their neighbors because they _____.
    a. subsisted on animal food
    b. inhabited a large amount of territory
    c. grew corn and had permanent settlements
    d. hunted for deer

103. Among the Iroquois tribes, all property belonged to _____.
    a. tribal elders
    b. young men
    c. women
    d. tribal leaders

104. The _____ peoples, who carried remnants of the Mississippian culture, lived throughout the Southeast, south of the Ohio River and east of the Mississippi.
    a. Cayuga
    b. Muskogean
    c. Algonquian
    d. Penobscot

105. Upon Columbus's arrival in the Western Hemisphere, many Great Plains tribes were increasing their reliance on _____.
    a. buffalo
    b. agriculture
    c. tobacco
    d. small game

106. Tribes in the Pacific coast region and the Great Basin fed themselves by _____.
    a. hunting buffalo
    b. implementing agricultural practices
    c. using earlier subsistence practices
    d. fishing

107. In the Southwest, most Native Americans lived in _____.
   a. nomadic tribes
   b. small, seasonally migratory groups
   c. cedar longhouses
   d. settled agricultural communities

108. The Athapascans, principally _____, were skillful warriors who preyed on the sedentary pueblo Indians.
   a. Apache and Comanche
   b. Comanche and Navajo
   c. Apache and Navajo
   d. Navajo and Shoshone

109. By the time Columbus arrived, most Native Americans depended on _____ for a major portion of their food.
   a. hunting and gathering
   b. farming
   c. fishing
   d. scavenging

110. The great similarity that underlay the cultural diversity of Native American tribes was that they all _____.
   a. used large domesticated animals
   b. had developed the wheel
   c. followed the same burial practices
   d. had adapted to the natural environment local to each tribe

111. By 1492, the indigenous population of the New World was about the same as the population of
   a. the British Isles.
   b. Europe.
   c. China.
   d. Spain and Portugal.

112. The empire of the Mexica was located in
   a. southern Texas.
   b. Peru.
   c. Guatemala.
   d. central Mexico.

113. Historians know more about the fifteenth-century Mexica than any other Native American society of the time because of
   a. their written sources and monuments.
   b. the records of Spanish conquerors.
   c. both of the above.
   d. neither of the above.

114. The empire of the Mexica had its origins around A.D. 1325, when the Mexica began to
   a. mine for gold.
   b. sacrifice humans to the war god Huitzilopochtli.
   c. be hired as mercenaries by other tribes.
   d. domesticate horses.

115. The central values of the Mexica revolved around
   a. war.
   b. the cultivation of corn.
   c. fertility.
   d. art.

116. The ultimate act of bravery among the Mexica was to
   a. die in battle.
   b. sacrifice oneself for others.
   c. capture prisoners.
   d. endure pain.

117. The empire of the Mexica was basically a
   a. system of slavery.
   b. labor system.
   c. religious expression.
   d. way to collect tribute.

118. When the Mexica conquered a tribe, they
   a. removed its ruling elite.
   b. did not interfere much with its government.
   c. killed all its young men.
   d. kidnapped its children.

119. In exchange for tribute, the Mexica gave conquered provinces
   a. military protection.
   b. military training.
   c. trade goods from the Mexica.
   d. very little.

120. The achievements of Mexican society were made possible by
   a. scientific advances.
   b. the massive redistribution of wealth.
   c. the cultivation of food crops.
   d. the discovery of gold mines.

121. Europeans were amazed by Mexican society's
   a. overall egalitarianism.
   b. extremes of poverty and wealth.
   c. significant wealth.
   d. cultural weakness.

122. The weakness of the empire of the Mexica was
   a. the discontent among subject peoples.
   b. the high rate of attrition among warriors.
   c. the short life span of its subjects.
   d. high levels of infant mortality.

123. In 1492, about four million of the _____ indigenous people of the New World lived in North America.
   a. five million
   b. ten million
   c. twenty million
   d. eighty million

124. Historians and archaeologists know a great deal about the Mexica because their _____.
   a. oral tradition survived the Spanish conquest
   b. elaborate cave paintings still exist
   c. written sources interested the Spanish conquerors
   d. influence was more important than that of any other tribe

125. The Mexica expanded their empire by _____.
   a. discovering new territories
   b. taking over other governments
   c. enslaving conquered peoples
   d. military force

126. By 1500, the Mexican empire encompassed a larger area than _____ combined and contained almost three times as many people.
   a. North America and Siberia
   b. Spain and Portugal
   c. Africa and Australia
   d. Europe and the British Isles

127. _____ held the most exalted positions in the Mexican social hierarchy.
   a. Priests
   b. Lawmakers
   c. Artisans
   d. Warriors

128. Mexicans used captured prisoners as _____.
   a. a source of ransom money
   b. adoptees for high-ranking families
   c. slaves
   d. sacrifices to the war god.

129. A tribe conquered by the Mexica would have to pay the empire tribute in _____.
   a. money
   b. labor
   c. goods
   d. allegiance

130. Tribute redistributed to the Mexica as much as _____ of the goods produced by conquered tribes.
   a. one eighth
   b. one sixth
   c. one fifth
   d. one third

131. Conquered provinces received _____ from the Mexica in return for their tribute.
   a. a say in the governance of the empire
   b. kickbacks
   c. constant harassment
   d. immunity from punitive raids

132. The Mexica failed to create among their subjects a belief that their rule was legitimate because they based their authority on _____.
   a. military conquest
   b. distant governors
   c. local elites
   d. extreme cruelty

***Short Answer*** Write a paragraph response to each question.

1. What is the difference between archaeologists and historians?
2. To what does the term *prehistory* refer? Is it an accurate label?
3. How and why did humans migrate into the Western Hemisphere?
4. What are Clovis points? What do they suggest about Paleo-Indian culture?
5. What caused Paleo-Indians to diversify their cultures beginning about 11,000 years ago?
6. Where was the Great Basin? How did the Archaic cultures that lived there adapt to their environment?
7. How did the availability of food shape the culture of the Archaic peoples of the Pacific Northwest coast?
8. What changes occurred among Woodland cultures around 2000 B.C.? How did those changes affect the Woodland peoples?
9. Why did Southwestern cultures turn to agriculture? What impact did the shift have on their way of life?
10. What are burial mounds? What do they reveal about the Woodland culture of the time?
11. What were the Iroquoian tribes, and how did they differ from other eastern tribes?
12. What common features of fifteenth-century European life did Native Americans not have? How significant was the lack of these cultural and technological resources?
13. Why do the Mexica stand out among other Central and South American cultures?
14. What was the fundamental purpose of the empire the Mexica? Who benefited from it?

***Building Historical Skills*** Historians use a variety of sources to think and talk about the past, including maps, illustrations, and written records. Maps provide a variety of different kinds of comparative information in a condensed visual format; reading them requires learning how to sort through this information. To deepen our understanding of the past by supplementing written records, historians frequently interpret material culture, such as a vase or a painting, with techniques borrowed from art history, archaeology, or anthropology. Written records, though familiar as sources, raise their own problems of interpretation. Every document reflects someone's particular perspective or assumptions. It is the historian's task to study and compare each document to other records with other perspectives. The following exercise introduces you to using written documents as sources of information.

***Analyzing Sources Activity*** Answer the following questions in a paragraph based on "Historical Question: Did the Mexicans Practice Human Sacrifice?" on page 20 of *The American Promise*, Second Edition.

1. What sorts of people were sacrificed in Mexican religious rituals? Was sacrifice always a matter of taking a human life?
2. What were the bases of Mexican religious belief?

3. How did Mexican religious beliefs encourage human sacrifice?
4. How did the Mexica see human sacrifice?

**WEB LINKS** To explore the topics discussed in the exercise above, visit the Web links noted below.

"Civilizations in America: The Mexica/Aztecs"
http://www.wsu.edu:8080/~dee/CIVAMRCA/AZTECS.HTM

"Chronological Table of Mesoamerican Archaeology"
http://weber.ucsd.edu/~dkjordan/arch/mexchron.html
Choose "Aztecs"

"Middle American Culture"
http://www.ibiblio.org/expo/1492.exhibit/a-America/midAmerica.html

# Answer Key

## Prologue: Ancient America, Before 1492

### *Chapter Overview*

#### *Chronology*

1. b
2. c
3. a
4. c
5. d
6. c
7. b
8. c
9. d
10. a

#### *Defining Terms*

1. archaeologists
2. historians
3. writing
4. *Homo sapiens*
5. prehistory
6. Pangaea
7. continental drift
8. Wisconsin glaciation
9. Paleo-Indians
10. Clovis points
11. Archaic
12. Folsom hunters
13. Great Basin
14. Chumash
15. totems
16. corn
17. Anasazi
18. burial mounds
19. chiefdoms
20. Cahokia
21. Algonquian
22. Iroquoian tribes
23. League of Five Nations
24. Muskogean
25. Athapascans
26. Mexica
27. Huitzilopochtli
28. tribute

### *Chapter Review*

#### *Multiple-Choice*

1. c
2. b
3. b
4. c
5. a
6. c
7. d
8. c
9. a
10. c
11. b
12. d
13. c
14. c
15. d
16. b
17. c
18. a
19. c
20. a
21. d
22. c
23. b
24. a
25. c
26. c
27. a
28. b
29. d
30. c
31. b
32. b
33. c
34. d
35. a
36. a
37. d
38. d
39. a
40. b
41. c
42. d
43. a
44. a
45. a
46. c
47. b
48. c
49. d
50. a
51. c
52. d
53. b
54. d
55. c
56. b
57. c
58. b
59. b
60. a
61. c
62. d
63. d
64. c
65. b
66. a
67. d
68. a
69. a
70. d
71. c
72. d
73. b
74. d
75. a
76. c
77. a
78. c
79. d
80. c
81. a
82. b
83. b
84. b
85. d
86. c
87. d
88. b

89. c
90. c
91. d
92. d
93. a
94. a
95. d
96. d
97. d
98. b
99. b
100. c
101. a
102. c
103. c
104. b
105. a
106. d
107. d
108. c
109. a
110. d
111. b
112. d
113. c
114. c
115. a
116. c
117. d
118. b
119. d
120. b
121. c
122. a
123. d
124. c
125. d
126. b
127. d
128. d
129. c
130. d
131. d
132. a

### *Short Answer*

1. Both archaeologists and historians use various kinds of evidence to learn about and understand people who lived in the past. However, they use different kinds of evidence. Archaeologists focus on the long period of time before human beings left written records; they use physical objects like bones, pots, baskets, textiles, graves, and buildings, and the natural environment in which they were made. Historians, on the other hand, consider mostly writings, including private correspondence, legal texts, official speeches, newspapers, court records, and censuses. This means that archaeologists and historians concentrate on different time periods.
2. *Prehistory* is the label used for the 97 percent of human existence during which no systems of writing existed. It is not an accurate term insofar as ancient peoples used oral communication and had both an individual and a collective history. Ancient peoples did what modern peoples do, moving around, surviving in the natural environment, learning, and adapting to change. Yet the absence of written records means that much of that history is entirely lost to us. In that sense, using *prehistory* is correct.
3. Beginning about 80,000 years ago the earth entered a global cold spell called the Wisconsin glaciation, during which snow piled up in glaciers without melting and caused the sea level to drop by as much as 350 feet. This was enough to uncover the seafloor that is submerged 120 feet below the surface of the Bering Strait. Beringia, the land that was revealed, stretched between Asian Siberia and American Alaska. Siberians probably moved onto Beringia to hunt the herds of mammoth, bison, and other game animals that lived off of its grasses and shrubs, eventually reaching North America.
4. Clovis points were distinctively shaped spearheads, named after the place in New Mexico where they were first excavated. The points were used for hunting large mammals and have been found throughout North and Central America in sites dated between 11,500 and 11,000 years ago. The fact that they were used over such an immense amount of land indicates that Paleo-Indians shared a common ancestry and way of life, providing support for the idea that they migrated from a single area, Siberia.
5. Paleo-Indians throughout the Americas specialized in hunting big game animals. However, about 11,000 years ago the animals upon which they depended became extinct. This was probably the result of the climate changes that occurred when the Wisconsin glacial period ended, leading to warmer temperatures. It may also have been exacerbated by overhunting. When these animals disappeared, peoples were forced to adapt to the many different environments in which they lived, producing a wide variety of cultures.
6. The Great Basin was the area between the Rocky Mountains and the Sierra Nevada. It was a region of great environmental diversity, spanning marshes and lakes, arid deserts, and treeless mountain heights. The Archaic Indians of the region moved around constantly, depending on the amount of rainfall. They took all kinds of game animals, including bison, rabbits, and rodents, and fished with hooks and nets. However, they relied primarily on plant food, which could be collected in large quantities and stored in baskets to protect against the shortages caused by the unreliable rainfall.
7. The Pacific Northwest coast had a rich natural environment. In particular, there were abundant supplies of fish and other marine life. The peoples of the region would catch and dry large quantities of fish, which left them with a substantial amount of time to devote to activities other than gathering food. They turned their attention to woodworking, fashioning enormous canoes for fishing, hunting, and warfare, multifamily houses in more or less permanent villages, and totems that honored lineages and displayed a family's wealth and status.

8. Around 2000 B.C., agriculture and pottery became incorporated into the Woodland cultures' hunter-gatherer lifestyle. The Mexican crops of gourds and pumpkins were introduced into parts of Missouri and Kentucky, and after that Woodland peoples began to cultivate local species like sunflowers. Techniques for making ceramic pots were probably introduced from Mexico as well; the pots were more durable than baskets, but their heaviness made them impractical for nomadic cultures. Although agriculture and pottery were both convenient for the Woodland peoples, allowing them to add to the quantity, variety, and predictability of food sources, they did not fundamentally alter their hunting and gathering practices.
9. The Southwestern climate was very dry, and the unpredictable rainfall meant that the supply of wild-plant food was erratic. Probably in response to this, sometime around 1500 B.C. Southwestern hunters and gatherers began to cultivate corn, a crop that was already grown in Mexico. The turn to agriculture meant that Southwestern peoples had to give up their migratory ways because they had to develop complicated irrigation systems and also the crops needed constant tending. They began settling in permanent villages, first in pit houses and later, in some places, in cliff dwellings and walled pueblos.
10. Around 500 B.C., Woodland cultures throughout the drainage of the Mississippi River began to build burial mounds, which were large quantities of earth deposited over a grave containing a body and grave goods. The size of the mounds, the labor and organization required to erect them, and the differences in artifacts buried with certain individuals suggest that Woodland peoples had developed a social and political hierarchy called a chiefdom. For example, analysis of the Hopewell culture that existed between 100 B.C. and A.D. 400 shows that the most important graves contained men who were hunters, indicating that they were the most valued members of the society. A later Mississippian mound at Cahokia, Illinois, covered a man who had been buried with a large retinue of other people who presumably had been sacrificed on his death, implying that he was able to command a great deal of power and loyalty.
11. The Iroquoian tribes were centered in Pennsylvania, upstate New York, and the upland regions of the Carolinas and Georgia. They were unusually successful at cultivating corn and other crops, which allowed them to settle in permanent villages. The tribes were also matriarchal: property, including children and inheritance, belonged to women, women headed family clans, and women selected the male chiefs who governed the tribes. Finally, several of the Iroquoian tribes had joined together in a confederation, the League of Five Nations, which was a powerful influence in war and diplomacy well into the eighteenth century.
12. Native Americans did not possess many things common to European life. They did not have sailing ships; they had not invented the wheel; they did not use large domesticated animals like horses or cows; they had no metal other than copper and no knowledge of metallurgy. Yet while these technologies were essential to Europeans, they were not particularly relevant to Native Americans. Their cultures had developed in response to the varied natural environments in which they lived and did not require many of the things that Europeans could not imagining foregoing.
13. The Mexica stand out for a number of reasons, the first being the sheer size of their empire. Starting from a marshy island on Lake Texcoco in A.D. 1325, the Mexica conquered land stretching from coast to coast across central Mexico and covering as many as twenty-five million people. Moreover, the Mexica, unlike most of the other cultures in the Western Hemisphere up to that time, left written sources and massive monuments that historians can use to recreate their lives and customs. Finally, the Spanish interest in subduing them in the sixteenth century provides another source of information.
14. At a fundamental level, the empire of the Mexica was a military and political system for collecting tribute from conquered peoples. Defeated tribes paid the Mexica in tribute rather than money, and tribute could be anything from people to be used as sacrifices to food products to luxury items. The system was designed to redistribute wealth from nonnoble Mexicans and subject peoples to the relatively small nobility of Mexican warriors and priests. It was remarkably effective, giving as much as a third of the goods produced by conquered tribes to the Mexica.

### *Analyzing Sources*

1. The Mexica usually sacrificed prisoners who had been captured in battle or rendered as part of the payment of tribute. Yet Mexican citizens were sacrificed as well, particularly young men, women, and children; for example, an honored young man was sacrificed to Tezcatlipoca, the god of human fate, every eighteen months. Sacrifice did not always have to be dramatic. All Mexicans did ritual bloodletting by piercing themselves with stingray spines or cactus thorns to show their religious devotion. While wealthy and noble Mexicans engaged in ritualistic canni-

balism, every Mexican participated in symbolic cannibalism by eating small cakes made of flour mixed with blood and shaped into human forms.

2. Mexicans believed that the world was suffused with the power of supernatural beings, with a particular deity overseeing every important activity. These gods communicated with human beings through various omens that communicated whether the gods were happy or not. Humans were obliged to demonstrate their own reverence for the gods by observing appropriate rituals. Since every occurrence could be interpreted as an omen, Mexicans believed that the events of daily life had a supernatural dimension.
3. According to Mexican theology, the most powerful gods were Huitzilopochtli, the war god, and Quetzalcoatl, the god who sustained human beings: the Mexica believed that these two gods had created the universe and everything in it. The current epoch of existence, the Fifth Sun, had been created when two gods sacrificed themselves to make the sun and the moon. To keep the light of the sun strong and keep it in motion, the Mexica were convinced that they needed to follow the example of the gods and feed it with human blood. If that blood were not provided, the world would be destroyed by earthquakes, and humans would be ravaged by supernatural monsters. Thus, human sacrifice was necessary to maintain life on earth.
4. The Mexica saw human sacrifice as part of their religious rituals and therefore as an act of worship. Given their theology, it was a perfectly normal and reasonable activity, one that staved off the end of the world. Thus, sacrificial victims performed a sacred duty: they gave themselves so that others might live and thrive. As such, they were treated with reverence; the eating of victims was considered a sign of respect.

CHAPTER

# EUROPEANS AND THE NEW WORLD, 1492–1600

# 1

## Chapter Overview

### *Chapter Summary*

***Introduction*** The chapter opens with a description of Christopher Columbus's encounter with the Taino people on the island of San Salvador in October of 1492. Columbus's landfall in the Caribbean signaled the beginning of the transformative impact European cultures would have on the New World and its inhabitants. But that impact cut both ways, and the encounter would change the history of Europe and the rest of the world as well. Europeans slowly began to understand that what Columbus had found was a whole New World (as they called it) separated from their own by vast oceans. After 1492, neither of these worlds would ever be the same again.

***Europe in the Age of Exploration, pp. 4–8*** Though Viking explorers reached eastern Canada around the year 1000, their settlements were short-lived and had no significant impact on subsequent European expansion or the New World. Historically, Europeans had turned to the East to pursue an expanding trade with Asia and Africa.

**MEDITERRANEAN TRADE AND EUROPEAN EXPANSION** The Mediterranean trade in exotic goods carried overland by traders from the East was dominated by Italian bankers and merchants from the twelfth through the fifteenth centuries. By the fifteenth century, various factors both impeded and stimulated further European expansion. The bubonic plague—the Black Death—wiped out about a third of the European population, causing great hardship and distress. While the insecurity and dislocation caused by the plague led some to avoid taking risks, paradoxically it encouraged others to venture out on voyages of exploration, especially those who sought to better their position within European society. The desire for overseas expansion was further heightened by advances in geographic knowledge and navigational aids. In the end it was the Portuguese who took the lead in venturing out beyond the borders of the known world.

**A CENTURY OF PORTUGUESE EXPLORATION** Although Portugal was small and relatively poor, the nation was located on the fringes of the thriving Mediterranean trade and had participated in zealous crusades against Muslims. Prince Henry the Navigator was an influential advocate of

Portuguese exploration. From 1415 to 1460 he amassed information about sailing techniques and geography and encouraged the explorations and conquests down the west coast of Africa that would eventually lead to a discovery of a sea route to the rich trade of the East. A key development in this quest was the Portuguese invention of the caravel, a ship whose sturdy construction enabled it to survive long and stormy voyages. By 1480, the Portuguese were trading with Africans, obtaining gold, slaves, and ivory, and venturing further down the African coast. In 1488, Bartolomeu Dias rounded the southern tip of Africa—the Cape of Good Hope—and ten years later, Vasco da Gama led the first Portuguese fleet to India. By the early sixteenth century, the Portuguese had established trading posts throughout the East Indies and controlled a widespread empire. The sea route they had discovered to the East destroyed the monopoly of the old Mediterranean trade, as it eliminated the need for overland travel and the role of middlemen merchants.

***A Surprising New World in the Western Atlantic, pp. 8–12*** Inspired by the example of the Portuguese, other Europeans reasoned that alternative routes to the Indies might be possible. One such European was Christopher Columbus, born in Genoa in 1451. After years as a sailor learning from Portuguese maritime innovations, Columbus became obsessed with the possibility that by sailing west instead of east, one could eventually reach Asia.

**THE EXPLORATIONS OF COLUMBUS** Although Columbus, like most other Europeans, believed the earth was spherical, he parted company with many of his fellow mariners in his certainty that the circumference of the earth was much smaller than commonly believed and thus that an expedition west was feasible. In 1492, after years of seeking a sponsor, he persuaded King Ferdinand and Queen Isabella of Spain to provide backing for such an expedition. Columbus's initial voyage to the New World and his reports of the new land's abundance excited the overseas ambitions of the Spanish monarchs, who hastened to assert their control by asking for the Pope's official confirmation of their right to the lands Columbus had discovered. Alarmed by this move, the Portuguese negotiated the Treaty of Tordesillas with Spain in 1494, which established that all land discovered to the east of an imaginary line belonged to Portugal, while all land to the west of that line would be the province of Spain. Columbus returned to the New World three more times and died in 1506 still convinced that what he had explored was part of Asia.

**THE GEOGRAPHIC REVOLUTION AND THE COLUMBIAN EXCHANGE** Within thirty years of Columbus's landfall at Guanahani, European perceptions of world geography had undergone a revolution. Journeys of other explorers in the wake of Columbus's voyage confirmed the presence of several large masses of land in the western Atlantic, but gradually it became clear that these were not parts of Asia at all. In 1507, Martin Waldseemüller, a German cartographer, published the first map to show the New World as a continent distinct from Asia, which he dubbed America after Amerigo Vespucci. Subsequent discoveries by Vasco Núñez de Balboa, who crossed the isthmus of Panama to reach the Pacific Ocean in 1513, and Ferdinand Magellan, who led an expedition to circumnavigate the globe in 1519, provided conclusive geographic evidence that Columbus had stumbled on a whole new world—but they also demonstrated the unfeasibility of sailing west to gain access to Asia. Columbus's arrival in the Caribbean had other revolutionary effects as well. The reconnection of the two hemispheres introduced new items and technologies into the New World, including iron, sailing ships, horses, and deadly diseases that caused epidemics among Indian tribes. American goods made the reverse trip, introducing Europeans to pineapples, corn, potatoes, and syphillis. However, it took another generation for the Spanish to find the material wealth for which they longed.

***Spanish Exploration and Conquest, pp. 12–28*** The early period of Spanish colonization in the New World (1492–1519) took place primarily in the Caribbean islands, where Spanish settlers enslaved local tribes and forced them to grow crops and mine the limited gold available. Far more enticing to the Spanish monarchs were rumors of great wealth to be had in the interiors of Mexico and Central and South America. The mainland phase of exploration, which began with Hernán Cortés's expedition into Mexico in 1519, lasted until about 1545.

**THE CONQUEST OF MEXICO** In 1519, Hernán Cortés, who would become the most famous conquistador of all, led an expedition of Spaniards from Cuba into Mexico in search of a rumored kingdom of fabulous wealth. Montezuma, the emperor of the Mexica, who had heard of Cortés's approach, became convinced that the Spaniard was the god Quetzalcoatl returning to the capital city Tenochtitlán and sent emissaries bearing gifts to meet the intruders. When the Spaniards finally reached Tenochtitlán in November of 1519, they took Montezuma hostage, hoping to use him as a puppet through whom they could rule. However, after the Spanish brutally massacred some Mexica nobles, the population revolted, killed Montezuma, and began a ferocious assault on the Spaniards. Cortés and his men fought their way out of the city, now determined to conquer Tenochtitlán. In the spring of 1521, with the support of tens of thousands of Indian allies, Cortés and his men besieged the city. Within two months they had completed the systematic looting and destruction of Tenochtitlán and the total subjugation of the Mexica people.

**THE SEARCH FOR OTHER MEXICOS** Urged on by an insatiable lust for gold, conquistadors moved out to search for other Mexicos. In the next few years, Francisco Pizarro brutally conquered the huge Inca empire in Peru, capturing a huge treasure of gold and silver. In the 1520s, Juan Ponce de León and Lucas Vásquez de Allyón led coastal expeditions north to Florida, the Gulf coast, and beyond as far as South Carolina. In the 1540s, Hernando de Soto and Francisco Vásquez de Coronado separately explored parts of the North American interior in search of gold. De Soto led his men on a brutal three-year march through the southeastern United States in search of riches but perished empty-handed along the Mississippi River in 1542. Coronado moved northward out of Mexico, traveling as far as Kansas in search of the legendary Seven Cities of Cíbola. After several years of wandering through the Southwest and Great Plains, he never located the fabulously rich cities. Juan Rodríguez de Cabrillo sailed along the coast of California; his men made it as far as Oregon but were forced to turn back by a storm. The expeditions of conquistadors like de Soto, Coronado, and many others convinced Spaniards that, although extensive land stretched northward from Mexico and Peru, its inhabitants had few riches worth pursuing.

**NEW SPAIN IN THE SIXTEENTH CENTURY** Spain dominated the New World in the sixteenth century. Spain's rivals, most notably England and France, could only sit back in envy at Spain's remarkable conquest of the Western Hemisphere. The Spanish created the colonial society of New Spain that provided other Europeans with an excellent example of how the New World could be exploited to serve the purposes of the Old.

After 1519, Cortés and the Spanish monarchy compensated Cortés's men by giving them Mexica towns rather than gold. This action established the system of *encomienda*, which gave the conquistadors the right to control the Indians and the lands surrounding the towns they were granted. In theory they were obliged to care for the Indians materially and spiritually. In practice, the *encomenderos* often mistreated the Indians, abusing and overworking them. The Catholic missionaries who sought to convert the Indians were guilty of similar maltreatment, especially when the Indians were not receptive to their message. One clergyman, Bartolomé de Las Casas, spoke out against the cruel treatment. The Spanish crown itself sought reform, though for a different reason: the desire to reduce the growing autonomy of the *encomenderos*. This they attempted in part through a reform of

1549 known as the *repartimiento*, which limited the labor an *encomendero* could require from his Indians. The *reparimiento* may have improved the lot of Indians slightly, but it could not alter the crucial fact that exploited Indian labor had now replaced gold as the most important New World treasure the Spaniards could plunder.

Throughout the sixteenth century, silver mining provided the most immense wealth to the Spanish empire. The mines were usually supervised by a handful of Spaniards and worked by Indians and later by enslaved Africans. The mining industry embodied the basic relationship between the colonists and Spain: the Indians worked for local Spanish bosses to produce silver for export to Spain, thus benefiting Spain, not the colony. New Spain had a rigid class and caste system. At the top were the *peninsulares*, individuals born in Spain, followed by the *criollos*, or creoles, offspring born in the Americas of Spanish parents. These two groups comprised only 1 or 2 percent of the population. Below them were the mestizos, people born of Spanish men and Indian women, and at the bottom of the social pyramid were the pure Indians, who made up the bulk of the population. This type of strict social stratification by race and origin would become common in European colonies throughout the New World.

**THE TOLL OF SPANISH CONQUEST AND COLONIZATION** Conquest and colonization of New Spain devastated Indian cultures. By 1560, the main centers of Indian civilization had been destroyed, and the remaining people completely subjugated. Adding to the culture shock of conquest was the deadly devastation wrought by European diseases, such as smallpox and measles, against which the Indians had no immunities. By 1570, the Indian population of New Spain had dropped to just 10 percent of what it had been prior to Columbus's arrival. Since the Indian deaths left New Spain with a shortage of laborers, the colonists began to import African slaves; in later centuries, the African slave trade would replace Indians as the major source of New World labor.

**NORTHERN OUTPOSTS IN FLORIDA AND NEW MEXICO** After the explorations of de Soto, Coronado, and others, North America was of little interest to Spanish officials. In the mid-sixteenth century, however, the Spanish monarchy ordered the establishment of a few settlements in North America to give reality to its claim over the area. Thus, in the latter half of the sixteenth century, the Spanish attempted to establish outposts along the vast Atlantic coastline but only one—St. Augustine, founded in Florida in 1565—proved viable. Sixteen hundred miles west of St. Augustine, another Spanish outpost was founded in 1598 by Juan de Oñate in New Mexico, but attempts there to establish more than one settlement also failed because of Indian revolts against Spanish rule. By the beginning of the seventeenth century, New Mexico was nothing more than a dusty symbol of Spanish claims to the North American Southwest.

***The New World and Europe, pp. 28–31*** The sixteenth century was considered the Golden Age of Spain. Using the vast wealth of New Spain, King Charles I fought dynastic and religious battles in Europe and used bribes to have himself selected as the Holy Roman Emperor Charles V. But still another challenge confronted the Catholic king in the form of Martin Luther and the Protestant Reformation.

**THE PROTESTANT REFORMATION AND THE EUROPEAN ORDER** In 1517, Martin Luther started the Protestant Reformation by publicizing his criticisms of the Catholic Church. Luther wanted to reform what he thought were unscriptural practices. He insisted that people did not need priests to interpret the Bible for them and that faith in God, not good works, was essential for salvation. Though Luther's ideas caught on quickly, the new theology faced a formidable adversary in Charles V, King of Spain and Holy Roman Emperor, who swore to commit all his efforts to extinguish the Protestant heresies.

**NEW WORLD TREASURE AND SPANISH AMBITIONS** New World wealth allowed Charles V and his son and successor, Philip II, to maintain Spanish supremacy throughout the sixteenth century. American treasure, however, encouraged the empire to pursue its great-power ambitions to a degree that ultimately caused the empire's ruin. The monarchy's incessant warfare ultimately outstripped even the seemingly inexhaustible New World revenues, bringing the Spanish empire to the brink of bankruptcy. Furthermore, to help finance their military ambitions, both kings continually raised taxes in Spain, thus further impoverishing the majority of Spain's peasant population, on whom the major tax burden fell. Ultimately, Spain's New World wealth proved a great short-term benefit but a long-term burden.

**EUROPE AND THE SPANISH EXAMPLE** Spain's example proved that a New World empire could make a major contribution to a nation's power and prestige in Europe. France and England tried to follow Spain's example. In 1524, France authorized Italian explorer Giovanni da Verrazano to sail westward. Verrazano searched the coast of North America from North Carolina to Canada for the fabled Northwest Passage to the East Indies. More important for later French claims, Jacques Cartier mounted expeditions to the St. Lawrence River area beginning in 1535 and established a colony in 1541 that survived only briefly. English attempts to establish North American settlements in the sixteenth century were no more successful. Sir Humphrey Gilbert led two expeditions in 1578 and 1583 to establish colonies in Newfoundland, until Gilbert himself disappeared at sea. In 1585, Sir Walter Raleigh explored the North Carolina coast and later sent a colony of over one hundred settlers to the island of Roanoke. When the next supply ship reached Roanoke, the colonists had disappeared mysteriously. Nothing was left except the word "Croatoan" carved on a tree.

## *Conclusion: The Legacy of the Sixteenth Century*

The establishment of the "Columbian exchange" became the most important legacy of the European presence in the New World. This exchange, initiated by the Spanish, saw the introduction into the New World of European "products" and especially diseases. The exchange also demonstrated another sixteenth-century event of momentous significance: after millions of years, the Atlantic Ocean no longer constituted an unbridgeable barrier separating the Eastern and Western Hemispheres. After almost a century of unchallenged dominion over the New World, the Spanish would find themselves having to contend with other European interlopers. In the seventeenth century, as Spain's new rivals began to challenge its hegemony and to make colonial forays of their own, they would have to learn how to differ from and improve on Spain's example.

## *Chronology Activity*

Read the annotated chronology, and answer the multiple-choice questions.

1415 Portugal conquers Cueta at the Strait of Gibraltar, gaining access to the western coast of Africa. This gave the Portuguese the basic, physical access to the ocean that they needed to begin their exploration of the African coast.

1444 Portuguese explorers reach Cape Verde.

1451 Columbus born in Genoa.

1480 Portuguese ships reach Congo.

1488 Bartolomeu Dias rounds Cape of Good Hope. This achievement was a major step in the establishment of the Portuguese East Indian empire. By rounding the southern tip of Africa, Dias proved that it was possible to sail around Africa and therefore to gain access to the Asian spice trade.

1492 Columbus lands on the Caribbean island that he names San Salvador. This contact represented the first meeting between the hemispheres in centuries. Although Columbus insisted to the end of his life that he had landed somewhere in Asia, it became apparent to other explorers that he had come across a previously unknown continent.

1493 Columbus makes second voyage to the New World.

1494 Portugal and Spain negotiate the Treaty of Tordesillas to divide the New World between them. This treaty gave Spain title to most of South America and protected Portugal's claim to its African trade route. It was indicative of the European attitude toward the New World — that Europeans could dispose of its land as they saw fit.

1497 John Cabot searches for Northwest Passage.

1498 Vasco da Gama sails to India. This was the culmination of Portuguese exploration of the coast of Africa. Vasco da Gama's trip accomplished what the Portuguese had hoped for all along: an ocean route to the Indies and Asia.

1500 Pedro Alvares Cabral makes landfall in Brazil.

1507 German mapmaker Waldseemüller names New World *America.*

1513 Vasco Núñez de Balboa crosses the isthmus of Panama.

1517 Protestant Reformation begins in Europe. The Protestant Reformation gave a religious motivation to exploration. Catholic leaders saw the Reformation as an assault on their own authority and sought New World converts and riches to uphold their position and religion.

1519 Hernán Cortés leads expedition to find and conquer Mexico. His success demonstrated that the New World contained more than people and crops: it harbored gold mines and immense material wealth. Cortés's victory over the Mexicans inspired a generation of conquistadors to search for another Tenochtitlán and catapulted the Spanish monarchy to a position of great power within Europe.

Ferdinand Magellan sets out to sail around the world. Magellan died in the Philippines, but his crew managed to reach Asia by means of sailing west. However, the enormous rate of casualties convinced most Europeans that the westward route was too long and dangerous to be profitable and that the wealth of the Americas was a better reason to sail that direction than access to the spice trade.

Charles I of Spain becomes Holy Roman Emperor Charles V.

1521 Cortés conquers the Mexica at Tenochtitlán.

Juan Ponce de León lands in Florida.

1524 Guatemala, El Salvador, and Nicaragua come under Spanish control.

1526 Lucas Vázquez de Allyón establishes San Miguel de Gualdape on Georgia coast.

1528 Pánfilo de Narváez leads expedition to survey the Gulf Coast from Florida to Texas.

1532 Francisco Pizarro begins conquest of Peru. Peru was the second Mexica empire for which other explorers had been searching in vain. The conquest of the Incan empire opened large silver mines to Spanish control and further increased the wealth of Spain.

1539 Hernando de Soto launches exploration of the Southeast.

1540 Francisco Vásquez de Coronado starts to explore the Southwest and Great Plains.

1542 Juan Rodríguez Cabrillo explores California coast.

1549 *Repartimiento* reforms begin to replace *encomienda.*

1565 Pedro Menéndez de Avilés establishes St. Augustine, Florida.

1587 English colonists settle Roanoke Island. The English colonizing experiment was a disaster: the colonists fought with local Indians and eventually disappeared entirely. It was a symbol of everything that could go wrong with New World settlements.

1598 Juan de Oñate leads expedition into New Mexico. This was one of the last Mexican attempts to find another wealthy empire in the inland of North America. All Oñate got for his labors was battles with Indians and the establishment of a dusty garrison town in New Mexico.

## *Chronology Questions* Choose the letter of the best answer.

1. Portugal gained access to the Strait of Gibraltar and to trade with the western coast of Africa in
   a. 1415.
   b. 1444.
   c. 1488.
   d. 1492.

2. What is the correct order for the following events?
   1. Portuguese explorers reached Cape Verde.
   2. Bartolomeu Dias rounded the Cape of Good Hope.
   3. Columbus lands on San Salvador.
   4. Cabral made a landfall in Brazil.

   a. 2, 3, 4, 1
   b. 4, 3, 1, 2
   c. 1, 2, 3, 4
   d. 3, 2, 4, 1

3. All of the following happened in 1519 except
   a. Cortés conquered Mexico.
   b. Magellan set out to sail around the globe.
   c. Da Gama sailed to India.
   d. Charles I of Spain became the Holy Roman Emperor.

4. What is the correct order for the following events?
   1. Pizarro defeated Peru.
   2. The English settled Roanoke Island.
   3. Oñate led an expedition into New Mexico.
   4. De Coronado explored the Southwest and the Great Plains.

   a. 1, 4, 3, 2
   b. 4, 3, 2, 1
   c. 1, 3, 2, 4
   d. 2, 4, 1, 3

5. Bartolomeu Dias rounded the Cape of Good Hope in
   a. 1480.
   b. 1492.
   c. 1497.
   d. 1500.

6. In 1497,
   a. Hernando de Soto explored the Southeast.
   b. Franciscan missionaries arrived in Mexico.
   c. Juan Ponce de León landed in Florida
   d. John Cabot searched for the Northwest Passage.

7. What is the correct order for the following events?
   1. Columbus landed in Venezuela.
   2. Columbus landed on San Salvador in the Caribbean.
   3. Balboa crossed the isthmus of Panama.
   4. Cabral made landfall in Brazil.

   a. 4, 2, 1, 3
   b. 3, 1, 4, 2
   c. 2, 4, 3, 1
   d. 2, 1, 4, 3

8. Portugal and Spain divided the New World with the Treaty of Tordesillas in
   a. 1444.
   b. 1494.
   c. 1517.
   d. 1540.

9. What is the correct order for the following events?
   1. *Repartimiento* reforms replaced the *encomienda* system.
   2. Cortés conquered the Aztec empire.
   3. Spanish exploration of the Great Plains began.
   4. Columbus landed in Venezuela.

   a. 4, 2, 3, 1
   b. 1, 2, 4, 3
   c. 2, 4, 3, 1
   d. 3, 4, 1, 2

10. The Protestant Reformation began in
    a. 1444.
    b. 1517.
    c. 1532.
    d. 1587.

***Defining Terms*** Match each term with the correct definition.

✓ Incan empire
✓ astrolabe
✓ *encomienda*
Cathay Company
✓ Martin Luther
✓ *portunlanos*
✓ Vasco da Gama
Jacques Cartier
✓ Amerigo Vespucci
✓ Columbian exchange
✓ quadrant
✓ East Indies
✓ royal fifth
✓ Ferdinand Magellan
✓ caravels
✓ Treaty of Tordesillas
✓ *criollo*
✓ Giovanni da Verrazano
Roanoke
✓ Hernán Cortés

1. A device for determining latitude, which helped set the stage for western exploration.
astrolabe

2. A device for determining latitude, which helped set the stage for western exploration.
quadrant

3. Charts that included detailed drawings of the shoreline and compass settings for sailing from one point to another. portunlanos

4. Small Portuguese ships that could carry enough supplies for a long sea voyage. caravels

5. The collective name for India, Indonesia, and China where Europeans traded for luxury items.
East Indies

6. This explorer commanded the first Portuguese fleet to sail to India. Vasco da Gama

7. The Spanish and the Portuguese negotiated this in 1494 to delineate their overseas holdings.
Treaty of Tordesillas

8. An Italian businessman and amateur geographer who accompanied a Spanish expedition to South America. The German cartographer Martin Waldseemüller named the New World in his honor. Amerigo Vespucci

9. Under the sponsorship of the King of Spain, this explorer set out to circumnavigate the globe in 1519. Ferdinand Magellan

10. The transatlantic exchange of goods, peoples, and ideas that began when Columbus arrived in the Caribbean, bringing the hemispheres together after centuries of separation. Columbian exchange.

11. The most famous Spanish conquistador, in 1519 he undertook an expedition mainland Mexico.
Hernan cortes

12. An empire spanning a region containing more than nine million people and stretching along the western coast of South America for two thousand miles. Incan empire

13. The Spanish crown's share of any wealth plundered by the conquistadors. This land and money catapulted the Spanish monarchy to a position of immense power in sixteenth-century Europe.
royal fifth

14. The system that gave entire towns and their inhabitants to individual conquistadors and their followers. encomienda

15. The Spanish root word for a term referring to the children who were born in the New World to parents who were Spanish immigrants to New Spain. Criollo

16. The Catholic priest who initiated the Protestant Reformation. Martin Luther

17. The explorer dispatched by the French to scout the Atlantic coast of North America for a Northwest Passage to the East Indies. Giovanni da Verrazano

18. The French explorer who made a voyage up the St. Lawrence River. Jacques Cartier

19. The English company that sponsored Martin Frobisher's attempt to find a Northwest Passage in Newfoundland. Cathay Company

20. England's first attempt at American colonization, located off the coast of North Carolina. Roanoke

## Chapter Review

***Multiple-Choice*** Choose the letter of the best answer.

1. The first European settlers in the New World were the
   a. Spanish.
   b. Portuguese.
   c. Norse.
   d. English.

2. Prior to the fifteenth century, luxury and exotic goods traveled to Europe
   a. by sea from Greece and Africa.
   b. overland from Persia, Asia Minor, India, and Africa.
   c. by river from central Europe.
   d. overland from Italy.

3. From the twelfth century through the fifteenth century, Mediterranean trade was dominated by
   a. Persia.
   b. Asia Minor.
   c. Italian cities.
   d. Africa.

4. In the late thirteenth century, Genoese ships carried goods from
   a. southern Europe to eastern Europe.
   b. southern Europe to northern Europe.
   c. northern Europe to southern Europe.
   d. eastern Europe to northern Europe.

5. A major reason for the increase in western exploration in the fifteenth century was
   a. the Black Death.
   b. a famine.
   c. financial depression.
   d. competition from non-European traders.

6. Explorers like Columbus hoped to
   a. be elevated to the aristocracy.
   b. convert natives to Christianity.
   c. expand human knowledge.
   d. eventually live abroad.

7. Astrolabes and quadrants were used to
   a. determine the lapse of time between hoisting sails and reaching maximum speed.
   b. estimate speed.
   c. determine latitude.
   d. map the shoreline.

8. The first Europeans to use new maritime technology to sail outside the limits of the known world were the
   a. Spanish.
   b. Italians.
   c. French.
   d. Portuguese

9. Prince Henry the Navigator was famous for
   a. advocating Portuguese expansion.
   b. inventing *portulanos.*
   c. sailing around the Cape of Good Hope.
   d. exploring Africa.

10. Traders were interested in Africa because of its
    a. size.
    b. wheat and gold.
    c. non-Christian population.
    d. climate.

11. The Portuguese discovered that the most profitable way to use Africa was to
    a. conquer areas violently.
    b. colonize inland territory.
    c. establish coastal trading posts.
    d. mine for their own gold.

12. By the early sixteenth century, the Portuguese controlled a major empire in
    a. Africa.
    b. Europe.
    c. the East Indies.
    d. South America.

13. Historically, Europeans were the most interested in traveling to the _____.
    a. east
    b. west
    c. north
    d. south

14. The ______ were the first known Europeans to settle in North America.
    a. Portuguese
    b. Spanish
    c. English
    d. Norse

15. From the ______ to the fifteenth century, luxury goods came into Europe from the east through Mediterranean trade routes.
    a. tenth century
    b. eleventh century
    c. twelfth century
    d. thirteenth century

16. The dissemination of information among literate Europeans was aided by the invention of _____.
    a. quadrants
    b. the postal service
    c. maps
    d. movable type

17. Major aids to ______ were developed in the fifteenth century.
    a. health problems
    b. church attendance
    c. shipbuilding
    d. navigation

18. The Portuguese and the Spanish cooperated in the _____, which expelled Muslims from the Iberian peninsula.
    a. peninsulares
    b. Reconquest
    c. geographical exploration of the world
    d. Crusades

19. The most influential advocate of Portuguese exploration was _____.
    a. Prince Henry the Navigator
    b. Bartolomeu Dias
    c. Vasco da Gama
    d. ordinary fishermen

20. The ______ enabled Portuguese sailors to round Cape Verde.
    a. support of the king
    b. invention of the compass
    c. caravel
    d. lure of wealth

21. In the 1460s, the Portuguese began using ______ on plantations in the Cape Verde islands.
    a. African gold
    b. ivory
    c. sugar
    d. slaves

22. The ______ developed new methods of sailing the ocean that allowed Christopher Columbus to make his voyage west.
    a. Spanish
    b. Genoese
    c. English
    d. Portuguese

23. Most Europeans adhered to the teachings of the Greek philosopher Ptolemy, who held that Asia could not be reached from the west because
    a. the Atlantic was too rough.
    b. the earth was too vast.
    c. the earth was flat.
    d. the Atlantic was filled with monsters.

24. Columbus's estimate of the circumference of the globe was off by
    a. 10 percent.
    b. 15 percent.
    c. 25 percent.
    d. 50 percent.

25. Columbus's initial journey was sponsored by the government of
    a. Genoa.
    b. Spain.
    c. Portugal.
    d. England.

26. Columbus and his men were disappointed by San Salvador because
    a. the native Tainos were hostile.
    b. the weather was too warm.
    c. it took too long to sail there.
    d. it was not filled with riches.

27. Columbus's first journey
    a. enriched the Spanish treasury.
    b. produced a shipload of spices.
    c. made Spain into a serious challenger of Portugal.
    d. was not very important.

28. Within thirty years of Columbus's discovery of San Salvador, Europeans understanding of ______ was revolutionized.
    a. agriculture
    b. world geography
    c. medicine
    d. metallurgy

29. King Henry VII of England funded a voyage to discovered a Northwest Passage to India under the leadership of
    a. Amerigo Vespucci.
    b. Pedro Alvars Cabral.
    c. John Cabot.
    d. Ferdinand Magellan.

30. The Portuguese explorer Pedro Alvars Cabral accidentally made a landfall at
    a. Mexico.
    b. Guatemala.
    c. Peru.
    d. Brazil.

31. In 1507, Martin Waldseemüller
    a. circumnavigated the globe.
    b. landed in Mexico.
    c. published a map showing the New World separate from Asia.
    d. found Venezuela.

32. In 1519, Ferdinand Magellan
    a. set out to circumnavigate the globe.
    b. died in the Philippines.
    c. marched over the isthmus of Panama.
    d. returned to Spain with a cargo of spices.

33. After Magellan's voyage, most Europeans who crossed the Atlantic
    a. intended to get to Asia.
    b. were geographers and cartographers.
    c. were headed for the New World.
    d. hoped to recreate Magellan's route.

34. Europeans procured a number of valuable items from the New World, including
    a. iron technology.
    b. corn and potatoes.
    c. horses.
    d. microorganisms.

35. Columbus believed he could reach Asia by sailing west because he rejected the teachings of _____.
    a. Henry the Navigator
    b. the Grand Khan of the Mongols
    c. Ptolemy
    d. Bartolomeu Moniz

36. Columbus believed that the earth was a sphere and that it was possible to reach the East Indies by sailing _____.
    a. north
    b. south
    c. east
    d. west

37. _____ granted to the Spanish all land discovered west of an imaginary line three hundred miles west of the Azores.
   a. Pope Alexander VI
   b. King Ferdinand
   c. Queen Isabella
   d. The Tainos

38. In 1493, Ferdinand and Isabella sent Columbus on a second journey west to locate _____.
   a. the men he had left behind
   b. South America
   c. new peoples
   d. mainland Asia

39. King Henry VII of England sent John Cabot to look for a northwest passage _____ in 1497.
   a. Newfoundland
   b. Brazil
   c. the Indies
   d. Venezuela

40. _____ was the first European to circumnavigate the globe.
   a. Ferdinand Magellan
   b. Vasco Núñez de Balboa
   c. Amerigo Vespucci
   d. Pedro Alvars Cabral

41. Magellan's voyage took him _____ and into the Pacific Ocean.
   a. across the isthmus of Panama
   b. around Cape Horn
   c. around the Cape of Good Hope
   d. through the Northwest Passage

42. After Magellan, most Europeans who sailed west were intending to go to _____.
   a. China
   b. India
   c. the New World
   d. Africa

43. The _____ exchange refers to the transatlantic exchange of goods, people, and ideas.
   a. Spanish
   b. Portuguese
   c. Columbian
   d. American

44. The most catastrophic aspect of the Columbian exchange was the introduction of _____ into the New World.
   a. horses
   b. microorganisms
   c. firearms
   d. iron technology

45. Initial Spanish ventures in the New World were _____.
   a. unprofitable
   b. somewhat profitable
   c. extremely profitable
   d. financially ruinous

46. Hernán Cortés was greatly aided in his search for the Aztec kingdom by the services of his translator _____.
   a. Quetzalcoatl
   b. Montezuma
   c. Tenochtitlán
   d. Malinali

47. Montezuma feared that the Spanish were led by the god _____, who was expected to return to Tenochtitlán.
   a. Quetzacoatl
   b. Marina
   c. Tlaxcala
   d. Maya

48. _____ was a "second Mexico" for the Spanish.
   a. Peru
   b. Guatemala
   c. El Salvador
   d. Nicaragua

49. _____ led a major Spanish expedition to find another Peru in North America.
   a. Marcos de Niza
   b. Hernando de Soto
   c. Francisco Vásquez de Coronado
   d. Juan Rodriguez Cabrillo

50. Francisco Vásquez de Coronado explored all the way from northern Mexico to _____ in search of treasure.
   a. central Kansas
   b. eastern Georgia
   c. southern Oregon
   d. northern Michigan

51. France and Europe were involved in ______ in the sixteenth century, giving the Spanish a monopoly over the New World and its development.
    a. Asian trade
    b. African trade
    c. European affairs
    d. financial schemes

52. The Spanish monarchy took ______ of everything confiscated by conquistadors.
    a. two-thirds
    b. one-half
    c. two-fifths
    d. one-fifth

53. Spanish ______ received the tribute towns had previously paid to the Mexican empire.
    a. conquistadors
    b. *encomenderos*
    c. bureaucrats
    d. royalty

54. Major ______ were discovered in Bolivia and Mexico in the 1540s.
    a. emerald mines
    b. diamond mines
    c. gold deposits

55. Prior to 1519, Spanish efforts to colonize the New World
    a. were very profitable.
    b. were moderately profitable.
    c. barely broke even.
    d. were a drain on the Spanish treasury.

56. When visiting Tenochtitlán, Hernán Cortés accepted Montezuma's hospitality and
    a. reciprocated.
    b. left Tenochtitlán peacefully.
    c. kidnapped his wife.
    d. captured him and held him hostage.

57. By 1524, Spain controlled all of the following except
    a. Brazil.
    b. Guatemala.
    c. El Salvador.
    d. Nicaragua.

58. The largest treasure produced by Spanish conquests in the New World came from
    a. Peru.
    b. Mexico.
    c. New Mexico.
    d. Cuba.

59. In 1539, Hernando de Soto led an expedition of six hundred men to find
    a. California.
    b. another Peruvian empire.
    c. missing Spaniards.
    d. better geographic information about North America.

60. The Spanish distributed lands to conquistadors through the system of
    a. the royal fifth.
    b. *repartimiento.*
    c. *peninsulares.*
    d. *encomienda.*

61. The most important treasure the Spanish plundered from their New World holdings was
    a. tobacco.
    b. gold.
    c. land.
    d. Indian labor.

62. One of the foremost critics of the Spanish treatment of Indians was
    a. Bartolomé de Las Casas.
    b. Bernadino de Sahagún.
    c. Juan Rodríguez de Cabrillo.
    d. Zacatecas.

63. Royal officials were disturbed by the brutal treatment of the *encomenderos* of Indians because
    a. it signaled the autonomy of the *encomenderos.*
    b. of their Christian scruples.
    c. the pope objected to it.
    d. it was a poor use of the labor force.

64. After 1540, the most important economic activity in New Spain was
    a. raising sugar.
    b. cattle ranching.
    c. gold mining.
    d. silver mining.

65. Society in New Spain was
    a. stratified by social origin and race.
    b. relatively egalitarian.
    c. identical to that of Spain.
    d. patterned on that of the native Indians.

66. When Indian labor dwindled, the Spanish began to import
    a. free laborers from Spain.
    b. indentured servants from Spain.
    c. African slaves.
    d. indentured servants from Africa.

67. In 1519, Charles I of Spain used the wealth of New Spain to
    a. decorate his court and lavish his wife with goods from Asia.
    b. finance expeditions to North America.
    c. invest in slavery in New Spain and San Salvador.
    d. finance his defense of the Catholic Church and fight dynastic battles.

68. Monarchs like Charles V were threatened by the Protestant Reformation because they believed that
    a. Luther's doctrines were immoral.
    b. Luther advocated the overthrow of kings and queens.
    c. the pope was infallible.
    d. the church spoke for God and they ruled for God.

69. According to Martin Luther, the only true source of information about God's will was
    a. the Bible.
    b. himself.
    c. the church.
    d. priests.

70. Luther intended to
    a. reform the church.
    b. cause a schism in the church.
    c. start a civil war.
    d. get rid of the pope.

71. Between 1527 and 1598, Spanish taxes
    a. decreased.
    b. increased somewhat.
    c. doubled.
    d. increased fivefold.

72. By the end of the sixteenth century, the Spanish monarchy spent two-thirds of its annual revenue on
    a. the military.
    b. exploration.
    c. interest payments.
    d. the church.

73. In the sixteenth century, European nations realized that colonization had given Spain
    a. a huge economic problem.
    b. power and prestige.
    c. steady economic growth.
    d. a complicated social structure.

74. The first French settlement in North America was
    a. Jacksonville, Florida.
    b. in northern Canada.
    c. along the St. Lawrence River.
    d. in Newfoundland.

75. The Cathay Company sent Martin Frobisher to the New World to
    a. fish off the coast of Newfoundland.
    b. take New Spain.
    c. explore the Southeast.
    d. open trade with China.

76. The English colonization of Roanoke Island was organized by
    a. Sir Walter Raleigh.
    b. Sir Humphrey Gilbert.
    c. John White.
    d. Martin Frobisher.

77. Who publicly challenged the authority of the Catholic Church in 1517?
    a. Holy Roman Emperor Charles V
    b. King Charles I
    c. Martin Luther
    d. Martin Frobisher

78. The New World commercial endeavors of which country proved to other European countries that this new land was a new arena for commerce?
    a. England
    b. Spain
    c. Portugal
    d. The Netherlands

79. The ______ century was Spain's Golden Age.
   a. fourteenth
   b. fifteenth
   c. sixteenth
   d. seventeenth

80. In 1519, Charles I of Spain used his New World wealth to secure his selection as Charles V of _____.
   a. France
   b. Germany
   c. Portugal
   d. the Holy Roman Empire

81. Martin Luther initiated the ______ in 1517.
   a. Holy Roman Empire
   b. Protestant Reformation
   c. Spanish Golden Age
   d. Counterreformation

82. Luther preached the doctrine of justification by _____.
   a. the Bible
   b. ritual
   c. the priesthood
   d. faith

83. Charles V pledged to ______ the new Protestant ideas.
   a. exterminate
   b. ignore
   c. tolerate
   d. actively support

84. The Spanish nobility was exempt from _____.
   a. military service
   b. taxation
   c. religious services
   d. debts

85. The territorial ambitions of the Spanish monarchy brought Spain close to _____.
   a. bankruptcy
   b. controlling southern Europe
   c. dominating the Asian market
   d. taking over the slave trade

86. Spain's example showed that a North American empire could make a large contribution to a nation's ______ in Europe.
   a. domestic happiness
   b. religious authority
   c. peaceful existence
   d. power and prestige

87. In 1564, French Huguenots established a settlement in Florida that was quickly destroyed by the _____.
   a. English
   b. Indians
   c. Spanish
   d. Italians

88. The English colonists at Roanoke intended to ______.
   a. convert Indians to Christianity
   b. return to England as soon as possible
   c. found a thriving settlement
   d. intermarry with local Indians

***Short Answer*** Write a paragraph response to each question.

1. What kind of trade routes existed in Europe between the twelfth century and the fifteenth century?
2. What factors encouraged Europeans to begin looking for new trade routes in the fifteenth century?
3. Why did the Portuguese play a key role in European exploration?
4. Why did Christopher Columbus believe that Asia could be reached easily by a westward route, and what was the significance of his voyage?
5. Did Columbus's initial discoveries live up to Spanish hopes and expectations? What was the value of his discoveries?
6. What impact did Columbus's journeys have on Europeans' understanding of the geography of the world?

7. On what land had Spain established settlement prior to Cortés's expedition to Mexico, and why did Cortés go to Mexico in 1519?
8. What methods did Spain use to rule its New World colonies in the sixteenth century?
9. Who settled New Spain, and what kind of social system did the colonists create?
10. How did Martin Luther initiate the Protestant Reformation? What doctrine did he preach, and how did it threaten the established church?
11. How did New World treasure affect the Spanish monarchy and people?
12. In the sixteenth century, what did France and England do to try to imitate Spanish colonization in the New World? Was either country as successful as Spain?

***Building Historical Skills*** Historians use a variety of sources to think and talk about the past, including maps, illustrations, and written records. Maps provide a variety of different kinds of comparative information in a condensed visual format; reading them requires learning how to sort through this information. To deepen our understanding of the past by supplementing written records, historians frequently interpret material culture, such as a vase or a painting, with techniques borrowed from art history, archaeology, or anthropology. Written records, though familiar as sources, raise their own problems of interpretation. Every document reflects someone's particular perspective or assumptions. It is the historian's task to carefully study and compare each document to other records with other perspectives. The following exercises introduce you to using maps, illustrations, and written documents as sources of information. Use these sources as well as the material in the chapter to think about different themes and topics discussed in the text.

***Map Activity*** Answer the following questions in a paragraph based on Map 1.2: European Explorations in Sixteenth-Century America on page 10.

**READING THE MAP** Which countries were most actively exploring the New World? Which countries were exploring later than others?

**CONNECTIONS** What were the motivations behind explorations? What were the motivations for colonization?

**WEB LINKS** To explore the topics discussed in the exercise above, visit the Web links noted below.

"European Voyages of Exploration"
http://hist.ucalgary.ca
Choose "Multimedia History Tutorials"

"1492: An Ongoing Voyage"
http://www.ibiblio.org/expo/1492.exhibit/Intro.html

***Visual Activity*** Huejotzingo Codex on page 15 in *The American Promise*, Second Edition, is a listing of the items the Nahua of Huejotzingo were forced to give to other Spanish conquistadors while their *encomendero* Cortés was visiting Spain. The objects in the upper left-hand corner represent the various sorts of grain the Nahua handed over as tribute. The round yellow disks stand for gold, which was mined in large quantities in central Mexico. The gold and the feathers at the top right-hand corner are related to the picture of the Madonna and child underneath. This is a depiction of a military banner the Spanish made for a campaign, using feathers and gold they exacted from the Nahua. The human figures depicting Nahua laborers are placed below both the crops and the banner and are depicted as hunched over. This seems like a pictoral rendition of the weight the Nahua carried as they worked to advance Spanish goals for which they likely had little sympathy.

Answer the following questions in a paragraph each based on Huejotzingo Codex.

**READING THE IMAGE** What does this image say about the relationship between the Spanish *encomenderos* and the Indians they conquered?

**CONNECTIONS** Why did the Spanish conquer the Mexican mainland? Does this image indicate that they found what they hoped they would?

**WEB LINKS** To explore the topics discussed in the exercise above, visit the Web links noted below.

http://lcweb.loc.gov/exhibits/treasures/tr00.html

http://marauder.millersv.edu/~columbus/data/art/KICZA-1.ART

http://www.bradley.edu/academics/las/his/His105/Reading.2

***Analyzing Sources Activity*** Answer the following questions in a paragraph based on "Documenting the American Promise: Justifying Conquest" on page 22 in *The American Promise,* Second Edition.

1. How did the *requerimiento* answer the criticisms of Montecino? According to the *requerimiento,* why was conquest justified? What was the source of Indian resistance to conquest?
2. What arguments might a critic like Montecino have used to respond to the *requerimiento*'s justification of conquest? What arguments might the Mexican leader Montezuma have made against those of the *requerimiento*?
3. Was the *requerimiento* a faithful expression or a cynical violation of the Spaniard's Christian faith?

**WEB LINKS** To explore the topics discussed in the exercise above, visit the Web links noted below.

"Religious Orders, the Indians, and the Conquest"
http://marauder.millersv.edu/~columbus/data/art/
Choose "HARO-01.ART"

"Bartolomé de Las Casas and the Tradition of Medieval Law"
http://www.maxwell.syr.edu/maxpages/classes/His381/LasCasas2.html

"Modern History Sourcebook: An Aztec Account of the Conquest of Mexico"
http://www.fordham.edu/halsall/mod/aztecs1.html

"World History Chronology"
http://campus.northpark.edu/history//WebChron/Americas/Cortes.htm

# Answer Key

## Chapter 1: Europeans and the New World, 1492–1600

### *Chapter Overview*

#### *Chronology*

1. a
2. c
3. c
4. c
5. a
6. d
7. d
8. b
9. a
10. b

#### *Defining Terms*

1. astrolabe or quadrant
2. quadrant or astrolabe
3. *portunlanos*
4. caravels
5. East Indies
6. Vasco da Gama
7. Treaty of Tordesillas
8. Amerigo Vespucci
9. Ferdinand Magellan
10. Columbian exchange
11. Hernán Cortés
12. Incan empire
13. royal fifth
14. *encomienda*
15. criollo
16. Martin Luther
17. Giovanni da Verrazano
18. Jacques Cartier
19. Cathay Company
20. Roanoke

### *Chapter Review*

#### *Multiple-Choice*

1. c
2. b
3. c
4. b
5. a
6. a
7. c
8. d
9. a
10. b
11. c
12. c
13. a
14. d
15. c
16. d
17. d
18. b
19. a
20. c
21. d
22. d
23. b
24. c
25. a
26. d
27. c
28. b
29. c
30. d
31. c
32. a
33. c
34. b
35. c
36. d
37. a
38. d
39. c
40. a
41. b
42. c
43. c
44. b
45. c
46. d
47. a
48. a
49. b
50. d
51. d
52. a
53. a
54. d
55. a
56. c
57. a
58. d
59. a
60. a
61. b
62. a
63. c
64. d
65. b
66. d
67. d
68. d
69. a
70. a
71. d
72. c
73. b
74. c
75. d
76. a
77. c
78. b
79. c
80. d
81. b
82. d
83. a
84. b
85. a
86. d
87. c
88. c

#### *Short Answer*

1. Exotic goods like spices, silk, carpets, ivory, and gold were the primary focus of European trade between the twelfth and fifteenth centuries. These traveled overland from Persia, Asia Minor, India, and Africa and then were dispersed throughout

Europe by means of Mediterranean trade routes. Italian merchants and bankers dominated the trade and were willing to fight to protect their monopoly. In the late thirteenth century, Genoese merchants began to ship goods to northern Europe by sailing through the Strait of Gibraltar and sailing up the Atlantic coastline, a route that allowed them to carry larger quantities less expensively than the overland route permitted.

2. There were a number of factors that encouraged Europeans to look for new ways to travel to the East in the fifteenth century. The bubonic plague of the mid-fourteenth century killed about a third of the European population, giving survivors greater chances for social advancement and creating a willingness to take risks in return for large rewards. Monarchs hoped to increase the size of their lands and increase the number of taxable subjects under their rule. Ambitious nonnobles hoped that they could gain entrance into the aristocracy as a reward for their exploits. Finally, technological advances helped as well, as new navigational aids like compasses, hourglasses, the astrolobes, and the quadrant made it easier for sailors to keep track of their location even on the open ocean.
3. Located on the western tip of Europe, Portugal had excellent access to the Atlantic and the Mediterranean. In 1415, Portugal expelled Muslims from the Strait of Gibraltar, which gave traders access to the Atlantic coast of Africa. At the same time, Prince Henry the Navigator, the son of the Portuguese king, took an active interest in exploration, collecting up-to-date information about sailing techniques and geography in the hopes of spreading Christianity and finding new sources of trade. The Portuguese developed a type of ship called a caravel, which could store enough supplies for long periods at sea. These factors provided Portugal with the financial and technical means to round the southern tip of Africa and eventually reach India by sea.
4. Christopher Columbus believed—incorrectly—that Asia lay about 2,500 miles away from the edge of Europe, which was a shorter distance from Europe than Lisbon was from southern Africa. He did not realize that the voyage was actually 11,000 miles or that North and South America existed. His voyages were important because they led to the discovery of the Americas, even though Columbus himself never acknowledged that he had found a New World.
5. Initially, the Spanish monarchy was disappointed by Columbus's discoveries. The crown wanted to find either access to the Asian spice trade or large quantities of gold and silver. Their first New World holdings provided neither. The real value of the New World for the first generation that knew of it was the stimulation of geographical knowledge and the Columbian exchange, which provided Europeans with new crops like corn, potatoes, and pineapples.
6. Within about thirty years, Columbus's discovery of the New World had radically altered Europeans' understanding of world geography, although it took a great deal of additional exploration to make the magnitude of his find clear. Columbus believed that he was exploring the outer reaches of Asia. However, by 1500, it was clear that there were several large chunks of land in the western Atlantic, and in 1507 the German cartographer Martin Waldseemüller published the first map showing the New World separate from Asia. In 1513, his speculation was confirmed when Núñez de Balboa crossed the isthmus of Panama and reached the Pacific Ocean, demonstrating that more water lay between the New World and Asia. In 1519, Ferdinand Magellan showed just how much water when he attempted to circumnavigate the globe.
7. During the early sixteenth century, Spain had surveyed the Caribbean, scouted stretches of the mainland coast of South America, and established settlements on Hispaniola, Puerto Rico, Jamaica, and Cuba. None of these outposts provided the wealth the Spanish had hoped for. Hernán Cortés went into Mexico in 1519 to find riches. Only recently had Europeans determined that this land mass was not Asia but an entirely different continent. Spain and Cortés both were eager to make claims on the riches rumored to be there.
8. Initially, the Spanish crown used the *encomienda* system to distribute land to conquistadors. A conquistador, the *encomendero*, would be given control of a town and its inhabitants, who would be forced to work for their new owners. However, Catholic missionaries disliked the system because it was brutal and therefore hindered conversions, and the monarchy felt that it gave too much autonomy to the *encomenderos*. To regain control, in 1549, Spain instituted a reform called the *repartimiento*, which limited the amount of labor an *encomendero* could demand to forty-five days per year from each adult male.
9. About 225,000 Spaniards settled in New Spain over the course of the sixteenth century, most of whom were poor commoners. Because few Spanish women migrated, many Spanish men married Indian women. The highest social status was given to Spanish natives, called *peninsulares*; below them were creoles, who were the New World children of Spanish couples; and below them were the mestizos, the offspring of Spanish men and Indian women. Indians were at the bottom of the social heap. All in all, the society of

New Spain was stratified by class and race, with Europeans of any social origin considered superior to Indians.

10. In 1517, Martin Luther began the Protestant Reformation by publicizing his criticisms of the Catholic Church. He believed in the doctrine of justification by faith, which held that individuals could obtain salvation only by having faith that God would save them. Luther charged that the Catholic Church fraudulently claimed that priests were necessary for salvation, that it had neglected its proper role of helping individual Christians understand faith as it was revealed in the Bible, and that it wasted its resources interfering in the worldly realm of wars and politics. Luther hoped that he could reform the church. However, the church did not take kindly to his criticisms, which undermined its power and influence.
11. The Spanish monarchy did not employ the riches of New Spain wisely. For the most part, Spanish kings used the gold and silver they mined to pursue expensive European wars. This resulted in higher taxes for ordinary Spaniards: nobles were exempt from taxation, so the burden fell primarily on peasants. When taxes did not provide enough money for military adventures, the Spanish crown turned to loans from European bankers and by the end of the sixteenth century paid out two-thirds of its annual revenue on interest.
12. In 1524, the French sent Giovanni da Verrazano to look for a Northwest Passage on the Atlantic coast of North America. Nothing came of the trip, but in 1535 they funded Jacques Cartier's expedition up the St. Lawrence River, where they tried to establish a colony in 1541. Neither that colony nor a later one in Florida survived. In 1576, the English also searched unsuccessfully for a Northwest Passage around Newfoundland. They tried to establish colonies in Newfoundland and on Roanoke Island, none of which lasted for long. Neither the French nor the English were able to find the wealth that Spain had in Mexico and Peru.

### *Map Activity*

Reading the Map: Spain, England, and France were the most active in exploring the New World. Spain was the most dynamic, sending explorers over much of the North American southwest, the Caribbean islands, Central America, and the western seaboard of South America. Spain was also the earliest, beginning its journeys in 1492. England and France started much later. England's first voyage was in 1497, but it did little more until Gilbert's trip to Labrador in 1583. France's first expedition was in 1524.

Connections: Most European nations ventured overseas because they were interested in increased trading opportunities with Asia and incidentally in converting people to Christianity. When it became clear that the land mass Columbus discovered was not Asia but was in fact an obstacle between Europe and Asia, Europeans began to look at what goods the Americas had to offer. After the discovery of rich gold and silver mines in Central and South America, Spain colonized its holdings to exploit the natural resources its adventurers found. Other European nations colonized in hopes of finding wealth of their own.

### *Visual Activity*

Reading the Image: This image shows that the Spanish *encomenderos* saw the Indians as a source of commodities. They wanted the gold the Indians mined, the crops they grew, the textiles they wove, and the labor they could contribute to Spanish commercial enterprises. There is no sign in this image that the Indians were seen as the proper possessors of the results of their hard work. Instead, they are used as slave labor and beaten down by the task of producing for the Spanish.

Connections: The Spanish hoped to find riches in Mexico. It is clear from the image that they did: the drawing of the gold, crops, and goods that the Nahua provided make that obvious. They also saw their possessions as a way to increase their martial might, as can be seen from the military banner. Yet the banner also demonstrates the religious motivations behind the conquest. The picture is, ironically, of the Madonna and Child, indicating both the Spanish belief that God was protecting them and their desire to spread Christianity among peoples they considered heathens.

### *Analyzing Sources*

1. The *requerimiento* denied the basis of Montecino's case—that Indians had committed no crimes against the Spanish—by arguing that the Indians failed to concede the Spaniards their rights as conquerors and to convert to Christianity. The *requerimiento* justified conquest on the basis of papal grants. Because Christianity was the only valid faith, Indians had a responsibility to accept it and the rulers who imposed it on them. According to the logic of the *requerimiento,* Indians resisted because they did not accept God or papal or Spanish authority.
2. Montecino might have argued that Indians could not possibly have understood the sovereignty of the Christian God and his representatives on earth. He could also have pointed out that

slaughtering and enslaving Indians was not a good way to convince them that the god of the Spanish was a benign and merciful one; or, for that matter, that the Spanish monarchs were concerned about the welfare, spiritual or physical, of the Indians they conquered.

Montezuma could have argued that Indians did not accept the authority of the pope or the Spanish monarchy, since they had lived for centuries without knowing of either. Montezuma could have said that it was hardly the pope's place to give away territory he had never owned himself. He might have argued that it was ridiculous for the Spanish to expect Indians to submit tamely to Spanish declarations of domination, since most of them could not understand the language in which the *requerimiento* was made. Beyond that, he could have pointed to the warlike behavior of the Spanish, which did little to bolster their claims that Indians might theoretically be left in peace.

3. Likely there were elements of both in the Spanish attitude. Certainly, the Spanish believed that they had a responsibility to convert the peoples they encountered. However, they also wanted access to Indian land and labor, and that gave them an investment in interpreting Indian behavior as signs of resistance, which could be punished. The delivery of the *requirimiento*, in Spanish and with armed soldiers standing guard, cannot have done much to assuage Indian fears of the new Spanish regime.

CHAPTER

# 2 THE SOUTHERN COLONIES IN THE SEVENTEENTH CENTURY, 1601–1700

## Chapter Overview

### *Chapter Summary*

***Introduction*** This chapter begins with a description of Captain John Smith's capture by the warriors of Powhatan, the chief of about fourteen thousand Algonquian peoples who lived along the coast of Virginia. Smith believed that Powhatan had been ready to kill him by smashing his head between two rocks but that he was fortuitously saved by Powhatan's daughter, Pocahontas. However, it is far more likely that she was playing a part in a ceremony designed to express Powhatan's power of life and death. In the century after 1607, however, Powhatan's people would be decimated by English settlers and their diseases. Powhatan's world of hunters and gatherers would be replaced by one of settlers with weapons, tools, and ideas foreign to the Native Americans.

***An English Colony on the Chesapeake, pp. 40–45*** Impressed by Spain's successes in the New World, by 1600 King James I of England was eager to establish colonies of his own in North America. Though colonization was an expensive and risky undertaking, Spain's example had shown how profitable it could be. Thus, in 1606, the king granted a charter to the Virginia Company of London, a joint stock company of adventurers, authorizing their occupation of over six million acres in North America. These men and other proponents of colonization hoped settlements would benefit the empire, both by yielding goods and by providing a convenient destination for masses of unemployed English people.

**THE FRAGILE JAMESTOWN SETTLEMENT** In December 1606, 144 Englishmen sailed for Virginia aboard three ships. In May 1607, the 105 survivors of the journey put ashore on a small peninsula in the James River, about sixty miles in from the coast in the heart of Powhatan's chiefdom. They hastily built a fort as protection from the Indians and named the settlement Jamestown. The settlers soon discovered that disease and famine were greater killers than the Indians' spears and arrows. Despite Powhatan's overtures and John Smith's forays to trade with the

Indians, by January 1608, only 38 of the original settlers were alive to welcome the Virginia Company's supply ships and new colonists. Although the Virginia Company sent hundreds of new settlers each year to Jamestown, few survived these early years.

**ENCOUNTERS BETWEEN NATIVES AND NEWCOMERS** Given the colonists' vulnerability, it is perhaps surprising that Powhatan did not attack Jamestown and drive the English out of the Chesapeake. Several factors probably contributed to his hesitation. The Indians were impressed by the English God, which they felt must be very powerful, and even more by English goods. They were eager to trade corn to get these valuable items. Moreover, Powhatan and his *werowances* probably concluded that such powerful strangers would make better allies than enemies. Despite receiving food from the Indians, Jamestown failed to thrive not only because of the settlers' weakened physical condition but because the majority were gentlemen and their servants, who considered cultivating the land beneath them. Nevertheless, over time, the colony slowly expanded. Its continued existence changed Indian society, introducing new tensions over resources. After fifteen years of an uneasy truce, in 1622, Opechancanough, Powhatan's brother, launched an all-out assault on the colony, killing 347 settlers, nearly one-third of the English population. The attack failed to drive the English out. From this point on, the colonists no longer deemed the Indians necessary for their survival; instead, they concluded that their settlement's existence depended on the destruction of all Indians in the vicinity.

**FROM PRIVATE COMPANY TO ROYAL GOVERNMENT** The shocking mortality rate and evidence of mismanagement led to the Virginia Company's dissolution in 1624, and Virginia became a royal colony governed directly by the crown. The king now appointed the governor, but most features of local government established under the company remained in effect, such as the House of Burgesses, first convened in 1619. By 1624, it was evident that English settlers were in Virginia to stay: new settlers were still arriving, the crown was committed to the colony, and steady progress was being made in the cultivation of tobacco.

***A Tobacco Society, pp. 45–52*** In 1612, John Rolfe's experiments with West Indian tobacco seeds showed that the plant could be cultivated successfully in Virginia. The first shipment of Virginia-grown tobacco arrived in England in 1617 and sold for a handsome price. Ironically, the same Virginia colonists who could not or would not grow food for themselves quickly learned how to harvest as much tobacco as possible. Tobacco cultivation proved a crucial turning point for the Virginia colony, as the crop changed the aimless settlers into a community of dedicated planters.

**TOBACCO AGRICULTURE** Tobacco was a demanding crop requiring close year-round attention and intensive hand labor. Primitive tools and methods made the labor cycle even more difficult. English settlers, however, were willing to work hard because they could expect to do much better in the Chesapeake than in England. A hired laborer in a Virginia tobacco field earned in one year what it took his counterpart in England to earn in two to three. More important, land was so plentiful in Virginia that even laborers could hope to obtain it. New settlers to the area who paid their own passage received fifty acres of free land known as a *headright*. This policy, begun by the Virginia Company, was continued by the royal government to attract settlers.

**A SERVANT LABOR SYSTEM** The seventeenth-century Chesapeake was fundamentally a servant society, with about 80 percent of new arrivals working as indentured servants. Although headrights, cheap and abundant land, and relatively high wages enticed many poor English folk to immigrate to the New World, many would-be colonists did not have enough money to pay for their voyage across the Atlantic. As indentured servants, English workers contracted their labor for a period of four to seven years in return for passage to Virginia and the chance to acquire land and wealth. As many as 40 percent of the indentured servants died before their servitude ended, but those who survived were likely to acquire their own farms. More than two-thirds of the servants were young, unskilled males between the ages of fifteen and twenty-five. Many were orphans. Women were rare, and indentured servitude perpetuated this gender imbalance. Although female servants cost about the same as males and generally served for the same length of time, only about one servant in four was a woman because employers preferred men for field work. Servant life was very harsh by the standards of England and the Chesapeake. Servants had no control over who purchased their labor and could be sold from owner to owner. Laws often stretched the period of indenture, punishing servants who ran away or female servants who got pregnant with additional time on their contract. Given the shortage of other kinds of workers, masters had little choice but to rely on indentured servants.

***The Evolution of Chesapeake Society, pp. 52–59*** Tobacco cultivation propelled the evolution of Chesapeake society. The demands of tobacco agriculture dictated settlement patterns, transforming the Chesapeake colonial landscape into something very different from rural England. The varying degrees of success among tobacco growers created a hierarchical society, in which wealth and status among colonists were quite disparate. Social stratification led to political polarization that climaxed in 1676 with Bacon's Rebellion. Amid this political and social change, tobacco cultivation remained a constant.

**LIFE, FAITH, AND LABOR** Settlement in the Chesapeake was determined by the demands of tobacco. Settlements were dispersed; because tobacco exhausted the land quickly, farms consisted of cultivated land surrounded by virgin forest. Moreover, planters preferred land on navigable rivers to ease the transporting and loading of the tobacco. Houses were serviceable but not grand, the average being a four-hundred-square-foot, two-room box. Most Chesapeake settlers were nominally Protestants, but few were very observant. They preferred blood sports, games of chance, and good tobacco crops. Even the colony of Maryland, which was intended as a haven for persecuted English Catholics, devoted more attention to tobacco cultivation than religion.

Until midcentury, societal divisions in the Chesapeake were less between rich and poor planters than between free farmers and indentured servants, and a rough frontier equality characterized free families. After 1650, however, three developments contributed to a growing social polarization. First, tobacco prices declined as production increased, making it more difficult for freed servants to save enough to become landowners. Second, as the mortality rate of freed servants decreased, the number of freedmen seeking land increased. Finally, the drop in mortality also contributed to a rising planter elite class whose members were living longer, acquiring more land, and making more money. By the 1670s, Chesapeake society had become polarized: Landowners—the planter elite and the more numerous yeoman farmers—comprised one group; landless settlers, mostly freed servants, comprised the other. Each group looked on the other with mistrust.

**GOVERNMENT, POLITICS, AND POLARIZATION** In general, government and politics intensified rather than reduced socioeconomic distinctions. Discrepant laws governed masters and servants: masters were largely exempt from punishment for brutalizing their servants, while servants suffered harsh reprisals for the slightest transgressions. Moreover, the planter elite dominated the government, from membership in the House of Burgesses to the governor's council. In the late seventeenth century, the franchise became more restricted, voting limited to landowners and householders. Colonial officials not only administered government but profited from it as well, especially through revenue collecting. Beginning in 1660, the Navigation Act allowed the crown to extract revenue from the Chesapeake, and subsequent acts would be applied to other colonies as well. These measures were designed to give English merchants, shippers, and even seamen a monopoly on the colonial import trade. The acts reflected English mercantilist assumptions—the idea that the colonies existed to benefit the mother country. Hierarchy and stratification defined not only the relationship between king and colonies but also that between the planter and the lower classes. The severity of this order was mitigated by the expectation among both rulers and subjects that government was to be administered for the good of the commonweal. Chesapeake rebels did not challenge inequality and hierarchy but rather rose up when they believed their rulers failed to govern for the benefit of all.

**BACON'S REBELLION** In 1676, Bacon's Rebellion erupted as a dispute over Indian policy. Opechancanough, the chief who had led the Indian uprising of 1622, had attacked again in 1655. In two years of bitter fighting, colonists captured and killed him and forced the Indians to relinquish all claims to land already settled by the English. The wilderness beyond English settlement was reserved for exclusive Indian use. But as the Chesapeake population grew, the land-hungry poor pushed beyond the treaty limits and encroached on Indian land. Violence between and Indians erupted. The government tried to maintain the peace, but frontier settlers, led by the ambitious Nathaniel Bacon wanted revenge. They saw the colonial government, headed by William Berkeley, as corrupt officials and as much their enemies as the Indians.

Nathaniel Bacon was part of the elite. However, he was outside the inner circle of established planters. He insisted that Berkeley allow him to lead an army against the Indians. Berkeley refused and called for elections, which Bacon and his supporters swept. They passed Bacon's Laws, giving local settlers a greater voice in the government and cracking down on corruption. Berkeley authorized Bacon's campaign of frontier warfare and then changed his mind. Bacon declared war on Berkeley and the other Chesapeake "grandees." Bacon's forces routed Berkeley's, burned Jamestown, and caused Berkeley's flight from the colony. The rebellion ended suddenly when Bacon died of dysentery. Bacon had not intended to overturn the hierarchy. Instead, he challenged the ruthless and callous exploitation of the many "outsiders" by the few "insiders." After Bacon's Rebellion, political stability slowly returned to the Chesapeake. Improving economic conditions in England in the late seventeenth century led to the decline of indentured servitude and a concomitant decrease in the number of poor newly freed servants. By 1700, the Chesapeake was changing from a system of predominantly white indentured servitude to a system of African slave labor; this minimized the differences between plain folk and rich planters and, instead, magnified the differences between whites and blacks.

***Toward a Slave Labor System, pp. 59–65*** African slavery was introduced into the New World by the Spanish and Portuguese during the sixteenth century. In the seventeenth century, West Indian English planters followed the Iberian example and developed sugar plantations with slave labor. However, in English North America, African slavery was not adopted until the last quarter of the seventeenth century. Beginning in the 1670s, slavery slowly made its way out of the English Caribbean, and by the end of the century, slave labor systems were found in the Chesapeake as well as in Carolina.

**THE WEST INDIES: SUGAR AND SLAVERY** England's most profitable seventeenth-century colonies were not found on the North American mainland but in the Caribbean. English planters developed a profitable sugarcane industry, which by the end of the century exported nearly fifty million pounds a year to the mother country. Sugar plantations demanded a large initial investment, driving poor farmers from the island in search of better opportunities. The planters' immense profits came from the sweat and toil of African slaves. By 1700, the island of Barbados was literally a slave society controlled by white men. The plantation regime was extremely brutal for slaves, who were often worked to death. Although sugar plantations did not develop on the North American mainland, the Indies nonetheless exerted a powerful influence on the development of slavery in North America.

**CAROLINA: A WEST INDIAN FRONTIER** In 1663, a Barbadian planter named John Colleton and seven other men obtained a charter from King Charles II to colonize the region south of Virginia. The proprietors planned to siphon settlers from Barbados and other colonies and encourage them to develop an export crop. They established a permanent English beachhead in the southern part of the colony at Charles Towne (later Charleston) in 1670. The Barbadian immigrants brought their slaves with them, thus establishing African slavery in South Carolina from its inception. During the first generation of the colony, Carolina served primarily as an economic colony of Barbados, exporting everything from livestock to timber back to the island. In the mid-1690s, the colonists hit upon a hardy strain of rice that thrived in the region, and rice would be the industry that dominated Carolina in the future.

**THE CHESAPEAKE: TOBACCO AND SLAVES** By 1700, more than eight out of ten people in England's mainland southern colonies lived in the Chesapeake, and one out of eight was black. In 1650 slavery was still a relatively minor institution in Virginia and Maryland, but beginning in the 1670s, tobacco planters began a transition from servant to slave labor that portended slavery's full adoption and institutionalization in the American South. Africans were favored over indentured servants as laborers for a number of reasons. First, since they and their descendants were slaves for life, they constituted a potentially never-ending and self-perpetuating labor supply for planters. Also, since the majority of slaves purchased by Chesapeake planters in the seventeenth century came from the West Indies, they were already "seasoned," accustomed to their slave status, and perhaps knew some English as well. Furthermore, unlike indentured servants, African slaves could be controlled politically. Whereas servants came to the Chesapeake with expectations of eventual liberty and ownership of land, slaves had no hope of attaining the privileges of freedom. Unlike the previous divided between landless colonists on the one hand and planter elites and yeoman planters on the other hand, this change from a servant to a slave labor system polarized Chesapeake society along lines of race and status. Although there were still large economic differences among whites, the rights enjoyed by poorer white farmers made them feel that they too had a stake in the existence of slavery, even if they could not afford to own slaves themselves.

***Conclusion: Status and Race in the Southern Colonies*** By the end of the seventeenth century, the English colonies of Virginia, Maryland, and Carolina were firmly established in North America, producing staples such as tobacco for export. Export crops made a handful of colonists wealthy and provided a livelihood for many. Southern colonial society differed significantly from that of England, yet the colonists considered themselves English subjects, claiming the rights and privileges of English citizens. The English believed themselves superior to Indians and Africans; thus colonists did not hesitate to deny these groups the same rights and privileges. The English colonies differed from New Spain as well. The Chesapeake did not harbor gold or silver mines, and the *encomienda* system did not develop because Indians were too few and too hostile toward each other to organize effectively. However, the Chesapeake developed its own system of forced labor and racial distinctions. Only a remnant of Powhatan's powerful confederation existed by 1700. The English colonists were in North America to stay.

***Chronology Activity*** Read the annotated chronology, and answer the multiple-choice questions.

1588 England defeats Spanish Armada. This achievement helped convince England's King James I that it would be possible to colonize parts of North America that Spain claimed, as long as English settlement was located outside the major centers of Spanish population.

1606 Virginia Company of London receives royal charter to establish colony in North America.

1607 English colonists found Jamestown settlement; Pocahontas "rescues" John Smith.

1609 Starvation plagues Jamestown. The winter of 1609 nearly marked the end of the Jamestown settlement, as settlers who had neglected to grow their own food crops died in large numbers of hunger and disease.

1612 John Rolfe begins to plant tobacco in Virginia. Tobacco was the profitable export crop that transformed Virginia from a shaky society of adventurers to an established one of dedicated tobacco planters.

1617 First commercial tobacco shipment leaves Virginia for England. Although tobacco had not figured in the Virginia Company's original plans, the high price fetched by the first shipment to England was pivotal in turning Virginia into a society of dedicated tobacco planters.

Pocahontas dies in England.

1618 Powhatan dies, and Opechancanough becomes supreme chief.

1619 First Africans arrive in Virginia. The twenty Africans who came to Virginia in 1619 remained a distinct minority until the last quarter of the seventeenth century, when African slavery began to replace the servant labor system.

House of Burgesses begins to meet in Virginia. This was the first representative assembly in the British colonies, and it had a broader and more representative constituency than did its English counterpart.

1622 Opechancanough leads Indian uprising against Virginia colonists. Opechancanough's campaign to dislodge the settlers came close to destroying the Virginia colony. A third of the settlers died over the course of the conflict, and the event sparked a royal investigation into the affairs of the Virginia Company of London. Evidence of widespread mismanagement led to the king's revocation of the company's charter.

1624 Virginia becomes royal colony.

1632 King Charles I grants Lord Baltimore land for colony of Maryland.

1634 Colonists begin to arrive in Maryland. Although the colony was intended to be a haven for Catholics, the population grew slowly, and most of the settlers were Protestants. Like Virginia, most of the settlers were more interested in tobacco cultivation than spiritual concerns.

1644 Opechancanough leads Indian uprising against Virginia colonists. Opechancanough's second major attack led to two years of bitter fighting, during which the English captured and murdered Opechancanough and gained the upper hand. The treaty that resulted from the Indians' defeat set policies toward Indians that the government tried to maintain for the next thirty years, pushing Indians beyond the fringe of English settlement.

1660 Navigation Act requires colonial tobacco to be shipped to English ports and to be assessed customs tax. This act was representative of the mercantalist assumptions about the colonies: that what was good for England should determine policies toward the colonies.

1663 Carolina proprietors receive charter from King Charles II for Carolina colony. Carolina was unusual in that it was settled by people from another colony—Barbados—who were used to having slaves and consciously intended to recreate a slave society on mainland North America.

1670 Charles Towne, South Carolina, founded. Slave labor system emerges first in Carolina and more gradually in Chesapeake colonies. The spread of the slave labor system eventually shifted the main political concern of the Chesapeake from controlling the discontent poor white population to keeping slaves subjugated to whites.

1676 Bacon's Rebellion convulses Virginia. Bacon's Rebellion crystallized the grievances of landless former servants against the Virginia government. After the rebellion was suppressed, the English government strengthened the position of the Virginia elite, and the elite themselves relied more and more on what they saw as safer slave labor.

## *Chronology Questions* Choose the letter of the best answer.

1. The Navigation Act requiring colonial tobacco to be shipped to English ports and to be assessed customs tax was passed in
   a. 1607.
   b. 1618.
   c. 1634.
   d. 1660.

2. In 1622
   a. English colonists founded the Jamestown settlement.
   b. Opechancanough led an Indian uprising against Virginia colonists.
   c. King Charles I granted Lord Baltimore land for colony of Maryland.
   d. John Rolfe planted tobacco in Virginia.

3. Bacon's Rebellion broke out in
   a. 1612.
   b. 1624.
   c. 1644.
   d. 1676.

4. What is the correct order for the following events?
   1. England defeats the Spanish Armada.
   2. Virginia becomes a royal colony.
   3. English colonists found Jamestown.
   4. Opechancanough leads an Indian uprising against Virginia colonists.

   a. 1, 3, 2, 4
   b. 3, 2, 4, 1
   c. 4, 1, 2, 3
   d. 2, 3, 1, 4

5. What is the correct order for the following events?
   1. A slave labor system emerges first in Carolina and then more gradually in the Chesapeake colonies.
   2. John Rolfe begins to plant tobacco in Virginia.
   3. The first Africans arrive in Virginia.
   4. Carolina proprietors receive a charter from King Charles II.

   a. 2, 3, 4, 1
   b. 1, 2, 3, 4
   c. 4, 2, 1, 3
   d. 3, 4, 2, 1

6. Charles Towne, South Carolina, was founded in
   a. 1606.
   b. 1619.
   c. 1644.
   d. 1670.

7. What is the correct order for the following events?
   1. The first commercial tobacco shipment leaves Virginia for England.
   2. The Navigation Act is passed.
   3. Starvation plagues Jamestown.
   4. Colonists begin to arrive in Maryland.
   a. 4, 3, 1, 2
   b. 3, 1, 4, 2
   c. 2, 4, 3, 1
   d. 3, 1, 2, 4

8. The Virginia Company of London received its royal charter in
   a. 1606.
   b. 1612.
   c. 1618.
   d. 1622.

9. What is the correct order for the following events?
   1. Pocahontas "rescues" John Smith.
   2. Powhatan dies.
   3. Virginia becomes a royal colony.
   4. Opechancanough leads an Indian uprising against Virginia colonists.
   a. 4, 1, 3, 2
   b. 2, 4, 3, 1
   c. 1, 4, 2, 3
   d. 1, 2, 4, 3

10. England defeated the Spanish Armada in
   a. 1588.
   b. 1606.
   c. 1622.
   d. 1632.

## *Defining Terms* Match each term with the correct definition.

✓ John Colleton
✓ Richard Hakluyt
✓ yeoman planter
✓ tobacco
✓ Bacon's Laws
✓ indenture
✓ freedom dues
✓ servant labor system
✓ headright
going abroad
✓ Opechancanough
✓ Barbados
✓ seasoning
✓ grandees
✓ free status
✓ Lord Baltimore
✓ Powhatan
✓ Navigation Acts
✓ joint stock company
✓ House of Burgesses

1. A way for English merchants to pool capital and share risks in trading voyages and colonial ventures. joint stock company

2. An English proponent of colonization who argued that colonization would provide an outlet for the poor, a source of goods, and a market for England. Richard Hakluyt

3. Algonquian chief who headed a confederacy of tribes in the Chesapeake region. During this time, the colonists depended on the Indians'corn for food, which the Indians traded for European goods, including iron and steel. Powhatan

4. Powhatan's brother. He replaced Powhatan as supreme chief after Powhatan's death in 1618 and shortly thereafter led an all-out assault on the English settlers in an attempt to prevent the colony from becoming a permanent settlement. From then on, most colonists considered Indians their perpetual enemies. Opechancanough

5. Virginia's assembly, which was elected by the colony's inhabitants. This was the first representative assembly in the British colonies, although the laws proposed had to be approved first by the Virginia Company and later by the king's bureaucrats in England. House of Burgesses

6. Land given to free settlers to encourage migration to the Chesapeake. head right

7. A contract in which poor immigrants traded four to seven years of labor in exchange for passage to the colonies and food and shelter once they were there. indenture

8. The payment, usually of corn and clothes, that a colonial employer was obligated to give an indentured servant on the expiration of his or her contract. freedom dues

9. A type of labor in which employers rely on paid employees rather than family labor or slaves. In seventeenth-century Chesapeake, servants were usually indentured or unfree for a limited amount of time, and their payment was the cost of passage, food, and shelter, not cash wages. Servant labor system

10. This plant provided the economic underpinning of the Chesapeake economy and determined patterns of settlement and the social structure of the region. tobacco

11. In 1632, Charles I gave this Catholic friend six and a half million acres in the Chesapeake region, which he used to establish the colony of Maryland. Lord Baltimore

12. A farmer who owned a small plot of land sufficient to support a family and tilled largely by family members and perhaps a few servants. Yeoman Planter

13. Legislation passed in England in the 1650s and 1660s. These laws required that colonial goods had to be shipped through British ports on British ships to funnel trade into the hands of English merchants, shippers, and seamen. Navigation Acts

14. The elite planters who dominated Virginia's economy and government. They were greatly resented by ordinary Virginians, who felt that they operated the government for their own benefit and ignored the needs and concerns of the poor. grandees

15. Laws passed in Virginia in June of 1676, giving local settlers more power over the government and controlling the ability of officeholders from using their positions for personal gain. Bacon's laws

16. A small island in the West Indies, which became the most profitable part of the British New World empire as the result of a flourishing sugar industry. Barbados

17. The Barbadian planter who, along with seven other men, founded Carolina, the first colony on mainland North America to rely extensively on slave labor. John Colleton

18. The privileges of poor white farmers in Chesapeake society. This status included owning property, marrying, having families, bequeathing property and freedom to descendants, moving and associating with others freely, serving on juries, voting, and holding political office. free status

19. In reference to African slaves, a term that means acclimation to the natural environment of the New World and the repressive confines of slavery. Chesapeake planters tended to purchase slaves from the West Indies, where they had already adjusted to their status and learned some English. Seasoning

20. African slaves' practice of seeking out the company of other slaves on neighboring plantations. This was a source of difficulty for masters because slaves might go from innocent socializing to planning to run away or rebel. going abroad

## Chapter Review

***Multiple-Choice*** Choose the letter of the best answer.

1. The first English monarch to seriously consider settling North America was
   a. King James I.
   b. Queen Elizabeth I.
   c. King Philip II.
   d. Emperor Charles V.

2. The Virginia Company of London was a
   a. group of settlers.
   b. bank.
   c. tobacco-importing firm.
   d. joint stock company.

3. Richard Hakluyt argued that colonies would give the English
   a. international prestige.
   b. an outlet for poor laborers.
   c. a place to send criminals.
   d. gold and silver mines.

4. Investors in the Virginia Company of London hoped to
   a. convert Indians to Christianity.
   b. contribute to the wealth of the English crown.
   c. make quick profits.
   d. raise cash crops.

5. When the English first settled in Jamestown, they faced strong resistance from the
   a. local Indians.
   b. Spanish.
   c. French.
   d. Portuguese.

6. The greatest threats the English settlers faced were from
   a. disease and starvation.
   b. disease and Indians.
   c. starvation and Indians.
   d. starvation and the climate.

7. When Indians did not want to trade for corn with Captain John Smith, he
   a. negotiated with them.
   b. paid them in gold.
   c. took hostages or killed them.
   d. begged.

8. Powhatan and his people were suspicious of English intentions because they
   a. bullied Indians to make them follow English norms.
   b. converted Indians to Christianity.
   c. intermarried with Indian women.
   d. adopted Indian children.

9. During the early years of the Virginia colony, most of the settlers were
   a. gentlemen.
   b. artisans.
   c. laborers.
   d. farmers.

10. In March of 1622, an all-out assault on English settlers in Virginia was organized by
    a. Opechancanough.
    b. Powhatan.
    c. the Spanish army.
    d. the Algonquian.

11. The 1622 uprising prompted
    a. most of the remaining settlers to leave Virginia.
    b. the Virginia Company of London to invest more money in the settlement.
    c. the Virginia Company of London to improve its management practices.
    d. a royal investigation of affairs in Virginia.

12. Under royal government in Virginia, all free adult men could vote for
    a. members of Parliament.
    b. taxation measures.
    c. the colony's governor.
    d. local burgesses.

13. English merchants used _____ to pool capital and share risks in trading voyages to Europe, Africa, and Asia.
    a. banks
    b. the royal treasury
    c. Italian financiers
    d. joint stock companies

14. James I's charter giving the Virginia Company of London over six million acres of land was in effect a royal license to poach on _____ claims.
    a. Portuguese
    b. Algonquian
    c. French
    d. Spanish

15. The first building the Jamestown settlers built was a _____.
    a. church
    b. government house
    c. fort
    d. house

16. After repeated skirmishes with settlers, Powhatan _____ the Jamestown settlement.
    a. traded with
    b. fought with
    c. invaded
    d. made peace with

17. Settlers sent _____ to trade for corn with Indian tribes upriver from Jamestown.
    a. Captain John Smith
    b. George Percy
    c. Powhatan
    d. Pocahontas

18. All of our information about Chesapeake Indians comes from _____.
    a. oral histories
    b. the Spanish
    c. Indian records
    d. distorted English sources

19. Indians traded _____ for European goods like iron and steel weapons and tools.
    a. women
    b. protection
    c. labor
    d. corn

20. The 1622 Indian uprising killed _____ of the English population of Jamestown.
    a. very little
    b. a sixth
    c. a third
    d. all

21. In 1624, King James revoked the charter of the Virginia Company and made Virginia _____.
    a. an autonomous region
    b. self-governing
    c. the possession of Lord Baltimore
    d. a royal colony.

22. The House of Burgesses was _____ Virginia's inhabitants.
    a. imposed on
    b. drawn by lot from
    c. elected by
    d. irrelevant to

23. In 1612, John Rolfe
    a. married Pocahontas.
    b. planted the first West Indian tobacco seeds.
    c. saved Jamestown from extinction.
    d. was captured by Powhatan.

24. English settlers in the Chesapeake worked hard in their tobacco fields because they were
    a. bored.
    b. expecting better financial returns than they could get in England.
    c. forced to by investors.
    d. forced to by the king.

25. Initially, poor English people did not go to the Chesapeake in large numbers because
    a. it was mostly used as a penal colony.
    b. the land was too expensive.
    c. they were afraid of Indians.
    d. they could not afford the fare to sail across the Atlantic.

26. The seventeenth-century Chesapeake was fundamentally a society of
    a. servants.
    b. slaves.
    c. free farmers.
    d. aristocrats.

27. The cost of passage from England to the Chesapeake was about £5, or the equivalent of an English servant or laborer's
    a. week's wages.
    b. month's wages.
    c. year's wages.
    d. lifetime earnings.

28. After serving his or her indenture, an employer was required to give a servant
    a. freedom dues.
    b. free land.
    c. a share of the master's crop.
    d. nothing.

29. Most indentured servants were
    a. female.
    b. skilled craftsmen.
    c. men between thirty-five and forty-five.
    d. men between fifteen and twenty-five.

30. In 1622, an official of the Virginia Company wrote that Chesapeake plantations would not flourish until
    a. slaves were imported in large numbers.
    b. there were enough women to establish families.
    c. there were more indentured servants.
    d. more money was invested in it.

31. A servant in the Chesapeake was
    a. bound to a single master for the whole period of indenture.
    b. subject to being sold.
    c. able to request a new master.
    d. treated like a member of the family.

32. Female servants were prohibited from
    a. working in the fields.
    b. working while pregnant.
    c. marrying.
    d. owning land.

33. Masters in the Chesapeake were so hungry for labor that they
    a. did not hesitate to devise legal ways to keep servants under their control.
    b. convinced England to send convicts over for long-term servitude.
    c. captured Indians and forced them to work.
    d. bought up small farmers' land, forcing the farmers to work for them.

34. In the Chesapeake, masters could not easily hire free men and women because they chose to
    a. live in idleness.
    b. hire themselves out to farmers.
    c. work as domestic servants.
    d. work their own land.

35. The first commercial shipment of _____ left Virginia in 1617.
    a. cotton
    b. tobacco
    c. sugar
    d. furs

36. English settlers expected to _____ in Virginia than they could in England.
    a. receive a better education
    (b.) earn more money
    c. create a better society
    d. worship more freely

37. About 80 percent of immigrants to the Chesapeake during the seventeenth century were _____.
    a. slaves
    b. gentlemen
    (c.) indentured servants
    d. free laborers

38. Servants under indenture usually worked _____ without pay.
    a. six months
    b. one two two years
    c. two to three years
    (d.) four to seven years

39. The biggest risk to planters was that servants would _____before serving out the term of indenture.
    a. marry
    b. run away
    c. return to England
    (d.) get sick and die

40. Most indentured servants had some experience with _____.
    a. carpentry
    b. iron working
    (c.) agricultural work
    d. tailoring

41. Female servants did _____.
    a. field work
    b. not have indentures as long as men
    (c.) household work
    d. not have to serve indentures if they married

42. Some Englishmen were alarmed by the colonial practice of treating servants like _____.
    (a.) property
    b. family members
    c. equals
    d. royalty

43. Women servants were not allowed to _____.
    a. work in the fields
    (b.) get married
    c. eat with masters
    d. become free unless they were married

44. Masters did not hesitate to devise legal ways to _____ the period of servitude.
    a. ease
    (b.) extend
    c. shorten
    d. protect

45. Tobacco cultivation resulted in the absence of
    (a.) community life.
    b. religious sentiment.
    c. food crops.
    d. family life.

46. Ideally, a tobacco planter wanted land that
    a. faced the wilderness.
    (b.) fronted a navigable river.
    c. was near other planters.
    d. had already been used for a tobacco farm.

47. Maryland was intended as a haven for
    a. Protestants.
    (b.) Catholics.
    c. criminals.
    d. farmers.

48. Until the middle of the seventeenth century, the principal social division in the Chesapeake was between
    a. servants and slaves.
    b. rich and poor planters.
    (c.) free farmers and unfree servants.
    d. the English and the Indians.

49. The decline in the price of tobacco in the third quarter of the seventeenth century contributed to the
    (a.) end of the rough equality of the Chesapeake population.
    b. stability of the rough equality of the Chesapeake population.
    c. increase in the number of servants surviving their indenture.
    d. bankruptcy of the Virginia Company of London.

50. Indentured servants in the Chesapeake believed that the local government
    a. treated them fairly.
    b. promoted their interests.
    c. favored the interest of masters.
    d. taxed them unreasonably.

51. After 1670, voting for the Virginia House of Burgesses was open to
    a. landowners and householders.
    b. every free white male.
    c. every free white male over twenty-one.
    d. English royalty.

52. The Navigation Act of 1660 required that all colonial products be sent
    a. anywhere they were wanted.
    b. only to European ports.
    c. only to colonial destinations.
    d. only to English ports.

53. During the 1660s and 1670s, violence between settlers and Indians increased because
    a. Indians wanted to regain their old land.
    b. the local government encouraged it.
    c. settlers were encroaching on Indian land.
    d. the king wanted to control more territory.

54. Bacon's Laws were not intended to
    a. limit the holding of multiple offices.
    b. give settlers a voice in tax levies.
    c. restore the vote to all freemen.
    d. overturn property rights.

55. Ultimately, Bacon's Rebellion
    a. removed Indians from Virginia.
    b. strengthened the position of freemen.
    c. overturned the power of elite planters.
    d. strengthened the position of elite planters.

56. The most important contribution to the renewal of stability in the Chesapeake was
    a. King James's reforms in the aftermath of Bacon's Rebellion.
    b. the declining importance of the servant labor system.
    c. the decimation of the Indian population.
    d. increasing prosperity.

57. Farmers needed a great deal of land to farm tobacco because it _____.
    a. quickly exhausted the soil's fertility
    b. needed a great deal of room to grow
    c. took a very long time to mature
    d. was so extensive to grow that it had to be planted in excess.

58. Arrangements for marketing tobacco contributed to the _____ of settlements.
    a. density
    b. dispersion
    c. seacoast location
    d. inland location

59. In 1632, King Charles II granted his friend _____ about six and a half million acres in the Chesapeake region.
    a. Lord Baltimore
    b. Captain John Smith
    c. Richard Hakluyt
    d. Lord Thomas Culpepper

60. Most Chesapeake colonists were nominally Protestant, but their daily lives _____.
    a. did not involve religion
    b. often included cutting timber for building new churches
    c. reflected their extreme piety
    d. often included trying to convert Indians

61. A declining rate of mortality led to the formation of a _____ in the Chesapeake.
    a. large class of yeoman farmers
    b. democratic government
    c. large class of merchants
    d. planter elite

62. In the 1670s, when planters viewed the landless as dangerous, the governor's council did not like to _____ masters who brutalized their servants.
    a. grant land to
    b. support
    c. censure
    d. execute

63. In 1670, the House of Burgesses limited voting rights to landowners to limit _____ political rights.
  a. slaves'
  b. servants'
  c. Catholics'
  d. freemen's

64. In 1676, Bacon's Rebellion erupted as a dispute over _____.
  a. taxation
  b. slavery
  c. Indian policy
  d. the Navigation Act of 1660

65. A _____ required all colonial exports to go to British ports.
  a. Navigation Act
  b. House of Burgesses decision
  c. group of planter elites
  d. group of new merchant settlers

66. After Bacon's Rebellion, _____ replaced Berkeley with a new governor.
  a. the voters
  b. the king personally
  c. royal officials
  d. Bacon's supporters

67. In the seventeenth century, the most profitable part of the British New World empire was in
  a. Virginia.
  b. Maryland.
  c. the Caribbean.
  d. Newfoundland.

68. The sugar industry transformed the British Caribbean by
  a. encouraging the migration of indentured servants.
  b. leading to massive revolts.
  c. driving out poor farmers.
  d. reducing the population to penury.

69. By 1700, three-quarters of the population of Barbados consisted of
  a. black slaves.
  b. white servants.
  c. free white farmers.
  d. Indians.

70. In Barbados, the slave population grew because of the
  a. rate of reproduction among slaves.
  b. number of Africans purchased by Caribbean plantation owners.
  c. purchase of West Indians as slaves.
  d. import of slaves from North America.

71. Barbadian John Colleton established the colony of
  a. Carolina.
  b. Roanoke.
  c. Maryland.
  d. Virginia.

72. The first profitable export crop grown in Carolina was
  a. tobacco.
  b. cotton.
  c. indigo.
  d. rice.

73. In 1700, one out of eight people in the Chesapeake was
  a. English.
  b. Indian.
  c. African.
  d. a servant.

74. By 1700, an advantage of slave labor over servant labor was that
  a. the initial cost of obtaining slaves was lower than indenturing servants.
  b. servants had a high death rate.
  c. slaves never went out of bondage.
  d. servants could run away more easily than slaves.

75. The slave labor system polarized Chesapeake society along the lines of
  a. slaveowning status.
  b. wealth.
  c. race.
  d. education.

76. In contrast to Barbados, slaves in the seventeenth-century Chesapeake
  a. had to work hard.
  b. experienced constant exposure to white surveillance.
  c. did not suffer mistreatment.
  d. were permitted to keep their children.

77. Most of the slaves purchased by Chesapeake planters in the seventeenth century came from
    a. the West Indies.
    b. Africa.
    c. Carolina.
    d. England.

78. Planters did not like, but permitted, slaves'
    a. working with white servants.
    b. visiting other plantations.
    c. having children.
    d. having close contact with masters.

79. By the middle of the seventeenth century, exports of _____ from the British Caribbean totaled about 150,000 pounds.
    a. sugar
    b. tobacco
    c. corn
    d. olives

80. The average sugar baron in Barbados in 1680 owned 115 _____.
    a. pigs
    b. acres of land
    c. indentured servants
    d. African slaves

81. The _____ exerted a powerful influence on the development of slavery in the mainland colonies.
    a. Spanish
    b. English
    c. Portuguese
    d. West Indies

82. John Colleton and the proprietors of Carolina hoped to develop a _____.
    a. gold mining industry
    b. fur trade
    c. society of gentlemen
    d. profitable export crop

83. English officials associated Carolina with _____.
    a. Santo Domingo
    b. Barbados
    c. London
    d. the Chesapeake

84. Slaves cost _____ servants.
    a. the same as
    b. slightly more than
    c. three to five times more than
    d. ten times more than

85. The emerging slave labor system _____ economic differences among whites.
    a. did not affect
    b. lessened
    c. increased
    d. got rid of

86. By 1700, more than three-quarters of white families in the Chesapeake _____.
    a. owned slaves
    b. did not own slaves
    c. had indentured servants
    d. owned their own land

87. African slaves and _____ performed the same tasks on tobacco plantations, working side by side in the fields.
    a. masters
    b. Indians
    c. yeomen
    d. white servants

88. By 1700, the most pressing political issue in the Chesapeake was _____.
    a. the decline in tobacco production
    b. keeping small farmers from rebelling
    c. nurturing the resurgence of the servant labor system
    d. nurturing the growing slave labor system

***Short Answer*** Write a paragraph response to each question.

1. What were the primary threats to the survival of the Jamestown colony?
2. For what reasons did the Powhatan and his Algonquian confederacy refrain from eliminating the Jamestown colony while it was in a weakened condition?
3. Why did James I revoke the Virginia Company of London's charter? What were the results of the reorganization?

4. What made tobacco such a demanding crop? Why were colonists in the Chesapeake willing to devote the effort to growing it?
5. What factors encouraged the development of the indenture system in the Chesapeake?
6. Describe the conditions of the indentured servant system. What were the additional risks for women?
7. How did tobacco cultivation shape the settlement of the Chesapeake?
8. How did the structure of the government amplify inequality between masters and slaves in the Chesapeake?
9. What issues sparked Bacon's Rebellion?
10. How did the development of the sugar industry transform the social structure of Barbados?
11. In what way was the colony of Carolina a West Indian frontier?
12. What caused planters in the Chesapeake to shift from a servant labor system to a slave labor system?

***Building Historical Skills*** Historians use a variety of sources to think and talk about the past, including maps, illustrations, and written records. Maps provide a variety of different kinds of comparative information in a condensed visual format; reading them requires learning how to sort through this information. To deepen our understanding of the past by supplementing written records, historians frequently interpret material culture, such as a vase or a painting, with techniques borrowed from art history, archaeology, or anthropology. Written records, though familiar as sources, raise their own problems of interpretation. Every document reflects someone's particular perspective or assumptions. It is the historian's task to study and compare each document to other records with other perspectives. The following exercises introduce you to using maps, illustrations, and written documents as sources of information. Use these sources as well as the material in the chapter to think about different themes and topics discussed in the text.

***Map Activity*** Locate the following places on Map 2.2: The West Indies and Carolina in the Seventeenth Century on page 60 in *The American Promise*, Second Edition.

1. Charles Towne
2. Barbados
3. Virginia
4. James River
5. the West Indies
6. the Carolina Grant

Answer the following questions in a paragraph based on Map 2.2: The West Indies and Carolina in the Seventeenth Century.

**READING THE MAP** Locate English colonies in America and English holdings in the Caribbean.

**CONNECTIONS** Why were colonists in Carolina so interested in Barbados? What goods did they export? Describe the relationship between Carolina and Barbados in 1700.

**WEB LINKS** To explore the topics discussed in the exercise above, visit the Web links noted below.

"South Carolina Colonial Maps"
http://www.sciway.net/hist/maps/mapscolonial.html

"The Abbreviated History of Barbados"
http://www.barbados.org/history1.htm

***Visual Activity*** "Secotan Village" on page 39 of *The American Promise*, Second Edition, is an engraving based on a drawing by John White, one of the English explorers of the island of Roanoke. It shows the layout of an Indian village called Secotan, located along the coast of North Carolina. This picture highlights the village practices of the coastal Indians of the sixteenth and seventeenth centuries. The houses in the middle part of the engraving are clustered together, demonstrating a close-knit society. The fields are located around the perimeter of the houses, a model not unlike the one that was common in England but that was abandoned by English migrants to the Chesapeake. Indians are shown eating together, an indication of the communal practices that were typical of the area's tribes. Indians are portrayed hunting deer in the upper left hand side of the image, which shows that they lived on a combination of agriculture and hunting. Their worship, while apparently sex-segregated, is undertaken in a group as well: two separate companies of men are kneeling, while a third dances around in a circle. There are no forts or fences in the engraving, a sign that the inhabitants of the village did not fear outside attack.

Answer the following questions in a paragraph based on "Secotan Village."

**READING THE IMAGE** What does this image say about Indian life in Secotan?

**CONNECTIONS** How did Indian society differ from the English tobacco society that emerged later?

**WEB LINKS** To explore the topics discussed in the exercise above, visit the Web links noted below.

"Close Encounters of the First Kind, 1585–1767"
http://www.mdarchives.state.md.us/msa/stagser/S1259/121/4198/html/0000/html
Choose "Guide to Documents" and then "MSA SC 2221-17-3."

"John White"
http://www.nps.gov/
Choose "Search," type in "John White," and select the first option, "John White."

***Analyzing Sources Activity*** Answer the following questions in a paragraph based on "Historical Question: Why Did English Colonists Consider Themselves Superior to Indians and Africans?" on page 54 of *The American Promise*, Second Edition.

1. What kinds of words did the English use to describe Indians, and what did the terms imply about English attitudes?
2. How did the English view of Africans differ from their view of Indians?
3. What kinds of social hierarchies did the Chesapeake colonists construct to differentiate servants, slaves, and freemen?

**WEB LINKS** To explore the topics discussed in the exercise above, visit the Web links noted below.

"Introduction to Colonial African-American Life"
http://www.history.org/people/african/aaintro.htm

"The Roots of American Slavery"
http://www.stratfordhall.org/schwarz.htm

"Jamestown 16071630"
http://ab.mec.edu/jamestown/jamestown.html

# Answer Key

## Chapter 2: The Southern Colonies in the Seventeenth Century, 1601–1700

### *Chapter Overview*

#### *Chronology*

1. d
2. b
3. d
4. a
5. a
6. d
7. b
8. a
9. d
10. a

#### *Defining Terms*

1. joint stock company
2. Richard Hakluyt
3. Powhatan
4. Opechancanough
5. House of Burgesses
6. headright
7. indenture
8. freedom dues
9. servant labor system
10. tobacco
11. Lord Baltimore
12. yeoman planter
13. Navigation Acts
14. grandees
15. Bacon's Laws
16. Barbados
17. John Colleton
18. free status
19. seasoning
20. going abroad

### *Chapter Review*

#### *Multiple-Choice*

1. a
2. d
3. b
4. c
5. a
6. a
7. c
8. a
9. a
10. a
11. d
12. d
13. d
14. d
15. c
16. d
17. a
18. d
19. c
20. c
21. d
22. c
23. b
24. b
25. d
26. a
27. c
28. a
29. d
30. b
31. b
32. c,
33. a
34. d
35. b
36. b
37. c
38. d
39. d
40. c
41. c
42. a
43. b
44. b
45. a
46. b
47. b
48. c
49. a
50. c
51. a
52. d
53. c
54. d
55. d
56. b
57. a
58. b
59. a
60. a
61. d
62. c
63. d
64. c
65. a
66. c
67. c
68. c
69. a
70. b
71. a
72. d
73. c
74. c
75. c
76. a
77. b
78. b
79. a
80. d
81. d
82. d
83. b
84. c
85. c
86. b
87. d
88. d

#### *Short Answer*

1. Colonists at Jamestown faced three major threats: the local Indians, hunger, and disease. Although James I had given the Virginia Company of London millions of acres of Virginia, the settlers discovered on their first night in North America

that the local Algonquian Indians were prepared to defend their own claim to the land. More dangerous was the fact that settlers did not plant their own food, causing them to rely on Indians, sources for grain. Although they were able to barter for, or sometimes steal, corn, many starved to death as a result. Others died of diseases.

2. The Algonquian Indians were very suspicious of the English because they found their new neighbors both friendly and willing to use superior weapons to force Indians to trade for food. The Algonquian did not organize an all-out assault on Jamestown for fifteen years, probably for several reasons. For one thing, they were impressed by the power of the Christian God. For another, they likely concluded that they could benefit from an alliance with the English; Powhatan's own dominance over regional tribes was strengthened by his relationship with the English, which provided him access to superior European iron and steel weapons and tools.
3. The near-success of an Indian uprising in 1622 caused James I to launch a royal investigation of affairs in Virginia. The investigators discovered that the high death rate among colonists was caused by disease and mismanagement rather than Indian raids, prompting James I to revoke the Virginia Company's charter and make Virginia a royal colony. Although the shift made the colony subject to royal law rather than that of the investors, Virginia retained most of the features of local government that had been established under the Virginia Company. The king appointed the governor and his council, but colonists retained the right to elect the Council of Burgesses, a representative assembly that proposed local laws.
4. Tobacco was an unusually difficult plant to grow because it required close attention and hand labor year-round. When one crop was being readied for market, the next needed to be in the ground already; and food crops had to be planted and tended during the tobacco crop cycle, which left little time for leisure. However, English colonists were willing to work hard to reap the benefits of tobacco—a better living than they could hope to achieve in England. In the Chesapeake, a hired man could earn in a year what would take him two or three years in England. Land was so abundant and cheap that it was relatively easy for ordinary workers to save money and purchase farms of their own.
5. Poor English people had many incentives to migrate to the Chesapeake, including headrights, affordable land, and high wages caused by the extreme shortage of labor in the colonies. It was not easy for the poor to get to the Chesapeake, however. Passage across the Atlantic cost about a year's wage for servants or laborers. An indenture allowed a potential immigrant to sell his or her ability to work for the cost of transportation; and planters were willing to pay twice the cost of transportation to a contract broker to get more hands to grow tobacco.
6. The indentured servant system was quite harsh, even by the rough standards of the Chesapeake: servants could not choose an employer, they could be bought and sold throughout the period of indenture, the work was very demanding, and servants had little control over the conditions under which they labored. Employers used the law to extend the period of servitude, causing punishments for petty crimes like running away or stealing food to add as much as six extra years to a servant's indenture. Women faced special risks: they could not marry while indentured but were often pressured into sexual relationships. Pregnancy and childbirth added a fine and extra time to a woman's service.
7. Tobacco farms disrupted the patterns of community life to which settlers had been accustomed. In England, people clustered together in villages and small towns that were surrounded by fields, but tobacco did not accommodate itself to that type of settlement. Instead, colonists spread out. A tobacco farm demanded a total of five to ten acres under cultivation. However, it exhausted the fertility of the soil rapidly, causing farmers to buy far more land than they initially needed, contributing to a dispersed pattern of settlement. Tobacco farmers also wanted to settle along navigable rivers, adding to the dispersal.
8. The most vital social distinction in seventeenth-century Chesapeake was between masters and servants. The governor's council protected masters who abused their servants by refusing to punish them but responded harshly to servants who disobeyed their masters. After 1640 no former servant was in either the council or the House of Burgesses, and in 1670, the House of Burgesses limited voting rights to landowners and householders, denying poor men suffrage.
9. There were two basic issues involved in Bacon's Rebellion. The first was Indians; as land grew scarce, former servants were unable to purchase their own farms. They came to resent that the government reserved land for Indian settlements on the fringes of English habitation. They also resented the elite planters who dominated government but had no sympathy for their concerns. When the government refused to allow them to wage a frontier war against the Indians, they revolted.
10. Poor white farmers could not afford the expensive machinery needed to process sugar. Many of them left for better opportunities elsewhere, lowering the number of whites on the

island and increasing the wealth of those who had the resources to remain. By 1680, the average sugar planter on Barbados was four times richer than the average Chesapeake tobacco planter. Also, sugar planters relied on slave labor, purchasing thousands of African slaves. By 1700, slaves constituted more than three-quarters of the island's population.

11. Carolina was founded by a Barbadian planter named John Colleton and a group of seven other proprietors. They intended from the beginning to siphon settlers from Barbados and other colonies and encourage the development of an export crop. Most of the colonists to Carolina did come from Barbados, and they brought their slaves with them; by 1700, half the population of Carolina was black. During the first generation of settlement, before the beginning of a profitable rice industry, Carolinians relied economically on trade with the West Indies, selling livestock, timber, and captured local Indians.
12. Although slaves cost three to five times more than indentured servants, they were never freed, and given the declining mortality rate in the 1680s, planters calculated that slaves would live longer than a servant's period of indenture. Slaves constituted a perpetual labor force because the children of slave mothers inherited the status of slavery. Servants expected land after their indentures and became discontent when their avenues to success were blocked. Slaves, however, would never be freed.

### *Map Activity*

Reading the Map: English land claims reflected King James I's concerns about trespassing too close to Spain's colonial holdings. On the North American continent, the English held a large swath of the eastern coastline, including Delaware, Maryland, Virginia, and Carolina, but the Spanish still possessed Florida and the bulk of Central and South America. The same was true in the Caribbean. The English had settled in the Bahamas and on Jamaica, St. Kitts, Nevis, and Barbados. However, the Spanish controlled the larger islands of Cuba, Hispaniola, Puerto Rico, and Trinidad.

Connections: Barbadians established the colony of Carolina in 1663. They intended to model their colony after the West Indies, basing the economy on the cultivation of a profitable export crop. Most of the early migrants, both free whites and black slaves, came from Barbados. Early trade centered on Barbados as well.

What goods did they export? During the first generation of settlement, Carolina colonists exported the bulk of their goods to Barbados. They sold livestock and timber to the West Indies. They also captured local Indians and sold them to Caribbean planters as slaves. After some experimentation with tobacco, cotton, indigo, olives, and rice, Carolinians found a hardy strain of rice and worked out methods of cultivation that provided the foundation for a flourishing rice industry.

Describe the relationship between Carolina and Barbados in 1700. Carolina was essentially a frontier outpost of the West Indian sugar economy. Barbados migrants populated the colony, bringing their slaves with them. Like Barbados, Carolina had a large population of blacks—by 1700, about half of the settlers were enslaved blacks. The Carolina economy was based on the same export model as Barbados, and much of its trade was with the West Indies.

### *Visual Activity*

Reading the Image: This image shows that Secotan was a highly communal society. People lived near one another, ate together, worshipped communally, hunted in groups, and tended fields in close proximity. The society appears to be peaceful, insofar as there are no fortifications against attack. There also are no obvious signs of social stratification. The people in the image are dressed similarly, and none of the dwellings are larger than the others.

Connections: Indians lived close together, in a fashion similar to that of English village-dwellers. However, the Indians practiced subsistence agriculture: they grew food for themselves, not for resale, so their plots of land were only as large as they needed to be for raising a sufficient quantity of food. English tobacco farmers in the Chesapeake bowed to the demands of producing crops for a market. Tobacco farms were huge because the plant exhausted the soil rapidly; thus, tobacco farmers lived far apart from one another. Tobacco eventually created a wide gap between the rich and the poor, particularly when land became scarce and the poor could no longer afford to purchase their own farms. Indian societies were led by chiefs and *werowances* who held political control over their own tribes and sometimes other tribes as well, but they did not have the same gap between the rich and the poor that existed in European communities.

### *Analyzing Sources*

1. The English adopted the word *Indian* from the Spanish, who had themselves used it as a result of their initial failure to realize that Columbus had not landed on the Asian subcontinent. Not only was the label inaccurate, but it also homogenized the enormous diversity of the residents of the Americas. The English also referred to Indians as *savages*, largely because Indians did not behave according to the tenets of English civilization.

Both terms showed a lack of respect for Indians; however, neither was based on differences in skin tone. The English felt that Indian social practices, not their color, produced their inferiority.

2. The English colonists identified Africans by their skin color more often than by their un-English ways; they had adopted the term *Negro* from the Spanish label, which meant "black." Moreover, black was not a neutral color in the minds of the English. It was associated with evil and set up as a direct opposite of white, which was the color of goodness and purity. By the 1680s, English colonists referred to themselves as white, rather than strictly English, making the contrast between themselves and their slaves more readily apparent.

3. In general, colonists took preexisting English ideas about "us" and "them" and exaggerated them to prevent themselves from sliding into an uncivilized state. Colonists drew distinctions between supposedly savage Indians and Africans and their own Christianity, which they believed was intrinsically better than other beliefs. They certainly felt that there was a hierarchy of skin color, in which white was preferable to black. However, they also drew distinctions between free and unfree people. Black slaves were debased in English eyes by the existence of black slavery, and that debasement in turn reinforced racial prejudice. But better-off colonists were contemptuous of all servants, feeling that poor white servants and landless workers were nearly as contemptible as black servants.

CHAPTER

# THE NORTHERN COLONIES IN THE SEVENTEENTH CENTURY, 1601–1700

# 3

## Chapter Overview

### *Chapter Summary*

***Introduction*** Chapter 3 begins with a discussion of the role of Anne Hutchinson, one of the most vocal and devout Puritans to emigrate to America in the seventeenth century. Hutchinson was a well-educated, well-spoken woman in the Massachusetts Bay Colony whose in-home discussions of the previous week's sermons were initially well received. In time, however, increasing numbers of both men and women came to listen to her, and the meetings alarmed her nearest neighbor, the former governor of the colony, John Winthrop. Fearing that she was subverting the good order of the colony, Winthrop and others brought forth charges of heresy against her, and she was excommunicated from the Boston church. She and her family were banished, first to Rhode Island and then to Long Island, where all but her ten-year-old daughter were killed by Indians.

***Puritan Origins: The English Reformation, pp. 72–74*** The English Reformation began less as a result of doctrinal revolts than because of a political dispute between the king and the pope. In 1534, King Henry VIII, angered by the power of the Catholic Church, broke England's ties with Rome and established himself as head of his nation's Christian faith. Henry made relatively few other changes in his "new" church, which remained very Catholic in theology and worship. Many English Protestants clamored for reforms that would "purify" the church of its Catholic trappings; these Protestants came to be called Puritans. The survival of English Protestantism was still in doubt when Elizabeth I came to the throne in 1558 and attempted to consolidate a position midway between the extremes of Catholicism and Puritanism. Continued Puritan agitation for further reform of the church continued during the reigns of Elizabeth's successors, James I and Charles I, neither of whom were at all receptive to Puritan ideas. Indeed, both monarchs' anti-Puritan policies made many Puritans believe that if they were to be free to live and worship in peace, then they would have to leave England. For example, King Charles I's dissolution of Parliament in 1629 caused great anxiety among English Puritans who, now without political representation, could not defend themselves legally against Charles's anti-Puritan policies.

***Puritans and the Settlement of New England, pp. 74–79*** The sixteenth-century religious and political turmoil engendered by the English Reformation led many Puritans to emigrate to New England. The colonies they established at Plymouth and Massachusetts Bay were shaped by their faith and by their desire to create a new society that conformed to God's plan for humankind.

**THE PILGRIMS AND PLYMOUTH COLONY** Plymouth colony was settled by the Pilgrims, separatist Puritans who had fled England in 1608 and had lived for several years in Holland. Though able to worship freely there, the Pilgrims became alarmed when their children began to drift away from their families and their church, and thus they decided to emigrate to Virginia. They left for the New World aboard the Mayflower in August 1620, landing at Cape Cod in present-day Massachusetts in November. To provide order, security, and legitimacy for the new colony, the Pilgrims created their own government by consent, drawing up the Mayflower Compact. They also elected William Bradford as their governor. Though survival was difficult in the early years, the Pilgrims were lucky in their Indian friends—like Squanto and Chief Massasoit—who showed them how to gather seafood and cultivate corn. After the first harvest in the fall of 1621, the settlers invited the Indians to celebrate a thanksgiving feast. Plymouth remained a small colony, attracting few immigrants, but that did not bother the Pilgrims, who wanted to live quietly and simply according to their faith.

**THE FOUNDING OF MASSACHUSETTS BAY COLONY** Shortly before Charles I dissolved Parliament in 1629, a number of Puritans had formed the Massachusetts Bay Company and been granted a charter for colonization in New England. In 1630, this group sailed for the New World with elected governor John Winthrop to lead them and a key provision in their charter that would allow them self-government in Massachusetts. Aboard the ship *Arbella,* Winthrop delivered a sermon to his followers about the significance of their journey and their duty as settlers to follow a righteous path and to adhere strictly to God's laws. He and his followers established settlements around Boston in 1630, and despite early hardships, the Massachusetts Bay colony enjoyed a steady stream of migration during its first decade. Unlike the Virginia colonists, most immigrants to New England were farmers or tradesmen of middle-class origin and came as part of a family.

***The Evolution of New England Society, pp. 79–88*** New Englanders did not scatter themselves across the land like their Chesapeake counterparts but instead settled in numerous small towns located either on the coast or river, ensuring access to water. The townspeople's strong piety, sustained by the institutions of local government, enforced remarkable religious and social conformity in these communities, though tensions and changes would later test and even splinter that conformity.

**CHURCH, COVENANT, AND CONFORMITY** God's word—not elaborate ceremony—was the focus of Puritan services. Puritans considered the church to be not an actual building but the men and women who entered into a solemn covenant with each other and with God to lead a holy and righteous life. Since Puritans were Calvinists, they believed Christians must discipline their behavior to conform strictly to their religious ideas. Calvinism also preached the doctrine of predestination whereby individuals were either saved or damned according to God's choice. The Puritan covenant required the disciplining of the entire community; church members were to watch the behavior of others and report any transgressions, such as improper observation of the Sabbath, to church elders, whose job it was to punish violators of the community's covenant. Though the church had no direct role in civil government, Puritans believed the government was ultimately subordinate to the church. As much as possible, they sought to make public life conform to their view of God's law.

**GOVERNMENT BY PURITANS FOR PURITANISM** The Puritans created a civil government that was governed by Puritans for Puritanism. The leading officials in the towns of the Massachusetts Bay Colony were the "freemen," who had to be male church members. All the other men were designated "inhabitants" and could vote and take part in the town government. At the town meetings, every man—whatever his status—could speak up, a level of popular participation that was unprecedented in the seventeenth century. When new town governments distributed land among their inhabitants, each family was given a house lot, a garden, and a portion of agricultural land on the edge of town. Typical land allocations were clustered in the middle, which meant New England had a more equitable distribution of wealth than the Chesapeake had. The house lots were set close together near the center, a physical layout that enabled colonists to keep an eye on their neighbors' activities and enforced godly behavior.

**THE SPLINTERING OF PURITANISM** Puritanism's emphasis on individual Bible study soon resulted in dissension among some of the faithful who believed that God's ways could be interpreted differently from the interpretation mandated by ministers. The two most important dissidents in early Massachusetts Bay were Roger Williams and Anne Hutchinson. Williams believed the church and government should be completely separated. He was expelled from Massachusetts and helped found the colony of Rhode Island.

**GROWTH, CHANGE, AND CONTROVERSY** New England's rocky soil and harsh winters made the growing and export of crops such as tobacco and rice impossible. Instead, a fur trade with the Indians and a timber industry developed, but the most important export was fish, which found ready markets abroad. The fish trade also stimulated colonial shipbuilding and trained generations of fishermen and sailors; it also contributed to the growth of trade networks and a merchant class. New England's population boomed during the seventeenth century, owing to high marriage, high birth rates, and a healthy climate relatively free of diseases. And as the children of the original founders began to have children themselves, Puritan leaders worried about their falling away from the faith. Thus, in 1662, they drew up the Halfway Covenant by which unconverted children of saints could become halfway church members. The Puritans also had to content with the arrival of new religious groups, most notably the Quakers, whose views were very different from their own.

***The Founding of the Middle Colonies, pp. 88–95*** No section of the English empire in North America was more diverse in its history, its ethnic and religious pluralism, or its political institutions than the proprietary colonies of New York, New Jersey, and Pennsylvania.

**FROM NEW NETHERLAND TO NEW YORK** The Dutch settled New York after the voyages of Henry Hudson in 1609. The colony became the property of the Dutch West India Company, which struggled to govern the settlement and sent officials who set policies many colonists deeply resented. New Netherland was Dutch in little more than ownership, as few immigrants came from Holland, and the population remained small. It was a linguistically and religiously diverse colony. Immigrants from Sweden, France, Germany, Holland, and many other places made up sizable minorities in the colony, and these people felt no loyalty to the Dutch West India Company. When England sent a fleet to take New Netherland in 1664, the colony fell. Charles II gave the colony as part of an enormous land grant to his brother, James the Duke of York, and New Netherland became New York.

**NEW JERSEY AND PENNSYLVANIA** New York's creation led indirectly to the founding of two other middle colonies, New Jersey and Pennsylvania. New Jersey first belonged to the Duke of York, but he gave it to two friends who became the colony's proprietors. Conflicts between these men and some preexisting settlers led one of the proprietors to sell his interest to two Quakers. These Quaker proprietors themselves had a conflict and called in English Quaker William Penn, who arbitrated an agreement whereby New Jersey was able to maintain its proprietary government. Penn himself became interested in establishing a colony in the New World to provide a safe haven for the Quakers, an unpopular and persecuted sect whose members were imprisoned and executed in great numbers. Penn intended to settle Pennsylvania as a "Holy Experiment"—a society based on Quaker principles. The Quakers believed that all individuals could communicate directly with God. They refused to accept hierarchical status or deference to those of rank and title, since in God's eyes all humans were equal. In 1681, Charles II, eager to rid England of this troublesome religious minority, made Penn the proprietor of a new colony called Pennsylvania.

**TOLERATION AND DIVERSITY IN PENNSYLVANIA** Between 1682 and 1685, almost eight thousand immigrants came to Pennsylvania, most of them members of the Society of Friends, or Quakers. Quaker ideals showed in the fair Indian policy and the tolerance of religious diversity in the new colony. Pennsylvania and its capital, Philadelphia, soon rivaled New York as a center of commerce, exporting flour and other foodstuffs to the West Indies and importing textiles and manufactured goods. As the colony's proprietor, Penn had extensive power, but he proposed a more representative government in which property owners could vote for a council and an elected assembly, both of which were subject to an appointed governor's veto. Penn believed that the form of government mattered less than the people in it, but Quakers found points of disagreement. There were many struggles in the assembly, and in 1701 a new Charter of Privileges gave the assembly extensive new powers.

***The Colonies and the British Empire, pp. 95–98*** Until the 1660s, the English crown largely ignored the colonies. The king then realized the profits to be made by regulating colonial trade; he moved to consolidate royal control over colonial governments.

**ROYAL REGULATION OF COLONIAL TRADE** The Navigation Acts of 1650, 1651, and 1660 were the heart of England's system of regulation. They restricted trade within the empire to English (including American) ships and enumerated certain colonial goods—such as tobacco—which could be shipped only to England or to other English colonies. This did not interfere with New England and the middle colonies, whose main exports were not enumerated. Another act, the Staple Act of 1663, required that all goods imported into the colonies pass through England. By the end of the seventeenth century, colonial trade flowed in channels defined and regulated by the British empire.

**CONSOLIDATION OF ROYAL AUTHORITY** The middle colonies, Maryland, and South Carolina were all proprietary colonies closely linked to the crown, and Virginia had been a royal colony since 1624. The monarchy now directed its efforts toward the New England colonies, which had developed their own distinctively independent Puritan governments. A devastating war with the Indians (King Philip's War, 1675–1676) created the pretext for a royal investigation of whether New England adhered to English laws. This resulted in the crown's decision to revoke the Massachusetts Bay Company's charter and to incorporate all the colonies stretching from Maine to Maryland into one entity called the Dominion of New England, appointing Sir Edmund Andros as royal governor. When news reached America of James II's ouster in the Glorious Revolution, a rebellion broke out in Boston, and Andros and his followers were arrested. However, the days of Puritan independence and complete self-rule were over.

***Conclusion: The Seventeenth-Century Legacy of English North America*** At the close of the seventeenth century, the English New World colonies were firmly established. The English empire in North America was quite different from its Spanish counterpart. The settlers relied on agriculture and trade rather than precious metals. Religious, political, social, and economic diversity could be seen throughout the settled areas, and free white males enjoyed an unusual degree of political influence for that time. Over the next half-century, the colonies would experience surprising changes.

***Chronology Activity*** Read the annotated chronology, and answer the multiple-choice questions.

1534 Henry VIII breaks with Roman Catholic Church and initiates English Reformation. Henry VIII's decision to break with the Catholic Church would have major repercussions for the English people. Many of those who opposed the Church of England and who wanted a true reformation began to study the Protestant ideas found on the continent and became Puritans. Eventually, a group of those Puritans would set sail for America and become known as pilgrims.

1609 Henry Hudson searches for Northwest Passage for Dutch East India Company.

1620 English Puritans found Plymouth colony. The Puritan colony at Plymouth suffered many setbacks, but its leaders were able to develop strong relationships with the local Indian tribes.

1626 Peter Minuit purchases Manhattan island for Dutch West India Company and founds New Amsterdam.

1627 Massachusetts Bay Company receives royal charter for colony. The colony thus received the right to govern itself from the colony rather than having to report back to England.

1629 John Winthrop leads Puritan settlers to Massachusetts Bay. Winthrop remained a major influence over the lives of the Puritan settlers long after his retirement.

1635 Roger Williams, banished from Massachusetts, establishes Rhode Island colony.

1636 Thomas Hooker leaves Massachusetts and helps found Connecticut colony.

1637 Anne Hutchinson accused of Antinomianism. The next year she was excommunicated from Boston church. Hutchinson would travel to Rhode Island and then to Long Island, where almost her entire family was killed during an Indian attack.

1642 Civil war inflames England, pitting Puritans against royalists. Disputes between King Charles I and Parliament escalated until war finally broke out. The king and his supporters were defeated politically and militarily by Puritan parliamentary forces led by Oliver Cromwell.

1649 English Puritans win civil war and execute King Charles I. The execution meant that Puritans were firmly in control of the English government; in fifty years they went from being a harassed group of religious dissidents to a dominant power in the English government.

1650 Quakers arrive in Massachusetts, persecuted there. The Quakers were one of the only Protestant sects to allow women to preach, which was part of the reason for their persecution.

1660 Monarchy restored in England; Charles II becomes king. Navigation Act requires colonial goods to be shipped in English vessels through English ports. The Navigation Act was one of the first passed by the English government to try to impose greater control over the colonies.

1662 Many Puritan congregations adopt Halfway Covenant. The original New England Puritans allowed their children to be baptized before becoming full members of the church on the theory that sainthood was inherited. However, during the 1650s and 1660s, children of visible saints increasingly did not experience the inward transformation that would allow them to become full members of the church. When they began to have babies themselves, those children could not be baptized. By Puritan theology, they would go to hell if they died, but churches could not allow anybody to become a church member without conversion. The solution was the Halfway Covenant, which allowed the unconverted children of saints to become halfway church members, with the ability to baptize their children but not to participate in communion or have voting privileges.

1663 Staple Act requires all colonial imports to come from England. This act required all goods imported into the colonies to pass through England. This gave English merchants a monopoly on exports to the colonies and, by raising the prices of non-English goods, provided English manufacturers with a competitive edge in the colonial marketplace.

1664 English seize New Netherland colony from Dutch, rename it New York.
Duke of York subdivides his colony, creating new colony of New Jersey. Unlike many of the colonies of the New World, the New Netherland colony had been ethnically and religiously diverse. Despite the English seizure of the colony, this did not change, and New York remained a diverse, powerful colony.

1675 Indians and colonists clash in King Philip's War. The English colonists won the war, but it gave the English crown an excuse to launch an investigation into the New England colonies to determine whether they abided by English law. Discovering numerous violations, royal officials revoked the Massachusetts charter.

1681 King Charles II grants William Penn charter for colony of Pennsylvania. Penn's colony became a model for enlightened behavior, especially toward the Indian tribes.

1686 Royal officials create Dominion of New England. The Dominion of New England encompassed Massachusetts and the other colonies north of Maryland. Colonists were offended by the new English governor Edmund Andros's flouting of Puritan traditions like keeping the Sabbath, and by invalidating all land titles, every property owner in New England faced the prospect of losing his or her land.

1688 James II overthrown by Glorious Revolution; William III becomes king. When Charles II died in 1685, he was succeeded by his brother James II, a staunch Catholic. James's attempt to appoint Catholics to government posts caused a group of Protestant noblemen to invite William of Orange to take the throne.

1691 Massachusetts becomes royal colony. When the Glorious Revolution broke out, colonists in Massachusetts took the opportunity to seize Andros and other English officials and put them in jail. The rebels reestablished the old charter, but that was replaced by a royal charter, which changed the Puritan nature of the colony. The governor was appointed by the king rather than elected by the colonists' representatives, and possession of property replaced church membership as a prerequisite for voting.

1692 Witch trials flourish at Salem.

## *Chronology Questions* Choose the letter of the best answer.

1. In 1534, Henry VIII
   a. became king of England.
   b. broke from the Roman Church.
   c. fathered Edward VI.
   d. commissioned a new translation of the Bible.

2. The royal Charter for the Massachusetts Bay Company was granted in
   a. 1603.
   b. 1610.
   c. 1615.
   d. 1629.

3. What is the correct order for the following events?
   1. Massachusetts Bay Company receives royal charter for colony.
   2. Quakers arrive in Massachusetts.
   3. English Puritans found Plymouth colony.
   4. Many Puritan congregations adopt Halfway Covenant.

   a. 2, 3, 1, 4
   b. 3, 1, 2, 4
   c. 4, 1, 3, 2
   d. 1, 3, 2, 4

4. The group which first arrived in Massachusetts in 1656 were the
   a. Puritans.
   b. Quakers.
   c. Catholics.
   d. Pilgrims.

5. Charles II came to throne following the English civil war in
   a. 1680.
   b. 1600.
   c. 1660.
   d. 1628.

6. One of the first attempts by the English to impose control over the colonies, passed in 1660, was the
   a. Sugar Act.
   b. Tea Act.
   c. Intolerable Act.
   d. Navigation Act.

7. The English seized New Netherland from the Dutch in
   a. 1637.
   b. 1649.
   c. 1664.
   d. 1686.

8. The first major war between the colonists and Indians, fought in 1675, was known as
   a. King Philip's War.
   b. the French and Indian War.
   c. the Seven Years War.
   d. Queen Anne's War.

9. What is the correct order for the following events?
   1. Navigation Act requires colonial goods to be shipped in English vessels through English ports.
   2. Royal officials create Dominion of New England.
   3. Massachusetts becomes royal colony.
   4. Staple Act requires all colonial imports to come from English

   a. 1, 4, 2, 3
   b. 4, 3, 1, 2
   c. 3, 2, 4, 1
   d. 1, 2, 3, 4

10. John Winthrop led Puritan settlers to Massachusetts Bay in
    a. 1609.
    b. 1620.
    (c.) 1630.
    d. 1649.

***Defining Terms*** Match each term with the correct definition.

✓ Glorious Revolution
✓ English Reformation
✓ Staple Act
✓ Navigation Acts
✓ Act of Supremacy
✓ Charter of Privileges
✓ royal charter
✓ Parliament
✓ "invisible saints"
✓ "little commonwealth"
✓ freemen
✓ colonial council
✓ proprietary colonies
✓ Quakers
✓ Pilgrims
✓ Puritanism
✓ Halfway Covenant
✓ Mayflower Compact

1. The parliamentary act by which Henry VIII became head of the Church of England. This also outlawed the Catholic Church in England and gave all holdings of the Catholic Church to the king. Act of supremacy
2. The set of ideas and religious principles that appealed to dissenters from the English Church, including the belief that the church needed to be purified by eliminating the elements of Catholicism from its practices. puritanism
3. The legislative body in England. Parliament
4. Henry VIII's break with the Roman Catholic Church, which established the nominally Protestant Church of England. Henry VIII's decision was politically motivated; he had no particular quarrel with Catholic theology and remained an orthodox Catholic in most matters of religious practice. English reformation
5. English Protestants who sought to withdraw and separate from the Church of England. Because these actions would be severely punished in England, they migrated first to Holland and then to North America in search of a place where they could establish the pious life they envisioned. Pilgrims
6. The document signed by the Pilgrims when they realized that they had landed far north of the Virginia grant they had been given by their charter. This document was intended to provide order, security, and a claim to legitimacy until the king granted them formal legal rights. May flower compact
7. John Winthrop's description of how families should be run. Each family was considered this because it mirrored the hierarchy of God's creatures, with humankind being subordinate to God. "little commonwealth"

8. A Protestant sect that believed that the individual was spoken to directly by God. Their refusal to keep the Sabbath, along with their belief that preachers and the Bible were not needed, made them outcasts in America and frequent targets of abuse. This sect developed in England and spread through the country and into America. Quakers

9. Those individuals who were fortunate enough to be among the handful of people predestined by God to receive eternal life. Puritans thought these believers could be identified by their behavior and that membership in a Puritan church was a sign of salvation. "invisible saints"

10. The term used for the Massachusetts Bay Company's stockholders. These individuals made up the General Court that made the laws governing the company's affairs and were able to vote for the civil government of the colony as well. Freemen

11. The compromise that allowed the unconverted children of Puritan saints to be members of the church. This marked a decline in Puritan religious fervor. Halfway covenant

12. Colonies granted by the English crown to an individual or a group. proprietary colonies

13. Pennsylvania's civil government, which was elected by property owners who possessed at least one hundred acres of land or who paid taxes and had the power to originate laws and administer the affairs of the government. Colonial Council

14. Legislation passed in Pennsylvania in 1701, giving the proprietor the power to appoint the council but stripping the council of its powers and turning those powers over to the elected assembly. Charter of privileges

15. These were issued by a king to exercise greater control over colonial governments. In many cases, these replaced the proprietary claims that had previously been made on lands in America. royal charter

16. This overthrew James II and placed William of Orange on the throne of England. James II, a Catholic, had an aggressive campaign to put Catholics in government posts. In reaction, a group of Protestant noblemen asked William to be the king of England. In 1688, William and Mary became co-monarchs. Glorious Revolution

17. Legislation passed by Parliament in 1650, 1651, and 1660 that set forth the fundamental regulations governing colonial trade because they specified that goods imported into England had to be transported in English ships and enumerated specific colonial products that could be shipped only to England or the English colonies. Navigation Acts

18. Parliamentary legislation passed in 1663, requiring that all goods imported into the colonies pass through England. This raised the price of foreign goods and gave English merchants and manufacturers a competitive edge in the colonial market. Staple Act

## Chapter Review

***Multiple-Choice*** Choose the letter of the best answer.

1. What era began in Germany in 1517?
   a. The Restoration
   b. The Catholic Unification
   (c.) The Protestant Reformation
   d. The Weimar Republic

2. The honorific title "Defender of the Faith" was bestowed on
   a. Elizabeth I.
   (b.) Henry VIII.
   c. James I.
   d. Isabella of Spain.

3. When Parliament passed the Act of Supremacy, the properties of the Catholic Church in England became the property of
   a. the king.
   b. the pope.
   c. the nobility.
   d. the bishops.

4. The English Reformation ultimately
   a. caused political and religious turmoil.
   b. spared England political and religious turmoil.
   c. caused the pope to declare war on England.
   d. was permanently reversed.

5. During the sixteenth century, Puritanism was
   a. less an organized movement than a set of religious ideas shared by some dissenters.
   b. a very organized movement that effectively challenged the king.
   c. dying out; more and more people were returning to Catholicism.
   d. spreading throughout Europe as people interacted during war.

6. When Henry VIII died in 1547, the English Reformation was
   a. complete.
   b. not yet entrenched.
   c. popular with most English people.
   d. opposed by his successor.

7. Protestantism was outlawed in England by
   a. Henry VIII.
   b. Mary I.
   c. Elizabeth I.
   d. Edward VI.

8. Puritans wished to do all of the following except
   a. abolish the church hierarchy.
   b. emphasize the individual's relationship with God.
   c. study the Bible closely.
   d. increase the number of church rituals.

9. The monarch who legalized Protestantism in England was
   a. Elizabeth I.
   b. Mary.
   c. Edward I
   d. Henry VII.

10. Charles I, who enforced conformity to the Church of England,
    a. instituted policies requiring baptism.
    b. was receptive to Puritan ideas.
    c. instituted aggressive anti-Puritan policies.
    d. wanted to start colonies in the New World and encouraged Puritans to move there.

11. James I and his son Charles I
    a. followed Elizabeth I's policies toward Puritans.
    b. encouraged religious dissenters.
    c. espoused Roman Catholicism.
    d. moved the Church of England away from Puritanism.

12. As a reform of the Church of England, new translation of the Bible was authorized by
    a. Charles I.
    b. Martin Luther.
    c. James I.
    d. Elizabeth.

13. The Roman church was a catholic, or, _____ church.
    a. Jewish
    b. Roman
    c. universal
    d. holy

14. The Protestant Reformation first arose in _____ in 1517.
    a. France
    b. Germany
    c. England
    d. Holland

15. At Henry VIII's insistence, Parliament's Act of outlawed the Catholic Church in England.
    a. Supremacy
    b. Anglicanism
    c. Protestantism
    d. Lutheranism

16. The privilege of appointing _____ in England became the privilege of the king after the English Reformation.
    a. the pope
    b. nobles
    c. local governors
    d. members of the church hierarchy

17. The _____ were English people who insisted on a thorough reformation.
    a. Catholics
    b. Anglicans
    c. Puritans
    d. bishops

18. Queen Mary I married Philip II of Spain and tried to return England to _____.
    a. Spain
    b. Catholicism
    c. Protestanism
    d. a monarchy

19. By 1603, when Elizabeth I died, many people in England looked on _____ as a defining feature of national identity.
    a. theology
    b. the monarchy
    c. imperialism
    d. Protestantism

20. Elizabeth I was succeeded by _____.
    a. Charles I
    b. Mary
    c. James I
    d. James II

21. James I authorized a new version of _____.
    a. Parliament
    b. the Magna Carta
    c. the Bible
    d. the Mayflower Charter

22. In 1629, _____ dissolved Parliament.
    a. James I
    b. Charles I
    c. Elizabeth
    d. Henry VIII

23. Life in New England was shaped by the colonists' strong belief in
    a. Protestantism.
    b. Puritanism.
    c. Catholicism.
    d. democracy.

24. Separatists, known as Pilgrims, moved to Holland because
    a. their ancestors came from there.
    b. they knew Holland would provide a good place to raise their children.
    c. they could make large profits and establish many churches there.
    d. if they stayed in England, they would be severely punished.

25. The capital that was provided for the Pilgrims to travel to America came from
    a. investors in a joint stock company.
    b. King James I.
    c. the electors of Holland.
    d. the pope.

26. The Pilgrims left Holland on the Mayflower and settled in
    a. Jamestown, Virginia.
    b. Charles Towne, South Carolina.
    c. Plymouth, Massachusetts.
    d. Salem, Massachusetts.

27. The first governor of the Massachusetts Bay Colony was
    a. John Winthrop.
    b. Martin Luther.
    c. Cotton Mather.
    d. John Calvin.

28. The royal charter for the Massachusetts Bay Company included the following provision:
    a. a governing body located in England.
    b. land to colonize Virginia.
    c. land to colonize Massachusetts.
    d. a governing body located in the colony.

29. When Winthrop and his followers arrived in America, they made it clear that they did not want to be associated with
    a. England.
    b. Indians.
    c. the Pilgrims at Plymouth.
    d. Puritanism.

30. John Winthrop believed that the Puritans had a duty to
    a. set an example of godliness.
    b. renounce the Church of England.
    c. actively agitate for reform in England.
    d. encourage religious toleration in their new colony.

31. For the most part, immigrants to New England were from which rank of English society?
    a. Highest
    b. Lowest
    c. Middle
    d. There was a mixture of all classes.

32. The typical New England immigrants were
    a. a family.
    b. a couple.
    c. women.
    d. men.

33. According to Winthrop, each family was a
    a. democracy.
    b. partnership.
    c. commune.
    d. little commonwealth.

34. The social order of early New England was defined by
    a. a zeal for independence.
    b. constraints of servitude.
    c. family, church, and community.
    d. the tobacco market.

35. The Pilgrims sailed to America aboard the _____.
    a. *Mayflower*
    b. *Pinta*
    c. *Nina*
    d. *Santa Maria*

36. The first governor of the Plymouth colony was _____.
    a. Cotton Mather
    b. John Calvin
    c. William Bradford
    d. Squanto

37. The tribe whose territory included Plymouth was the _____.
    a. Massasoit
    b. Squanto
    c. Wampanoag
    d. Samoset.

38. By _____, Plymouth had become a permanent settlement.
    a. 1603
    b. 1610
    c. 1617
    d. 1630

39. The area that John Winthrop and his followers settled in became known as _____.
    a. New Haven
    b. Boston
    c. New York
    d. Pennsylvania

40. While aboard the *Arbella*, John Winthrop gave one of the most famous sermons in history, during which he discussed the idea of a "_____ upon a hill."
    a. house
    b. church
    c. castle
    d. city

41. By 1640, New England had one of the highest to population ratios in all of Christendom.
    a. Indian
    b. preacher
    c. bishop
    d. bureaucrat

42. The vast majority of immigrants to the Massachusetts Bay Colony were either _____ or farmers.
    a. servants
    b. slaves
    c. nobles
    d. tradesmen

43. According to Winthrop, humankind was subordinate to _____.
   a. no one
   b. the government
   c. him
   d. God

44. Families who immigrated to New England were sometimes accompanied by a few _____.
   a. horses
   b. servants
   c. cows
   d. patrons

45. Puritans believed that the church was the
   a. same thing as civil government.
   b. rituals of baptism and marriage.
   c. men and women who had entered a covenant with each other and God.
   d. building where the services were preached.

46. Puritan views on church membership derived from the theology of
   a. John Calvin, who stressed the doctrine of predestination.
   b. Martin Luther, who stressed the doctrine of the watchmaker god.
   c. John Winthrop, who stressed the doctrine of the watchmaker god.
   d. St. Augustine, who stressed the doctrine of predestination.

47. Ministers in Puritan communities were prohibited from
   a. soliciting new immigration.
   b. proclaiming fasting days.
   c. proclaiming days of humiliation.
   d. holding government office.

48. In matters of civil government, the Puritan churches of New England
   a. had no influence.
   b. made all decisions.
   c. had no direct role.
   d. played varied roles from town to town.

49. One of the most important functions of New England government was
   a. regulating religious practices.
   b. controlling family life.
   c. deciding church laws.
   d. land distribution.

50. The founder of Rhode Island was
   a. Cotton Mather.
   b. Arthur Rhodes.
   c. William Penn.
   d. Roger Williams.

51. Thomas Hooker founded a major dissenting community at
   a. Hartford.
   b. Boston.
   c. Providence.
   d. Long Island.

52. Puritan leaders saw dissent as
   a. a natural outgrowth of individual Bible study.
   b. a serious error in judgment.
   c. something to be tolerated.
   d. healthy.

53. The success of the Puritan Revolution
   a. caused New Englanders to return to England.
   b. decreased immigration to New England.
   c. increased immigration to New England.
   d. gave New England an important voice in British politics.

54. The Quakers believed that God spoke to individuals through
   a. the Bible.
   b. Preachers.
   c. an inner light.
   d. temporal authorities.

55. The Halfway Covenant
   a. made unconverted Puritans full members of the church.
   b. denied baptism to the children of unconverted Puritans.
   c. gave limited voting rights to unconverted Puritans.
   d. allowed the unconverted children of saints to become halfway church members.

56. Quakers were often branded with the letter
   a. Q, which stood for Quaker.
   b. H, which stood for heresy.
   c. A, which stood for accepted.
   d. P, which stood for Pilgrim.

57. To Puritans, a church was a solemn _____.
   a. edifice
   b. covenant
   c. group of men
   d. rebellion

58. According to Calvin, only God knew who the _____, or invisible saints, were.
   a. elect
   b. sinners
   c. bishops
   d. covenant keepers

59. To bring public life into conformity with their view of God, the Puritans refused to observe _____.
   a. baptism
   b. Sabbath
   c. formal churchgoing
   d. Christmas

60. Company stockholders of the Massachusetts Bay Company were also known as _____.
   a. indentured servants
   b. bureaucrats
   c. freemen
   d. gentry

61. All men other than freemen were classified as _____ according to the Massachusetts Bay Colony.
   a. inhabitants
   b. servants
   c. citizens
   d. slaves

62. The community Thomas Hooker founded was located in the _____ River Valley.
   a. Silicon
   b. Connecticut
   c. Red
   d. Cape Cod

63. The leaders of the parliamentary forces during the clash between King Charles I and Parliament were _____.
   a. monarchists
   b. Catholics
   c. Dutch
   d. Puritans

64. By the 1680s, the majority of full church members in New England were _____.
   a. freemen
   b. indentured servants
   c. women
   d. inhabitants

65. The Halfway Covenant, created in 1662, allowed the unconverted children of saints to _____ their children.
   a. marry
   b. baptize
   c. kill
   d. excommunicate

66. Quakers were members of the Society of _____.
   a. Friends
   b. God
   c. Jesus
   d. Puritans

67. New York, New Jersey, and Pennsylvania originated as
   a. fishing docks.
   b. proprietary colonies of England.
   c. property of the West India Company.
   d. Dutch colonies.

68. The most important outpost in the region north of the Chesapeake was
   a. Pennsylvania.
   b. New Amsterdam.
   c. New Netherland.
   d. Massachusetts Bay Colony.

69. The principal trading center in New Netherland was
   a. Manhattan.
   b. New Netherland.
   c. New Amsterdam.
   d. Boston.

70. In 1664, New Netherland became
   a. Vermont.
   b. New Amsterdam.
   c. New Jersey.
   d. New York.

71. Charles II gave William Penn a land grant to found a colony in America for
   a. Puritans.
   b. Quakers.
   c. Shakers.
   d. Catholics.

72. After New York, the most diverse colony in North America was
   a. Pennsylvania.
   b. Boston.
   c. Plymouth.
   d. Chesapeake.

73. In 1609, Henry Hudson was dispatched to North America by the Dutch East India Company to search for
   a. a suitable colony to shelter Quakers.
   b. a good harbor.
   c. gold.
   d. a Northwest Passage to the Orient.

74. In Pennsylvania, the civil government
   a. was used to enforce morality.
   b. had no effective power.
   c. was removed from the Quaker faith.
   d. was completely democratic.

75. The capital of Pennsylvania, Philadelphia, rivaled New York as a center of
   a. export.
   b. government.
   c. shipbuilding.
   d. religious thought.

76. As proprietor of Pennsylvania, Penn's powers were subject to review only by
   a. the West India Company.
   b. the king.
   c. the colonial assembly.
   d. God.

77. Penn stressed that the exact form of government mattered less than
   a. religion.
   b. the king.
   c. the men who served in government.
   d. the citizens of the colony.

78. The Quaker-dominated assembly in Pennsylvania wanted to have the ability to debate and amend
   a. laws.
   b. religious regulations.
   c. land grants.
   d. assembly appointments.

79. New York, New Jersey, and Pennsylvania were originally _____ colonies: that is, they were granted to one or more proprietors.
   a. free
   b. merchant
   c. Middle
   d. proprietary

80. Peter Minuit, the resident director of the West India Company, purchased _____ from the Manhate Indians.
   a. Manhattan Island
   b. Long Island
   c. Plymouth
   d. the Hudson River

81. The inhabitants of _____ were remarkably diverse.
   a. New Netherland
   b. Plymouth
   c. Boston
   d. the Chesapeake

82. William Penn's "holy experiment" was the establishment of a _____ colony in America.
   a. Quaker
   b. Puritan
   c. Catholic
   d. Methodist

83. The Quakers were highly unusual in that they allowed _____ to obtain positions of religious leadership.
   a. children
   b. women
   c. slaves
   d. men

84. Pennsylvania's capital city, ________, became a center of commerce.
   a. Boston
   b. Philadelphia
   c. Pittsburgh
   d. New York

85. Pennsylvania's assembly was the only _____ legislature in the British colonies.
    a. bicameral
    b. unicameral
    c. independent
    d. standing

86. Property owners who possessed _____ or who paid taxes elected the colonial council in Pennsylvania.
    a. a house
    b. a business
    c. 10 acres of land
    d. 100 acres of land

87. The Charter of _____ stripped the colonial council of Pennsylvania of its powers and gave those powers to the assembly.
    a. Quakers
    b. England
    c. William Penn
    d. Privileges

88. William Penn granted every settler in Pennsylvania _____.
    a. a job.
    b. a farm.
    c. church membership
    d. freedom of religion

89. After 1660, the English crown began to
    a. make royal colonies into proprietary ones.
    b. lose interest in the colonies.
    c. consolidate royal authority over colonial governments.
    d. encourage migration to the colonies.

90. The Navigation Acts of 1650, 1651, and 1660 interfered most with the economy of
    a. the Chesapeake.
    b. New England.
    c. the middle colonies.
    d. all of the colonies.

91. The Staple Act of 1663 required that
    a. goods imported to England pass through the colonies.
    b. all merchants pay a tithe to the state.
    c. the colonies trade directly with the French and the Dutch.
    d. all goods imported to the colonies pass through England.

92. By the end of the seventeenth century, colonial merchants and shippers
    a. were treated unfairly by the English government.
    b. had been driven out of business by English merchants.
    c. had access to markets throughout the British empire on the same terms as residents of England.
    d. were ready to rebel against English regulations.

93. King Philip's War broke out in 1675 largely because
    a. Massachusetts settlers were randomly killing Wampanoag Indians.
    b. Massachusetts settlers were trying to convert Wampanoag Indians.
    c. the crown encouraged it.
    d. Massachusetts settlers were encroaching on Indian land.

94. King Philip's War left New England colonists with all of the following except
    a. a devastated frontier.
    b. a renewed religious faith.
    c. an enduring hatred of Indians.
    d. a large war debt.

95. King Philip represented the interests of the
    a. French.
    b. British.
    c. Dutch.
    d. Indians.

96. The Dominion of New England was formed after a royal investigator found that
   a. New Englanders were not following English laws.
   b. New Englanders were incapable of self-rule.
   c. England could get more tax monies out of one large colony.
   d. England would find it easier to administer one large colony.

97. Massachusetts colonists were horrified that the Dominion invalidated
   a. royal charters.
   b. rental agreements.
   c. the Navigation Acts.
   d. land titles.

98. The Glorious Rebellion reasserted
   a. royal control over the colonies.
   b. Protestant influence in England.
   c. tax laws on the colonies.
   d. Catholicism within England.

99. Within the colonies, the Glorious Revolution led to
   a. the destruction of the Dominion.
   b. the strengthening of the Dominion.
   c. a revolt against all royal authority.
   d. political chaos.

100. King William's War made it clear to many colonists that
   a. they could do without English help.
   b. English trade regulations were onerous.
   c. the English government provided necessary military security.
   d. the English government engaged its colonies in pointless wars.

101. The _____ Acts set forth two fundamental regulations governing colonial trade.
   a. Navigation
   b. Colonial
   c. Free Trade
   d. Shipping

102. While the Navigation Acts did not affect New England's principal exports, they did affect the Chesapeake exportation of _____.
   a. fish
   b. flour
   c. tobacco
   d. lumber

103. Colonial commerce benefited from coming under the protection of the _____.
   a. local militia
   b. British navy
   c. Canadian army
   d. Parliament

104. The colony of _____ had been a royal colony since 1624.
   a. Maryland
   b. Pennsylvania
   c. South Carolina
   d. Virginia

105. The New England colonies possessed _____ but had developed their own governments.
   a. diplomatic immunity
   b. the Mayflower Compact
   c. colonial legislatures
   d. royal charters

106. In 1676, Edward Randolph, an agent of the king's, arrived to investigate the adherence of the colonies to English _____.
   a. official religion
   b. laws
   c. monetary systems
   d. holidays

107. In 1684, in a move to govern New England more directly an English court revoked the charter of _____.
   a. Puritans
   b. New Jersey
   c. Virginia
   d. Massachusetts

108. In 1686, Massachusetts and the other colonies north of Maryland were incorporated into the Dominion of New England, which invalidated all _____.
   a. land titles
   b. religious freedoms
   c. Vermont
   d. North Carolina

109. Rebels from the colony of _____ rebelled against the royal government and held control of the colony for over a year.
   a. Vermont
   b. New York
   c. Massachusetts
   d. Virginia

110. In 1691, Massachusetts became a _____ colony.
   a. proprietary
   b. royal
   c. Dutch
   d. Puritan

***Short Answer*** Write a paragraph response to each question.

1. Why did Henry VIII choose to break with the Roman Catholic Church?
2. What was Puritanism?
3. Why did Puritans begin to immigrate to New England?
4. How were the Pilgrims different from other Puritans?
5. What was the Massachusetts Bay Company, and how was it founded?
6. What kind of people immigrated to the Massachusetts Bay Colony?
7. What was the government system in New England under Puritanism?
8. Why did Puritanism splinter?
9. What was the Halfway Covenant, and why was it adopted by Puritan churches in the 1660s?
10. Why was New Netherland so different from the British colonies?
11. Why was Pennsylvania founded?
12. What were the toleration policies in early Pennsylvania?
13. How did the Navigation Acts affect the colonies in America?
14. How did the monarchy attempt to consolidate royal authority after King Philip's War (1675–1676)?
15. What was the Glorious Revolution?

***Building Historical Skills*** Historians use a variety of sources to think and talk about the past, including maps, illustrations, and written records. Maps provide a variety of different kinds of comparative information in a condensed visual format; reading them requires learning how to sort through this information. To deepen our understanding of the past by supplementing written records, historians frequently interpret material culture, such as a vase or a painting, with techniques borrowed from art history, archaeology, or anthropology. Written records, though familiar as sources, raise their own problems of interpretation. Every document reflects someone's particular perspective or assumptions. It is the historian's task to study and compare each document to other records with other perspectives. The following exercises introduce you to using maps, illustrations, and written documents as sources of information. Use these sources as well as the material in the chapter to think about different themes and topics discussed in the text.

***Map Activity*** Locate the following places on Map 3.3: American Colonies at the End of the Seventeenth Century on page 96 of *The American Promise,* Second Edition.

1. New England Colonies
2. Middle Colonies
3. Chesapeake Colonies
4. Lower South Colonies
5. Areas of European Settlement
6. New France
7. Boston

Answer the following questions in a paragraph based on Map 3.3: American Colonies at the End of the Seventeenth Century.

**READING THE MAP** What geographic feature acted as the boundary for colonial territorial claims? Which colonies were the most settled and which the least?

**CONNECTIONS** The map divides the colonies into four regions. Can you think of an alternative organization? On what criteria would it be based?

**WEB LINKS** To explore the topics discussed in the exercise above, visit the Web links noted below.

"The Cartographic Creation of New England"
http://www.usm.maine.edu/~maps/exhibit2/sec4.htm

"Samuel Champlain's Chart of Port St. Louis (Plymouth)"
http://etext.lib.virginia.edu/users/deetz/Plymouth/champlain.html

***Visual Activity*** The Massachusetts Bay Colony seal pictured on page 76 of *The American Promise,* Second Edition, was used for official documents and records from the colony. The seal, which depicts an Indian man inviting the English to "Come Over and Help Us," was intended to demonstrate the superiority of the English and the inferiority of the Indian people. The Indian's inferiority is demonstrated by his lack of clothing: he is wearing nothing but a loincloth made of leaves, not unlike the wardrobe Adam and Eve were supposed to have put together after eating the apple, a Biblical reference that would not have been lost on a Puritan viewer. He is shown as living in a state of almost unadulterated nature, with no housing or society depicted. There are only a couple of trees, a bow, and an arrow, implying that what society the eastern Indians had developed revolved around warfare. The irony of the seal is that, in fact, the English settlers generally had no interest in helping the Indians and the Indians did not want English "help." Of course, the Indians were not in a position to impede the English settlers from achieving their vision of settling America, and as a result the English helped themselves to the land, usually at the expense of the native tribes.

Answer the following questions in a paragraph based on "Seal of Massachusetts Bay Colony."

**READING THE IMAGE** What does the seal demonstrate regarding the English view of the Indians?

**CONNECTIONS** How did the viewpoint represented by the seal affect colonization in the Americas? What were the English expecting when they traveled to America, and in what ways were those expectations not met?

**WEB LINKS** To explore the topics discussed in the exercise above, visit the Web links noted below.

"The 1629 Charter of Massachusetts Bay"
http://www.law.ou.edu/hist/massbay.html

"Excerpt of Hutchinson's *History of the Massachusetts-Bay*"
http://www.people.virginia.edu/~rwm3n/webdoc9.html

***Analyzing Sources Activity*** Answer the following questions in a paragraph based on "Documenting the American Promise: King Philip Considers Christianity" on page 80 of *The American Promise*, Second Edition.

1. To what degree is Eliot's dialogue a reliable guide to Philip's doubts about the wisdom of becoming a praying Indian?
2. According to Eliot, was Philip's religion a stumbling block to his acceptance of Christianity? What made Philip fear that he would "fall down the precipice"?
3. If Philip had written a dialogue proposing that Eliot convert to the Wampanoag way of life, what arguments might it have made?

**WEB LINKS** To explore the topics discussed in the exercise above, visit the Web links noted below.

"The Wampanoag in 'King Philip's War' and After"
http://www.plimoth.org/Library/Wampanoag/wamppost.htm

"Edward Randolph's Description of King Philip's War (1685)"
http://www.swarthmore.edu/SocSci/bdorsey1/41docs/45-ran.html

# Answer Key

## Chapter 3: The Northern Colonies in the Seventeenth Century, 1601–1700

### *Chapter Overview*

#### *Chronology*

1. b
2. d
3. b
4. b
5. c
6. c
7. c
8. a
9. a
10. c

#### *Defining Terms*

1. Act of Supremacy
2. Puritanism
3. Parliament
4. English Reformation
5. Pilgrims
6. Mayflower Compact
7. "little commonwealth"
8. Quakers
9. "invisible saints"
10. freemen
11. Halfway Covenant
12. proprietary colonies
13. colonial council
14. Charter of Privileges
15. royal charters
16. Glorious Revolution
17. Navigation Acts
18. Staple Act

### *Chapter Review*

#### *Multiple-Choice*

1. c
2. b
3. a
4. a
5. a
6. b
7. b
8. d
9. a
10. c
11. d
12. c
13. a.
14. b.
15. a
16. d
17. c
18. b
19. d
20. b
21. c
22. b
23. b
24. d
25. a
26. c
27. a
28. d
29. c
30. a
31. c
32. a
33. d
34. c
35. a
36. c
37. c
38. d
39. b
40. d
41. b
42. d
43. d
44. b
45. c
46. a
47. d
48. c
49. d
50. d
51. a
52. b
53. b
54. c
55. d
56. b
57. b
58. a
59. d
60. c
61. a
62. b
63. d
64. c
65. b
66. a
67. b
68. c
69. c
70. d
71. b
72. a
73. d
74. a
75. a
76. b
77. c
78. a
79. d
80. a
81. a
82. a
83. b
84. b
85. b
86. d
87. d
88. d
89. c
90. a
91. d
92. c
93. d
94. b
95. d
96. a
97. d
98. b
99. b
100. c
101. a
102. c
103. b
104. d
105. d
106. b
107. d
108. a
109. b
110. b

### *Short Answer*

1. Henry's decision to break with Rome was based on several factors. He recognized that the Protestant Reformation offered him the opportunity to break free from the control of the Pope and to take control of the church in England. Thus he could seize control of the considerable wealth that the church possessed there. The break also gave Henry power over who was appointed to bishoprics and other positions of power within the hierarchy in England, and this enabled Henry to retain greater control over the country.
2. Puritanism was a branch of Protestantism that developed after the Reformation. The Puritans believed that the church needed to be subjected to a thorough reformation and that the changes that Henry and his successors had introduced were not substantial enough. They believed that the church hierarchy should be abolished; that the rituals of Catholic worship be eliminated; and that the emphasis in religion should instead be placed on an individual's relationship with God.
3. Following the accession of James I to the throne, the government in England turned increasingly hostile against Puritanism. He and his son, Charles I, enforced conformity to the Church of England and punished dissenters. Then, in 1629, Charles I dissolved Parliament, where Puritans were well represented. His anti-Puritan policies convinced many Puritans that they could no longer defend their faith in England.
4. The Pilgrims were also known as Separatists. They wanted to separate themselves completely from the Church of England rather than remain part of the Church. Most Puritans, including the later immigrants that settled in the Massachusetts Bay Colony, wanted to reform the Church from within and sought to make changes that way. The Pilgrims wanted to be completely apart from the Church, and this was one of the reasons that they were not discouraged with the rather limited number of immigrants who settled in Plymouth.
5. The Massachusetts Bay Company was founded as a joint stock venture between a group of Puritans and investors. Led by John Winthrop, the company traveled to Massachusetts and established a settlement on the peninsula that is modern day Boston. The joint stockholders had managed to sneak a provision into the charter that allowed the colony to be run from the colony, rather than in England, which was significant because it provided the colony much more freedom.
6. The Massachusetts Bay Colony was deeply religious, based on Puritan ideas, but the founders were not separatists and as such welcomed immigrants to the settlement. Like English Puritans, most of the immigrants came from the middle ranks of English society: they were primarily farmers and tradesmen who were able to finance their journeys themselves. The bulk of Puritans immigrated as part of a family group, in contrast to settlers in the Chesapeake.
7. The government created by the Puritans in New England was designed to keep Puritanism alive and well. The number of citizens grew too large for all of the men to meet together, so many towns elected deputies to serve as representatives. All men, regardless of social standing, were allowed to vote and speak out at town meetings (where locals officials were elected), but other members of the community, notably women, were prohibited from doing so. Popular participation by men was routinely practiced in Puritan communities at a time when it was rarely exercised elsewhere, making the communities appear far more democratic than their contemporaries.
8. The Puritans comprised many different groups. Puritanism defined dissent as an error, and so anyone who did not hold to the exact teaching of the Puritan leaders found himself (or occasionally herself) outside the community. Roger Williams, Anne Hutchinson, and Thomas Hooker are all examples of pious individuals who were not able to conform to Puritanism in the way the leadership demanded. As these individuals left the fold and founded their own communities, they were joined by others, and in time, major groups of dissenters emerged all over New England.
9. In the 1650s, the children of the original New England settlers were becoming adults and having their own families. However, unlike their parents, they were not undergoing the conversion experience that would allow them to become full members of their churches. This meant that they could not have their offspring baptized, a serious concern given the rate of infant and child mortality. The Halfway Covenant was intended to deal with this problem by allowing the unconverted children of saints to become partial church members: they could baptize their infants, but they could not take communion or vote on church issues.
10. New Netherland was unusual for several reasons. Unlike most of the other colonies, it was not founded specifically for religious reasons; rather, it was a primarily economic colony. The colony did not attract many European immigrants and was not profitable. In addition, the colony was remarkably diverse, in that those who did immigrate to the colony were religiously and ethnically heterogeneous.
11. Pennsylvania was founded as a "holy experiment." William Penn, the proprietor of Pennsylvania, had been granted 45,000 square

miles of land by King Charles II. The grant was given partially because Charles II hoped that Penn's colony would attract Quakers—the religious group that Penn belong to—thereby reducing their numbers in England. The colony welcomed peoples of all Christian faiths and as a result became one of the most successful colonies in America.

12. Pennsylvania prided itself on its toleration. Even the Indian tribes were treated fairly within the colony. Any individual was welcome to reside in Pennsylvania, although only Christians could vote and hold office. Women were allowed to be religious leaders. Immigrants from all over Europe traveled to Pennsylvania to be allowed to practice their religions in peace.
13. The Navigation Acts were designed to allow the British government to benefit economically from the colonies. Certain "enumerated" (listed) goods, such as tobacco, could be shipped only to England or to other English colonies. In addition to the rules regarding enumerated products, goods being shipped to England could be sent only in English ships. Some of the colonies, such as those in New England, were not impacted severely, but others, such as the Chesapeake colonies, were dramatically affected.
14. After King Philip's War, Charles II, whose father had been executed by Puritan Parliamentary rebels, initiated a royal investigation to determine whether New England abided by English rules. His agent concluded that New England was out of line, and Charles II decided to govern New England more directly. In 1684, the Crown revoked the Massachusetts charter and sent governors to oversee the colonies. Two years later, royal officials created the Dominion of New England, which combined several colonies into one large colony, and also revoked proprietary rights in some areas and invalidated all land titles. All of these acts were designed to further English control over the colonies.
15. The Glorious Revolution was the bloodless uprising that overthrew King James II of England. James was a devout Catholic and wanted to return England to Catholicism. When the Protestant nobility found out about his plans, they made their own plans to overthrow him and replace him with the Dutch ruler, William of Orange. James II found out about the plan and fled to France, and William became the king of England.

### *Map Activity*

Reading the Map: The major geographic feature that bounded the colonial territories was the Appalachian mountain range, which ran north to south from New Hampshire to Georgia. The most settled colonies were those in the north and in the Chesapeake region. Massachusetts, New York, Pennsylvania, Maryland, and Virginia were relatively highly populated, while North Carolina, South Carolina, and Georgia had only a handful of settlements. The coastal regions harbored far more people than the inland territories, and most of the inland areas that were inhabited were along major rivers like the James and the Hudson.

Connections: The map divides the colonies along the lines of English settlement. However, there would be numerous other ways to organize the colonies. For instance, it would be possible to consider them in light of Indian tribes, many of which still had significant claims to the land that Europeans inhabited. That map would show the Iroquois confederacy in New York and Pennsylvania, the Algonquians along the Atlantic seaboard, and the Muskogeans in the Southeast. The colonies could also be divided into economic zones, with New England's distinctive fish and timber industry constituting one area, the Middle colonies' importing and exporting another, and the Chesapeake and Lower South's tobacco crops a third.

### *Visual Activity*

Reading the Image: The seal clearly depicts the Indian as inferior. Not only is he asking for help, but he is barely clothed, which in Puritan minds was a sign of sinfulness. He is holding a bow and arrow, which were inferior to the English firearms. He is speaking English; however, few English settlers took the time to learn the language of the native tribes, so his words would need to be in English for anyone to understand them. Overall, the impression created by the seal is one of inferiority and even childlike behavior: the only Puritans who traveled around nearly naked were children.

Connections: The seal's depiction of the native peoples was clearly misleading. The trip to the Americas was undertaken by many who believed that, in fact, the Indians were friendly and desired help from the British. In fact, as many colonists discovered when they arrived, many of the indigenous tribes did not trust the English (with good reason). After all, the colonists sought to expel the Indians from their traditional lands. The English settlers who traveled to the Americas were expecting an inferior, desperate people, and instead they encountered men and women who were willing to fight to retain their traditional holdings. Some tribes remained open to helping the settlers, but as King Philip's War indicated, many others were not willing to allow themselves to be overrun completely by English settlers.

### *Analyzing Sources*

1. Clearly, Eliot had a certain level of insight into the reasons that Indians chose not to become Christians, and he had no doubt heard most of the arguments himself. However, the dialogue was created, at least in part, to remove those arguments and establish clear reasons for the conversion of Indians to Christianity. By the end of the dialogue, it is obvious that Philip is in the wrong; he admits that he is afraid of excommunication, and promises to "ponder and consider of these things." In that sense, the reliability of the dialogue must be questioned.
2. Yes, Philip's religion a stumbling block to his acceptance of Christianity. One of his first arguments against becoming a praying Indian is that if he does so and the other members of his tribe do so, they will no longer respect him as a sachem, and he will become a common man rather than one possessed of great authority and power. Philip also argues that if he does convert, he will be a poor and weak sachem and will be easily trodden on by others. Ultimately, according to Philip, "the way I am now, I am full and potent, but if I change my way and pray to God, I shall be empty and weak."

   Philip feared that he would fall down the precipice if he attempted to overcome the hurdles that prevented his conversion: that is, dealing with his loss of power, and becoming a "common" man rather than a great sachem. He feared that climbing over the hurdles that stood in his way of conversion would lead him to fall and that his fall would be a deadly one.
3. One of the strongest arguments would have been that Eliot would be seen as a great leader in the eyes of the Wampanoag. Their hierarchy was similar in many ways to the traditional Christian hierarchy, so a comfort factor might have existed as well. Philip might have made the point to Eliot that their belief systems were not all that different and that by becoming a Wampanoag, Eliot would be worshipped as a chief. Power can be a very persuasive device, especially when wielded by someone as talented as Philip was.

# COLONIAL AMERICA IN THE EIGHTEENTH CENTURY, 1701–1770

4

## Chapter Overview

### Chapter Summary

***Introduction*** Chapter Four begins with a portrait of Benjamin Franklin's early life in Boston and his arrival in Philadelphia. Franklin's experience reveals much about the everyday lives of ordinary people in the eighteenth-century North American colonies. But his story also illustrates some of the major changes taking place in the eighteenth century as social and economic forces continued to emphasize the differences among the colonies at the same time that cultural and political developments began to unify them.

***A Growing Population and Expanding Economy, pp. 107–108*** The most important fact about eighteenth-century colonial America was its remarkable population growth. The number of colonists rose over the century from 250,000 in 1700 to 2 million by 1770. At the same time, the ethnic and religious profile of the thirteen colonies diversified substantially, owing to increasing immigration from places other than England. The availability of cheap, abundant land, the concomitant surplus of food, and ample work opportunities engendered a social and economic environment that allowed the majority of free colonists to prosper to a degree unusual in the eighteenth century.

***New England: From Puritans to Yankee Traders, pp. 108–112*** Though New England's population increased during the eighteenth century, its growth fell behind that of the other colonies. The main reasons were New England's higher ratio of settlers to land and Puritan communities' reputation for hostility to non-Puritan religions. But Puritan orthodoxy was on the wane, and the growth of a vibrant commercial network in New England meant that trade became a faith that often competed with Puritan traditions.

**NATURAL INCREASE AND LAND DISTRIBUTION** Natural increase was mostly responsible for the growth of New England's population during the eighteenth century, much as it had been during the previous century, owing to high marriage rates and large family size. The growing population of New Englanders sought new land by expanding their holdings west and north, increasingly pressing up against the lands of hostile Indian and French neighbors. Also beginning in the eighteenth century, the colonial governments of Massachusetts and Connecticut, in need of revenue, stopped the practice of granting land to towns and instead began selling it directly to individuals. These new landowners tended to settle on individual farms rather than congregating in towns or villages, as seventeenth-century settlers had. As a result, the influence of churches and towns over people's behavior began to decline.

**FARMS, FISH, AND TRADE** The scarcity of land in New England resulted in agricultural diversification. Farmers grew a variety of crops rather than one major crop for the market, which was often hard to access. Although New England was not a good place to get rich, farmers were at the base of a diversified commercial economy. As they had since the seventeenth century, New Englanders made their fortunes at sea. Their main commodity was codfish, most of which was exported to markets in southern Europe or the West Indies. The entire New England economy benefited from this Atlantic commerce, which created a host of jobs ranging from laborers and sailors to ship captains and merchants. The merchants were the link at the hub of trade between local folk and the international market. By the middle of the century, a wealthy merchant aristocracy had emerged in New England, the richest and most successful of whom lived in Boston: at the same time, a small percentage of people in the region lived in genuine poverty. New England also remained the most English and most homogeneous of all the colonial areas.

***The Middle Colonies: Immigrants, Wheat, and Work, pp. 112–118*** No section of the North American colonies was more diverse ethnically, politically, or religiously than the middle colonies—New York, New Jersey, Pennsylvania, and Delaware. This heterogeneity was largely the result of the influx of non-English immigrants—notably Germans and Scots-Irish—whose arrival by 1770 had increased the population of the middle colonies by a factor of ten.

**GERMAN AND SCOTS-IRISH IMMIGRANTS** Germans made up the largest group of immigrants from the European continent to the middle colonies. Most German immigrants came from a region in southwestern Germany known as the Palatinate. A good number were peasants seeking to escape a harsh political and economic environment. However, the majority of these Germans were "middling" folk, neither the poorest nor the better off. Similar motives impelled the Scots-Irish, who considerably outnumbered German immigrants. The label "Scots-Irish," like "Pennsylvania Dutch," was a misnomer because the Scots-Irish actually came from northern Ireland, Scotland, and England. Most were poor farm laborers or tenant farmers who were exploited by greedy landlords or compelled to flee to the colonies by droughts, crop failures, high food prices, and rising rents. The process of immigration was miserable and expensive. Many Germans and Scots-Irish, particularly young males who migrated alone, paid for their passage by becoming redemptioners, a kind of indentured servant.

**PENNSYLVANIA: "THE BEST POOR [WHITE] MAN'S COUNTRY"** Immigrants came to the middle colonies for the perceived economic opportunities. Because of a scarcity of labor, hired workers could get high wages. Most bound servants worked in cities and towns. Masters prized them because they were much cheaper than hired day laborers, and the strictures of bondage were rigorously enforced. African slavery existed in the middle colonies, albeit on a very small scale, since only the more affluent white colonists could afford slaves and there was little use for their labor on family-operated farms. Slaves were treated much more harshly than were white servants; even when slaves obtained their freedom white racism often made African Americans the victims of reprisals for white Europeans' suspicions and anxieties.

Immigrants were interested in the middle colonies because of the availability of land and relatively peaceful frontier relations with Indians. However, even Pennsylvania, with its policy of negotiating with Indian tribes to purchase land, pushed its agreements with the Indians to the limit. Few colonists went beyond the northern boundary of Pennsylvania, where landlords and Iroquois Indians controlled land. Most people with limited funds moved just beyond already improved farms, where land was cheaper. Flour milling was the number one industry, and flour the number one export of the middle colonies, which allowed many middle colonists to enjoy a fairly secure and stable existence. The comparatively widespread prosperity of the middle colonies allowed its inhabitants to buy more English imports between 1720 and 1770 than either New England or the South could buy. At the center of trade in wheat exports and English imports stood Philadelphia, the largest colonial city in North America and second only to London in the British empire. A wealthy merchant elite, most of whom were Quaker, ruled the city. Quaker beliefs in industry, thrift, honesty, and sobriety encouraged the accumulation of wealth, a goal earnestly recommended in works like Benjamin Franklin's *Poor Richard's Almanack*. The widespread conviction that good things came from work led to the reputation of the middle colonies as the best poor man's country in the world.

***The Southern Colonies: Land of Slavery, pp. 118–127*** For most of the eighteenth century, the southern colonies (Virginia, Maryland, North and South Carolina, and Georgia) contained more colonists than either the middle colonies or New England. Many European immigrants funneled from the middle colonies into the backcountry or came as indentured servants, and African slaves made important contributions to population growth and southern culture.

**THE ATLANTIC SLAVE TRADE AND THE GROWTH OF SLAVERY** Involuntary immigrants in the form of African slaves contributed to the burgeoning population in the southern colonies. During the eighteenth century, slavery became the defining characteristic of the southern colonies. Southern colonists lived in two distinct geographic and agricultural areas. The Chesapeake colonies of the upper South — Virginia and Maryland — specialized in tobacco cultivation, while the lower South of the South Atlantic coastal region specialized in the production of rice and indigo.

The southern colonies' black population grew enormously because of a combination of natural increase and the flourishing African slave trade to British North America during the eighteenth century. The slaves were primarily West Africans who had been kidnapped or captured in war and sold into bondage to other Africans, who in turn sold them to the European slavers who brought them over on slave ships. Perhaps even worse than being sold into lifelong bondage was the ordeal of crossing the Atlantic — the infamous Middle Passage — when on the average about 15 percent of a ship's human cargo died from dehydration, malnutrition, diseases, or other maladies incurred from the filth, pollution, and overcrowding below deck. The slaves were then sold to colonial slave merchants or to southern planters who put them to work on tobacco or rice plantations. The small number of slaves purchased by individual planters reflected in part the comparatively high price of slaves as the demand for their labor increased. Despite a fairly high mortality rate — especially in the first two years of slave life in the colonies — the natural increase of slaves during the eighteenth century meant that more slaves were becoming acculturated and that the majority of slaves were native-born.

**SLAVE LABOR AND AFRICAN AMERICAN CULTURE** Planters extracted as much work as possible from their slaves. Eighteenth-century masters preferred slaves over indentured servants not only because slaves served for life but also because colonial laws did not hinder masters from using force to keep their slaves working and tractable. Although the likelihood of brutal retaliation made most slaves cautious about resisting, rebellion did occur once in the eighteenth century with the 1739

Stono uprising in South Carolina. Its outcome illustrated that slaves, no matter how determined, had no chance of overturning slavery and that open rebellion amounted to suicide since all the power resided with slave owners.

Despite these limitations, slaves did what they could to retain their humanity, protect themselves from abuse, and gain a measure of autonomy. In South Carolina, on larger plantations, a task system of labor developed that allowed individual slaves who finished their work before the end of the day to use the remainder as they pleased—fishing, hunting, sewing, cooking, or gardening. The concept of kinship, which structured slaves' relations with each other, created a network of extended family relationships, giving slaves a sense of belonging, and giving their lives meaning and purpose. Slaves also expressed other features of their West African origins by giving their children African names, growing familiar crops, and building similar types of houses.

**TOBACCO, RICE, AND PROSPERITY** African slave labor increased the prosperity of planters, British merchants, and the monarchy. Rice and indigo, the main staples of Carolina planters, made up three-fourths of lower South exports, with the majority of the crops going to England and the rest to the West Indies. Together with Chesapeake tobacco, these products made the southern colonies the richest in North America. The per capita wealth of free southern whites was three times greater than that of the middle colonists and four times more than that of New Englanders. The wealthiest were the rice grandees of the lower South and the tobacco gentry of the Chesapeake who owned large estates that were maintained and supported by slaves. The gap in wealth among white Southerners caused envy and sometimes tension, but a shared sense of white supremacy mitigated the potential for rebellion or resentment. The planter/slaveholding class also dominated southern colonial politics. In both the Chesapeake and the lower South, landholding determined voting rights, and the requirement was set high enough to deny about 40 percent of white men in Virginia the right to vote.

***Unifying Experiences, pp. 127–136*** While all three colonial groups became increasingly different during the eighteenth century, colonists throughout British North America shared certain unifying economic, religious, and political experiences. Economically, all three regions were agrarian and sold their staples in similar external and internal markets that offered essentially the same array of goods to consumers throughout the colonies. Religiously, the colonists became more secular during the eighteenth century, and politically, they became aware that despite having thirteen different local governments, they all owed allegiance to the same king and Parliament and all shared distinctive identity as British colonists.

**COMMERCE AND CONSUMPTION** Colonial products stimulated the development of mass markets throughout the Atlantic world and helped to establish an important feature of the eighteenth-century commercial revolution: Ordinary people, not just the wealthy elite, bought not only essentials for basic survival but also things they desired. The Atlantic commerce that took colonial goods to English markets brought the desired consumer goods back to the colonies. English exports to North America became increasingly important, multiplying by a factor of eight between 1700 and 1770. The consumption of English exports created a material uniformity among all colonial classes and made the colonists look and feel more British, even though they lived three thousand miles away. It also accustomed them to defining their own wishes and acting on them.

**RELIGION, ENLIGHTENMENT, AND REVIVAL** It was possible to find virtually every form of Protestant Christianity in the colonies and even Catholicism in Maryland. But churches argued over fine points of doctrine, convincing many colonists that toleration of religious differences was desirable. Other colonists became deists. Influenced by the Enlightenment, an intellectual movement, a new climate developed, characterized by an optimistic view of human nature and a belief that the universe was an orderly and functional mechanism. Enlightenment ideas encouraged people to think for themselves and to study the world around them to find ways to improve society. Ministers were concerned about widespread religious indifference. The Great Awakening, a wave of religious revivals that swept the colonies, fulfilled many people's need for a strong, emotional religion. Its greatest proponent, Anglican minister George Whitefield, was a riveting speaker who preached sermons to thousands of people in nearly every colony. The Great Awakening did not tend to make permanent converts, but it did convince people that each individual soul mattered and that each person could decide whether or not to be saved.

**BONDS OF EMPIRE** The British empire's colonial policies provided a common framework of political expectations and experiences to the diversity of peoples, religions, and communities that existed in eighteenth-century North America. British power defended the colonists from foreign enemies and Indians, and although each colony had its own militia, the British army and navy bore the responsibility of colonial defense. No coherent policy toward the Indians developed before the 1760s, but the colonists and British shared the view that the Indians were useful as trading partners, were powerful allies at times, and on occasion, were deadly enemies.

By and large, the empire's economic policies were effectively enforced through the Navigation Acts. When royal officials attempted to exercise political power in colonial governments, they often met with fierce opposition and resentment. Royal governors were hamstrung by instructions from England and had so little patronage with which to buy votes that in effect they were given the task of ruling without having the power to force their will on the colonists. Americans liked to think that their colonial governments were replicas of Parliament, but they were not. In short, the colonial assemblies provided numerous checks on the power of royal governors while simultaneously trying to preserve as many colonial privileges as possible.

## *Conclusion: The Dual Identity of British North American Colonists*

The eighteenth-century colonists had a distinctive dual identity as American colonists and as British subjects that would soon create conflict and controversy for them. By 1776, the thirteen colonies would be forced to decide whether they were American or British.

## *Chronology Activity*

Read the annotated chronology, and answer the multiple-choice questions.

1702 Queen Anne's War triggers large German immigration to American colonies. About 85,000 fled the German principalities, particularly the southwestern region called the Palatinate, after a French invasion made ordinarily bad conditions intolerable. By 1770, Germans made up 15 percent of immigrants and represented the largest contingent of migrants from the European continent.

1715 Yamasee War pits South Carolina colonists against Yamasee and Creek Indians. A bloody frontier conflict, the Yamasee War was the kind of uprising that caused North American colonists to be nervous about their safety and to depend on the British for military defense.

1717 Scots-Irish immigration to American colonies begins to increase. The Scots-Irish came largely from the north of Ireland, northern England, and Scotland, and constituted 36 percent of all immigrants in 1770. Most of them were farm laborers or tenant farmers facing poor agricultural conditions and high rents in their native countries.

1721 *New England Courant* begins publication. James Franklin's paper was one of the earliest American papers and the first to refuse to submit its copy to the governor for official approval. It served as a medium through which to disseminate dissenting opinions publicly, stimulating the growth of the newspaper industry.

1723 Benjamin Franklin arrives in Philadelphia. Franklin's experiences in Philadelphia illustrated the changes that were transforming the British colonies in the eighteenth century—his desire to make something of himself, his eagerness to challenge orthodoxy, his self-confidence in his own abilities, and a marked decline in religious observance.

1730s Jonathan Edwards leads New England religious awakening. Edwards preached about humanity's depravity and God's vengefulness in a fiery style designed to encourage greater religious zeal in his listeners. He was in the forefront of the Great Awakening, the wave of evangelical revivals that proponents hoped would end the colonial tendency toward religious indifference.

1732 Georgia founded. Georgia was only the second British colony along the South Atlantic coastline. Despite the late start, by 1770 the lower South had 15 percent of the southern population, with blacks outnumbering whites in many counties.

1733 Benjamin Franklin begins to publish *Poor Richard's Almanack. Poor Richard's Almanack* was a popular calendar of weather predictions, astrological alignments, and epigrams, which reflected the concerns of eighteenth-century Pennsylvanians. Pennsylvania, which began as a Quaker utopia, came to epitomize the desirability of ambition and wealth as spurs to work, discipline, and good behavior.

1737 The Penn family takes advantage of "Walking Purchase" to claim twice as much land as originally agreed on with Indians. Although the Penns followed a policy of negotiating with Indians to purchase land to reduce frontier clashes, they did not always make fair deals. The Walking Purchase was a 1686 agreement granting the Penns land as far as a man could walk in a day and a half; however, they sent out runners and approximately doubled the size of their claim.

1739 Slave insurrection occurs at Stono, South Carolina. In September, a group of twenty slaves attacked a country store, killed its attendants, confiscated weapons, and headed toward Spanish Florida. They persuaded other rebel slaves to join them and burned half a dozen plantations and killed more than twenty whites before they were stopped and killed themselves. The rebellion demonstrated that even the most determined slaves could not effectively resist or overturn the slave system.

1740s George Whitefield preaches revival of religion throughout the colonies. Whitefield was the most famous revivalist in the eighteenth-century Atlantic world. His preaching attracted tens of thousands of listeners and often roused people to a state of religious ecstasy. Without having a significant effect on church membership, revivalists helped give colonists a set of common experiences and foster the democratic and egalitarian ideas that every soul mattered and individuals could decide about everlasting life.

Majority of southern slaves are born in colonies rather than in Africa. The rate of natural increase among slaves set the southern colonies apart from other New World slave societies, although the continued importation of Africans meant that African culture remained very influential.

1741 New York officials suspect slave conspiracy and execute thirty-one slaves. The slave conspiracy was supposedly revealed by arson and several unexplained thefts. This incident was typical of the attitude of whites in the middle colonies, who used blacks as scapegoats for their own suspicions and anxieties.

1745 Olaudah Equiano born in present-day Nigeria. *The Interesting Narrative,* Equiano's 1789 book about his kidnapping in Africa, voyage to America, and experiences as a slave, is a rare account of the process of enslavement.

1750s Colonists begin to move down Shenandoah Valley from Pennsylvania into southern backcountry. Settlers in Pennsylvania tended to move just beyond already improved farms. Shunning the northern regions, which were controlled by large landholders and the Iroquois, they went farther and farther to the south and west.

Colonists increasingly became indebted to English merchants. As the European market for English exports tightened, colonial markets became increasingly important to British merchants; exports to North America multiplied eightfold between 1700 and 1770, outpacing the rate of population growth. When the colonists could not pay for English goods, English exporters extended them liberal credit, causing colonial debts to soar.

1769 American Philosophical Society founded in Philadelphia. The American Philosophical Society was the outgrowth of an earlier discussion group organized by Benjamin Franklin. It was the center of Enlightenment thought in the American colonies and fostered communication among leading colonial thinkers, especially discussions on ways to improve society.

## *Chronology Questions* Choose the letter of the best answer.

1. The Yamasee War, which strengthened the colonists' dependence on British military aid, broke out in
   a. 1702.
   b. 1715.
   c. 1732.
   d. 1739.

2. What is the correct order for the following events?
   1. George Whitefield preaches the revival of religion throughout the colonies.
   2. Benjamin Franklin begins to publish *Poor Richard's Almanack.*
   3. The American Philosophical Society is founded in Philadelphia.
   4. Jonathan Edwards leads a New England religious awakening.

   a. 1, 3, 4, 2
   b. 2, 4, 1, 3
   c. 4, 2, 1, 3
   d. 3, 1, 2, 4

3. The *New England Courant*, one of the earliest American newspapers, began publication in
   a. 1721.
   b. 1733.
   c. 1739.
   d. 1745.

4. In 1741,
   a. the American Philosophical Society is founded in Philadelphia.
   b. New York officials suspect a slave conspiracy and execute thirty-one slaves.
   c. Benjamin Franklin arrives in Philadelphia.
   d. Olaudah Equiano is born in present-day Nigeria.

5. The majority of southern slaves were born in the colonies rather than in Africa beginning in the
   a. early 1800s.
   b. 1780s.
   c. 1760s.
   d. 1740s.

6. What is the correct order for the following events?
   1. Queen Anne's War triggers large German immigration to American colonies.
   2. Scots-Irish immigration to American colonies begins to increase.
   3. The Penn family takes advantage of the "Walking Purchase."
   4. Colonists begin to move down the Shenandoah Valley into Pennsylvania.

   a. 1, 2, 3, 4
   b. 3, 1, 2, 4
   c. 4, 3, 1, 2
   d. 4, 1, 2, 3

7. The Stono slave rebellion occurred in South Carolina in
   a. 1702.
   b. 1723.
   c. 1739.
   d. 1769.

8. During the 1750s,
   a. Olaudah Equiano was born in present-day Nigeria.
   b. Georgia was founded.
   c. George Whitefield preached the revival of religion throughout colonies.
   d. the colonists increasingly became indebted to English merchants.

9. What is the correct order for the following events?
   1. A slave insurrection occurs at Stono, South Carolina.
   2. New York officials suspect a slave conspiracy and execute thirty-one slaves.
   3. The Yamasee War pits South Carolina colonists against Yamasee and Creek Indians.
   4. Georgia is founded.
   a. 4, 2, 1, 3
   b. 1, 4, 3, 2
   c. 2, 1, 4, 3
   d. 3, 4, 1, 2

10. Scots-Irish immigration to the American colonies began to increase in
   a. 1717.
   b. 1737.
   c. 1757.
   d. 1777.

## *Defining Terms* Match each term with the correct definition.

Scots-Irish
Pennsylvania Dutch
Yamasee War
Middle Passage
Stono Rebellion
"Walking Purchase"
Atlantic commerce
redemptioner
agricultural diversification
task system
newspapers
deist
indigo
partible inheritance
George Whitefield
Olaudah Equiano
Enlightenment
American Philosophical Society
*Poor Richard's Almanack*
free colonists
natural increase
squatters

1. Population growth through reproduction. This was the major source of population growth in the colonies in the eighteenth century. natural increase

2. People who settled on unoccupied land without paying for it in the hopes that it might eventually become theirs. squatters

3. Colonists who were not indentured servants or slaves. free colonists

4. The subdivision of land more or less equally among sons. By the eighteenth century, this practice had created farms too small to support a family. partible inheritance

5. The growing of many small crops rather than a single large crop for market. This was characteristic of colonial New England. agricultural diversification

6. The trade carried on between the colonies, the Caribbean, and Europe. The goods involved included New England fish, livestock, and timber; Caribbean refined sugar and molasses; and European luxury goods. Atlantic commerce

7. The colonial name for the Germans who settled in the middle colonies. Pennsylvania Dutch

8. The colonial name for immigrants from the north of Ireland, Scotland, and northern England. Scots-Irish

9. A variant of indentured servants. A captain would agree to transport an impoverished immigrant, who would then obtain the money to pay for his or her passage from colonial relatives or by selling his or her labor as a servant. redemptioner

10. The Penn family's agreement with Indian tribes guaranteeing the Penns land as far as a man could walk in a day and a half. The Penns managed to double the size of their claim by sending out three runners. "walking Purchase"

11. Benjamin Franklin's calendar of weather predictions, astrological alignments, and pithy epigrams. Promising long-term rewards for tireless labor, its popularity suggested that Pennsylvanians were more concerned about worldly profits than piety. Poor Richard's Almanack

12. A plant used to make blue dye. Farmers in the lower South specialized in the production of this crop. indigo

13. A slave in the mid-eighteenth century and author of *The Interesting Narrative*, a rare account of the process of enslavement. Olaudah Equiano

14. The crossing of the Atlantic in the hold of a slave ship. On average, 15 percent of slaves died during this voyage, with mortality rates sometimes reaching 50 percent or higher. Middle Passage

15. A slave rebellion that broke out in South Carolina in 1739. It was put down with great violence and demonstrated that eighteenth-century slaves had no real chance of overturning the slave system or defending themselves in a strike for freedom. Stono Rebellion

16. The way that Southern slaveowners structured their slaves' work. A slave would be given a specific responsibility—an area of ground to be planted or a job to be completed, for instance—and when the slave had finished, he or she could garden, fish, hunt, spin, weave, sew, or cook. task system

17. The eighteenth-century innovation that transformed news from information conveyed privately through letters and conversations into something public. newspapers

18. People who believed that God's plan could be found in nature rather than the Bible. The belief had a major impact on educated colonists. deists

19. An eighteenth-century intellectual movement that challenged conventional wisdom and encouraged people to study the world around them and think for themselves. Enlightenment

20. A group formed in 1769 out of an earlier discussion group formed by Benjamin Franklin. The institution fostered communication among leading colonial thinkers searching for ways to improve society. American Philosophical Society

21. The most famous revivalist in the eighteenth-century Atlantic world. George whitefield

22. A frontier war between the Yamassee and Creek Indians and English colonial settlements. It was typical of frontier fighting in that it involved numerous complicated alliances and was very bloody. Yamasee war

## Chapter Review

### *Multiple-Choice* Choose the letter of the best answer.

1. The most important fact about eighteenth-century colonial America was its
   a. economic underdevelopment.
   b. shortage of available land.
   c. phenomenal population growth.
   d. level of violence.

2. By 1770, the thirteen colonies were
   a. varied in people and environments.
   b. as homogeneous as Virginia.
   c. all subject to what amounted to a colonial "state" religion.
   d. all under one colonial government.

3. In general, the growth and diversity of the eighteenth-century population derived from
   a. immigration.
   b. natural increase.
   c. both immigration and natural increase.
   d. Indian assimilation.

4. About 33 percent of all eighteenth-century immigrants came from
   a. England.
   b. Africa.
   c. the German principalities.
   d. Scotland.

5. In 1770, half the colonists were of
   a. African descent.
   b. English descent.
   c. Native American descent.
   d. Scots-Irish descent.

6. By 1770, the people of the colonies were distinctively
   a. Native American.
   b. colonial.
   c. English.
   d. Irish.

7. In addition to the growth in population, one of the major features of eighteenth-century colonial society was the
   a. depressed economy.
   b. expanding economy.
   c. lack of food.
   d. low birth rate.

8. In 1700, most colonists lived on the edge of a
   a. small town.
   b. vast wilderness.
   c. city.
   d. river.

9. Land in the colonies was
   a. much cheaper than in Europe.
   b. beyond the means of average people.
   c. given away for free.
   d. difficult to farm.

10. The mushrooming colonial population was sustained by the
    a. pleasant climate.
    b. abundant land.
    c. support of the English government.
    d. insatiable demand for labor.

11. The abundance of land meant that it was possible for the colonial population to grow
    a. rapidly and with widespread poverty.
    b. slowly and without widespread poverty.
    c. slowly and with widespread poverty.
    d. rapidly and without widespread poverty.

12. The unique achievement of the eighteenth-century colonial economy was
   a. the wealth of most colonists.
   b. the poverty of most colonists.
   c. the modest economic welfare of most of the colonists.
   d. its similarity to the European economy.

13. The growth and diversity of the eighteenth-century colonial population derived from two sources: _____.
   a. immigration and natural increase
   b. immigration and internal migration
   c. Native American assimilation and immigration
   d. Native American assimilation and natural increase

14. _____ made up about three-fourths of colonial population growth.
   a. Immigration
   b. Indentured servants
   c. Natural increase
   d. Transported convicts

15. Of the following eighteenth-century immigrant groups, the smallest number came from _____.
   a. Africa
   b. the German principalities
   c. northern Ireland
   d. England

16. By 1770, the people of the colonies had a distinctive _____ profile.
   a. German
   b. English
   c. colonial
   d. African

16. Eighteenth-century colonial society's booming population was accompanied by _____.
   a. an expanding economy
   b. widespread hunger
   c. a shortage of consumer goods
   d. a shortage of affordable land

18. After almost a century of settlement, most colonists lived within fifty miles of _____.
   a. Virginia
   b. Massachusetts
   c. navigable rivers
   d. the Atlantic coastline

19. Compared with the Old World, land in the colonies was _____.
   a. cheap
   b. very expensive
   c. scarce
   d. hard to farm

20. Newcomers who lacked the money to buy land often lived as _____ along the frontiers of settlement.
   a. wage laborers
   b. squatters
   c. beggars
   d. tenant farmers

21. Without _____, land was almost worthless.
   a. improvements
   b. livestock
   c. transportation
   d. labor

22. The standard of living of free colonists _____ during the eighteenth century.
   a. remained static
   b. declined
   c. improved
   d. was miserable

23. The most important reason that immigrants avoided New England was its
   a. cold winters.
   b. high ratio of people to land.
   c. high cost of living.
   d. high mortality rate.

24. When settlers dispersed from New England towns in search of farmland,
   a. they often died alone in the wilderness.
   b. they were almost always financially successful.
   c. Puritan communities lost their cohesiveness.
   d. Puritan communities regained their cohesiveness.

25. The New England population grew by natural increase in large part because
   a. most married women had children.
   b. almost no children died before reaching adulthood.
   c. almost no women died in childbirth.
   d. the church encouraged childbearing.

26. When passing on land, New England families
    a. left all land to the eldest son.
    b. divided the land equally among sons.
    c. divided the land equally among all children.
    d. gave land to the neediest child.

27. During the eighteenth century, the colonial governments of Connecticut and Massachusetts started selling land to
    a. churches.
    b. groups of settlers.
    c. individuals.
    d. towns.

28. When colonists moved into western Massachusetts and Connecticut and north into New Hampshire and Maine, they tended to settle
    a. in towns.
    b. on large plantations.
    c. on individual farms.
    d. on religious communes.

29. The major agricultural product the New England colonies exported was
    a. corn.
    b. cotton.
    c. livestock.
    d. wheat.

30. Many New Englanders made a living
    a. growing rice.
    b. exporting whiskey.
    c. at sea.
    d. refining sugar.

31. The commercial economy of New England was dominated by
    a. ship captains.
    b. merchants.
    c. bankers.
    d. lawyers.

32. In the late seventeenth century, the richest 5 percent of Bostonians owned about one-third of the city's wealth; by 1770, they owned
    a. a quarter of the city's wealth.
    b. the same proportion of the city's wealth.
    c. half of the city's wealth.
    d. two-thirds of the city's wealth.

33. Most New Englanders traced their ancestry to
    a. Africa.
    b. England.
    c. France.
    d. the German principalities.

34. Most of the slaves in New England were concentrated
    a. among clergymen.
    b. in towns.
    c. on family farms.
    d. on large plantations.

35. New England's population growth was lower than that in other colonies because it _____.
    a. had a less desirable ratio of people to land
    b. was extremely cold
    c. had a lot of wild animals
    d. had very poor land

36. The perils of _____ gave wives a shorter life expectancy than husbands.
    a. childbirth
    b. housework
    c. parenting
    d. disease

37. During the seventeenth century, New England towns gave out land to _____.
    a. speculators
    b. individuals
    c. stockholders
    d. families

38. Starting in the eighteenth century, _____ determined whether a person could obtain land.
    a. money
    b. church membership
    c. personal reputation
    d. political ties

39. The relative scarcity of land in New England encouraged _____.
    a. extreme poverty and hunger
    b. slavery and indentured servitude
    c. urban dwelling and crowding
    d. agricultural diversification and individualism

40. By 1770, New Englander farmers had _____ wealth as free colonists in the southern colonies.
    a. much less
    b. double the
    c. lost interest in
    d. about the same

41. _____ tended to do better than other artisans because they served the most dynamic sector of the New England economy.
    a. Tanners
    b. Tailors
    c. Wheelwrights
    d. Shipbuilders

42. The _____ commerce benefited the entire New England economy.
    a. Pacific
    b. Mexican
    c. Atlantic
    d. colonial

43. By the 1770s, wealth in Boston and other seaport cities was becoming _____.
    a. more polarized
    b. less polarized
    c. much higher overall
    d. scarce

44. Because New England's farms were small and primarily raised livestock, they were not suited for _____ labor.
    a. family
    b. wage
    c. slave
    d. indentured

45. In 1770, the population of the middle colonies had multiplied tenfold, mainly from
    a. an influx of European immigrants.
    b. natural increase.
    c. the importation of African slaves.
    d. intercolonial immigration.

46. The first large-scale migration of German immigrants from the southwestern Palatinate region was spurred by
    a. crop failures.
    b. French invasions during Queen Anne's War.
    c. a long drought.
    d. a repressive new government.

47. Economically, German immigrants represented the
    a. very poor.
    b. middling folk.
    c. prosperous.
    d. rich.

48. German and Scots-Irish immigrants both tended to be
    a. Protestant and clannish.
    b. practicing Lutherans.
    c. members of dissenting churches.
    d. from urban areas.

49. Immigrants from northern Ireland, Scotland, and England usually left their homes because of
    a. deteriorating economic conditions.
    b. religious persecution.
    c. warfare.
    d. high taxes.

50. "Redemptioners" paid their way to the colonies
    a. by selling their labor under contract.
    b. by obtaining church sponsorship.
    c. themselves.
    d. with discounted tickets.

51. Masters purchased servants because they were
    a. a bargain.
    b. the only labor available.
    c. obligated to by the colonial government.
    d. generous.

52. Most farms in the middle colonies operated using
    a. family labor.
    b. slave labor.
    c. a single worker.
    d. gangs of day laborers.

53. The conditions under which a slave labored were legally set by
  a. the master's commands.
  b. colonial law.
  c. local custom.
  d. a written contract.

54. The major export from the middle colonies was
  a. fish.
  b. flour.
  c. rum.
  d. milling equipment.

55. Because of the comparatively widespread prosperity, residents of the middle colonies
  a. saved a lot of money.
  b. gave unusually high tithes to their churches.
  c. invested in risky joint stock corporations.
  d. indulged in English imports.

56. The popularity of Benjamin Franklin's *Poor Richard's Almanack* demonstrated that Pennsylvania's Quakers had
  a. remained committed to the idea of a divine inner light.
  b. made work into a secular faith.
  c. become very lazy.
  d. changed their outward behavior entirely.

57. The _____ made up the largest contingent of migrants from the European continent to the middle colonies.
  a. Swedes
  b. French
  c. Germans
  d. Scots-Irish

58. Scots-Irish immigrants tended to be militant _____ who seldom hesitated to swear oaths or bear arms.
  a. Quakers
  b. Mennonites
  c. Presbyterians
  d. Catholics

59. Most immigrants from northern Ireland, Scotland, and England were _____ or tenant farmers.
  a. farm laborers
  b. industrial workers
  c. merchants
  d. artisans

60. Because they were weak and unskilled, children ten years old or younger who traveled as redemptioners usually had to become servants until they were _____ years of age.
  a. thirteen
  b. fifteen
  c. twenty-one
  d. thirty-five

61. Slavery did not become entrenched in the middle colonies because _____.
  a. Quakers opposed the practice
  b. farmers could bring in their crops with family labor
  c. slaves were seen as incompetent workers
  d. indentured servants resisted the importation of slaves

62. Slave codes punished slaves _____ servants for the same transgressions.
  a. less than
  b. the same as
  c. somewhat more severely than
  d. much more severely than

63. Despite the middle colonies' reputation as a haven for the poor, _____ faced serious discrimination and poor treatment.
  a. redemptioners
  b. white farmers
  c. squatters
  d. slaves

64. The _____ dominated the lucrative fur trade of the St. Lawrence Valley and the eastern Great Lakes.
  a. French
  b. Dutch
  c. English
  d. Iroquois

65. In the eighteenth-century middle colonies, _____ was the number one industry.
   a. fishing
   b. flour milling
   c. meat processing
   d. shipping

66. In Philadelphia, _____ dominated local government during the eighteenth century.
   a. merchants
   b. lawyers
   c. planters
   d. ministers

67. By 1770, the most populous region of the British colonies was
   a. New England.
   b. the South.
   c. the middle colonies.
   d. the far West.

68. African slaves in the South
   a. always were imported from the West Indies.
   b. came from different African cultures.
   c. came from the same African culture.
   d. spoke the same language.

69. During the Middle Passage, the long trip across the Atlantic from Africa to the Americas, African slaves were
   a. allowed to move about the slave ship.
   b. forced to help sail the ship.
   c. confined to the hold.
   d. beaten constantly.

70. Normally, an individual planter purchased
   a. a single slave at a time.
   b. a relatively small number of slaves at a time.
   c. complete slave families.
   d. large gangs of slaves.

71. The process of acculturation was helped by
   a. planters' kindly treatment of their slaves.
   b. the limited number of languages spoken in Africa.
   c. planters' preferences for slaves from specific regions of Africa.
   d. the closeness of the southern climate to that of Africa.

72. The southern colonies were set apart from other New World slave societies by the
   a. growing number of babies born into slavery.
   b. kindness of many masters.
   c. high rate of death among slaves.
   d. violence of slave rebellions.

73. Masters preferred black slaves over white indentured servants because they
   a. served for life and could be freely disciplined.
   b. served for life and were believed to be better workers.
   c. could be freely disciplined and were believed to be better workers.
   d. served for life and were believed to be smarter.

74. The Stono Rebellion demonstrated that
   a. in the eighteenth century, determined slaves could escape their masters.
   b. eighteenth-century slaves had no chance of overturning slavery.
   c. slaves could kill whites and get away with it.
   d. the slave regime was lax about discipline.

75. Slaves often recreated West African kinship ties by
   a. marrying close relatives.
   b. rebelling against their masters.
   c. performing ritualistic ceremonies.
   d. adopting one another.

76. Slaves' labor financially benefited all of the following groups except
   a. their masters.
   b. poor whites.
   c. British merchants.
   d. the monarchy.

77. The vast differences of wealth among white southerners engendered
   a. open hostility.
   b. armed rebellion.
   c. only occasional tension.
   d. cross-racial alliances.

78. The politics and economy of the southern colonies was dominated by
a. numerically superior poor whites.
b. the middle classes.
c. the slaveholding gentry.
d. urban merchants.

79. The colonies in the upper south, surrounding the Chesapeake Bay, specialized in growing _____, as they had in the seventeenth century.
a. tobacco
b. wheat
c. indigo
d. sugar

80. Until Georgia was founded in 1732, _____ was the sole British colony along the South Atlantic coast.
a. Florida
b. Virginia
c. Maryland
d. South Carolina

81. Of the 300,000 Africans who came to British North America between 1619 and 1780, 95 percent arrived in _____.
a. New England
b. New York
c. Georgia
d. the South

82. Most of the slaves transported to British North America were _____.
a. young adults
b. female
c. children
d. older adults

83. During the Middle Passage, many slaves died from _____, and also of disease.
a. depression
b. suicide
c. dehydration
d. beatings

84. In 1740, the majority of southern slaves were born in _____.
a. Africa
b. the colonies
c. the West Indies
d. South America

85. In the South, as in West African societies, _____ structured slaves' relations with one another.
a. owners
b. tribal leaders
c. personal affinity
d. kinship

86. The southern colonies provided 90 percent of all North American exports to _____.
a. France
b. Canada
c. the West Indies
d. England

87. _____ made the grandees of the lower South very rich.
a. Rice
b. Indigo
c. Cotton
d. Commerce

88. Politically, the eighteenth-century southern gentry became _____.
a. extremely democratic
b. more committed to enforcing a state religion
c. a self-perpetuating oligarchy
d. increasingly corrupt

89. The European market for colonial goods made it clear that
a. only the elite would buy luxury items.
b. the colonies would never provide a market for English goods.
c. ordinary people would buy luxury items.
d. most people were not interested in purchasing unnecessary goods.

90. Despite considerable regional differences, colonists throughout British North America shared
a. the desire for a slave system.
b. economies based on commerce.
c. economies based on agriculture.
d. a commitment to religious faith.

91. In both New England and the South, adherents of different faiths were
    a. persecuted by the state-supported church.
    b. excused from taxes that supported the state-sponsored church.
    c. given equal status with the state-supported church.
    d. permitted to worship publicly.

92. In the Newtonian universe, order was maintained by
    a. basic mathematical laws.
    b. the constant intervention of God.
    c. human behavior.
    d. nature.

93. The center of Enlightenment thought in British North America was
    a. Philadelphia, Pennsylvania.
    b. Boston, Massachusetts.
    c. New York City, New York.
    d. Charleston, South Carolina.

94. Many eighteenth-century ministers were especially concerned by the spread of
    a. Catholicism.
    b. evangelical faiths.
    c. Deism.
    d. religious indifference.

95. Revivals were important because they
    a. halted the long-term decline in church membership.
    b. imparted the message that every soul mattered.
    c. discouraged the consumption of luxury items.
    d. focused colonial discontent with the ruling order.

96. Since the Puritan revolution of the mid-seventeenth century, British rulers had
    a. ignored the colonies.
    b. exploited the colonies.
    c. micromanaged the colonies.
    d. encouraged the development of the colonies.

97. At a minimum, British power
    a. kept intercolonial strife to a minimum.
    b. defended the colonists from foreign enemies.
    c. organized the militia.
    d. regulated the state churches.

98. The principal medium of exchange between Indians and British colonists was
    a. corn.
    b. furs.
    c. tobacco.
    d. slaves.

99. When royal officials tried to wield their authority on issues other than those relating to sea trade,
    a. they met with stiff resistance from colonists.
    b. colonists obeyed them.
    c. the British monarchy discouraged them.
    d. state legislatures cooperated with them.

100. During the eighteenth century, colonial assemblies
    a. became stronger than royal governors.
    b. grew weaker than royal governors.
    c. lost their influence with their constituents.
    d. reflected the economic makeup of their communities.

101. For most eighteenth-century colonists, _____ mattered less than in the seventeenth century.
    a. commercial undertakings
    b. religion
    c. politics
    d. economic concerns

102. Over the course of the eighteenth century, _____ markets became increasingly important to English exporters.
    a. domestic
    b. European
    c. colonial
    d. Asian

103. In eighteenth-century America, Protestantism became more _____.
   a. varied
   b. belligerent
   c. unified
   d. nationalized

104. Many educated eighteenth-century colonists became _____.
   a. Roman Catholics
   b. deists
   c. Presbyterians
   d. Quakers

105. Most eighteenth-century colonists went to _____ seldom or not at all.
   a. town
   b. taverns
   c. stores
   d. church

106. In Massachusetts during the mid-1730s, the fiery Puritan minister Jonathan Edwards inspired religious fervor by emphasizing _____.
   a. hard work
   b. the Puritan belief that humans were sinful
   c. the idea of a watchmaker God
   d. that all men were created equal

107. France's policy of excluding Protestants and foreigners meant that the population of New France was _____.
   a. large
   b. small
   c. old
   d. poor

108. The shifting alliances and complex dynamics of the _____ struck a fragile balance along the frontier
   a. plantation system
   b. missionaries
   c. fur trade
   d. tobacco trade

109. Colonial governors were hampered in their ability to develop relations of trust and respect with influential colonists because they _____.
   a. always insisted on remaining in England
   b. had short terms in office
   c. were often Roman Catholic
   d. did not have the power to veto colonial legislation

110. By 1720, colonial assemblies had won the power to _____.
   a. choose the governor
   b. initiate legislation
   c. overturn royal policy
   d. control foreign trade

***Short Answer*** Write a paragraph response to each question.

1. What caused the growth and diversity of the population of eighteenth-century colonial America?
2. How did the abundance of land affect the growth of colonial society?
3. How and why did patterns of settlement change in eighteenth-century New England?
4. Describe the economic and trade activity of eighteenth-century New England.
5. How did the distribution of wealth change in Boston over the course of the eighteenth century?
6. Which Europeans immigrated to the middle colonies and why?
7. Why was Pennsylvania labeled "the best poor man's country"? Were any groups denied its benefits?
8. What factors controlled the price of farmland in Pennsylvania? How did price influence patterns of settlement?

9. What did Africans undergo in the process of being enslaved, transported, sold, and acculturated to southern planters?
10. What kinds of traditions did West African slaves maintain?
11. How did slave labor enrich the fortunes of both white colonists and the British empire?
12. What were the consequences of rising colonial consumption?
13. How did the Great Awakening begin, and what was its importance?
14. In what areas did colonists rely on the British empire? When did they resist British power?

***Building Historical Skills*** Historians use a variety of sources to think and talk about the past, including maps, illustrations, and written records. Maps provide a variety of different kinds of comparative information in a condensed visual format; reading them requires learning how to sort through this information. To deepen our understanding of the past by supplementing written records, historians frequently interpret material culture, such as a vase or a painting, with techniques borrowed from art history, archaeology, or anthropology. Written records, though familiar as sources, raise their own problems of interpretation. Every document reflects someone's particular perspective or assumptions. It is the historian's task to study and compare each document to other records with other perspectives. The following exercises introduce you to using maps, illustrations, and written documents as sources of information. Use these sources as well as the material in the chapter to think about different themes and topics discussed in the text.

***Map Activity*** Locate the following places on Map 4.2: Atlantic Trade in the Eighteenth Century on page 110 in *The American Promise*, Second Edition.

1. Philadelphia
2. Ivory, Gold, and Slave Coasts
3. Boston
4. New France
5. New York
6. England
7. Charleston
8. West Indies
9. Norfolk

Answer the following questions in a paragraph based on Map 4.2: Atlantic Trade in the Eighteenth Century.

**READING THE MAP** What were the major markets for trade coming out of Europe? What goods did the English colonies import and export?

**CONNECTIONS** In what way did the flow of raw materials from the colonies affect English industry? How did English colonial trade policies influence the Atlantic trade?

**WEB LINKS** To explore the topics discussed in the exercise above, visit the Web links noted below.

"West Africa during the Eighteenth Century"
http://www.loc.gov/exhibits/odyssey/educate/guinea.html

"The Atlantic Neptune Online"
http://mercator.cogs.nscc.ns.ca/neptune.html
Choose "CHART"

"The English Fishery and Trade in the Eighteenth Century"
http://www.heritage.nf.ca/exploration/18fishery.html

***Visual Activity*** This painting of Bethlehem, Pennsylvania, executed in 1757, demonstrates the extent to which human habitation influenced the natural environment of North America. Toward the back of the painting, the artist has depicted a thick forest. The trees along the river have been largely cleared away, though, and replaced with farms, gardens, livestock pens, houses, and public buildings. The residents of Bethlehem did not remove all of the trees: instead of representing uncontrolled nature, though, they are used to mark human boundaries. For instance, trees line the road to the left and front the house in the foreground. The gardens in front of the public buildings in the center of the image reinforce the settlers' desire for controlled nature. They are neatly laid-out plots of grass divided by geometric walkways. Moreover, Bethlehem is clearly well linked to the outside world, with roads running into and out of town and a river in the foreground.

Answer the following questions in a paragraph based on "Bethlehem, Pennsylvania" on page 116 in *The American Promise*, Second Edition.

**READING THE IMAGE** What does this painting indicate about settlers' priorities?

**CONNECTIONS** Why might Pennsylvanians have been so concerned about maintaining order?

**WEB LINKS** To explore the topics discussed in the exercise above, visit the Web links noted below.

"Hargrett Library Rare Map Collection"
http://www.libs.uga.edu/darchive/hargrett/maps/colamer.html
Choose map number 30, "A view of Savannah (1734)"

"William Penn, Visionary Proprietor"
http://xroads.virginia.edu/~CAP/PENN/pnhome.html
Choose "Boom Town: 1821–1861"

"The Moravians in Georgia, 1735–1740"
http://www.cviog.uga.edu/Projects/gainfo/mora-toc.htm

***Analyzing Sources Activity*** Answer the following questions in a paragraph based on "Documenting the American Promise: Regulating Slavery" on page 124 in *The American Promise*, Second Edition.

1. Why did legislators believe laws like these were necessary?
2. Did these laws apply only to slaves? To what degree were the laws designed to regulate the behavior of slave owners?

3. According to the laws, what kinds of slave behavior were most threatening?
4. Why did legislators pass special laws that governed slaves instead of simply governing them by the same laws that applied to all other colonists?

**WEB LINKS** To explore the topics discussed in the exercise above, visit the Web links noted below.

"The Ten Precepts of American Slavery Jurisprudence"
http://www.udayton.edu/~race/02rights/precepts.htm

"North American and South American Slavery"
http://www.rit.edu/~nrcgsh/bx/bx03b.html

"Chronology of the History of Slavery and Racism"
http://innercity.org/holt/slavechron.html
Choose "1619–1798" after the introductory text.

# Answer Key

## Chapter 4: Colonial America in the Eighteenth Century, 1701–1770

### *Chapter Overview*

#### *Chronology*

1. b
2. c
3. a
4. b
5. d
6. a
7. c
8. d
9. d
10. a

#### *Defining Terms*

1. natural increase
2. squatters
3. free colonists
4. partible inheritance
5. agricultural diversification
6. Atlantic commerce
7. Pennsylvania Dutch
8. Scots-Irish
9. redemptioners
10. "Walking Purchase"
11. *Poor Richard's Almanack*
12. indigo
13. Olaudah Equiano
14. Middle Passage
15. Stono Rebellion
16. task system
17. newspapers
18. deists
19. Enlightenment
20. American Philosophical Society
21. George Whitefield
22. Yamasee War

### *Chapter Review*

#### *Multiple-Choice*

1. c
2. a
3. c
4. b
5. b
6. b
7. b
8. b
9. a
10. d
11. d
12. c
13. a
14. c
15. d
16. c
17. a
18. d
19. a
20. b
21. d
22. c.
23. b
24. c
25. a
26. b
27. c
28. c
29. c
30. c
31. b
32. c
33. b
34. b
35. a
36. a
37. d
38. a
39. d
40. a
41. d
42. c
43. a
44. c
45. a
46. b
47. b
48. a
49. a
50. a
51. a
52. a
53. a
54. b
55. d
56. b
57. c
58. c
59. a
60. c
61. b
62. d
63. d
64. d
65. b
66. a
67. b
68. b
69. c
70. b
71. c
72. a
73. a
74. b
75. d
76. b
77. c
78. c
79. a
80. d
81. d
82. a
83. c
84. b
85. d
86. d
87. a
88. c
89. c
90. c
91. d
92. a
93. a
94. d
95. b
96. d
97. b
98. b

| | |
|---|---|
| 99. a | 105. d |
| 100. a | 106. b |
| 101. b | 107. b |
| 102. c | 108. c |
| 103. a | 109. b |
| 104. b | 110. b |

### *Short Answer*

1. The population growth of eighteenth-century colonial America was caused by two factors: natural increase and immigration. Natural increase caused about three-fourths of the population increase. Immigration contributed the remaining quarter and also accounted for the diversity of the colonial population. Fewer than 10 percent of immigrants came from England, about 36 percent were Scots-Irish from northern Ireland, 33 percent were African, 15 percent were from the German principalities, and 10 percent were Scottish. By 1770, only about half of all colonists were of English descent, and 20 percent were descended from Africans.
2. In most countries, a fast-growing population leads to hunger and poverty because there are more people than resources. In the North American colonies, however, there was a low ratio of people to land. Laborers were desperately needed to work farms and thus could command unusually high wages; and land was cheap enough that a relatively high number of people could purchase it themselves. This meant that the population could grow quickly without producing widespread poverty. According to economic historians, the standard of living of free colonists improved over the course of the eighteenth century, making most colonists far from rich but decidedly comfortable.
3. During the seventeenth century, New England towns gave land to families, who settled near one another in close-knit towns and villages. Over time, the practice of partible inheritance—the subdivision of land more or less equally among sons—caused the system to collapse, as farms became too small to support a family. Sons who wished to farm had to move away from the towns of their birth. Also, colonial governments in New England stopped granting land for towns and began selling directly to individual settlers to raise revenue. The new purchasers tended to settle on farms rather than in towns, where they were further from the eyes of their neighbors and more able to regulate their conduct according to their own dictates.
4. While many New Englanders farmed, they did not raise cash crops; instead, they raised food for their own consumption or for trade. The ocean, however, provided a major economic stimulus. Fish alone made up over a third of New England's exports in the eighteenth century. New Englanders caught fish, especially cod, which made up a large part of slaves' diet. The rest of New England's exports went to England and continental Europe, to the benefit of a broad range of New Englanders, including ship captains, clerks, laborers, tradesmen, and merchants.
5. New England was not as prosperous as the rest of the colonies, but it did harbor a handful of very rich merchants. The most successful lived in Boston, where they bought and sold imported goods and also owned and insured ships involved in the Atlantic trade. They became richer over the course of the eighteenth century. In the late seventeenth century, the wealthiest 5 percent of Bostonians controlled a third of the city's wealth, while the poorest two-thirds had a sixth. By 1770, the wealthiest 5 percent owned about half of the city's wealth, while the poorest two-thirds possessed less than a tenth.
6. Germans and Scots-Irish were the most numerous of the European immigrant groups to relocate to the middle colonies. Throughout Europe, peasants suffered from exploitation by the government and landowners, but those from the German Palatinate faced unusually harsh conditions. French invasions of the area during Queen Anne's War in the early eighteenth century worsened their problems and spurred the first great migration from the area. Scots-Irish immigrants (a misnomer for immigrants from the north of Ireland, Scotland, and northern England) confronted economic difficulties, including droughts, crop failures, high food prices, and rising rents. Most of them headed for the middle colonies in hopes of escaping current conditions and improving their lot in life.
7. Poor immigrants to Pennsylvania perceived unparalleled opportunity for betterment. Although many arrived as indentured servants facing years of restrictive bondage, the shortage of labor in the area meant that free workers commanded extremely high wages. After the term of indenture was completed, a poor person had an unusual amount of opportunity. But despite being quite poor, blacks were denied the opportunities that even poor whites expected. Black slaves in Pennsylvania were treated much more harshly than the colony's white indentured servants, and free blacks were limited by whites' entrenched racism.
8. At a basic level, the price of farmland was determined by soil quality, access to water, and the distance to a market town. The price could be increased by improvements—whether the land

already had been cleared, plowed, fenced, and ditched or had a house and barn already in place. Improved land cost three or four times as much as the same acreage of unimproved land. The cheapest land always lay at the margin of settlement, so new purchasers tended to migrate just beyond already improved farms, where the land was still relatively cheap. Ultimately, this led to a dispersed pattern of settlement, with colonists moving along the Delaware, Schuykill, and Susquehanna Rivers and toward the eastern slopes of the Appalachian Mountains.

9. Generally, free-born people in the inland villages of West Africa became slaves when they were captured in war, kidnapped, or sold into slavery by other Africans. After that, they were taken to the coast and sold to African traders, who resold them to European or colonial slave traders. Then the shocked and disoriented slaves were shipped from Africa to the New World via the Middle Passage, the cross-Atlantic trip that killed on average 15 percent of the involuntary migrants. Once they arrived in North America or the Caribbean, they were sold, usually in small groups, to planters. At that point, they underwent the process of "seasoning," which involved acclimation to the routines of slavery and the environment of the colonies.

10. Slaves had a limited amount of control over their own lives, but they managed to keep West Indian culture alive in the southern colonies nonetheless. In West Africa, kinship structured people's relationships and linked individuals to their ancestors. Although slaves often arrived alone and without family, they recreated kinship ties through a process of informal adoption; slaves who went through the Middle Passage together declared themselves siblings, and new slaves on established plantations were incorporated into existing families. Slaves also maintained the material culture of West Africa by growing familiar food crops, including yams and okra, constructing African-style huts, recreating African instruments, and following African funeral rites.

11. Slave labor fueled the development of southern cash crops like rice, indigo, and tobacco, and those crops in turn created immense wealth for whites. The southern colonies provided 90 percent of North American exports to England, with output increasing enormously over the eighteenth century. The money gained from agriculture made the southern gentry by far the richest in the colonies. However, the monarchy and the British empire benefited as well. Under the provisions of the Navigation Acts, nearly all colonial goods went to England, where the monarchy collected tax on them and British merchants reexported them with a healthy markup.

12. The eighteenth century witnessed the rise of mass markets, spurred by colonial products like tobacco and sugar that were within the reach of ordinary people, not just the elite. The English received most colonial exports and sent English goods back. Thus, the colonies exhibited a level of material uniformity, and colonists looked and felt remarkably British despite the fact that they lived on the wrong side of the Atlantic. The rising level of consumption also offered people an unusual array of choices. While the decisions to be made were relatively trivial—what to purchase and when—they accustomed colonists to thinking of themselves as individuals who had the ability to come to their own conclusions about things that influenced the quality of their lives.

13. Eighteenth-century colonists were, on the whole, nominally Christian but religiously indifferent. Clergymen from many different denominations were profoundly concerned about what they saw as a lack of piety and faith. To combat it, they unleashed a wave of revivals called the Great Awakening by historians; emotional styles of preaching were used to attempt to convert unbelievers and revitalize the faithful. The revivalists seldom made lasting converts, but they did impart an important message to colonists by preaching that every soul mattered and that individuals could make important choices about their own salvation. The revivals of the Great Awakening expressed democratic and egalitarian values and bridged the class, faith, and regional differences that separated colonists.

14. Most colonists expected the British to protect them from foreign enemies, including New France and New Spain. Those who lived toward the edges of settlement were always concerned about threats from Indians and counted on the British to keep the menace at bay while protecting the flow of furs between Indians and European intermediaries. Colonists accepted, though they did not always comply with, British regulation of trade, including the collection of customs duties and the inspection of cargoes. But colonists resisted British attempts to control the internal affairs of their colonies. Royal governors, who were generally English rather than colonial, found it increasingly difficult to keep a reign on colonial assemblies, which demanded the right to pass legislation (including tax laws and public spending) and often flouted the authority of the monarch's colonial representatives.

### *Map Activity*

Reading the Map: European products went to the major port cities of the North American colonies (Boston, New York, Philadelphia, Norfolk, and Charleston) and also to the West Indies and the Ivory, Gold, and Slave Coasts of western Africa. The most common items that colonists imported from England were manufactured goods, although there was some trade in linens and horses as well. There was, however, a thriving trade between the colonies and both Africa and the West Indies, with the colonies exchanging fish, livestock, flour, lumber, rice, and rum for slaves and sugar. Most other exports went to England and revolved around raw materials and foodstuffs. Boston, for instance, sent out fish, furs, and naval stores, while Norfolk provided tobacco and the West Indies shipped molasses and fruit.

Connections: The raw materials provided by the colonies provided a spur to the growth of the mass market. Colonial flour, sugar cane, and tobacco leaf could be processed into relatively inexpensive consumer commodities, like crackers, sweets, and pipe tobacco, which were within the reach of a broad range of purchasers. Colonial trade policies guaranteed that the English benefited from the Atlantic trade; they had a virtual monopoly over colonial raw materials, and so collected customs duties on them and also reexported them at considerable profit.

### *Visual Activity*

Reading the Image: This painting of Bethlehem, Pennsylvania, shows an orderly settlement dominated by straight lines and right angles. Crops (to the right of center) and garden areas (center) are laid out in tidy rows; the houses and buildings are rectangular. The only exceptions are the roads that follow the banks of waterways: presumably even the industrious residents of Bethlehem could not convince the channels to change course. Settlers in the town clearly believed in keeping things in their places, with penned livestock separated from fields and forested areas banished to well beyond the outskirts of human habitation. It is also evident from the multistory, centrally located town buildings that residents appreciated communal life, even if they did settle on individual farms like the one in the foreground.

Connections: Moravian immigrants, members of a dissenting Protestant sect who were persecuted in Europe for their refusal to bear arms and swear to oaths, founded the town of Bethlehem. For immigrants like these, it was very important to establish control over their lives and also over their surroundings. The name "Bethlehem" indicates that they saw their new town as a sanctuary or the birthplace of something holy. They would not have wished to encourage disorder in their symbolic new beginning. Moreover, many Europeans reacted to being surrounded by wilderness by working extremely hard to maintain what they saw as civilized standards of behavior and life, including the imposition of "rational" towns on an inherently irrational landscape.

### *Analyzing Sources*

1. Legislators responded to uprisings like the slave rebellion at Stono, South Carolina, with new laws designed to protect whites from the consequences of slavery. They argued that repressive laws were necessary because slaves were "prone to such cruel practices" as rising up against their masters, as South Carolina's 1740 slave patrol law put it. The 1740 act taxing imported slaves contended that African slaves were "barbarous" and could be dangerous to white settlers in the colony. Their general belief was that Africans who had not been exposed to the supposedly civilizing influence of white culture were more likely to rebel than those who had been born and raised under the slave system.
2. The laws were designed solely to keep slaves in line, although they affected whites as well. Patrols, for instance, required white men to help police the behavior of slaves whether they owned human property or not. Whites who owned taverns or were suspected of harboring or interacting with blacks were subject to inspection by the patrols. Taxes on imported Africans took a direct financial toll on large slave owners. As a general rule, the laws were designed to encourage owners to deal harshly and strictly with their slaves; there were almost no regulations limiting the violence that whites could mete out to slaves. The thrust of the laws was to enforce strict discipline and thus protect whites.
3. The tax law makes it clear that legislators saw the mere presence of slaves as a constant, if low-grade, threat that could be contained only by the presence of greater numbers of whites. The slave patrol law indicates that whites were concerned about slaves who went out without permission or white accompaniment and it mandated whippings for slaves who disobeyed. However, the 1740 slave code provisions show that destruction of property and physical violence against whites were the most feared slave behaviors, both acts punishable by death. The danger that slaves represented was tolerable because of the goods they produced; if those goods were ruined, the slaves were simply a liability. And any manifestations of violence against whites were seen as a sign of impending rebellion, demanding immediate and severe retaliation.

4. Legislators clearly believed that slaves needed to be subject to strict controls to protect southern whites and the southern economy. If two whites got into a fight, they were not going to undermine the racial hierarchy on which the colony's labor system depended, nor was a fight between an elite and a poor white likely to encourage other poor whites to turn against the ruling classes. Legislators did not feel that the punishment of whites always had to serve as a warning to other whites, whereas the punishment of blacks should. Furthermore, they felt that slaves were inherently less reasonable and more violent than whites and so demanded especially harsh punishments.

CHAPTER

# THE BRITISH EMPIRE AND THE COLONIAL CRISIS, 1754–1775

5

## Chapter Overview

### *Chapter Summary*

***Introduction*** The chapter begins with an account of loyalist governor Thomas Hutchinson. As governor of Massachusetts, Hutchinson presided over Boston's most turbulent years, witnessing the Stamp Act, Townshend duties, and the Boston Massacre and Boston Tea Party—all of the main events that preceded and helped to precipitate the American Revolution. Unlike many Americans, though, he did not believe that the British government was determined to deprive colonists of their traditional English liberty.

***The French and Indian War, pp. 144–151*** From the late seventeenth to the late eighteenth centuries, whenever England and France fought wars for European domination, their respective colonists in North America were affected. In the 1750s, tensions heightened as the French began to encroach south from Canada into lands the British colonists coveted for themselves. The result was the French and Indian War, which laid the groundwork for the crisis between British leaders and American colonists in the 1760s.

**FRENCH-ENGLISH RIVALRY IN THE OHIO VALLEY** In 1753, the French moved south with the objective of building a solid, fortified defense to protect their trading relationship with Indians from Pennsylvania traders. Virginia claimed the territory as well as France, and a group of powerful Virginia planters had organized the Ohio Company, obtaining a royal grant to a large tract of land in the Ohio Valley. The Virginian governor sent George Washington to warn the French to leave the region; but in 1754, in the first battle of the French and Indian War, French troops drove out the American militia, capturing Washington and killing a third of his men.

**THE ALBANY CONGRESS AND INTERCOLONIAL DEFENSE** The British knew that they would need help from the colonists and Indian neutrality to win the war with the French. Twenty-four delegates from seven colonies met in Albany, New York, to discuss the feasibility of a united colonial effort deal to more effectively with the French threat. Led by Benjamin Franklin and Thomas Hutchinson, the Albany Congress also proposed that a new arrangement between Great Britain and the colonies be created that would allow for a more centralized and autonomous united colonial government. However, neither Parliament nor the colonies liked the idea (known as the Albany Plan of Union). Representatives from the Iroquois League collected presents from the English but refused to pledge themselves to fight against the French, who they believed would win the war.

**THE WAR AND ITS CONSEQUENCES** In 1755, General Edward Braddock was sent from England to attack the French at Fort Duquesne and drive them from the Ohio Valley. Though Braddock's force was completely routed and the first two years of the conflict went badly for England, the tide began to turn in 1757 as Prime Minister William Pitt committed a huge number of troops and much money to the war effort. The decisive English victory came in 1759, when the British defeated the French forces holding the city of Quebec. The loss of Quebec demoralized the French army, and within a year's time, the war was over in North America. As a result of England's victory, all of North America east of the Mississippi River now belonged to Great Britain. However, the Treaty of Paris allowed France to retain its islands in the Caribbean, and French territory west of the Mississippi River was transferred to Spain. Indians lost more than colonists, since their lands were assigned to English rule, and they had lost the ability to play the European opponents off of each other. Americans were unhappy that England credited its own soldiers for the victory, disparaging colonial contributions and pointing to continued American trade with the French. Americans believed that they had fought bravely despite the contempt of the British, and many families suffered losses. But in the long run, what affected the American colonists most was the huge debt the war had caused.

***Tightening the Bonds of Empire, pp. 151–154*** Over the course of the 1760s, the new king, George III, and his revolving-door of ministers attempted to formulate policies that would address the problem of the huge British war debt. These interventions would be met with increasing consternation on the part of Americans.

**BRITISH LEADERSHIP AND THE INDIAN QUESTION** King George III came to the throne at the age of twenty-two and in the middle of the French and Indian War. He trusted only his tutor, Lord Bute, who disliked Pitt's policy of aggressively pursuing the war against the French. He negotiated the unfavorable Treaty of Paris and then decided to keep an expensive standing army in America. This was largely due to fighting between Indians and colonists. Indians were unhappy about the outcome of the war and, inspired by Delaware prophecies, started a pan-Indian movement that rejected whites and their trading goods. In 1763, the Ottawa chief Pontiac began attacking British forts. The British handled most of the fighting, although in western Pennsylvania the Paxton Boys "defended" themselves by killing friendly Indians. In an effort to control the situation, the British issued the Proclamation of 1763. This established a line drawn from Canada to Georgia, along the Appalachian Mountains, to the west of which colonists were forbidden to settle and beyond which all territory was reserved for the Indians. Settlers and land speculators alike were incensed at this restriction on westward movement.

**GROWING RESENTMENT OF BRITISH AUTHORITY** It fell to Bute's successor as prime minister, George Grenville, to formulate policies to deal with the war debt. Grenville discovered that customs officers' salaries were four times greater than the revenue they collected, in large part due to bribery and smuggling. Americans were particularly unwilling to pay a high duty on French molasses, which they used to make rum. Grenville devised the Revenue Act of 1764, or Sugar Act, which lowered the molasses duty but increased the penalties for smuggling, allowing British naval crews to board and examine ships and send smugglers to a vice-admiralty court in Halifax, Nova Scotia. He also pushed through the Currency Act, which prohibited the colonists from issuing any more paper money. While the British viewed these measures as appropriate and necessary for administering the colonies, the colonists found this increased British interference in their affairs disturbing and unwelcome.

***The Stamp Act Crisis, 1765, pp. 154–159*** Continued evasion prevented the Revenue Act of 1764 from becoming the moneymaker Grenville had envisioned. Thus, in 1765, he secured passage of the Stamp Act, which led to conflict over Parliament's right to tax the colonies at all.

**TAXATION AND CONSENT** The Stamp Act was simple: Americans were to pay a tax on all printed or official papers, a special stamp being embossed on all such documents to show the tax had been paid. Unlike the Sugar Act, which levied an indirect tax as part of a trade regulation, the new tax was direct and intended simply to raise money. Anticipating opposition, he stipulated that all stamp distributors be from the colonies. He was warned by Thomas Hutchinson that because colonists had not paid taxes before, they could reasonably conclude that Parliament had conceded the right to tax to local legislatures. English tradition held that taxes were a gift of the people to their rulers, approved by their representatives. However, Grenville believed that colonists were virtually represented in Parliament, while Americans argued that they were represented only in their own legislative bodies.

**RESISTANCE STRATEGIES AND CROWD POLITICS** Colonial reaction to the Stamp Act assumed various forms. In Virginia's House of Burgesses, Patrick Henry submitted a series of resolutions—the Virginia Resolves—two of which intimated strongly that neither king nor Parliament had the right to legislate for the colonies. Local communities also responded to the Stamp Act's passage. In the summer of 1765, the Boston Sons of Liberty—a group formed under politician Samuel Adams—engaged in demonstrations, while mobs ransacked the future Boston stamp distributor's home and inflicted other increasingly violent forms of intimidation on those suspected of supporting the tax. By November 1, 1765, the day the act took effect, no American was foolish enough to become a distributor and enforce the act. It seemed that the colonists, at least temporarily, had won the day.

**LIBERTY AND PROPERTY** Soon groups calling themselves the Sons of Liberty were protesting the Stamp Act in almost every colony. In the fall of 1765, nine colonies sent representatives to a Stamp Act Congress in New York to discuss possible united colonial opposition to the act. They were extremely cautious in addressing the issue of parliamentary sovereignty, however, and in the end sent only a polite petition requesting the act's repeal. Up to 1765, the majority of colonists accepted Parliament's status as a government that represented them for legislative purposes. However, they saw the right to own property as a special kind of liberty, requiring security against greedy rulers who might try to strip them of their property. This fear led the colonists to conclude that only a governing body in which they were directly represented could tax them. They believed the Stamp Act violated this principle of liberty and property, and some began to speak and write of a conspiracy among British leaders to enslave them. English politicians and merchants were concerned about trade disruption and pressed for the repeal of the Stamp Act. In the summer of 1765, Grenville was replaced by the marquess of Rockingham, who pushed for repeal. The Stamp Act was finally rescinded in March 1766. However, George III and Parliament were determined to uphold parliamentary sovereignty and thus simultaneously issued the Declaratory Act. In asserting Parliament's right to legislate for the colonies "in all cases whatsoever," the act upheld Parliament's power to tax.

***The Townshend Acts and Economic Retaliation, 1767–1770, pp. 159–163*** The marquess of Rockingham was replaced by William Pitt in the summer of 1766. Pitt appointed Charles Townshend to be the empire's chief financial minister, making it his job to deal with the war debt and the continuing cost of stationing the British army in America. Unfortunately, his simple plan to raise revenue quickly in the colonies turned into a major political and economic blunder.

**THE TOWNSHEND DUTIES** Townshend proposed a tax in the form of a navigation act, establishing new duties on tea, glass, lead, paper, and painters' colors. Townshend assumed that duties levied on trade would be more acceptable than internal taxes, but although the duties were not burdensome, the fact that they were intended solely to raise money grated on colonists. The duties also provided that some of the money generated would go to paying royal governors' salaries to end their dependence on state legislatures. Then Townshend came down hard on the New York assembly when it refused to implement the 1765 Quartering Act, mandating that colonists furnish shelter and provisions for British soldiers. Americans began to worry that their representative legislative government was not secure. Protest was spearheaded by Massachusetts, which issued a circular letter for all the colonies to endorse protesting the Townshend duties. In Great Britain, Lord Hillsborough denounced Massachusetts's circular letter and ordered the dissolution of the Massachusetts assembly.

**NONCONSUMPTION AND THE DAUGHTERS OF LIBERTY** Boston retaliated against the British by organizing a consumer boycott of all British-made goods. All the colonies eventually established similar policies, called nonconsumption agreements, and then nonimportation agreements, which barred British imports entirely. These strategies were difficult to enforce because merchants were concerned about the financial impact. However, in late 1768 Boston merchants agreed to suspend trade, and other major cities followed suit. As keepers of their households, women played an important role in nonconsumption, and home manufacture like the spinning of homespun cloth became symbolic of American patriotism. Nonconsumption of British goods proved an effective colonial weapon because, as predicted, it hurt British merchants and manufacturers.

**MILITARY OCCUPATION AND "MASSACRE" IN BOSTON** In the midst of the uproar over the Townshend duties, the English government sent troops to Boston to help keep the peace. The presence of British troops exacerbated the already hostile relationship between British officials and city inhabitants. Until 1770, things were quiet, but the end of the nonimportation agreements began a new round of controversy in Boston. First, a low-level customs official fired on a crowd and accidentally hit an eleven-year-old boy. Then, largely as a result of American provocation, compounded by British soldiers' arrogant behavior, on March 5, 1770, there was a violent confrontation between the troops and Bostonians. When the smoke cleared, five Americans lay dead. Bostonians were outraged and demanded retribution for what they called the Boston Massacre. Further violence was avoided and the Boston lawyers, John Adams and Josiah Quincy, defended the British troops, hoping to demonstrate to the empire that most colonists were not lawless but interested in preserving liberty and justice. Adams and Quincy won a full acquittal for the British commander and for all but two of the soldiers.

***The Tea Party and the Coercive Acts, pp. 163–171*** Around the time of the Boston Massacre crisis, a new ministry in London, headed by Lord Frederick North, sought to ease tensions and end the boycott of British goods caused by the Townshend duties. In 1770, Lord North repealed all of the Townshend duties except the one on tea, which he hoped would serve as a reminder of parliamentary supremacy. There were two years of relative calm, convincing people that further trouble might be avoided.

**THE CALM BEFORE THE STORM** After the repeal of the Townshend duties, trade boomed and relations with the empire were relatively peaceful. However, the 1772 *Gaspée* incident and the royal commission of inquiry that followed fed colonial suspicions by suggesting that if suspects were arrested, they would be sent to England to be tried for treason. In the same year, a proposal for paying the salaries of superior court justices out of the tea duty created alarm. In response, the

Boston town meeting helped organize committees of correspondence throughout the colonies that created a political network independent of royal colonial governments and allowed the colonial assemblies to coordinate better resistance to British threats. The calm was finally shattered entirely by the 1773 Tea Act, which was designed to relieve the financially strapped East India Company by allowing the company to sell its tea through its own agents directly to the Americans, many of whom purchased and drank cheap smuggled Dutch tea.

**TEA IN BOSTON HARBOR** Radicals argued that the Tea Act was an insidious trick to make Americans buy dutied tea. Colonists could not use nonimportation to combat the threat because the trade was lucrative and it was impossible to distinguish dutied tea from smuggled tea once it was brewed. Once again, the Sons of Liberty turned to pressuring agents to resign. In Boston, a standoff took place between city inhabitants who refused to unload tea shipments and the royal governor who refused to send the tea back to England. In December 1773, a group of the Sons of Liberty, dressed as Indians, boarded the company's ships and dumped the tea into Boston harbor.

**THE COERCIVE ACTS** Outraged at the colonists' vandalism and their contempt for British property rights, Lord North persuaded Parliament to issue the Coercive Acts. These acts closed the port of Boston, altered the colony's charter, allowed royal officials accused of capital crimes to be tried in England, and instituted a new amendment to the Quartering Act. In effect, these acts placed Boston and the colony of Massachusetts under martial law. Massachusetts colonists were further outraged by the subsequent passage of the Quebec Act, which gave the French Catholic province of Quebec control of the Ohio Valley and the lucrative fur trade. The acts alarmed other colonists, who saw them as a sign of England's ability to override local government.

**THE FIRST CONTINENTAL CONGRESS** In response to the Coercive Acts, the colonies called for the convening of the First Continental Congress, which met in Philadelphia in the fall of 1774. Men of all political persuasions were there, from radicals to moderates. The congress met for seven weeks and eventually hammered out a declaration of rights that asserted that each colonial government had the sole right to legislate for and tax its own people. Delegates also approved the formation of a Continental Association to implement a unified boycott of English trade. These bodies became functioning political bodies despite their lack of formal authority, in large part because they were composed of the same men who had been in the colonial legislatures.

***Domestic Insurrections, 1774–1775, pp. 171–176*** General Thomas Gage, the military commander and governor of Massachusetts, initially thought that he was facing a domestic insurrection that would be easily quelled by a show of force. Americans, however, felt that they were defending themselves from an enslaving government. In the south, slaves took the patriot rhetoric of slavery to mount their own kind of insurrection in the name of liberty.

**LEXINGTON AND CONCORD** Thomas Gage believed that the British position was bad; he requested twenty thousand troops and also advised that the Coercive Acts be repealed. English leaders refused to back down, so he began organizing troops for a decisive strike against rebel "minutemen" who were gathering in the countryside. In April 1775, his attempt to organize a surprise attack on a suspected ammunition storage site at Concord was ruined when his forces were met by American militia at Lexington, five miles east of their destination. The British dispersed the men, went to Concord, where they found no ammunition, and then exchanged shots with more militiamen at the Old North Bridge. As the British returned to Boston, they were fired on by militia units from both sides of the road. The war had begun.

**ANOTHER REBELLION AGAINST SLAVERY** Besides marking the military beginnings of the American rebellion, the battles at Lexington and Concord also aroused a more profound issue that the rhetoric and ideology of rebellion had brought to the forefront: black slavery. Lord Dunmore, the governor of Virginia, threatened to arm slaves to fight the colonists, and in November of 1775 he issued an offer to able-bodied male slaves, promising freedom to those who would fight. He did not want to start a slave rebellion and in fact returned slaves who did not meet his requirements. In the northern colonies, slaves understood the implications of colonists' rhetoric and seized the moment to press for their own liberation. The challenge was stronger in the south, where the numerical preponderance of slaves caused owners considerable misgivings. By the end of the war, as many as thirty thousand slaves had taken up Dunmore's offer and as many as eighty thousand slaves escaped bondage on their own over the course of the war. Slaves were often treated quite badly by the army, and others were recaptured by their owners.

## *Conclusion: How Far Does Liberty Go?*

American resistance to imperial policies grew slowly, but as misunderstandings escalated, so did the level of tension and violence. By the 1770s, the colonists were convinced that Parliament meant to deprive them of their liberties and to reduce them to "abject slavery." To gain support for their cause, patriotic leaders had to infuse the masses with a keen sense of their own rights and liberties; black Americans also picked up on this rhetoric, hoping to free themselves from slavery and oppression. By 1775, with the outbreak of fighting and the specter of slave rebellions, American leaders turned to the king to resolve the question of who had actual authority over the colonies.

## *Chronology Activity*

Read the annotated chronology, and answer the multiple-choice questions.

1747 Ohio Company of Virginia formed. The Ohio Company was put together by wealthy Virginians who wanted to capitalize on Virginia's expansive charter and sell land in the Ohio Valley. The British government agreed to give them a grant of 200,000 acres to create a hedge against French claims to the same area.

1754 French and Indian War begins in America. The French and Indian War was the name for the American setting of a major worldwide conflict. It eventually drove the French out of Canada, but the cost of the war caused enormous tension between Great Britain and its North American colonies.

Albany Congress proposes Plan of Union and courts Iroquois support. The Albany Congress marked the first real attempt to create an intercolonial governmental agency to coordinate defense and Indian affairs. On the whole, the meeting was not a success: The plan was not popular with either delegates or the British government, and the Iroquois refused to commit to fighting the French.

1755 General Braddock defeated by French and Indians in Pennsylvania. Braddock's defeat at Fort Duquense had a chilling effect on the war effort. British leaders were disheartened by the loss and failed on their other campaigns as a result.

1757 William Pitt, prime minister in Britain, fully commits to war effort. Pitt was willing to commit massive resources to an all-out war against the French and their allies in America. His elevation to power resulted in a string of successes that turned the tide of the war in favor of the British.

1759 Quebec falls to British. Quebec was a seemingly invincible fortress city. Its fall to the young British general James Wolfe broke French resistance and led to the end of the war.

1760 George III becomes king. George III was young and unprepared for his duties as king of England. His inability to find a prime minister he liked contributed to the worsening relations between Great Britain and its colonies.

1763 Treaty of Paris ends French and Indian War. The treaty negotiations were complex and gave England a great deal of territory but failed to capitalize on the decisive victory. The French lost Canada to Great Britain but retained their Caribbean islands, while their territory west of the Mississippi River went to Spain. English title was confirmed for the eastern half of North America.

Pontiac's uprising provokes fear and destruction in western frontier settlements. Pontiac was angry about the British government's claim to Indian lands in the Ohio region, and inspired by Delaware prophecies, he formed a pan-Indian movement rejecting white ways and especially white settlers. Although the uprising was defeated, its high cost in money and lives demonstrated to the British the importance of maintaining peace on the frontier.

Proclamation of 1763 prohibits settlement west of Appalachians. The Proclamation was intended to ease frontier tensions and protect the fur trade by keeping Indians and colonists apart. However, it created discontent among colonial settlers and land speculators and demanded the installation of a standing army of British soldiers to uphold the law.

1764 The Revenue (Sugar) Act lowers tax on foreign molasses to promote compliance with trade duty. Although the act was seen by the British as a way of enforcing previously existing laws, American colonists were upset by the provision allowing the British to prosecute smugglers in a vice-admiralty court in Nova Scotia rather than in local civil courts. Reaction to the act foreshadowed questions about England's right to tax Americans, although most of the response came from Americans in the shipping trades.

Currency Act prohibits issuance of colonial paper money. This act added to the growing colonial resentment of British authority by prohibiting the printing of paper currency in the colonies. British merchants supported the measure because it meant they would no longer be paid in depreciated money, but colonists, who depended on printed money to lubricate the economy, were left with no short-term financing flexibility.

1765 Stamp Act imposes tax on documents. The Stamp Act imposed a tax on paper used for various colonial documents. It was the first British legislation to impose a direct tax on a colonial item; moreover, it had to be paid in sterling silver, a hardship for cash-poor Americans. The act caused uproar among Americans.

May. Patrick Henry sponsors Virginia Resolves. The resolves went from obvious statements about Virginians' status as British citizens and the tradition of self-taxation to making the radical contention that only the Virginia legislature represented Virginians and so was the only body that could tax them. While the resolves were not passed in the House of Burgesses, they were widely reprinted and inspired other colonial legislatures to debate the issue.

August. Crowd actions in Boston inaugurate Sons of Liberty. The Sons of Liberty devised the strategy of direct action against the Stamp Act, organizing street demonstrations designed to intimidate Andrew Oliver, the stamp distributor. Their August 14 gathering convinced Oliver to resign, showed the royal authorities in Boston that they had little power without a supportive police force or militia, and taught hundreds of ordinary Bostonians that they could have an impact on politics.

October. Stamp Act Congress meets in New York City. The Stamp Act Congress was called in response to riots surrounding protests over the Stamp Act. Colonial leaders met to issue a more moderate challenge to Parliament, submitting a petition couched in traditional language but maintaining that Parliament could not tax the colonies. The meeting advanced the radical notion of intercolonial political activity and echoed the demonstrators' contention that liberty and property were linked.

1766 Stamp Act repealed; Declaratory Act asserts Parliament's control over colonies. English merchants were alarmed by the trade disruptions surrounding the Stamp Act and put pressure on Parliament to repeal the measure. To back down with a measure of dignity, Parliament repealed the Stamp Act but also passed the Declaratory Act, asserting the Parliamentary right to legislate for the colonies.

1767 Townshend duties reinstate revenue-raising taxes. While the Townshend duties simply established taxes paid by importers and passed on indirectly to colonists, they were designed for the purpose of raising money, not regulating trade. This demolished the colonial distinction between internal and external taxes. Also, money from the duties was to be used to pay governors' salaries, thus increasing their independence from local assemblies.

1768 Fall. British troops stationed in Boston. By 1768, Townshend's new customs commissioners had been forced to flee to an island in Boston harbor for safety, and a celebration of the Stamp Act demonstration of 1765 put huge crowds in the streets. Governor Francis Bernard realized that he could not depend on the loyalty of the Massachusetts militia, so he requested British soldiers to keep the peace.

1769 Year of nonimportation agreements; Daughters of Liberty appear. In response to the Townshend duties, colonial merchants agreed to boycott British goods entirely. This gave women a new outlet for political expression, as the home manufacture of prohibited items took on a wider and more public meaning.

1770 March 5. Boston Massacre. After January 1, 1770, some merchants refused to extend the expired nonimportation agreements. This led to crowd action and violence, culminating in an incident in which British soldiers protecting the Boston customs house fired on a hostile crowd and killed five people.

Townshend duties repealed; Lord North comes to power. Lord North concluded that the decrease in trade caused by the Townshend duties was not worth the trouble and recommended repeal. However, he maintained the tax on tea as a symbolic expression of Parliamentary authority.

1772 June. *Gaspée* attacked off Rhode Island. The incident involved a Royal Navy ship that was burned while it chased down suspected smugglers off the coast of Rhode Island. The British decision to transport suspects, if any were found, to England for trial seemed contrary to the traditional right to a trial by a jury of one's peers.

Committees of correspondence formed. In response to the *Gaspée* incident, American legislatures formed a network of standing committees to report and publicize news of English outrages. This was the first serious effort to create semiofficial links among the American colonial governments.

1773 Tea Act lowers price of tea to encourage Americans to purchase legal rather than smuggled tea. American colonists had been drinking English tea and paying the duty on it but also had smuggled in large quantities of Dutch tea, causing the British East India Company to suffer from sagging sales. The Tea Act was intended to remedy this problem by allowing East India Company agents to sell directly through special agents rather than public auction, lowering the price to make it competitive with the illegal variety.

December 16. Boston Tea Party. Americans believed that the Tea Act was a trick to get them to buy more British tea and thus pay more taxes to the British government. In Boston, a crisis emerged when three ships bearing tea arrived in late November. They sat in the harbor for twenty days, and then the impasse was broken by the Sons of Liberty, who stole onto the ships and destroyed the tea by dumping it overboard.

1774 Parliament passes Coercive Acts (Intolerable Acts): Boston Port Act, Massachusetts Government Act, Impartial Administration of Justice Act, Quartering Act, Quebec Act. The Coercive Acts were meant to punish Massachusetts. However, they seemed to colonists to indicate the arbitrary nature of British imperial rule and simply increased American resistance.

September. First Continental Congress meets. Continental Association formed. The Congress responded to the Coercive Acts by making a declaration of rights, insisting on the colonial right to self-taxation and imposing a staggered and limited boycott of trade with England. The Continental Association was formed to enforce the boycott. The Congress, the Association, and the local bodies charged with monitoring commerce and confronting violators all became functioning political bodies despite their lack of formal authority.

1775 April 19. Battles of Lexington and Concord. General Thomas Gage, the military governor of Boston, planned a surprise attack on Concord, which he suspected of harboring stores of ammunition. However, news of the march got out, and his troops were faced by armed Americans at Lexington, five miles east of their final destination. Fighting broke out and continued throughout the day in Lexington and Concord, as well as on the return to Boston.

Virginia's Lord Dunmore promises freedom to defecting slaves. Dunmore's offer was designed to frighten slaveowners and prevent them from rebelling against British rule, not lead to emancipation; he rejected all but the young, male, and able-bodied. However, as many as thirty thousand slaves had taken him up on the offer by 1778, despite the ill treatment they received from the British army.

## *Chronology Questions* Choose the letter of the best answer.

1. The Revenue (Sugar) Act lowered the tax on foreign molasses and antagonized some Americans in
   a. 1755.
   b. 1759.
   c. 1764.
   d. 1766.

2. Which one of the following events did not occur in 1763?
   a. The Treaty of Paris ends the French and Indian War.
   b. George III becomes king.
   c. Pontiac's uprising breaks out in the west.
   d. British legislation prohibits settlement west of the Appalachians.

3. What is the correct order for the following events?
   1. British troops are stationed in Boston.
   2. The Boston Massacre occurs.
   3. Townshend duties reinstate revenue-raising taxes.
   4. The nonimportation agreements are signed.
   a. 3, 1, 4, 2
   b. 4, 2, 3, 1
   c. 1, 3, 2, 4
   d. 3, 2, 4, 1

4. Lord Dunmore promised freedom to defecting slaves in
   a. 1760.
   b. 1768.
   c. 1770.
   d. 1775.

5. In 1773, the
   a. Boston Tea Party occurred.
   b. Stamp Act was repealed.
   c. Coercive Acts were passed by Parliament.
   d. Daughters of Liberty appeared.

6. What is the correct order for the following events?
   1. The Ohio Company of Virginia is formed.
   2. William Pitt, prime minister in Britain, fully commits to the war effort.
   3. Quebec falls to the British.
   4. The French and Indian War begins in America.
   a. 2, 4, 3, 1
   b. 4, 3, 1, 2
   c. 2, 3, 1, 4
   d. 1, 4, 2, 3

7. The *Gaspée* incident occurred off the coast of Rhode Island in
   a. 1764.
   b. 1769.
   c. 1772.
   d. 1775.

8. What is the correct order for the following events?
   1. The Stamp Act imposes a tax on documents.
   2. The Declaratory Act asserts Parliament's control over the colonies.
   3. The Currency Act prohibits the issuance of colonial paper money.
   4. The Tea Act lowers the price of tea.
   a. 2, 1, 4, 3
   b. 1, 4, 3, 2
   c. 3, 1, 2, 4
   d. 1, 2, 4, 3

9. The Albany Plan of Union was proposed in
   a. 1747.
   b. 1754.
   c. 1767.
   d. 1774.

10. Which one of the following events did not occur in 1765?
    a. Patrick Henry sponsors the Virginia Resolves.
    b. General Braddock is defeated by the French and Indians in Pennsylvania.
    c. The Stamp Act Congress meets in New York City.
    d. Crowd actions in Boston inaugurate the Sons of Liberty.

***Defining Terms*** Match each term with the correct definition.

nonconsumption agreements
Quartering Act
Townshend Duties
Declaratory Act
Stamp Act Congress
Currency Act
Sugar Act
Virginia Resolves
Coercive Acts
Paxton Boys
Lord Dunmore
John Stuart, Earl of Bute
Phillis Wheatley
Frederick North
Fort Necessity
Fort Duquense

Lexington and Concord
Ohio Valley
*Letters from a Farmer in Pennsylvania*
British East India Company
Continental Association
Albany Plan of Union
Treaty of Paris
Ohio Company
Sons of Liberty
Daughters of Liberty
Pontiac
General Thomas Gage
minutemen
virtual representation
committees of correspondence

1. The area encompassing present-day western Pennsylvania and eastern Ohio. Claimed by France and Virginia, the region was the center of a thriving, and very profitable, fur trade. Ohio Valley

2. A group of wealthy Virginians with a grant from the English king to 200,000 acres of forests in the Ohio Valley in 1747. The investors hoped to profit from resale of the land, while the English wanted to use English settlers to block the French. Ohio Company

3. The fort built by George Washington and his Virginian militia in 1754 in the aftermath of a disastrous military altercation with the French in the Ohio Valley. The French attacked the fort, killing or wounding a third of the fort's occupants and forcing Washington to surrender. The conflict proved the first in the French and Indian War. Fort Necessity

4. An outline for a more unified colonial government presented at the Albany Congress by Benjamin Franklin and Thomas Hutchinson. The plan called for a limited governmental agency, representing all the colonies, that would coordinate defense and Indian affairs. Neither the Albany delegates nor the British government liked the plan. Albany Plan of Union

5. The first target of the British offensive against the French in the French and Indian War. In 1755, General Edward Braddock led a combined army of British and Virginian troops to the French outpost in western Pennsylvania but was ambushed a day short of the fort and badly beaten by the French and their Indian allies. The defeat demoralized the other British armies and cast a pall over the first couple years of fighting. Fort Duquense

6. The 1763 agreement that ended the French and Indian War. England gained Canada and all of North America east of the Mississippi River, but in spite of the overwhelming British victory, the French retained their Caribbean islands and the English returned Cuba to Spain. The Indians' claim to any of the disputed land was completely ignored. Treaty of Paris

7. This man, George III's tutor and first prime minister, did not approve of his predecessor's strategy of aggressively pursuing the war with the French. He squandered the victory by negotiating the unfavorable Treaty of Paris and then made the expensive and unpopular decision to keep a standing army in North America. John Stuart, Earl of Bute

8. The chief of the Ottawa tribe in the northern Ohio region. In 1763, he led a pan-Indian uprising against the British in protest over their claims to Indian land. Although the rebellion was suppressed, it resulted in nearly 2,500 casualties and convinced the British that they would have to keep an army in America to prevent further outbreaks of frontier warfare. Pontiac

9. Scots-Irish inhabitants of central Pennsylvania who believed that the colonial government was not doing enough to protect them against the Indian threat. They took matters into their own hands by murdering twenty friendly Indians in the town of Conestogaand then marched toward Philadelphia to demand a greater voice in the state assembly. They were finally turned back by Benjamin Franklin, who promised not to prosecute them for their crimes. Paxton Boys

10. Prime Minister George Grenville's attempt to fund the huge British war debt by clamping down on smuggling and encouraging the collection of customs duties. This, which was also called the Revenue Act of 1764, lowered the duty on French molasses and increased penalties for smuggling. It led to ugly confrontations at port cities and annoyed shippers. Sugar Act

11. A piece of British legislation that prohibited the printing of paper money in the colonies. Currency Act

12. The idea that the British Parliament represented all British subjects, wherever they were and whether or not they were able to vote. George Grenville used this idea to argue that the Stamp Act, or other Parliamentary taxes on colonists, did not constitute taxation without representation. Visual Representation

13. A series of seven resolutions authored by Patrick Henry and debated by the Virginia House of Burgesses in 1765. They took the protest over the Stamp Act to its logical conclusion, arguing that the Virginian assembly alone had the right to tax Virginians and that tax laws originating outside of Virginia were not legitimate. These resolutions did not pass, but they were widely reported in newspapers and encouraged further resistance. Virginia resolves

14. A group formed to protest the Stamp Act by Boston shopkeepers and craftsmen under the leadership of Samuel Adams. They defied the Stamp Act by using street demonstrations to convince the Massachusetts stamp distributor to resign. Sons of liberty

15. A meeting of delegates from nine colonial assemblies in October 1765. The group came together in the wake of street demonstrations against the Stamp Act, in the hopes of issuing a measured and moderate challenge to Parliamentary authority. While it wrote up a cautious petition, its dismissal of Parliament's claim to represent the colonies was quite radical. Stamp Act Congress

16. Legislation passed by Parliament in March 1766, at the same time that the Stamp Act was repealed. It stated Parliament's right to legislate for the colonies "in all cases whatsoever," thus reinforcing Parliament's authority and showing the colonists that Parliament upheld the power to tax them. Declaratory Act

17. Taxes on tea, glass, lead, paper, and painters' colors levied in 1767 by the chancellor of the exchequer. These taxes were in the tradition of the navigation acts, levying taxes on goods imported into the colonies, but they roused colonial ire because they were intended to raise revenue rather than regulate trade. Townshend duties

18. Philadelphia lawyer John Dickinson's 1768 response to the Townshend duties. Dickinson contended that the Townshend duties constituted taxation without representation and were therefore a sign of the British desire to enslave the colonies. Letters From a farmer in Pennsylvania

19. A 1765 British rule directing the colonies to furnish shelter and provisions for the British army. The New York assembly refused to enforce the act on the grounds that it was a tax measure, requiring New Yorkers to pay money by order of Parliament. Townshend's decision to suspend the assembly until it complied caused other colonists to wonder if their legislative government was secure. Quartering Act

20. Consumer boycotts of British goods called in response to the Townshend duties. These boycotts gave women an unprecedented opportunity to express their political affiliations because they relied on women's willingness to manufacture at home what they had previously purchased ready-made. non consumption agreements

21. Female patriots who emerged during the boycotts of British goods. These women showed that women could play a role in the public sphere. Daughters of Liberty

22. The British prime minister who recommended the repeal of the Townshend duties. He convinced Parliament to do away with all of the duties except that on tea in order to cool tensions while maintaining the principle of Parliamentary authority. Frederick North

23. Bodies formed by colonial assemblies in the aftermath of the *Gaspée* incident to link the colonies and pass on news of British misdeeds. They represented the first effort to create semiofficial links among the American colonial governments. Committees of correspondence

24. The major British exporter of tea to the colonies, which had been losing money because of competition from smuggled Dutch tea. In response, Lord North proposed the Tea Act of 1773, giving favored status to this commercial organization. Although the move lowered the price of tea, Americans interpreted it as another attempt to increase revenue to pay royal governors and judges.
British East India company

25. Lord North's response to the destruction of tea in the Boston harbor. The acts suspended civil government in Massachusetts, closed the Boston harbor, allowed royal officials trial in England, and mandated the civilian quartering of British troops if necessary. The acts frightened colonists, who understood that what could be implemented against Massachusetts could be used in the other colonies too. Coercive Acts

26. A mechanism created by the First Continental Congress to enforce a staggered boycott against British trade. Local groups would monitor commerce and confront violators. Although the groups had no formal authority, they were accepted as legitimate governmental bodies by many Americans. Continental Association

27. The military governor of Massachusetts who, after the passage of the Coercive Acts, recommended repealing the acts but was ignored by political leaders in England. General Thomas Gage

28. Militia units that formed in Massachusetts in the wake of the Coercive Acts. They were supposed to be prepared to respond quickly to any threat from the British army in Boston. minutemen

29. The locations of the first fighting of the Revolutionary War, which broke out on April 19, 1775. Lexington and Concord

30. The royal governor of Virginia when the revolution started, he threatened to arm slaves to defend imperial authority. Although he had no desire to emancipate slaves or start a slave rebellion, his challenge highlighted the divergence between planters' claims to liberty and their own slaveholding practices. Lord Dunmore

31. An enslaved domestic servant and poet owned by a Boston merchant. Her writings showed that slaves understood the inherent irony of revolutionary rhetoric. Phillis Wheatley

## Chapter Review

### *Multiple-Choice* Choose the letter of the best answer.

1. The French and Indian War broke out over
   a. contested land in Massachusetts.
   b. contested land in the Ohio Valley.
   c. religious differences.
   d. trade policies.

2. In the late 1740s, the French began building forts in the Ohio Valley in response to
   a. Spanish threats.
   b. Pennsylvania traders' incursions.
   c. Virginian land speculation.
   d. Indian attacks.

3. In 1747, the British government authorized speculative real estate development of Virginia's unsettled western lands in order to
   a. make some money.
   b. block French expansion.
   c. gain popularity with colonial residents.
   d. expand the supply of fresh land.

4. George Washington's first armed expedition against the French in the Ohio Valley
   a. was a stunning military success.
   b. won him fame as a military strategist.
   c. ended disastrously.
   d. convinced the French to abandon their fort.

5. To win their war against the French in the New World, the British needed
   a. intercolonial cooperation and Indian support.
   b. help from colonists and colonial tax monies.
   c. help from colonists and Indian support.
   d. intercolonial cooperation and colonial tax monies.

6. Colonies from Virginia northward were instructed by the British to send delegates to the Albany Congress, which was supposed to
   a. coordinate the mutual defense of the colonies and woo Indians.
   b. raise money for the war.
   c. draft a peace treaty.
   d. demonstrate symbolic support for the war effort.

7. The Albany Plan of Union proposed a unified
   a. but limited agency to coordinate defense and Indian affairs.
   b. and powerful agency to coordinate defense and Indian affairs.
   c. but limited agency to enforce British laws.
   d. and powerful agency to enforce British laws.

8. The Albany Plan of Union was approved by
   a. none of the colonies.
   b. most of the colonies.
   c. the British Parliament.
   d. the king.

9. During the first two years of the French and Indian War, the British
   a. did quite well on the American front.
   b. stumbled quite badly on the American front.
   c. successfully won Indian support.
   d. won battles because the French were not prepared to fight.

10. In the French and Indian War, French resistance was finally broken after
    a. a lengthy siege of Cuba.
    b. Quebec fell to the British.
    c. Indians massacred the defenders of Montreal.
    d. the Spanish invaded Canada.

11. The Treaty of Paris that ended the French and Indian War
    a. gave Cuba to Great Britain.
    b. returned Caribbean Islands to Spain.
    c. permitted the French to retain Quebec.
    d. assigned Indian lands to the English.

12. In the wake of the French and Indian War, American colonists
    a. were ashamed of trading furs with the French during the conflict.
    b. appreciated British military support.
    c. admired the British military leaders who had won the war.
    d. believed that their contributions had not been appreciated by the British.

13. Competition over land in _____ touched off nearly a decade of war between France and England.
    a. New York
    b. New Jersey
    c. the Ohio Valley
    d. Canada

14. The French built a series of forts to create a barrier to _____ expansion.
    a. too rapid
    b. Spanish
    c. British-American
    d. Indian

15. Under the terms of its seventeenth-century charter, _____ claimed all lands west of the Mississippi River and north to Lake Superior.
    a. Pennsylvania
    b. Massachusetts
    c. Virginia
    d. Connecticut

16. After a third of his soldiers were killed or wounded in a French attack on Fort Necessity, Washington _____ as he began his military career.
    a. capitulated
    b. retreated
    c. escaped
    d. continued fighting

17. Benjamin Franklin and Thomas Hutchinson drew up the Albany Plan of Union, proposing a _____ governmental agency to coordinate defense and Indian affairs.
    a. regionalized colonial
    b. royal
    c. unified colonial
    d. New York

18. The Iroquois League's strategy in the French and Indian War was to _____ the two sides.
    a. ignore
    b. play off
    c. encourage
    d. discourage

19. The British hoped to defeat the French quickly by attacking them in three _____.
    a. continental European sites
    b. strategic places
    c. heavily armed ships
    d. ways—by land, by sea, and by a trade boycott

20. The French and Indian War finally turned around after the rise to power in 1757 of _____, England's Secretary of State.
    a. William Pitt
    b. Edward Braddock
    c. William Shirley
    d. William Johnson

21. As a result of the peace negotiations at the end of the French and Indian War, _____ was turned over to England.
    a. Cuba
    b. Martinique
    c. Canada
    b. New Orleans

22. In the wake of the French and Indian War, American colonists were _____.
    a. very grateful to England
    b. uncertain about what to do with the new land they had gained
    c. resentful over the British army's treatment of American troops
    d. in terrible debt

23. In the 1760s, the basic idea underlying British policy making was that
    a. colonists did not deserve the protection of British law.
    b. taxes on residents of England should be raised.
    c. colonists should help service the huge war debt.
    d. cabinet leadership was unusually stable.

24. Prime Minister Bute's most significant decision while in office was to
    a. deliberately isolate the king.
    b. keep a standing army in the colonies.
    c. remove the army from the colonies.
    d. refuse to negotiate the Treaty of Paris.

25. The ostensible reason for keeping British troops in America in the early 1760s was to
    a. subdue colonial uprisings.
    b. watch for signs of French military resurgence.
    c. maintain peace between colonists and Indians.
    d. prevent the Spanish from moving into British territory.

26. In the 1760s, a religious revival sparked by several Delaware Indian prophecies encouraged tribes from western New York to the Great Lakes to
    a. capitulate to white dominance.
    b. act more like Europeans.
    c. form an alliance with the Americans.
    d. return to old Indian customs.

27. Pontiac, the chief of the Ottawa tribe, became famous after he
    a. created the Delaware prophecies.
    b. rejected the Delaware prophecies.
    c. inaugurated an uprising against the British.
    d. became wealthy trading European goods.

28. The Paxton Boys were responsible for
    a. ending the Indian uprising.
    b. sparking the Indian uprising.
    c. overturning the Pennsylvanian legislature.
    d. murdering friendly Indians.

29. The Proclamation of 1763 was issued to
    a. protect colonists.
    b. end Pontiac's uprising.
    c. raise revenue for the British government.
    d. avert costly frontier warfare.

30. The boundary for western settlement set out in the Proclamation of 1763 was opposed by
    a. the British military and eastern speculators.
    b. western settlers and eastern speculators.
    c. Indians and western settlers.
    d. New England farmers and the British military.

31. George Grenville, George III's second chief minister, was determined to
    a. enforce the proclamation line.
    b. suppress Indian uprisings.
    c. tackle the war debt from the French and Indian War.
    d. keep the French out of North America.

32. The hardest duty for Grenville to enforce was the one
    a. on molasses.
    b. on grain and whiskey.
    c. on enumerated manufactured goods.
    d. on sugar from the Caribbean.

33. The Sugar Act stipulated that smugglers caught without proper paperwork be
    a. executed without trial.
    b. prosecuted by a local court.
    c. prosecuted by a vice-admiralty court in Nova Scotia.
    d. deported to England.

34. Grenville persuaded Parliament to pass the Currency Act of 1764 in response to
    a. persistent counterfeiting in the colonies.
    b. British merchants who wanted to get full value for their goods.
    c. the excessive amount of currency in circulation in the colonies.
    d. the excessive amount of gold and silver in circulation in the colonies.

35. In the 1760s, George III's many ministers wrestled with the issue of _____.
    a. paying French war reparations
    b. whether to impose the Anglican religion on the colonists
    c. how to service the war debt without violating what the colonists saw as their rights
    d. how to deal with slavery

36. As prime minister, John Stuart, the earl of Bute, negotiated the Treaty of Paris and decided to keep _____.
    a. the Indians from practicing their traditional forms of worship
    b. the boundary of Virginia as it had been before the war
    c. a standing army in the colonies
    d. the tax on tea

37. In the early 1760s, Indians in the northwest were influenced by a _____, encouraging them to give up white culture.
    a. wave of disease
    b. lengthy famine
    c. financial crisis
    d. religious revival

38. Three months after the Treaty of Paris was signed, Pontiac, chief of the Ottawa tribe, attacked a _____ garrison.
    a. French
    b. British
    c. Shawnee
    d. colonial

39. The Paxton Boys were responsible for _____ twenty Christian Indians in response to Pontiac's uprising.
    a. converting
    b. befriending
    c. educating
    d. murdering

40. The Proclamation of 1763 promised to protect both Indians and _____.
    a. colonists
    b. British forts
    c. the environment
    d. the fur trade

41. George Grenville hoped to solve the English government's financial difficulties by
    a. raising the taxes levied on residents of Great Britain
    b. raising the taxes levied on colonists
    c. enforcing existing customs duties
    d. printing large quantities of paper money.

42. The Sugar Act raised revenue by _____ the duty on molasses.
    a. enacting
    b. raising
    c. lowering
    d. removing

43. The vigilant enforcement of the Sugar Act annoyed _____.
    a. American shippers
    b. Parliament
    c. colonial assemblies
    d. French companies with molasses interests in the Caribbean

44. George Grenville's Currency Act of 1764 reduced the colonies' _____.
    a. flow of money
    b. war debts
    c. gold and silver coin
    d. dependence of British banks

45. The Stamp Act differed from earlier legislation because it
    a. was a trade regulation.
    b. was imposed by Parliament.
    c. was created by the colonial legislatures.
    d. was intended simply to raise money.

46. The Stamp Act was unpopular for many reasons, including the condition that the tax be paid for with
    a. agricultural surpluses.
    b. paper currency.
    c. letters of credit.
    d. sterling silver.

47. Prime Minister Grenville defended the Stamp Act by arguing that
    a. colonists did not need to be represented in Parliament.
    b. colonists were virtually represented in Parliament.
    c. taxation did not require consent.
    d. the king could tax at will.

48. The challenge to the Stamp Act was led by
    a. colonial governors.
    b. colonial assemblies.
    c. customs collectors.
    d. ordinary people.

49. Local communities decided that the most effective way to protest the Stamp Act was to
    a. defy the law.
    b. refuse to use paper at all.
    c. prevent the distribution of stamped paper.
    d. riot in the streets.

50. Boston, the capital of Massachusetts, instituted the first concerted effort to resist the Stamp Act because its
    a. governor was supportive.
    b. major occupational groups relied on paper.
    c. legislature was unusually radical.
    d. leaders were in close communication with Virginia's Patrick Henry.

51. Samuel Adams and the Sons of Liberty decided to oppose the Stamp Acts by means of
    a. legislative resolutions.
    b. petitions of protest.
    c. a large street demonstration.
    d. nonviolent resistance.

52. The Boston demonstration against the Stamp Act showed colonists that
    a. without police to call on, the royal authorities would use the army.
    b. street action was ineffective.
    c. stamp collectors were determined to stay in their posts.
    d. resistance would not result in massive retaliation.

53. When the Stamp Act took effect on November 1, 1765, royal authorities
    a. regained control of Boston.
    b. allowed ships to pass through the harbor without stamped papers.
    c. halted trade by refusing to allow ships without stamped papers into the harbor.
    d. all resigned their offices.

54. The Stamp Act Congress was radical because it
 a. denied colonial submission to Parliament.
 b. rejected the authority of the king.
 c. dismissed the notion of private property.
 d. advanced the idea of intercolonial political action.

55. American colonists believed that, as English citizens, their social, political, and economic freedom was protected by
 a. having an elected monarch.
 b. refusing to obey laws.
 c. having representative governments pass laws.
 d. allowing every adult male to vote.

56. The repeal of the Stamp Act by Parliament in 1776 showed that
 a. Parliament gave up on taxing the colonies.
 b. economic considerations won out.
 c. the king supported the colonists.
 d. Parliament decided that virtual representation was not workable.

57. The Stamp Act imposed a tax on _____ used for various colonial documents.
 a. paper
 b. postage
 c. painters' colors
 d. lawyers' fees

58. George Grenville delegated the administration of the Stamp Act to _____ agents, hoping to blunt hostility.
 a. royal
 b. shipping
 c. American
 d. foreign

59. Prior to the Stamp Act, colonists were taxed only by _____.
 a. the British Parliament
 b. the king
 c. their assemblies
 d. their customs houses

60. The Virginia Resolves stated that Virginians, as _____, enjoyed the right of self-taxation.
 a. British citizens
 b. colonists
 c. voters
 d. landowners

61. According to colonists, Parliament had the right to impose _____ taxes to regulate trade.
 a. sales
 b. stamp
 c. income
 d. external

62. In Boston, resistance to the Stamp Act was spearheaded by _____, a town politician.
 a. Thomas Hutchinson
 b. Francis Bernard
 c. John Adams
 d. Samuel Adams

63. On the day that the Stamp Act went into effect, customs officials _____ ships to pass through the harbor without properly stamped clearance papers.
 a. dared
 b. encouraged
 c. allowed
 d. did not allow

64. The Stamp Act Congress declared that colonists were _____ Parliament.
 a. better than
 b. contemptuous of
 c. submissive to
 d. not beholden to

65. Americans believed that the right to _____ was a special kind of liberty requiring special safeguards.
 a. vote
 b. self-defense
 c. legislative representation
 d. own property

66. When Parliament simultaneously repealed the Stamp Act and passed the Declaratory Act in 1766, it upheld the power to _____.
 a. declare war in Indian territories
 b. make colonial laws
 c. appoint colonial assemblies
 d. tax

67. Charles Townshend, the chancellor of the exchequer, proposed new taxes in the form of
    a. a revamped Sugar Act.
    b. a navigation act.
    c. a sales tax.
    d. an income tax.

68. The Townshend duties imposed by the Revenue Act of 1767 were unpopular because they
    a. embodied the idea of taxation through trade duties.
    b. were burdensome.
    c. made tea and sugar very expensive.
    d. were internal taxes.

69. One very controversial aspect of the Townshend duties was that some of the revenue would
    a. support members of Parliament.
    b. go directly to the king.
    c. help English paupers.
    d. pay the salaries of royal governors.

70. Charles Townshend, England's chief financial minister, responded to New York's resistance to the Quartering Act with
    a. fines.
    b. the New York Suspending Act.
    c. jail sentences for legislators.
    d. military occupation.

71. Francis Bernard, the governor of Massachusetts, dissolved the colony's assembly in 1768 after it
    a. refused to implement the Quartering Act.
    b. denied the validity of parliamentary taxation.
    c. protested the Suspending Act.
    d. publicly celebrated the repeal of the Stamp Act.

72. In 1767 and 1768 many colonial towns passed nonconsumption agreements, which were intended to
    a. hurt trade with Great Britain.
    b. encourage more people to buy French goods.
    c. help American farmers.
    d. lower British customs revenues.

73. The colonists found that nonimportation agreements were even more difficult to implement than nonconsumption agreements because
    a. they were perceived as less effective.
    b. assemblies avoided them.
    c. merchants liked them less.
    d. consumers resisted them.

74. The Townshend duties provided the colonists an unparalleled opportunity for developing
    a. merchants' selflessness.
    b. lawyers' patriotism.
    c. artisans' activism.
    d. women's patriotism.

75. On the whole, the colonial boycotts of 1769
    a. failed to have an impact on British merchants.
    b. were a success.
    c. did not influence the British government.
    d. ended the controversy over taxes.

76. In the fall of 1768, three thousand British troops occupied Boston because
    a. of the nonimportation agreements.
    b. there were threats against the royal governor's life.
    c. of a public celebration of the Stamp Act demonstration of 1765.
    d. Indians were mounting attacks on the surrounding countryside.

77. On March 5, 1770, colonial tensions came to a climax after
    a. shops carrying British goods were attacked by crowds.
    b. Ebenezer Richardson fired on a crowd.
    c. the Boston Massacre.
    d. Thomas Hutchinson's appointment as governor.

78. After the Boston Massacre, Sons of Liberty members John Adams and Josiah Quincy famously
    a. defended colonists who had participated in riots.
    b. defended the soldiers who had been involved.
    c. disrupted the trials of the soldiers who had been involved.
    d. made orations at the funerals of the colonists who had died.

79. Charles Townshend, the chancellor of the exchequer, turned to _____ to pay for the war debt and the cost of stationing the British army in America.
    a. force
    b. the colonial assemblies
    c. duties levied on transatlantic trade
    d. property taxes

80. By the time Charles Townshend implemented the Revenue Act of 1767, colonists had started objecting to external taxes intended only to _____.
    a. annoy them
    b. assert Parliamentary authority
    c. hamper trade
    d. raise money

81. Before the Townshend duties of 1767, local assemblies set the _____ of their own officials.
    a. privileges
    b. salaries
    c. terms
    d. powers

82. Charles Townshend suspended the New York assembly after it refused to implement the _____ Act, which it claimed was a tax measure in disguise.
    a. Quartering
    b. Sugar
    c. Revenue
    d. Stamp

83. The _____ assembly tried to coordinate the protest against the Townshend duties.
    a. Massachusetts
    b. New York
    c. Georgia
    d. Pennsylvania

84. Many of the British goods prohibited by nonconsumption agreements were _____ items.
    a. agricultural
    b. medical
    c. industrial
    d. household

85. The protest over the Townshend duties provided an unparalleled opportunity for _____ patriotism.
    a. male
    b. female
    c. colonial
    d. black

86. _____ had become a prominent symbol of patriotism by the end of 1769.
    a. Cornmeal
    b. Homespun cloth
    c. Tea
    d. Coffee

87. By the summer of 1768, Massachusetts's governor Francis Bernard determined that he needed _____ to keep the peace.
    a. a militia
    b. British soldiers
    c. a police force
    d. the navy

88. _____ the Boston Massacre remains obscure to this day.
    a. The death toll in
    b. The number acquitted in
    c. The cause of the tension leading up to
    d. Who was responsible for

89. Just after the Boston Massacre, the new British prime minister, Frederick North, recommended
    a. reimposing the Stamp Act.
    b. repealing the Townshend duties.
    c. taxing coffee.
    d. strictly enforcing the Townshend duties.

90. The *Gaspée* investigation seemed to violate the British tradition of
    a. trade regulation.
    b. trial by jury.
    c. representative government.
    d. prosecuting smugglers.

91. The British handling of the *Gaspée* incident had the unintended effect of
   a. creating semiofficial links among the colonial governments.
   b. disrupting relations between colonial governments.
   c. encouraging smugglers to resist capture.
   d. reducing smuggling activity along the American coast.

92. The Tea Act of 1773 was intended to
   a. increase the tax on tea.
   b. convince Americans to drink tea rather than coffee.
   c. raise the overall price of tea.
   d. give favored status to the East India Company.

93. The revived Sons of Liberty combated the Tea Act by
   a. nonimportation agreements.
   b. pressuring tea agents to resign.
   c. consumer boycotts.
   d. threatening tea drinkers.

94. The Boston Port Act punished the city for the Tea Party by
   a. rerouting trade through New York.
   b. raising customs duties.
   c. closing the harbor to all shipping.
   d. using all taxes to pay for the destroyed tea.

95. The Massachusetts Government Act
   a. promised an eventual return to representative government.
   b. altered the colony's charter.
   c. augmented the power of the state's assembly.
   d. established martial law in Boston.

96. The fourth of the Coercive Acts, the Quartering Act, permitted military commanders to
   a. build new houses to shelter soldiers.
   b. directly tax residents for the support of soldiers.
   c. take over public accommodations.
   d. lodge soldiers wherever necessary.

97. The Quebec Act frightened colonists because it
   a. returned the city to the French.
   b. was seen as an affront to Protestants.
   c. overturned the city's French civil law.
   d. established new colonial taxes.

98. Nearly all of the delegates to the First Continental Congress were
   a. interested in provoking a crisis with England.
   b. in agreement on what liberties they claimed as English subjects.
   c. unified in their ideas about how to respond to the Coercive Acts.
   d. the leading statesmen of their localities.

99. The declaration of rights the First Continental Congress produced made the radical claim that
   a. colonists were not subject to any British laws.
   b. colonists would no longer accept trade regulations.
   c. colonial governments had the sole right to legislate for their residents.
   d. the king was not a legitimate ruler.

100. To put pressure on England, the Continental Congress agreed to
   a. harass British soldiers.
   b. encourage smuggling.
   c. impose a staggered and limited boycott of trade.
   d. demand a complete boycott of trade.

101. In 1770, Lord North removed all of the Townshend duties except for the tax on _____, a pointed reminder of Parliament's ultimate power.
   a. painters' colors
   b. lead
   c. tea
   d. paper

102. The colonial nonimportation agreements _____ after the repeal of the Townshend duties.
   a. ended
   b. were strengthened
   c. were ignored
   d. continued

103. The decision of the investigation commission after the *Gaspée* incident was seen as a curtailment of the right to _____.
   a. trade with the French
   b. taxation without representation
   c. trade with the Indians
   d. trial by jury

104. By spring 1773, half the towns in Massachusetts had set up their own _____, providing local forums for debate.
   a. legislatures
   b. committees of correspondence
   c. customs houses
   d. taverns

105. The Tea Act embodied the power of Parliament to _____ the colonies.
   a. tax and make laws for
   b. financially help
   c. choose representatives for
   d. supply luxury items for

106. The Boston Sons of Liberty dumped £10,000 sterling worth of tea into the Boston harbor to protest the _____.
   a. presence of British troops
   b. newly enacted sales tax
   c. duties imposed on tea
   d. continued importation of African slaves

107. The Impartial Administration of Justice Act stipulated that any royal official accused of a capital crime in the colonies would be _____.
   a. tried in court in England
   b. tried in court in the colonies
   c. dismissed immediately
   d. automatically acquitted

108. The Quebec Act gave Quebec control of the fur trade in _____.
   a. the Ohio Valley
   b. Canada
   c. the Appalachians
   d. New York

109. Delegates to the First Continental Congress created the Continental Association, with chapters in each town, to enforce a _____.
   a. curfew to quell mob action
   b. coordinated smuggling movement
   c. move toward home rule
   d. limited trade boycott

110. The key reason that committees of public safety, committees of correspondence, regrouped colonial assemblies, and the Continental Congress were able to wield authority over American colonists was that they _____.
   a. were acknowledged as legitimate by the British government
   b. threatened dissenters with violence
   c. were composed of the same men who had been in disbanded government bodies
   d. had the support of the British army

111. When armed confrontation broke out in Massachusetts, Thomas Gage, the military commander and new governor, believed he was facing a
   a. major revolt.
   b. domestic insurrection.
   c. long war.
   d. dispute between local factions.

112. Over the winter of 1774 to 1775, pessimistic Americans who were unhappy with the Coercive Acts and the British presence in Boston
   a. agitated for further boycotts.
   b. joined the British army.
   c. accumulated arms and ammunition.
   d. left the colonies.

113. In 1775, General Thomas Gage, the military commander and governor of Massachusetts, advised the British government to
   a. march on the American rebels.
   b. repeal the Coercive Acts.
   c. arrest the troublemakers.
   d. reduce the number of troops in the colony.

114. Paul Revere's role in the American turmoil of 1775 was to
   a. call the people to the Old North Church.
   b. urge the militia to hold their fire.
   c. warn the minutemen of British troop movements westward.
   d. give General Gage information about minutemen strategy.

115. When the British army arrived in Lexington in April 1775, it found
   a. ill-trained American minutemen on the village green.
   b. the ammunition it was supposed to confiscate.
   c. a large American army.
   d. that everybody had fled the village.

116. The fighting at Lexington and Concord in April 1775
   a. left both the British and the Americans apprehensive.
   b. allowed the British to confiscate American ammunition stores.
   c. showed that the Americans could stop a British raid.
   d. demonstrated British military superiority.

117. The royal governor of Virginia, Lord Dunmore, responded to the outbreak of excitement over the battles at Lexington and Concord by
   a. removing stockpiles of gunpowder.
   b. threatening to arm slaves.
   c. both of the above.
   d. neither of the above.

118. In 1775, Lord Dunmore, the royal governor of Virginia, offered freedom to
   a. any able-bodied slave who would fight for the British.
   b. his own slaves.
   c. any slave who could make it behind British lines.
   d. any slave who would begin a general slave rebellion.

119. In a 1774 newspaper essay, the poet Phillis Wheatley drew attention to
   a. the artistic achievements of slaves.
   b. the unjustness of slavery.
   c. a planned slave rebellion.
   d. the hypocrisy of northern slave owners.

120. At the start of the war, slaves in the northern colonies
   a. fought for the British.
   b. were freed in large numbers by their masters.
   c. sued colonial governments for their freedom.
   d. conspired to free themselves.

121. To communicate important information among themselves, southern blacks in 1775 depended on
   a. word of mouth.
   b. southern newspapers.
   c. sympathetic planters.
   d. northern blacks who infiltrated the plantations.

122. Blacks who fled to the British army during the Revolutionary War were
   a. treated fairly by British commanders.
   b. treated poorly by British commanders.
   c. almost always recaptured by their owners.
   d. used as soldiers.

123. Assessing the British position in Boston in early 1775, General Thomas Gage became concerned because the Boston rebels were very angry _____.
   a. day laborers
   b. jobless and homeless people
   c. freeholders and farmers
   d. malcontents and former convicts

124. In April 1775, English leaders ordered General Thomas Gage to _____ trouble-makers quickly.
   a. arrest
   b. deport
   c. negotiate with
   d. placate

125. Gage planned a surprise attack on a suspected _____ at Concord.
   a. smuggler's hideout
   b. treasonous town government
   c. rebel militia
   d. ammunition storage site

126. As the British soldiers marched from Concord to _____, militia units attacked them from both sides in the bloodiest fighting of the day.
   a. the western frontier of Massachusetts
   b. Boston
   c. Lexington
   d. the Old North Bridge

127. Lord Dunmore, the royal governor of Virginia, threatened to arm _____ if necessary to ward off militia attacks like the ones in Lexington and Concord.
   a. royal officials
   b. slaves
   c. loyalists
   d. women

128. Slaves in the Northern colonies saw the Revolution as an ideal time to _____, although many whites did not agree.
   a. demand their own freedom
   b. support their white masters against the British
   c. run away in large numbers
   d. purchase their freedom

129. Phillis Wheatley was a slave and an accomplished _____ by the age of sixteen.
   a. cook
   b. poet
   c. seamstress
   d. lecturer

130. In Ulster County, New York, at least twenty slaves in four villages were planning to _____.
   a. petition for freedom
   b. undertake an armed rebellion
   c. fight for the British
   d. fight for the Americans

131. As many as thirty thousand slaves in Virginia joined _____.
   a. a slave rebellion
   b. a northern colonial militia
   c. the British army
   d. the Church of England

132. The Revolution led to _____ for thousands of blacks.
   a. freedom
   b. indentured servitude
   c. reparations
   d. a stronger political voice

***Short Answer*** Write a paragraph response to each question.

1. Why did Virginians object to French incursions into the Ohio Valley in the 1750s?
2. What were the goals of the Albany Conference? Did the delegates achieve those goals?
3. What was the early British strategy for defeating the French in the French and Indian War? Was the strategy successful?
4. How did Pontiac's uprising affect British policy toward the colonies?
5. Why was the Sugar Act passed, and how did it work?
6. How did George Grenville interpret the role of Parliament in taxing the colonies? On what basis did colonists disagree?
7. What were the Virginia Resolves? What made them radical?
8. How were the concepts of liberty and property related? How were these two concepts related?

9. What were the Townshend duties? What was the source of American outrage over them?
10. How did the Townshend duties encourage female patriotism?
11. After the Boston Massacre, what happened to the British soldiers involved in the conflict? Why did Americans involved with the patriot cause decide to defend them?
12. What role did the *Gaspée* incident play in undermining the relatively calm relationship between the English and their American colonies?
13. What were the Coercive Acts intended to do? Why did they frighten colonists outside of Massachusetts?
14. How did the First Continental Congress view its responsibilities? What was its outcome?
15. Why did General Gage march on Concord in April 1775? What was the outcome of the planned attack?
16. In 1775, why did Lord Dunmore, the governor of Virginia, offer freedom to slaves who would fight for the British?

***Building Historical Skills*** Historians use a variety of sources to think and talk about the past, including maps, illustrations, and written records. Maps provide a variety of different kinds of comparative information in a condensed visual format; reading them requires learning how to sort through this information. To deepen our understanding of the past by supplementing written records, historians frequently interpret material culture, such as a vase or a painting, with techniques borrowed from art history, archaeology, or anthropology. Written records, though familiar as sources, raise their own problems of interpretation. Every document reflects someone's particular perspective or assumptions. It is the historian's task to study and compare each document to other records with other perspectives. The following exercises introduce you to using maps, illustrations, and written documents as sources of information. Use these sources as well as the material in the chapter to think about different themes and topics discussed in the text.

***Map Activity*** Locate the following places on Map 5.2: North America before and after the French and Indian War on page 150 in *The American Promise*, Second Edition.

1. Louisiana
2. Proclamation Line of 1763
3. Spanish Florida
4. New Orleans
5. Quebec
7. Ohio River
8. Great Lakes
9. British colonies

Answer the following questions in a paragraph based on Map 5.2: North America before and after the French and Indian War.

**READING THE MAP** How did European land claims change from 1750 to 1763? Which country's claims did not change?

**CONNECTIONS** What was the goal of the Proclamation Act of 1763?

**WEB LINKS** To explore the topics discussed in the exercise above, visit the Web links noted below.

"Digital History Ltd."
http://www.digitalhistory.org
Choose "Table of Contents" and explore.

"North America, as Divided amongst the European Powers (1774)"
http://scarlett.libs.uga.edu/darchive/hargrett/maps/maps.html
Choose "Colonial America" and then map number 65.

"Treaty of Paris 1763"
http://grid.let.rug.nl/~usa/D/1751-1775/7yearswar/paris.htm

***Visual Activity*** Paul Revere's engraving of the Boston Massacre shows a middle-class crowd composed of well-dressed, respectable men in knee breeches, white stockings, and powdered wigs. These men are not rabble-rousers, as the viewer can tell from the small and harmless dog in the foreground of the picture, which is intended to represent the mild intentions of the colonists who had gathered in front of the customs house that day. The British soldiers, however, are extremely aggressive, leaning into the crowd as they fire. Although there are more colonists than soldiers, the soldiers are drawn as being much larger than the colonists and thus, visually at least, their equals in might. To reinforce the wanton nature of the attack, Revere has placed the sign "Butcher's Hall" on the customs house building.

Answer the following questions in a paragraph each based on "The Bloody Massacre Perpetrated in King Street, Boston, on March 5, 1770," on page 163 of *The American Promise*, Second Edition.

**WEB LINKS** To explore the topics discussed in the exercise above, visit the Web links noted below.

"The Murder of Crispus Attucks"
http://www.loc.gov/exhibits/treasures/trr046.html

"Anonymous Account of the Boston Massacre"
http://www.ukans.edu/carrie/docs/texts/bostanon.html

"Transcript of the Trial of Captain Thomas Preston"
http://www.ilt.columbia.edu/k12/history/blacks/masacre.html

***Analyzing Sources Activity*** Answer the following questions in a paragraph each based on "Documenting the American Promise: The Destruction of the Tea" on page 168 in *The American Promise*, Second Edition.

1. Does Thomas Hutchinson persuade you that he had no other option than to refuse to let the ship either leave or land? Why did he reject the use of troops to guard the tea?
2. How might men like Hewes be politicized by hacking open chests of tea?

3. John Adams says that Hutchinson took a malicious pleasure in forcing the tea crisis to its conclusion. Was he right or wrong in your judgment? Why?
4. What is at stake for John Adams in the showdown over tea when he speaks of ten years of struggle by "the Continent" and poverty and servitude to "Egyptian Taskmasters"? How does he feel about the possibility of deaths in the building struggle?
5. Who does Samuel Adams think is really responsible for the destruction of the tea? Why?

**WEB LINKS** To explore the topics discussed in the exercise above, visit the Web links noted below.

"Documents on the American Revolution 1764 to 1776"
http://www.carleton.ca/~pking/doc.htm
Choose "Documents for 1773 and the *Boston Tea Party*"

"The Boston Tea Party, 16 December 1773"
http://www.adw03.dial.pipex.com/peel/c-eight/bostontp.htm

"The Tea Party"
http://jefferson.village.virginia.edu/seminar/unit1/mob.html
Choose "viewed the incident differently."

# Answer Key

## Chapter 5: The British Empire and the Colonial Crisis, 1754–1775

### *Chapter Overview*

#### *Chronology*

1. c
2. b
3. a
4. d
5. a
6. d
7. c
8. c
9. b
10. b

#### *Defining Terms*

1. Ohio Valley
2. Ohio Company
3. Fort Necessity
4. Albany Plan of Union
5. Fort Duquense
6. Treaty of Paris
7. John Stuart, Earl of Bute
8. Pontiac
9. Paxton Boys
10. Sugar Act
11. Currency Act
12. virtual representation
13. Virginian Resolves
14. Sons of Liberty
15. Stamp Act Congress
16. Declaratory Act
17. Townshend duties
18. *Letters from a Farmer in Pennsylvania*
19. Quartering Act
20. Nonconsumption agreements
21. Daughters of Liberty
22. Frederick North
23. committees of correspondence
24. British East India Company
25. Coercive Acts
26. Continental Association
27. General Thomas Gage
28. minutemen
29. Lexington and Concord
30. Lord Dunmore
31. Phillis Wheatley

### *Chapter Review*

#### *Multiple-Choice*

1. b
2. b
3. b
4. c
5. c
6. a
7. a
8. a
9. b
10. b
11. d
12. d
13. c
14. c
15. c
16. a
17. c
18. b
19. b
20. a
21. c
22. c
23. c
24. b
25. c
26. d
27. c
28. d
29. d
30. d
31. c
32. a
33. c
34. b
35. c
36. c
37. d
38. b
39. d
40. d
41. c
42. c
43. a
44. a
45. d
46. d
47. b
48. b
49. c
50. b
51. c
52. d
53. b
54. d
55. c
56. b
57. a
58. c
59. c
60. a
61. d
62. d
63. c
64. c
65. d
66. d
67. b
68. a
69. d
70. b
71. b
72. a
73. c
74. d
75. b
76. c
77. c
78. b
79. c
80. d

81. b
82. a
83. a
84. d
85. b
86. b
87. b
88. d
89. b
90. b
91. a
92. d
93. b
94. c
95. b
96. d
97. b
98. d
99. c
100. c
101. c
102. a
103. d
104. b
105. a
106. c
107. a
108. a
109. d
110. c
111. b
112. c
113. b
114. c
115. a
116. a
117. c
118. a
119. d
120. d
121. a
122. b
123. c
124. a
125. d
126. b
127. b
128. a
129. b
130. b
131. c
132. a

### *Short Answer*

1. Virginia claimed the Ohio Valley on the basis of its seventeenth-century charter, which had granted the colony all lands west to the Mississippi River and north to Lake Superior. In keeping with the charter, in 1747 a group of wealthy Virginians formed the Ohio Company and got a grant from the king to 200,000 acres in the Ohio Valley. The British were interested in blocking the French, whereas the speculators hoped to profit from reselling the land. By 1753 Virginians had built an eighty-mile road and a trading post near modern-day Pittsburgh. The royal governor of Virginia and many prominent planters were shareholders in the company, giving them a definite stake in the long-term control of the region.
2. The Albany Conference was formed in response to British leaders' realization that they would need colonial help to win the war against France. Delegates were supposed to construct an inter-colonial agency to coordinate mutual defense and to gain the support of the tribes of the powerful Iroquois Nation of western New York. Neither goal was accomplished. Benjamin Franklin and Thomas Hutchinson proposed the Albany Plan of Union, which called for a unified governmental agency to meet these goals, but they could not gain the support of either the colonies or the British government. The Iroquois Nation accepted thirty wagons of gifts but refused to commit themselves to fighting the French, whom they believed the more likely victors.
3. Initially, the British planned to use their armies against the French in three strategic places. The English general Edward Braddock was assigned to attack the French at Fort Duquense in western Pennsylvania. In Massachusetts, Governor William Shirley was to aim for Fort Niagara, and forces under William Johnson of New York were given the job of heading toward Lake Champlain to push the French back into Canada. However, Braddock's assault was a disaster; he died, and almost half of his troops were killed or wounded. The defeat in turn alarmed the other two armies. Shirley's troops gave up, and Johnson's troops were routed before they made it to Lake Champlain.
4. Pontiac's uprising, a major pan-Indian movement against the British army and British colonists in the far West, convinced the British government that continued war with Indians was would be too costly in terms of lives and money. Therefore, the government issued the Proclamation of 1763, forbidding colonists from settling west of a line running from Canada to Georgia along the crest of the Appalachian Mountains. Ten thousand British troops were left in the colonies to police the line in the hopes of protecting the lucrative fur trade. Settlers had already moved west of the line, however, and speculators stood to lose the money they expected to make on the resale of their claims. The result was increased tensions between royal officials and colonists.
5. George Grenville, the British prime minister, needed to lower the war debt, which stood at £123 million in 1763. He discovered that customs officers' salaries were four times higher than the revenue they brought in, due largely to bribery and smuggling, and determined that he needed to tighten customs procedures. The Sugar Act (the Revenue Act of 1764) was part of Grenville's campaign to raise revenue by enforcing the laws. It lowered the duty on French molasses, a popular commodity for smugglers, and raised penalties for smuggling. The idea was that the act would make it more attractive to obey the law than to flout it, although in practice it did little but inflame colonial opinion.

6. Both Grenville and most colonists believed in the English tradition that saw taxes as a gift of the people to the king offered freely by their representatives. English citizens had the liberty to enjoy their property without fear of unjust confiscation because the king could not simply demand money; Parliament granted it instead. The difference between Grenville and the colonists was that Grenville felt that Parliament represented all British citizens, regardless of where they lived. Thus, any taxes Parliament chose to levy on colonists (the stamp tax, for example) did not infringe on their liberty. Colonists, however, argued that Parliament could not adequately represent the colonies and that as a result Parliamentary taxes on colonists were inherently unjust.

7. The Virginia Resolves were resolutions presented to Virginia's House of Burgesses by Patrick Henry in response to the Stamp Act. The first three uncontroversial resolves stated that Virginians were British citizens and therefore enjoyed the same rights and privileges, including the right to self-taxation, as any other British citizens. The fourth resolve pointed out that Virginians always had taxed themselves through the House of Burgesses, and the fifth took these relatively obvious maxims and pushed them to their logical extreme by concluding that the Virginia assembly had the sole right to tax Virginians. The sixth denied the validity of any tax originating outside of Virginia, and the seventh declared that anybody who opposed the resolves was an enemy of the colony. By essentially denying that Parliament had any authority over the colony, the Virginia Resolves went further than most colonists were willing to go, but their message was widely publicized and debated in the other colonies.

8. American colonists claimed the prerogatives of British liberty, which to them meant that they had the right to be free from interference by other people. Life in civil society demanded some interference with freedom of action in the form of laws, but as long as those laws were passed by representative government, they remained compatible with liberty. The right to own property was also viewed as an essential part of liberty—one that required strict safeguards because of the likelihood that a greedy ruler would deprive citizens of their property through unfair taxation (again, only a representative body could tax British subjects fairly). To Americans in the 1760s, however, Parliament did not seem particularly representative, and the Stamp Act in particular struck many as a plot to deny them both liberty and property.

9. The Townshend duties were a return to the tradition of the Sugar Act. They were not direct taxes, like the Stamp Act, but instead established new duties on various items imported into the colonies. The money would be paid by the shipper, although it would be passed on to colonists in the form of higher prices. Americans had insisted that they did not object to external taxes (that is, money the British government raised in the course of regulating trade), so the British assumed that acceptance of the duties would be a matter of course. But despite the fact that the duties were not particularly burdensome, they aroused a storm of controversy because of the principle they embodied. To Americans who were already upset about the Stamp Act, trade regulation intended only to raise money was as bad as direct taxes intended for the same purpose.

10. American colonists responded to the Townshend duties by imposing nonconsumption and nonimportation agreements, which were consumer and merchant boycotts of British goods. Many of the products Americans imported were household items and therefore under the control of women. Colonial leaders understood that women's cooperation was essential because women would have to begin to make at home many of the things they had been purchasing as ready-made imports. Thus, women had the opportunity to express their affiliation with colonial protest by complying with the nonconsumption agreements and taking up home manufacture. Refusing to drink tea and weaving cloth were private, domestic acts that became signs of political defiance in the context of the boycott.

11. In the immediate aftermath of the Boston Massacre, Thomas Hutchinson, the governor of Massachusetts, jailed British Captain Thomas Preston and the eight soldiers involved in the incident, both for their own protection and to appease angry Bostonians. He also promised that they would be held accountable for their actions, and in fact the soldiers were brought to trial in the fall of 1770. Their defense was taken on by two young lawyers, John Adams and Josiah Quincy, both of whom had ties to the Boston Sons of Liberty. However, John Adams in particular was committed to the notion that all defendants, regardless of their popularity, deserved a fair trial. It also made strategic sense, trying to impress the British government with the idea that the Boston leadership was not composed of lawless rioters but instead was committed to the defense of British liberty and law.

12. In 1770 and 1771, trade boomed between the British and the Americans, and patriot leaders

seemed to be losing their power. Then, in 1772, a Royal Navy ship called the *Gaspée* was burned while chasing down suspected smugglers off of the Rhode Island coast. A royal investigating committee made no arrests, but it did announce that any suspects it found would be sent to England to stand trial for high treason. This action upset Americans because it seemed to undermine the traditional English right to a trial of a jury by one's peers. Representatives in the Virginia House of Burgesses proposed the creation of committees of correspondence, which linked the colonies and provided a channel by which to pass on further distressing news in 1773.

13. Most of the Coercive Acts were designed to punish the colony of Massachusetts for its participation in the destruction of ninety thousand pounds of East Indian Company tea. To reassert royal authority, one of the acts declared that Boston's harbor was closed to all shipping traffic until such time as the tea was paid for and another act altered Massachusetts's colonial charter to strengthen royal authority. The other acts were more general: the Quartering Act was amended to allow military commanders to lodge soldiers wherever necessary, royal officials accused of capital crimes were guaranteed trials in England rather than the colonies, and the continuation of French civil law in Quebec was confirmed and Canada was given control of the Ohio Valley. Although the acts had the greatest direct impact on Massachusetts, they struck other colonists as a sign of England's tyrannical leanings. Most assumed that what applied to Massachusetts could somebody apply to them as well—that if England could change Massachusetts's government, inaugurate military rule, and then arbitrarily privilege French Quebec, no liberties were secure.

14. The First Continental Congress had two basic jobs: delegates needed to agree on what liberties they claimed as English subjects and what rights Parliament held over them, and they also had to construct a unified response to the Coercive Acts. This was complicated by the fact that delegates did not agree on either major issue. Some delegates opposed all Parliamentary control, while others wanted to create a miniparliament in America to aid the British one in its dealings with the colonies. Many delegates favored a ban on trade with England to force the repeal of the Coercive Acts, but colonies that depended on exports refused to support a complete stoppage. In the end, the Congress wrote a careful declaration of rights, couched in traditional language but containing the radical (from the British point of view) proposition that Americans were represented not in Parliament but in their own legislatures and so would submit only to trade regulation, not taxation, from the imperial government.

15. General Thomas Gage, the military governor of Massachusetts, encouraged the British government to repeal the Coercive Acts, but was commanded to arrest troublemakers instead. To carry out the order, he planned surprise attack on a suspected ammunition depot at Concord, a village eighteen miles west of Boston. However, news of the march spread, and British soldiers were met at Lexington, five miles east of Concord, by armed American men. Gunfire broke out, and the British continued on to Concord, where they did not find the ammunition they expected. There was more fighting in Concord, and American militia attacked the British as they returned to Boston. The day's fighting marked the official outbreak of the war.

16. After the battles at Lexington and Concord, Lord Dunmore, Virginia's royal governor claimed he would arm slaves to ward off attacks by colonists if such a move proved necessary. He clearly understood that the specter of armed slaves was certain to produce panic among planters. At the same time, he had no interest in producing a full-blown slave rebellion. Thus, when he finally carried out his threat several months later, he limited the offer to able-bodied adult male slaves, going so far as to return slaves who did not meet his criteria to their angry owners.

### *Map Activity*

Reading the Map: Between 1750 and 1763, the English and the Spanish both increased their holdings substantially, at the expense of France, which lost a great deal of territory. In 1750, the French held eastern Canada and the Louisiana, a territory that covered much of the modern-day Midwest from the Great Lakes to New Orleans, and pressed its ownership of the Ohio Valley against competing English claims. The Spanish possessed Mexico, Florida, and Cuba, and the English commanded the east coast of North America and western Canada. All three powers owned scattered islands in the Caribbean. However, as a result of the war, France lost all of its holdings except for its Caribbean islands and fishing rights and small islands in the far north, while Spain got French territory west of the Mississippi and England got Canada and French land east of the Mississippi. The only European power that did not undergo a shift in its colonial fortunes as a result of the war was Russia, which continued to hold a thin line of territory along the northwest coast.

Connections: The Proclamation Act of 1763 was announced in the aftermath of Pontiac's uprising in northern Ohio following the French and Indian War. Treaty negotiations assigned the land to the English, but the Indians who lived there and had fought with the French were not consulted and did not acknowledge English sovereignty. The fighting was expensive and bloody, and the English decided to limit contact between colonists and Indians and protect the lucrative fur trade as well. Their solution was the Proclamation Line, which set a boundary down the ridge of the Appalachians from Canada to Georgia, beyond which colonists could not move. The problem was that both settlers and speculators refused to respect the line, and even an expensive standing army could not prevent them from infringing on territory the British were trying to reserve for the Indians.

### *Visual Activity*

Reading the Image: Paul Revere's depiction of the Boston Massacre is a clear attempt to rouse political support for the colonial resistance to British trade policies. The scene is one of clear aggressors and victims, with the British filling the former role and the colonists the latter. One of the colonists has raised his hand as if to implore the soldiers to stop firing; others are already turning around to leave the scene. The British, by way of contrast, are on the attack. The captain in the far right lower corner, is actively ordering his troops to fire, and they are complying happily: the third soldier from the right seems to be smiling, and the one at the far end of the line is lunging forward with his bayonet.

Connections: In Paul Revere's version of the Boston Massacre, the British are guilty of unprovoked violence against innocent and unarmed colonists, who want nothing more than to get away from the gunfire. Nothing in the picture explains what so many colonists were doing around so few soldiers or why the firing started in the first place. In reality, the mob had descended on a single British sentry guarding the customs house. He was later joined by a seven-man guard under the command of the British Captain Thomas Preston. The crowd threw sticks and snowballs at the guards, finally hitting one. The soldier fired, then the rest of the guard followed his lead. The British attack was neither planned nor unprovoked; but Revere, a supporter of the patriot cause, had every reason to downplay the American contribution to the melee.

### *Analyzing Sources*

1. For a man as law-abiding and upstanding as Thomas Hutchinson, it is unlikely that there were any options other than leaving the tea ships in a state of suspended animation. Given his position, he certainly could have allowed the understandably nervous captain to leave without unloading his tea or paying the duty. However, many of the problems with the colonies stemmed from the inconsistent enforcement of past trade policies and customs duties, and, as an officer of the empire, Hutchinson seems to have felt a genuine obligation to follow the rules. He also could not know whether the English authorities would approve of his flouting of the law, given the political situation in London, where the crown was attempting to reinforce its authority over the colonies. He was not insensitive to the political ramifications of his actions; he refused to use troops to guard the tea because he feared "a greater convulsion" than that surrounding the Boston Massacre.
2. George Robert Twelves Hewes was a shoemaker, an occupation that involved skilled labor but in all likelihood would not have provided a sufficiently lavish income to permit him to vote or serve in the government. However, in taking part in extralegal protests like the Tea Party, Hewes was raised to a position of leadership. He describes himself as the "boatswain" of his division, the man delegated to get the keys to the hatches and candles for lighting from the ship's captain. The act of dumping the tea overboard was itself a political statement, indicating displeasure with the Tea Act of 1773. It also exposed the participants to a certain amount of danger for their political beliefs, since he mentions that the vandals were surrounded by "British armed ships," although they did not interfere. The experience demanded a certain level of commitment and confidence and doubtless raised both qualities in the participants as well.
3. Adams assumed that Hutchinson refused to allow the tea to leave Boston out of a desire to deliberately upset both Bostonians and the captains of the tea ships. In Adams's opinion, it was fortunate that only property, not human life, was destroyed, demonstrating beyond a shadow of a doubt the maliciousness of Hutchinson and the customs officials. It is not impossible that Hutchinson wanted to force a showdown over the Tea Act. At the same time, it is clear from Hutchinson's account that he could not count on the support of the British administration if he chose to return the tea; the tax on tea was a holdover from the Townshend duties, retained for the purpose of reminding colonists that Parliament could impose taxes on them if it so wished. Adams does not acknowledge the complexity of Hutchinson's situation.
4. Adams was referring to the protests that had been occurring throughout the colonies ("the

Continent") since the passage of the Sugar Act in 1764. He felt that the Tea Party was necessary to assert the American opposition to Parliamentary taxation. If the colonists had given in and accepted the tea tax, they would have tacitly undermined their contention that Parliament did not rightfully represent them and so could not legally tax them. For colonists to accept Parliamentary taxes would be to sign away their traditional English right to liberty and control over their own property, hence reducing them to a state of slavery not unlike that of the Jews in Egypt. He did not seem particularly distressed by the prospect of casualties, although he did comment that a few select deaths would be as productive of beneficial results as hundreds of random deaths.

5. Samuel Adams argued in his letter to Arthur Lee that Thomas Hutchinson and the Boston's other royal officials were responsible for the destruction of the East India Company Tea. His logic was that Hutchinson had the power to determine whether the ships would be allowed to leave Boston harbor without unloading or paying the duty on the tea they carried. When Hutchinson decided not to grant the captains' request, he "encouraged and provoked" the colonists to their act of vandalism. They had, in his view, two choices: they could destroy the tea or submit to losing their liberty and their property through the acceptance of unfair taxation. Naturally, the colonists chose the latter, leaving Hutchinson at fault for forcing the confrontation.

CHAPTER

# THE WAR FOR AMERICA, 1775–1783

# 6

## Chapter Overview

### *Chapter Summary*

***Introduction*** The chapter opens with Abigail Adams managing the family farm while her husband, John, was serving at the Second Continental Congress in Philadelphia. Abigail Adams eagerly awaited word that the Congress had "declared an independency" and admonished her husband to "Remember the Ladies." While her husband humorously chastised her for her "saucy" suggestion, she seemed to understand very early in the conflict that the events that were occurring could let loose a dynamic of equality and liberty that would affect the country for generations to come.

***The Second Continental Congress, pp. 184–192*** In 1775, nearly a month after the fighting at Lexington and Concord, the Second Continental Congress assembled in Philadelphia. It was faced with the contradictory tasks of raising and supplying an army, while trying to negotiate a reconciliation with England.

**ASSUMING POLITICAL AND MILITARY AUTHORITY** The Second Continental Congress had no legal authority. At the town and colony levels, governments subverted British authority by assuming power. Royal administrators could do little to stop these transfers of power, and most simply left for England. While the delegates at the congress were well-established political figures in their own colonies, they had to learn to work together despite being of different minds about many political topics. Most of the delegates who attended the Second Continental Congress were not yet prepared for a total break with England. Most eager for independence were the Massachusetts men, whose colony had been stripped of civil government by the Coercive Acts. Delegates from the middle and southern colonies were more inclined toward reconciliation, fearing that fighting for independence would disrupt trade, create civil unrest, and leave the colonies vulnerable to enemies like France and Spain.

Despite hopes to contain the conflict, all agreed that a military buildup was necessary to counter the invading British army. Congress created the Continental army, named George Washington of Virginia the commander in chief, and authorized a currency issue of $2 million to pay military expenses. Despite taking on the traditional functions of government, the Second Continental Congress did not declare independence for another year and had no basis to compel compliance from Americans.

**PURSUING BOTH WAR AND PEACE** In June 1775, the Battle of Bunker Hill took place. It was the bloodiest engagement of the entire war, with heavy casualties, especially on the British side. The British won but failed to pursue the Americans back to their headquarters at Cambridge. A week later, George Washington arrived in Cambridge to take command of the Continental army, an undisciplined, ragtag outfit, which he quickly sought to transform into a more cohesive fighting force. Meanwhile, the Congress continued to pursue reconciliation with England with congressional moderates, led by John Dickinson, issuing the Olive Branch Petition to the king. George III rejected the petition, labeling the Americans rebels and traitors, which made it difficult to maintain the fiction that only the king's ministers were to blame for the troubles.

**THOMAS PAINE AND THE CASE FOR INDEPENDENCE** It was an English writer newly arrived in America who broke the logjam of public sentiment regarding independence or reconciliation. In his 1776 pamphlet *Common Sense*, Thomas Paine attacked the monarchy, not just the king's ministers, and called on Americans to separate from England and establish a republic. *Common Sense* was widely read, and public opinion shifted rapidly after its publication. By May, the prospect of an alliance with France and news that the British were hiring German mercenaries had further solidified support for independence. On July 2, the Congress adopted the Virginia delegation's Resolution of Independence. After wrangling over some of the specific grievances, particularly one condemning slavery, a final public draft of the Declaration of Independence was formally signed on July 4, 1776. Independence finally had been launched, but the outcome was far from certain.

***The First Year of War, 1775–1776, pp. 192–195*** Both sides approached war with caution. The Americans were keenly aware of England's military might, and the British, after Bunker Hill, had more respect for the rebels' fighting abilities. Compounding England's problem of fighting in hostile territory were the logistics of long-distance supply and their desire to regain the allegiance of the colonists, not destroy and conquer them.

**THE AMERICAN MILITARY FORCES** The American forces had the advantage of being highly mobilized to fight and could theoretically mobilize considerable manpower. However, Americans traditionally had relied on militia, which were good for limited engagements but not lengthy wars requiring military campaigns far from home. To attract potential recruits, the colonies had to resort to cash and land bounties and the draft. Close to twenty thousand women served in the Continental army as cooks, washerwomen, and nurses. Despite Washington's initial prohibition against black recruits, about five thousand eventually served in the war as well. Military service helped politicize Americans, making neutrality seem as dangerous as commitment to the cause.

**THE BRITISH STRATEGY** The American task was relatively simple: to defeat an invading army. Britain's objective was not so straightforward: to restore loyalist regimes to power in the colonies, while not destroying the enemy completely. Counting on substantial pockets of loyalist support in the Carolinas and the middle colonies, the British assumed this goal would not be too difficult to achieve. They initially focused their military campaigns on New York, Pennsylvania, and New Jersey. Strategically, the overall British plan was to divide and conquer—to separate the rebellious colonies from those believed to be still loyal.

**QUEBEC, NEW YORK, AND NEW JERSEY** In late 1775, an American expedition into Canada succeeded in capturing Montreal but failed to take Quebec. The main action of the first year of the war, however, took place in the summer of 1776, when the British decided to seize heavily loyalist New York as their headquarters. Washington's outnumbered and inexperienced troops who met the

British at the Battle of Long Island were badly defeated and driven in slow retreat across New Jersey, over the Delaware River, and into Pennsylvania. Despite his heavy losses, on Christmas night 1776, Washington daringly recrossed the icy Delaware River with a force of 2,400 men and surprised and scattered the Hessians holding Trenton. That victory and a subsequent one at Princeton did much to lift patriot morale, but what had really enabled the Continental army to survive this first year was the continued reluctance of British troops to press their advantage when they had the opportunity.

***The Home Front, pp. 195–203*** Battlefield victories alone did not determine the war's outcome; struggles behind the lines were equally vital. One of the most important issues on the home front was the contest between patriots and loyalists for the hearts and minds of the thousands of neutrals.

**PATRIOTISM AT THE LOCAL LEVEL** Committees of correspondence, safety, and inspection became the revolution's most important political agencies at the local level, supporting the war effort in many ways—from the procurement of arms and men to the rounding up and prosecuting of suspected traitors. These committees could sometimes be oppressive in their treatment of loyalists. Also at the local level, increasing numbers of white women not only assumed many traditional male occupations but also, in the process, became politicized.

**THE LOYALISTS** Between 20 to 30 percent of Americans remained loyal to the British monarchy in 1776. Their motivations varied. Some were royal officeholders; others were merchants whose businesses were linked to the imperial system; still others were cultural, ethnic (most notably Native Americans and African slaves), and religious groups that had no reason to believe they would fare better under an independent American government than they had under the British. Loyalist strongholds thus could be found everywhere, although the largest pockets were in the middle colonies and in the South.

**WHO IS A TRAITOR?** In June 1775, the First Continental Congress passed a resolution declaring loyalists to be traitors. Over the course of the war, hounded by patriots in their communities, harassed by legislative and judicial actions, many loyalists found their position intolerable. For women, the position was less clear because there was no consensus on whether women had the political will to decide to be loyalists or not, particularly if they were married. Thousands of loyalists eventually fled the country, seeking sanctuary in England or Canada. The British military strategy depended on using loyalists to hold occupied territory, but in many colonies that strategy was poorly implemented and ended in disaster when the British decided to withdraw and left loyalists in the hands of their enemies.

**FINANCIAL INSTABILITY AND CORRUPTION** One of the nation's biggest problems was finding ways to finance the war. The Continental Congress printed money, but its value fell rapidly. One way to pay for the war was through borrowing hard money from wealthy men, who were given certificates of debt in return. Congress also resorted to paying soldiers with promises of land. As the war progressed, prices rose to exorbitant levels, and a brisk black market in prohibited imports emerged. In vain, the Congress tried to stem the inflationary spiral by instituting price controls.

***The Campaigns of 1777–1779: Highs and Lows, pp. 203–208*** Though Washington had skillfully avoided outright defeat the first year of the campaign, the Continental army would face a tough challenge as the British implemented their strategy to isolate New England by controlling the Hudson River.

**BURGOYNE'S ARMY AND THE BATTLE OF SARATOGA** The commander of the British army in Canada, General John Burgoyne, had been directed to capture Albany. Proceeding down the upper Hudson with his enormous and slow-moving army, he stopped first to seize Fort Ticonderoga, which had been abandoned by American troops when they saw the size and firepower of his army. The British immediately gave chase but lost a crucial month cutting through the thick forest to the north of Albany. The British strategy called for General Howe to move up the Hudson from New York City and join forces with Burgoyne in Albany. But Howe changed his mind and instead attacked Philadelphia, which he took with relative ease. A third group of troops was supposed to move east from the Great Lakes down the Mohawk River, but they were held back at Fort Stanwix. This left Burgoyne to fight the Americans in the north alone. After two costly engagements at Saratoga, New York, Burgoyne's forces were surrounded by General Horatio Gates. His food supplies dwindling and his men demoralized, Burgoyne officially surrendered on October 17, 1777, giving the Continental army its first decisive victory over a major British force. The British offered a negotiated settlement, but the Americans refused. During the winter after Saratoga (1777–1778), spirits ran high, but finances and supplies ran perilously low. Washington's army at Valley Forge witnessed some of the worst privations of the entire war due to corrupt suppliers and greedy farmers, who preferred to sell grain to the British—who could pay in hard currency—rather than to their own army.

**THE WAR IN INDIAN COUNTRY** By 1779, most Indians had concluded that they could not remain neutral. However, Indians who attempted to ally themselves with the Americans discovered that American commanders often could not distinguish between friends and enemies. A group of Delaware and Shawnee Indians negotiated a treaty with Americans at Fort Pitt, promising support for supplies. However, the promised goods did not arrive, and American militiamen captured and killed friendly Indian leaders. In some places, pervasive anti-Indian campaigns emerged. The Indians who supported the American side generally did so because they felt that the Americans were unstoppable in their westward pressure and that it was better to work out an alliance than lose the war entirely.

**THE FRENCH ALLIANCE** As a result of the American victory at Saratoga, in February 1778, the Americans and the French drafted a formal alliance against England. The treaty offered the United States full diplomatic recognition and complete military, commercial, and financial support until independence was won. France, as a monarchy, was concerned about the alliance with the antimonarchical revolutionaries but wanted desperately to defeat England. The French navy arrived off the coast of Virginia in 1778 and began threatening British New York. For the first few months the alliance did not bring any dramatic victories, although it would become vital in 1781.

***The Southern Strategy and the End of the War, pp. 208–214*** Despite the desire of many of his ministers and military commanders to end the war quickly, George III was determined to crush the rebellion and pushed his generals into formulating a new strategy for victory, focusing on the South.

**GEORGIA AND SOUTH CAROLINA** The British shifted their efforts to the south for a number of reasons. Loyalist sentiment was considered to be strongest in the southern colonies, and planters' nervousness about the war's impact on trade and their slave populations meant they might be more amenable to coming over to the British side. Also important was the colonies' economic value to the empire. During the first few years of the campaign, the southern strategy seemed to be working, as first Georgia in 1778 and then South Carolina in 1780 fell to the British.

**BENEDICT ARNOLD'S TREASON** The new British strategy succeeded in 1780 partly as a result of information about American troop movements and supplies secretly furnished to General Henry Clinton by Benedict Arnold. Arnold had been one of the war's early heroes, but now feeling betrayed by his own government, he conspired with British agents to turn over the patriot stronghold at West Point on the Hudson River. The scheme was exposed and foiled; Arnold fled to the safety of the British camp. News of his behavior galvanized the American public, giving Americans a scapegoat on which to heap their own concerns.

**THE OTHER SOUTHERN WAR: GUERRILLAS** In the southern backcountry the conflict assumed a new dimension of fighting: guerrilla warfare. In hit-and-run attacks, partisan bands from both sides attacked opponents and anybody claiming to be neutral. The war in the backcountry proved that there was not enough loyalist support in the South to allow the British to hold reconquered territory as the army moved north.

**SURRENDER AT YORKTOWN** In 1781, the British general Cornwallis moved into North Carolina, hoping to prevent the colony from providing patriot guerrillas in South Carolina with arms and men. Although he was not successful, he decided to move into Virginia, capturing Williamsburg and Charlottesville and ultimately making his way to Yorktown. The fortunes of war turned in the rebels' favor with the arrival of the French navy. While French ships sealed off any retreat by sea, Washington surrounded Cornwallis on land. After a short siege, Cornwallis surrendered on October 19, 1781.

**THE LOSERS AND THE WINNERS** Though the surrender at Yorktown marked the official end of the war, it would be two more years before a peace treaty was signed. It took time for both sides to acknowledge that the end had finally arrived, and neither wanted to withdraw from the field until the other side had as well. The American diplomats Benjamin Franklin, John Adams, and John Jay, who negotiated the peace treaty, secured favorable terms: official recognition of American independence and of the United States and transfer of all territory east of the Mississippi River, between Canada and Florida, to the new nation. The Treaty of Paris did not recognize Indians as players in the war and turned over land to the United States as though it were uninhabited. Many tribes saw the outcome of the war as a disaster.

## *Conclusion: Why the British Lost*

Many factors contributed to the British defeat. It was hard for the British to supply their army, especially since they did not want to ravage the countryside. At the same time, the British failed to back loyalists and use their energies effectively. The French alliance and military support throughout were crucial to the American victory. Finally, after abdicating civil power in the colonies in 1775 and 1776, the British were never able to regain it.

## *Chronology Activity*

Read the annotated chronology, and answer the multiple-choice questions.

1775 May 10. Second Continental Congress convenes in Philadelphia. The Congress lacked legal authority. Nonetheless, it undertook the traditional functions of government, including creating and army, financing war, and negotiating for peace.

June 14. Continental Congress creates Continental army. The creation of an army fulfilled one of the Congress's contradictory tasks—making war while trying to reconcile with Great Britain.

June 17. Battle of Bunker Hill. Bunker Hill was the first real battle of the war. The British won but with very high casualties. Perhaps because of their losses, they failed to follow up on their victory by pursuing the Continental army to its headquarters in Cambridge.

July. Congress offers the Olive Branch Petition in attempt at reconciliation with king. This was the other side of Congress's job in 1775—trying to negotiate a settlement with the king. When the king rejected the petition, moderates found their position in the Congress undermined. American armies march on Montreal and Quebec.

1776 January 1. Americans lose assault on Quebec. The assault on Quebec was a terrible failure. The march there was undersupplied, and the assault itself resulted in heavy losses.

January. Thomas Paine's *Common Sense* published. *Common Sense*'s antimonarchical message was instrumental in rousing the public desire for complete independence.

March. British evacuate Boston.

July 4. Declaration of Independence adopted. The Declaration was the culmination of pro-independence desires. It was a dangerous undertaking, however, since the British government could define the signers as treasonous. If caught, signers would have been subject to execution.

August 27. Battle of Long Island. This battle was another loss for the Continental army, one that sent it into a lengthy retreat across New Jersey and Pennsylvania.

September 15. British take Manhattan.

November. Americans retreat to Philadelphia.

December 26. Washington surprises British and Hessians at Trenton. This attack was one of the few American victories of 1776. It was important to restoring morale.

1777 January. Washington winters at Morristown, New Jersey.

July. Burgoyne takes Fort Ticonderoga for British. American troops at Fort Ticonderoga, short on food and supplies, spotted the British approach and abandoned the fort without a fight.

August 6. Fort Stanwix ambush. The Fort Stanwix ambush prevented a column of British troops from reinforcing Burgoyne at Saratoga, contributing to the British loss there.

September. British occupy Philadelphia. General Howe's decision to advance on Philadelphia rather than join General Burgoyne also contributed to Burgoyne's lack of troops and his eventual surrender. However, the British felt that Howe's success counterbalanced Burgoyne's failure and offered to negotiate and end to the war, which the Americans refused.

October 17. Burgoyne surrenders at Saratoga. The surrender was the first major American victory of the war. It helped convince the French to join the war openly.

December. Washington goes into winter quarters at Valley Forge, Pennsylvania. At Valley Forge, insufficient and shoddy supplies undermined the morale of the Continental army, causing some to wonder whether the country was worth the fight.

1778 February. France enters war on American side. The French recognized the United States as an independent nation and promised full military and commercial support. The effects were not immediately evident, but as the war progressed the French contribution became increasingly valuable.

July–August. French fleet threatens New York and Newport, Rhode Island.

December. Savannah, Georgia, falls to British. This was the first success of the new southern strategy. It gave the British hope that they would be able to win the war by grabbing Southern states, with their sizable loyalist populations.

1779 January–June. Skirmishes in South Carolina and Georgia.

1780 Philadelphia Ladies Association raises money for soldiers. The Ladies Association showed the increasing politicization of white women.

October. British evacuate Newport.

March–May. British lay siege to Charleston, South Carolina.

July. Rochambeau and French army arrive at Newport. This signaled the beginning of French naval support for the war, which was very important to the eventual American victory.

August 16. Battle of Camden, South Carolina, dims hopes for Americans. Camden was a major defeat: there was a panic, and soldiers simply ran from the battlefield. The following day, only seven hundred out of three thousand troops showed up to regroup.

September–October. Benedict Arnold's treason exposed. Arnold's treacherous behavior represented all of the bad behavior that the patriots feared the most. However, he provided a scapegoat, providing a kind of displacement of American anxieties, and actually revitalized patriotism.

September–December. Guerrilla warfare in South. The guerrilla war demonstrated that the southern strategy of using loyalists to hold southern states was not going to work after all.

October 7. Battle of Kings Mountain, South Carolina. This battle was a massacre of loyalist militiamen that forced General Cornwallis to remove his troops from North Carolina and return to South Carolina. It demonstrated that the British forces were stretched too thin.

1781 January 17. Battle of Cowpens, South Carolina.

May–August. Cornwallis in Virginia. Cornwallis decided to take a more aggressive approach toward the South. He declared that North Carolina was secure, even though it was not, and moved up into Virginia.

August. Cornwallis occupies Yorktown, Virginia. This followed a successful series of assaults on Williamsburg and Charlottesville and seemed to indicate the success of Cornwallis's plan.

September 5. French fleet takes Chesapeake Bay. The French victory over the British navy at Chesapeake Bay allowed the French to control the coastline of the upper South and made a sea retreat impossible for Cornwallis.

September 28–October 19. Siege of Yorktown. A large combined force of French and British soldiers cut off Cornwallis's land routes, thus preventing the British from escaping by either land or sea. He was more or less trapped in Yorktown with dwindling food supplies and no means of withdrawal.

October 19. Cornwallis surrenders. Cornwallis's surrender was the last straw for the British public. King George III was under more and more pressure to end the war, and he finally agreed to do so.

1783 The Treaty of Paris ends the war. The Treaty of Paris took six months to negotiate. It gave the United States formal independence and defined its new boundaries. However, it did not include input from any of the Indian nations who had fought in the war.

## *Chronology Questions* Choose the letter of the best answer.

1. What is the correct order for the following events?
   1. Thomas Paine's *Common Sense* is published.
   2. The Declaration of Independence is signed.
   3. The Battle of Bunker Hill is fought.
   4. The Second Continental Congress convenes in Philadelphia.

   a. 1, 2, 4, 3
   b. 3, 2, 1, 4
   c. 2, 4, 3, 1
   d. 4, 3, 1, 2

2. In 1778, after Burgoyne surrendered at Saratoga,
   a. British evacuated Newport.
   b. American armies marched on Montreal and Quebec.
   c. France entered the war on the American side.
   d. Washington went into winter quarters at Valley Forge, Pennsylvania.

3. The Continental Congress created the Continental army in
   a. 1775.
   b. 1776.
   c. 1777.
   d. 1778.

4. In 1777, the British army was unable to reinforce Burgoyne's troops at Saratoga because
   a. Cornwallis occupied Yorktown, Virginia.
   b. the French fleet took the Chesapeake Bay.
   c. of the siege of Yorktown.
   d. Fort Stanwix was ambushed.

5. What is the correct order for the following events?
   1. The Americans retreat to Philadelphia.
   2. The Battle of Long Island is fought.
   3. Washington surprises the British and Hessians at Trenton.
   4. The British take Manhattan.
   a. 4, 3, 2, 1
   b. 1, 3, 2, 4
   c. 2, 4, 1, 3
   d. 1, 2, 3, 4

6. In 1776, the Continental army lost the
   a. Battle of Long Island.
   b. Battle of Bunker Hill.
   c. Battle of Camden.
   d. siege of Yorktown.

7. The Treaty of Paris ended the Revolutionary War in
   a. 1780.
   b. 1781.
   c. 1782.
   d. 1783.

8. What is the correct order for the following events?
   1. Savannah, Georgia, falls to the English.
   2. Guerrilla warfare takes place in the South.
   3. The Battle of Camden, South Carolina, is fought.
   4. The British lay siege to Charleston, South Carolina.
   a. 2, 4, 3, 1
   b. 1, 4, 3, 2
   c. 4, 3, 1, 2
   d. 3, 1, 2, 4

9. The Comte de Rochambeau and the French army arrived in Rhode Island in
   a. 1776.
   b. 1778.
   c. 1780.
   d. 1783.

10. In 1775,
    a. Congress offered the Olive Branch Petition to King George.
    b. the British evacuated Boston.
    c. the Declaration of Independence was adopted.
    d. the Battle of Kings Mountain, South Carolina, occurred.

***Defining Terms*** Match each term with the correct definition.

Ladies Association
the southern strategy
Treaty of Paris
*Common Sense*
treasonable acts
Hessians
General John Burgoyne
Thayendanegea
muskets
loyalists
certificates of debt
Battle of Long Island
Valley Forge
Trenton
Declaration of Independence
Fort Stanwix
Camden
divide and conquer
White Eyes
General William Howe
General Charles Cornwallis
Benedict Arnold
Second Continental Congress
Olive Branch Petition
militias

1. The elective body that gathered in Philadelphia on May 10, 1775, and was responsible for both the war effort and the attempts at reconciliation with Great Britain. Second continental congress

2. The British commander at the Battle of Bunker Hill. He won the engagement, but his insistence on a frontal attack led to very high casualties. General william Howe

3. An appeal to King George drafted by John Dickinson and congressional moderates in July 1777, after the battles of Lexington, Concord, and Bunker Hill. It demonstrated the continued interest in repairing the breach with England, particularly among delegates from the middle colonies. Olive Branch Petition

4. Thomas Paine's 1776 pamphlet outlining the case against monarchy. This work galvanized antimonarchical sentiment in the colonies and contributed to support for full independence. common sense

5. The Second Continental Congress's formal statement of independence from Great Britain, adopted on July 4, 1776. Declaration of Independence

6. The local military forces that dominated colonial defense, which were effective in short campaigns but less useful for long-term ones. militias

7. The British strategy during the first years of the war, this relied on Great Britain's ability to cut New England off from the rest of the colonies. divide and conquer

8. German mercenary soldiers hired by the British to supplement their regular troops. Hessians

9. A serious defeat for the Continental army, with 1,500 casualties. The loss forced Washington out of Long Island, across New Jersey, and into Philadelphia. Battle of Long Island

10. The location of the Continental army's Christmas attack on Hessian soldiers in their winter quarters along the Delaware. The victory did a great deal to restore patriot morale after the defeats of 1776. Trenton

11. A group formed by women from prominent Philadelphia families to collect money for the Continental soldiers. This was a manifestation of women's growing political engagement. Ladies Association

12. Americans who remained committed to the British monarchy. In 1776, this group constituted between 20 and 30 percent of the American population. loyalists

13. A Mohawk leader, known as Joseph Brant to Americans, who supported the English in the Revolutionary War. He was unhappy about the treatment his tribe had received from Americans, in particular their tendency to pay very little for Indian land. Thayendanegea

14. By June of 1775, the First Continental Congress had defined loyalty to the British government to constitute treason and loyalists to be traitors. As the Revolutionary War continued, some states made it treasonous to join the British army or provide it with food or ammunition, while others defined treason as discouraging enlistment in the Continental army or undermining patriot morale. treasonable acts

15. A means used by Congress to finance the war. Congress borrowed hard money from rich men and gave them these (also called public securities), which promised repayment with interest. certificates of debt

16. The commander of the large army of British soldiers who were forced to surrender to the Continental army at Saratoga in the first decisive victory for the Continental army. General John Burgoyne

17. This was the location of a 1777 battle between American and British forces. The British believed that the Palatine Germans of the Mohawk valley were loyalists and would not block their advance down the Mohawk River to Albany. Instead, they were defeated by American troops, including Palatine Germans and Oneida Indians, a loss that prevented Burgoyne from getting necessary reinforcements and contributed to his loss at Saratoga. Fort Stanwix

18. A sixteenth-century gun still in use in the seventeenth century. While soldiers in militia units were supposed to have their own firearms, they rarely had up-to-date guns. A shortage of weapons was a problem throughout the Revolutionary War. muskets

19. Washington's quarters for the winter of 1777 to 1778. This marked a low point of the war, as soldiers found themselves housed in drafty sheds and short of blankets, boots, and stockings. Valley Forge

20. A Delaware leader who allied with the Americans at Fort Pitt in exchange for supplies. He was ambushed and killed by militiamen. White Eyes

21. The British attempt to recapture the South after France joined the war. They believed that the large numbers of loyalists presumed to be there would make it an easy task. the southern strategy

22. The British general responsible for pacifying South Carolina and later for the campaign into Virginia. Although he was able to defeat the Americans in battle, he had difficulty holding onto the territory he won. General Charles Cornwallis

23. The scene of a devastating American defeat in South Carolina. The militiamen at the center of the battle panicked and ran at the sight of the British cavalry. Camden

24. An American general who acted as a British informant. The disclosure of his treachery spurred a renewal of patriotism. Bendict Arnold

25. The official settlement that ended the war. The treaty granted the United States full independence, defined its boundaries, gave creditors on both sides the right to collect unpaid debts, and specified Great Britain's military withdrawal. It was signed nearly two years after the fighting ended. Treaty of Paris

## Chapter Review

***Multiple-Choice*** Choose the letter of the best answer.

1. When the colonies began to break away from Great Britain, many American towns instituted
   a. government by decree.
   b. mob rule.
   c. rule by lottery.
   d. government by committee.

2. By the end of 1775, most royal governors in the American colonies had
   a. been killed.
   b. used the militia to resist the colonists.
   c. joined the colonists.
   d. sailed for England.

3. Most of the delegates to the Second Continental Congress
   a. believed that the colonies would function better without a king.
   b. opposed total independence for the colonies.
   c. did not want to change the colonies' relationship with Great Britain.
   d. felt that the colonial economy would be stronger if the colonies declared independence.

4. The Second Continental Congress chose George Washington to command the Continental army because he
   a. was already commanding the soldiers massed around Boston.
   b. was widely famed for his military prowess.
   c. was liked most by the delegates.
   d. had a Virginian background.

5. The "Declaration of the Causes and Necessity of Taking Up Arms," a document justifying the outbreak of the Revolutionary War, was written by
   a. Thomas Jefferson.
   b. John Dickinson.
   c. Samuel Adams.
   d. John Adams.

6. The continental dollars used to fund the 1775 military buildup were backed by
   a. trust.
   b. gold.
   c. silver.
   d. overseas investment.

7. The Battle of Bunker Hill, the bloodiest of the entire Revolutionary War, was a victory for the
   a. Americans.
   b. British.
   c. Loyalists.
   d. Second Continental Congress.

8. After the Battle of Bunker Hill, the British commanders
   a. ran more raids into the countryside.
   b. took to impressing food from colonial farmers.
   c. destroyed the core of the Continental army.
   d. sat in Boston and did nothing.

9. The Olive Branch Petition, written in July of 1775, was authored by
   a. congressional radicals.
   b. congressional moderates.
   c. Anglican clergymen.
   d. Parliament.

10. Thomas Paine's pamphlet *Common Sense* argued that
    a. the British monarchy was an absurd institution.
    b. the British monarchy was a praiseworthy institution.
    c. Parliament was an absurd institution.
    d. Parliament was a praiseworthy institution.

11. One factor that hastened an official American declaration of independence was the
    a. discovery of a gold mine.
    b. aid of German mercenaries.
    c. prospect of an alliance with France.
    d. mass emigration of loyalists to Canada.

12. In the course of formally adopting the Declaration of Independence, congressional delegates wrangled over Thomas Jefferson's denunciation of
    a. Parliament.
    b. slavery.
    c. the king.
    d. inequality.

13. On May 10, 1775, nearly a month after the fighting at Lexington and Concord, the _____ assembled in Philadelphia.
    a. First Continental Congress
    b. Second Continental Congress
    c. House of Burgesses
    d. Committee of Public Safety

14. By 1775, _____ was a moderate, seeking reconciliation with England.
    a. John Dickinson
    b. Samuel Adams
    c. John Adams
    d. George Washington

15. Delegates from _____ were among the few men at the Second Continental Congress who believed that independence from England was desirable.
    a. Virginia
    b. Massachusetts
    c. Pennsylvania
    d. New York

16. To pay for the expenses of putting together an army, the Congress authorized a $2 million currency issue based on _____.
    a. trust
    b. gold
    c. silver
    d. government bonds

17. The British suffered terrible casualties at the Battle of Bunker Hill because General Howe insisted on a _____.
    a. frontal assault.
    b. siege
    c. retreat
    d. nighttime attack

18. After the battle of Bunker Hill, General Howe insisted on pulling his troops back to Boston, where they _____.
    a. raided the surrounding countryside
    b. lingered for more than nine months
    c. harassed American shipping
    d. nearly starved

19. Even after fighting broke out, delegates from the _____ colonies urged that channels for negotiation with Great Britain remain open.
    a. southern
    b. New England
    c. frontier
    d. middle

20. _____ wrote *Common Sense*, a pamphlet that helped destroy the automatic deference most Americans still had for the monarchy.
    a. Benjamin Franklin
    b. Abigail Adams
    c. Thomas Paine
    d. Thomas Jefferson

21. By May 1776, all but four of the colonies were agitating for _____ Great Britain.
    a. full reconciliation with
    b. a trade boycott against
    c. partial reconciliation with
    d. independence from

22. Printed copies of the Declaration of Independence did not include the _____.
    a. preamble
    b. date it was written
    c. list of grievances
    d. signers' names

23. The strength of the colonial militias before the Revolutionary War lay in
    a. lengthy engagements.
    b. limited engagements.
    c. overseas engagements.
    d. shooting practice.

24. To raise a strong army for the long term, soldiers who committed for the duration of the war against the British were promised a
    a. steady paycheck.
    b. good diet.
    c. one hundred acre land grant.
    d. $20 bonus.

25. Typical draftees into the Continental army tended to be a community's
    a. prominent men.
    b. professional soldiers.
    c. middling merchants.
    d. marginal men.

26. On his fifth day as commander in chief, George Washington ruled that black Americans
    a. could not enter army camps.
    b. who served in the army were considered free.
    c. could not serve in the Continental army.
    d. who were enslaved could serve in the army with the permission of their masters.

27. The Continental army failed in
    a. winning any battles.
    b. drafting soldiers.
    c. disciplining its troops.
    d. developing the precision and discipline of European professional armies.

28. To end the colonial rebellion, the British had to defeat
    a. the Continental army.
    b. the local militias.
    c. both of the above.
    d. neither of the above.

29. England's task in the war for America was to
    a. destroy an enemy country.
    b. pacify an enemy country.
    c. restore the old governments.
    d. negotiate with the rebels.

30. Because of the colony's large number of loyalists and geographic advantage, the British strategy focused first on
    a. Virginia.
    b. New England.
    c. Pennsylvania.
    d. New York.

31. In late 1775, the Americans launched an offensive to capture
    a. Montreal and Quebec.
    b. Boston and Philadelphia.
    c. Boston and Montreal.
    d. Philadelphia and Quebec.

32. After the Battle of Long Island, General Washington decided to
    a. hold Manhattan against a British attack.
    b. strip Manhattan of ammunition and supplies.
    c. burn Manhattan to the ground.
    d. return to Long Island for another fight.

33. After capturing two critical Hudson River forts in November 1776, General Howe
    a. attacked Washington's army at Philadelphia.
    b. put his German troops in winter quarters.
    c. captured the Continental Congress in Baltimore.
    d. took the city of Philadelphia.

34. What really saved the American army in 1776 was
    a. mediocre British troops.
    b. the reluctance of the British to follow through when they had the advantage.
    c. the excellence of American troops.
    d. the inability of the British to get supplies.

35. From the earliest days of settlement, local defense in the colonies rested with a _____.
    a. militia
    b. professional army
    c. extensive police force
    d. town sheriff

36. To encourage longer periods of service, a soldier who signed up for a _____ enlistment received an up-front bonus of $20.
    a. six-month
    b. one-year
    c. three-year
    d. five-year

37. The total number of individual enlistments over the course of the war totaled roughly _____ of the white male population over sixteen.
    a. one-eighth
    b. one-quarter
    c. half
    d. three-quarters

38. Black soldiers were sometimes put into _____ units.
   a. integrated
   (b) segregated
   c. spy
   d. draft

39. Military service helped Americans become _____ during the early stages of the Revolutionary War.
   a. apathetic
   b. afraid of the British
   (c) politicized
   d. disciplined

40. During the course of the war, the British captured and for a time occupied every _____ with no significant gain.
   a. sizeable village
   b. county in New England
   c. county in the South
   (d) major port city

41. One key ingredient of the British strategy rested on the assumption that large numbers of Americans were too _____ to support the war effort.
   (a) loyal
   b. apathetic
   c. incompetent
   d. greedy

42. In August 1776, the British sent _____ mercenary soldiers to fight with the English troops.
   a. French
   (b) German
   c. Swiss
   d. Italian

43. Immediately after the Battle of Long Island, Washington evacuated his troops to _____.
   a. New Jersey
   b. the Delaware River
   c. Fort Lee
   (d) Manhattan Island

44. The Christmas Battle of _____ did a great deal to restore the sagging morale of the Continental army.
   a. Morristown
   b. Princeton
   c. Hudson River
   (d) Trenton

45. Committees of correspondence in patriot communities dismayed loyalists by their
   a. ability to tax.
   b. neutrality.
   c. enforcement of boycotts.
   (d) exercise of excessive and arbitrary power.

46. During the Revolutionary War, many white women
   a. fought disguised as men.
   b. retreated into housework.
   (c) demonstrated a capacity for patriotism.
   d. served in the Continental Congress.

47. Tories were afraid of
   a. Parliament.
   b. the monarchy.
   (c) democratic tyranny.
   d. the aristocracy.

48. The most visible and dedicated loyalists in the Revolutionary War were very seldom
   a. merchants.
   b. royal officials.
   (c) yeoman farmers.
   d. conservative lawyers.

49. During the Revolutionary War, many Indians
   a. remained completely neutral.
   b. fought with the Hessians.
   c. supported the Americans.
   (d) supported the British.

50. Loyalists were most vocal
   a. after the victories later in the war.
   b. after they moved to England.
   c. after an Indian raid.
   (d) before the war.

51. When a loyalist husband fled but his wife stayed in the colonies, she was usually
    a. allowed to keep her dower rights.
    b. given all of her husband's property.
    c. jailed.
    d. deported.

52. After the Revolution, the descendants of some loyalist refugees sued to regain property that had entered the family through the mother's line of inheritance on the grounds that
    a. women did not have the independent will to make political decisions.
    b. confiscation of property was illegal.
    c. the mothers were secretly patriots.
    d. the children were secretly patriots.

53. In 1776, Richard Stockton of New Jersey
    a. signed the Declaration of Independence.
    b. swore an oath of allegiance to the king.
    c. both.
    d. neither.

54. The Continental Congress funded the war effort by
    a. printing paper money.
    b. voluntary donations.
    c. involuntary donations.
    d. trade and barter.

55. Because of currency devaluation, Continental soldiers were often paid with
    a. paper money
    b. land bounties.
    c. hard currency.
    d. foodstuffs.

56. Shortly after the Continental Congress began to print money, depreciating currency led to
    a. rising prices.
    b. a brisk black market.
    c. an increase in debt.
    d. all of the above.

57. The contest for the allegiance of _____ was a major factor in determining the outcome of the war.
    a. women
    b. blacks
    c. loyalists
    d. Indians

58. Various _____ dominated the political landscape in patriot communities.
    a. generals
    b. clergymen
    c. delegates to the Continental Congress
    d. committees

59. In 1780, the women of the Philadelphia Ladies' Association collected _____to support the Continental soldiers.
    a. food
    b. socks
    c. blankets
    d. money

60. The loyalists feared _____ most of all.
    a. tax increases
    b. religious persecution
    c. democratic tyranny
    d. the Indians

61. The Oneida leader Thayendanegea complained to _____ about the colonists' treatment of his tribe.
    a. France
    b. the Second Continental Congress
    c. King George
    d. Parliament

62. In backcountry areas of America, loyalism was spread largely by means of _____.
    a. pamphlets
    b. speeches
    c. newspapers
    d. Committees of Correspondence

63. Throughout the war, about 28,000 loyalists found haven in _____.
    a. England
    b. the British West Indies
    c. South Carolina
    d. Canada

64. At its lowest point, the dollar bottomed out at _____ of its face value.
    a. one-fifth
    b. one-tenth
    c. one-twentieth
    d. one-fortieth

65. One method Congress used to fund the war was to borrow _____ from wealthy men.
    a. stocks
    b. land
    c. hard money
    d. paper money

66. The wartime black market primarily sold _____.
    a. food
    b. cotton cloth
    c. luxury items
    d. military supplies

67. In the 1777 campaign, a major weakness of General John Burgoyne's army was
    a. its ineptitude.
    b. a shortage of cannon.
    c. a lack of pack horses.
    d. its large size.

68. The goal of the British strategy in 1777, which began with Burgoyne's capture of Fort Ticonderoga, was to
    a. capture Charleston.
    b. isolate New England from the rest of the colonies.
    c. enlist the help of Indian tribes.
    d. capture seaports and thus ensure supply lines.

69. The first Battle of Saratoga was won by the
    a. British.
    b. Americans.
    c. Seneca.
    d. Oneida.

70. After the second Battle of Saratoga, General Burgoyne
    a. committed suicide.
    b. surrendered.
    c. retreated.
    d. was promoted.

71. In September of 1777, proposals for a negotiated settlement were rejected by
    a. the Americans.
    b. the British.
    c. both.
    d. neither.

72. Army suppliers often
    a. provided extra goods free of charge.
    b. provided defective food, clothing, and gunpowder.
    c. sold food to the British.
    d. were paid in land bounties.

73. The Americans lost the support of the Delaware and Shawnee Indians because the
    a. Delaware and Shawnee were secretly agents of the British.
    b. Delaware and the Shawnee did not want to fight.
    c. Americans captured, held, and killed friendly chiefs.
    d. Americans refused to reinstate the 1763 Proclamation Line.

74. American military leaders and militias' attitude toward Indians was
    a. often quite hostile.
    b. cautious but friendly.
    c. welcoming and enthusiastic.
    d. generally neutral.

75. Indian support for the American side in the Revolution persisted because Indians
    a. were forced to support the Americans at gunpoint
    b. felt that the British were worse than the Americans.
    c. believed that Americans sincerely wanted to work with them.
    d. preferred to work out an alliance than lose the war.

76. The most crucial support the French provided the American side in the Revolutionary War was
    a. a steady supply of specie.
    b. agricultural goods.
    c. divisions of soldiers.
    d. the French navy.

77. The French were convinced to enter the war by the American
    a. formalization of alliances with Indian tribes.
    b. victory at the Battle of Trenton.
    c. victory at the Battle of Saratoga.
    d. suffering at Valley Forge.

78. The French entered the war because of their
    a. commitment to democratic principles.
    b. desire to test their navy.
    c. interest in the strategy of the war.
    d. traditionally hostile relationship with England.

79. In 1777, British General _____ assumed command of an army of 7,800 soldiers and an enormous number of accompanying people and horses in Canada.
    a. John Burgoyne
    b. Joseph Brant
    c. William Howe
    d. Henry Clinton

80. American troops who spotted the approach of General Burgoyne's troops abandoned Fort _____ without a fight.
    a. Lee
    b. Ticonderoga
    c. Washington
    d. Stanwix

81. General Howe disrupted British plans when he decided to try to capture _____ rather than moving his troops up the Hudson to meet General Burgoyne.
    a. New York
    b. Philadelphia
    c. Baltimore
    d. Princeton

82. The American commander _____ was in charge at the Battle of Saratoga.
    a. George Washington
    b. Artemas Ward
    c. Benedict Arnold
    d. Horatio Gates

83. The second Battle of Saratoga was the first _____ for the Continental army.
    a. serious loss
    b. draw
    c. near-win
    d. decisive victory

84. During the winter of 1777 to 1778, Washington's aide-de-campe _____ wondered if the country was too corrupt to be worth fighting for.
    a. John Adams
    b. Benjamin Franklin
    c. Thomas Jefferson
    d. Alexander Hamilton

85. In 1778, a Delaware leader named White Eyes negotiated a treaty with the Americans at Fort Pitt, pledging Indian support in the war in exchange for _____.
    a. protection
    b. farming expertise
    c. guarantees of land
    d. supplies

86. The pro-American Indians of Coshocton were attacked by _____ in 1781.
    a. British troops
    b. militiamen
    c. Cherokees
    d. backcountry guerrilla troops

87. The most crucial support France offered to the United States was its _____.
    a. advisors
    b. army
    c. cavalry
    d. navy

88. By late fall of 1778, French ships had sailed away from the mainland United States and toward _____ to defend their interests there.
    a. the West Indies
    b. Canada
    c. Florida
    d. Louisiana

89. After the French entered the Revolutionary War in 1778, one of the only British leaders who wanted to continue the conflict was
   a. the commander of the British navy.
   b. King George III.
   c. Lord North.
   d. General Burgoyne.

90. After France joined America in the Revolutionary War in 1778, the British inaugurated a new war strategy that focused on
   a. the West Indies.
   b. New England.
   c. the Middle Atlantic region.
   d. the South.

91. In its Southern campaign, the British army quickly subdued
   a. Georgia and Virginia.
   b. Georgia and South Carolina.
   c. South Carolina and Virginia.
   d. Virginia and Delaware.

92. The British army's 1780 strategy worked in part because
   a. the loyalists were a strong and coherent force.
   b. the French and American troops were arguing among themselves.
   c. Benedict Arnold furnished information about troop movements and supplies.
   d. Benedict Arnold was given a command at West Point.

93. Public knowledge of Benedict Arnold's betrayal inspired
   a. confidence among loyalists.
   b. cynical despair among patriots.
   c. mass executions.
   d. a renewal of patriotism.

94. In South Carolina, the response to Gates's defeat at Camden and Benedict Arnold's treason was
   a. a guerrilla war.
   b. the pacification of the area.
   c. a religious revival.
   d. increased cotton production.

95. The American campaign in the South succeeded because the
   a. Americans won battles.
   b. Americans murdered all the loyalists in the area.
   c. Americans prevented the British from foraging for food.
   d. French won battles.

96. In the spring of 1781, the American plan to defeat the British gained momentum when the
   a. Indians joined the American forces in Virginia.
   b. New York harbored reopened.
   c. French sent a fleet to the Chesapeake Bay.
   d. Pennsylvania militia became more organized.

97. After the 1781 naval battle that gave the French the control of the Chesapeake Bay,
   a. Cornwallis's army lost its water escape route.
   b. the Americans ran low on food.
   c. Washington's troops began to move south.
   d. the Indians raided British strongholds.

98. The end of the Revolutionary War was first signaled by
   a. Horatio Gates's loss at Camden.
   b. Cornwallis's surrender at Yorktown.
   c. the Battle of Saratoga.
   d. Benedict Arnold's treason.

99. In the negotiations for the settlement of the Revolutionary War, the British
   a. stirred up loyalists in the former colonies.
   b. threatened to go back to war if their demands were not met.
   c. exploited differences between French and American interests.
   d. bribed the American commissioners.

100. In the Treaty of Paris, Indians were
   a. given reservation lands.
   b. treated as full negotiators.
   c. not officially recognized as players in the war.
   d. pushed into Canada.

101. After France joined the war British sentiment turned in favor of ending the conflict quickly, with the exception of the _____.
   a. commander of the navy
   b. commander of the army
   c. king
   d. prime minister

102. The British believed that Southerners could not afford the cost of an all-out war because of its potential to destabilize _____.
   a. trade
   b. gender relations
   c. slavery
   d. political hierarchies

103. The first two southern targets for the British were _____.
   a. Georgia and North Carolina
   b. Virginia and South Carolina
   c. Georgia and South Carolina
   d. North Carolina and South Carolina

104. At the Battle of Camden, General Gates put the _____ into the center of the battle, where they panicked at the sight of the enemy's cavalry.
   a. militiamen
   b. regular soldiers
   c. officers
   d. labor units

105. Benedict Arnold lobbied General Washington for the command of _____.
   a. Philadelphia
   b. West Point
   c. Saratoga
   d. Albany

106. Benedict Arnold got into trouble when he began to _____ the British.
   a. lie to
   b. negotiate for payment from
   c. withhold information from
   d. cheat

107. The British left North Carolina after receiving news of a massacre of _____ at Kings Mountain in South Carolina.
   a. allied Indians
   b. patriot militia
   c. loyalist units
   d. British soldiers

108. Cornwallis had the upper hand in Virginia until the American army received an infusion of _____.
   a. French military support
   b. morale
   c. money from wealthy Americans
   d. new American recruits

109. It took _____ for three American commissioners to negotiate a three-way settlement in Paris.
   a. two weeks
   b. one month
   c. three months
   d. six months

110. For Indian tribes, especially those in the _____, the Treaty of Paris signaled the beginning of a new and longer war with the United States.
   a. South
   b. New England region
   c. Northwest Territory
   d. Southwest region

***Short Answer*** Write a paragraph response to each question.

1. How did American rebels subvert British colonial authorities?
2. How did the Second Continental Congress pursue both war and peace in 1775?
3. What factors hastened the Second Continental Congress's declaration of independence from Great Britain?
4. What problems did the Americans face when they tried to put together the Continental army? How did they try to solve those problems?
5. Why was British military strategy in the Revolutionary War more complicated than that of the Americans?
6. Was the military performance of the Americans in the first year of the war a success? Why or why not?
7. How did white women respond to the Revolutionary War?
8. What did people hold loyalist sentiments?
9. How did the American revolutionaries treat loyalists?
10. Why did the British lose the second Battle of Saratoga?
11. How did Americans treat their Indian allies in the war?
12. Why did France decide to support the Americans in the Revolutionary War?
13. Why did Great Britain shift its strategic focus from New England to the South?
14. How did the guerrilla war in the South undermine the British southern strategy?
15. What happened at Yorktown in 1781?

***Building Historical Skills*** Historians use a variety of sources to think and talk about the past, including maps, illustrations, and written records. Maps provide a variety of different kinds of comparative information in a condensed visual format; reading them requires learning how to sort through this information. To deepen our understanding of the past by supplementing written records, historians frequently interpret material culture, such as a vase or a painting, with techniques borrowed from art history, archaeology, or anthropology. Written records, though familiar as sources, raise their own problems of interpretation. Every document reflects someone's particular perspective or assumptions. It is the historian's task to study and compare each document to other records with other perspectives. The following exercises introduce you to using maps, illustrations, and written documents as sources of information. Use these sources as well as the material in the chapter to think about different themes and topics discussed in the text.

***Map Activity*** Locate the following places on Map 6.2: Loyalist Strength and Rebel Support on page 199 in *The American Promise,* Second Edition.

1. Charleston
2. Boston
3. New York City

4. Philadelphia
5. Savannah
6. Newport
7. Norfolk

Answer the following questions in a paragraph based on Map 6.2: Loyalist Strength and Rebel Support.

**READING THE MAP** What forces were stronger, those loyal to Britain or those rebelling? What areas were contested? If the contested areas ultimately sided with the British, how would the balance of power change?

**CONNECTIONS** Who was more likely to be a loyalist, and why? How many loyalists left the United States, and where did they go?

**WEB LINKS** To explore the topics discussed in the exercise above, visit the Web links noted below.

"The American Revolution"
http://revolution.h-net.msu.edu/
Choose "Essays," then "'Despise the mean Distinctions [these] Times Have Made': The Complexity of Patriotism and Quaker Loyalism in One Pennsylvania Family."

"Thomas Hutchinson and Loyalists"
http://www.pbs.org/ktca/liberty/chronicle/hutchinson-loyalists.html

"The Road to Independence"
http://grid.let.rug.nl/~usa/H/1994/ch3_p13.htm
Choose "Loyalists during the American Revolution."

***Visual Activity*** After the Declaration of Independence was approved by the Second Continental Congress in July of 1776, printed copies were distributed and often read aloud to crowds. This engraving depicts a scene of this kind of public reading and serves as a piece of propaganda in support of the patriot cause. The reader is seated on a white horse and carries a long, thin pole; the pose is reminiscent of a medieval knight. The crowd to which he reads is enthusiastic. One man in the front is waving his hat around in delight, and there is already a flag flying from a window. The gathering also is resolutely middle class. All of the individuals are well dressed, tidy, and clean, even though the people who would most likely rely on a public reading for their news would have been the less presentable poor. The engraver is clearly conveying that revolutionaries do not have to be hooligans but are in fact eminently respectable sorts. Although they are less demonstrative in their job, there are women as well as men in the crowd, showing that the appeal of the revolution cuts across sex as well as class.

Answer the following questions in a paragraph based on "Declaration of Independence Read to a Crowd" on page 192 in *The American Promise,* Second Edition.

**READING THE IMAGE** What does this image say about the desirability of independence?

**CONNECTIONS** How accurate is this representation of the reception of independence?

**WEB LINKS** To explore the topics discussed in the exercise above, visit the Web links noted below.

"The Declaration of Independence"
http://www.nara.gov/exhall/charters/
Choose "Declaration of Independence"

"The Rough Draft of the Declaration of Independence"
http://grid.let.rug.nl/~usa/D/1776-1800/independence/doitj.htm

***Analyzing Sources Activity*** Answer the following questions in a paragraph based on "Documenting the American Promise: The Issue of Independence" on page 190 in *The American Promise*, Second Edition.

1. What reasons did the men of Scituate, Massachusetts, give for favoring immediate independence? Who asked them to vote on this matter?
2. Did the mechanics of New York agree in their reasoning with the men of Scituate? What evidence is there in this document that the New York Assembly was not friendly to their petition?
3. Document 3 alludes to petitions circulating in Virginia that make these elite men uneasy. Why?
4. Why do the two Philadelphia merchants in Document 4 oppose independence at this juncture?

**WEB LINKS** To explore the topics discussed in the exercise above, visit the Web links noted below.

"Declaring Independence: Drafting the Documents"
http://lcweb.loc.gov/exhibits/declara/declara1.html

"A Biography of Robert Morris, 1734–1806"
http://grid.let.rug.nl/~usa/B/rmorris/rmorris.htm

# Answer Key

## Chapter 6: The War for America, 1775–1783

### *Chapter Overview*

#### *Chronology*

1. d
2. c
3. a
4. d
5. c
6. a
7. d
8. b
9. c
10. a

#### *Defining Terms*

1. Second Continental Congress
2. General William Howe
3. Olive Branch Petition
4. *Common Sense*
5. Declaration of Independence
6. militias
7. divide and conquer
8. Hessians
9. Battle of Long Island
10. Trenton
11. Ladies Association
12. loyalists
13. Thayendanegea
14. treasonable acts
15. certificates of debt
16. General John Burgoyne
17. Fort Stanwix
18. muskets
19. Valley Forge
20. White Eyes
21. the southern strategy
22. General Charles Cornwallis
23. Camden
24. Benedict Arnold
25. Treaty of Paris

### *Chapter Review*

#### *Multiple-Choice*

1. d
2. d
3. b
4. d
5. a
6. a
7. b
8. d
9. b
10. a
11. c
12. b
13. b
14. a
15. b
16. a
17. a
18. b
19. d
20. c
21. d
22. d
23. b
24. c
25. d
26. c
27. d
28. c
29. c
30. d
31. a
32. b
33. b
34. b
35. a
36. c
37. b
38. b
39. c
40. d
41. a
42. b
43. d
44. d
45. d
46. c
47. c
48. c
49. d
50. d
51. a
52. a
53. c
54. a
55. b
56. d
57. c
58. d
59. d
60. c
61. c
62. b
63. d
64. d
65. c
66. c
67. d
68. b
69. a
70. b
71. a
72. b
73. c
74. a
75. d
76. d
77. c
78. d
79. a
80. b

81. b
82. d
83. d
84. d
85. d
86. b
87. d
88. a
89. b
90. d
91. b
92. c
93. d
94. a
95. c
96. c
97. a
98. b
99. c
100. c
101. c
102. c
103. c
104. a
105. b
106. b
107. c
108. a
109. d
110. c

### *Short Answer*

1. As a general rule, the political leadership in the colonies subverted British authority by simply assuming power on its own. Neither the First nor the Second Continental Congress had any legal authority to exist; the legislatures that selected delegates did not possess formal power either. These bodies gained power by acting as if they had it already. The same process applied at the local level, where selectmen and town councilors simply renamed themselves and took the task of ruling the town on themselves. Royal administrators could do little to stop such actions because they did not have police forces or reliably loyal militias.
2. The Second Continental Congress pursued war by engaging in it directly. In June 1775, militias from Massachusetts and Connecticut engaged British troops at the Battle of Bunker Hill. A week later, General George Washington took over command of the Continental army and set about making it into a disciplined, professional army, showing that more engagements could be expected. Simultaneously, moderates in the Congress appealed to the king with the Olive Branch Petition, affirming loyalty to the monarchy and blaming all colonial difficulties on the king's ministers and Parliament. The peace sentiment began to collapse only after King George personally rejected the petition.
3. Public pressure for full independence was galvanized in January of 1776, following the publication of Thomas Paine's pamphlet *Common Sense*. Paine believed that the institution of kingship was irrational and ridiculous because it gave a single man enormous power over others by an accident of birth, not demonstrated talent. The pamphlet sold 150,000 copies in a matter of weeks, and his arguments helped undermine the automatic deference most Americans had for the monarchy. The prospect of an alliance with France helped as well, and the French made it clear that they would help only if the Americans separated from England. Finally, news that the English were hiring German mercenaries solidified support for independence.
4. The greatest difficulty facing the American military establishment was that no standing army existed in the colonies. Colonial defense had rested on local militia, which required the participation of every able-bodied man over the age of sixteen. The militia functioned well when faced with local Indian attacks but were not really capable of fighting long-term campaigns far away from home. Congress attempted to solve the weakness of the militia system by giving bonuses for longer periods of enlistment, to give commanders time to adequately train their troops and carry out campaigns. They also assigned troop quotas to each state, causing local governments to draft soldiers to fill out the army.
5. The Americans had to repulse and defeat an invading army, but the British wanted to put down the American rebellion and restore monarchical power to the colonies. This meant that they had to win back thirteen discrete political entities without alienating the colonial population. They needed a huge army but hesitated to confiscate food from colonial citizens, which forced the British to supply their troops from overseas. Moreover, the British had to defeat both the Continental army and the militia units scattered about the countryside. It was not feasible for them to take a single political nerve center and end the war that way because 95 percent of Americans lived outside of urban centers.
6. The performance of the Americans was mixed: there were a handful of high spots but quite a few failures as well. The Christmas Day victory at the Battle of Trenton was a stunning success, as was an attack on the British at Princeton, where the Continental army successful captured supplies. However, at the beginning of the year the Americans had launched an expedition to capture Montreal and Quebec; they obtained their first goal but failed to take Quebec and suffered heavy casualties in the process of losing. The Continental army lost the Battle of Long Island, again with heavy casualties, and had then been driven out of Manhattan, across New Jersey, and into Pennsylvania. Overall, the Americans had been able to continue fighting largely because the British did not follow through militarily when they had the advantage.
7. For many white women, the war offered a chance to become politicized. Women whose husbands

were away on military or political service took over family farms and businesses, and their increased competence apparently encouraged them to speak their minds on politics as well. Women avidly discussed politics with each other and defended their patriotism. Some supported the war effort more directly by collecting money for the Continental army.

8. Loyalists tended to be people who were attached to the idea of the British empire; many of them feared that in a society without a king, all notions of deference and hierarchy would be destroyed, and chaos would result. People with direct ties to Great Britain espoused the loyalist cause as well—merchants, royal officials, and conservative lawyers. The religious liberty the British had granted to dissident groups like the Palatine Germans had engendered loyalty, too. There were also loyalists who simply disliked leading patriot politicians and slaves in the South who resented their owners and often decamped to the British when given the opportunity. Indians also tended to side with the British, feeling that their treatment at the hands of American settlers had been unfair.

9. The loyalist felt that the treatment that they received at the hands of the patriots demonstrated a tyrannical denial of liberty of conscience and freedom to own private property that was worse than any actions undertaken by the king or Parliament. State laws defined treason as joining the British army or providing it with food or ammunition, saying or printing anything that undermined patriot morale, or discouraging enlistments in the Continental army. Punishments ranged from house arrest to the suspension of political privileges to the confiscation of property and deportation. Loyalists were also sometimes subject to extralegal punishments like tarring and feathering.

10. A number of factors caused the British to lose at Saratoga. For one thing, General Burgoyne's army was extremely large; when it was held up north of Albany, its supply lines were stretched. Second, Burgoyne expected reinforcements from General Howe in New York and a third body of troops moving east from the Great Lakes. However, Howe decided to invade Philadelphia rather than meeting up with Burgoyne in Albany, and the troops arriving from the east were stopped by the Americans at Fort Stanwix. By the time the Battle of Saratoga occurred, Burgoyne was short on both soldiers and food, and when his retreat was blocked, he was forced to surrender.

11. Because of the poor treatment they had traditionally received at the hands of Americans, most Indian tribes allied with the English. Some, however, tried to throw their lot in with the Americans. A significant group of Delaware and Shawnee made an alliance with the Americans. However, they were very poorly treated: their several of their leaders were kidnapped and killed. Anti-Indian campaigns were a regular feature of the war, and American soldiers often failed to distinguish between friendly and enemy tribes.

12. France was ruled by a king and was therefore hesitant about entering the war on the side of the antimonarchical Americans. However, the French wanted to defeat the English, who were traditional rivals and had quite recently taken Canada. They also hoped that an American victory would open new trade opportunities and perhaps even give France the opportunity to grab the British West Indies. Beyond that, the French felt that an American defeat would not be an unmitigated loss for France, since an ongoing war would drain England of men and resources.

   The South had many valuable crops, including tobacco, rice, and indigo, which the British wanted to keep under their control. British leaders believed that the high slave population in the South would act as a potentially destabilizing element that would work to their advantage: they felt that southerners would prefer surrender to the potential of a slave uprising. Finally, the British assumed that the South harbored large pockets of loyalists, which would make it possible for them to conquer an area, leave it in loyalist hands, and move on to the next colony.

   The British southern strategy counted on sufficient loyalist strength to hold reconquered territory as the British army moved north. The guerrilla war demonstrated that this strategy was untenable. Patriot guerrilla bands were able to make life dangerous for loyalists, burning and looting their property and sometimes murdering them. Guerrillas also harassed British forces, preventing them from foraging for food.

   In 1781, General Cornwallis decided to move the war north into Virginia. He successfully captured Williamsburg and raided Charlottesville, and it looked like the campaign was going well for the British. However, an infusion of French military support upset the balance. The French navy blocked the Chesapeake Bay, and a combined French and American army trapped Cornwallis's army at Yorktown. Cornwallis was forced to surrender after a twelve-day siege, and the military war in America quickly came to a halt.

### *Map Activity*

Reading the Map: The patriot forces enjoyed greater overall strength. The rebels dominated almost all of

New England, including Massachusetts, Rhode Island, Connecticut, and New Hampshire. They also held most of Delaware, Pennsylvania, and Virginia, and the coastal areas of the southern colonies. The British, by way of contrast, had isolated pockets of strength within several of the colonies, often centered around urban areas. For example, New York City was a loyalist stronghold, as was Newport, Norfolk, Charleston, Savannah, and even Philadelphia, where the Second Continental Congress met for much of the war. There were a few contested areas, mostly coastal or far inland, along the Appalachian Mountains. The coastal regions of North Carolina and South Carolina were firmly patriot, but about halfway inland the areas became contested. New Jersey was fought over, as were parts of Maryland and a bit of western Virginia. Unlike the rest of solidly patriot New England, Vermont did not firmly favor independence from Great Britain. If the contested areas had sided firmly with the British, they would have been able to move outside of their urban bases in those colonies. It probably would have helped their overall supply situation: one problem the British encountered repeatedly was that they could not venture into the countryside to get food. The patriots still would have commanded the allegiance of a greater swathe of territory. However, the British would have received a definite strategic advantage if they could have swung contested regions in their favor.

Connections: Loyalists were people who had ties to the British empire. In some cases, those ties were ideological or cultural, such as people who believed that hierarchy kept society together; in other cases, they were strictly financial, including royal officials and merchants involved in transatlantic trade. Those who felt themselves to be outsiders were drawn to loyalism as well. Indians, for instance, saw the British government as a hedge between themselves and land-hungry colonists. Black slaves in the South had no reason to support an independence that did not affect their own status. In the southern backcountry, planters resented the political dominance of the lowlands gentry who were closely identified with the Revolution. Over thirty-five thousand loyalists fled the United States over the course of the war. Between seven and eight thousand relocated to England. Another twenty-eight thousand emigrated to Canada. Others tried to remain in the United States but were often hurt by the British practice of invading and then abandoning colonies, leaving loyalists exposed to retaliation from patriots.

### *Visual Activity*

Reading the Image: This engraving implies that independence is the salvation of the nation: the messenger looks like a knight rescuing a maiden, but in fact he's saving the whole country. The people hearing the news are clearly delighted by it. They're cheering and smiling, and one is even holding up a placard bearing the happy news. Even the men and women depicted in the windows in the background have smiles on their faces. The obvious implication is that independence is welcomed by one and all and will be universally beneficial.

Connections: Certainly many Americans were in favor of independence by the time the Second Continental Congress made it official in 1776. However, the engraving leaves out some important information. For one thing, the reading is being made to a thoroughly enthusiastic audience in an urban area. Cities tended to be more loyalist than the countryside, and loyalists were still quite vocal in 1776, but nobody in the crowd looks unhappy or upset. The distinct members of the audience are all middle class, although plenty of poor people lived in cities. They are also exclusively white, despite the presence of blacks in urban areas.

### *Analyzing Sources*

1. According to the men of Scituate, immediate independence was necessary because the British government was plotting to govern the colonies tyrannically, allowing colonists no say in their own affairs. They charged that the government had been using devious methods to destroy colonial liberty for years, which was bad enough. However, the British recourse to military action, and in particular their use of mercenaries and Indian allies, made it vital for the colonies to break free of Great Britain entirely. They claimed to have deliberated this issue on the recommendation of the town's General Assembly, and they directed their remarks toward the delegates of the Continental Congress.
2. The New York mechanics wanted independence for many of the same reasons the men of Scituate did, although they focused more on the issue of taxation and less on the introduction of soldiers into the colonies. They believed that the British government was oppressive and tyrannical and that the king was unwilling to hear petitions for redress from taxation, which was turning colonists into slaves. It is clear from the report that the New York Assembly was not convinced by the mechanics' reasoning. For one thing, the Assembly did not want the paper to be read to the entire gathering; the document states that the House was cleared and the paper read to the Chair of the Assembly, who was to determine whether it should be passed on to the larger gathering. According to the last paragraph, the chair apparently decided not to let the petition go any further, arguing that the Assembly did not have the power to declare in favor of independence. Only the Continental Congress could, but there is no evidence that the Chair chose to

forward the petition to that body to show New York's sentiments on the subject.

3. According to Landon Carter, one of the definitions of independence circulating in Virginia in 1776 involved the overthrow of all hierarchical authority, particularly that of the rich over the poor. This was by itself a threat to a rich planter like Carter. However, one of the things to which the poor objected was the funding of slave patrols, groups of men who patrolled southern roads and plantations to control slaves' behavior, which were publicly funded but beneficial only to those with the resources to own slaves. Southern slave societies depended on bridging the gap between rich and poor whites by means of racially designated slavery. If poor whites decided that they were not getting any advantage out of the slavery, the whole system could be undermined.

4. Merchants often benefited from close relations with Great Britain, and many of them disliked the revolutionary movement. Joseph Reed argues in his letter to Robert Morris that more will be lost from independence than gained. In particular, he points out that under British rule, colonists did not bear any of the internal taxes to which British citizens were subject and also did not have to pay for the cost of their own governance. Robert Morris agrees that independence will not be in the overall interest of America as a whole and further contends that independence has increased divisions rather than drawing colonists together.

CHAPTER

# BUILDING A REPUBLIC, 1775–1789

# 7

## Chapter Overview

### *Chapter Summary*

***Introduction*** Chapter 7 opens with a discussion of patriot James Madison's political development during the 1770s and 1780s. Madison was the son of a wealthy plantation master and had an excellent education. He became involved in Revolutionary politics and served in the Continental Congress, where he became frustrated by the practical limitation of the Articles of Confederation. In 1787, he organized the Philadelphia convention, which rewrote the entire governmental structure of the nation by producing the Constitution. His personal growth from an aimless young man to a leading political thinker mirrored the path of the developing United States.

***The Articles of Confederation, pp. 222–226*** From 1776 until 1781, the Second Continental Congress governed without any constitutional basis. Members found it hard to establish a government on principles congruent with the themes of the Revolution. Eventually the congress promulgated the Articles of Confederation, which they found difficult to implement.

**CONGRESS AND CONFEDERATION** After much debate and many revisions, in November 1777, the Congress approved the Articles of Confederation, which set forth the powers and structure of the Congress. The Congress would remain the central institution of national authority, with the power to make war and conduct foreign affairs and to appropriate, borrow, and issue money. However, taxes and troops were to be requisitioned from the states, and there was to be no national executive branch. All thirteen state legislatures would have to approve any measure intended to amend or ratify the Articles. In short, the Articles allowed the states considerable power and sovereignty.

**THE PROBLEM OF WESTERN LANDS** The main delay in the ratification of the Articles of Confederation was the problem regarding ownership of western lands. Some states had no claim to land beyond their boundaries and argued that the western lands should be given to the Congress for the benefit of all citizens. In 1781, Virginia finally broke the impasse by agreeing to renounce its claims to the West, which convinced Maryland, the last holdout, to sign. The western lands issue showed that powerful interests separated the states and that their unity of purpose, formerly directed against England, would not be a given in the future.

**RUNNING THE NEW GOVERNMENT** Not much exultation greeted the inauguration of the new government. The Congress continued lurching along, its myriad problems unresolved by the Articles. Daily activities were handicapped by the lack of a quorum to conduct business; state legislatures were slow to select delegates, and those appointed were often reluctant to come. The attempt to avoid an executive branch proved untenable, and executive departments were created to handle administrative functions. By the time the Articles were fully functioning, another problem emerged: the best political talent was no longer participating at the national level but at the state level, where the most important tenets of revolutionary ideology were being promulgated in state constitutions.

***The Sovereign States, pp. 226–233*** In the first decade of nationhood, the states were sovereign and all-powerful. Americans' main affiliation was at the state level, with people identifying themselves as Virginians or New Yorkers, for example, rather than as Americans. State government was therefore the laboratory where the Revolution's principles would first be tested.

**THE STATE CONSTITUTIONS** To avoid the flaws of the British system, in particular its unwritten constitution, Americans insisted that their own governments rest on clearly stated and permanently inscribed laws so that no individual or group could subvert them. All state constitutions embraced the concept of republicanism, which could suggest both envisioning leaders as autonomous and public-minded and direct democracy, with very little standing in the way of the will of the people. Either way, republicanism suggested government that promoted the people's welfare. An important decision in almost all state constitutions was to sharply limit the governor's powers and greatly expand the powers of the lower houses. Six of the state constitutions included bills of rights, which were lists of basic individual liberties that governments could not abridge.

**WHO ARE "THE PEOPLE"?** Despite the rhetoric of "the authority of the people," under the new state constitutions the only people allowed political participation, whether in the form of voting or office holding, were property holders. The justification for such a restricted franchise, which few questioned, was that only property owners possessed the independence of mind and purse to make wise political decisions. Moreover, the authors of the new constitutions were themselves wealthy property owners who viewed the Revolution as an effort to guarantee people the right to own property and to prevent unjust governments from appropriating it through taxation. About one-quarter to one-half of the adult white male population was disfranchised by property qualifications.

**EQUALITY AND SLAVERY** More difficult to resolve than the issue of white males' political participation was the question of slavery. Revolutionary rhetoric that emphasized the importance of liberty and the danger of enslavement directed attention to America's own institution of bondage. In southern states, legislatures included specific language in the constitution disbarring slaves from basic human rights. Slavery was cast into disrepute in places such as New England, where it was to be abolished in a very short time, and the middle Atlantic, where it was slowly phased out. However, it survived in all the southern and border states. Few southern whites could envision any alternative to slavery.

***The Critical Period, pp. 233–239*** From 1781 to 1786, many American worried that the Articles of Confederation were too weak. Others, however, defended the Articles as the best guarantee of individual liberty. The topic of the proper form of government remained controversial throughout the period.

**FINANCIAL CHAOS AND PAPER MONEY** As a result of the war years, the confederation and the individual states had enormous debts. They had printed virtually worthless money to take care of these debts, causing a serious postwar depression. Congress turned to Philadelphia financier Robert Morris. Morris's first strategy for saving the government from economic disaster—establishing a 5 percent duty on imported goods, to be used to fund the debt—was defeated. His other brainchild—the creation of the Bank of North America—was too limited in its scope to solve the confederation's economic problems. Because the Articles of Confederation reserved most key economic functions to the states, Congress was helpless to tax trade, control inflation, stop the flow of state-issued paper money, or pay the debt. But the confederation had one source of potential revenue, the national domain.

**LAND ORDINANCES AND THE NORTHWEST TERRITORY** Thomas Jefferson drafted the original policy for handling the national domain, the territory north of the Ohio River and east of the Mississippi River. He wanted to give land to settlers to encourage rapid and democratic settlement and avoid land speculation, provide that states have representative governments equal in value with the original states after they reached a certain population, and prohibit slavery. The Ordinance of 1784 adopted his ideas about surveying the land but rejected free land and abolition. The Ordinance of 1785 stipulated that land be sold in 640-acre parcels for $640 in cash or debt certificates, a very large sum that favored wealthy land speculators. The Northwest Ordinance promised territories eventual self-government, devised an interim plan, and prohibited slavery.

**SHAYS'S REBELLION, 1786–1797** Most Americans liked low taxes, cheap money, and easy credit, but social elites preferred high taxation and expensive money. Massachusetts elites were able to get the state's legislature to raise taxes, which were to be paid in hard money. Western farmers were hard-pressed to comply and often lost their property and were sent to jail. In response, in the fall of 1786 a former Continental army captain, Daniel Shays, led farmers in a tax revolt, challenging the idea that a popularly elected government was always fair and just. Shays and his followers were denounced as rebels and traitors by the Massachusetts legislature, which was horrified by the idea that people would dare to rebel against the laws of a republican government. At Springfield in January 1787, a state militia scattered Shays's troops. This tax rebellion created an ironic predicament for old rebels now taking a hard line against civil disorder. It also caused leaders throughout the country to worry about whether the confederation could handle similar uprisings in the future.

***The United States Constitution, pp. 239–243*** Events like Shays's Rebellion caused many Americans to conclude that the central government created by the Articles was indeed too weak to deal with the nation's pressing problems. They thus called for a meeting to augment the powers of the Articles, little realizing that they would end up totally reworking the national government.

**FROM ANNAPOLIS TO PHILADELPHIA** Led by Virginian James Madison, a general meeting of all the states was planned at Annapolis in September 1786 to empower the confederation government to regulate trade. When only five states showed up, it was agreed to adjourn the convention with a call for another to meet in Philadelphia the following May but with a much broader agenda for expanding the Articles' power. Fifty-five delegates from every state except Rhode Island assembled in Philadelphia, most of them concerned with the weaknesses of the Articles. The men who assembled at Philadelphia represented property-holding interests and harbored fears of democratic disorder; they all shared serious concerns about the weaknesses of the confederation government and a willingness to take bold action.

**THE VIRGINIA AND NEW JERSEY PLANS** Virginia laid out the Virginia Plan, which proposed the scrapping of the Articles and the creation of a whole new three-branch government consisting of a judiciary, a strong executive, and a legislature with representation based on population. Small-state delegates came up with a plan of their own, known since as the New Jersey Plan. It allowed for Congress's powers to be greatly augmented and for a plural presidency of three men. But their stipulation that Congress would remain a single house with each state having one vote met with opposition from most delegates because it based representation on states rather than population. The Great Compromise, which broke the impasse, employed features from both plans. There would be a bicameral legislature in which the House of Representatives would be apportioned by population and the Senate would represent each state. A "three-fifths clause" allowed for "all other persons" (that is, slaves) to be counted as three-fifths of the population. This language reflected the discomfort of the constitution's framers in mentioning slavery in a republican document, although the issue arose in three separate places.

**DEMOCRACY VERSUS REPUBLICANISM** Though the Philadelphia delegates still professed unswerving faith in republicanism, the new government reflected their concern that pure democracy was a dangerous thing. Only in the House of Representatives was a popular will to be seen, and that body could be checked by the Senate. Still, the delegates had devised a government with "checks and balances" among all the branches, with the idea that this arrangement would prevent tyranny by any one sector. Before leaving Philadelphia, the delegates specified that only nine of thirteen states' approval would be needed to ratify the Constitution. They also agreed that the Constitution would be submitted to special state ratifying conventions rather than to existing state legislatures, many of which would be sure to reject it out of hand.

***Ratification of the Constitution, pp. 243–249*** If the people had voted on the Constitution in the fall of 1787, it probably would not have passed, since substantial majorities opposed the document in Massachusetts, Virginia, and New York. In only a few of the remaining states could the Federalists count on support; to obtain ratification by nine states, they faced a daunting task.

**THE FEDERALISTS** The Constitution's supporters had a number of advantages over those who opposed the document, not the least of which were their superior organization and the fact that many of them were members of the established political elite. They also seized control of an appealing label, calling themselves Federalists, a term that once had described opponents of centralization. They called their critics Antifederalists, a label that made them sound as though they stood for nothing constructive. Due a combination of practical concerns on the part of small states and voter apathy, by May 1788, eight states had ratified the Constitution. Still, one more was needed.

**THE ANTIFEDERALISTS** The Antifederalists were a diverse group that drew support from rural and backcountry areas with a long tradition of antipathy toward eastern elites; nevertheless, there were elite Antifederalists. The new government, they claimed, could not effectively represent the interests of the individual states and their populations. It would increase taxes, wield dictatorial powers, favor the elites over the common people, and put an end to individual liberties. Above all, they protested the document's lack of a bill of rights.

**THE BIG HOLDOUTS: VIRGINIA AND NEW YORK** Although the decisive ninth vote for ratification had been cast by New Hampshire, a new government could not hope to succeed without the participation of Virginia and New York, whose conventions were closely divided. George Mason and Patrick Henry led the Antifederalist opposition in Virginia's ratifying convention. After Federalists promised a carefully worded bill of rights, the Virginia convention ratified the Constitution by a ten-vote margin. The New York Antifederalists argued that such a large and powerful state as New York did not need to yield so much authority to a new federal government. But New York Federalists counted among their ranks two key leaders, Alexander Hamilton and John Jay, who coauthored with James Madison *The Federalist Papers*, a brilliantly argued case for the Constitution. The Federalist #10, one of the most compelling essays, challenged the Antifederalists' conviction that republican government had to be small-scale. Newspaper support and heavy lobbying, combined with news of Virginia's decision, finally convinced New York. In less than twelve months, the United States Constitution had been written and ratified.

***Conclusion: Decade of Decision*** In the 1780s, the American people confronted the challenges of self-government. They wrestled with the problem of how much democracy to permit while still maintaining a workable system. When they discovered that demanding unanimity made it impossible to function, they created a stronger, national government regulated by a system of checks and balances. The ratification of the Constitution ended a decade of protest, revolution, and political experimentation. However, there was still opposition to the Constitution, and conflict between its supporters and opponents continued into the 1790s.

***Chronology Activity*** Read the annotated chronology, and answer the multiple-choice questions.

1775 May. Second Continental Congress begins. Despite having no formal authority, the Second Continental Congress served as the nation's central government for six years, until the Articles of Confederation were ratified by all thirteen states.

1776 Virginia adopts state bill of rights. Virginia passed the first bill of rights in the nation, based on the wording of the Declaration of Independence. It lists the basic individual liberties that governments could not abridge, and its example was followed by five other states.

John Dickinson of Pennsylvania drafts Articles of Confederation. The Articles of Confederation became the nation's first formal, constitutional government. Dickinson's plan gave sweeping powers to the federal government.

1777 November. Final draft of Articles of Confederation approved by Congress and sent to states. The final draft reduced the power of the federal government substantially and reserved most real authority for the states.

1778 State constitutions completed.

1780 Pennsylvania abolishes slavery. Pennsylvania was the first state to abolish slavery by statute. However, it provided for a very gradual emancipation, in which only slaves born after March 1, 1780, would be freed and then only after the age of twenty-eight.

1781 Articles of Confederation ratified. It took six years to ratify the Articles, largely because small states did not want to ratify unless unsettled land was turned over to the national government and used for the benefit of the nation as a whole. The situation was resolved only after Virginia agreed to turn over most of its western holdings.

Creation of executive departments; Robert Morris appointed superintendent of finance. Although the Articles of Confederation did not include the formation of any executive branch at all, some administrative departments turned out to be necessary. Depending on the head administrator, the departments could become quite powerful. Robert Morris, as superintendent of finance brought in to try to fix the national government's financial affairs, wielded a great deal of influence.

Bank of North America formed. The Bank of North America was supposed to help the government create economic stability and augment its revenue by providing a place to deposit its monies and a source of reliable banknotes.

Slave Quok Walker sues for freedom in Massachusetts. Walker's lawyer argued that the Massachusetts constitution's preamble made slavery illegal by stating that all men are born free and equal. Quok won his case and was set free. By 1789, slavery had been effectively abolished by judicial decision in Massachusetts.

1782 Virginia relaxes state manumission law. Upper South states like Virginia were unwilling to provide for even gradual emancipation, in which only slaves born in the future would be freed and then only on reaching a certain age. However, they did encourage owners to free their slaves by making manumission easier, leading to the emancipation of thousands of slaves in the 1780s.

1783 Treaty of Paris signed.

1784 Gradual emancipation laws passed in Rhode Island and Connecticut.

Treaty of Fort Stanwix with Iroquois. The Treaty of Fort Stanwix coerced partial cessions of land from the Iroquois. It also spurred a united Indian meeting near Detroit in 1786 at which participants declared that no further cessions of land would be valid without unanimous consent.

1785 Gradual emancipation in New York.

1786 Gradual emancipation in New Jersey.

Bank of North America expires. The Bank of North America had never issued enough banknotes to have a significant impact on the economy, but it had enriched Robert Morris and his two partners in the bank to a degree that struck many as suspicious.

Virginia adopts Statute of Religious Freedom.

Farmer Shays leads rebellion in western Massachusetts. Shays's Rebellion deepened national leaders' sense of crisis by demonstrating that democratically elected popular majorities could be perceived as oppressive by minority groups.

Annapolis meeting proposes convention to revise Articles of Confederation. The Annapolis meeting was sparsely attended, but delegates agreed to meet again for the purpose of trying to rework the federal government.

1787 Northwest Ordinance allows self-government and prohibits slavery in Northwest Territory. This was the third land act that attempted to deal with the issue of how to deal with the northwest portion of the national domain. It was closer to Jefferson's vision of the territory's development than the previous versions had been.

May–September. Constitutional convention meets in Philadelphia. The Constitutional convention laid out a much more powerful national government than had existed under the Articles of Confederation, in the hopes of controlling what delegates saw as the evils of excessive democracy.

1788 United States Constitution ratified. Despite opposition from rural, backcountry voters and politicians who feared that centralized government was a sure recipe for tyranny, Federalists were able to mobilize supporters and win ratification.

## *Chronology Questions* Choose the letter of the best answer.

1. In November of 1777, the
   a. Treaty of Paris was signed.
   b. Second Continental Congress began to meet.
   c. Bank of North America expired.
   d. final draft of the Articles of Confederation was sent to the states.

2. The Treaty of Fort Stanwix, which spurred an Indian union against the Americans, was signed in
   a. 1776.
   b. 1782.
   c. 1784.
   d. 1787.

3. What is the correct order for the following events?
   1. The state constitutions are completed.
   2. Pennsylvania abolishes slavery.
   3. Virginia relaxes its state manumission law.
   4. Slave Quok Walker sues for freedom in Massachusetts.

   a. 1, 3, 4, 2
   b. 1, 3, 2,4
   c. 4, 2, 3, 1
   d. 1, 2, 4, 3

4. The Northwest Ordinance allowing self-government and prohibiting slavery in the Northwest Territory passed in
   a. 1784.
   b. 1785.
   c. 1787.
   d. 1788.

5. In 1788
   a. the United States Constitution was ratified.
   b. Virginia adopted the Statute of Religious Freedom.
   c. executive departments were created.
   d. the Treaty of Paris was signed.

6. In 1781, the year Robert Morris was appointed superintendent of finance, the
   a. Annapolis meeting occurred.
   b. Articles of Confederation were ratified.
   c. Constitutional Convention met in Philadelphia.
   d. Bank of North America expired.

7. What is the correct order for the following events?
   1. The United States Constitution is ratified.
   2. Farmer Shays leads a rebellion in western Massachusetts.
   3. The Articles of Confederation are ratified.
   4. State constitutions are completed.

   a. 4, 2, 3, 1
   b. 4, 3, 2, 1
   c. 2, 4, 1, 3
   d. 2, 3, 1, 4

8. Pennsylvania began the gradual emancipation of slaves in 1780, and Virginia relaxed its state manumission law in
   a. 1782.
   b. 1783.
   c. 1784.
   d. 1785.

9. In 1786
   a. Shays's Rebellion occurred.
   b. gradual emancipation laws passed in Rhode Island and Connecticut.
   c. the Bank of North America expired.
   d. all of the above occurred.

10. What is the correct order for the following events?
    1. The Annapolis meeting is held.
    2. Virginia adopts a state bill of rights.
    3. The Articles of Confederation are ratified.
    4. State constitutions are completed.
    a. 1, 4, 2, 3
    b. 3, 4, 2, 1
    c. 3, 4, 1, 2
    d. 2, 4, 3, 1

***Defining Terms*** Match each term with the correct definition.

| | |
|---|---|
| ✓Northwest Ordinance | ✓Federalists |
| ✓Virginia Plan | ✓executive departments |
| ✓New Jersey Plan | ✓Alexander Hamilton |
| ✓Federalist #10 | ✓George Mason |
| ✓republicanism | ✓Paul and John Cuffe |
| ✓quorum | ✓John Dickinson |
| ✓bill of rights | ✓impost |
| ✓Great Compromise | ✓national domain |
| ✓Disqualifying Act | ✓Northwest Territory |
| ✓Bank of North America | ✓gradual emancipation |
| ✓Articles of Confederation | ✓property qualifications |
| ✓Antifederalists | ✓three-fifths clause |

1. The moderate congressman from Pennsylvania who drafted the Articles of Confederation. His original outline gave a great deal of power to the federal government, but it was heavily amended before it was accepted by the states. John Dickinson

2. The first formal United States government. These defined the union as a loose confederation of states and gave the national government little ability to interfere with state decisions and actions. The national government had rotating personnel, no executive branch, no power of taxation, and the requirement of unanimity for any major change. Articles of confederation

3. The western lands up to the Mississippi River. At the time that the Articles of Confederation were being debated, some states, including Virginia, the Carolinas, and Georgia, claimed that land as part of their original colonial charters. Small states with firmly set boundaries refused to ratify the Articles of Confederation until the land was turned over to the federal government. national domain

4. The number of delegates required to conduct legislative business. The confederation congress required two delegates from at least seven states to fulfill its day-to-day activities but often could not meet the minimum of fourteen. quorum

5. These departments were set up by the Continental Congress to handle purely administrative governmental functions. executive departments

6. The idea that government needs to rest on the consent of the governed and work in the interest of the public at large. To some people in the 1770s, it invoked a way of thinking about leaders as autonomous, virtuous, public-minded citizens who placed civic values above private interests. republicanism

7. A list of basic individual liberties that governments cannot abridge. bill of rights

8. Standards demanding that voters and officeholders be worth a set amount of money. This reflected the commonly held eighteenth-century notion that property holders alone had the independence of mind to participate in government. property qualifications

9. Two free black brothers from Massachusetts who refused to pay state taxes on the grounds that they were not allowed to vote and so were being taxed without their consent. They went to jail for tax evasion, but their petition eventually spurred the state legislature to extend the suffrage to tax-paying free black men. Paul and John cuffe

10. The process of slowly freeing slave populations by allowing only future generations to be freed and then only after they hit a specified age. States like Pennsylvania and New York, which had sizeable slave populations, phased the practice out this way. This method was seen as balancing the civil rights of blacks and the property rights of their owners by delaying the promise of freedom. gradual emancipation

11. A tax levied on imports. Robert Morris suggested one to finance the national government after the Revolutionary War but was unable to gain the consent of states such as Rhode Island and New York, which had active ports. impost

12. A private bank proposed by Robert Morris to augment the revenue of the confederation government. The bank enjoyed a special relationship with the national government, holding its hard money deposits, making short-term loans, and issuing banknotes backed by hard money. The bank had little impact on the nation's overall financial health, however, because it issued so little currency. Bank of North America

13. The national domain north of the Ohio River and east of the Mississippi River. North west Territory

14. The 1787 land act that promised eventual self-government for a territory with a white male population of five thousand and prohibited slavery in the Northwest Territory. Northwest ordinance

15. The legislation passed by Massachusetts in the wake of Shays's Rebellion. The measure made it illegal for the rebels to vote, hold public office, work as schoolmasters, or operate taverns. The idea was that these prohibitions would make it impossible for the rebels to express their political opinions or work in fields in which they could influence others. Disqualifying Act

16. A New Yorker and the delegates at the Annapolis meeting who wanted to expand the limited mandate of the Philadelphia meeting and use it to do whatever was necessary to expand the power of the federal government. Alexander Hamilton

17. James Madison's plan for a new central government. It repudiated the principle of a confederation of states and set out a three-branch government with the power to veto state legislation and coerce states militarily to obey national laws. Virginia Plan

18. The central government suggested by delegates from the smaller states of New Jersey, Connecticut, Delaware, and New Hampshire. This plan called for a plural presidency and a stronger national congress in which each state would have one vote. New Jersey Plan

19. The agreement that broke the logjam over whether representation should be apportioned by population or given equally to each state, regardless of size. This agreement based the number of delegates to the House of Representatives on population and gave each state two delegates to the Senate. Great Compromise

20. The agreement that settled the issue of what constituted population for the purposes of representation, specifically whether slaves counted as property or as people. three-fifths clause

21. Supporters of the Constitution. The name was not very logical, since it came from a Latin root meaning "league," and the supporters were opposed to the confederation concept. However, it had positive Revolutionary-era associations and forced the supporters' opponents to take on a negative-sounding designation. Federalists

22. Opponents of the Constitution. They feared that the new national government would become corrupt or tyrannical and objected to the Constitution's lack of a bill of rights. They tended to be from rural and backcountry areas, with a strong suspicion of the motives of eastern elites, and were strong in states like New York, which had a strong economy and could afford to remain independent. Anti Federalists

23. One of the leaders of the Antifederalists in Virginia. He had been a participant in the Philadelphia convention and was one of the three delegates who refused to sign the Constitution. Federalists won his support for the Constitution only by including a resolution that certain individual rights and republican principles were inviolate in the new government and by proposing twenty specific measures that the new government would promise to consider. George Mason

24. James Madison's revolutionary argument that republican government did not have to be small scale but would in fact benefit from a large and diverse population. Federalist #10

## Chapter Review

### *Multiple-Choice* Choose the letter of the best answer.

1. From 1776 until 1781, the Second Continental Congress existed without any
   a. popular support.
   b. internal conflict.
   c. formal constitutional basis.
   d. financial problems.

2. John Dickinson drafted the Articles of Confederation when the delegates to the Second Continental Congress felt the need to specify the powers, authority, and makeup of the
   a. judiciary branch.
   b. executive branch.
   c. Congress.
   d. state legislatures.

3. The controversial points in the first draft of the Articles of Confederation were the congress's ability to
   a. settle disputes between states and administer unsettled western lands.
   b. settle disputes between states and run a postal service.
   c. run a postal service and administer unsettled western lands.
   d. run a postal service and borrow money.

4. Under the Articles of Confederation, each state delegation cast
   a. one vote.
   b. two votes.
   c. votes proportionate to the geographical size of the state.
   d. votes proportionate to the population of the state.

5. To approve or amend the Articles of Confederation required the consent of
   a. half of the states.
   b. two-thirds of the states.
   c. three-quarters of the states.
   d. all of the states.

6. To derive revenue to fund the government, under the Articles of Confederation each state was to contribute to the common treasury
   a. a set amount determined by lottery.
   b. in proportion to the current property value of the state's land.
   c. whatever the state determined was appropriate.
   d. the same amount, regardless of size.

7. Many state leaders liked the lack of centralized authority in the confederation government in the late 1770s because they
   a. felt it would avoid the potential tyranny of government.
   b. wanted no united governmental body whatsoever.
   c. wanted to avoid paying taxes.
   d. hoped it would lead to the eventual abolition of slavery.

8. Virginia, Connecticut, the Carolinas, and Georgia all claimed their western boundaries lay at the
   a. Hudson River.
   b. Pacific coast.
   c. Mississippi River.
   d. Appalachian Mountains.

9. Delaware and Maryland refused to sign the Articles of Confederation because of
   a. the slavery issue.
   b. land disputes.
   c. religious differences.
   d. trade policy disagreements.

10. In the dispute over the Articles of Confederation, James Madison and Thomas Jefferson finally agreed to give up Virginia's western lands because they
    a. were tired of arguing.
    b. saw the concession as being in their state's economic interests.
    c. decided that their land claims were unfair.
    d. worried that a large state would be contrary to republican principles.

11. After the Revolutionary war, active politicians often devoted their talents to
    a. state government.
    b. national government.
    c. county government.
    d. the judiciary.

12. In the absence of an executive branch under the Articles of Confederation, Congress developed
    a. nothing.
    b. a chief of staff.
    c. executive departments.
    d. a judiciary advisory committee.

13. The Second Continental Congress met in Philadelphia and other cities for five years without any _____.
    a. enthusiasm
    b. representation from most states
    c. delegates from New England
    d. formal constitutional basis

14. The task of drafting a new constitution fell to _____ of Pennsylvania.
    a. John Dickinson
    b. Robert Morris
    c. Benjamin Franklin
    d. James Madison

15. The final draft of the Articles of Confederation proposed _____ the states.
    a. no relationship between
    b. a loose confederation of
    c. a tight confederation of
    d. getting rid of

16. The structure of the proposed government under the Articles of Confederation paralleled that of the _____.
    a. Continental Congress
    b. British Parliament
    c. Virginia House of Burgesses
    d. modern Senate

17. Under the Articles of Confederation, the Congress was to receive funding from taxes levied by _____ government.
    a. federal
    b. town
    c. county
    d. state

18. In the final debate over the Articles of Confederation, five small states proposed that Congress be given administrative control over _____ lands.
    a. southern
    b. northern
    c. western
    d. eastern

19. Eight states with _____ were ready to sign the Articles of Confederation as approved by the Congress in 1777.
    a. urban centers
    b. port cities
    c. western land claims
    d. sizeable slave populations

20. In 1781, the Virginia congressmen _____ and Thomas Jefferson agreed to cede all lands to the confederation except what would later become West Virginia.
    a. George Washington
    b. James Madison
    c. Patrick Henry
    d. George Mason

21. Before the Congress could conduct business, the Articles of Confederation required a quorum of at least two representatives from _____ states to conduct business, which it often did not have.
    a. two
    b. five
    c. seven
    d. ten

22. The Articles of Confederation deliberately refrained from setting up _____ branch, but a modest one was invented by necessity.
    a. an executive
    b. a legislative
    c. a judicial
    d. a military

23. In the first decade of independence from Great Britain, American citizens felt the most allegiance to their
    a. state governments.
    b. national government.
    c. families.
    d. schools.

24. A shared feature of all the postcolonial state constitutions was the conviction that government should
    a. be expensive.
    b. involve the input of all adults over the age of twenty-one.
    c. rest on the consent of the governed.
    d. be very powerful.

25. Most political writers of the 1770s and 1780s believed that republics could succeed only if they were
    a. well funded.
    b. large.
    c. small.
    d. heterogeneous.

26. Soon after the Revolution, the most important decisions the lower houses of state governments made were
    a. economic.
    b. judicial.
    c. legislative.
    d. executive.

27. There was widespread agreement in the 1780s that the only legitimate participants in government were the
    a. politically gifted.
    b. artisan classes.
    c. propertied classes.
    d. descendants of the original colonial settlers.

28. Writers of the new state constitutions viewed the Revolution as an effort to guarantee
   a. all white adult males the right to vote.
   b. the right to own property, undisturbed by government interference.
   c. freedom from taxation.
   d. the abolition of slavery.

29. Virginia's bill of rights, like those of other states, applied to all individuals who had "entered into a state of society," meaning
   a. individuals who could read and write.
   b. white individuals.
   c. free people.
   d. mannerly white males.

30. The ideals of the Revolution spurred seven Massachusetts freemen to refuse to pay taxes for three years because they
   a. were protesting the continuation of slavery.
   b. were loyalists.
   c. did not have any money.
   d. were protesting their inability to vote.

31. By 1789, slavery in Massachusetts had been effectively abolished by
   a. judicial decision.
   b. petition.
   c. statute.
   d. civil disobedience.

32. In the debate over slavery engendered by the Revolution, bills for general emancipation in the Upper South states of Maryland and Virginia were
   a. debated and defeated.
   b. debated and passed.
   c. never considered.
   d. rejected in favor of gradual emancipation.

33. Slaves who ran away during the Revolutionary war went to
   a. Canada.
   b. England.
   c. Indian tribes.
   d. all of the above.

34. In the 1780s, George Washington freed
   a. none of his slaves.
   b. a handful of his slaves.
   c. half of his slaves.
   d. all of his slaves.

35. Under the Articles of Confederation, the _____ were sovereign and all-powerful.
   a. cities
   b. judgeships
   c. federal agencies
   d. states

36. After the Revolution, Americans felt that they had been injured by the _____ nature of political British traditions; this attitude shaped the construction of their new state constitutions.
   a. unwritten
   b. unfair
   c. overly specific
   d. hierarchical

37. In the late 1770s, republicanism was widely thought to succeed only in _____.
   a. a large, centralized power center
   b. a three-branch government
   c. relatively small units
   d. town meetings

38. Property qualifications disenfranchised probably _____ all adult white males.
   a. one-sixth to one-third
   b. one-quarter to one-half
   c. one-third to two-thirds
   d. one-half to three-quarters

39. Writers of the new state constitutions saw the Revolution as an effort to prevent unjust governments from appropriating their _____.
   a. personal liberty
   b. savings
   c. right to vote
   d. property

40. Virginia's constitution, in its bill of rights, gave all _____ the right to life, liberty, property, and freedom of conscience.
   a. people
   b. women
   c. adults
   d. free people

41. Delaware's 1777 constitution explicitly made _____ illegal, basing its logic on the equality phrase.
    a. franchise restrictions
    b. slavery
    c. imbalances of wealth
    d. land ownership

42. Pennsylvania was the first state to end slavery by _____.
    a. judicial decision
    b. popular vote
    c. executive action
    d. statute

43. More than ten thousand slaves from South Carolina _____ in 1783 by leaving with the British army.
    a. were hanged
    b. achieved immediate freedom
    c. were returned to their masters
    d. were shipped to the West Indies

44. Beginning in the 1780s, the North-South pattern was _____.
    a. freedom versus slavery
    b. cities versus villages
    c. factories versus farms
    d. Germans versus Moravians

45. During the Revolutionary War, the confederation and individual states ran up huge war debts, financed by
    a. minting gold coins.
    b. the French government.
    c. printing money and borrowing from private sources.
    d. mining in the Northwest Territories.

46. To solve the confederation's postwar economic problems, the superintendent of finance, Robert Morris, suggested
    a. an income tax.
    b. a 5 percent import tax.
    c. a sales tax.
    d. a stamp tax.

47. Robert Morris, the new confederation's superintendent of finance, proposed creating
    a. the federal treasury.
    b. the stock market.
    c. a new constitution.
    d. a private bank.

48. Thomas Jefferson advocated dealing with the national domain after 1784 by
    a. giving the land to settlers.
    b. loaning the land to settlers.
    c. selling the land to settlers.
    d. selling the land to speculators.

49. Jefferson insisted that the new states created out of the Northwest Territory have representative governments equal in status with the original states once they
    a. had existed for a set number of years.
    b. reached a certain population.
    c. sheltered a specific number of very wealthy men.
    d. improved half of the available land.

50. The Ordinance of 1784
    a. did not use a rectangular grid.
    b. prohibited slavery.
    c. guaranteed self-government and eventual statehood.
    d. set aside land for the Indians.

51. The Northwest Ordinance of 1787 prohibited slavery and also
    a. encouraged the gradual manumission of slaves.
    b. prohibited free blacks from settling in the Northwest Territory.
    c. demanded that slavery be abolished all over the nation.
    d. warned that fugitive slaves caught in the Northwest Territory would be returned.

52. The most serious obstacle to settlement in the Northwest Territory was
    a. Indian resistance.
    b. transportation to the area.
    c. the isolation of the area.
    d. the cheapness of eastern land.

53. Most wealthy people were in favor of the new confederation's raising revenue through
    a. easy credit.
    b. heavy taxation.
    c. printing paper currency.
    d. bond issues.

54. In 1786, a Massachusetts farmer and onetime captain in the Continental army named Daniel Shays
   a. considered revolting against high taxes but changed his mind.
   b. led a tax revolt.
   c. condemned protests against high taxes.
   d. argued in favor of high taxes.

55. The governor of Massachusetts, James Bowdoin, responded to the 1786 tax revolt by
   a. expressing sympathy for the farmers.
   b. promising to argue for lower taxes in the future.
   c. characterizing the protestors as illegal rebels.
   d. ignoring it.

56. After Shays's Rebellion, the tax rebels were
   a. exiled as traitors.
   b. executed as traitors.
   c. fully pardoned and given all their civil rights.
   d. prevented from voting, holding office, working as schoolmasters, or operating taverns.

57. During the Revolutionary War, some $400 million to $500 million in _____ had been injected into the economy, causing prices and wages to fluctuate wildly.
   a. credit
   b. gold and silver
   c. paper currency
   d. foreign goods

58. By 1781, it took _____ continental dollars to buy what one had purchased in 1775.
   a. 15
   b. 72
   c. 146
   d. 239

59. Congress turned to _____ to fix the nation's financial woes, even though he had been forced to resign from Congress in 1778 for suspected profiteering.
   a. Samuel Adams
   b. Robert Morris
   c. George Mason
   d. Alexander Hamilton

60. Banknotes from the Bank of North America held their value better than currency because they were backed by _____.
   a. public confidence
   b. hard money
   c. Thomas Jefferson's personal guarantee
   d. France

61. Thomas Jefferson drafted the original policy for handing the _____, which was a large part of the national domain.
   a. Northwest Territory
   b. Mississippi River
   c. Appalachian Mountains
   d. Ohio River

62. Jefferson's original policy draft for the national domain prohibited _____ in the Northwest Territory.
   a. free blacks
   b. speculators
   c. industry
   d. slavery

63. Under the Ordinance of 1785, state boundaries conformed to _____.
   a. a rectangular grid
   b. Indian holdings
   c. geographic features
   d. French territorial boundaries

64. The Confederation Congress expected states to contribute revenue to the national government _____.
   a. voluntarily
   b. under threat of force
   c. when they could afford to
   d. not at all

65. In the postwar period, the upper house of Massachusetts wanted to retire the state debt by _____.
   a. issuing paper
   b. forcing the national government to excuse the state from paying taxes
   c. raising taxes
   d. lower the pay in the lower house of the legislature

66. Shays's Rebellion showed that _____.
   a. rebel leaders could reform the government
   b. popularly elected governments were not always fair and just
   c. the government could not raise taxes
   d. slavery was still a powerful force

67. The delegates meeting in Philadelphia in 1787 were supposed to
   a. disband the national government.
   b. replace the Articles of Confederation.
   c. increase the power of the state governments.
   d. revise the Articles of Confederation.

68. The fifty-five men who assembled in Philadelphia in 1787 generally
   a. were troubled by the weaknesses in the confederate government.
   b. liked the Articles of Confederation as they stood.
   c. were elder statesmen.
   d. had radical, antiauthoritarian leanings.

69. Two-thirds of the delegates to the 1787 Philadelphia meeting were
   a. artisans.
   b. day laborers.
   c. farmers.
   d. lawyers.

70. At the 1787 Philadelphia meeting, the Virginia Plan for restructuring the government called for
   a. an extremely strong national government.
   b. a moderate revision to the existing Articles of Confederation.
   c. a more direct democracy.
   d. a plural presidency.

71. The 1787 New Jersey plan to restructure the government differed from the Articles of Confederation in calling for
   a. sweeping congressional power to tax, regulate trade, and use force on state governments.
   b. representation of states, not people.
   c. giving each state a single vote.
   d. the creation of a single-house congress.

72. In the debate over the United States Constitution, the Great Compromise adopted the bicameral legislature to
   a. end the logjam over how to apportion representation.
   b. pacify James Madison.
   c. provide for a more representative government.
   d. distance the new government from the old one.

73. The proposed constitution at the Philadelphia convention touched on but never directly mentioned the words
   a. "slaves" or "slavery."
   b. "slavery" or "service."
   c. "slaves" or "labor."
   d. "service" or "labor."

74. The delegates at the Philadelphia convention saw political danger in too much
   a. republicanism.
   b. democracy.
   c. centralized government.
   d. elitism.

75. In the final version of the Constitution, senators were to be elected by
   a. the House of Representatives.
   b. voters.
   c. state legislatures.
   d. an electoral college.

76. The framers of the Constitution curbed the excesses of democracy by
   a. devising a government with limits and checks on all branches.
   b. keeping the executive branch weak.
   c. giving a lot of power to the House of Representatives.
   d. limiting the right to vote for representatives and senators.

77. James Madison, who had initiated the Philadelphia convention, was initially
   a. entirely satisfied with the Constitution.
   b. appalled by the Constitution.
   c. worried that the Constitution would not solve the government's problems.
   d. actively opposed to the passage of the Constitution.

78. The Constitution specified a mechanism for ratification that demanded that
   a. a majority of voters in each state had to agree to it.
   b. nine out of thirteen state legislatures had to agree to it.
   c. nine out of thirteen special ratifying conventions had to agree to it.
   d. the special ratifying convention in every state had to agree to it.

79. The impetus for the Philadelphia convention came from a small circle of Virginians who wanted to augment the power of the _____.
   a. state governments
   b. national government
   c. executive branch
   d. Bank of North America

80. While the Philadelphia convention was supposed to revise the Articles of Confederation, _____ hoped that delegates would go further in strengthening the national government.
   a. James Madison
   b. Alexander Hamilton
   c. Thomas Jefferson
   d. Patrick Henry

81. The majority of delegates to the Philadelphia convention had been _____.
   a. foot soldiers in the war
   b. in the Continental Congress
   c. state governors
   d. farmers

82. The Virginia Plan at the Philadelphia convention called for a _____ national government.
   a. weak
   b. single chamber
   c. three-branch
   d. slightly altered

83. The New Jersey Plan at the Philadelphia convention retained the principle that the national government was to be an assembly of _____.
   a. states
   b. people
   c. strong executives
   d. representatives of the judiciary

84. At the Philadelphia convention, the _____ broke the deadlock over the issue of representation.
   a. three-fifths clause
   b. Great Compromise
   c. plural presidency
   d. bicameral legislature

85. To avoid using the word *slaves*, the Constitution's framers substituted the term _____.
   a. "all other Persons"
   b. "permanently indentured"
   c. "Persons of African descent"
   d. "unfree Persons"

86. The final draft of the Constitution gave _____ a six-year term of office.
   a. the president
   b. representatives
   c. Supreme Court justices
   d. senators

87. The final draft of the Constitution specified that _____ would be used to elect the president and vice president.
   a. a direct vote
   b. the House of Representatives
   c. state legislatures
   d. an electoral college

88. When the final vote was taken at the Philadelphia convention in September 1787, _____ dissenters refused to endorse the Constitution.
   a. no
   b. three
   c. twenty
   d. fifty

89. After the delegates to the Philadelphia convention drafted the Constitution, they sent it to the
   a. Continental Congress.
   b. state legislatures.
   c. state voters.
   d. ratifying conventions.

90. In the fight over ratification, the pro-Constitution forces referred to themselves as the
   a. Republicans.
   b. Madisonians.
   c. Federalists.
   d. Antifederalists.

91. Georgians passed the Constitution rapidly because they
   a. thought it would lower taxes.
   b. were apathetic.
   c. wanted the government to regulate trade.
   d. felt it would provide greater protection.

92. Antifederalists in Connecticut, Maryland, and South Carolina tended to be
   a. urban artisans.
   b. rural westerners.
   c. large landholders.
   d. merchants.

93. The only state in which the Federalists encountered difficulty early in the ratification process was
   a. Delaware.
   b. New Jersey.
   c. Massachusetts.
   d. Pennsylvania.

94. The Antifederalists could be characterized as coming from
   a. elite social backgrounds.
   b. states with solid economic footing.
   c. rural and backcountry areas.
   d. all of the above.

95. Antifederalists were convinced that under the Constitution, elected representatives would always be
   a. corrupt.
   b. upper class.
   c. middle class.
   d. lower class.

96. Federalists wanted power to flow to
   a. laborers and mechanics.
   b. independent farmers.
   c. intelligent, virtuous, public-spirited leaders.
   d. a cross-section of the population.

97. The most widespread objection to ratifying the Constitution was that it
   a. gave too much power to the House of Representatives.
   b. lacked any guarantees of individual liberties.
   c. allowed too many people the right to vote in national elections.
   d. allowed too few people the right to vote in national elections.

98. Central to New York governor George Clinton's opposition to the Constitution was his conviction that
   a. it would cheat farmers.
   b. New York did not need it.
   c. New York Federalists were intellectually inferior.
   d. it was bad for artisans and workers.

99. In Federalist #10, James Madison challenged the Antifederalist conviction that
   a. republican government had to be small scale.
   b. Federalists were snobs.
   c. the Constitution would harm the interests of the lower classes.
   d. direct democracy was a beneficial form of government.

100. The last state to ratify the Constitution was
   a. New York.
   b. Virginia.
   c. Rhode Island.
   d. New Hampshire.

101. Both North Carolina and _____ refused to call constitutional ratifying conventions.
   a. New Hampshire
   b. Vermont
   c. Rhode Island
   d. South Carolina

102. In the debate over the ratification of the Constitution, the pro-Constitution forces called themselves _____.
   a. Antifederalists
   b. Shaysites
   c. Federalists
   d. Unionists

103. In Georgia, ratification of the Constitution was popular for protection against _____.
   a. Indians and Spanish Florida
   b. high taxes
   c. problems with piracy
   d. labor unrest

104. The Federalists' campaign was helped by the fact that the _____ tended to be in their camp.
   a. majority of voters
   b. largest states
   c. most populist states
   d. established political elite

105. Antifederalists were concerned that even the _____, the only directly democratic element of the new government, did not adequately represent its constituency.
   a. House of Representatives
   b. Senate
   c. presidency
   d. judiciary

106. The Federalists wanted power to flow to _____, who they believed to be intelligent, virtuous, and public-spirited.
   a. men like themselves
   b. yeomen farmers
   c. artisans
   d. small merchants

107. The absence of a _____ in the Constitution made many Antifederalists uneasy.
   a. bill of rights
   b. guarantee of slavery
   c. elected judiciary
   d. method of making amendments

108. _____ provided the decisive ninth vote for ratification of the Constitution.
   a. New Hampshire
   b. New Jersey
   c. Connecticut
   d. North Carolina

109. In Federalist #10, Madison made the novel argument that a _____ was a guarantee of liberty.
   a. small, homogeneous population
   b. large, diverse population
   c. powerful executive
   d. weak Congress

110. _____'s ratification of the Constitution ensured the solidity and legitimacy of the new government.
   a. Rhode Island
   b. Massachusetts
   c. New Jersey
   d. New York

***Short Answer*** Write a paragraph response to each question.

1. What kind of national government was instituted under the Articles of Confederation?
2. What issue complicated the passage of the Articles of Confederation? How was that issue solved?
3. Why was the government under the Articles of Confederation often inefficient and slow?
4. What philosophy underlay the state governments of the 1770s?
5. After the Revolutionary War, how did the new state constitutions define "the people"? On what basis did these constitutions exclude people from the democratic process?
6. How did language about the promise of freedom and equality for all men apply to slavery in the new state constitutions?
7. How did the Congress try to solve its financial problems in the early 1780s? Why did the measures fail?
8. How did the land ordinances of 1784, 1785, and 1787 reflect Thomas Jefferson's vision for the national domain? How did they depart from his vision?

9. What were the issues behind Shays's Rebellion? How did the former Revolutionary leaders react to it?
10. What kind of delegates attended the Philadelphia convention in 1787? Did they reflect the social composition and concerns of the nation?
11. How did the delegates at the Philadelphia convention deal with the issue of slavery?
12. How did the final Constitution reflect the framers' suspicion of democratic expression?
13. How did the Federalists overcome resistance to the Constitution and win a string of early ratifications?
14. Why did Antifederalists oppose the Constitution?
15. Why did the state of New York hold out against the Constitution, and what was the significance of this state's ratification?

***Building Historical Skills*** Historians use a variety of sources to think and talk about the past, including maps, illustrations, and written records. Maps provide a variety of different kinds of comparative information in a condensed visual format; reading them requires learning how to sort through this information. To deepen our understanding of the past by supplementing written records, historians frequently interpret material culture, such as a vase or a painting, with techniques borrowed from art history, archaeology, or anthropology. Written records, though familiar as sources, raise their own problems of interpretation. Every document reflects someone's particular perspective or assumptions. It is the historian's task to study and compare each document to other records with other perspectives. The following exercises introduce you to using maps, illustrations, and written documents as sources of information. Use these sources as well as the material in the chapter to think about different themes and topics discussed in the text.

***Map Activity*** Locate the following places on Map 7.1: Cession of Western Lands, 1782–1802 on page 225 in *The American Promise,* Second Edition.

1. Territory claimed by Virginia alone
2. Territory claimed by both Virginia and Connecticut
3. Territory claimed by both Virginia and Massachusetts
4. Territory claimed by South Carolina
5. Territory claimed by Georgia
6. Territory claimed by North Carolina
7. Territory claimed by Connecticut

Answer the following questions in a paragraph based on Map 7.1: Cession of Western Lands, 1782–1802 in *The American Promise,* Second Edition.

**READING THE MAP** Which states had the largest claims on western territory? What disputed territory became the fourteenth state?

**CONNECTIONS** In what context did the first dispute regarding western lands arise? How was it resolved? How did the experience of the 1760s and the institution of democratic rule influence the decision of Virginia to give up its western lands?

**WEB LINKS** To explore the topics discussed in the exercise above, visit the Web links noted below.

"Historical Maps of Illinois and the Northwest Territory"
http://images.library.uiuc.edu/projects/historical_maps/
Choose "Maps of North America and the Northwest Territory."

"The Articles of Confederation and the Constitution"
http://revolution.h-net.msu.edu/essays/bernstein.confederation.html

***Visual Activity*** Thomas Jefferson's map of the Northwest Territory details his ideas about dividing up the territory into new states. His proposed states are different from many of the established states in that they are all relatively angular. The lines that divide the states vertically are perfectly straight, as are the lines that divide them horizontally. Jefferson deviates from this pattern only in places where the natural geography of the area makes a tidy partition impossible. For example, in his proposed state number three, Lake Huron and Lake Michigan eat into what would otherwise be a rectangular piece of real estate, and he uses the Ohio River as a dividing line between states seven and ten. For the most part, Jefferson ignores the natural boundaries indicated by rivers and mountains, which in his map go through states rather than defining them. His map also depicts states that are similar in size. The older states varied wildly, depending on a combination of their original land grants and historical circumstance; the new ones, in Jefferson's vision, are of relatively equal size and so theoretically will carry similar political weight in the House of Representatives.

Answer the following questions in paragraphs based on "Jefferson's Map of the Northwest Territory" on page 232 of *The American Promise*, Second Edition.

**READING THE IMAGE** What does this map indicate about Jefferson's vision of the Northwest Territory?

**CONNECTIONS** What were the problems with Jefferson's design for the division of the territory? Why did Congress alter it in the land ordinances of 1784, 1785, and 1787?

**WEB LINKS** To explore the topics discussed in the exercise above, visit the Web links noted below.

"The Northwest Ordinance"
http://www.statelib.lib.in.us/www/ihb/docnword.html

"Indiana State Archives Collections Database"
http://www.state.in.us/icpr/webfile/archives/homepage.html
Choose "Land office records" and then "A fuller description."

***Analyzing Sources Activity*** Answer the following questions in paragraphs based on Documenting the American Promise: Blacks Petition for Freedom and Rights on page 230 of *The American Promise*, Second Edition.

1. What do these four Massachusetts petitioners mean when they congratulate state legislators for their recent efforts to "free themselves from slavery"? Are they contradictory when they claim a natural right "as men" to relief from slavery but then also "bow in submission" to the "governor of the universe" who has allowed their slavery? What is it they "disclaim" out of consideration to their present masters? Why do they raise the case of a Spanish version of slavery?
2. Is the Cuffe petition essentially a call for "no taxation without representation"? Does it differ from the revolutionaries' stand on taxation in relation to Britain? Do the petitioners want representation or relief from taxation? Why do they mention their military service?
3. Why do you think the Connecticut couple waited until 1784 to contact their former owner, who had left in 1774? Who might be scaring the family with threats to sell them out of state? What is the basis of their petition to the state government? On what grounds were they finally freed? How might you account for the assembly's additional five-year delay to arrive at this decision in 1789?
4. What can you conclude about the options available to northern blacks to secure freedom or rights under law? Are the petitioners confident about their rights or about the outcome they expect? How have they had to shape their petitions to appeal to an all-white legislature? Do you see instances of subtle irony or sarcasm employed?

**WEB LINKS** To explore the topics discussed in the exercise above, visit the Web links noted below.

"Africans in America"
http://www.pbs.org/wgbh/aia/home.html
Choose "Revolution" and then "Narrative"

"Amherst History Museum: African-Americans in Amherst"
http://www.amhersthistory.org/ahm_aa/ahm_aa4.htm

"Maryland State Archives: Descriptions of African American Records"
http://www.mdarchives.state.md.us/msa/refserv/html/afridesc.html

# Answer Key

## Chapter 7: Building a Republic, 1775–1789

### *Chapter Overview*

#### *Chronology*

1. d
2. c
3. d
4. c
5. a
6. b
7. b
8. a
9. d
10. d

#### *Defining Terms*

1. John Dickinson
2. Articles of Confederation
3. national domain
4. quorum
5. executive departments
6. republicanism
7. bill of rights
8. property qualifications
9. Paul and John Cuffe
10. gradual emancipation
11. impost
12. Bank of North America
13. Northwest Territory
14. Northwest Ordinance
15. Disqualifying Act
16. Alexander Hamilton
17. Virginia Plan
18. New Jersey Plan
19. Great Compromise
20. three-fifths clause
21. Federalists
22. Antifederalists
23. George Mason
24. Federalist #10

### *Chapter Review*

#### *Multiple-Choice*

1. c
2. c
3. a
4. a
5. d
6. b
7. a
8. c
9. b
10. d
11. a
12. c
13. d
14. a
15. b
16. a
17. d
18. c
19. c
20. b
21. c
22. a
23. a
24. a
25. a
26. a
27. c
28. b
29. c
30. d
31. a
32. a
33. d
34. a
35. d
36. a
37. c
38. b
39. d
40. d
41. b
42. d
43. b
44. a
45. c
46. b
47. d
48. a
49. b
50. c
51. d
52. a
53. b
54. b
55. c
56. d
57. c
58. c
59. b
60. b
61. a
62. d
63. c
64. a
65. c
66. b
67. d
68. a
69. d
70. a
71. a
72. a
73. a
74. b
75. c
76. a
77. c
78. c
79. b
80. b

81. b
82. c
83. a
84. b
85. a
86. d
87. d
88. b
89. a
90. c
91. d
92. b
93. c
94. d
95. b
96. c
97. b
98. b
99. a
100. c
101. c
102. c
103. a
104. d
105. a
106. a
107. a
108. a
109. b
110. d

### *Short Answer*

1. State leaders in the late 1770s were very wary of strong, centralized authority of the sort they believed the British empire epitomized. As a result, the Articles of Confederation identified the union as a loose confederation in which the states retained all powers and rights not expressly delegated to the congress. The national government did not have executive or judiciary branches. There was no mechanism by which the national government could force states to contribute their fair share of taxes or control states' legislation. The Articles themselves could be amended only by the unanimous agreement of all thirteen states.
2. The question of whether states or the national government would control unsettled western lands was the most divisive. Eight of the thirteen states claimed boundaries extending far to the west on the basis of their original British colonial charters. The remaining five states were small and lacked such expansive land grants. The smaller states wanted the national government to have administrative control over western lands so that every state could benefit from them, not just the states that claimed the territory. Two states, Delaware and Maryland, refused to sign the Articles of Confederation until a national domain policy was adopted. The issue was finally solved when Virginia agreed to renounce its western claims on the theory that too large a state could not be governed in a republican manner.
3. A number of problems hampered the national government under the Articles of Confederation. There were endless problems convincing delegates to attend sessions; the Articles required that two delegates from at least seven states be present to conduct business, but often fewer than fourteen men showed up. Because the national government was cumbersome and lacked prestige, state governments were slow to select delegates, and the delegates were themselves often unenthusiastic in performing what they saw as an unrewarding chore. Politicians of talent preferred to serve at the state level. Finally, few delegates remained for more than a short term, resulting in a membership that was often inexperienced.
4. States were sovereign and all-powerful in the 1770s, and their constitutions reflected the conviction that government properly rested on the consent of the governed. Republican leaders believed that the example of British colonial rule demonstrated that distant governments could easily become tyrannical; therefore, the best government was close to the people and gave them maximum voice. Nearly every state had a two-chamber assembly with a very strong lower house. Most restricted the power of the governor, restricting executive terms to one year and removing the ability to dismiss and convene legislatures, veto legislation, or use patronage to buy loyalty. Many states also included bills of rights in their constitutions, lists of basic individual liberties that governments could not abridge.
5. When state constitutions talked about "the people," they usually referred to white, male, adult property holders. Every state set property qualifications for voters and candidates because most believed that only the propertied classes could legitimately participate in the government. Only property owners could be guaranteed to have the independent political will to make intelligent public choices. Those who lacked property were held to be too dependent on others for the basics of life to vote their consciences. Between a quarter to a half of all white adult men were disenfranchised by property qualifications.
6. Language about freedom and equality affected slavery differently, depending on how important slaves were to a state's economy; a split between the North and the South was already developing. Virginia's constitution, for example, was written by slaveholders who believed that they were equal to British citizens, but these white men did not extend this idea of equality to their own human property. Delegates insisted that their bill of rights apply only to those who had entered the "state of society." In Massachusetts, a state with a marginal number of slaves, the constitution did not have any such exclusionary language, and slaves sued for their freedom with the argument that the constitution made slavery illegal. Vermont's 1777 constitution explicitly made slavery illegal, but there were almost no slaves in that state.

7. In 1781, Congress, desperate over the severe depreciation of its money and the postwar depression, named Robert Morris superintendent of finance. Morris proposed a 5 percent import tax (impost) to raise money for the national government; but the Articles of Confederation gave Congress no authority to levy such a tax, and Morris was forced to attempt to amend the Articles. He was unable to get unanimous consent for such a change, since several states with ports already collected import taxes and did not care to share their income. Morris's next proposition was a private bank, the Bank of North America, which would hold the government's hard money deposits, make short-term loans to the government, and provide stable currency in the form of banknotes. The bank did provide the government with a currency that held its value, but it issued so little that it had little financial impact; when its charter expired in 1786, the Pennsylvania legislature refused to renew it.

8. Thomas Jefferson recommended that the national domain be divided into ten states, divided into ten-mile-square townships, with land given free to settlers, slavery prohibited, and the promise of self-governance and eventual statehood. This would, he believed, encourage the orderly settlement of free farmers whose labors would benefit the nation. The land ordinances reduced the number of states from ten to three to five and shrank the size of townships to six miles square. They also rejected Jefferson's desire to give away land, demanding that purchasers pay a base price of $1 in hard cash or debt certificates an acre, and specifying a 640 acre minimum purchase. However, the ordinances did specify that territories be given self-governance and after 1787 prohibited slavery as well.

9. To retire the state debt, Massachusetts levied high taxes and demanded that they be paid in hard money. By 1786, cash-poor farmers in the western part of the state were losing their land because of what they saw as unfair and undemocratic taxes inspired by the selfish demands of eastern commercial powers. Under the leadership of Daniel Shays, a former Continental army captain, farmers called conventions, circulated petitions, and began marching on courthouses to demand relief. Revolutionary leaders were appalled by these acts of civil disobedience, characterizing the Shaysites as illegal rebels and even calling for their execution as traitors. They had refused to consider the possibility that popular majorities in democratic legislatures could be oppressive.

10. The fifty-five delegates at the Philadelphia convention were those most concerned about the weaknesses of the Articles of Confederation. Political leaders who were satisfied with the Articles tended to avoid the meeting, and most of the delegates opposed to revision left halfway through the convention. The delegates were wealthier and more socially prominent than most Americans: two-thirds were lawyers, half had been officers in the Continental army, and seven had been state governors. The majority had served in the Continental Congress. There were no artisans, farmers, or day laborers among them.

11. Slavery became a serious problem for the delegates in the context of apportioning representation. If slaves were counted as property, they added to the southern tax burden, but if they were people, they bulked up southern influence in the House of Representatives. Delegates settled on the three-fifths clause, under which all free persons plus "three-fifths of all other Persons" counted toward the apportionment of representatives. The euphemistic language showed the discomfort delegates felt in naming slavery in a republican document. However, the delegates also agreed not to end the importation of slaves until 1808 and agreed to return fugitive slaves from free to slave states, thus guaranteeing protection of the institution and helping to perpetuate it.

12. The Constitution was much less democratic than the Articles of Confederation. Only the House of Representatives was directly elected by the voters. Senators were put into office by the vote of state legislatures, given six-year terms to foster long-term service and protection from the whims of democratic majorities. The presidency was even more removed from ordinary voters; it was filled by means of an electoral college, again chosen by state legislatures. The president was a powerful position, with the ability to check the House of Representatives by means of the veto.

13. The Federalists identified the states most likely to ratify quickly and scheduled Constitutional conventions quickly there, before their opponents had a chance to campaign. They were aided in some cases by low voter turnout, which favored pro-Constitution forces. Federalists were often political elites and as such had power out of proportion to their overall number. There were also practical reasons for states to support the Constitution. Small states like New Jersey and Delaware were overshadowed by stronger neighbors and wanted a powerful federal government, whereas Georgia, threatened by Indians and Spanish Florida, hoped that for the enhanced protection of a centralized authority.

14. Antifederalists were concerned that the new government was so distant from voters that it would become corrupt and tyrannical, as the British government had. They pointed out that in

the House of Representatives, the only democratic arm of the government, one member represented thirty thousand people. Moreover, they worried that elected representatives would always be from the elite, a problem that had not been as serious under the Articles where power resided in state governments. They disliked the lack of a bill of rights, the regulation of the time and place of congressional elections (which could limit the ability of rural voters to express themselves politically) and the prohibition of state-issued money.

15. New York's governor, George Clinton, represented agrarian interests in upstate New York, which were largely opposed to the Constitution. Also, he felt that New York was such a large and powerful state that it would not benefit from relinquishing its authority to a central government. New York's ratification of the Constitution ensured the solidarity and legitimacy of the new government because it was a geographically and economically strategic state.

### *Map Activity*

Reading the Map: Virginia had the largest single claim on western territory. It asserted ownership to the land to the west of its southern border all the way to the Mississippi River. To the north, its territory extended all the way to the Great Lakes. Georgia, South Carolina, and North Carolina all claimed land west to the Mississippi River as well. Some land was contested: both Massachusetts and Virginia claimed land around Lake Michigan and Lake Huron, and Connecticut and Virginia both believed they owned the Western Reserve near Pennsylvania. Vermont was claimed by New York and New Hampshire but was ceded in 1791 and became the fourteenth state.

Connections: The first dispute over western lands broke out in 1777, when the Articles of Confederation were being debated in Congress. John Dickinson's original draft gave Congress authority over unsettled western lands. This power was removed in the final draft, at the insistence of states with western land claims. However, small states bounded by less grandiose colonial charters wanted the national government to administer western land to the benefit of all the states. On this basis, Delaware and Maryland refused to approve the Articles, which demanded the unanimous consent of the states. The impasse was finally resolved in 1781 when Virginia agreed to cede all lands to the confederation except the area that became West Virginia. Thomas Jefferson and other Virginian leaders decided to give up Virginia's western lands, even though the decision did not make economic sense: the state of Virginia could earn money from selling the land to settlers. However, Jefferson was concerned that extensive holdings would result in less democratic government. In particular, he argued that an enormous state could not be governed in a republican manner because the seat of government would simply be too far from its citizens to represent them properly. Obviously, he was influenced by the American experience of the British empire in the 1760s, when the British government seemed too distant and too out of touch with its colonial citizens to understand their concerns.

### *Visual Activity*

Reading the Image: Jefferson clearly saw the Northwest Territory as a place in which he could enact his vision of republicanism. The states are laid out in rational, linear shapes: they are not contorted geographical expressions like New York and Massachusetts. The map also shows an attempt to distribute natural resources among the proposed state. Almost all of the states have access to some body of water, although not all of them could get to a river, the most efficient means of transporting goods and people. One of the only places Jefferson uses a natural geographic feature as a boundary is between states seven and ten; if the river were not used, one of the states would not be able to access the Ohio River. Finally, the states are similar in size, guaranteeing that each can have a chance at roughly even representation in the national Congress.

Connections: The problem with Jefferson's design was that it did not take into account natural features and boundaries. For instance, while all of his states could get to water, not all of them enjoyed river access, which constituted a tremendous commercial disadvantage. Thus, Congress called for the territory to be divided into three to five states, conforming to natural geographic boundaries. Congress did, however, maintain Jefferson's strict, geometric plans for township divisions. Jefferson's plan also ignored Indian claims to the Northwest Territory, complicating the vital matter of forcing land cessions out of different tribes.

### *Analyzing Sources*

1. The petitioners begin by expressing their sympathy with the aims of the Revolutionary leaders, who often spoke of British attempts to "enslave" the colonies—a hint that their plight as slaves was similar to that of the Americans under British rule. The petitioners' demand for their rights and their willingness to accede to the will of God seems to be more conciliatory than submissive. They acknowledge that God has permitted them to become slaves but insist that their polite and reasonable behavior will cause him to aid them in their attempt to gain freedom. They make it clear that they are not demanding to be paid for their unremunerated past labors,

perhaps to avoid resistance on the grounds that owners could not afford to give their slaves what they deserved for a lifetime of work. They mention that the Spanish allow African slaves a day a week to perform their own work to capitalize on the traditional English hostility toward the Spanish. The English argued that although the Spaniards "have not those sublime ideas of freedom that English men have," the Spanish are more advanced in this case.

2. John and Paul Cuffe, two free Massachusetts blacks, protested the high taxes levied on them by the state, arguing that generations of involuntary servitude and prejudice have put Massachusetts blacks in a state of great poverty. The revolutionaries tended to argue that the problem was not taxation but rather taxation without representation. The Cuffe brothers touch on this issue but are more concerned with the long-term effects of discrimination, which make the taxes impossible to pay. They mention that do not have the franchise and so have no representation; the thrust of that argument, however, is that their lack of representation means that legislators have little sympathy for their plight, not that they inherently wish to vote. They mention their military service to demonstrate their claims to citizenship and by extension their claims on the Massachusetts government.

3. In 1784, Connecticut passed its gradual emancipation law; these laws often did not affect people who were currently defined as slaves but instead provided eventual freedom for those born to slave mothers after a certain date. The couple may have hoped that the new state constitution gave them de facto freedom and then learned that neither they nor their children were legally free. The petition says that, as property, the petitioners had been forfeited to the state when their owner fled, so it is possible that state or town officials wished to sell them or that patriot relatives of loyalists may have claimed their services. The petitioners argue that they deserve to be emancipated because they have demonstrated their ability to provide for themselves and a sizeable family and will thus not be a drain on the community. They were freed, however, because their former owner agreed to emancipate them, not strictly because they had managed on their own. The five-year delay could be related to the family's belief that the 1784 letter from their former owner guaranteed their status as free, which could have been unexpectedly challenged.

4. These petitions make it clear that northern blacks were often dependent on winning the sympathy of white lawmakers and officials to guarantee their freedom. They need to justify their right to freedom in language demonstrating their fitness as citizens—pointing out military service and the ability to support themselves—rather than using the strict natural rights arguments favored by white revolutionaries. Given the length and detail of the documents, the petitioners seem to feel that they deserve freedom but that they are not confident about the outcome of their requests. They have to use subtle arguments and in some cases appeal to the legislators' pride. For instance, the petitioners in the first document repeatedly declare themselves submissive, although they work in a bit of irony, particularly when they point out that even the supposedly despotic Spanish give their slaves time to work for themselves. The Cuffe brothers also use very respectful language but comment that as a people blacks are fair—something that their white legislators clearly are not.

CHAPTER

# THE NEW NATION TAKES FORM, 1789–1800

# 8

## Chapter Overview

### *Chapter Summary*

***Introduction*** This chapter opens with a discussion of the important role the first American president, George Washington, played in promoting national unity. The thirteen states had come through a turbulent decade, veering between fear of the divisive effects of party politics on the one hand and mistrust of executive power on the other. Washington's reputation for virtue and self-sacrifice increased confidence that executive power was not incompatible with the people's welfare. However, political divisions emerged around economic policy and foreign affairs, despite the best efforts of the era's politicians.

***The Search for Stability, pp. 257–260*** Leaders in the early 1790s believed that political parties were incompatible with national stability and harmony. They sought to heal the divisions of the 1780s, passing a Bill of Rights to satisfy Antifederalists and promoting the private virtue of women, which leaders hoped would increase the public virtue of male citizens.

**WASHINGTON'S CABINET** Washington appointed to his cabinet individuals whom he considered the best and the brightest, regardless of their ideological differences—men like Alexander Hamilton, who headed the Treasury and Thomas Jefferson, who became secretary of state. Few could have anticipated that fundamental disagreements resulting in twenty years of party divisions would be the outcome of Washington's diverse and talented cabinet.

**THE BILL OF RIGHTS** Convening in April 1789, the First Congress began to construct a bill of rights, which had been promised to Antifederalists by constitutional proponents. Final agreement on the first ten amendments to the Constitution—the Bill of Rights—came in September 1789. The first eight amendments dealt with individual liberties, while the ninth and tenth concerned the boundary between federal and state authority. Though ratifying these amendments took another two years, they had the immediate effect of solidifying a sense of national unity. The Constitution deliberately left all individual voting rights decisions to the states to avoid the complications in imposing one national voting law. Most states maintained some sort of property qualification for voting, the one exception being New Jersey, which for a time enfranchised all free inhabitants worth more than £50, including free blacks and unmarried women. By 1807, however, the New Jersey legislature had redefined voting rights to exclude women and blacks.

**THE REPUBLICAN WIFE AND MOTHER** Women's exclusion from politics did not mean that they had no civic role or responsibility. Courtship, marriage, and motherhood were all reevaluated in a republican context. Writers claimed that republican women's most important role was to reform and sustain the morality and manners of men and emphasized the importance of mothers as the teachers of virtuous sons. Thus, women's domestic obligations were instilled with political meaning, and literacy and knowledge for women were encouraged, but only in the service of improved maternal duty. Traditional gender relations remained unaltered.

***Sources of Economic Change, pp. 260–262*** The 1790s witnessed new prosperity and economic growth, with changes in finance and growth in agriculture and transportation.

**COMMERCIAL AGRICULTURE** For most of the eighteenth century, American farmers engaged in a local market economy, often bartering their produce for luxury and manufactured goods. Beginning in the 1790s, however, increasing numbers of farmers turned to large-scale commercial farming, especially in grain and cotton production. European population growth and the concomitant increase in the demand for food provided a market, as did the disruptions caused by the Napoleonic Wars. The increase in overseas grain trade generated a host of new jobs in related areas as the number of millers, coopers, and ship and wagon builders expanded. Thanks to Eli Whitney's invention of the cotton gin in 1793, the United States by the turn of the century was well on its way to becoming one of the largest exporters of cotton in the world.

**TRANSPORTATION** The prosperity brought by grain and cotton exports applied only to places within thirty miles of navigable waterways or the cost and thus highlighted the need to improve transportation systems. In the 1790s, road building commenced, and within a few years, a network of roadways had evolved, especially in southern New England and the mid-Atlantic states. Road building greatly facilitated westward migration, and by 1800, four new states became sufficiently populated to join the Union. Because of low passenger demand, road building and other forms of transportation in the South lagged far behind the North. Cotton and tobacco planters continued to rely on rivers to move their products, which reinforced the economic dominance of property owners fronting the eastern waterways.

**MERCHANTS AND CAPITAL** The increase in overseas trade stimulated the emergence of a commercial class in major port cities. Dominating this burgeoning class were wealthy merchants who imported and exported goods and owned some of the ships that carried the goods. The creation of the new federal government was a boon to business because all the obstacles to interstate trade were removed. New investment opportunities appeared not only in mercantile trade but also in such areas as road construction, stagecoach lines, and textile mills. The rise of commercial banks met the need for investment capital and further stimulated the growing economy.

***Hamilton's Political Economy, pp. 263–269*** In 1790, the government changed its temporary home from New York to Philadelphia. Long-range plans called for a capital on the Potomac River between Maryland and Virginia. Meanwhile, a major controversy over issues of economic policy was brewing, creating political fissures in the new government. At its center was Alexander Hamilton, head of the Treasury.

**THE PUBLIC DEBT AND TAXES** As Treasury secretary, Hamilton first turned his attention to the $52 million public debt. He proposed funding the depreciated certificates of debt that the old Congress had issued during and since the war. He also recommended that Revolutionary War state debts be "assumed" by the national government so that state as well as federal bondholders would look to the central government for eventual payment. Hamilton did not envision paying off and thus eliminating the debt but instead hoped to create a large and permanent national debt, new bonds being issued as old ones were paid off. The result, he believed, would be that creditors—the wealthy classes most likely to lend money to the government—would have a permanent stake in seeing the government survive. Though Congress ultimately passed Hamilton's funding and assumption plans, Jefferson, Madison, and others opposed his schemes, asserting that only a few already wealthy men would benefit.

**THE FIRST BANK OF THE UNITED STATES AND THE *REPORT ON MANUFACTURES*** Hamilton's economic agenda also called for the creation of a national Bank of the United States and a program to encourage domestic manufacturing. His proposed bank was a private financial corporation that would work for the public good. Once again his ideas provoked opposition, led by James Madison and Thomas Jefferson, who declared that the bank was unconstitutional. Hamilton countered by arguing that the "necessary and proper" constitutional clause implied that the federal government had the power to create such a bank. Washington agreed, and the bank was chartered for twenty years. Next, Hamilton turned his attention to the nation's long-term economic development and security, which he believed lay in manufacturing. His *Report on Manufactures* mobilized the new powers of the federal government to impose tariffs and grant subsidies on those enterprises engaged in manufacturing, although he had to be careful not to undercut the position of the merchants who were among his main allies. The plan did not pass Congress.

**THE WHISKEY REBELLION** To meet the interest payments on the national debt, Hamilton proposed a 25 percent excise tax on whiskey and other distilled spirits. Western farmers began protesting the measure soon after its passage. Opposition climaxed in 1794 with the so-called Whiskey Rebellion, when western Pennsylvania farmers refused to pay the tax and began terrorizing tax collectors. These actions represented a major challenge to federal authority. At Hamilton's urging, President Washington called out a militia of nearly fifteen thousand and personally accompanied the army into Pennsylvania. By the time the militia arrived, protesting farmers had dispersed and the rebellion quickly collapsed. Nevertheless, the Whiskey Rebellion was an initial example of what would be a continuing conflict: the tension between minority rights and majority rule.

***Conflicts West, East, and South, pp. 269–274*** Washington's second term, which began in 1793, proved to be one of constant challenges and crises, both at home and abroad. On the western frontier, a powerful confederation of Indians resisted white encroachments on their lands. Simultaneously, conflicts between France and England almost forced the United States into another war. To the South, the Haitian Revolution roused fears of racial war among southern slave owners.

**TO THE WEST: THE INDIANS** By the Treaty of Paris of 1783, England had ceded all land east of the Mississippi to the United States, but a substantial portion of that land was inhabited by Indian tribes. As the growing white population moved into western lands, skirmishes with the Indians increased. In the fall of 1791, General Arthur St. Clair led an army against the Miami and Shawnee Indians but was ambushed and completely routed in the worst U.S. defeat in the long history of Indian wars. In the 1794 Battle of Fallen Timbers, General Anthony Wayne, with some 3,500 men, soundly defeating the Indian confederation. The following summer, the tribes reluctantly agreed in the Treaty of Greenville to abandon most of their territory in Ohio in exchange for treaty goods.

**ACROSS THE ATLANTIC: FRANCE AND ENGLAND** European events exacerbated political polarization on the domestic front when England and Revolutionary France went to war in 1793, raising the question of whether the United States should support the French. During the American Revolution, the colonies had promised to aid France if that country were ever under attack; now, however, the Washington administration decided on a policy of neutrality. Many Americans, believing the United States was honor-bound and ideologically committed to the French cause, organized pro-French political clubs. Washington promulgated the Neutrality Proclamation, but Americans continued to trade with France and the French West Indies. In 1793 and 1794, England vented its anger at the United States's narrow interpretation of neutrality by seizing hundreds of American vessels in the vicinity of the French West Indies. Washington then dispatched John Jay to resolve the crisis and negotiate a treaty with Britain.

**THE JAY TREATY** As the administration's emissary, John Jay was to secure agreement about general commercial ties between the two countries and to negotiate compensation for the seizure of American ships. Jay negotiated a long and complex treaty in 1794 that was more favorable to Great Britain than to the United States. The opposition condemned the treaty unanimously, accusing the administration of betraying France and the American people in exchange for improved trading status that would benefit only merchants. In the end, the treaty just barely passed in Congress with the vote in both houses divided along precisely the lines of the Hamilton-Jefferson split on economic policy.

**TO THE SOUTH: THE HAITIAN REVOLUTION** French St. Domingue, the French-controlled western part of Hispaniola, erupted in a complicated revolution in 1791. Approximately 30,000 whites ruled St. Domingue, which also harbored a population of nearly half a million slaves, two-thirds of them of African birth. There were also 28,000 freed coloreds (*gens de couleur*) of mixed race, who had some economic power but no political clout. The French Revolution inspired white colonists to rebel against the royalist government; then the free coloreds rebelled; they were followed by an enormous slave uprising. By 1793, there was a civil war involving the French, the Spanish, and the British in addition to local inhabitants. Americans were horrified by the revolt, which heightened fears of a slave rebellion in the United States.

***Federalists and Republicans, pp. 275–281*** The Jay Treaty controversy proved to be the final catalyst for the formation of political parties, despite the widespread belief among the elite that parties were a curse to republican government. Washington's decision not to run again opened the door to serious partisan electioneering, as both factions, now known as Federalists and Republicans, sought the presidency for one of their own.

**THE ELECTION OF 1796** The 1796 election pitted Federalist candidate John Adams against Republican Thomas Jefferson. While the two contestants remained above the fray, their supporters worked to ensure their respective candidates' and parties' success. Since the people did not vote directly for the president, partisan maneuvering took place in the electoral college, where Alexander Hamilton tried to manipulate the election of Thomas Pinckney, Adams's "running mate." Not only did Hamilton's scheme fail, but it caused Adams to win and his rival Jefferson to become the vice president. Adams promised to rise above party strife, and to demonstrate his commitment, he retained Washington's cabinet, not realizing that all three members were Hamilton loyalists. Adams and Jefferson attempted to work together, but the influence of the Hamiltonian cabinet made such an alliance impossible.

**THE XYZ AFFAIR** Soon after taking office, Adams confronted angry French reaction to the Jay Treaty. In retaliation, France harassed American shipping, especially in the Caribbean where hundreds of U.S. vessels were seized. When negotiations with the French failed, Adams convened a special session of Congress, recommending military and defensive measures. He also continued attempts at negotiation, sending three commissioners to France. The French government, however, was still angered at the American betrayal and insulted the American diplomats by demanding bribes before talks could take place. The XYZ Affair, as it became known, led to public cries in the United States, especially among the Federalists, for war. As a result of American mobilization, an unofficial "Quasi War" with France broke out at sea, mostly in the Caribbean, with American ships seizing French merchant ships.

**THE ALIEN AND SEDITION ACTS** One of the most serious domestic ramifications of the Quasi War was the passage of the Alien and Sedition Acts, which Federalists argued were essential to maintain national security during this turbulent time. The Sedition Act punished "false" criticism of the government with jail times and fines and was used mostly against Republican newspaper editors. The Alien Acts imposed longer periods for naturalization and allowed the president to deport without trial foreigners thought to be a danger to the country. These acts were deployed to harass French immigrants in the United States and discourage others from coming. With the Virginia and Kentucky Resolutions, Jefferson and Madison opposed both the Alien and Sedition Acts on the grounds that they violated the Bill of Rights, but to little effect. In January 1799, peace overtures from France arrived, which Adams accepted, thus ending the Quasi War. However, in accepting peace, Adams lost the support of his own party and lost the election of 1800 to Thomas Jefferson.

## *Conclusion: Parties Nonetheless*

The foreign and domestic crises of the 1790s gave rise to political parties, a concept the writers of the Constitution abhorred for they believed factionalism would result in the Republic's demise. The Federalists grew out of the supporters of the Constitution in 1788, and they dominated Congress and the presidency through the 1790s, supporting initiatives to strengthen the economy and the federal government. Opposition to the whiskey tax, the Jay Treaty, and the Alien and Sedition Acts coalesced into the Republican Party, which was united by an Antifederalist wariness of a powerful national government. By 1800, the labels Federalist and Republican denoted not only competing philosophies of government but also the proper names of political parties.

## *Chronology Activity*

Read the annotated chronology, and answer the multiple-choice questions.

1789 Washington inaugurated president. Washington was elected unanimously by the electoral college. To many Americans, he embodied the republican ideal of disinterested, public-spirited leadership.

French Revolution begins. The French Revolution led to foreign-policy disagreements between Americans who supported the anti-monarchical revolution and those who felt that it was too radical and, eventually, too violent.

First Congress meets in New York City.

1790 Hamilton's funding and assumption plans approved. Hamilton's plans to bolster the American economy were extremely controversial. They benefited primarily the rich and raised the taxes of ordinary Americans.

Government moves from New York to Philadelphia.

1791 Bill of Rights ratified by states. The Bill of Rights had been demanded by seven states as a condition of ratifying the Constitution. The passage of the Bill of Rights was a unifying force in the new nation.

Bank of the United States chartered by Congress. The Bank of the United States was a part of Hamilton's economic plan. The bank was privately held but served the public functions of holding government revenues and regulating credit and interest and issuing reliable currency.

St. Clair's defeat by Ohio Indians. St. Clair's defeat in Ohio was the single worst American loss in the Indian-U.S. wars. It contributed to Americans' extreme fear of Indians.

Congress passes whiskey tax. The 25 percent whiskey tax was Hamilton's method of funding the expanded state debt. It was extremely unpopular with grain farmers, who were forced to pay it up-front to distilleries.

1793 Washington's second term begins. Washington's unanimous reelection to the presidency was a rare show of unity in the federal government.

War breaks out between France and England. The war between France and England increased domestic political woes, as Americans argued over which side, if either, to support.

1793 Washington issues Neutrality Proclamation. The Neutrality Proclamation was supposed to assure both France and England that the United States intended to stay out of the war between the two countries and so protect trading relationships with both countries. However, to the belligerents, trade itself looked like a contribution to the other side's war effort, and France and England both eventually seized American merchant ships in retaliation.

Battle of Fallen Timbers; U.S. victory over Indians in Ohio. The defeat at Fallen Timbers was a devastating loss for the Ohio Indians. It forced them to enter negotiations from a position of weakness and eventually cede most of Ohio to the Americans.

1794 Whiskey Rebellion in western Pennsylvania. This outbreak of violence was directed at John Neville, a tax collector who was overly enthusiastic about collecting the hated whiskey excise tax. The government responded with a show of force. While the rebellion dissipated without violence, it was a sign of the continued disagreement over how far citizens could go in protesting the actions of a republican government and how much the government could do in return.

1795 Treaty of Greenville with Indians. In the Treaty of Greenville, Ohio Indians ceded nearly all of their land to the Americans in exchange for treaty goods intended to increase Indian dependence on the United States government.

Jay Treaty with England. The Jay Treaty was a much-hated agreement between England and the United States, which offered major concessions to England and got few in return. It helped to crystallize the emerging American political parties.

1796 John Adams elected president, Thomas Jefferson vice president. Adams and Jefferson were rivals and represented different political points of view. Alexander Hamilton's meddling in the electoral college, however, caused them to be the first and second vote-getters, respectively, and thus in the two top administrative positions at the same time.

1797 XYZ affair with France. The XYZ affair with France involved the French government's demand of bribes in exchange for stopping the seizure of American ships. It mobilized public opinion against the French.

1798 Quasi War with France. This was John Adams's reaction to the XYZ Affair and the continued seizure of American ships. Twenty naval warships were launched in the Caribbean to fight French privateers, but war was never officially declared.

Alien and Sedition Acts. Because the United States did not declare war against France, the administration could not silence its critics under treason laws. Thus, congressional Federalists passed the Alien and Sedition Acts to serve the same purpose. They were used to fine, imprison, and deport dissenters.

Virginia and Kentucky Resolutions. Thomas Jefferson and James Madison believed the Alien and Sedition Acts were unconstitutional but did not have the congressional or judicial support to get them overturned at the national level. They turned instead to the states, drafting resolutions passed by the Virginia and Kentucky legislatures, which declared that the federal law violated state bills of rights.

1800 Election campaign between Adams and Jefferson. The 1800 election was openly conducted along partisan lines, with Federalist and Republican leaders meeting to pick candidates for president and vice president.

1801 Jefferson elected president. Adams had lost a great deal of support among Federalists because of his willingness to end the war with France by negotiation. His candidacy was doomed to failure.

***Chronology Questions*** Choose the letter of the best answer.

1. The ratification of the Bill of Rights, an action that helped unify the nation, occurred in
   a. 1785.
   b. 1791.
   c. 1799.
   d. 1804.

2. Which of the following events was the last to occur?
   a. The French Revolution begins.
   b. The First Congress meets in New York City.
   c. Washington is inaugurated president.
   d. War breaks out between France and England.

3. After George Washington's two terms, John Adams was elected president in
   a. 1791.
   b. 1793.
   c. 1796.
   d. 1800.

4. What is the correct order for the following events?
   1. The XYZ affair with France occurs.
   2. The Quasi War breaks out.
   3. Hamilton's funding and assumption plans are approved.
   4. The Bank of the United States is chartered by Congress.
   a. 2, 1, 4, 3
   b. 2, 4, 1, 3
   c. 1, 4, 3, 2
   d. 3, 4, 1, 2

5. In 1801, after Adams lost his Federalist support by negotiating to end the war with France,
   a. the government moved from New York to Philadelphia.
   b. Washington's second term began.
   c. the XYZ affair with France occurred.
   d. Jefferson was elected president.

6. What is the correct order for the following events?
   1. Washington issues the Neutrality Proclamation.
   2. The Jay Treaty with England is signed.
   3. War breaks out between France and England.
   4. The French Revolution breaks out.
   a. 4, 3, 1, 2
   b. 3, 1, 4, 2
   c. 3, 2, 1, 4
   d. 2, 4, 1, 3

7. The Quasi War with France broke out in
   a. 1789.
   b. 1793.
   c. 1798.
   d. 1805.

8. What is the correct order for the following events?
   1. The Treaty of Greenville is signed with the Indians.
   2. St. Clair is defeated by Ohio Indians.
   3. Jefferson is elected president.
   4. The Battle of Fallen Timbers is fought.
   a. 4, 1, 3, 2
   b. 2, 4, 1, 3
   c. 3, 2, 4, 1
   d. 1, 2, 4, 3

9. The whiskey tax of 1791 led to the Whiskey Rebellion in western Pennsylvania, which occurred in
   a. 1791.
   b. 1794.
   c. 1797.
   d. 1801.

10. What is the correct order for the following events?
   1. The Alien and Sedition Acts are enacted.
   2. The Jay Treaty is signed with England.
   3. The Quasi War with France occurs.
   4. The Virginia and Kentucky Resolutions are passed.
   a. 2, 3, 1, 4
   b. 4, 1, 3, 2
   c. 4, 2, 1, 3
   d. 1, 2, 4, 3

***Defining Terms*** Match each term with the correct definition.

✓XYZ Affair
✓*Report on Public Credit*
✓*Report on Manufactures*
✓Napoleonic Wars
✓Bank of the United States
✓Lancaster Turnpike
✓Little Turtle
✓assumption plan
✓public virtue
✓Alien and Sedition Acts
✓Bill of Rights
✓New Jersey Constitution
✓Neutrality Proclamation
✓Virginia and Kentucky Resolutions
✓Quasi War
✓Haitian Revolution
✓Whiskey Rebellion
✓Eli Whitney
✓Judith Sargent Murray
✓Thomas Pinckney
✓General Anthony Wayne
✓General Arthur St. Clair
✓Alexander Hamilton
✓banknotes
✓green-seed cotton

1. Washington's choice for Secretary of the Treasury who was a New Yorker known for his brilliance and financial astuteness. The position he took was the hardest, since revenue problems had been responsible for undermining the confederation government. Alexander Hamilton

2. The first ten amendments to the Constitution, passed through Congress in 1789 and ratified by the states in 1791. The amendments were a concession to Antifederalists and had the effect of cementing a sense of national unity. Bill of Rights

3. Until 1807, this was written in such a way that all free inhabitants worth over £50 could vote. This included free blacks and unmarried women: as long as they had the financial standing, they were enfranchised. This was in contrast to most states, which deliberately prevented slaves, servants, blacks, women, and other groups from voting. New Jersey constitution

4. The author of a series of essays on female education. At a time when most proponents of female education presented it as an act of duty to the family, she argued that women should be educated to make them rational and self-confident beings, poised to become the equals of men. Judith Sargent Murray

5. The masculine quality that allowed men to make the intelligent and selfless decisions that would ensure liberty in a republican government. Writers in the 1790s argued that women, while not possessors of public virtue themselves, could help instill it in men by reforming the morals and manners of the men in their lives. public virtue

6. Two decades of continental warfare centered around France and England, the consequences of which initially left the United States in the financially advantageous position of being the only neutral shipper in the Atlantic trade. Napoleonic wars

7. A strain of cotton that grew well in drier, inland regions of the southern United States but was extremely difficult to clean. After the invention of the cotton gin in 1793, the problem was solved, and cotton production grew rapidly. green-seed cotton

8. The inventor of the cotton gin, which solved the problem of cleaning hardy green-seed cotton fibers. The cotton gin increased southern cotton production but also spread slavery. Eli Whitney

9. The first private toll road in the United States, finished in 1794. Lancaster Turnpike

10. The paper currency that banks issued as loans. These were backed by the gold and silver paid into the bank by stockholders. Because banks issued two or three times as much money in these as they held in hard money, the spread of these fueled the American economy of the 1790s by creating new money. bank notes

11. Hamilton's proposal for dealing with the sizeable public debt. He suggested funding the debt at full value and paying interest on it to bondholders, a move that inspired a great deal of resentment because it benefited the wealthy speculators who had purchased IOUs cheaply from their original holders. Report on Public Credit

12. Hamilton's suggestion that the national debt should be widened to include the $25 million that state governments owed to farmers, merchants, and moneylenders. Although some states had paid off their debts, others had made almost no headway. The plan consolidated federal power over the states and also demanded that the federal government exercise its powers of taxation to meet the interest payments on the large national debt. assumption plan

13. One of Hamilton's proposals for strengthening the American economy. Hamilton wanted to establish a way to serve the public interest by serving as a repository for the federal government's revenues. Although Jefferson believed that this was unconstitutional, Washington approved of it, and it was chartered in 1791. Bank of the United States

14. Hamilton's proposal for improving the American economy, this was concerned with strengthening American manufacturing to reduce dependence on British imports. It was the only one of Hamilton's plans that was not approved by Congress. Report on Manufactures

15. The event that exploded in western Pennsylvania in 1791 after Hamilton convinced Congress to pass legislation funding the national debt by means of a 25 percent excise tax on whiskey. Western farmers had an abundance of wheat and rye, which they often converted into whiskey; they found themselves paying high taxes in cash at the distillery, a severe economic hardship for many of them, and they resented funding a national debt that benefited wealthy speculators. President Washington took this event so seriously that he personally headed an army to put it down, although it had dispersed by the time he arrived. This highlighted the question of what citizens of a republic could or could not do to protest what they saw as unjust governmental actions. Whiskey Rebellion

16. The American governor of the Northwest Territory who was appointed to displace the Indians and clear the way for permanent American settlement in Ohio in 1791. He led two thousand men into the worst American defeat in the entire history of the U.S.-Indian wars, losing 55 percent of his force in a few hours. General Arthur St. Clair

17. The second commander of the United States military in Ohio. He was headstrong and rambunctious, with a reputation for heavy drinking and strict discipline. He defeated a confederated army of Indians at the Battle of Fallen Timbers in August 1794 and forced the concession of most of the Ohio territory in the Treaty of Greenville. General Anthony Wayne

18. The chief of the Miami tribe who commented that the alcohol provided to Indians under the Treaty of Greenville had killed more Indians than the war had. Little Turtle

19. Washington's 1793 declaration of the American position in the war between Great Britain and France. This was undercut by the American practice of trading with the French in the West Indies and did not protect American merchant ships from harassment by the British. Neutrality Proclamation

20. A complex revolution that broke out in 1791 in Saint Domingue, the western part of the Caribbean island of Hispaniola. Starting as an antimonarchical revolution led by the islands whites, in 1793 it turned into a violent slave revolt involving French, Spanish, and British troops. The revolt caused Americans to fear the outbreak of a slave rebellion in their own society. Haitian Revolution

21. The Federalist who was John Adams's informal running mate in the 1796 election. Hamilton's attempts to get him elected president instead of Adams backfired and caused Thomas Jefferson to end up with the vice presidency instead. Thomas Pinckney

22. An attempt on the part of the French government to demand a large bribe and a loan from the American government in return for a treaty and an end to the French seizure of ships carrying British goods. It caused an anti-French backlash in the United States. XYZ Affair

23. The United States's first undeclared war. In 1798, after French officials attempted to force the American government to provide them with both a large bribe and a loan, twenty naval warships were launched into the Caribbean. The conflict ended in 1799 when President Adams responded to peace overtures from France but not before tensions between Federalists and Republicans had been considerably exacerbated. Quasi war

24. Legislation passed by the Federalist-dominated Congress to suppress criticism of the administration. The laws were designed to make false criticism of the government illegal and to ease the deportation of aliens. Both were used against opponents of the Quasi War. Alien and Sedition Acts

25. Responses condemning the Alien and Sedition Acts. They were drafted by Thomas Jefferson and James Madison and submitted to the federal government by means of the states in 1798. The responses tested the idea that state legislatures could judge the constitutionality of federal laws and nullify those that were in conflict with the Bill of Rights. Virginia and Kentucky Resolutions

## Chapter Review

***Multiple-Choice*** Choose the letter of the best answer.

1. When President George Washington picked heads for the departments of war, treasury, and state, he chose
   a. his supporters.
   b. only Federalists.
   c. only men who shared his philosophical views.
   d. talented and experienced individuals. (circled)

2. The hardest job in President George Washington's government was heading the
   a. Department of War.
   b. Treasury. (circled)
   c. Department of State.
   d. Supreme Court.

3. For attorney general, President George Washington picked Edmund Randolph, a Virginian who had
   a. been an Antifederalist. (circled)
   b. refused to attend the Constitutional Convention.
   c. neither.
   d. both.

4. Vice president John Adams's job was to
   a. coordinate the different departments.
   b. participate in legislative debates.
   c. preside over the Senate. (circled)
   d. preside over the House of Representatives.

5. Delegates at the 1787 Philadelphia convention had neglected to include a bill of rights on the grounds that
   a. the government would never become despotic.
   b. individual rights were not important.
   c. many states already protected individual rights.
   d. they did not have the time to write one.

6. The passage of the Bill of Rights had the immediate effect of
   a. causing divisions between Federalists and Antifederalists.
   b. sparking a series of rural uprisings.
   c. cementing a sense of national unity.
   d. creating a more democratic government.

7. One important omission in the Bill of Rights was the failure to include the right to
   a. freedom of speech.
   b. peaceable assembly.
   c. freedom of press.
   d. vote.

8. At the time the Bill of Rights was enacted, state property qualifications for voting excluded
   a. poor farmers, widows, and free blacks.
   b. free blacks and the urban middle class.
   c. the urban middle class, slaves, and tenants.
   d. slaves, tenants, wives, and propertyless wage laborers.

9. Married women in New Jersey owned no property and thus had no political rights because by law
   a. their husbands held title to everything.
   b. they could not inherit.
   c. their children held title to everything.
   d. the state held title to everything.

10. After 1807, New Jersey changed its voting law to
    a. enfranchise free black men.
    b. enfranchise women.
    c. disenfranchise both blacks and women.
    d. disenfranchise women.

11. According to writers in the 1790s, American women contributed to the nation's political liberty by
    a. upholding public virtue.
    b. voting sensibly.
    c. dutifully obeying their husbands and rulers.
    d. remaining ignorant.

12. Proponents of the 1790s model of womanhood based on republican ideals helped to legitimize female
    a. political participation.
    b. education.
    c. equality.
    d. employment.

13. Most of the writers of the Constitution believed that parties were a _____ force.
    a. dangerous
    b. neutral
    c. positive
    d. democratic

14. One powerful source of unity in the United States during the 1790s was veneration for the _____.
    a. Senate
    b. Supreme Court justices
    c. vice president
    d. president

15. To lead the Department of State, President Washington chose _____, who was serving as minister to France.
    a. Alexander Hamilton
    b. Thomas Jefferson
    c. General Henry Knox
    d. Edmund Randolph

16. Seven states had ratified the Constitution on the condition that a _____ be swiftly incorporated.
    a. bill of rights
    b. debt-funding bill
    c. amendment removing property restrictions on suffrage
    d. equal rights clause

17. The first U.S. Congress would not consider proposed amendments by state constitutional ratifying conventions that would change the _____ of the new government.
    a. pay scale
    b. location
    c. structure
    d. officials

18. The _____ constitution enfranchised all free inhabitants worth over £50, including free blacks and unmarried women.
    a. New York
    b. Massachusetts
    c. Virginia
    d. New Jersey

19. In the 1790s, male and female writers argued that _____ bound wives to their husbands.
    a. duty
    b. force
    c. affection
    d. nothing

20. In the 1790s, _____, a feminine quality, was seen as a way to encourage public virtue in men.
    a. obedience
    b. intelligence
    c. public power
    d. sexual chastity

21. A series of essays by Judith Sargent Murray of Massachusetts favored education that would make women into the equals of men but justified the measure on the basis of _____.
    a. economic necessity
    b. the creation of better voters
    c. the need for more teachers
    d. family duty

22. Proponents of the new republican motherhood argued that women must _____ their husbands.
    a. argue with
    b. defer to
    c. distrust
    d. be the social equals of

23. In the second half of the eighteenth century, country store owners were paid in
    a. cash at the time of the transaction.
    b. periodic cash payments.
    c. luxury items.
    d. "country goods" or periodic cash payments.

24. The traditional pattern of local market exchange was altered in the 1790s as a result of
    a. a dramatic decrease in the international price of grain.
    b. a dramatic increase in the international price of grain.
    c. food shortages in the eastern United States.
    d. increased imports from England and France.

25. Food prices in Europe rose sharply after 1793, when France and England entered two decades of
    a. natural disasters.
    b. economic depression.
    c. the Napoleonic Wars.
    d. urbanization.

26. Until the mid-1790s, cotton was an extremely labor-intensive crop in the inland South because
    a. the variety that thrived there was hard to clean.
    b. no variety of cotton thrived in drier, inland regions.
    c. even slave labor could not remove its seeds.
    d. it had little ready market.

27. Between 1792 and 1800, cotton production in the South increased from 138,228 to 35 million pounds due to
    a. an increase in the number of slaves to clean the cotton.
    b. a new variety of cotton that grew faster.
    c. improved farming technology.
    d. the invention of a machine to separate the seeds from the fiber.

28. The cash economy that prospered in the 1790s due to grain and cotton exports was initially confined to areas near
    a. the mountains.
    b. navigable waterways or the coast.
    c. major cities.
    d. local roads.

29. In the 1790s, many new roads were built to help transport people and goods
    a. from north to south.
    b. from east to west.
    c. toward the east coast.
    d. into Canada.

30. Road building and commercial stagecoach travel remained rudimentary south of the Potomac River in 1800 because
    a. there were no goods to be transported.
    b. there was no need to travel outside of the area.
    c. there was low passenger demand.
    d. southerners distrusted innovation.

31. The strength of the European grain and cotton trades contributed to the growth of the
    a. commercial classes in seacoast cities.
    b. propertyless working class.
    c. number of subsistence farmers.
    d. number of artisans.

32. The creation of the federal government affected merchants, transportation companies, and textile mills because it
    a. encouraged states to erect trade barriers.
    b. guaranteed the free movement of goods across state borders.
    c. stifled the creation of business opportunities.
    d. no longer allowed merchants to have ownership in seagoing vessels.

33. The need for investment capital grew in the 1790s because
    a. Americans had overcome their suspicion of banks.
    b. there were many new investment opportunities.
    c. there was a shortage of gold and silver.
    d. the economy was contracting.

34. As the need for capital rose in the 1790s, banks created new money for the economy by issuing
    a. hard currency.
    b. banknotes with no hard money backing.
    c. only as many banknotes as they could back with hard money.
    d. two to three times as much money in banknotes as they held in hard currency.

35. The economic _____ of the 1790s was in sharp contrast to the previous decade.
    a. instability
    b. prosperity
    c. depression
    d. stagnation

36. Beginning in the mid-eighteenth century, most farmers moved from self-sufficiency to _____ at local stores and in nearby towns.
    a. market transactions
    b. investment opportunities
    c. international banking
    d. cooperative ownership

37. In the late eighteenth century, _____ prices were generally rising in Europe because of war and population growth.
    a. manufactured items'
    b. clothing
    c. luxury goods
    d. food

38. The Napoleonic Wars left the United States with a near-monopoly on the _____ trade.
    a. Mediterranean
    b. Asian
    c. Indian fur
    d. Atlantic

39. Eli Whitney's invention of the cotton gin allowed faster _____.
    a. cotton picking
    b. production of cotton thread
    c. separation of cotton seeds from fiber
    d. cotton weeding in the fields

40. The _____ textile industry provided a ready market for the abundance of raw cotton after the invention of the cotton gin.
   a. English
   b. American
   c. French
   d. Spanish

41. Southern cotton and tobacco planters relied on _____ to move produce to market.
   a. new roads
   b. turnpikes
   c. stagecoaches
   d. rivers

42. The surge in overseas grain and cotton trade stimulated the growth of the commercial classes in _____.
   a. western towns
   b. seacoast cities
   c. the southern backcountry
   d. inland areas

43. The creation of _____ allowed for an increase in the volume of trade by finally removing all obstacles to interstate business alliances.
   a. large corporations
   b. a national bank
   c. new state governments
   d. the federal government

44. The development of _____ made it possible for American businesses to get the investment capital they needed.
   a. commercial law
   b. commercial banking
   c. a nationwide system of credit
   d. a national currency

45. As secretary of the treasury, Alexander Hamilton first tackled a public debt of nearly $52 million owed to
   a. foreign creditors.
   b. foreign and American creditors.
   c. American creditors.
   d. the American government.

46. Alexander Hamilton's 1790 *Report on Public Credit* recommended that the $52 million public debt be
   a. ignored.
   b. paid off as rapidly as possible.
   c. defaulted on.
   d. funded at full value.

47. Alexander Hamilton's plan for dealing with the problem of depreciated IOUs was calculated to appeal to
   a. members of the clergy who had loaned the government money during the war.
   b. speculators who had bet that they might rise in value.
   c. middling sorts who had invested in them to support the new government.
   d. the poor, who had accepted them as pay during the war.

48. The effect of Alexander Hamilton's "assumption plan" was to
   a. call for the federal government to assume state debts.
   b. consolidate federal power over the states.
   c. add $25 million to the federal debt.
   d. all of the above.

49. To meet the interest payments on his proposed $77 million national debt, Alexander Hamilton convinced Congress to
   a. tax distilled spirits.
   b. raise import duties.
   c. tax wine and beer.
   d. impose a stamp tax.

50. James Madison and other national leaders objected to Alexander Hamilton's financial plan because it would
   a. profit speculators and encourage spendthrift behavior.
   b. profit speculators and lead to high taxation.
   c. lead to high taxation and encourage spendthrift behavior.
   d. encourage spendthrift behavior and corrupt the legislature.

51. Alexander Hamilton intended for the Bank of America to be a
    a. windfall for the wealthy.
    b. public bank.
    c. way to bribe legislators.
    d. private bank that worked primarily for the public good.

52. Alexander Hamilton did not expect that the Bank of America would
    a. exert control over credit.
    b. give the wealthy an investment in the nation.
    c. stabilize the value of paper currency.
    d. equitably distribute financial resources.

53. Alexander Hamilton's unsuccessful *Report on Manufactures* was designed to encourage
    a. people to purchase European goods.
    b. cottage industries in people's homes.
    c. the production of American-made goods.
    d. greater agricultural output.

54. When Alexander Hamilton's whiskey excise tax was imposed on farmers, their most common response was to
    a. pay it willingly.
    b. pay it grudgingly.
    c. evade it.
    d. murder tax collectors.

55. When Alexander Hamilton realized that the revenue yield from his newly enacted whiskey excise tax was far less than anticipated, he
    a. tightened up prosecution of tax evaders.
    b. abandoned the law.
    c. modified the law.
    d. imposed martial law.

56. The Whiskey Rebellion foreshadowed a conflict that would plague the new nation,
    a. the right to consume spirits versus Christian values.
    b. the tension over tariffs on imported whiskey and rum.
    c. minority rights versus majority rule.
    d. the right to make domestic whiskey versus the importers of European spirits.

57. In the 1780s, paper IOUs and certificates of debt were worth as little as _____ of the original value.
    a. one-twentieth
    b. one-third
    c. one-half
    d. three-quarters

58. After the Revolutionary War, _____ held the largest portions of the national debt.
    a. the original purchasers of government bonds
    b. farmers
    c. shipping agents
    d. wealthy white speculators

59. Alexander Hamilton wanted the federal government to assume _____ debts.
    a. rich individuals'
    b. its own
    c. state
    d. no

60. Congressman and former ally James Madison objected to Alexander Hamilton's funding plan because it would give windfall profits to speculators and lead to _____.
    a. high taxes
    b. war with the Indians
    c. political wrangling along party lines
    d. higher prices

61. In Alexander Hamilton's proposed national bank, 20 percent of the bank's stock would be bought by _____ and the rest would come from private investors.
    a. the federal government
    b. the states
    c. local communities
    d. foreigners

62. According to Alexander Hamilton's plan, the national bank's directors who were not appointed by the government would be chosen from among the _____.
    a. voting public
    b. national representatives
    c. Treasury Department
    d. private stockholders

63. Thomas Jefferson advised President Washington that it was _____ to create a national bank.
    a. unconstitutional
    b. morally wrong
    c. wise
    d. pointless

64. Alexander Hamilton's 1791 *Report on Manufactures* mobilized the power of the federal government to encourage _____.
    a. the purchase of manufactured goods from abroad
    b. local manufacturing
    c. people to go into farming
    d. rapid industrialization in the South

65. _____ were extremely angry about the whiskey excise tax.
    a. Cotton farmers
    b. Urban drinkers
    c. New England congressmen
    d. Grain farmers

66. The Whiskey Rebels felt that their behavior was justified because they were being subject to _____.
    a. tyrannical government
    b. oppressive taxation
    c. military rule
    d. minority rule

67. After the Treaty of Paris, British Indian agents in southern Ohio assured the Shawnees and the Delawares that
    a. Indians had the right to occupy land over the claims of American settlers.
    b. the British maintained political control over the area.
    c. the British had not given the area to the American government.
    d. Americans would not want to move to the territory.

68. In the face of the strong desire of settlers to move westward, General Arthur St. Clair's mission was to
    a. displace Indians to allow permanent American settlement in Ohio.
    b. displace British Indian agents in Ohio.
    c. start a war with the Indians in Ohio.
    d. teach Indians and American settlers in Ohio how to coexist.

69. When General Anthony Wayne became the commander of the U.S. forces in Ohio, he asserted that a permanent peace with the Indians would be possible only when the
    a. American army was more disciplined.
    b. American government set up reservations.
    c. settlers learned to behave more cautiously toward the Indians.
    d. Indians were convinced of American superiority.

70. The 1794 Battle of Fallen Timbers was a
    a. major defeat for the Americans.
    b. moderate defeat for the Americans.
    c. major defeat for the Indians.
    d. draw.

71. The 1795 Treaty of Greenville caused widespread misery among Indians because the American government
    a. never observed its obligations under the treaty.
    b. often paid its annual allowance in liquor.
    c. took the entire Ohio territory.
    d. introduced guns to the Indian tribes in the region.

72. Many Americans reacted positively to the outbreak of the French Revolution in 1789 because
    a. it overthrew the Catholic Church.
    b. France almost immediately attacked England.
    c. it overthrew monarchy and privilege in the name of republicanism.
    d. it was so much more radical than the American Revolution.

73. The British government expressed its displeasure with the President George Washington's interpretation of neutrality by
    a. declaring war.
    b. ignoring the situation.
    c. capturing merchant ships near France.
    d. capturing merchant ships near the West Indies.

74. John Jay negotiated a treaty with England that was unpopular because
   a. it made no provision for reimbursement for captured ships or lost slaves.
   b. it granted the British eighteen months to withdraw from their western forts.
   c. it called for the repayment of debts Americans owed to the British.
   d. all of the above.

75. John Jay's treaty with the English was beneficial to
   a. American sailors.
   b. merchants in the overseas trade.
   c. western grain farmers.
   d. southern tobacco farmers.

76. The immediate catalyst for the revolution in Saint Domingue was the
   a. Whiskey Rebellion.
   b. French Revolution.
   c. American Revolution.
   d. Jay Treaty.

77. By 1793, the war on Saint Domingue included
   a. French, Spanish, and British troops.
   b. French, Spanish, and American troops.
   c. French and Spanish troops.
   d. French and American troops.

78. The Haitian Revolution sparked
   a. American fears of a slave rebellion.
   b. American slave rebellions.
   c. black conspiracies in the United States.
   d. a strong civil rights movement in the United States.

79. President Washington's second term began in 1793, after a _____ reelection.
   a. hotly contested
   b. narrow
   c. unanimous
   d. moderately favorable

80. General Arthur St. Clair, the governor of the Ohio Territory, was given the task of _____.
   a. making peace with aggrieved Indian tribes in the area
   b. reestablishing the lucrative fur trade
   c. organizing the settlers into townships
   d. clearing out the Indians so that Americans could settle in the area

81. After General Arthur St. Clair's defeat in the Northwest Territory, Washington appointed _____ as commander of the American forces in Ohio.
   a. himself
   b. General Henry Knox
   c. Alexander Hamilton
   d. General Anthony Wayne

82. The decisive action that defeated the confederated Indians in Ohio was the Battle of _____.
   a. Fort Recovery
   b. Fort Greenville
   c. Fallen Timbers
   d. the Maumee River

83. By the terms of the Treaty of Greenville, Northwestern Indian tribes were forced to cede most of _____ to the Americans.
   a. Kentucky
   b. Wisconsin
   c. Ohio
   d. Indiana

84. The French Revolution elevated _____ over monarchy and privilege.
   a. anarchy
   b. pure democracy
   c. republicanism
   d. communism

85. In May 1793, President Washington's _____ and the British capture of U.S. ships near the French West Indies showed that the question of loyalty to France or England was a delicate foreign policy issue.
   a. Neutrality Proclamation
   b. wartime alliance
   c. Democratic Society
   d. pro-British treaty

86. Americans were furious that the Jay Treaty gave the British eighteen months to _____.
   a. stop the impressment of American sailors
   b. vacate their western forts
   c. cease harassing American ships
   d. negotiate for peace with France

87. The western third of the large Caribbean island of _____ became engulfed in revolution starting in 1791.
   a. Hispaniola
   b. Cuba
   c. Barbados
   d. Santo Domingo

88. Haitian _____, led by Toussaint L'Overture, destroyed the northern regions of the island.
   a. slaves
   b. free coloreds
   c. poor whites
   d. rich whites

89. By the time of the election of 1796, a party contest emerged around the issue of
   a. slavery.
   b. support for either France or England.
   c. the national debt.
   d. industrialization.

90. Until the adoption of the Eleventh Amendment in 1804, the vice president was
   a. chosen by voters.
   b. picked by the president.
   c. the second highest vote-getter in the electoral college.
   d. appointed by caucus.

91. Alexander Hamilton exercised a great deal of influence in John Adams's administration because he
   a. was appointed Secretary of the Treasury.
   b. was appointed Secretary of State.
   c. and Adams were political allies.
   d. had influence over all three of Adams's cabinet members.

92. France responded to the Jay Treaty by
   a. accepting it graciously.
   b. attempting to work with pro-French elements in the American government.
   c. seizing American ships carrying British goods.
   d. declaring war on the United States.

93. The XYZ affair involved a
   a. British attempt to bribe American officials in treaty negotiations.
   b. French refusal to recognize the American minister to France.
   c. French attempt to bribe American officials treaty negotiations.
   d. rebellion in Haiti.

94. The Quasi War of 1798 got its name because it was
   a. not fought by a real military branch.
   b. too short to be a real war.
   c. not very important.
   d. of uncertain legal status.

95. Republicans feared that Federalists wanted to build up the army during the Quasi War to
   a. enter a European war.
   b. take more Indian land.
   c. threaten domestic dissenters.
   d. go after tax evaders.

96. Because the war with France was never made legal, pro-French Republicans could not be
   a. harassed.
   b. subject to treason laws.
   c. treated like criminals.
   d. deported.

97. The Sedition Act
   a. extended the waiting period for naturalization.
   b. set punishments for anyone convicted of falsely criticizing the government.
   c. required aliens to register with the federal government.
   d. empowered the president to deport foreigners.

98. The two Alien Acts passed by Congress in 1798 were intended to
   a. harass French immigrants to the United States.
   b. discourage British immigrants from coming to the United States.
   c. make it easier to deport native-born American citizens.
   d. strengthen immigrants' rights.

99. The main targets of the Sedition Act were
  a. foreigners.
  b. Republican politicians.
  c. Republican voters.
  d. Republican newspaper editors.

100. To work against the Alien and Sedition Acts, James Madison and Thomas Jefferson turned to the
  a. Supreme Court.
  b. state courts.
  c. Senate.
  d. state legislatures.

101. By the early 1790s, rival politicians were given the distinctive labels of Federalists and _____.
  a. Antifederalists
  b. Republicans
  c. Democrats
  d. Patriots

102. In 1796, presidential candidates were chosen by _____ and then elected by the electoral college.
  a. informal caucus
  b. popular vote
  c. state legislatures
  d. the Senate

103. In the election of 1796, _____ became president and vice-president.
  a. chief rivals
  b. running mates
  c. John Adams and Thomas Pinckney
  d. Thomas Jefferson and Aaron Burr

104. On becoming president, John Adams retained the same three cabinet members from George Washington's administration without realizing that they were _____ loyalists.
  a. Jay
  b. Hamilton
  c. Pinckney
  d. Jefferson

105. Throughout the 1790s, Federalists and Republicans disagreed most strongly about _____ policy.
  a. foreign
  b. domestic
  c. economic
  d. military

106. The Quasi War's action took place most in the _____.
  a. Atlantic
  b. Caribbean
  c. Chesapeake Bay
  d. English Channel

107. In 1798, when the Federalist-dominated Congress appropriated funds to recruit an army of ten thousand men, the Republicans _____.
  a. supported the measure enthusiastically
  b. objected that the real aim was to quell domestic dissent
  c. had a "wait and see" reaction
  d. trusted the Federalists to do what was best for the nation

108. In 1798, the Federalists hammered out a _____ to muffle opposition to their policies in regard to France.
  a. constitutional amendment
  b. Alien Act
  c. suspension of the Bill of Rights
  d. Sedition Act

109. Thomas Jefferson and James Madison drafted a set of resolutions condemning the Alien and Sedition Acts and had _____ present them to the federal government.
  a. state legislatures
  b. Alexander Hamilton
  c. French immigrants
  d. Supreme Court justices

110. By responding to the French peace initiative in late 1799, John Adams _____ the support of a significant part of his own party.
  a. won
  b. consolidated
  c. lost
  d. did not change

***Short Answer*** Write a paragraph response to each question.

1. How did George Washington go about making appointments to government posts when he became president?
2. What important right did the Bill of Rights omit, and why?
3. What impact did republican ideals of motherhood have on women's position in society in the 1790s?
4. What factors changed grain farmers' patterns of local market exchange in the 1790s?
5. What led to the increase in road building in the 1790s? What effect did the new roads have?
6. How did Americans meet the need for investment capital as the volume and scope of trade, manufacturing, and transportation increased in the new nation?
7. What did Hamilton's *Report on Public Credit* propose doing with the national debt? Why was his plan controversial?
8. How did Hamilton envision the workings of the Bank of the United States, and what did he hope it would contribute to the nation's welfare?
9. What immediate issues sparked the outbreak of the Whiskey Rebellion, and what larger issues did it represent?
10. What happened at the Battle of Fallen Timbers? What were its long-term effects on the confederated Indians who fought there?
11. Why was the outbreak of the French Revolution problematic for the United States?
12. What made the Jay Treaty so unpopular with the American public?
13. How were the rivals John Adams and Thomas Jefferson elected president and vice president in 1796?
14. What was the XYZ Affair? What events caused it?
15. How did the Quasi War lead to the Alien and Sedition Acts?

***Building Historical Skills*** Historians use a variety of sources to think and talk about the past, including maps, illustrations, and written records. Maps provide a variety of different kinds of comparative information in a condensed visual format; reading them requires learning how to sort through this information. To deepen our understanding of the past by supplementing written records, historians frequently interpret material culture, such as a vase or a painting, with techniques borrowed from art history, archaeology, or anthropology. Written records, though familiar as sources, raise their own problems of interpretation. Every document reflects someone's particular perspective or assumptions. It is the historian's task to study and compare each document to other records with other perspectives. The following exercises introduce you to using maps, illustrations, and written documents as sources of information. Use these sources as well as the material in the chapter to think about different themes and topics discussed in the text.

***Map Activity*** Locate the following places on Map 8.2: Western Expansion and Indian Land Cessions to 1810 on page 270 of *The American Promise,* Second Edition.

1. Ohio River
2. Fort Recovery
3. Fallen Timbers
4. Fort Greenville
5. Muskingum River
6. Cincinnati
7. St. Clair's defeat
8. Fort Washington
9. Indiana Territory
10. Michigan Territory

Answer the following questions in paragraphs based on Map 8.2: Western Expansion and Indian Land Cessions to 1810.

**READING THE MAP** Locate the Appalachians. What line of 1763 ran along the mountains? What was that line's purpose, and how well was that purpose met?

**CONNECTIONS** How much did the population of the United States grow between 1770 and 1790? How did this growth affect western settlement?

**WEB LINKS** To explore the topics discussed in the exercise above, visit the Web links noted below.

"Indian Wars in the Northwest Territory"
http://users.anderson.edu/~roebuck/war.html

"Treaty of Greenville, 1795"
http://www.yale.edu/lawweb/avalon/greenvil.htm

***Visual Activity*** The cartoonist depicts a representative body that bears an unfortunate resemblance to a barroom brawl. The two men fighting—Roger Griswold of Connecticut, with the cane, and Matthew Lyon of Vermont, with the fire tongs—are depicted as animalistic. Their hair is standing on end, their noses are elongated into snouts, and their eyes are deeply circled in black. Their audience is no better than they are. The dog in the lower left-hand corner adds to the apparent informality of what ought to be a august gathering, and the man depicted to the dog's left bears a marked resemblance to the canine spectator. Some of the other congressmen are waving their arms, as if to express their enthusiasm for the spectacle.

Answer the following questions in paragraphs based on "Cartoon of Matthew Lyon Fight in Congress," on page 277 of *The American Promise,* Second Edition.

**READING THE IMAGE** What is the cartoonist trying to convey about the tone of Congress and its members?

**CONNECTIONS** How did the Constitution's political ideals contrast with the actual behavior of politicians in the 1790s?

**WEB LINKS** To explore the topics discussed in the exercise above, visit the Web links noted below.

"A More Perfect Union: Symbolizing the National Union of States"
http://www.loc.gov/exhibits/us.capitol/s1.html

"The House Of Representatives Educational Resources"
http://www.house.gov/house/Educat.html
Choose "Early Congressional Documents."

***Analyzing Sources Activity*** Answer the following questions in paragraphs based on "Documenting the American Promise: The Crisis of 1798: Sedition" on page 278 of *The American Promise,* Second Edition.

1. Why did Federalists believe a Sedition Act was necessary? What exactly was the threat, according to Abigail Adams? According to James Bayard? What is the threat implied by the wording of the act?
2. Does Matthew Lyon's criticism of President Adams rise to the level of threat that Federalists feared? How do you explain his guilty verdict? His reelection to Congress?
3. What might Madison have meant by "interpose" as the desired action by states? What could states actually do? What is the check today on federal laws deemed to be unconstitutional?
4. How would Adams and Bayard square the Sedition Act with the First Amendment's protection of free speech? Did critics of the law invoke freedom of speech and press?
5. Which side had the stronger argument in 1798 and 1799? Do you think there should be limits on what can be said publicly about high government officials?

**WEB LINKS** To explore the topics discussed in the exercise above, visit the Web links noted below.

"The Alien and Sedition Acts"
http://www.yale.edu/lawweb/avalon/alsedact.htm

"Virginia Resolution: 1798"
http://www.yale.edu/lawweb/avalon/virres.htm

"James Madison and the Sedition Acts"
http://www.columbia.edu/~pen3/aha/gl/madisbg.html

# Answer Key

## Chapter 8: The New Nation Takes form, 1789–1800

## *Chapter Overview*

### *Chronology*

1. b
2. d
3. c
4. d
5. d
6. a
7. c
8. b
9. b
10. a

### *Defining Terms*

1. Alexander Hamilton
2. Bill of Rights
3. New Jersey Constitution
4. Judith Sargent Murray
5. public virtue
6. Napoleonic Wars
7. green-seed cotton
8. Eli Whitney
9. Lancaster Turnpike
10. banknotes
11. *Report on Public Credit*
12. assumption plan
13. Bank of the United States
14. *Report on Manufactures*
15. Whiskey Rebellion
16. General Arthur St. Clair
17. General Anthony Wayne
18. Little Turtle
19. Neutrality Proclamation
20. Haitian Revolution
21. Thomas Pinckney
22. XYZ Affair
23. Quasi War
24. Alien and Sedition Acts
25. Virginia and Kentucky Resolutions

## *Chapter Review*

### *Multiple-Choice*

1. d
2. b
3. a
4. c
5. c
6. c
7. d
8. d
9. a
10. c
11. a
12. b
13. a
14. d
15. b
16. a
17. c
18. d
19. c
20. d
21. d
22. b
23. d
24. b
25. c
26. a
27. d
28. b
29. b
30. c
31. a
32. b
33. b
34. d
35. b
36. a
37. d
38. d
39. c
40. a
41. d
42. b
43. d
44. b
45. b
46. d
47. b
48. d
49. a
50. b
51. d
52. d
53. c
54. c
55. a
56. c
57. a
58. d
59. c
60. a
61. a
62. d
63. a
64. b
65. d
66. b
67. a
68. a
69. d
70. c
71. b
72. c
73. d
74. d
75. b
76. b
77. a
78. a
79. c
80. d
81. d
82. c
83. c
84. c

85. a
86. b
87. a
88. a
89. b
90. c
91. d
92. c
93. c
94. d
95. c
96. b
97. b
98. d
99. d
100. d
101. b
102. a
103. a
104. b
105. a
106. b
107. b
108. d
109. a
110. c

### *Short Answer*

1. The new Congress set up departments of war, treasury, and state but left Washington to choose secretaries and other administrative positions. Because he, like other politicians of the time, distrusted political partisanship, he picked talented and experienced individuals for the posts, even though they were separated by deep philosophical differences. As a result, his cabinet represented a variety of opinions. For example, Alexander Hamilton, a moving force behind the Constitution, was his secretary of the treasury, while he selected Edmund Randolph, an Antifederalist, as his attorney general.
2. The Bill of Rights neglected to include the right to vote, which was not seen as a fundamental liberty requiring government protection until much later. In fact, the 1788 Constitution deliberately allowed the states to define voters to promote stability in the new federal government. States used different criteria to exclude some classes of voters. As a result, any uniform federal voting law could exclude people who were already able to vote in state elections or include new voters that a given state deemed undesirable. Most states maintained property qualifications for voting, which made slaves, servants, apprentices, tenants, wives, and propertyless wage earners ineligible.
3. Republican ideals centered on the importance of mothers as the teachers of virtuous sons. This had the effect of legitimizing female education, which was still a controversial notion, in the name of guaranteeing a well-educated and moral future male citizenry. Republican motherhood thus gave women's domestic obligations a political meaning. It did not, however, overturn traditional gender relations. Women's role in the state was still filtered through the family, and their education was presented as a form of subordination to family needs.
4. Until the 1790s, most farmers' experiences of market transactions involved bartering "country goods" like agricultural surpluses for manufactured items. In the 1790s, they began to grow grain for the international market as a result of sharply rising European food prices. When the Napoleonic Wars broke out in 1793, the United States benefited in two ways: the war caused food prices to increase even more than they had as a result of population growth, and it left the United States as virtually the only neutral shipper, with a near monopoly on the Atlantic trade. American grain farmers responded with larger crops.
5. The cash economy spurred by commercial agriculture was limited to people who lived closet to waterways or ports because the cost of transporting goods over primitive American roads was simply too high. The market for grain was increasing, however, so in the 1790s, east-to-west roadbuilding commenced, linking eastern cities with western towns. By 1800, there was a dense network of roadways connecting cities and towns in southern New England and the Middle Atlantic. While agricultural shipping remained too expensive, the roads encouraged the migration of settlers to the territories.
6. In the 1790s, Americans were putting money into investment opportunities that involved long commitments and large sums. Investment capital of this sort was provided by commercial banks, an innovation that had not existed in America before the Revolution. Banks got money through the sale of stock. They then loaned out the money in the form of banknotes, which were paper currency backed by the gold and silver paid in by stockholders. Because banks issued two to three times as much money in currency as they held in gold and silver, they were actively increasing the money available for new ventures.
7. Hamilton wanted to fund the public debt by rolling over old IOUs and certificates of debt at their original face value into new bonds and making regular interest payments to the holders. This would make the bonds into a stable medium of exchange and inject new money into the economy. However, wealthy speculators had purchased IOUs cheaply, and the plan would benefit them rather than the original owners. Hamilton also suggested adding states' debts to the federal debt, an "assumption plan" that was to be funded by an extremely unpopular excise tax on whiskey that hit grain farmers hard. Thus, Hamilton's plan was controversial because it greatly enhanced the fortunes of the wealthy while adding to the tax burden of ordinary Americans.

8. Hamilton modeled the Bank of the United States on the Bank of England, which was a private bank serving the public interest. He wanted the federal government to purchase 20 percent of the bank's stock, with the bank then acting as the government's fiscal agent. The bank would hold and handle government revenues from import duties, land sales, and the whiskey excise tax. The other 80 percent of the stock would be sold to private investors. Hamilton believed that the bank would help stabilize the economy by exerting control over credit, interest rates, and the value of currency.

9. The immediate motivation for the Whiskey Rebellion was Hamilton's deeply unpopular 25 percent excise tax on distilled spirits, a tax that was very high and had to be paid up front at the distillery by perpetually cash-poor grain farmers. Farmers generally responded by simply evading the law; but in western Pennsylvania an enthusiastic tax collector produced a violent revolt that President Washington responded to with force. In an underlying sense, the Whiskey Rebellion was about what citizens can do when they think a law is unjust and how the government can respond. To many people, the whiskey rebels were unlawfully rejecting the will of the people as expressed through Congress. The rebels, however, believed that they were entitled to protest and demonstrate against oppressive taxes.

10. The confederated Indians of the Ohio territory suffered a major defeat at Fallen Timbers, where they were dispatched by General Anthony Wayne's troops in a little over an hour. The loss, combined with the American practice of destroying cornfields and villages, forced them into negotiations that culminated in the Treaty of Greenville. Given their weak bargaining position, the treaty was highly disadvantageous for them. The Indians ceded most of Ohio to the Americans; in return, they received $25,000 of treaty goods up front, with additional shipments each year. The American government hoped to create an Indian dependence on American goods and very successfully created a severe alcohol problem by fulfilling the annual allowance with liquor.

11. Many Americans were enthusiastic about the French Revolution, which initially bore ideological similarities to the American Revolution. For the federal government, however, the Revolution created delicate political problems when France and England went to war. France had helped the United States during its war against Great Britain, and the confederated government had signed an alliance in 1778 promising to help France if it were ever under attack. Pro-French Americans wanted to deliver on that promise, but pro-British Americans were upset about the wave of French executions and often had commercial ties to England as well. Washington tried to steer a safe course by issuing the Neutrality Proclamation, assuring both sides of the United States's good intentions toward them.

12. John Jay was dispatched to England because the British were seizing neutral American merchant ships trading with the French West Indies. The United States saw these seizures as a strong bargaining chip, one that could be used to force concessions from the British on compensation for the ships and also on the matter of paying for escaped slaves and vacating western forts. Jay, however, returned to the United States with a treaty that made no provision for the lost ships or slaves and that gave the British another eighteen months to withdraw from their western forts, while guaranteeing their continued access to the fur trade. In exchange, Jay got some favorable commercial agreements, which were of value only to a handful of merchants in the overseas trade.

13. The election of both Adams and Jefferson was a result of the failure of the Constitution to anticipate parties and tickets. Until the passage of the Eleventh Amendment in 1804, the electoral college voter could cast two votes, both for president, on a single ballot. The top vote-getter became the president, and the next highest won the vice presidency. In 1796, Alexander Hamilton tried to influence the electors to support Thomas Pinckney, Adams's unofficial running mate. His plan backfired, with Adams winning the largest number of votes, and his rival, Thomas Jefferson, coming in second.

14. France was deeply upset about the Jay Treaty, which seemed to make the United States into a British satellite and retaliated by abandoning the 1778 alliance and allowing armed private vessels to seize American ships carrying British goods. Despite Federalist desires to go to war, John Adams, the newly elected president, sent a three-man commission to France to negotiate a treaty. First, French officials refused to receive the commissioners. Then Talleyrand, the French minister of foreign affairs, sent three agents, known to the American public as X, Y, and Z, to suggest that a $250,000 bribe might be in order and that a $12 million loan would secure a peace treaty. The horrified commissioners refused and returned to an angered United States.

15. Although the United States launched twenty naval warships into the Caribbean in 1798 in response to French attacks on American ships and the XYZ affair, war was never officially declared. If it had been, John Adams and the Federalists could have clamped down on

mounting internal dissent by subjecting their opponents to treason law. Thus, Congress passed the Sedition Act, which made it illegal for people to engage in conspiracies against the government or falsely criticize it—only there was disagreement over what made criticism false, of course. The Alien Acts extended the waiting period for naturalization and allowed the president to deport without trial any foreigner suspected of being a danger to the United States. They were used primarily to harass French immigrants already in the United States and discourage others from coming.

### *Map Activity*

Reading the Map: The Proclamation Line of 1763 ran along the ridge of the Appalachians. Its purpose was to prevent settlers from moving west of the mountains, a common behavior that stirred up expensive Indian wars. The map makes it clear that the Proclamation Line failed in its intent. By 1783, Americans had forced Indians to cede a great deal of land west of the mountains, and they had more than doubled their Indian holdings by 1810. The forts and battles demonstrate that, as the British had been aware, expansion led to armed hostilities with Indian tribes that held prior claim to the land.

Connections: The population of the United States doubled in the twenty years between 1770 and 1790, from 2 million to nearly 4 million. This population growth created a great deal of pressure for the opening of fresh western lands. By the mid-1780s, several thousand settlers a year were moving down the Ohio River, some headed for Kentucky and others for eastern Ohio. The opening of east-west roads and stagecoach lines helped carry settlers to these western regions. By 1800, Vermont, Kentucky, Tennessee, and Ohio were sufficiently populated to join the Union.

### *Visual Activity*

Reading the Image: The cartoonist has shown a gathering of men with neither the dignity nor the self-control expected of them. The fact that two Representatives are engaging in a physical fight is shameful, but as awful as their behavior is, their fellow congressmen are equally bad. Nobody is intervening or attempting to break up the fight. Instead, the other congressmen are watching and grinning; one man, who can be seen between Griswold and Lyons, appears to be practically hoisting himself over the table in his excitement.

Connections: According to the political ideals of the 1780s, when the Constitution was drafted, politicians were supposed to be disinterested and nonpartisan, using their superior wisdom to determine the best course of policy for the nation. The notion that elected officials might experience conflicts that were too deep to be resolved was not considered. However, despite the unanimous election of George Washington as the president, the leaders of the first Congress found a great deal about which they differed. Not only did they not agree on many subjects, but because they all believed themselves to be wise and disinterested, it followed that their opponents could only be selfish and corrupt. As the party system coalesced around these divisions, it was easy for tempers to get out of hand.

### *Analyzing Sources*

1. Federalists argued that criticism of the president and the government was a threat to the stability of the nation. Abigail Adams contended to her sister that because the American government was representative, the insult leveled against her husband were actually aimed at the whole American people; she also argued that the "unfounded" criticism, if ignored, would lead to a civil war, whereas its suppression would contribute to "the Peace and harmony of our country." James Bayard made a similar defense of the Sedition Act. Since the government depended on "the good will of the people," the spreading of false information willfully and untruthfully subverted the government. The actual wording of the Act threatens anybody who publicly or in print opposes and encourages others to oppose the laws and policies of the government with heavy fines and jail time—without making any exception for legitimate dissent.
2. Matthew Lyon's criticism of President Adams was not any immediate call for an overturning of the government. He did not advocate removing Adams from the presidency illegally, nor did he demand armed rebellion. However, he did contend that Adams was not behaving in the manner appropriate to a wise, disinterested republican ruler. Instead, he was selfishly augmenting his own power at the expense of the public good and discarding valuable advisors and appointees and replacing them with toadies. His guilty verdict can be explained by the fact that the Federalists interpreted any criticism of Adams as unmerited and unfair and therefore meeting the requirements set out under the Sedition Act. Lyon's reelection to Congress from jail demonstrates that many Vermont voters did not agree with the Federalist interpretation of malicious and untrue criticism.
3. Madison wanted the states to try to stop the workings of the federal government by demonstrating that the Alien and Sedition Acts were contrary to the Bill of Rights and so infringed on the liberties of the people. In reality, while the federal government can nullify state laws, there is no provision in the constitution for the states to

nullify federal laws. States' laws must conform to a federal standard, but the relationship is not two-way. In reality, the protest was little more than symbolic and had little effect on the application of the Alien and Sedition Acts. Today, states challenge federal law in the Supreme Court. That was an option in 1798 as well, but the judiciary was dominated by Federalist sympathizers, and Madison felt that a court case would be pointless.

4. Adams and Bayard would both insist on a vital distinction between just and unjust criticism of the government. Just as people do not have the freedom to yell "fire" in a theater when there is not one burning, so, Adams and Bayard would claim, there is no natural right to stir up unjustifiable resentment toward the government. Madison's objection to the Sedition Act in the Virginia Resolution does invoke the protection of the Bill of Rights with the comments that the Act is "expressly and positively forbidden by one of the amendments" to the Constitution. Even more dangerously, Madison also believes, the right of free speech and free press is a guarantee of democracy, not a threat to it, because republics rely on the ability of citizens to freely discuss and comment on their public officials.

5. The critics of the Alien and Sedition Acts had the stronger argument. The problem with the Federalists' argument is that they were already on the shaky side of legislative behavior when they effectively went to war against France without making an official declaration. Many people feel that in times of war, the need for national support overrides the right to object. However, the Federalists were not willing to risk the public controversy of declaring war, nor were they willing to work to gain public support. Instead, they simply squelched their critics. There need to be some limits on what can publicly be said about high officials, simply because a great deal of information is irrelevant to the fulfillment of the duties of office; but criticism of government decisions and policies ought to be protected.

CHAPTER

# REPUBLICAN ASCENDANCY, 1800–1824

# 9

## Chapter Overview

### *Chapter Summary*

***Introduction*** This chapter begins with an account of the life of the Shawnee chief Tecumseh. Born in 1768 into a family of six sons and one daughter in the Ohio country, Tecumseh grew up during the American Revolution, which killed his father and two of his brothers and led to repeated raids on his family's home. As a young man, he witnessed and fought against the incursion of white settlers into Indian territory. While many Indians tried to accommodate themselves to the new realities, Tecumseh rejected assimilation and the temptation of alcohol. He looked to traditional Indian practices instead and tried to join tribes in a pan-Indian confederacy. His dissolute younger brother, Tenskwatawa, had a spiritual rebirth and preached against the adoption of white ways. The two were a threat to the stability of Thomas Jefferson's administration, especially after they allied themselves with Canada. War finally broke out between the United States and the British-Indian forces. It was a disaster for the Indians, who lost Tecumseh and much of their land.

***Jefferson's Presidency, pp. 289–296*** Thomas Jefferson would look back on his election as the "revolution of 1800," a moment when he would impose a new vision of republican simplicity on the federal government. At the same time, a different kind of revolution was in the making as a slave named Gabriel, perhaps inspired by the rhetoric of the presidential campaign, plotted a rebellion to strike for freedom.

**THE ELECTION OF 1800** In 1800, John Adams faced competition from Republicans and his own Federalist Party. Not only did he lose the election, but the electoral college produced a tie vote between Jefferson and his running mate, Aaron Burr. Some Federalists preferred Burr because he was seen as subject to Federalist pressure, but Hamilton threw his support behind Jefferson. In February 1801, when the House met to choose the new president, it took thirty-seven separate ballots to get Jefferson elected.

**GABRIEL'S REBELLION** In Virginia in 1800, a twenty-four-year-old enslaved blacksmith named Gabriel plotted a massive slave revolt. Inspired by the Haitian Revolution, Gabriel and his followers planned to march on Richmond, set fires, capture an arsenal, and take James Monroe, the governor, hostage. They believed that Monroe would be sympathetic toward their cause because he was known to be pro-French, therefore proliberty. The slave revolt was aborted because of a massive thunderstorm. Scores of alleged conspirators were quickly rounded up and tried, and twenty-seven were hanged for taking to heart the rhetoric of revolutionary rights and contemplating rebellion. The rebellion scared politicians into secretly looking for a site to which they could deport future troublesome slaves. However, the idea was dropped out of fear that deportation would encourage defiance from slaves who were willing to risk their lives for freedom.

**THE JEFFERSON VISION OF REPUBLICAN SIMPLICITY** Jefferson believed his mission was to direct the nation back to the principles of the Revolution, from which the Federalists had strayed. He believed the independent farmer was the source of true freedom in America and that widespread landownership would make for a virtuous citizenry. As president, Jefferson repudiated many of the programs of his Federalist predecessors, especially Alexander Hamilton, emphasizing instead simplicity and informality. To achieve economy in government, he cut military spending, eliminated all federal internal taxes, and drastically reduced the number of employees of the executive branch.

**THE JUDICIARY AND THE MIDNIGHT JUDGES** Within a few months of taking office, Jefferson found himself embroiled in a constitutional confrontation with the judicial branch. Infuriated by outgoing president John Adams's last minute appointment of "midnight judges," Jefferson denied appointment to many of these individuals. A power showdown between the executive and judicial branches ensued when William Marbury brought suit against the executive for attempting to deny his judicial appointment. In the landmark decision *Marbury v. Madison*, Federalist Chief Justice John Marshall ruled that Marbury had a right to his appointment but that ordering Secretary of State Madison to make it would be unconstitutional. Marshall had sidestepped the confrontation but in the process established the concept of judicial review.

**THE PROMISE OF THE WEST: THE LOUISIANA PURCHASE AND THE LEWIS AND CLARK EXPEDITION** Since the end of the French and Indian War in 1763, the Louisiana Territory had belonged to Spain. However, in 1800, Spain secretly ceded the territory back to France, a situation that aroused American fear. Having weak Spain controlling the Mississippi was one thing, but France was powerful. An American delegation was sent to France to try to purchase New Orleans, and the United States eventually bought the entire Louisiana Territory for $15 million. The Louisiana Purchase added 828,000 square miles to the United States. Even before the purchase had been made, Jefferson had been interested in the trans-Mississippi west. In 1803, he had arranged for his personal secretary, Meriwether Lewis, and Kentuckian William Clark to go on a secret journey into the area to satisfy his scientific interests. Congress had more traditional aims, asking the expedition to scout out locations for military posts, to initiate trade agreements with the Indians, and to seek a Northwest Passage waterway to the West. Lewis and Clark and their party reached the Pacific in November of 1805 and returned as heroes carrying invaluable information about the unknown West.

***Republicans in a Dangerous World, pp. 296–303*** After his easy reelection in 1804, Jefferson faced the repercussions of the renewed war between France and England and the problem of a powerful new Indian confederacy to the west.

**TROUBLES AT SEA AND THE EMBARGO ACT OF 1807** Though both France and England placed a host of restrictions on American trade with the enemy, the British policy of impressment proved most egregious to the United States. Between 1807 and 1812, around 2,500 men were captured by British commanders and impressed into royal naval service. Events reached a crisis point when three American sailors were killed when a British frigate fired on the *Chesapeake*, an

American ship that had picked up some British deserters, in American territorial waters. Though many Republicans clamored for war, the American army and navy were unprepared, and Jefferson had to resort to economic means to punish the British. In 1807, Jefferson persuaded Congress to pass a drastic measure known as the Embargo Act, prohibiting American ships from engaging in any trade with any foreign port. He thought it would punish the British by denying them American agricultural goods, but instead it was a complete disaster for the American economy. The act hit New England merchants and southern planters particularly hard, bringing trade to a standstill. It was also difficult to enforce and had little of the intended impact on the British, who simply turned to South American countries for agricultural goods. The embargo stayed in place until Jefferson left office but was then replaced by the Non-Intercourse Act of 1809, which prohibited trade only with Great Britain, France, and their colonial possessions.

**MADISON GETS ENTANGLED** The 1808 presidential election came in the midst of an embargo-induced depression. James Madison, Jefferson's secretary of state, was elected president, but the Federalist candidate, Charles Pinckney, ran much more strongly than he had in 1804. In 1810, the Non-Intercourse Act expired and was replaced by a new law that reopened free commercial relations with either Great Britain or France, whichever stopped restrictions on neutral shipping first. Napoleon, wanting to entice the United States into reimposing its embargo against England, declared that France would no longer interfere with American shipping. Madison believed the French and reinstated the embargo against England, but French leaders continued to seize American ships. Many Americans felt that the nation was on the verge of war but were unsure whether the correct target was France or England. Young congressional Republicans called War Hawks encouraged a military response to foreign challenges.

**INDIAN TROUBLES IN THE WEST** Maritime issues were only part of the reason for the conflict between the United States and Britain. In the face of constant encroachments of white settlers west onto Indian lands, Indians had begun consolidating alliances with British Indian agents. American concern at this was compounded by the two dynamic Shawnee Indian leaders, the war chief Tecumseh and his mystical brother Tenskwatawa, known as the "Prophet," who united the many tribes of Indiana, Ohio, and Michigan in a confederation to protect their lands. The governor of the Indiana Territory, William Henry Harrison, negotiated a treaty with unrepresentative Indians to purchase three million acres of territory at bargain prices, causing Tecumseh to work with Southern tribes as well. In 1811, alarmed at the brothers' growing power, Harrison, met the Shawnees at Tippecanoe Creek and captured and destroyed their stronghold, Prophetstown. The Battle of Tippecanoe was heralded as a great victory for the Americans and made Harrison a national hero, although it antagonized the Indians.

***The War of 1812, pp. 303–306*** After Tippecanoe, Tecumseh allied with British military commanders in lower Canada, and U.S. conflicts with the Indians soon merged into a broader confrontation with England known as the War of 1812.

**THE WAR BEGINS** The War Hawks urged the country to go to war, which they felt would legitimize attacks on western Indians, end impressment, and preserve national honor. In June 1812, Congress declared war on Great Britain in a sectionalized vote, with New Englanders largely opposed. The war did not go well: a proposed invasion of Canada failed, and the British grabbed forts on the Great Lakes. On the home front, New Englanders, led by Federalist merchants, openly opposed the war and carried on illegal trade with England. Federalists gained political strength in the election of 1812, demonstrating discontent with the war. American fortunes improved somewhat with General Harrison's victory at the Battle of the Thames in 1813 and Andrew Jackson's defeat of the Creeks at the Battle of Horseshoe Bend in 1814.

**THE BRITISH OFFENSIVES OF 1814** The lowest point for Americans in the war came in August 1814 when British troops landed and marched on Washington, putting the government to flight and setting fire to several public buildings, including the Capitol. The invading army then proceeded up toward Baltimore, where it was turned back by the Maryland militia. At the same time, the Americans were halting other offensives in northern New York at Plattsburgh and in the South at New Orleans, where General Andrew Jackson once again led American forces to a decisive victory—ironically, after peace negotiators had concluded a treaty.

**THE WAR ENDS** The 1814 Treaty of Ghent that ended the War of 1812 resulted in the Americans giving in on impressment and relinquishing any claims to Canada. For their part, the British agreed to abandon their western forts and aid to Indians. The Federalist Party was disgraced because in December 1814, New England Federalists had met in Hartford, Connecticut, to discuss their grievances and propose amendments to the Constitution designed to protect New England from the growing southern and western influence. But in the changed atmosphere produced by American victories and the peace treaty, the Hartford Convention and the Federalist Party itself came to seem irrelevant and even treasonous. The war's biggest winners were the Republican War Hawks, who redefined the Republican Party along more expansive lines. Its biggest losers were the Indians; their leader, Tecumseh, had been killed, and they could no longer count on support from the British.

***Women's Status in the Early Republic, pp. 306–309*** Unlike the American Revolution, the War of 1812 had little impact on women. What advances in rights and status women gained during the early Republic came incrementally as a result of local action in courts, legislatures, and religious organizations.

**WOMEN AND THE LAW** Despite the United States's independence, American law, especially regarding gender, continued to reflect its English past. The English common law doctrine of *feme covert* prevailed in most cases regarding white women. Under coverture, a married woman's rights, status, and property were subsumed into her husband, whom she was obligated to obey. Women could not control their wages, make contracts, sue, or be sued. State legislatures did not rewrite British laws that applied to women, nor did they challenge the notion that marriage was defined by unequal power relations. Divorce was the one aspect of family law that changed. By 1820, every state except South Carolina allowed for divorce. It was still difficult and uncommon, though, because states felt that they had an obligation to protect women and children and to regulate the use and inheritance of property. Life was somewhat freer for single females, who in most instances could own and convey property, initiate suits, and pay taxes. However, they could not vote, serve on juries, or practice law, and unless they had inherited money, they were likely to be poor. Slaves were not subject to the laws that shaped free peoples' marriages because, as property, they could not enter freely into contracts, including marriage. As a result, slave unions did not establish unequal power relations backed by force of law.

**WOMEN AND CHURCH GOVERNANCE** By 1800, the majority of congregants in Protestant denominations were women. The churches' hierarchies, however, were dominated by men. Yet in some smaller Baptist sects and in the Quaker church, women increasingly played more active and visible roles, including serving with men on governance committees. In some Methodist and Baptist congregations, women even served as preachers or "exhorters," although they were not ordained ministers. Jemima Wilkinson, the best-known female preacher, believed that she was neither male nor female, wore her hair in the masculine style, and did not use gender-specific pronouns. She established a settlement in western New York with more than 250 followers. As women exhorters became more common, they were subject to criticism from established church authorities who believed that women should remain silent. They were countered by defenders of women's preaching like Deborah Pierce; but in the majority of Protestant congregations, individual churches reinstated gendered patterns of dominance and subordination.

***Madison's Successors, pp. 309–315*** Beginning with Madison's election in 1808 and through the elections of James Monroe in 1816 and 1820, Virginians dominated the presidency. The Federalists never recovered from the stigma of disloyalty after the Hartford Convention. Called the "Era of Good Feelings," Monroe's two terms nonetheless were hardly devoid of controversy.

**THE MISSOURI COMPROMISE** When Missouri applied for admission to the Union as a state in 1819, slavery was already well established there. Even so, a New York representative, James Tallmadge Jr., proposed two amendments to the Missouri statehood bill, one prohibiting the further introduction of slaves into Missouri and the other providing for the gradual emancipation of those already there. These amendments alarmed southerners because they feared that admitting Missouri as an eventual free state would signal the increasing political power of the North at the expense of the South. Maine's desire for statehood helped to resolve the impasse, and what became known as the Missouri Compromise was proposed to maintain the balance of power. Maine would gain admission as a free state and Missouri as a slave state. In addition, to assuage northern fears that slavery would continue to expand north, the Missouri Compromise prohibited slavery above the southern latitude of Missouri at the 36°30′. The Compromise passed largely because a handful of northern representatives believed that minimizing sectional controversy was in the best interests of the nation as a whole; the need to bridge the differences between the North and the South remained an important issue for political parties.

**THE MONROE DOCTRINE** The United States faced foreign policy problems. Andrew Jackson's 1816 invasion of Florida, while of dubious legality, led to the purchase of that territory from Spain in 1819. Meanwhile, the threat of Spanish interference in South American revolutions resulted in President James Monroe's promulgation of the Monroe Doctrine. The doctrine declared the Americas closed to further colonization and stipulated that the United States would consider any foreign challenge to the sovereignty of existing American nations as an unfriendly act toward the United States. In return, the doctrine pledged noninterference by the United States in European affairs.

**THE ELECTION OF 1824** In 1824, there were four candidates competing for the presidency: William Crawford, John Quincy Adams, Henry Clay, and Andrew Jackson. Jackson received more popular and electoral votes than any other candidate but not the constitutionally mandated majority of electoral votes. This threw the election to the House, where Henry Clay's support of John Quincy Adams led to the latter's election. Jackson's supporters, believing their candidate deserved the presidency, were enraged when he lost and became even angrier when Adams named Clay his secretary of state. The outrage the Jacksonians expressed at what they called a "corrupt bargain" haunted Adams throughout his tenure.

**THE ADAMS ADMINISTRATION** John Quincy Adams's term of office was largely a failure. He proposed a sweeping plan of federal funding for internal improvements. However, he refused to use patronage to gain support for his programs, most often awarding positions in his administration to the opposition to placate political enemies. His failure to create a loyal base of support spelled doom for most of his programs.

***Conclusion: From Jefferson to Adams*** Though the beginning of the nineteenth century saw Jeffersonian Republicans seeking to limit the size and power of government, this trend had to yield to the realities of a growing nation. The Louisiana Purchase expanded the United States dramatically, while the War of 1812 renewed Americans' confidence in their independence from England and undermined the ability of Indians in the Northwestern Territory to protect themselves from white settlers. The war also raised General Andrew Jackson to such prominence that he won the popular, if not the electoral, vote in 1824, upsetting the one-party rule of the Republican Party.

***Chronology Activity*** Read the annotated chronology, and answer the multiple-choice questions.

1789 Judiciary Act establishes six Supreme Court justices who preside over circuit courts.

1800 Thomas Jefferson and Aaron Burr tie in electoral college. Although Burr was running for the position of vice president, when he tied in the electoral college he refused to concede the election to Jefferson. As a result, the election was thrown into the House of Representatives.

1800 Gabriel's Rebellion fails in Virginia. Gabriel, a twenty-four-year-old blacksmith, plotted an elaborate slave rebellion involving hundreds of coconspirators from five different Virginia counties. The rebellion was discovered, and twenty-seven of the plotters were hanged, but Virginia's politicians were unnerved by the plotters' comparison of themselves to Revolutionary leaders. The politicians considered finding a suitable place to which they could deport the rebellious slaves, the closest they came to embracing a plan to reduce the number of slaves in the state.

1801 Judiciary Act reduces Supreme Court justices to five and allows for sixteen circuit judges. This act allowed John Adams and John Marshall to make numerous appointments to the court system in the final days of Adams's presidency and thus maintain federal influence in the national government. The appointment of these "midnight judges" infuriated Jefferson.

Jefferson elected president by House of Representatives. It took thirty-seven ballots to determine the outcome of the election. Some Federalist representatives preferred Burr to Jefferson because they believed that his lack of principles would make him easier to control. Ultimately, Alexander Hamilton put his support behind Jefferson, and he was elected. The election demonstrated that the constitutional system could accommodate a change in leadership without resorting to violence.

1802 Judiciary Act of 1801 repealed. After Adams's appointment of the "midnight judges," Republicans turned their attention to revoking the Judiciary Act of 1801 that had allowed for the creation of so many new slots. The question was one of the power relation between Congress and the judiciary: congressional Republicans argued that the new courts were expensive and that if Congress could create courts, it could abolish them too.

1803 *Marbury v. Madison* declares part of Judiciary Act of 1789 unconstitutional. This case established the concept of judicial review. By declaring that Marbury's suit was based on an act that was itself unconstitutional, the Court assumed the legal authority to nullify acts of the other branches of the federal government.

Embargoes on American shipping by England and France. During the previous war between England and France, American shippers had benefited from trade with both sides. The belligerents were determined to avoid that mistake and so established independent restrictions on American trade, backed by threats of blockades and seizure. This caused enormous political headaches for Jefferson and his successor, James Madison.

Louisiana Purchase from France. The Louisiana Purchase covered a huge swathe of land from New Orleans to Canada and was made for the bargain price of $15 million. Jefferson was concerned about the constitutional implications of making so large a purchase (he was not convinced that he had the authority), but his desire for the land outweighed his abstract principles.

1804 Jefferson reelected president. Jefferson's reelection was an easy victory, with the Federalist candidate, Charles Cotesworth Pinckney, receiving only fourteen votes in the electoral college. The Republicans would continue in the presidency for twenty more years.

Burr-Hamilton duel. Burr killed Hamilton, robbing the Federalist party of its shrewdest statesman. In June 1804, Hamilton made public his low opinion of Burr. Burr was convinced that Hamilton's remarks deprived him of the governorship of New York and challenged him to a duel if he refused to renounce his comment. Hamilton would not back down from his position, nor could he refuse to duel without damaging his reputation for integrity and bravery. The public outcry over Hamilton's death helped squelch the custom of dueling in the North.

1804–1806 Lewis and Clark expedition. Even before the Louisiana Purchase, Jefferson had secured funding for an exploratory journey into Spanish and Indian territory to study the region's science and also find locations for military posts, negotiate commercial agreements for the fur trade, and look for a water route between the East and West coasts. The expedition was a huge success, resulting in favorable relations with dozens of Indian tribes and invaluable information about the flora and fauna of the west.

1807 June. *Chesapeake* attacked and searched by British in Chesapeake Bay. The attack by the British on an American ship occurred in American territorial waters and killed three American citizens. Jefferson was outraged but also limited by the reduced size of the American army and navy.

December. Embargo Act forbids any American ship from engaging in trade with any foreign port. The Embargo Act was Jefferson's response to the *Chesapeake* incident. It was intended to punish England by denying it even indirect access to American agricultural goods, but it devastated the American economy instead.

1808 James Madison elected president. While Madison won the election by a wide margin, the Federalist candidate, Charles Cotesworth Pinckney, picked up a great deal of support because of the unpopularity of the Embargo Act.

1809 Treaty of Fort Wayne with Indians in Indiana Territory. The treaty was negotiated by William Henry Harrison, governor of the Indiana Territory. By dealing with chiefs who had, in some cases, no claim to the land in question and falsely promising that the United States would seek no more cessions of land, he was able to purchase over three million acres of land in exchange for two cents per acre.

Non-Intercourse Act passed. This act replaced the Embargo Act. It forbade American trade with England and France and their colonies and so opened the way for legal, indirect trade with the belligerents. This eased the financial suffering of New England shippers and southern planters.

1811 Battle of Tippecanoe won by William Henry Harrison's troops. Harrison decided to attack Tecumseh's brother Tenskwatawa's village, Prophetstown, while Tecumseh was on a recruiting trip in the south. Harrison's victory undermined Tenskwatawa's influence but increased Tecumseh's desire to make war on Americans.

1812 June. War declared on Great Britain. Young Republican congressmen called War Hawks pushed for a declaration of war on Great Britain because of the seizure of ships and impressment of sailors, British alliances with western Indians, and their belief that Great Britain had insulted the United States. The declaration was opposed by nearly every New England representative and some of those from the Middle Atlantic states.

Madison reelected president. Madison won the election; his opponent was DeWitt Clinton, another Republican, albeit one with Federalist support. Madison's margin of victory was slimmer than it had been in 1808, largely as a result of discontent with the war.

1814 British attack Washington, D.C., burning several buildings. Badly trained Maryland militia units fled from the British advance, marking a low point in the war effort.

Treaty of Ghent ends War of 1812. Since neither side won a decisive victory, the Treaty of Ghent did not settle the issues that had started the war in the first place. Instead, both the United States and Great Britain agreed to give up longstanding goals.

Hartford Convention. This convention was called by Federalists who were upset about the war's unhappy impact on New England interests and their inability to stop it. Delegates proposed a variety of constitutional amendments designed to protect their influence against the South and West and make it impossible for a single party or group to lead the country into war again. When the war was concluded shortly after the meeting, the Federalists ended up looking unpatriotic.

1815 Battle of New Orleans won by Andrew Jackson's forces. Although the battle took place after the peace treaty had been signed, it was one of the only rousing American victories of the war.

1816 James Monroe elected president. Monroe's time in office was called "the Era of Good Feelings" by a contemporary newspaper, but in fact it was marked by a variety of disagreements over domestic and foreign politics.

1819 Spain cedes Florida to United States. General Andrew Jackson invaded the northern part of Spanish Florida in 1818, ostensibly in search of Seminole Indians who had been protecting escaped slaves. He declared himself the commander of northern Florida and executed two British subjects as a demonstration of his power. President Monroe considered a court martial but was dissuaded by Jackson's popularity. Instead, John Quincy Adams, the secretary of state, negotiated the Adams-Onis Treaty with Spain, exchanging Florida for the promise to abandon any claim to Texas or Cuba.

1820 Missouri Compromise admits Missouri as slave state and Maine as free state. The admission of Missouri to statehood became complicated after James Tallmadge Jr. of New York offered amendments designed to gradually end slavery in the state. The result was a huge congressional debate dividing along sectional lines. It was resolved only when the balance of power between slave and free states was maintained with the admission of Maine at the same time as Missouri and the latitude 36°30′ was made the permanent dividing line between slave and free territory.

Monroe reelected president. Monroe was reelected with all but one electoral college votes. This was evidence of the eclipse of the Federalists, but it did not demonstrate voter satisfaction: barely a quarter of all eligible voters participated in the election.

1823 Monroe Doctrine asserts independence of Western Hemisphere from European intervention. Monroe was concerned that Spain, and perhaps France and Prussia as well, might try to reclaim the colonies that were declaring independence in South and Central America. In response, Monroe formulated a statement of principles prohibiting Europeans from colonizing nations in the Western Hemisphere. In exchange, he promised that Americans would stay out of European conflicts.

1824 "Corrupt bargain" election of John Quincy Adams. General Andrew Jackson won the popular vote but not a majority of the electoral votes. The election was thrown into the House of Representatives, where Adams won by a single vote. However, Adams's presidency was undermined by rumors that he had made a deal with Henry Clay, trading the secretary of state position for Clay's support in the House of Representatives during the election.

## *Chronology Questions* Choose the letter of the best answer.

1. What is the correct order for the following events?
   1. The Embargo Act forbids American trade with any foreign port.
   2. Madison is elected president.
   3. Embargoes are imposed on American shipping by England and France.
   4. The Non-Intercourse Act is passed.
   
   a. 1, 4, 3, 2
   b. 3, 1, 2, 4
   c. 4, 2, 1, 3
   d. 4, 1, 3, 2

2. In 1800, in response to the Haitian Revolution,
   a. the Judiciary Act established six Supreme Court justices.
   b. Jefferson was elected by the House of Representatives.
   c. the Louisiana Purchase was made.
   d. Gabriel's Rebellion occurred, but failed, in Virginia.

3. James Monroe was elected for his first term as president by a wide margin in
   a. 1804.
   b. 1808.
   c. 1812.
   (d.) 1816.

4. In 1814, which one of the following did not occur?
   a. The British attacked Washington, D.C., burning several buildings.
   (b.) Spain ceded Florida to the United States.
   c. The Treaty of Ghent ended the War of 1812.
   d. The Hartford Convention met.

5. The Monroe Doctrine asserted the independence of the Western Hemisphere from European intervention in
   a. 1812.
   b. 1816.
   (c.) 1823.
   d. 1839.

6. What is the correct order for the following events?
   1. The Battle of Tippecanoe is won by William Henry Harrison's troops.
   2. Madison is elected president.
   3. War is declared on Great Britain.
   4. The Treaty of Fort Wayne is signed with Indians in Indiana Territory.
   a. 2, 3, 1, 4
   (b.) 2, 4, 1, 3
   c. 4, 3, 1, 2
   d. 1, 2, 3, 4

7. What is the correct order for the following events?
   1. The Judiciary Act establishes six Supreme Court justices.
   2. *Marbury v. Madison* declares part of Judiciary Act of 1789 unconstitutional.
   3. The Judiciary Act of 1801 is repealed.
   4. The Judiciary Act reduces the number of Supreme Court justices to five.
   a. 3, 1, 4, 2
   (b.) 1, 4, 3, 2
   c. 4, 2, 1, 3
   d. 3, 2, 1, 4

8. The Missouri Compromise admitted Missouri as a slave state and Maine as a free state in
   a. 1804.
   b. 1811.
   c. 1815.
   (d.) 1820.

9. What is the correct order for the following events?
   1. The Battle of New Orleans is won by Andrew Jackson's forces.
   2. The Treaty of Ghent ends the War of 1812.
   3. War is declared on Great Britain.
   4. The *Chesapeake* is attacked and searched by the British.
   (a.) 4, 3, 2, 1
   b. 1, 2, 4, 3
   c. 2, 4, 1, 3
   d. 3, 1, 2, 4

10. In 1824, the presidential race was marred by
    a. the "corrupt bargain" election of John Quincy Adams.
    b. the Burr-Hamilton duel.
    c. the reelection of Monroe.
    d. the reelection of Madison.

***Defining Terms*** Match each term with the correct definition.

✓ "Era of Good Feelings"
✓ War Hawks
✓ Tecumseh
✓ Sacajawea
✓ Robert R. Livingston
✓ Jemima Wilkinson
✓ *feme covert*
✓ *Chesapeake* incident
✓ "corrupt bargain"
✓ *Report on the Causes and Reasons for War*
✓ *Marbury v. Madison*
✓ Adams-Onis Treaty
✓ Gabriel's Rebellion
✓ Hartford Convention
✓ Monroe Doctrine
✓ Missouri Compromise
✓ Freewill Baptists
✓ Non-Intercourse Act of 1809
✓ Treaty of Ghent
✓ Embargo Act of 1807
✓ midnight judges
✓ impressment
✓ divorce
✓ Plattsburgh

1. A slave revolt that was planned in 1800 in Virginia. Although it was not carried out, southern whites were unnerved by the plan and the fact that the plotters compared their struggle for freedom to that of Revolutionary leaders. Gabriel's Rebellion
2. These sixteen men were appointed with lifetime tenure by Adams under the Judiciary Act of 1801 during the last few weeks of his presidency. His intention was to maintain a stronghold of Federalist influence in the new Republican government. midnight judges
3. An 1803 Supreme Court case that established the concept of judicial review when Chief Justice John Marshall argued that parts of the Judiciary Act of 1789 were in conflict with the Constitution. The Supreme Court assumed legal authority to nullify acts of other branches of the government in this power struggle between Congress and the judiciary. Marbury v. Madison
4. America's minister to France in 1802, he was instructed by Jefferson to try to buy the city of New Orleans from France. When he was offered the entire Louisiana Territory, he made the purchase for the bargain price of $15 million. Robert R. Livingston
5. A sixteen-year old Indian woman who accompanied the Lewis and Clark expedition. Her presence was unexpectedly helpful because the Indian tribes the party encountered believed that women never accompanied war parties. Sacajawea
6. The British practice of seizing and forcing into service sailors whom they accused of being deserters from the British navy. This became a major issue leading to the War of 1812 because many impressed sailors were native-born Americans. impressment

7. An event that occurred in 1807 when the British fired upon an American ship, killing three Americans in American territorial waters. Jefferson was furious but unable to retaliate militarily because of prior cuts in the army and navy. Chesapeake incident

8. Jefferson's response to the *Chesapeake* incident. This banned American ships from engaging in trade with any foreign port to cut off British access to American agricultural goods. It had disastrous effects on the United States's economy but did not have much of an impact on Great Britain, which simply began trading with South American countries. Embargo Act of 1807

9. The act that replaced the Embargo Act. This banned trade only with Great Britain, France, and their colonial holdings and so opened the way to legal, indirect trade. This move helped the economic standing of New England shippers and southern planters, who had suffered greatly under the Embargo Act. Non-Intercourse Act of 1809

10. A charismatic Shawnee leader who worked to form a pan-Indian federation to combat American divide-and-conquer strategies for exacting Indian land. He argued that no Indian tribe should sell land to anybody because it was rightfully held in common by all tribes. Tecumseh

11. Young Republicans elected to the national Congress in the fall of 1810. They were eager for war to legitimize attacks on Indians, end impressment, and avenge foreign insults and so pushed for the 1812 declaration of war against Great Britain. War Hawks

12. A document written by John C. Calhoun, a congressman from South Carolina and War Hawk, to justify the American declaration of war against Great Britain. The report did not merely condemn Great Britain's naval actions but focused extensively on English insults in treating the United States like a third-rate power. Report on the causes and Reasons for war

13. A minor 1814 naval engagement on the northern end of Lake Champlain, which the British lost. The loss caused the British military leadership to withdraw a large army without engaging American troops and convinced British political leaders that a land invasion was an impractical way to fight the war. Plattsburgh

14. The agreement that ended the War of 1812. Since neither side had decisively won, it reflected a mutual agreement to give up certain goals. The Americans yielded on impressment and Canada, while the British evacuated western forts and ended their Indian alliances. The most concrete result was an agreement to set up a commission to determine the exact boundary between the United States and Canada. Treaty of Ghent

15. A meeting called by New England Federalists in December 1814 to discuss constitutional amendments that would limit the power of the South and West. After General Andrew Jackson's victory at the Battle of New Orleans and the conclusion of the Treaty of Ghent, the convention looked unpatriotic, and the Federalists' fortunes never recovered. Hartford convention

16. A legal doctrine resting in British common law that subsumed a wife's civic identity to her husband's. A wife was obligated to obey her husband, render him domestic and sexual services, and turn over all of her property to him. It gave state backing to the unequal power relations within marriage. feme covert

17. The one aspect of family law that changed in the early Republic. Prior to the Revolution, only New England jurisdictions recognized the legality of this practice; by 1820, every state except for South Carolina allowed this practice. divorce

18. Small groups of Baptists centered in Maine, New Hampshire, Vermont, and upstate New York. The sect was unusual in that it allowed women to openly preach, although it did not give them the formal ordination that would allow them to preach officially or perform baptisms.
Freewill Baptists

19. An "exhorting woman" who claimed that she was neither male nor female but the embodiment of the "Spirit of Light." She eventually withdrew to her own settlement in western New York with more than 250 followers of both sexes. Jemima Wilkinson

20. A newspaper's appellation for James Monroe's presidency. The paper was referring to the apparent subsidence of party feelings—the Federalists were spent as a national force, and in 1820 Monroe only lost one electoral vote—but there were still differences of opinion over a wide assortment of topics. "Era of Good Feelings"

21. The congressional legislation that allowed Missouri to enter the Union as a slave state by coupling its admission with that of Maine and declaring that the southern boundary of Missouri would became a permanent line dividing slave and free. The dispute demonstrated southerners' increasing concern about the national balance of power between slave and free states. Missouri Compromise

22. The agreement that delivered Florida to the United States in 1819 in exchange for the United States repudiating any claim to Texas or Cuba. Southerners saw this as a concession, since they had seen both places as potential slave states. Adams-Onis Treaty

23. The 1823 assertion that the Western Hemisphere was closed to any further colonization by European powers. In exchange, Madison pledged that the United States would not become involved in European struggles. Although he could not back his policy with action, it was an important formulation of national goals. Monroe Doctrine

24. The deal in which John Quincy Adams supposedly gave Henry Clay the secretary of state position in exchange for Clay's support in the House of Representatives in the runoff presidential election of 1824. While there probably was not a formal bargain, Clay's appointment looked bad, and Jackson's supporters were able to get political mileage out of it. "corrupt bargain"

## Chapter Review

### *Multiple-Choice* Choose the letter of the best answer.

1. In the 1800 presidential election, Hamilton revealed the deep divisions in the Federalist camp by
   a. supporting Thomas Jefferson.
   b. nominating himself as a presidential candidate.
   c. campaigning for Aaron Burr.
   d. going public with an abusive condemnation of Adams.

2. The presidential election of 1800 was thrown into the House of Representatives because
   a. Adams objected to the outcome.
   b. Hamilton's meddling threw the outcome into doubt.
   c. Jefferson and Pinckney got an equal number of votes.
   d. Jefferson and Aaron Burr got an equal number of votes.

3. The presidential election of 1800 demonstrated that
   a. Jefferson was a very popular candidate.
   b. under the Constitution, leadership could transfer from one group to another peacefully.
   c. the House of Representatives was indecisive.
   d. the Federalists were a very strong force in American politics.

4. The slave leader Gabriel believed that the governor of Virginia, James Monroe, would be
   a. willing to grant slaves their freedom under a direct threat to his life.
   b. sympathetic to his views because of his pro-French politics.
   c. forced by planters to end slavery to prevent future rebellions.
   d. killed as an example to other slave owners.

5. After Virginia judges hanged twenty-seven black men for participating in Gabriel's Rebellion, Thomas Jefferson counseled James Monroe to
   a. continue with the executions.
   b. deport other rebellious blacks.
   c. brand the suspects instead.
   d. free the remaining suspects.

6. Thomas Jefferson's presidency was marked by
   a. an extremely formal style.
   b. his exorbitant spending.
   c. his personal sloppiness.
   d. a casual style of simplicity and frugality.

7. In Thomas Jefferson's vision, the source of true freedom in the United States was the
   a. banker.
   b. merchant.
   c. wage laborer.
   d. independent farmer.

8. According to Thomas Jefferson, the federal government should not
   a. run a postal system.
   b. collect internal taxes.
   c. maintain federal courts.
   d. collect customs duties.

9. In the final weeks before Jefferson became president, President Adams worked to maintain Federalist of the government control by
   a. changing federal laws in the Federalists' favor.
   b. using the Sedition Act to dismiss Republican legislators.
   c. appointing Federalist men to judicial, diplomatic, and military posts.
   d. challenging the results of the election.

10. The 1803 Supreme Court decision in *Marbury v. Madison* was a landmark because it
    a. allowed the House of Representatives to determine the constitutionality of laws.
    b. increased the power of the president.
    c. forced President Jefferson to honor President Adams's appointments.
    d. established the concept of judicial review.

11. Jefferson was reluctant about the Louisiana Purchase because he
    a. was afraid that it would upset the geographic balance of power.
    b. thought that he was stretching his constitutional prerogatives.
    c. worried about strong Federalist opposition.
    d. felt that the United States already had enough farmland.

12. The Lewis and Clark expedition
    a. set up military posts throughout the Midwest.
    b. gave the United States complete control over the fur trade.
    c. discovered a waterway linking the east and west coasts.
    d. collected important information on the peoples and environment of the West.

13. As president, Thomas Jefferson aimed for a more _____ federal government than his predecessors.
    a. expansive
    b. formal
    c. limited
    d. democratic

14. In the presidential election of 1800, John Adams received the support of _____.
    a. Southern Republicans
    b. New England Federalists
    c. western farmers
    d. urban workers

15. One of the jailed participants in Gabriel's Rebellion distressed southern whites by comparing himself to _____.
    a. George Washington
    b. James Monroe
    c. Tecumseh
    d. Toussaint L'Overture

16. After Gabriel's Rebellion, Thomas Jefferson toyed with the idea of _____ rebellious slaves.
    a. executing
    b. jailing
    c. deporting
    d. manumitting

17. Thomas Jefferson believed that widespread _____ was the cornerstone of liberty.
    a. wage labor
    b. slaveholding
    c. tenant farming
    d. land ownership

18. With the consent of Congress, President Jefferson abolished all federal _____.
    a. revenue
    b. construction projects
    c. external duties
    d. internal taxes

19. In the 1803 *Marbury v. Madison* decision, the Supreme Court found that the grounds of Marbury's suit were _____.
    a. frivolous
    b. in conflict with the Constitution
    c. in keeping with the Constitution
    d. in conflict with the Judicary Act of 1789

20. In 1800, the land west of the Mississippi River was claimed by _____.
    a. Spain
    b. France
    c. England
    d. the United States

21. All but one representative from _____ voted against the Louisiana Purchase.
    a. the west
    b. the south
    c. New England
    d. the middle Atlantic

22. The Lewis and Clark expedition reached the Pacific Northwest in 1805, and the explorers returned home as _____.
    a. official diplomats
    b. failures because they did not find a Northwest Passage to the Orient
    c. national heroes
    d. very wealthy men

23. When France and England went to war in the early 1800s, Jefferson experimented with different responses, including
    a. economic sanctions and military threats.
    b. economic sanctions and trade embargoes.
    c. trade embargoes and military threats.
    d. none of the above.

24. When France and England went to war in the 1803, they
    a. agreed to respect American neutrality.
    b. ignored the issue of trade with the United States.
    c. established independent restrictions on American trade with the enemy.
    d. both stopped trading with the United States.

25. Under the Embargo Act, American ships were forbidden from engaging in trade with
    a. France.
    b. England.
    c. France and England.
    d. any foreign port.

26. After the passage of the Embargo Act, England
    a. apologized to American shippers for the *Chesapeake* incident.
    b. made reparations to the United States government.
    c. made peace with France.
    d. turned to South America for agricultural goods.

27. The Embargo Act of 1807 hurt
    a. farmers.
    b. shippers.
    c. the federal government
    d. all of the above.

28. The Non-Intercourse Act of 1809
    a. prohibited trade with France, England, and their colonial possessions.
    b. extended the Embargo Act.
    c. prohibited trade with France and England's colonial possessions.
    d. established free trade with all nations.

29. James Madison did not receive universal Republican support in his 1808 presidential bid because
    a. Republicans from the South were upset about the Embargo Act of 1807.
    b. he was associated with John Adams.
    c. Republicans from the North were tired of having southern presidents.
    d. his positions were moving closer to those of the Federalists.

30. When the Non-Intercourse Act expired in 1810, Congress
    a. passed a law permitting conditional trade with either France or England.
    b. declared war on England.
    c. declared war on France.
    d. renewed the Embargo Act.

31. In 1811 James Madison was forced to reactivate an embargo on trade with England and France because
    a. French leaders continued to seize American ships.
    b. the English made no move to end impressments or repeal trade restrictions.
    c. both of the above.
    d. neither of the above.

32. A fundamental part of Shawnee chief Tecumseh's beliefs was that
    a. tribes should demand better prices for their land.
    b. only legitimate chiefs should negotiate sales to the American government.
    c. settlers in the Northwest Territory should be killed.
    d. all Indian lands were held in common by all tribes.

33. In the 1809 Treaty of Fort Wayne, the Indiana territorial governor William Henry Harrison got three million acres of Indian land by
    a. killing Tecumseh and Tenskwatawa.
    b. negotiating with unrepresentative chiefs.
    c. offering a good price.
    d. threatening to starve Indians who would not negotiate.

34. The November 1811 Battle of Tippecanoe had the effect of
    a. undermining William Henry Harrison's military reputation.
    b. destroying Tecumseh's Indian alliance.
    c. increasing Tecumseh's readiness to make war on the Americans.
    d. enhancing Tenskwatawa's power over his followers.

35. In the Northwest Territory, a powerful Indian confederacy led by the Shawnee Tecumseh mounted a challenge to _____.
    a. American settlers
    b. the British fur trade
    c. competing tribes in the area
    d. the eastern Indian confederacy

36. After the *Chesapeake* incident, Jefferson and Madison pushed for a _____, passed by Congress in December 1807.
    a. nonimportation law
    b. declaration of war
    c. total embargo
    d. ban on British goods

37. The Embargo Act had the immediate effect of _____.
    a. boosting the New England shipping industry
    b. helping American manufacturing
    c. increasing American commerce
    d. wiping out American commerce

38. The NonIntercourse Act of 1809 opened the way for _____ trade with France and England.
    a. legal, indirect
    b. illegal, indirect
    c. legal, direct
    d. illegal, direct

39. James Madison, the _____ for eight years, was Jefferson's obvious successor to the presidency.
    a. secretary of the treasury
    b. secretary state
    c. secretary of war
    d. postmaster general

40. In 1810 Madison reopened trade with _____ after a declaration that it would stop harassing American ships.
    a. the West Indies
    b. Spain
    c. England
    d. France

41. The Congress of 1810 was dominated by representatives who were _____, like Henry Clay.
    a. Federalists
    b. War Hawks
    c. pro-French
    d. peace-minded

42. Indiana's territorial governor, William Henry Harrison, used _____ to extract Indian lands.
    a. vigilante violence
    b. a divide-and-conquer strategy
    c. cash payments
    d. threats of war

43. The Treaty of Fort Wayne secured _____ for the United States.
    a. a peace treaty with Tecumseh
    b. Indian military aid
    c. title to over three million acres of land
    d. access to the Ohio River

44. The November 1811 Battle of _____ was a complete defeat for Tenskwatawa and heralded as a glorious victory for Americans.
    a. Tippecanoe
    b. Prophetstown
    c. Fort Wayne
    d. Wabash River

45. The defeat of the Indians at Tippecanoe propelled
    a. Tecumseh into an alliance with British military commanders.
    b. Americans into war with England.
    c. the War Hawks into renewed commitment.
    d. all of the above.

46. According to the *Report on the Causes and Reasons for War*, the war was necessary because the
    a. United States needed Canada and Florida.
    b. rate of impressments was rising.
    c. British were treating the United States like a third-rate power.
    d. trade between Britain and South America hurt the American economy.

47. After war was declared against England in 1812, congressional War Hawks proposed
    a. invading Canada.
    b. accepting British peace overtures.
    c. increasing the American naval presence on the Great Lakes.
    d. invading Great Britain.

48. The New England states responded to the declaration of war with England in 1812 by
    a. raising troops very reluctantly.
    b. contributing the services of state militia.
    c. raising taxes to support military spending.
    d. refusing to send troops.

49. The presidential election of 1812 demonstrated
    a. Federalist discontent with the war.
    b. Republican support for the war.
    c. widespread American support for the war.
    d. Madison's personal lack of popularity.

50. After a year of military blunders, in 1813 the war
    a. stalled.
    b. turned in favor of the British.
    c. turned in favor of the Americans.
    d. none of the above.

51. When the British invaded Washington, D.C., in August 1814, the Americans
    a. began peace negotiations.
    b. fled in disorder as the British advanced.
    c. put up a stiff resistance.
    d. successfully drove the British toward Baltimore.

52. After the American defeat of the British at Plattsburgh, British leaders decided to
    a. replace their military leadership.
    b. redouble their efforts at invading the United States.
    c. avoid incursions by land into the United States because they were costly and difficult.
    d. surrender unconditionally.

53. The December 1814 Battle of New Orleans had the effect of
    a. ending the war.
    b. leading to enormous American casualties.
    c. undermining General Andrew Jackson's military career.
    d. making General Andrew Jackson an instant hero.

54. The 1814 Treaty of Ghent reflected
    a. Jackson's stunning victory at New Orleans.
    b. American divisions over the war.
    c. a mutual agreement to give up certain goals.
    d. the British sense of victory in the conflict.

55. Delegates to the Hartford Convention in December 1814 proposed
    a. amending the Constitution to protect New England's sectional interests.
    b. refusing to pay for the war.
    c. rejecting the Treaty of Ghent.
    d. giving westerners more power in Congress.

56. The biggest winners in the War of 1812 were the
    a. Indians.
    b. British.
    c. War Hawks.
    d. Federalists.

57. Tecumseh's alliance with British military commanders in lower Canada propelled _____ to urge the United States to go declare war on the English.
    a. French trappers
    b. Southerners
    c. New Englanders
    d. Westerners

58. In June 1812, Congress declared war on Great Britain in a vote that divided along _____ lines.
    a. no discernible
    b. party
    c. sectional
    d. personal

59. The 1812 invasion of Canada, encouraged by the War Hawks, failed because _____.
    a. volunteers refused to cross the border
    b. the United States was unprepared for war
    c. the Canadian militia was very good
    d. the weather was bad

60. During the War of 1812, New England merchants carried on _____ with Great Britain.
    a. peace negotiations
    b. battles
    c. illegal trade
    d. legal trade

61. DeWitt Clinton of New York, James Madison's rival for the presidency in 1812, was able to attract the _____ vote.
   a. undecided
   b. southern
   c. Republican
   d. Federalist

62. In the South, General Andrew Jackson led 2,500 Tennessee militiamen in a successful attack on Creek Indians at _____.
   a. Horseshoe Bend
   b. the Thames
   c. York
   d. Lake Erie

63. In the August 1814, the British attacked _____, then headed for the port of Baltimore.
   a. the *Chesapeake*
   b. New York
   c. Washington, D.C.
   d. Philadelphia

64. The Hartford Convention's proposals were intended to _____ the political power of the South.
   a. increase
   b. decrease
   c. uphold
   d. destroy

65. The most concrete result of the Treaty of Ghent that ended the War of 1812 was an agreement to _____.
   a. regulate the fur trade
   b. determine the exact boundary between the United States and Canada
   c. end the British impressment of American sailors
   d. respect American neutrality in future wars

66. The biggest losers in the War of 1812 were the _____.
   a. British
   b. War Hawks
   c. Federalists
   d. Indians

67. In the early Republic, women's status changed
   a. as a result of wartime emergency.
   b. because of agitation on the part of women.
   c. because of agitation on the part of male politicians.
   d. in incremental steps.

68. Under the legal doctrine of *feme covert*, wives had
   a. limited property rights.
   b. no independent legal or political personhood.
   c. full custody of their children.
   d. no right to work for pay.

69. When state legislatures codified their laws, they generally
   a. addressed women's unequal status.
   b. gave women the right to vote in state elections.
   c. passed up the opportunity to change women's unequal status.
   d. worsened women's unequal status.

70. In the early years of the nation, the one aspect of family law that changed was
   a. divorce.
   b. marriage.
   c. custody of children.
   d. property rights.

71. In many states, divorce could be obtained only by
   a. mutual agreement between the husband and wife.
   b. church decree.
   c. paying lawyers large fees.
   d. petition to the state's legislature.

72. Single women in the early Republic were not able to
   a. serve on juries.
   b. own and convey property.
   c. initiate suits.
   d. pay taxes.

73. Single women in the early Republic often
   a. were lawyers.
   b. were wealthy.
   c. had fewer rights than married women.
   d. were poor.

74. Gender relations among black slaves were
   a. just like those among whites.
   b. affected by the same legal institutions.
   c. not affected by the legal institutions that applied to whites.
   d. unequal by force of law.

75. Around 1800, the church hierarchy of most Protestant denominations was
   a. dominated by women.
   b. exclusively male.
   c. elected by church members.
   d. composed of elderly men and women.

76. Quaker women who felt a special call were
   a. persecuted.
   b. ignored.
   c. tolerated.
   d. accorded the status of ministers.

77. In 1776, Jemima Wilkinson declared that
   a. she was the "Spirit of Light."
   b. women should not be able to preach publicly.
   c. she had become male.
   d. women were better preachers than men.

78. By the 1820s, many churches were responding to female preachers by
   a. reinstating patterns of gender dominance.
   b. encouraging them.
   c. refusing to acknowledge them.
   d. allowing them to be officially ordained.

79. Changes in women's status in the early Republic came in _____.
   a. incremental steps
   b. response to the war
   c. a sudden rush
   d. with great public support

80. Under coverture, a wife was legally obligated to _____ her husband.
   a. vote like
   b. obey
   c. respect
   d. financially support

81. In the early nineteenth century, very few people questioned the assumption that _____ lay at the heart of marriage.
   a. love
   b. equality
   c. unequal power relations
   d. religion

82. States made divorce difficult and upheld the institution of marriage to _____.
   a. regulate the use and inheritance of property
   b. force women to have a lot of children
   c. collect higher taxes
   d. simplify their record-keeping procedures

83. A single adult woman in the early Republic was likely to be poor unless she had _____.
   a. sympathetic relatives
   b. a good career
   c. inherited adequate property
   d. good looks

84. Slaves were denied the protective features of _____.
   a. separation
   b. baptism
   c. medical care
   d. marriage

85. In most Protestant denominations around 1800, white women were _____ of congregants.
   a. the minority
   b. the majority
   c. just half
   d. a tiny fraction

86. Traditionally, _____ women who felt a spiritual call were officially allowed to lead and speak in religious meetings.
    a. Methodist
    b. Lutheran
    c. Quaker
    d. Baptist

87. After recovering from a fever in 1776, Jemima Wilkinson believed that she was no longer _____.
    a. human
    b. alive
    c. male or female
    d. sane

88. Between 1790 and the 1820s, the tradition of _____ came into question among some radically democratic churches.
    a. communion
    b. the trinity
    c. gender subordination
    d. scriptural arguments

89. During Monroe's two terms as president, the nation
    a. enjoyed an unprecedented level of amity.
    b. developed a two-party system.
    c. underwent a major constitutional crisis.
    d. agreed on major foreign policy issues.

90. Missouri's admission to statehood was complicated because
    a. of the ten thousand slaves in the territory.
    b. it lacked the proper number of residents.
    c. southerners opposed its entrance.
    d. it wanted to remain independent.

91. James Tallmadge Jr.'s amendments to the Missouri statehood bill caused controversy because they proposed
    a. gradually emancipating all American slaves.
    b. gradually emancipating all slaves in Missouri.
    c. ending the sale of slaves between states.
    d. ending the sale of slaves in the United States.

92. The Missouri Compromise package passed because
    a. some southerners were willing to compromise.
    b. some northerners wanted to minimize sectional conflict.
    c. it was a foolproof solution.
    d. Henry Clay was popular with representatives.

93. James Monroe and Thomas Jefferson were worried that the Missouri crisis would
    a. lead to secession.
    b. cause congressional action to grind to a halt.
    c. reinvigorate the Federalist Party.
    d. inspire an abolitionist movement.

94. Southerners saw the 1819 Adams-Onis Treaty giving the United States Florida as a concession on their part because
    a. the climate was bad for growing cotton.
    b. it was supported by northern politicians.
    c. Florida was populated by antislavery settlers.
    d. the Americans abandoned any claim to Texas or Cuba.

95. Monroe formulated the Monroe Doctrine in response to
    a. the possibility that European nations would try to regain lost colonies.
    b. Jackson's invasion of Florida.
    c. the furor over Missouri.
    d. the Adams-Onis Treaty.

96. In 1824, the caucus system that had largely determined each party's leading presidential candidate
    a. worked according to nonpartisan ideals.
    b. nominated two candidates.
    c. tried to reelect Monroe for a third term.
    d. splintered.

97. In the 1824 presidential election, Henry Clay promoted the American System, which consisted of
   a. governmental noninterference in the economy.
   (b.) tariffs and federal expenditures on internal improvements.
   c. high internal taxes.
   d. a smaller military.

98. The 1824 election was the first presidential contest in which popularity with ordinary voters could be measured because in all but six states
   a. voters voted for the president directly.
   (b.) voters voted for the electoral college.
   c. voters voted for the state senators who elected the electoral college.
   d. there were public opinion polls.

99. John Quincy Adams's victory in the 1824 election was characterized as a "corrupt bargain" on account of
   (a.) his appointment of Henry Clay as secretary of state.
   b. his shameless pandering to the House of Representatives.
   c. the liberal use of bribes and payments.
   d. his use of patronage positions to secure support.

100. John Quincy Adams's presidency was marked by
   a. legislative success.
   b. a reduction in partisan bickering.
   c. the resurgence of the Federalists.
   (d.) his inability to implement his program.

101. _____ remained in the presidency through the elections of 1812, 1816, and 1820.
   (a.) Virginians
   b. New Englanders
   c. South Carolinians
   d. New Yorkers

102. In 1819, a constitutional crisis arose over _____'s application for statehood.
   a. Indiana
   (b.) Missouri
   c. Mississippi
   d. Illinois

103. Southerners objected to _____'s proposed amendments to the Missouri statehood bill because they drew extra political strength from the slave population.
   a. Henry Clay
   b. John C. Calhoun
   (c.) James Tallmadge Jr.
   d. James Madison

104. In 1820, the Senate agreed that the southern boundary of _____ would become the permanent line dividing slave from free.
   a. Ohio
   (b.) Missouri
   c. Illinois
   d. Kentucky

105. In 1816, General Andrew Jackson led American troops in an invasion of Florida in search of _____ who had been harboring escaped slaves.
   a. Spanish civilians
   (b.) Seminole Indians
   c. British officers
   d. American abolitionists

106. The Adams-Onis Treaty gave the United States Florida, but in exchange the United States agreed to abandon any claims to _____.
   a. Cuba or California
   b. Texas or California
   c. Cuba or Arizona
   (d.) Texas or Cuba

107. President Monroe's cabinet was filled with Republicans who espoused _____ philosophies.
   (a.) different
   b. similar
   c. identical
   d. impractical

108. _____ was the most popular candidate with voters in the 1824 presidential election.
   (a.) Andrew Jackson
   b. John Quincy Adams
   c. William H. Crawford
   d. Henry Clay

109. John Quincy Adams appointed his _____ to his cabinet.
   a. opponents
   b. close friends
   c. political allies
   d. family members

110. President Adams's opponents worried that he was using federal power to advance _____.
   a. the Supreme Court
   b. his own family
   c. commercial interests
   d. the military

***Short Answer*** Write a paragraph response to each question.

1. What was remarkable about the election of 1800?
2. What was Gabriel's Rebellion? How did white political leaders respond to it?
3. What was *Marbury v. Madison*, and why was it significant?
4. Why did Jefferson impose the Embargo Act of 1807? Did it have the desired effect on Great Britain?
5. What were the ongoing difficulties between the United States, France, and Great Britain in 1810 and 1811? How did James Madison deal with them?
6. What caused the Indian troubles in the Northwest Territory? How did they contribute to the outbreak of the War of 1812?
7. What groups opposed the War of 1812, and why? How was its unpopularity manifested?
8. What were the British offensives of 1814? What did they demonstrate to British leaders?
9. What was the outcome of the War of 1812 for the British, the Americans, and the Indians?
10. What was the legal doctrine of *feme covert*, and what did it assume about the nature of marriage?
11. Was the membership of most Protestant denominations around 1800 reflected in the church hierarchy? Why were changes in church hierarchy and governance short-lived?
12. What amendments did James Tallmadge Jr. propose to the Missouri statehood bill? Why did southerners oppose them?
13. Why did James Monroe formulate the Monroe Doctrine, and what did it say? What military and congressional support was available for the policy?
14. How did Andrew Jackson lose the presidency in 1824, despite his popular support? Why did his supporters claim that a "corrupt bargain" had been made?

***Building Historical Skills*** Historians use a variety of sources to think and talk about the past, including maps, illustrations, and written records. Maps provide a variety of different kinds of comparative information in a condensed visual format; reading them requires learning how to sort through this information. To deepen our understanding of the past by supplementing written records, historians frequently interpret material culture, such as a vase or a painting, with techniques borrowed from art history, archaeology, or anthropology. Written records, though familiar as sources, raise their own problems of interpretation. Every document reflects someone's particular perspective or assumptions. It is the historian's task to study and compare each document to other records with other perspectives. The following exercises introduce you to using maps, illustrations, and written documents as sources of information. Use these sources as well as the material in the chapter to think about different themes and topics discussed in the text.

***Map Activity*** Locate the following places on Map 9.5: The Missouri Compromise, 1820, on page 311 of *The American Promise*, Second Edition.

1. Missouri Compromise Line
2. Missouri
3. Maine
4. Arkansas Territory
5. Unorganized Territory
6. Spanish Territory
7. Adams-Onis Treaty Line

Answer the following questions in a paragraph based on Map 9.5: The Missouri Compromise, 1820.

**READING THE MAP** How many free and how many slave states were there prior to the Missouri Compromise? What did the admission of Missouri as a free state threaten to do?

**CONNECTIONS** Who precipitated the crisis over Missouri, what did he propose, and where did the idea come from? What was the Missouri Compromise and who proposed it?

**WEB LINKS** To explore the topics discussed in the exercise above, visit the Web links noted below.

"The Missouri Compromise"
http://169.147.169.151/genweb/archives/1918ks/v1/ch12p1.html

"Westward Expansion and Regional Differences"
http://odur.let.rug.nl/~usa/H/1994/ch5_p2.htm

"Africans in America: The Missouri Compromise"
http://www.pbs.org/wgbh/aia/part3/3h511.html

***Visual Activity*** This painting shows a view of St. Louis, Missouri, from the Illinois side of the Mississippi River. The men untying the ferry's ropes are both black and, presumably, free, since they are on the free side of the river. The ferry has a mixed clientele, indicating that the city attracts a wide range of visitors. There is a well-dressed woman on a horse, which is led by a man in a suit and a top hat, and another gentleman can be seen in the background, but there are also men with livestock. The picture makes the city look almost celestial. The foreground of the painting is dark, but the city is painted mostly in whites, with puffy clouds overhead and a muted landscape off toward the left-hand side.

Answer the following questions based on "A View of St. Louis from an Illinois Town" on page 310 of *The American Promise*, Second Edition.

**READING THE IMAGE** What kind of city was St. Louis?

**CONNECTIONS** Does this image of St. Louis conform to the usual depiction of the slave states as agricultural?

**WEB LINKS** To explore the topics discussed in the exercise above, visit the Web links noted below.

"Jefferson National Expansion Memorial"
http://www.nps.gov/jeff/
Choose "In Depth," then "St. Louis History," then scroll down to "St. Louis: The Early Years" and select "Learn More."

"Physical Growth of the City of St. Louis"
http://stlouis.missouri.org/heritage/History69/index.html
Choose "Boom Town: 1821–1861"

***Analyzing Sources Activity*** Answer the following questions based on "The Promise of Technology: Eli Terry's Clock" on page 316 of *The American Promise,* Second Edition.

1. How did Eli Terry revolutionize the manufacture of clocks in the United States? What were his distinctive contributions to the field?
2. How did the widespread availability of clocks affect American life?
3. In what ways did the spread of accurate timepieces cause problems as Americans became increasingly mobile in the nineteenth century?

**WEB LINKS** To explore the topics discussed in the exercise above, visit the Web links noted below.

"Domestic Products, Domestic Commodities"
http://www.columbia.edu/~bjb5/domestic.html

"Keeping Watch: A History of American Time"
http://www.chnm.gmu.edu/courses/jackson/mill/1R.html

"A Walk through Time: A Revolution in Timekeeping"
http://physics.nist.gov/GenInt/Time/revol.html

# Answer Key

## Chapter 9: Republican Ascendancy, 1800–1824

### *Chapter Overview*

#### *Chronology*

1. b
2. d
3. d
4. b
5. c
6. b
7. b
8. d
9. a
10. a

#### *Defining Terms*

1. Gabriel's Rebellion
2. midnight judges
3. *Marbury v. Madison*
4. Robert R. Livingston
5. Sacajawea
6. impressment
7. *Chesapeake* incident
8. Embargo Act of 1807
9. Non-Intercourse Act of 1809
10. Tecumseh
11. War Hawks
12. *Report on the Causes and Reasons for War*
13. Plattsburgh
14. Treaty of Ghent
15. Hartford Convention
16. *feme covert*
17. divorce
18. Freewill Baptists
19. Jemima Wilkinson
20. "Era of Good Feelings"
21. Missouri Compromise
22. Adams-Onis Treaty
23. Monroe Doctrine
24. "corrupt bargain"

### *Chapter Review*

#### *Multiple-Choice*

1. d
2. d
3. b
4. b
5. b
6. d
7. d
8. b
9. c
10. d
11. b
12. d
13. c
14. b
15. a
16. c
17. d
18. d
19. b
20. a
21. c
22. c
23. b
24. c
25. d
26. d
27. d
28. a
29. a
30. a
31. c
32. d
33. b
34. c
35. a
36. c
37. d
38. a
39. b
40. d
41. b
42. b
43. c
44. a
45. d
46. c
47. a
48. a
49. a
50. c
51. b
52. c
53. b
54. c
55. a
56. c
57. d
58. c
59. b
60. c
61. d
62. a
63. c
64. b
65. b
66. d
67. d
68. b
69. c
70. a
71. d
72. a
73. d
74. c
75. b
76. d
77. a
78. a
79. a
80. b
81. c
82. a

83. c
84. d
85. b
86. c
87. c
88. c
89. c
90. a
91. b
92. b
93. c
94. d
95. a
96. d
97. b
98. b
99. a
100. d
101. a
102. b
103. c
104. b
105. b
106. d
107. a
108. a
109. a
110. c

### *Short Answer*

1. The election of 1800 showed that the constitutional government could effect a transfer of power from one group to another without bloodshed. In 1800, the incumbent president, John Adams, was renominated by a Federalist caucus, but lack of support from prominent party-mates, including the influential Alexander Hamilton, led to his defeat. Federalists had hoped that his running mate, Charles Cotesworth Pinckney, would take the election. However, the final tally resulted in a tie between the Republican Thomas Jefferson and his running mate, Aaron Burr. The election went to the House of Representatives, where Jefferson won after thirty-seven ballots.
2. Gabriel's Rebellion was a major uprising planned by an enslaved Virginian blacksmith. The uprising alarmed white leaders because the plotters drew on the Revolutionary-era rhetoric of liberty and freedom to defend themselves. They planned to capture Virginia governor James Monroe and hold him hostage because he was known to hold pro-French, and therefore pro-liberty, views and one rebel compared himself to George Washington. Virginia courts initially responded by hanging the conspirators, but Monroe and Vice President Jefferson were disturbed by the idea of executing men for wanting to be free. Virginian politicians toyed with the idea of deporting rebellious slaves but were afraid that such a solution would encourage defiance.
3. After the 1800 election, John Adams and John Marshall, a Federalist judge, made a series of last-minute appointments to try to undermine the incoming Republican administration. Once Jefferson took office, he canceled nontenured appointments and refused to honor commission that had not been sent out. One of the men in that group, William Marbury, sued James Madison, the secretary of state, to demand that he make good on the appointment. The case went to the Supreme Court, where John Marshall, by then the Chief Justice, ruled that the commission was valid, that the president should have delivered it, but that the Court could not force him to do so. What made the case extraordinary was that the Court found the grounds of Marbury's suit, resting in the Judiciary Act of 1789, in conflict with the Constitution, thus setting the precedent for judicial review.
4. In 1806, an American ship, the *Chesapeake*, was ordered to stop for inspection by a British frigate. The *Chesapeake* refused and the British opened fire, killing three Americans in U.S. territorial waters. President Jefferson was furious, but the United States could not possibly go to war: the army and navy had been seriously reduced over the course of several years. Therefore, Jefferson decided on a total embargo, one that would prevent Americans from trading with any foreign port to prevent the British from obtaining American agricultural goods, even indirectly. The Embargo Act did not work as it was intended to; American shippers and planters suffered economically, while the British simply purchased food from South America.
5. When President Madison took office in 1809, the Embargo Act had been replaced by the Non-Intercourse Act, barring trade with France and England and their colonial possessions but not other ports. When that act expired in 1810, it was replaced by a law that permitted trade with either France or England, whichever first assured the United States that it would stop harassing American shipping. When the French leader Napoleon offered to comply with the new terms, Madison accepted his offer a little too hastily and notified England that he would reinstate the embargo unless it rescinded its own search and seizure policy. Unfortunately, Napoleon did not end French depredations on American shipping, and the English ignored Madison, forcing him to reenact the highly unpopular embargo. By 1811, it seemed to Madison and many other Americans that war was on the horizon, although which country was the appropriate target was far from obvious.
6. The difficulties in the Northwest Territory revolved around Indiana governor William Henry Harrison's attempts to purchase land from Indians cheaply, even if it meant negotiating with individuals who were not authorized to dispose of land. Harrison was quite unhappy when the Shawnee chief Tecumseh encouraged tribes to join in a pan-Indian alliance and stop selling their land. When Harrison, concerned about Tecumseh

and his brother Tenskwatawa's growing influence, attacked Tenskwatawa's village, Prophetstown, Tecumseh threw his support behind the British in lower Canada. This alliance infuriated western Americans and congressional War Hawks, who then pushed for war against Great Britain rather than France.

7. While southern and western representatives supported the declaration of war, New Englanders and some of the Middle Atlantic states were strongly opposed to it, feeling that the war would be against their best economic interests. The New England states were slow to provide troops for the army, and New England merchants engaged in an illegal trade with Great Britain. The fighting went poorly during the first two years of the war, which decreased support even further. By the fall of 1812, there was enough discontent over the unsuccessful war that Federalists picked up considerable support in the national elections.

8. The British offensives of 1814 started with a dramatic, if largely symbolic, victory when British forces invaded Washington, D.C., and burned public buildings, dockyards, and an arsenal. However, they were turned back at Baltimore by the Maryland militia and a steady barrage of gunfire from Fort McHenry in the harbor. Another offensive heading from Canada into New York was halted after the British lost a minor naval engagement at Plattsburgh on Lake Champlain. This was a decisive moment for British leaders in England, who concluded that land invasions of the United States were likely to be costly, difficult, and ineffective.

9. The English agreed to evacuate their western forts and stop helping the area's Indians; the United States yielded on impressment and gave up their claims to Canada. Despite this, the War Hawks gained a great deal from the war, taking up the banner of the Republican Party and reshaping it along more expansive lines, while the Federalists were practically destroyed by the outcome since the Hartford Convention, called to protect New England's sectional interests against the South and the West, looked unpatriotic. The Indians of the Northwest Territory, however, lost the most. The powerful chief Tecumseh died at the Battle of the Thames, and the British were no longer available to serve as a counterbalance against seemingly endless American land claims.

10. The doctrine of *feme covert* was implanted in British common law and retained in American law, even in the post-Revolutionary period when states rewrote their laws in accordance with Republican ideals. The underlying principle of coverture was that wives had no independent legal or political personhood. The civic life of a married women was subsumed by her husband's; she was legally obligated to obey him, and her property, wages, sexual services, and children belonged exclusively to him. Married women could not sue or be sued or make contracts, and their husbands could be charged with most kinds of crimes their wives committed in their presence. Coverture assumed that men did and should control their wives and that marriage was fundamentally a relationship between unequals.

11. By 1800, the majority of Protestant congregants were women, but church leadership, including ordained ministers, elders, and governing boards, were almost exclusively male. The few exceptions were mostly in small evangelical groups in New England that had been influenced by the Great Awakening. In these congregations, women served with men on governance committees, giving them a role in hiring ministers, admitting new members, disciplinary proceedings, sometimes debates over doctrinal points. Quakers also allowed women an expanded role in the church, permitting them to lead and speak in religious meetings, although church governance was sex-segregated. These were exceptions to the rule, however; the idea of male authority over women was deeply entrenched in American culture and some churches that had given women a greater say reversed their policies in the 1820s.

12. James Tallmadge Jr., a representative from New York, proposed that Missouri be allowed into the Union on two conditions: that slaves born in Missouri after the enactment of the statehood law be freed at the age of twenty-five and that no new slaves be imported into the state. Through this gradual emancipation, owners could use their old slaves until they died, and their slaves' children could be worked through their prime years and then sold South before the date of emancipation. Southerners, however, objected strongly to the proposed amendments. They were increasingly concerned about the national balance of power between slave and free states and did not want free states to outnumber slave states. Moreover, their slave population added to their representation in Congress, which they did not want to lose.

13. In the early 1820s, many of Spain's colonies in South and Central America were declaring their independence. James Monroe was concerned that Spain, perhaps joined by France and Prussia, might intervene to retake their holdings. In 1823, he incorporated a declaration of principles into his annual message to Congress: the Western Hemisphere was no longer open to European colonization, and attempts to establish colonies

would be taken by the United States as a sign of unfriendly intent. His statements, which became known as the Monroe Doctrine, were made without any real force behind them: the United States did not have the military might to intervene if a European power did decide to colonize, and Congress did not back Monroe's statements. Rather, the Monroe Doctrine was an abstract policy that Monroe chose to make public.

14. Andrew Jackson won a clear majority of votes in the 1824 presidential election; he had 153,000 votes to runner-up John Quincy Adams's 109,000. The problem was that with four candidates for the spot, Jackson did not win a clear majority of electoral college votes. This meant that the election was thrown into the House of Representatives, where only the top three vote-getters could enter the runoff. Henry Clay, with the fewest votes, threw his support behind John Quincy Adams, thus ensuring Adams's victory. When Adams offered Henry Clay the position of secretary of state three days after the election, Jackson's supporters howled that the two men had made a backroom deal, or corrupt bargain, with Clay trading his support for a cabinet position.

### *Map Activity*

Reading the Map: In 1819, there were an even number of slave and free states—eleven of each. The admission of Missouri threatened to upset the balance of power between slave and free states by giving slave states two more senators and bolstering southern strength in the House of Representatives. Ex-Federalists had already been concerned about the power of other sections' representatives to pass legislation detrimental to the Northeast. The prospect of another slave state seemed to worsen a problem that already existed.

Connections: James Tallmadge Jr., a representative from New York, began the crisis over Missouri's admission to the Union. He proposed amending Missouri's statehood bill to ensure the gradual emancipation of its slave population by means of laws modeled on New York's 1799 gradual emancipation law. Tallmadge wanted to prohibit the importation of new slaves into Missouri. His amendment also stipulated that all slaves born after statehood be freed after the age of twenty-five. The Missouri Compromise passed the House of Representatives with the help of deal-brokering by Henry Clay, a Kentucky representative and former War Hawk. The compromise resolved the furor over Missouri's statehood by balancing Missouri's entrance into the Union with that of Maine, a free state. To calm northern concerns about Missouri reaching so far into the North, it stipulated that in the future, slavery would be confined to the area south of Missouri's southern border, latitude 36°30′ (the Missouri Compromise Line). All of the Louisiana Territory north of that line, except for Missouri, would be free.

### *Visual Activity*

Reading the Image: It is clear from the painting that St. Louis was a busy commercial center and a major urban center in the area. There are commercial buildings and ports lining the St. Louis shore of the Mississippi. Several steamboats are shown already docked there, and more are on the river, indicating heavy traffic of people and goods. There are also several men depicted herding oxen that they likely intend to sell in St. Louis. The city is depicted as being quite large, with buildings that stretch back into the horizon and seem to fill the entire horizontal length of the canvas.

Connections: While much of the slave South was agricultural, there were a handful of urban centers. St. Louis was typical of nineteenth century southern cities in that it was located along a major waterway, making trade its major economic activity. As can be seen from the painting, the docks were at the center of St. Louis's commercial life: the only smokestacks are those on the steamboats, and there are no other signs of manufacturing enterprises. It is interesting that none of the passengers or crew traveling on the ferry are black. The only blacks depicted seem to be staying away from what would have to be for them the dangerous side of the river.

### *Analyzing Sources*

1. In the eighteenth century, clocks were extremely expensive items manufactured by hand for a limited and wealthy clientele. Terry trained as an artisan clockmaker, but he was determined to make clocks and affordable household fixtures and thus began to experiment with combining wooden and brass parts to lower the price of the finished product. In 1807, when the Embargo Act made brass impossible to obtain, he used all-wood parts. That year, he contracted to deliver 4,000 tallcase clocks in three years and spent the following twelve months developing the machinery to mass-produce their parts. His factory marked the first successful implementation of a system of manufacturing with interchangeable parts. He then designed a compact shelf clock, which was smaller and cheaper and brought a fairly accurate measurement of time into much wider distribution.

2. Before the nineteenth century, very few people had any need to know the exact time, so they relied on the position of the sun and the moon to give them a general calculation; in larger towns, public clocks and bells were employed. Clocks, however, made it possible for people to be more

accurate. As they become more common, families could coordinate their household schedules with a factory starting bell, businessmen could make and keep more appointments, and stagecoaches and canals could leave on scheduled times. Clocks allowed employers to expect and demand punctuality and made it possible to speed up the pace of life.

3. Clocks gave people the ability to be much more accurate about time. However, because people calculated the correct time by the sun, each town and village operated on its own time. As a result, anything scheduled over significant distances from east to west had to determine what time to use—that of the point of origin or of the stops along the way. This was particularly troublesome for railroads. For instance, Worcester, Massachusetts was forty miles west of Boston and operated on a five-minute time differential. In setting schedules, a train company had to determine whether to standardize time to the home city, with the necessity of displaying multiple clocks in each station, or calculate the local time in each town in which it stopped. The problem was not solved until the adoption of standardized time zones in the 1880s.

# THE EXPANDING REPUBLIC, 1815–1840 10

## Chapter Overview

### *Chapter Summary*

***Introduction*** Chapter 10 begins with an account of the rise of Andrew Jackson, who symbolized for many the self-confident and expanding nation that was emerging. As president from 1828 to 1836, Andrew Jackson presided over a multitude of changes in the economy, society, and politics of the United States, changes that profoundly affected American men and women, both in the workplace and in their personal lives.

***The Market Revolution, pp. 324–334*** After 1815, powerful economic and social forces dramatically changed the domestic marketplace. Major innovations in transportation aided the movement of commodities, information, and people, while the growth of textile mills and other factories created many new jobs, especially for women. Changes in banking, legal practices, and tariff policies encouraged rapid economic growth.

**IMPROVEMENTS IN TRANSPORTATION** Between 1815 and 1840, growing networks of roads, canals, steamboats, and finally railroads lowered the costs and raised the speed of travel significantly. Improved transportation had clear economic benefits because products could now be sold more cheaply to a wider market; however, it also had profound social and political effects, as news, mail, and people traveled farther and farther. The development of the steamboat transformed water travel, as did the ongoing building of canals, and by the 1830s, private railroad companies were competing with both for passengers and freight.

**FACTORIES, WORKINGWOMEN, AND WAGE LABOR** As markets developed, entrepreneurs reorganized their operations to increase production. New England textile manufacturers began using new machines driven by water power, and the factory system they developed spread rapidly in the 1820s to shoemaking and other industries. The Waltham system, which spread throughout New England, employed young single women who lived and worked for a few years in the mills. Though labor conditions were often trying, many women workers welcomed the relative freedom of living away from home and the opportunity to earn real wages. In the increasingly competitive textile market, owners soon cut wages and lengthened shifts. Women millworkers responded with strikes in 1834 and 1836, but their easy replaceability undermined their bargaining power. By midcentury, mill owners had shifted to a cheaper and more pliant source of labor—immigrant families. Manufacturing enterprises like shoemaking also employed women. The work was transformed by separating shoemaking into different tasks, some done by men and others, especially shoebinding, by much cheaper women. Female shoebinders also tried to strike in protest over decreasing pay, but their isolation made organization very difficult.

**BANKERS AND LAWYERS** Factory entrepreneurs relied increasingly on innovations in the banking system to finance their ventures. Thus, the number of state-chartered banks increased in the years after 1815, to several hundred by 1840. Banks aided economic expansion by making loans to various businesses and real estate enterprises and by increasing the money supply. The market revolution was also accompanied by a revolution in commercial law as a growing sector of entrepreneurial lawyers increasingly shaped the legal system to promote and protect the interests of commercial activity and private investment.

**BOOMS AND BUSTS** In 1819, the United States endured its first economic downturn, the panic of 1819, which was caused by a number of factors including the credit contraction by the second Bank of the United States and a European financial crisis. The resulting depression saw mounting unemployment, bank failures, plummeting crop prices, and the collapse of western land investments. Though the economy had fully recovered by the mid-1820s, some Americans saw the panic as a warning that rapid economic growth and territorial expansion would destabilize the nation and threaten its survival. Strong resentment against banks and anxiety about rapid economic change persisted in the minds of many Americans, ready to be exploited by politicians in the decades to come.

***The Spread of Democracy, pp. 334–338*** Coinciding with the market revolution was an equally profound transformation of American politics. Between 1820 and 1840, a democratic revolution of sorts occurred, with increased voter participation and officeholding. Two important features of this democratization were the emergence of the second-party system of Democrats and Whigs and the importance of candidates' popularity with the "common man" in determining the outcome of elections.

**POPULAR POLITICS AND PARTISAN IDENTITY** The 1828 election was the first presidential contest where popular votes determined the victor; in twenty-two out of twenty-four states, voters now designated electors committed to a particular candidate. The election also inaugurated modern-day electioneering, as many state-level candidates gave speeches and held barbecues and banquets to woo voters. More informal and direct campaign rhetoric and blatantly partisan newspapers were also part of this new style. By 1828, party labels appeared, with Andrew Jackson's followers assuming the name of Democratic Republicans, and those in the Adams–Henry Clay coalition calling their party the National Republicans. By 1836, Jacksonians simply referred to their organization as the Democratic Party, and the National Republicans had evolved into the Whig Party.

**THE ELECTION OF 1828 AND THE CHARACTER ISSUE** The 1828 election was also the first national election in which both candidates engaged in vicious character assassination. Jacksonians charged that John Quincy Adams was an elitist and extravagant aristocrat who had only won the election of 1824 by the "corrupt bargain." Adams's supporters called Jackson a sinful and impulsive man, guilty of murders during the War of 1812 and of bigamy. The stories became the real issues in the election, giving voters a choice between two different styles of masculinity. In the end, Jackson soundly defeated Adams, carrying most of the South and West, as well as New York and

Pennsylvania. The election showed a new approval of political parties and solidified a party loyalty that transcended individual candidates.

**JACKSON'S DEMOCRATIC AGENDA** Jackson's inauguration epitomized his public image as a man of the people, with an open reception at the White House that turned into a near-riot. He deviated from precedent by appointing party loyalists to his cabinet. Jackson also differed from his predecessors (especially Thomas Jefferson) in that he exercised full presidential powers over Congress and used the veto power more often than had all of the previous presidents combined.

***Cultural Shifts, pp. 338–343*** The market revolution was making the United States and particularly its more industrialized regions dramatically more wealthy by the year. It also transformed society and culture at almost every level, from the family to the world of leisure.

**THE FAMILY AND SEPARATE SPHERES** The growing separation between public and private life, between the workplace and the home, caused increasingly sharp distinctions between the social roles of men and women in Jacksonian America. In the middle-class family of the new industrial society, the husband was assumed to be the principal income producer, and the wife was expected to remain in the home and to engage in largely domestic activities. Within this context, women were to be the custodians of morality and benevolence; they were to provide religious and moral instruction to their children and to counterbalance the acquisitive, materialistic impulses of their husbands. The image never described reality: while most women did not perform paid work, they had to do heavy household labor, and wealthy women who hired servants became employers. They could not escape market relations.

**THE EDUCATION AND TRAINING OF YOUTH** The new market economy meant new opportunities for educating and training the youth of the 1820s and 1830s. Northern states adopted public schooling between 1790 and the 1820s, and the South soon followed. The job of educating the nation's youth began to fall more and more to women in their late teens, who provided an inexpensive source of teachers. Remarkably, basic education was the same for girls as for boys. Higher education was a different story, with only Oberlin College accepting women in the 1830s, although a handful of top-notch seminaries offered college-level education to women who could afford it. While some male youths went on to college, the vast majority left school at fourteen to train for an occupation, often moving to the city to take entry-level business positions. Many youth were freed from family restrictions, a source of concern for moralists.

**PUBLIC LIFE, THE PRESS, AND POPULAR AMUSEMENTS** A widely shared but hardly monolithic national culture became possible in the Jacksonian era as the movement of books, newspapers, and people spread ideas and values. Rising rates of literacy and new printing methods led to an explosion of newspapers. "Penny papers" covered a variety of issues ranging from entertainment to local news and exposés. By the end of the decade, penny papers could be found in every metropolitan area of the nation as well as in smaller towns and villages. Beginning in the 1830s, traveling lecturers crisscrossed the country, entertaining small-town audiences with a variety of presentations, ranging from dramatic readings of poetry and plays to lectures on history, physiology, and anatomy. Theater also flourished in the 1830s, as audiences across the country applauded everything from Shakespeare to minstrel shows. Another popular diversion was public oratory. Huge audiences listened with rapt attention to speeches at trials and to political orations that sometimes lasted for hours.

***Democracy and Religion, pp. 343–349*** After gathering momentum for three decades, an unprecedented revival of evangelical religion known as the Second Great Awakening peaked in the early 1830s. This evangelical movement contributed to a growing belief that individuals could improve not only themselves but the general human condition as well. The men and women of the new mercantile classes were the most enthusiastic converts to evangelical Protestantism.

**THE SECOND GREAT AWAKENING** The early nineteenth century witnessed a wave of religious revivalism that became known as the Second Great Awakening. Revivalists saw the nation's redemption possible only through stronger Christian beliefs and practices that would eliminate sin. The emotionally charged revivals typically attracted more women than men. They were led by itinerant preachers like the ex-lawyer Charles Grandison Finney. From 1800 to 1820, largely as a result of the Second Great Awakening, church membership doubled in the United States.

**THE TEMPERANCE MOVEMENT AND THE CAMPAIGN FOR MORAL REFORM** One of the first specific reform impulses was temperance, the movement to limit or prohibit consumption of alcohol. Drinking had been rising and was common among all classes. Reformers identified liquor as the cause of a number of social and family problems, including spouse and child abuse, poverty, and lack of productivity on the job. The first national organization, the American Temperance Society, was founded in 1826 by the evangelical minister Lyman Beecher, and by the mid-1830s, over a million people, most of them from the middle class, had joined its affiliates throughout the nation. The campaign shifted from voluntary temperance to the legal banning of alcohol. More controversial than temperance was a movement called "moral reform," which initially applied to public morals in general but quickly became restricted to a campaign to eradicate sexual sin, especially prostitution, which they saw as an outgrowth of uncontrolled male sexuality. The reformers published a national newspaper, *The Advocate of Moral Reform*, which was the first completely woman-operated publication in the nation. Moral reform drew on evangelical themes of self-control and suppression of sin, but its advocates' belief that women had a responsibility to speak out about unspeakable things meant that male evangelicals often did not support the movement.

**ORGANIZING AGAINST SLAVERY** The cause of abolishing slavery—"abolitionism"—gathered strength in the 1830s. In 1831, Bostonian William Lloyd Garrison began publishing the *Liberator*, a newspaper devoted to putting an immediate end to slavery. Black abolitionists such as David Walker not only demanded immediate emancipation but also called on northern whites to rid themselves of their own prejudices. Many northerners disliked both slavery and blacks and so were opposed to abolition. Their animosity often took the form of violence, with attacks ranging from destruction of property to murder. Women played a prominent role in abolition movements, which became a natural corollary to their involvement in other reform causes. The women's rights movement came out of the sexism women experienced in antislavery campaigns.

***Jackson Defines the Democratic Party, pp. 349–358*** In his two terms as president, Andrew Jackson worked to enact his vision of a politics of opportunity for all white males. The primary issues of his tenure were westward expansion, Indian removal, nullification, and "war" with the second Bank of the United States.

**INDIAN POLICY AND THE TRAIL OF TEARS** When Jackson became president, substantial tribal enclaves remained east of the Mississippi River, and he wanted them removed. The government's attempt in 1832 to relocate reluctant western Illinois tribes erupted into war and led to a major defeat for the Indians. More troubling to Jackson were the southern tribes of Creek, Chickasaw, Choctaw, and Cherokee whom the federal government hoped to remove to the West to open their lands for white settlement and cotton cultivation. Through appeals to the Supreme Court, the Cherokee—one of the most "assimilated" tribes—tried to stop encroachments onto their land by Georgia. Jackson repudiated the Court's decisions in their favor, and in 1835, the government was able to make a treaty with a minority faction of the tribe, ceding to Georgia the Cherokee's land in return for $5 million and land in present-day Oklahoma. When the majority of the Cherokee who did not recognize the treaty refused to move, Jackson sent federal troops in the winter of 1838, to force them on a twelve-hundred-mile trek west. Along this "trail of tears," nearly a quarter of the Cherokee perished.

**THE TARIFF OF ABOMINATIONS AND NULLIFICATION** The federal government passed tariffs to protect American manufactures and raise revenue in 1816 and 1824, over the protest of southern congressmen who feared the effects the tariffs would have on the southern export economy. The final and most controversial tariff of the period, passed in 1828, was an agglomeration of dozens of tariffs from every section of the country and from every type of industry demanding protection. Southerners opposed the measure, labeling it the "tariff of abominations." In 1832, a crisis arose when South Carolinians, led by John Calhoun, decided to nullify, as of February 1, 1833, the despised federal tariffs they believed were responsible for their state's economic stagnation. In response, Jackson sent warships to Charleston and pushed through Congress a Force Bill granting him the authority to use military force if necessary to uphold the tariff laws. As tensions escalated, Henry Clay fashioned a compromise that got the South Carolinians the lower tariff they wanted. In the long run, though, the issue of federal power versus states' rights was far from resolved.

**THE BANK WAR AND THE PANIC OF 1837** The major political issue of Jackson's presidency was not the tariff but his war against the Bank of the United States. Though the bank had had a stabilizing effect on the economy, Jackson considered it a bastion of elitism, concentrating great power in the hands of a privileged few. When Henry Clay and Daniel Webster sought to recharter the bank four years early, Jackson's strongly worded veto roused popular antibank sentiment. Seeing his victory against Henry Clay in the 1832 election as a mandate for destroying the bank, Jackson ordered all federal deposits withdrawn and redeposited in selected state banks. Unbound and unregulated, the economy went into high gear, and a fury of speculation ensued, especially in land. In an attempt to control the economy, Jackson issued the Specie Circular, which, along with other factors, precipitated a financial panic of major proportions. Hundreds of banks and businesses failed in the wake of the panic of 1837, and another five years of economic hard times followed.

**VAN BUREN'S ONE-TERM PRESIDENCY** Martin Van Buren's political acuity earned him the nickname "the Little Magician." However, for all his cleverness, Van Buren lacked the forcefulness of his predecessor, Jackson. Elected in 1836, the new president spent the bulk of his four years attempting to deal with the panic of 1837. As the election of 1840 drew near, the Whigs smelled victory. They settled on candidate William Henry Harrison to oppose Van Buren. The 1840 campaign was one of the most dramatic, participatory, and exciting in American history. Harrison and the Whigs won a resounding victory in both the popular vote and electoral college. Democratic hegemony over American politics was temporarily over.

***Conclusion: Democrats and Whigs*** Democrats put together a coalition of farmers, laborers, commercial men, and slave owners who embraced personal liberty, free competition, and opportunity open to all white men. The opposition party, the Whigs, were moralistic and favored state-sponsored entrepreneurship. National politics were heated and divisive in the 1830s, and voter turnout was high because politics was where different choices about economic development and social change were made. Controversy over new forces like slavery, free labor, and women's rights, led to the growth of third parties in the 1840s and eventually undermined the Democratic-Whig party system.

***Chronology Activity*** Read the annotated chronology, and answer the multiple-choice questions.

1807 Robert Fulton develops first commercially successful steamboat, *Clermont.* The *Clermont*'s first voyage, up the Hudson River from New York City to Albany, took thirty-two hours against a headwind, as compared with two days for the land route. By 1820s, a dozen steamboats made the trip daily, and by the 1830s there were over seven hundred steamboats in operation all over the country.

1816 Second Bank of the United States chartered for twenty years. The second Bank of the United States was the most powerful bank in the United States and exercised a huge influence over the economy by its decisions about loans and discount rates.

Import tariff imposed on foreign textiles. The tariff placed duties as high as 33 percent on imports like textiles and iron goods, in an effort to favor new American manufacturers and protect them from foreign competition.

1817 American Colonization Society founded to promote gradual emancipation and removal of African Americans to Liberia. The American Colonization Society was quite conservative: it was founded by a group of Maryland and Virginia planters. Its program was not always popular with newly freed slaves, whose connection to Africa might be three or more generations in the past.

1818 National Road links Baltimore and Wheeling, West Virginia. The National Road was sponsored by the federal government during Jefferson's presidency. It reflected Jefferson's discomfort with federal funding for programs that would have uneven economic benefits, and the money had to come from the sale of Ohio public lands, the area that would ultimately reap the rewards of the road. Progress on the road was very slow, and it did not reach its final destination, Ohio, until the 1830s.

1819 Economic collapse and panic nationwide. The panic of 1819 was the first sharp, large-scale economic downturn in U.S. history. It was caused by the second Bank of the United States's withdrawal of credit to state banks, combined with a European financial crisis and a drop in the price of agricultural commodities. The panic affected thousands of Americans and created lasting anxiety about rapid economic change.

1824 Congress passes expanded tariff bill. Like the 1816 tariff, the 1824 tariff was intended to shelter American manufacturing. It met resistance from southerners, who worried about its impact on shipping and the South's export of raw cotton.

1825 Erie Canal spans 350 miles in New York State. The Erie Canal connected Albany on the Hudson River with Buffalo on Lake Erie. It effectively linked the Port of New York City with the inland western region of the state and, via the Great Lakes, the entire Northwest Territory. The canal created a large regional market for goods.

1826 Schuylkill Canal—108 miles long—opens in Pennsylvania. Like the Erie Canal, the Schuylkill Canal was intended to create a regional market by linking the western and eastern parts of the state.

1828 Tariff of Abominations passed. This tariff was a bundle of conflicting duties, with high tariffs that both benefited and disadvantaged every region. It was particularly hard on South Carolina, which was already suffering from a decline in the worldwide price of cotton.

Andrew Jackson elected president. Jackson was the first president to be elected by popular vote. His presidency seemed to epitomize a commitment to democracy and equality of opportunity for white men: he kept his office open to visitors and couched his political decisions in terms of equality and democracy.

1829 David Walker's *Appeal to the Colored Citizens of the World* published. David Walker was a black printer in Boston. His tract condemned racism, drew on the egalitarian language of the Declaration of Independence, and hinted at racial violence if whites did not change their attitudes. The piece galvanized William Lloyd Garrison, a white abolitionist.

1830 Indian Removal Act appropriates money to relocate Indian tribes west of Mississippi River. The Act was a reflection of Andrew Jackson's belief that Indians should not be treated as sovereign foreigners and that they had no right to their tribal lands. The Removal Act appropriated $500,000 to relocate tribes out of the way of white settlement, west of the Mississippi. Many tribes refused to go quietly, some turning to warfare and others to the courts.

1831 William Lloyd Garrison begins publishing abolitionist newspaper *Liberator.* The paper broke from the older abolitionist stance favoring gradual emancipation; it called for immediate abolition, describing slavery as a moral sin demanding an uncompromising solution.

Charles G. Finney stages evangelical revival in Rochester, New York. After the completion of the Erie Canal, Rochester swelled with new inhabitants, who brought both prosperity and urban ills like prostitution, drinking, and gaming. Finney saw these kinds of areas as ripe for conversion.

Supreme Court allows Georgia to continue to subject Indians to state laws. The Cherokee sued the state of Georgia after it announced that it would subject Indians to state law. While the Cherokees' suit was set aside on technical grounds, Chief Justice John Marshall encouraged the tribe to seek further legal redress.

1832 Supreme Court in *Worcester v. Georgia* recognizes Cherokee as distinct community outside legal jurisdiction of Georgia. When Georgia jailed two missionaries under an 1830 law forbidding missionary aid to Indians without state permission, the Cherokee brought suit against the state. In this decision, the court gave the Cherokee the decision they had wanted in 1831—a declaration of Cherokee sovereignty. Georgia and Jackson refused to honor the decision, however.

Jackson vetoes Bank of United States charter. Daniel Webster and Henry Clay, supporters of the bank, hoped to embarrass Jackson and damage his plans for reelection by forcing him to veto the bank's charter, which they assumed had popular support. Instead, Jackson was able to use the opportunity to denounce the bank as an instrument of elitism.

New England Anti-Slavery Society founded. The New England Anti-Slavery Society was the first antislavery organization to support immediate abolition.

Andrew Jackson reelected president. Jackson's campaign relied on the language of class antagonism and egalitarian ideals, using the controversy over the Bank of the United States as a lens for American fears. He won the election easily with 55 percent of the popular vote and an electoral college victory of 219 to 49 for his opponent, Henry Clay.

1833 Nullification crisis: South Carolina declares federal tariffs void in the state. When tariff revisions in 1832 failed to relieve southern financial suffering, South Carolina politicians decided to act on the doctrine of nullification that they had proposed in 1828, declaring the law to be null and void in the state as of February 1, 1833. Jackson sent armed ships to Charleston and got the Force Bill, which defined the South Carolinian stance as treasonous, through Congress. The situation was calmed by the passage of a revised tariff more acceptable to the South, but while South Carolina withdrew its nullification of the old tariff, it also nullified the Force Bill.

New York and Philadelphia Anti-Slavery Societies founded. These groups were founded in response to the formation of the New England Anti-Slavery Society. By 1837, there were thirteen hundred local antislavery societies with a quarter of a million members.

1834 Female mill workers strike in Lowell, Massachusetts. When worldwide changes in the cotton market impelled mill owners to increase productivity by adding more machines per worker and lowering wages, female workers, emboldened by their communal living arrangements and status as temporary employees, went on strike. While their assertiveness was surprising, their easy replaceability undermined their bargaining power, and they were not successful.

1836 Jackson issues Specie Circular. The Specie Circular was Jackson's attempt to halt the spiraling economy in the aftermath of the bank war. However, by ordering that public land could be purchased only with hard money, he caused a contraction of currency and credit that contributed to the panic of 1837.

Martin Van Buren elected president. Van Buren was more of a backroom politician than a public figure, and Whigs believed that he could be defeated. Their strategy of running three candidates backfired, though, and Van Buren narrowly won the election.

1837 Economic panic. The Specie Circular caused bankers to reduce their loans; then the Bank of England began to insist on hard-money payments for American loans, which had grown because of a trade imbalance. This, combined with short-run failures in various crop markets, a downturn in the price of cotton on the international market, and a silver glut, created a panic in 1837. The hard times lasted for more than five years.

1838 Trail of Tears: Cherokee forced to relocate west. For more than two years after the Supreme Court decision giving them independent status, the Cherokee remained in Georgia without violence. Then, in 1835, a small, unauthorized part of the tribe signed a treaty ceding all tribal lands to Georgia in return for $5 million and an equal acreage in present-day Oklahoma. Despite protests, when the deadline for involuntary evacuation arrived, federal troops deported the Cherokee to their new home. Nearly a quarter of the Cherokee died before they reached their destination.

1840 Independent Treasury Act. Martin Van Buren called a special session of Congress in 1837 to consider the creation of an independent treasury system. The system would be funded by the government and would deal only in hard money; commercial banks would have limits put on their issuance of paper currency. The new system would not make loans and so would avoid the danger of speculative meddling in the economy, creating a powerful influence on the credit market without being directly involved. It took three years for the measure to win approval.

## *Chronology Questions* Choose the letter of the best answer.

1. What is the correct order for the following events?
   1. The Indian Removal Act is passed.
   2. *Worcester v. Georgia* recognizes the Cherokee as a distinct community.
   3. Indians are forced to relocate west on the Trail of Tears.
   4. Andrew Jackson is first elected president.

   a. 2, 3, 4, 1
   b. 4, 1, 2, 3
   c. 3, 1, 4, 2
   d. 1, 3, 2, 4

2. The first commercially successful steamboat, Robert Fulton's *Clermont*, was developed in
   a. 1807.
   b. 1817.
   c. 1828.
   d. 1836.

3. Which of the following events was the first to occur?
   a. An import tariff was imposed on foreign textiles.
   b. There was an economic collapse and panic nationwide.
   c. Pennsylvania's Schuylkill Canal was completed.
   d. The New York and Philadelphia Anti-Slavery societies were founded.

4. In response to deteriorating working conditions and wages, female mill workers went on strike in Lowell, Massachusetts, in
   a. 1807.
   b. 1815.
   c. 1825.
   d. 1834.

5. What is the correct order for the following events?
   1. The nullification crisis occurs in South Carolina.
   2. Andrew Jackson is reelected president.
   3. Congress passes an expanded tariff bill.
   4. The Tariff of Abominations is passed.
   a. 2, 4, 3, 1
   b. 3, 4, 2, 1
   c. 2, 3, 1, 4
   d. 3, 2, 4, 1

6. In 1818,
   a. William Lloyd Garrison began publishing the abolitionist newspaper *Liberator.*
   b. the National Road linked Baltimore and Wheeling, West Virginia.
   c. the Supreme Court allowed Georgia to continue to subject Indians to state law.
   d. Charles G. Finney staged evangelical revival in Rochester, New York.

7. What is the correct order for the following events?
   1. Jackson issues the Specie Circular.
   2. The Independent Treasury Act is passed.
   3. The Second Bank of the United States is chartered for twenty years.
   4. Jackson vetoes the Bank of United States charter.
   a. 2, 4, 1, 3
   b. 3, 2, 1, 4
   c. 3, 4, 1, 2
   d. 1, 4, 2, 3

8. The Erie Canal, which effectively linked New York City with the Northwest Territory, was completed in
   a. 1807.
   b. 1818.
   c. 1825.
   d. 1830.

9. The New England Anti-Slavery Society was founded in 1832, and the New York and Philadelphia Anti-Slavery societies were founded in
   a. 1817.
   b. 1833.
   c. 1838.
   d. 1840.

10. What is the correct order for the following events?
   1. The American Colonization Society is founded.
   2. The New England Anti-Slavery Society is founded.
   3. William Loyd Garrison begins publishing the abolitionist newspaper *Liberator.*
   4. David Walker's *Appeal to the Colored Citizens of the World* is published.
   a. 1, 4, 3, 2
   b. 4, 3, 2, 1
   c. 3, 1, 4, 2
   d. 2, 4, 1, 3

***Defining Terms*** Match each term with the correct definition.

✓Second Great Awakening
✓Whig Party
✓separate spheres
✓Erie Canal
✓Trail of Tears
✓Waltham system
✓female seminaries
✓minstrelsy
✓nullification
✓Maria Stewart
✓Specie Circular
✓Andrew Lloyd Garrison
✓Charles Grandison Finney
✓"Old Hickory"
✓*Worcester v. Georgia*
✓*Gibbon v. Ogden*
✓market revolution
✓penny papers
✓Tariff of Abominations
✓American Temperance Union
✓Democratic Party
✓steamboats
✓normal schools

1. The greatly increased pace of economic activity and large-scale distribution of goods that transformed the United States starting in 1815. Contributing factors included changes in transportation, the proliferation of factories, and innovations in banking, law, and tariff policies. market revolution

2. An important advance in the technology of transportation. First introduced in 1807, by the early 1830s these cut the cost and time of transit on all the major eastern and western water routes. Steamboats

3. The 1824 Supreme Court decision that declared navigation on the Hudson River to be a form of interstate commerce and thus under the jurisdiction of the federal government. This invalidated state-sponsored monopolies on steamboat service that traversed two or more states and opened competition. Gibbon v. Ogden

4. Completed in 1825, this 350-mile-long structure linked Albany with Buffalo, New York. It was a major transit route, moving agricultural goods east and manufactured goods west, and helped to solidify New York City's status as the premier commercial center in the nation. Erie canal

5. Young, single women worked in textile mills for lower wages than men but higher wages than they could get doing other jobs, living in company-owned, closely supervised boarding houses and presumably leaving after a few years to marry. This new relationship between work and the labor force offered the workers unprecedented, although still limited, personal freedom. Waltham system

6. Andrew Jackson's popular nickname, meant to suggest resilience and toughness. Jackson was the first president to have an affectionate nickname, a sign of the growing importance of popular support in presidential races. "Old Hickory"

7. The shortened name of the Democratic Republicans, Andrew Jackson's party, which promised to be responsive to the will of the majority. Democratic Party

8. The name adopted by former National Republicans, widely used in the 1836 election. This party favored national action to promote commercial development. Whig Party

9. The Jacksonian-era concept of gender relations that held that men's proper place was in the public world of work and politics, while women were to remain in the private world of the home. Separate Spheres

10. Teacher training schools for women that began opening in the 1840s, in response to the demand for inexpensive female teachers. normal schools

11. Private schools for young women established in the 1820s and 1830s. Some of them were as educationally rigorous as the best men's colleges. female seminaries

12. Cheap newspapers that covered politics, current events, racetrack events, and crime reporting. They were circulated nationwide by means of the postal service, spreading a common culture from cities into towns and villages and creating undeferential attitudes toward politics. penny papers

13. A popular form of musical comedy in the Jacksonian era and beyond. White performers blackened their faces, trading on and reinforcing racist ideas about blacks. minstrelsy

14. A popular religious revival that peaked in the 1830s that emphasized that salvation was available to anybody who chose to take it. Its focus on social perfection inspired many of the reform movements of the Jacksonian era. Second Great Awakening

15. The leading exemplar of the Second Great Awakening. He was a lawyer–turned preacher who crafted his message for a middle-class audience, describing God and Satan as representatives of political parties and potential converts as a jury evaluating the arguments of a trial lawyer. He promised a reign of Christian perfection that depended on Christian benevolence on the part of believers to improve society. Charles Grandison Finney

16. An umbrella organization of antidrinking groups that formed in 1836 that demanded total abstinence rather than moderation and began using political means rather than individual moral suasion to stop the sale of alcohol. American Temperance Union

17. The person who was the center of the Boston antislavery movement. He supported immediate abolition, not the gradual variety that had been common in the earlier antislavery movement. His radical abolitionist views and support of women in prominent positions in the antislavery movement did not mesh with the views of most white northerners in the 1830s. Andrew Lloyd Garrison

18. A young black woman who gave lectures on slavery and racial prejudice to black audiences in Boston. The fact of her sex made her controversial, and she was convinced to give up her career. Maria Stewart

19. The 1832 Supreme Court case that recognized the Cherokee as an independent nation within a state. Worcester v. Georgia

20. The twelve-hundred mile forced journey to Oklahoma that the Georgia Cherokee undertook in 1838 after President Jackson refused to enforce the Supreme Court's decision in *Worcester v. Georgia* and thus allowed Georgia to take over Cherokee lands. Nearly a quarter of the migrants died en route. Trail of Tears

21. The 1828 federal tariff. The tariffs were as high as 50 percent, and the bundle of conflicted duties had something for and against every economic and sectional interest. South Carolinian unhappiness with this tariff led to the nullification crisis. Tariff of Abominations

22. The idea that states have the power to overturn federal laws when those laws represented an overstepping of congressional powers. The controversial idea was first proposed by South Carolina politicians in 1828 as a response to the Tariff of Abominations. The implied threat was that states could secede if they deemed a federal law unreasonable. nullification

23. Andrew Jackson's attempt to halt the wildly booming economy of the mid-1830s. This was an order declaring that the federal government would accept only gold and silver for land purchases. It caused a general contraction of credit and contributed to the panic of 1837. specie circular

## Chapter Review

***Multiple-Choice*** Choose the letter of the best answer.

1. Powerful economic and social forces propelled by the end of the War of 1812 revolutionized
   a. the market.
   b. military strategy.
   c. marriage practices.
   d. religious beliefs.

2. Although improved transportation after 1815 had many benefits, it did not mean that
   a. products could be sold more cheaply to a wider market.
   b. the flow of political information was facilitated.
   c. economic gains were spread evenly.
   d. cultural changes were encouraged.

3. The 1824 Supreme Court decision in *Gibbon v. Ogden* helped to
   a. protect consumers from dangerous steamboat explosions.
   b. end the granting of state monopolies for steam transportation.
   c. encourage the building of canal networks.
   d. improve the quality of privately built roads.

4. In the 1810s, Pennsylvania and New York hoped to create regional markets for goods by commencing major state-sponsored
   a. road-building.
   b. railroad construction.
   c. ocean shipping projects.
   d. canal enterprises.

5. In the early nineteenth century, textile jobs were popular with women because
   a. the working conditions were excellent.
   b. the pay was equal to that earned by a young man.
   c. they were easy.
   d. they allowed for unprecedented autonomy.

6. When mill owners felt raised work loads and lowered wages in the mid-1830s, female employees responded by
   a. going on strike.
   b. accepting the changes.
   c. taking domestic service jobs instead.
   d. sabotaging their machines.

7. In the 1820s and 1830s, the American shoemaking industry was transformed by new
   a. modes of organizing work.
   b. kinds of machinery.
   c. styles of shoes.
   d. competition from Europe.

8. In a transaction called a specie payment, the holder of a banknote could exchange it for
   a. its equivalent in gold or silver.
   b. its value in land.
   c. banknotes from a different bank.
   d. goods or services from merchants.

9. In response to the market revolution that began around 1815, lawyers fashioned an American legal system that advanced the interests of
   a. ordinary Americans.
   b. commercial activity.
   c. community values.
   d. public works.

10. In the nineteenth-century entrepreneurial marketplace, American courts began to interpret contracts as
    a. a means of enforcing fairness.
    b. legally binding agreements.
    c. unnecessary.
    d. required for all business.

11. One of the precipitating causes of the panic of 1819 was the
    a. legal system's weaknesses.
    b. strength of the European economy.
    c. extension of loans to the government.
    d. the Bank of the United States.

12. The panic of 1819 affected
    a. only the very wealthy.
    b. only the very poor.
    c. mostly bankers.
    d. everyone connected with the commercial economy.

13. Between 1815 and 1840, networks of roads, canals, steamboats, and railroads _____ of travel.
    a. raised the speed and the cost
    b. raised the speed and lowered the cost
    c. lowered the speed and the cost
    d. lowered the speed and raised the cost

14. In the 1810s and 1820s, the federal government hesitated to fund transportation programs because enhanced public transport like roads and canals produced _____ economic benefits.
    a. few
    b. no
    c. even
    d. uneven

15. In the early nineteenth century, _____ sponsored most transportation improvements.
    a. the federal government
    b. private investors
    c. state governments
    d. banks

16. Canals were an economically prudent form of transportation because of their _____.
    a. speed of transit
    b. steam-powered boats
    c. cheap construction
    d. increased loads

17. In the 1830s, state-sponsored canal enterprises began to face competition from _____.
    a. public trolleys
    b. steamboats
    c. stagecoaches
    d. private railroad companies

18. The "Waltham System" referred to a _____ labor force.
    a. family
    b. young
    c. female
    d. all-male

19. Women shoebinders earned _____ wages, which kept manufacturers' costs down.
    a. piecework
    b. no
    c. hourly
    d. men's

20. Starting in the boom years of 1814 to 1816, _____ became the currency of the nation.
    a. state-issued notes
    b. federally issued notes
    c. specie
    d. banknotes

21. In the years after the War of 1812, lawyers' attention focused on laws to _____.
    a. protect workers
    b. protect property ownership
    c. protect the environment
    d. govern commerce

22. About half a million people across the country lost their _____ as a result of the panic of 1819.
    a. livelihoods
    b. homes
    c. savings
    d. confidence

23. The presidential election of 1828 was unusual in that it
    a. had unusually low voter turnout.
    b. was determined by popular vote.
    c. extended the franchise to free blacks.
    d. extended the vote to women.

24. The high number of voters in the 1830s was the result of
    a. relaxed voting restrictions and more interesting candidates.
    b. increased political interest and better newspaper coverage.
    c. better newspaper coverage and more interesting candidates.
    d. relaxed voting restrictions and increased political interest.

25. The 1828 election inaugurated
    a. formal party rivalry.
    b. less partisanship.
    c. a less formal campaigning style.
    d. a return to more formal campaigning styles.

26. In the 1830s, political issues were defined and political personalities publicized by
    a. governmental agencies.
    b. nonpartisan editorialists.
    c. partisan newspapers.
    d. caucuses.

27. The National Republicans and the Democratic Republicans both
    a. promoted commercial development.
    b. claimed the mantle of Jefferson, Madison, and Monroe.
    c. promised to respond to the will of the majority.
    d. supported Andrew Jackson.

28. The National Republicans, who later called themselves the Whig Party, were in favor of
    a. responding to the will of the majority.
    b. promoting farming interests in the South and the West.
    c. allowing states to secede from the Union.
    d. using the federal government to promote commercial development.

29. John Quincy Adams was vilified in the 1828 election as
    a. stupid.
    b. hot-tempered.
    c. a bigamist.
    d. a hopeless elitist.

30. The stories that circulated about John Quincy Adams and Andrew Jackson during the 1828 election were
    a. real issues.
    b. smokescreens.
    c. entirely false.
    d. entirely true.

31. In the 1828 presidential election, Andrew Jackson gained support from
    a. New Englanders.
    b. bankers.
    c. investors.
    d. the South and the West.

32. After the election of 1828, national politicians
    a. began to see the value of political parties.
    b. continued to deplore the existence of parties.
    c. tried to downplay personality politics.
    d. shifted their efforts to the state level.

33. President Jackson's cabinet appointments
    a. encompassed men of all factions.
    b. ignored his most powerful supporters.
    c. included only Jackson loyalists.
    d. excluded shrewd political strategists.

34. Like President Jefferson, President Jackson favored a limited federal government, but he differed from his predecessor in that he
    a. exercised his full presidential powers over Congress.
    b. was willing to extend federal support to transportation.
    c. wanted to charter a national bank.
    d. did not want to encourage western settlement.

35. Between 1828 and 1836, more men could and did _____.
    a. vote
    b. go to college
    c. farm
    d. save money

36. The election of 1828 was the first presidential contest in which _____ determined the outcome.
    a. the electoral college
    b. popular votes
    c. state legislatures
    d. counties

37. More than half the electorate voted in _____.
    a. 1796
    b. 1800
    c. 1812
    d. 1828

38. _____ were a major force in defining issues and publicizing political personalities in the 1820s and 1830s.
    a. Political parties
    b. Partisan newspapers
    c. Voters
    d. Government officials

39. By 1834, a few state-level National Republicans had shortened their name to the _____ Party.
    a. Republican
    b. Whig
    c. Democratic
    d. National

40. In the campaign of 1828, Jackson's supporters targeted _____, who they saw as the chief architect behind anti-Jackson propaganda.
    a. James Monroe
    b. Henry Clay
    c. John Quincy Adams
    d. John C. Calhoun

41. Voters in the presidential election of 1828 used _____ to comprehend what kind of public officer each presidential candidate would make.
    a. public debates
    b. policy statements
    c. scandalous stories
    d. character testimonials

42. John Quincy Adams publicly supported _____ in the election of 1828.
    a. limiting federal powers
    b. western expansion
    c. a new Indian policy
    d. commerce through federal action

43. During his time in office, President Jackson _____ the public.
    a. was hospitable toward
    b. was distant from
    c. ignored
    d. blatantly catered to

44. President Jackson _____ an unprecedented number of times during his tenure in office.
    a. sponsored legislation
    b. declared war
    c. vetoed congressional actions
    d. replaced cabinet members

45. In the Jacksonian era, ideas about gender relations revolved around the idea that husbands and wives
    a. found status and authority at home.
    b. found status and authority at work.
    c. had separate spheres of activity—husbands at work and wives at home.
    d. divided labor as they pleased.

46. Beginning in 1815, men increasingly performed their jobs
    a. outside the home.
    b. within the home.
    c. near the home.
    d. for subsistence goods.

47. In the 1830s, women's work at home was
    a. rendered invisible.
    b. assigned a cash value.
    c. seen as extremely feminine.
    d. treated as a source of feminine resentment.

48. In the 1830s, upper-class wives involved themselves in the commercial relations of the marketplace by
    a. functioning as employers.
    b. engaging in outwork.
    c. taking in boarders.
    d. all of the above.

49. Idealized notions about separate masculine and feminine spheres gained acceptance in the 1830s because they
    a. accurately described most people's lives.
    b. lightened women's domestic load.
    c. blurred the boundaries between masculinity and femininity.
    d. were comforting to the culturally dominant middle classes of the Northeast.

50. The popular 1830s ideal of separate spheres in society worked to the benefit of
   a. men and women.
   b. men.
   c. women.
   d. nobody.

51. Between the 1790s and the 1830s, the curriculum of schools in both the North and the South produced pupils who could
   a. read and calculate.
   b. go to college.
   c. understand the political system.
   d. study the classics.

52. By the 1830s, northeastern school districts were hiring
   a. young male teachers.
   b. young female teachers.
   c. older, married teachers.
   d. college graduates.

53. In the 1820s and 1830s, most boys left common school at the age of fourteen to
   a. seek an apprenticeship or work in business.
   b. attend college.
   c. take mill jobs.
   d. go to private academies.

54. Because of the system of employment and training in the 1830s, many young people lacked
   a. spending money.
   b. a place to live.
   c. parental oversight.
   d. the chance to leave home before they were in their twenties.

55. Newspapers appealing to popular tastes proliferated in the 1830s due to
   a. rising literacy rates and advertising.
   b. advertising and innovations in printing technology.
   c. innovations in printing technology and the establishment of the postal service.
   d. rising literacy rates and innovations in printing technology.

56. As theater became wildly popular in the 1830s, it promoted a new vision of
   a. black culture.
   b. women.
   c. public speaking.
   d. elite culture.

57. In the highly commercialized _____, the standard of living rose considerably during the 1820s and 1830s.
   a. Southeast
   b. Southwest
   c. Northeast
   d. Northwest

58. New ideas about gender relations in the 1830s characterized the home as _____ the world of market relations.
   a. an extension of
   b. competition to
   c. encouraging
   d. a refuge from

59. Advice books of the Jacksonian era treated household tasks as _____.
   a. tedious work
   b. loving familial duties
   c. good exercise
   d. children's work

60. By the 1830s, _____ rates for white females climbed dramatically, rivaling white male rates for the first time.
   a. literacy
   b. death
   c. marriage
   d. employment

61. Oberlin College in Ohio was the only American college in the 1830s to admit _____ students.
   a. female
   b. poor
   c. older
   d. Catholic

62. According to women educators in the 1830s, women made better _____ than men.
   a. factory workers
   b. chefs
   c. teachers
   d. business decisions

63. In the 1830s, a small percentage of boys leaving common school went _____.
   a. to learn a trade
   b. into business
   c. to private boys' academies
   d. into the ministry

64. New York had three _____ by 1835, and Philadelphia, Boston, and Baltimore each had one or two.
   a. full-time writers
   b. professional speakers
   c. theaters
   d. penny papers

65. The theater audiences of the 1830s were comprised mostly of _____ of all classes.
   a. white men
   b. black men
   c. white women
   d. people

66. As theater became more and more popular in the 1830s, celebrated _____ enlarged the scope of the possible for female behavior.
   a. teachers
   b. lecturers
   c. actresses
   d. poets

67. The core of the Second Great Awakening was the message that
   a. individual sin was inevitable.
   b. ministers were necessary for salvation.
   c. salvation was available to anyone.
   d. salvation was available to very few people.

68. The evangelical Protestantism of the 1830s was especially popular among
   a. the urban poor.
   b. subsistence farmers.
   c. the very rich.
   d. the new mercantile classes.

69. Outdoor camp meetings attracted people who were searching for
   a. cheap entertainment.
   b. immediate access to spiritual peace.
   c. a long-term spiritual commitment.
   d. ministerial learning.

70. After the completion of the Erie Canal, towns in western New York
   a. became very poor.
   b. adopted state-supported evangelical churches.
   c. lost their population.
   d. swelled with new inhabitants.

71. Charles Grandison Finney, one of the leading ministers of the Second Great Awakening, preached using
   a. complicated biblical language.
   b. theological arguments.
   c. legal metaphors.
   d. female assistants.

72. According to Charles Grandison Finney, salvation needed to be fostered through
   a. giving up worldly pursuits.
   b. reaching out to the unsaved.
   c. following certain religious rituals.
   d. tolerance of the practices of others.

73. The Connecticut minister Lyman Beecher's American Temperance Society argued that
   a. moderate alcohol intake was healthy.
   b. drinking was a moral vice.
   c. women should not drink but men could.
   d. beer was an acceptable drink.

74. The American Temperance Union demanded
   a. abstinence from hard liquor.
   b. total abstinence from alcohol.
   c. stricter licensing requirements for taverns.
   d. government-sponsored temperance pledges.

75. Moral reformers believed that they were
   a. radicals.
   b. protecting the home.
   c. defying their ministers.
   d. risking their virtue.

76. William Lloyd Garrison launched a drive for
   a. gradual emancipation.
   b. the colonization of freed slaves.
   c. immediate abolition.
   d. the extension of slavery into the northern states.

77. Most white northerners in the 1830s were
    a. antiabolition.
    b. in favor of immediate abolition.
    c. supportive of blacks' civil rights.
    d. in favor of slavery.

78. The New England abolitionist movement of the 1830s contributed to the
    a. decline of racism in the North.
    b. spread of voluntary manumissions in the upper South.
    c. first organized women's rights movement.
    d. increase in job opportunities for blacks.

79. The evangelical religious revival that began in 1801 _____.
    a. concentrated on blacks
    b. was limited to the lower classes
    c. broke out mostly among Catholics
    d. democratized religion

80. From 1800 to 1820, church membership _____ in the United States.
    a. remained static
    b. doubled
    c. quadrupled
    d. decreased

81. The leading exemplar of the Second Great Awakening was a _____-turned-minister named Charles Grandison Finney.
    a. businessman
    b. professor
    c. shoemaker
    d. lawyer

82. Charles Grandison Finney preached that a _____ was imminent.
    a. natural disaster
    b. reign of Christian perfection
    c. political upheaval
    d. moral crisis

83. The evangelical religion of the 1830s offered women _____.
    a. new opportunities for paid work
    b. nothing but spiritual comfort
    c. an expanded sphere of influence
    d. the chance to become ministers

84. Prior to the 1830s, _____ classes of Americans drank alcohol.
    a. all
    b. the upper
    c. the middle
    d. the lower

85. The moral reform campaign of the 1830s was particularly concerned with ending _____.
    a. prostitution
    b. mail delivery on Sunday
    c. family violence
    d. drinking

86. In Boston, William Lloyd Garrison led a(n) _____ movement.
    a. antislavery
    b. temperance
    c. moral reform
    d. evangelical

87. Maria Stewart raised controversy because she was a young black woman who presumed to _____ publicly.
    a. act in plays
    b. sing
    c. preach
    d. lecture

88. In the late 1830s, the cause of abolition _____ the nation as no other issue did.
    a. bored
    b. united
    c. divided
    d. annoyed

89. From the 1790s to the 1820s, the federal government negotiated treaties with Indian tribes on the assumption that they were
    a. American citizens.
    b. foreign nations.
    c. resident aliens.
    d. potential converts to Christianity.

90. Andrew Jackson believed that Indians were
    a. mostly civilized.
    b. talented farmers.
    c. subjects of the United States.
    d. his equals.

91. Members of the Cherokee tribe of Georgia were unusually
   a. warlike.
   b. assimilated.
   c. segregated.
   d. supportive of Jackson.

92. The 1832 Supreme Court case *Worcester v. Georgia* found that the Cherokee
   a. were a distinct community within Georgia.
   b. were subject to Georgia s laws.
   c. deserved voting rights.
   d. would have to be relocated.

93. Steep federal tariffs passed in 1816 and 1824 were opposed by
   a. New England merchants.
   b. middle state wheat farmers.
   c. the urban working classes.
   d. southern planters.

94. The 1828 Tariff of Abominations set
   a. a precedent by being the first duty enacted by the federal government.
   b. relatively low duties.
   c. consistent duties.
   d. conflicting duties.

95. In response to the 1828 Tariff of Abominations, South Carolina politicians promulgated the
   a. Force Bill.
   b. new tariff of 1833.
   c. doctrine of nullification.
   d. panic of 1837.

96. Senators Daniel Webster and Henry Clay believed that forcing a vote on rechartering of the Bank of the United States would
   a. lead to economic stability.
   b. destroy the anti-Jackson forces in Congress.
   c. cause President Jackson to lose the 1823 election.
   d. spur an economic recession.

97. President Jackson s veto of the Bank of the United States s recharter used
   a. sophisticated economic theories.
   b. the language of class divisions.
   c. strict constitutional arguments.
   d. Supreme Court precedents.

98. After Jackson removed federal deposits from the Bank of the United States he put them into
   a. pet banks.
   b. the newly-created federal treasury.
   c. national bonds.
   d. railroad investments.

99. In 1836, the Treasury Department issued the Specie Circular, which
   a. ordered that public land could be purchased with paper currency.
   b. ordered that public land could be purchased only with hard money.
   c. rechartered the Bank of the United States.
   d. increased the supply of gold and silver.

100. Martin Van Buren s chance for a second term as president was undermined by his
   a. desire to reinstate the Bank of the United States.
   b. unwillingness to support Indian removal.
   c. reputation for corrupt behavior.
   d. inability to end the economic depression.

101. Improved transportation after 1815 greatly accelerated the _____ flow of white settlers.
   a. northward
   b. southward
   c. westward
   d. eastward

102. Presidents from Monroe to Jackson preferred Indian _____ over warfare.
   a. removal
   b. coexistence
   c. assimilation
   d. slavery

103. In 1831, the Cherokee _____ the state of Georgia when the state declared that they were subject to state law.
   a. went to war against
   b. sued
   c. peacefully left
   d. became citizens of

104. In 1832, the _____ recognized the Cherokees' existence as a community separate from the state of Georgia.
   a. Removal Act
   b. president
   c. United States Congress
   d. Supreme Court

105. In response to _____, South Carolina politicians formulated the doctrine of nullification.
   a. Indian removal
   b. *Worcester v. Georgia*
   c. abolitionist agitation
   d. the Tariff of Abominations

106. The nullification crisis highlighted the problem of _____.
   a. economic legislation
   b. the excessive use of the presidential veto
   c. partisan politics
   d. federal power versus states' rights

107. By 1830, the Bank of the United States provided the nation with its most _____ circulating currency.
   a. secure and steady
   b. unreliable
   c. easily obtainable
   d. controversial

108. On his reelection, President Jackson felt that he had a popular mandate to _____ the Bank of the United States.
   a. refuse to renew the charter of
   b. harass
   c. reconcile with
   d. destroy

109. Bankers' response to the Specie Circular contributed to _____.
   a. an increase in the number of loans
   b. the panic of 1837
   c. a short-term economic boom
   d. lowered interest rates

110. Martin Van Buren suggested _____ to deal with the economic crisis.
   a. creating an independent treasury system
   b. rechartering the Bank of the United States
   c. restoring the pet bank system
   d. revoking the Specie Circular

## *Short Answer* Write a paragraph response to each question.

1. How did improved transportation after 1815 affect the economic, political, and social development of the United States?
2. What caused the Lynn shoebinders' protests of the 1830s? What did the protestors want, what methods did they use, and why weren't they successful?
3. Why did the panic of 1819 occur?
4. In what ways was the presidential campaign of 1828 different from previous races?
5. What was the "character issue" in the campaign of 1828? How did stories about the candidates mold the election?
6. What was Jackson's presidential agenda? How did he differ from previous presidents?
7. What ideas about gender relations circulated in the Jacksonian era? How accurately were these cultural prescriptions carried out?
8. How did education change in the 1820s and 1830s?

9. How did newspapers evolve between the 1790s and the 1830s?
10. What was the Second Great Awakening? What did it offer adherents?
11. What was the moral reform movement ? Why was it controversial?
12. How popular was abolition as a cause in the 1830s? Why were northerners hostile to it?
13. What was Andrew Jackson's Indian policy? How was it a departure from previous policy?
14. Why did South Carolina propose the doctrine of nullification? What problem was it intended to remedy?
15. How did Andrew Jackson destroy the second Bank of the United States? What were the economic ramifications?

***Building Historical Skills*** Historians use a variety of sources to think and talk about the past, including maps, illustrations, and written records. Maps provide a variety of different kinds of comparative information in a condensed visual format; reading them requires learning how to sort through this information. To deepen our understanding of the past by supplementing written records, historians frequently interpret material culture, such as a vase or a painting, with techniques borrowed from art history, archaeology, or anthropology. Written records, though familiar as sources, raise their own problems of interpretation. Every document reflects someone's particular perspective or assumptions. It is the historian's task to study and compare each document to other records with other perspectives. The following exercises introduce you to using maps, illustrations, and written documents as sources of information. Use these sources as well as the material in the chapter to think about different themes and topics discussing in the text.

***Map Activity*** Locate the following places on Map 10.3: Indian Removal and the Trail of Tears on page 351 in *The American Promise,* Second Edition.

1. Indian Reservations
2. Chickasaw ceded lands
3. Sac and Fox ceded lands
4. Creek ceded lands
5. Georgia
6. Choctaw ceded lands
7. Cherokee ceded lands

Answer the following questions in paragraphs based on Map 10.3: Indian Removal and the Trail of Tears.

**READING THE MAP** What states were most of the Native Americans removed from? Through what states did the Trail of Tears go?

**CONNECTIONS** Before Jackson's presidency, how did the federal government view Native Americans, and what policy initiatives were undertaken by the government and private groups? How did Jackson change the government's Native American policies?

**WEB LINKS** To explore the topics discussed in the exercise above, visit the Web links noted below.

"Cherokee Letter Protesting the Treaty of New Etocha"
http://www.pbs.org/wgbh/aia/part4/4h3083.html

"Indian Removal Act (1830)"
http://www.english.upenn.edu/~kajohnso/removal.html

***Visual Activity*** This engraving of the evangelist Charles Finney's New York church, the Broadway Tabernacle, gives a glimpse into Finney's stature as a preacher. He is not wearing robes or any other kind of clerical garb; he is distinct from the crowd on the basis of his charisma, not his uniform. Finney's popularity is evident: the pews, including those facing Finney's back and directly behind pillars, are packed, and there are even people standing behind the last row. The figures that are rendered distinctly reflect the nature of Finney's audience: They are wearing nice, middle-class clothes, the men in suits and carrying top hats and the women in bonnets, full skirts, and shawls. The audience is appears to be evenly divided between men and women, although the figures seated on the stage—presumably the officials of the church—are mostly male.

Answer the following questions in paragraphs based on "Charles G. Finney's Broadway Tabernacle" on page 345 in *The American Promise*, Second Edition.

**READING THE IMAGE** How does the engraving of Charles Finney's sermon at the Broadway Tabernacle reflect Finney's preaching style?

**CONNECTIONS** How did Charles Finney's preaching style differ from that of ministers in more established sects?

**WEB LINKS** To explore the topics discussed in the exercise above, visit the Web links noted below.

"Religion and the Founding of the American Republic"
http://www.lcweb.loc.gov/exhibits/religion/
Choose "Religion and the New Republic"

"Charles Grandison Finney (1792–1875)"
http://www.oberlin.edu/~EOG/images/CharlesGrandisonFinney.html

***Analyzing Sources Activity*** Answer the following questions in paragraphs based on "Documenting the American Promise: The Panic of 1837" on page 356 of *The American Promise*, Second Edition.

1. How could Martineau, a foreigner, so readily predict that the economic bubble would soon burst? Do you think the buyers and sellers in Chicago whom she describes could also predict it? Who was really making money in the Chicago she describes?

2. What does Hone's diary entry tell you about the interconnections between many businesses? Who or what does Hone blame for the crash?

3. In the *Christian Examiner*'s interpretation of the Panic, what caused the crash? Are American enterprise and ambition good or bad, in this view? What characteristics of American society stimulated this "lust of accumulation"?

**WEB LINKS** To explore the topics discussed in the exercise above, visit the Web links noted below.

"Deaths, Disturbances, Disasters and Disorders in Chicago"
http://www.chipublib.org/004chicago/chidisaster.html
Choose "1837–41, 1857–58: Financial Panics"

"Martin Van Buren"
http://www.whitehouse.gov/history/presidents/mb8.html

# Answer Key

## Chapter 10: The Expanding Republic, 1815–1840

### *Chapter Overview*

#### *Chronology*

1. b
2. a
3. b
4. d
5. b
6. b
7. c
8. c
9. b
10. a

#### *Defining Terms*

1. market revolution
2. steamboats
3. *Gibbon v. Ogden*
4. Erie Canal
5. Waltham system
6. "Old Hickory"
7. Democratic Party
8. Whig Party
9. separate spheres
10. normal schools
11. female seminaries
12. penny papers
13. minstrelsy
14. Second Great Awakening
15. Charles Grandison Finney
16. American Temperance Union
17. Andrew Lloyd Garrison
18. Maria Stewart
19. *Worcester v. Georgia*
20. Trail of Tears
21. Tariff of Abominations
22. nullification
23. Specie Circular

### *Chapter Review*

#### *Multiple-Choice*

1. a
2. c
3. b
4. d
5. d
6. a
7. a
8. a
9. b
10. b
11. d
12. d
13. b
14. d
15. b
16. d
17. d
18. c
19. a
20. d
21. d
22. a
23. b
24. d
25. c
26. c
27. b
28. d
29. d
30. a
31. d
32. a
33. c
34. a
35. a
36. b
37. d
38. b
39. b
40. b
41. c
42. d
43. a
44. c
45. c
46. a
47. a
48. a
49. d
50. a
51. a
52. a
53. a
54. c
55. d
56. b
57. c
58. d
59. b
60. a
61. a
62. c
63. c
64. d
65. a
66. c
67. c
68. d
69. b
70. d
71. c
72. b
73. b
74. b
75. b
76. c
77. a
78. c
79. d
80. b

81. d
82. b
83. c
84. a
85. a
86. a
87. d
88. c
89. b
90. c
91. b
92. a
93. d
94. d
95. c
96. c
97. c
98. a
99. b
100. d
101. c
102. c
103. b
104. d
105. d
106. d
107. a
108. d
109. b
110. a

### *Short Answer*

1. Economically, improved transportation helped fuel the market revolution of the 1820s and 1830s by making it faster and cheaper to transport goods and allowing products to be sold to a wider market. New methods of transportation facilitated the flow of political information in the form of mostly partisan newspapers, which defined political issues and publicized political personalities. The cheapness of travel had an impact on social life as well, allowing men and women from rural communities access to urban areas, where they sought jobs and goods.
2. In the 1830s, shoe entrepreneurs moved to cut shoebinders' wages as a cost-saving measure. Female shoebinders in the town of Lynn, Massachusetts, joined together to protest the cuts, using churches as meeting sites and religious newspapers to spread news. They drew on their collective sense of themselves as women, arguing that men and women should enjoy equal rights. Nonetheless, the women did not achieve the higher wages they wanted. For one thing, isolated shoebinders in other parts of New England continued to accept low wages; for another, even in Lynn, many shoebinders were uncomfortable with organized protest. They saw their work as part of their familial duties and did not like to see themselves primarily as paid workers.
3. A number of factors contributed to the panic of 1819. In 1818, the second Bank of the United States became concerned about state banks suspending specie payments. It started to call in its loans and insisted that state banks do the same, taking currency out of circulation. Then Europe underwent a financial crisis, and the overseas price of agricultural products dropped. This meant that when banks called in their loans, debtors involved in the commodities trade could not pay. Because of the complex network of credit and debt relationships, nearly everyone connected to the commercial economy was affected: thousands of Americans lost their savings and property, and hundreds of thousands lost their jobs.
4. The 1828 presidential campaign was the first in which popular votes determined the outcome; in twenty-two out of twenty-four states, voters chose electors committed to a particular candidate. Voter turnout was much higher as well, with more than half of the electorate voting. Although presidential candidates did not campaign directly, their supporters responded to the need to woo voters by attending informal picnics and banquets and giving informal, blunt speeches. Newspapers were increasingly and blatantly partisan, defining issues and publicizing personalities to a greater extent that had been possible in the past. For the first time, presidential campaigns were coordinated in the national arena.
5. In 1828, both Adams and Jackson's supporters deliberately spread scandalous stories about the opposition. Jackson men characterized Adams as an elitist and a snob and played up the "corrupt bargain" that supposedly catapulted him into office in 1824. Adams men decried Jackson as an illegitimate, immoral, uncontrolled adulterer. The stories became the real issues in the election, largely because voters believed that character issues conveyed larger questions about morality, honor, and discipline and used them to determine what kind of president each candidate would make; they believed that personal behavior would determine political choices.
6. Prior to taking office, Jackson was vague about his presidential objectives, calling for a judicious tariff, western expansion, and limited federal power. Once he became president, it became clear that he favored a Jeffersonian style of limited federal government because he feared that intervention in the economy provided some groups with unfair advantages. He did not support federal funding for internal improvements or monopolies. As a proponent of western expansion, he believed that land sales would spread political democracy. But Jackson was willing to exercise full presidential powers over Congress, employing the veto twelve times, whereas all previous presidents combined had used the veto a total of only nine times.
7. By the 1830s, husbands were expected to gain their status and authority at work, and wives were expected to find their happiness by devoting themselves to home and family. This

doctrine, known as separate spheres, allowed people to adjust to the market revolution: men displayed market values like selfishness and acquisitiveness, while women maintained older, noncommercial values. However, it did not reflect women's reality. While most married women did not work outside of the home, many contributed to household income by taking in boarders or outwork. Even wealthy married women participated in the market when they hired and supervised servants to do their heavy household tasks.

8. The market economy demanded a more educated workforce and new ways of training youth. In response, first northern and later southern states adopted public schooling, which produced boys and girls who could read and do basic arithmetic by the age of twelve or fourteen. Because taxpayers were footing the bill for the new schools, many turned to young, female teachers who were considerably cheaper than their male counterparts. Some female educators argued that women were better teachers than men, citing their natural patience and communication skills.

9. In the 1790s, there were fewer than ninety American newspapers, each printing a few thousand copies per issue. By the 1830s, steam-driven rotary presses with automatic paper feed devices made much larger print runs both possible and economical, a burgeoning postal system that carried papers throughout the nation, and rising literacy rates provided an audience. By the 1830s, there were eight hundred papers, and some cheap "penny papers" gained circulations of ten to twenty thousand copies daily.

10. The Second Great Awakening was an evangelical religious movement that began in Kentucky in 1801 and peaked in the 1830s. Its basic message was that anybody could achieve salvation by eradicating individual sin and accepting faith in God's grace. By lowering the bar for acceptance to salvation, the movement offered immediate access to spiritual peace. Moreover, it gave comfort to people in areas that were affected by the new social ills created by industrialization and commercialization by offering adherents with market ambitions a message of self-discipline in pursuit of spiritual and social perfection. The Second Great Awakening also expanded women's sphere of influence by demanding an active commitment to spiritual outreach.

11. The moral reform campaign began as a drive by women to improve public morals generally, but it narrowed to a focus on sexual sin, especially prostitution. In 1833, the New York Female Moral Reform Society formed and began to argue that male sexuality was a threat to society; they published their own paper, *The Advocate of Moral Reform*, which publicized first-person stories and advice about curbing sin. In New York, members undertook surveillance of brothels to intimidate patrons and urged women to marry only sexually chaste men. The women involved in the movement felt that they were simply protecting their homes from bad male behavior. Men in the evangelical movement did not agree, feeling that the women had overstepped the bounds of female propriety.

12. The movement for the abolition of slavery got organized in1832 and 1833, with antislavery societies forming in Boston, New York, and Philadelphia. The societies used print media and lecturers to spread their message, and by 1837 there were thirteen hundred antislavery societies in the North with a quarter of a million members. While the rate of growth was impressive, it by no means compromised a large proportion of the northern population. Most northerners opposed slavery because they felt that it ran counter to the nation's ideals, or they saw it as a rival to the free-labor system. However, they were also antiblack and thus antiabolition.

13. From the 1790s to the 1820s, the federal government treated Indian tribes as foreign nations: legally, their lands constituted independent countries within state borders. Within their own territory, Indians asserted their sovereignty and communal rights to their land. Jackson, however, felt that it was ridiculous to treat Indians as foreigners, when they were in his opinion subjects of the United States. In his first message to Congress in 1829, he announced that Indians could not remain independent and in sovereign control of tribal lands. Instead, he proposed relocating all Indians within the United States to the territory west of the Mississippi, which Congress agreed to by passing the Removal Act of 1830.

14. South Carolinians suffered a great deal from the 1828 Tariff of Abominations, a federal tariff that set conflicting, very high, duties and hurt the state's export market. In response to the imposition of the financially injurious federal policy, South Carolinians headed by John C. Calhoun proposed that the Union was a federation of states that had yielded some but not all power to the federal government. When Congress went too far, the states had the right to nullify its acts. The South Carolinians argued that the federal tariff represented an overstepping of that sort because Congress was using the tariff improperly to benefit specific industries rather than to raise revenue. They saw the measure as a way of increasing the power of states to challenge abuses of federal power.

15. When Andrew Jackson started his second term in office, the second Bank of the United States's charter was due to expire in 1836; because of Jackson's previous veto of a new charter, it was widely assumed that the bank would die at that point. But Jackson saw his reelection as a mandate to rid the nation of the bank as soon as possible and ordered his secretary of the treasury to withdraw federal deposits from the bank. The money was put into Democrat-controlled banks instead, where, unregulated, it caused the economy to boom. A nervous Jackson then passed the Specie Circular, demanding that land be paid for in hard money. Banks responded by reducing their loans, and this, compounded by international financial problems and weak markets for crops, led to the panic of 1837.

### *Map Activity*

Reading the Map: The majority of Native Americans who were forced to abandon their tribal lands under the Removal Act of 1830 were from southern states. Florida, Georgia, Alabama, and Mississippi had the largest concentrations of removed Indians, although the Sac and the Fox were forced out of unorganized territory in the Northwest. All of the Indian land traversed state boundaries: the Cherokee held territory in Georgia, Tennessee, Alabama, and North Carolina, the Choctaw and Chickasaw were in both Mississippi and Alabama, the Creek were in Georgia and Alabama, and the Sac and Fox spilled into Illinois. The Trail of Tears took Indians out of the Deep South and through the middle part of the country. It started in Georgia, headed through Tennessee and Kentucky, went through a bit of Illinois, and over the south part of Missouri before heading back south into modern-day Oklahoma.

Connections: From the 1790s until the 1820s, the federal government had negotiated with Indian tribes as if they were sovereign nations. The government purchased land, often through misleading or fraudulent treaties, and also encouraged a policy of assimilation, attempting to "civilize" Indians by Christianizing them. As late as 1819, Congress granted interdenominational missionaries $10,000 to instruct Indians in religion, reading, writing, and European styles of agriculture. The missionaries had limited success, in large part because Indian women did not wish to be forced into a gender system that lessened their social power. Jackson felt that assimilation was futile and that Indians were subjects of the United States, not foreign powers in their own right. He adopted a plan of removal, forcing Indians off of their traditional tribal lands and into unsettled territory west of the Mississippi River.

### *Visual Activity*

Reading the Image: The Broadway Tabernacle had been a theater, an appropriate venue given Finney's emotional oratorical style. Finney is not standing behind a pulpit of any sort. Instead, like an actor, he is giving his sermon extemporaneously, gesticulating toward heaven to make his point. The crowd listening to Finney is immense, but he is not overwhelmed. He stands out as the distinct center of attention, holding his own against the sheer mass of humanity that has come to hear his message.

Connections: Ministers from the more traditional strains of Protestantism, including Episcopalians, Congregationalists, Unitarians, Dutch Reformed, Lutherans, and Catholics, were intensely suspicious of the emotionalism of the evangelical movement. These were sects that relied on learned sermons that dissected biblical texts or on established liturgy as the source of worship and that drew distinctions between the clergy and the layperson. Charles Finney obviously rejected that model of Christian worship. He was much less formal in his preaching style, eschewing written notes or ministerial clothing, and he was dynamic, striding freely in front of his flock rather than confining himself behind a lecturn. This was in keeping with his belief that salvation depended on little more than a decision to accept God's grace. His job as a minister was not, in his view, to dispense a specialized sort of knowledge but to convince people to accept the salvation that was already available.

### *Analyzing Sources*

1. Martineau, as a foreigner, was not caught up in the prevalent Jacksonian belief that opportunity was around every corner, just waiting for a brash, bold person to grab it. As a result, she was able to see the speculative mania in terms of realistic risks and profits and to understand that the bubble could not grow indefinitely. Yet she also understands that the men buying land were unable to see as clearly as she did, in part because of their own naivete and inexperience and in part because of the excitement drummed up by the speculators who wanted to fleece them. She makes it clear that the people making money are not the purchasers of the land, who were buying as long-term investments, but those who were selling it for short-term profits and also the lawyers who wrote up the titles for the property.
2. Hone's diary demonstrates the extent to which businesses relied on other businesses for their cash flow and their ability to make their own payments. He mentions that the New York bank

of I. and L. Joseph went under because of news received from New Orleans about the failure of a different business, which had borrowed $2 million from the New York firm. His own son's failure likely created similar shock waves: He lost his father's money but also the money of his creditors, with whom he will have to meet. Hone, however, does not place the bulk of the blame on individual investors or banking policies. Instead, he feels that the fault lies with the government, which interfered with the nation's currency. As a Whig, he probably opposed Jackson's war against the second Bank of the United States and disapproved of the Specie Circular and its effect on credit.

3. According to the *Christian Examiner*, the economic collapse of 1837 was caused by greed, overconfidence, and laziness. In the editorialist's opinion, the government encouraged ambition, and people responded because, in a nation without set classes, wealth provided social status. This ambition was not necessarily bad because it led to the expansion of human civilization and control over nature. However, Americans had lost their sense of balance. They stopped working hard for long-term rewards, instead looking for immediate, if unstable, profits; they believed that the economy could never crash and that careful investment would simply mean losing out on opportunities for wealth.

# THE FREE NORTH AND WEST, 1840–1860 11

## Chapter Overview

### *Chapter Summary*

***Introduction*** This chapter begins with the story of how Thomas Lincoln (Abraham's father) and his family struggled to survive in antebellum America. Abraham Lincoln worked his way up from poverty to become president of the United States, and millions of Americans believed that with hard work, they too could make something of themselves, regardless of their origins. As Lincoln's father's experience showed, however, hardship and risk were ever present in that struggle.

***Economic and Industrial Evolution, pp. 366–372*** Americans in the 1840s and 1850s witnessed economic growth that transformed the nation into a bustling transcontinental giant. The phenomenal economic growth in the United States between 1800 and 1860 was the result of many factors: an increase in movement to the cities, an increase in Americans working in factories, the availability of new sources of energy—steam and coal—to fuel those factories, and a major increase in agricultural productivity. While cities and the number of factories and steam engines grew throughout the country, the heart of American economic growth during this period lay in agriculture.

**AGRICULTURE AND LAND POLICY** Settlement in the Midwest increased agricultural productivity, first because the lack of trees meant that land demanded less energy to clear and second because the rich soil gave higher crop yields. Farmers increased their production by adopting new agricultural techniques that greatly reduced the labor necessary for producing a crop. Most important were improved tools and farm machines, such as the John Deere steel plow, introduced in 1837 and continually improved thereafter, and the McCormick Reaper. The federal government made land available to settlers at the relatively low cost of $1.25 per acre, a policy that underlay the agricultural expansion of the nineteenth century.

**MANUFACTURING AND MECHANIZATION** Because the United States was land rich and labor poor, manufacturers constantly had to find ways to save labor. Mechanization offered the best prospects. The essential features of this mode of production became the use of interchangeable parts. Within a factory setting, standardized parts could be efficiently and rapidly assembled into a final product. This practice, known as the "American system," spread from industry to industry.

Manufacturing and agriculture meshed into a dynamic national economy, as New England—which led the nation in manufacture—shipped products like clocks, axes, and guns west and south in exchange for southern and western goods like wheat, pork, whiskey, tobacco, and cotton.

**RAILROADS: BREAKING THE BONDS OF NATURE** The rise of railroads during the 1840s and 1850s had an enormous effect on the economy as a whole. Railroads not only offered a mode of transport and travel faster than any other, but they provided the means for cities and communities not linked by rivers or canals to participate in trade. Railroads stimulated the growth of the iron and coal industries and fostered the growth of the telegraph industry, which was used to improve communication between railroad lines and to avoid collisions. Almost all the railroads were built and owned by private corporations, but government aid did come in the form of massive land grants to railroad entrepreneurs. An 1850 law provided a grant of six square miles of federal land to companies for each mile of track they built.

***Free Labor: Promise and Reality, pp. 372–377*** Prosperity and advancement during the antebellum period were not accessible to all Americans. Antebellum America was a white man's world, with women and free blacks overwhelmingly excluded from most opportunities. Discrimination against these two groups did not bother most white males, who took it for granted as the accepted order of things. There was concern in some quarters, however, about the varying nature of white men's experiences: how poverty could exist in the midst of prosperity, how some failed while others succeeded.

**THE FREE-LABOR IDEAL: FREEDOM PLUS LABOR** As northern society became more industrialized, leaders felt compelled to explain why the changes in the region's economy benefited some more than others. They developed the concept of "free labor," which meant that northern society was open to all individuals—that is, all white males—who were hard-working, self-reliant, and independent. If one maintained these qualities throughout life, they argued, material success would result. The free-labor system applied not only landowners but to wage laborers as well, with the reasoning that if they worked hard they could rise to the class of independent property owners. In northern public schools, textbooks and teachers attempted to instill students with free-labor values: self-reliance, discipline, and above all, hard work.

**ECONOMIC INEQUALITY** Free-labor apologists considered the gaps between rich and poor to be the inevitable when some individuals simply were harder workers, more able, and luckier than others. Though many men obtained the free-labor ideal, more Americans did not—that is, they remained landless and worked for wages. As with any such ideal, those who believed in it and did not succeed suffered great anxiety. The free-labor ideal led countless Americans, both rural and urban, to move every few years, searching for an opportunity that might never present itself. Thus, reality for many Americans, no matter how hard they worked, was not material success and security but a life of perpetual self-doubt and personal dissatisfaction.

**IMMIGRANTS AND THE FREE-LABOR LADDER** The risks and vagaries of free labor did not prevent millions of immigrants, mainly from Germany and Ireland, from coming to the United States during the 1840s and 1850s. The majority of German immigrants were artisans or tradesmen who settled in urban areas, especially in midwestern cities. On the whole, German Americans attained the free-labor ideal, becoming middle-class, independent producers. Irish immigrants were driven to the United States by destitution caused by famine. They entered at the bottom rung of the free-labor ladder and had difficulty climbing up. Approximately three out of four Irish immigrants worked as laborers or domestic servants. Most settled in northeastern cities, surviving on whatever low-paid menial labor they could find. The Irish were looked down on and discriminated against by most native-born Americans, and their Catholicism aroused Protestant resentment. Still, in America they found abundant (if low-paying) work and could earn in one day wages that would require several weeks of work in Ireland.

***Reforming Self and Society, pp. 377–382*** Free labor's emphasis on self-discipline and individual achievement dovetailed nicely with reformers' beliefs that many social problems were caused by insufficient self-control (see Chapter 10). Evangelical Protestants sought to eradicate sin and convert people, while temperance advocates fought against alcohol. Other groups sought perfection and personal fulfillment by rejecting established institutions, prescribing new modes of living, and founding utopian communities to put their ideas into practice. Abolitionists and women's rights activists perhaps faced the most overwhelming obstacles in their efforts to eliminate slavery and gain rights for women.

**THE PURSUIT OF PERFECTION: TRANSCENDENTALISTS AND UTOPIANS** The fundamental tenet of the New England–based literary and philosophical movement known as transcendentalism was that individuals should reject the materialistic world and abstract religion and instead look to themselves for truth and guidance. Unlike the transcendentalists, a few reformers sought to change the world by founding experimental utopian societies. The purpose or philosophy of these communities varied. Many, like the Fourierist communities, maintained communal ownership of property. Some, like the Oneida community, rejected traditional marriage and advocated a system of complex marriage instead.

**WOMEN'S RIGHTS ACTIVISTS** Although women constituted the core membership of most reform groups, they were excluded from leadership positions. Yet their participation taught them basic political skills, and in 1848 the reformers Elizabeth Cady Stanton and Lucretia Mott organized an independent movement for women's rights. They launched their campaign at a convention at Seneca Falls, New York. The Declaration of Sentiments issued by this gathering charged that history was fraught with male abuse of women and that the goal of such injury was "the establishment of absolute tyranny" over women. The Declaration went on to demand universal female suffrage. Although it was ridiculed, the manifesto laid the foundation for the women's rights movement.

**ABOLITIONISTS AND THE AMERICAN IDEAL** During the 1840s and 1850s, abolitionists continued to agitate for emancipation, and prominent black abolitionists began taking a more visible and active part in the struggle against slavery and discrimination. Some black leaders, impatient with white abolitionists' appeals to the conscience of the white majority and with the persistence of racial discrimination in the North, demanded more immediate action. Although the majority of black abolitionists cooperated with white abolitionists, they nonetheless established their own newspapers, held their own conventions, and articulated their own uncompromising ideas.

Free blacks aided the cause by quietly helping fugitive slaves. Former slave Harriet Tubman risked her life by making repeated trips down south to lead slaves to freedom along the "underground railroad," which ran through black neighborhoods, churches, and homes.

***The Westward Movement, pp. 382–392*** Until the 1840s, the overwhelming majority of Americans lived east of the Mississippi River. The revolutions in markets and transportation, the swelling population, and a booming economy helped to propel a westward surge from the 1840s on, but settlers effectively grabbed the West by moving on their own and then demanding protection from the federal government.

**MANIFEST DESTINY** Manifest Destiny rested on the idea that the United States was destined by God and history to expand its boundaries over the vast North American continent and, in the process, bring to other cultures and people the benefits of American democracy and the free-labor ideal. Coined by New York journalist John L. O'Sullivan in 1845, the term spread rapidly throughout the nation. Despite the grandiose nature of the slogan, it was largely a shield for more base economic concerns. Settlers wanted land, and politicians believed that prosperity rested on controlling trade with the Far East, which required access to Pacific ports.

**"OREGON FEVER" AND THE OVERLAND TRAIL** One of the earliest targets of Manifest Destiny was the Oregon Country in the Pacific Northwest. Great Britain and the United States both claimed sovereignty in the region and, in 1818, agreed to a treaty allowing both countries' citizens equal access to the territory. By the late 1830s, white emigrants, lured by missionaries' descriptions of bountiful, fertile land, began to travel in wagon trains along the Oregon Trail to reach Oregon Country. On their journey, settlers encountered Plains Indians, the majority of whom were mounted, nomadic buffalo hunters and warriors. Although the Plains tribes could be fearsome, they were severely impacted by white migrants who brought alcohol and disease and killed the buffalo on which the Indians depended for survival. Yet as white migration increased, settlers demanded government protection. Forts were established along the western trails, and the government initiated a policy of concentration, confining Native Americans to specific areas, out of the way of white migration and settlement. Far more threatening to white settlers than Indian attacks was the reality of trail life—heat, drought, treacherous rivers, disease, and myriad other hardships. The journey was particularly challenging for women, many of whom took on some traditionally male tasks. Despite the difficulties, migrants kept coming, and by 1845, Oregon had a population of five thousand American settlers.

**THE MORMON MIGRATION** A distinctive group of pioneers followed the Oregon Trail, not to the Pacific Northwest but instead to the region of the Great Salt Lake. These people were the Mormons, members of the Church of Jesus Christ of Latter-Day Saints. The Mormon trek resulted from a history of persecution in the eastern states. Joseph Smith Jr., founder of Mormonism, encountered strong opposition from the time he promulgated the new religion in New York in 1830. When Smith was arrested for polygamy and murdered by a mob in 1844, Brigham Young took over the leadership and led the Mormons to establish a settlement in Utah. Under Young and other church leaders, the Mormons built a thriving community that was a model of discipline and cooperation.

**THE MEXICAN BORDERLANDS** In 1821, Spain granted independence to Mexico, which then encompassed areas extending from the Oregon Country to Guatemala. However, the new republic was beset with a multitude of problems: civil wars, economic crises, Indian depredations, and endemic political instability. Compounding these was the invasion of Anglo-Americans—first traders and settlers who entered Mexico's northern provinces in the 1820s and then settlers who flocked to Texas at the invitation of the Mexican government, which wanted to populate and develop this area. The thousands of Anglos in Texas—the majority of whom were white Southerners and their slaves—soon far outnumbered the Mexican population, and the Mexican government realized its mistake. A showdown ensued between the forces of General Antonio López de Santa Anna and Anglo Texans who had rebelled against Mexico, declaring Texas an independent republic. With six thousand troops, Santa Anna crushed the Texans at the Alamo and Goliad, but he was ultimately defeated at the battle of San Jacinto in April 1836 by troops commanded by General Sam

Houston. The Republic of Texas was recognized by the United States in 1837. Meanwhile, the Mexican province of California also had attracted thousands of Anglo Americans. Caught up in the frenzy of Manifest Destiny, Anglos began conspiring to "liberate" California from Mexican rule, much the same way Texans had. In 1845, a group of Anglos led by John C. Frémont initiated an independence movement called the Bear Flag Revolt.

***The Politics of Expansion, pp. 392–394*** The growing number of Anglo Americans in the trans-Mississippi West put great pressure on the government in Washington to annex Texas, Oregon, and other territory. In the 1840s, these expansionist pressures helped push the United States into diplomatic crises with Great Britain and Mexico. Even more ominous was the way the politics of expansion flamed the fires of sectionalism by reopening the slavery question.

**TYLER AND THE WHIG FIASCO** President John Tyler initiated the politics of expansion. He had been vice president when William Henry Harrison died in office in 1841 after serving only one month. Tyler was actually a states' rights Virginia Democrat who had been picked as Harrison's running mate to help broaden the Whigs' appeal in the South. Tyler was profoundly incompatible with the ideological mainstream of the Whig Party, which supported Henry Clay's American System. He soon broke with congressional Whigs, who had united behind Clay's nationalistic economic program. Despite his lack of a base in either of the major parties, Tyler hoped to be elected president in his own right in 1844. To accomplish that, he embraced the issue of territorial annexation, hoping to use it as a bridge back to his former party.

**TEXAS, OREGON, AND THE ELECTION OF 1844** In 1843, Tyler decided to put the full force of his administration behind the annexation of Texas—a popular move, especially in the South. However, it was a dangerous strategy: Northerners did not want to add another slave state, and Mexico had never relinquished its claim to the territory. But Texas had been exploring the possibility of allying with Great Britain, and Tyler worked vigorously to annex Texas before his term was up. His annexation treaty failed, however, when John C. Calhoun linked it to slavery, leading northern antislavery Whigs to charge that the whole scheme was a proslavery conspiracy to benefit the South. Consequently, the Senate rejected the annexation treaty in June 1844. The issue dominated the 1844 election. Henry Clay hoped to avoid the issue by focusing on his economic program but undercut his support in the South by coming out against annexation. Martin Van Buren lost his chance at the Democratic nomination by opposing annexation, and the Democrats chose James K. Polk as their nominee. Polk ran full force on an expansionist platform, calling not only for the annexation of Texas but for acquisition of all of the Oregon Country as well. By combining the Oregon and Texas questions, the Democrats hoped to appeal to both northern and southern expansionists. Whig candidate Henry Clay finally hinted at his support for annexing Texas, but he only undermined his popularity in the North: Polk won the election. Before he left office, Tyler won congressional approval for annexation in February 1845, and Texas entered the union as the fifteenth slave state. Polk himself resolved the Oregon question, agreeing with the British to divide the territory at the forty-ninth parallel.

***The Mexican War, 1846–1848, pp. 394–402*** When the United States annexed Texas, tensions between the two nations escalated, but it was President Polk's insistence on acquiring Mexico's other northern provinces that made war between the two countries inevitable.

**"MR. POLK'S WAR"** Initially, Polk had hoped to buy Mexico's northern territory, but his envoy was rudely rebuffed by the Mexicans. The president decided that completing his expansionist agenda would require military action and ordered General Zachary Taylor to move American troops into the disputed land between the Nueces River and the Rio Grande, which was claimed by both Mexico and the United States. A skirmish resulting in American casualties gave Polk the pretext he needed, and on May 13, 1846, Congress officially declared war on Mexico. The war had many opponents in the United States, Whig critics chief among them, who charged that from the beginning Polk had contrived the whole affair and that the war amounted to bullying of a weak nation by its greedy imperialist neighbor. Polk believed that the United States would occupy Mexican territory and force the Mexicans to sue for peace quickly. In May 1846, Polk ordered Taylor to cross the Rio Grande and seize parts of northeastern Mexico, which he did. In the meantime, other offensives were taking place against New Mexico and California. In the summer of 1846, a small army under Colonel Stephen W. Kearny occupied the town of Sante Fe with no opposition and proclaimed the annexation of New Mexico. Kearny proceeded on to California, where he joined a conflict already in progress, the Bear Flag Revolt, led by John C. Frémont. The United States now controlled the two territories for which it had gone to war. By the time of the American conquest of California, Taylor had driven deep into Mexico's interior. On Washington's birthday 1847, Taylor's army met Mexican troops commanded by Santa Anna at Buena Vista and won another American victory. The series of victories gave the American troops a sense of superiority, but they worried about other hazards, especially the disease that killed far more soldiers than battle wounds did.

**VICTORY IN MEXICO** Even though the United States controlled all the borderlands and much of northern Mexico, Mexico still refused to end the hostilities or cede the conquered territories. At this juncture, Polk and General Winfield Scott, the commanding general of the army, launched a bold new campaign. Scott staged an amphibious landing at Veracruz on the coast and fought his way west toward Mexico City, reaching its outskirts in August 1847. After a hard fight, Americans occupied the city. Polk's peace emissary concluded the Treaty of Guadalupe Hidalgo, under which Mexico agreed to cede California and New Mexico and to recognize the Rio Grande and the Texas border. The United States agreed to assume $3.25 million in American claims against Mexico and to pay the Mexicans $15 million. The war was over and the United States had gained a vast new territory. But it had also acquired a new set of troubling and divisive issues.

## *Conclusion: Free Labor, Free Men*

Americans saw the geographical expansion of the 1840s as a natural corollary to the nation's economic transformation. To Northerners, industrial expansion confirmed the superiority of the free-labor system, in which individuals could choose to exert themselves and succeed. Since Northerners believed that failure was self-induced, they celebrated the system. But Southerners argued that slavery was a better system; they claimed that slaves did not suffer and that their society was more advanced than that of the North. The division between the Northern and Southern labor systems increasingly meant that their economic interests, cultural values, and political aims were antithetical. The victory in Mexico was not sufficient to bridge the differences between the sections.

***Chronology Activity*** Read the annotated chronology, and answer the multiple-choice questions.

1828 America's first railroad, the Baltimore and Ohio, breaks ground. By 1850, there were 9,000 miles of track in the United States, and by 1860 that figure had grown to 30,000 miles, or about as much as the rest of the world combined. The massive railroad expansion helped make the United States the world's second leading industrial power, behind Great Britain.

1836 Texas declares independence from Mexico. Americans had started settling in Texas in the 1820s, after the Mexican government granted the American Stephen Austin an enormous tract of land along the Brazos River. The American newcomers had little interest in assimilating to Mexican culture, and after General Antonio López de Santa Anna seized the government and centralized authority in Mexico City, they rebelled. After winning a major victory at San Jacinto, the Texans declared the establishment of the Lone Star Republic.

1837 John Deere patents his steel plow. The "singing plow" was made of steel that was strong enough to cut through the thick soil of the midwestern prairies. It increased agricultural productivity by allowing farmers to cultivate more land.

1840s Americans begin harnessing steam power to manufacturing. Once extensive mining began in the Pennsylvania coal fields and created a cheap source of fuel, it became more and more practical to use steam engines in factories. The use of steam power contributed to overall American productivity. Steam power also fueled the railroads that incorporated the most advanced developments of the first half of the nineteenth century.

Cyrus McCormick and others create practical mechanical reapers. Mechanical reapers cost between $100 and $150, but they allowed farmers to harvest up to twelve acres a day. Nonetheless, they were unreliable in their early stage of development and depended on horses or oxen for power.

1841 First wagon trains set out for West on Oregon Trail. Inspired by missionaries' descriptions of the lush and fertile Oregon Country, increasing numbers of American settlers headed for the West Coast. The trek involved four to six months of grueling travel across what was known as the "Great American Desert" between the Mississippi River and the Rockies and was especially hard on women, who were often unwilling migrants.

Vice President John Tyler becomes president of the United States when William Henry Harrison dies in office after one month. Tyler was a Democrat until he broke with Andrew Jackson over nullification. He did not sympathize with Whigs' economic goals and had been placed on the ticket only to satisfy Southerners. His vetoes of key Whig legislation caused him to be expelled from the Whig Party; his attempts to win his way back into the Democratic Party by championing the annexation of Texas contributed to heightened sectional tensions in the 1840s.

1842 Webster-Ashburton Treaty settles all border issues with British Canada except Oregon. After Tyler was expelled from the Whig Party, his entire cabinet resigned except for Daniel Webster, who stayed as secretary of state to negotiate the Webster-Ashburton Treaty. His success was not sufficient to redeem Tyler's administration, though.

1844 Democrat James K. Polk elected president on platform calling for annexation of Texas and Oregon. The Democratic strategy in the 1844 election was to pull out all the stops on behalf of western expansion, demanding the "reannexation" of Texas and the "reoccupation" of Oregon. This meant that both Northerners and Southerners could support expansion without feeling that one section was being favored over another.

Samuel F. B. Morse invents telegraph. The first telegraph message went out over forty miles of wire between Washington and Baltimore, and the telegraph quickly spread alongside railroad tracks. It was used extensively by railroad managers who discovered the many advantages of instantaneous communication for scheduling trains and avoiding accidents.

1845 Term *manifest destiny* coined by New York journalist John L. O'Sullivan and used as justification for Anglo American settlers to take western land. O'Sullivan was an armchair expansionist, but he neatly summarized a grandiose excuse for expansion—the idea that the United States was destined to spread across the continent and in fact had a responsibility to do so to bring democratic civilization to areas suffering under the rule of foreign powers. While settlers and politicians liked to use manifest destiny as an excuse for taking other nations' land, most were motivated by simple economic considerations, like land hunger and access to Pacific ports and the Asian trade.

United States annexes Texas, which enters Union as a slave state. President Tyler used James K. Polk's presidential victory as a chance to declare a mandate in favor of Texas's annexation. In February of 1845, after a vehement debate between antislavery and proslavery congressmen, Texas was offered admission to the United States.

1846 Bear Flag Revolt, independence movement to secede from Mexico, takes place in California. As was the case in Texas, American settlers in California soon outnumbered Mexican citizens and became discontent with Mexican rule. Americans settlers in the Sacramento Valley were aware that the United States was interested in acquiring the territory, and, with the encouragement of former army captain John C. Frémont, they took matters into their own hands.

May 13. Congress declares war on Mexico. Polk used an attack on American forces as a pretext to declare war, ignoring the fact that the soldiers had been on disputed territory. While Americans supported the war, it was much more popular in the South than the North, and antislavery Whigs kept up a steady chorus of criticism of the president and the aims of the war.

United States and Great Britain agree to divide Oregon Country at forty-ninth parallel. During his campaign, Polk had promised to demand all of the Oregon Country as far north as the southern latitude of Russian Alaska. However, he was already at war with Mexico and could not afford to fight on two fronts. To the anger of many westerners, he agreed to a compromise settlement.

1847 Brigham Young leads advance party of Mormons to Great Salt Lake in Utah. Mormons had been persecuted by "gentiles" since the religion was first founded in 1830 by Joseph Smith Jr. Non-Mormons saw Smith's followers as heretics, and when church dissenters publicized Smith's advocacy of bigamy, Smith was arrested and shot dead when a mob stormed the jail. The church's new leader, Brigham Young, decided to move his adherents to a remote area. Leaving 12,000 Mormons in eastern Iowa, Young led an advance group to the edge of the Great Salt Lake in what was then Mexican territory. By means of discipline and communal labor, within ten years the Mormons had developed an irrigation system that allowed them to farm.

1848 Treaty of Guadalupe Hidalgo ends Mexican War. Mexico gives up all claims to Texas north of Rio Grande and cedes provinces of New Mexico and California to United States. General Winfield Scott's capture of Mexico City finally forced the Mexican government to sue for peace. The treaty was detrimental for the Mexicans, who lost an enormous amount of their land and did not benefit from the California gold rush, and it led to long-term hostility toward Yankees.

Oneida Community organized in New York. The Oneidans were led by John Humphrey Noyes, who believed that the saved were literally without sin. However, he also believed that private property could make even saints greedy and that the root of private property lay in marriage. Thus, he forbade individual marriages among his followers and practiced economic communalism.

First women's rights convention in United States held at Seneca Falls, New York. The convention, organized by reformers Lucretia Mott and Elizabeth Cady Stanton, produced a manifesto called the Declaration of Sentiments. Modeled after the Declaration of Independence, the Declaration of Sentiments demanded that women be given full rights of citizenship, including the vote. The demand was ridiculed by most Americans but provided the basis for the women's rights movement.

1849 California gold rush begins. The discovery of gold occurred almost simultaneously with the area's transfer to the United States. Thus, Mexico in no way benefited from the find.

Harriet Tubman escapes from slavery in Maryland. Tubman repeatedly risked her life and her freedom by returning to the South and escorting slaves to freedom. Free blacks in the North aided the enterprise by participating in what came to be known as the underground railroad, providing food and shelter to the fugitives.

1850 Mormon community of Deseret annexed to United States as Utah Territory. Mexico lost Utah to the Americans as part of the Treaty of Guadalupe Hidalgo. The area was largely ignored until Brigham Young's 1852 announcement that many Mormons practiced polygamy. The news caused an outcry that forced the American government to establish its authority in Utah.

1851 Conference in Laramie, Wyoming, between U.S. government and Plains tribes marks beginning of government policy of forcing Indians onto reservations. The American government rescinded the "permanent" frontier it had granted to Indians just to the west of the Mississippi River. Then, at the Laramie conference, it forced tribal leaders, who hoped to gain protection from wagons trains, to accept restriction to specific areas that whites promised never to violate. This laid the groundwork for the reservation system, although whites' unwillingness to stay out of Indian territory and Indians' unwillingness to give up their nomadic way of life meant years of further warfare.

1855 Massachusetts integrates public schools as a result of campaigns led by African American leaders. The black abolitionist leaders who rose to prominence in the 1840s and 1850s were much more aware of Northern discrimination than their white counterparts. They organized campaigns against segregation, with the victory in Massachusetts constituting their most notable success.

## *Chronology Questions* Choose the letter of the best answer.

1. In 1851
   a. the Webster-Ashburton Treaty settled most border issues with Canada.
   b. a meeting in Laramie, Wyoming marked the start of the reservation system.
   c. John Deere invented his steel plow.
   d. the term *manifest destiny* was coined.

2. The Bear Flag revolt, an independence movement to secede from Mexico, broke out in California in
   a. 1836.
   b. 1841.
   c. 1846.
   d. 1850.

3. In the first notable success of northern abolitionist leaders, Massachusetts integrated its public schools in
   a. 1828.
   b. 1837.
   c. 1845.
   d. 1855.

4. What is the correct order for the following events?
   1. Vice President John Tyler becomes president.
   2. The United States annexes Texas.
   3. James Polk is elected president.
   4. Texas declares independence from Mexico.
   a. 4, 1, 2, 3
   b. 3, 4, 2, 1
   c. 2, 3, 4, 1
   d. 4, 1, 3, 2

5. The first wagon trains set out for Oregon in
   a. 1828.
   b. 1837.
   c. 1841.
   d. 1849.

6. What is the correct order for the following events?
   1. The first wagon trains set out for the West on the Oregon Trail.
   2. The Webster-Ashburton treaty settles all border issues with Canada except Oregon.
   3. United States and Great Britain agree to divide Oregon Country at the forty-ninth parallel.
   4. James Polk is elected president.
   a. 1, 2, 4, 3
   b. 3, 2, 1, 4
   c. 1, 3, 4, 2
   d. 3, 2, 4, 1

7. Samuel F. B. Morse invented the telegraph in
   a. 1836.
   b. 1844.
   c. 1851.
   d. 1855.

8. Brigham Young led an advance party of Mormons to the Great Salt Lake in Utah in
   a. 1837.
   b. 1842.
   c. 1847.
   d. 1851.

9. Which one of the following did not occur in 1848?
   a. The Treaty of Guadalupe Hidalgo ends the Mexican War.
   b. The first women's rights convention in the United States takes place at Seneca Falls.
   c. America's first railroad, the Baltimore and Ohio, breaks ground.
   d. The Oneida community is organized in New York.

10. What is the correct order for the following events?
    1. The Bear Flag revolt takes place in California.
    2. Congress declares war on Mexico.
    3. The Mormon community of Deseret is annexed to the United States as the Utah Territory.
    4. The Treaty of Guadalupe Hidalgo ends the Mexican War.
    a. 4, 3, 1, 2
    b. 4, 2, 1, 3
    c. 3, 1, 4, 2
    d. 1, 2, 4, 3

***Defining Terms*** Match each term with the correct definition.

American system
free labor
potato blight
manifest destiny
cradle
underground railroad
singing plow
Fort Laramie, Wyoming
"Mr. Polk's War"
"Fifty-four Forty or Fight"
Treaty of Guadalupe Hidalgo
transcendentalists
Seneca Falls Declaration of Sentiments
Webster-Ashburton Treaty
Nueces River
telegraph
Buena Vista
James G. Birney
free-labor ideal
joint occupation
*ranchos*
coffin ships
John Humphrey Noyes
squatting
John Tyler
Deseret
Veracruz
Fourierists

1. John Deere's strong, smooth steel plow. Unlike the cast-iron plows that had been used since the 1820s, Deere's 1837 model could slice easily through thick prairie soil, hence its nickname. The steel plough allowed farmers to use their energy to break more ground and plant more crops. Singing plow

2. A frame attached to a scythe. By 1850, this innovation a allowed farmers to harvest two or three acres of wheat a day, in contrast to only three-fourths of an acre a day without a cradle. Cradle

3. The practice of farming unclaimed federal land without paying for it. In the nineteenth century, millions Americans who could not afford the going price of $1.25 an acre for federal land simply took it for their own use. Many of them had to move from place to place. squatting

4. The practice of manufacturing and then assembling interchangeable parts. This was one American response to the shortage of cheap labor in the nineteenth century; it spread quickly from gun-making into other industries and even extended to the making of machines. American system

5. A system of transmitting a series of dots and dashes that could instantly convey electronic messages along lengths of wire. The telegraph industry grew with the railroads, which used telegraphs to schedule trains and avoid head-on collisions. By making long-distance communication cheap, efficient, and fast, it changed American businesses, newspapers, government, and everyday life. telegraph

6. A system of labor in which workers were not slaves. In the nineteenth century, Northerners favorably contrasted their system of paid workers to that of the South, with its slave laborers. free labor

7. The notion that all American men who worked hard and saved their money could become independent producers or landowners. It was a popular way for Americans in the 1840s and 1850s to explain discrepancies in wealth and success without blaming the existing economic system. free-labor ideal

8. A blight that ruined Irish potato crops. Since millions of poor Irish farmers depended on potatoes for their food, tens of thousands starved to death; many others contributed to the large wave of Irish immigrants who entered the United States in the 1840s and 1850s. potato blight

9. A slang term for ships from Ireland, because so many malnourished Irish immigrants died crossing the Atlantic Ocean. coffin ships

10. A group of New England writers who argued that individuals should not conform to the materialistic world or abstract notions of religion but instead turn to themselves for truth and guidance. Transcendentalism was not so much an alternative to the value of mainstream society as an exaggerated form of the rampant individualism of the age. transcendentalists

11. Followers of the French social theorist who believed that individualism and competition were evils that could be eradicated by communal living. Small groups of Americans attempted to reform society by living in communities based on Fourier's ideas. Fourierists

12. The leader of the utopian Oneida community who believed that marriage and private property were the sources of greed and selfishness and eradicated both in his settlement. The Oneida community survived until long after the Civil War. John Humphrey Noyes

13. A manifesto based on the Declaration of Independence. It was produced by the first women's rights gathering in 1848 and demanded the immediate granting of full rights of citizenship to women, including the suffrage. Although no states took up the cause, this manifesto became the focus of the women's rights movement for the next seventy years. Seneca Falls Declaration of Sentiments

14. A system of help for fugitive slaves from the South. Running mainly through black neighborhoods northward, runaway slaves used this network to receive food and shelter from sympathizers. underground railroad

15. A term coined by journalist John L. O'Sullivan, who demanded that the United States fulfill what he saw as its God-given responsibility to take over the North American continent. The phrase provided an ideological shield for westward expansion and masked the economic motivations that inspired most people: settlers wanted land, and politicians wanted access to trade with Asia. manifest destiny

16. The 1818 agreement between Great Britain and the United States that established Oregon as "free and open" to settlement by both countries. The agreement was threatened by the increase in American migration that began during the 1830s. Joint occupation

17. The American fort at which members of the Plains Indian tribes were persuaded to sign agreements in 1851 that restricted them to specific areas. The policy of isolation set by this treaty was the genesis of the reservation system. Fort Laramie, Wyoming

18. The Mormon haven on the Great Salt Lake in Utah, established in 1847 after Joseph Smith Jr., the founder of the religion, was killed by a mob in Nauvoo, Illinois. The Mormons who settled at Deseret developed an efficient irrigation system through cooperative labor rather than the competition common among most emigrants. Deseret

19. The huge cattle-raising estates granted to California settlers by the Mexican government. The government hoped to encourage migration and economic growth but ended up with enough discontented Anglos that they lost the region entirely. California Indians were negatively affected as well; of the 300,000 who lived in the area when the Spanish arrived in 1769, only 150,000 were left in 1846. ranchos

20. The first vice president to become president when the elected president, William Henry Harrison, died in office in April 1841. Tyler was nominally a Whig but had been a member of the Democratic Party until the 1830s and had consistently opposed Whig measures. His decision to open the issue of Texas annexation contributed to the growth of sectional hostility and the outbreak of war with Mexico. John Tyler

21. The 1842 treaty that settled all border disputes with Canada except for Oregon. The treaty was negotiated by Daniel Webster, who remained secretary of state of Tyler's cabinet after the other members resigned. Even this success was not enough to make Tyler's administration successful, however. Webster-Ashburton Treaty

22. The presidential candidate of the fledgling Liberty Party in the 1844 election. When the Whig candidate, Henry Clay, waffled on the issue of annexing Texas, he picked up the votes of disillusioned Northern Whigs. This meant that Clay lost the state of New York and thus the presidency. James G. Birney

23. The Democratic campaign slogan in the 1844 election, which called for the "reoccupation" of the Oregon territory all the way to the southern latitude of Russian Alaska. Because President Polk, who was close to war with Mexico, was not willing to go to war with Great Britain over the issue, he accepted a division of the territory along the forty-ninth parallel instead. "Fifty-four Forty or Fight"

24. The boundary separating Texas from Mexico, according to the Mexicans. Americans disagreed; they placed the boundary at the Rio Grande, 150 miles to the south. President Polk's decision to move troops past the Rio Nueces and to the banks of the Rio Grande helped precipitate the Mexican War in 1846. Nueces River

25. Antiwar Whigs' label for the American war with Mexico. They claimed that the president had deliberately arranged the incident that sparked the war and hoped to undercut national support for the conflict. "Mr. Polk's war"

26. The scene of a major battle in 1847 between the American general Zachary Taylor and the Mexican general Antonio López de Santa Anna. Santa Anna had hoped to stop the American advance into Mexico by assembling a huge army of 21,000 soldiers; however, he lost the battle and withdrew his army during the night. Buena Vista

27. The beginning of General Winfield Scott's march to Mexico City in 1847. In a carefully planned maneuver, 8,600 American troops made an amphibious landing near here and took the city after eighty-eight hours of shelling. Veracuz

28. The February 1848 agreement that ended the Mexican War. The Mexicans agreed to give up all claims to Texas above the Rio Grande and cede the provinces of California and New Mexico to the United States. In return, the United States paid the Mexican government $15 million and assumed $3.25 million dollars in claims that American citizens had against Mexico. Treaty of Guadalupe Hidalgo

## Chapter Review

***Multiple-Choice*** Choose the letter of the best answer.

1. During the 1840s and 1850s, many Americans began to move from
   a. cities to farms.
   b. small towns to the wilderness.
   c. farms to cities.
   d. the wilderness to small towns.

2. American productivity increased in the 1840s and 1850s partly because a growing number of Americans worked
   a. on railroads.
   b. for themselves.
   c. on farms.
   d. in factories.

3. The transition to the use of steam power in manufacturing was slow because
   a. water and animal power was still effective.
   b. people were afraid of new technology.
   c. the machines were unreliable.
   d. workers did not like it.

4. Beginning in the 1830s, factories and railroads gained a cheap, plentiful fuel source in Pennsylvanian
   a. gasoline.
   b. timber.
   c. oil.
   d. coal mining.

5. As Americans began to move west, agricultural productivity was limited by
   a. federal land policies.
   b. farmers' laziness.
   c. the physical labor required to clear land.
   d. Indian encroachment.

6. Farmers found that greater agricultural productivity was possible in the Midwest because
   a. it was relatively treeless.
   b. its soil was richer than that of the east.
   c. both of the above.
   d. neither of the above.

7. John Deere's 1837 plow was revolutionary because it
   a. was made of cast iron.
   b. used steam power.
   c. was made of steel.
   d. had a radically new design.

8. Mechanical reapers and better plows permitted farmers to increase their crop productivity because they
   a. allowed more land to be brought into cultivation.
   b. increased the yield of a given acre of cultivated land.
   c. made farming more attractive to city dwellers.
   d. required so little human or animal energy to use.

9. Up to 1860, the nation continued to become a great deal richer in
   a. seed development.
   b. gold and silver.
   c. land.
   d. Indian trade.

10. The "American system" was a
    a. series of roads.
    b. manufacturing technique.
    c. style of teaching.
    d. new kind of banking.

11. The United States catapulted into a position as the world's second leading industrial power, behind Great Britain, because its
    a. railroads expanded massively.
    b. manufactured goods were so good.
    c. mining techniques were advanced.
    d. labor force was cheap.

12. In the early days of the industry, almost all railroads were owned by
    a. the federal government.
    b. state governments.
    c. private corporations.
    d. the public.

13. During the 1840s and 1850s, Americans lived amidst a profound _____ transformation that had been underway since the start of the nineteenth century.
    a. gender
    b. economic
    c. scientific
    d. political

14. The change from _____ as a source of energy permitted factories to be more productive beginning around 1840.
    a. water to steam
    b. coal to steam
    c. water to coal
    d. steam to water

15. The doubling of _____ productivity contributed more than any other single factor to the economic growth of the 1840s and 1850s.
    a. industrial
    b. artisans'
    c. agricultural
    d. miners'

16. During the 1850s, _____ added more people than any other state in the Union.
    a. New York
    b. California
    c. Illinois
    d. Virginia

17. The agricultural productivity of frontier farmers was increased by _____ farm implements.
    a. the total mechanization of
    b. the falling price of
    c. the invention of basic
    d. labor-saving improvements in

18. _____ permitted farmers to harvest two or three acres of wheat a day.
    a. Scythes with cradles
    b. Scythes
    c. Steel plows
    d. Mechanical reapers

19. _____ created the basic precondition for the increase in agricultural productivity that underlay the nation's economic growth in the mid-nineteenth century.
    a. Mechanical reapers
    b. Federal land policy
    c. Speculators
    d. Bankers

20. Between 1840 and 1869, New England led the nation in _____.
    a. agricultural output
    b. manufacturing
    c. land sales
    d. wheat processing

21. The _____ industry incorporated the most advanced developments of the mid-nineteenth century.
    a. coal mining
    b. gun manufacturing
    c. railroad
    d. textile

22. _____ permitted railroad managers to avoid deadly collisions.
    a. Human runners
    b. Careful scheduling
    c. Telephones
    d. Telegraph messages

23. In the northern and western states, discrimination against women and free blacks in the half century after the Revolution was
    a. uncommon.
    b. not a source of concern to most white men.
    c. a source of serious concern to most white men.
    d. not discussed publicly.

24. Proponents of free-labor ideas used them to explain the
    a. successes and shortcomings of American society.
    b. successes of American society.
    c. shortcomings of American society.
    d. existence of slavery in the South.

25. According to free-labor spokesmen, success was available to
    a. anyone who worked hard.
    b. only those who had inherited wealth.
    c. only the very brilliant.
    d. only the well educated.

26. The free-labor ideal argued that wage labor was a
    a. first step toward independence.
    b. dead end.
    c. sure route to success.
    d. good career.

27. In keeping with the free-labor ideal, communities throughout the North and the West funded
    a. welfare programs.
    b. cheap loans for small businessmen.
    c. saloons for workingmen.
    d. public schools.

28. In 1860, almost 60 percent of white adult men in the North
    a. had wealth of more than $2,000.
    b. remained single.
    c. retained servants.
    d. were propertyless.

29. Free-labor spokesmen considered the economic inequalities of the mid-nineteenth century
    a. a failing of the system.
    b. an advantage of the system.
    c. the fault of government policies.
    d. a natural outgrowth of freedom.

30. In the nineteenth century, the desire of Americans to get ahead economically led to
    a. social and geographic mobility.
    b. social and geographic stability.
    c. complete social disintegration.
    d. an increased reliance on networks of family and friends.

31. The majority of the immigrants who arrived between 1840 and 1860 came from
    a. Germany or France.
    b. France or England.
    c. Germany or Ireland.
    d. Ireland or France.

32. First-generation German Americans tended to work as
    a. wage laborers.
    b. farmers.
    c. professionals.
    d. independent producers.

33. Most of the Irish immigrants who arrived between 1840 and 1860 were
    a. rich.
    b. middle-class.
    c. industrial workers.
    d. desperately poor.

34. Most Irish immigrants in the mid-nineteenth century were
    a. skilled artisans.
    b. Protestants.
    c. entertainers.
    d. laborers or domestic servants.

35. Women had little opportunity to aspire to _____ during the first half of the nineteenth century.
    a. factory work
    b. men's jobs
    c. teaching
    d. domestic service

36. Most white men in the 1840s and 1850s considered _____ women and free blacks proper and just.
    a. discrimination against
    b. opening opportunities to
    c. the equal education of
    d. the physical mistreatment of

37. The free-labor system was expected to benefit _____, allowing them increased chances to succeed.
    a. the wealthy
    b. wage laborers
    c. black men
    d. women

38. The free-labor ideal affirmed _____ vision of human potential.
    a. an egalitarian
    b. an unrealistic
    c. an elitist
    d. a pessimistic

39. Free-labor supporters argued that all human problems stemmed from _____.
    a. an unfair economic system
    b. indolence and vice
    c. bad luck
    d. a lack of inherited wealth

40. In 1860, about a _____ of American men possessed $2,000 in overall wealth, which was the average amount of wealth held by adult white men in the North.
    a. tenth
    b. fifth
    c. quarter
    d. third

41. In 1860, about 90 percent of _____ were propertyless.
    a. free blacks
    b. women
    c. white men
    d. young men

42. The free-labor ideal pointed to _____ as the sources of both success and failure.
    a. the government
    b. families
    c. individuals
    d. schools

43. By 1860, _____ made up about one-eighth of the American population.
    a. Germans
    b. Indians
    c. foreign-born residents
    d. native-born residents

44. Slaveholders of the mid-nineteenth century preferred to use _____ for heavy, dangerous jobs.
    a. Irish laborers
    b. young slaves
    c. German laborers
    d. elderly slaves

45. The reform movements of the 1840s and 1850s were based on the common belief that social problems resulted from
    a. psychological repression.
    b. insufficient self-control.
    c. economic injustice.
    d. massive social change.

46. The transcendentalists were a group of New England writers who believed that people should
    a. practice Buddhism.
    b. look within themselves for truth and guidance.
    c. practice an evangelical religion.
    d. conform to social norms.

47. Utopian communities like those of the Fourierists wanted to
    a. become models of perfection.
    b. provide a steady living for participants.
    c. foster industrialization.
    d. start a working-class rebellion.

48. John Humphrey Noyes, the leader of the Oneida community, taught that individuals who had achieved salvation
    a. were without sin.
    b. still might suffer eternal damnation.
    c. had a responsibility to help others.
    d. should become hermits.

49. The Oneida community was organized to allow members to practice
    a. their public speaking skills.
    b. intensive meditation.
    c. vegetarianism.
    d. complex marriage.

50. In the first half of the nineteenth century, reform societies were normally headed by
    a. ministers.
    b. young unmarried people.
    c. women.
    d. men.

51. In 1848, about one hundred people gathered in Seneca Falls, New York, for the first American
   a. meeting of abolitionists.
   b. transcendentalist convention.
   c. literary conference.
   d. women's rights convention.

52. Although women's rights conventions before 1860 repeatedly called for it, no state even came close to permitting women to
   a. vote.
   b. divorce.
   c. own property.
   d. go to college.

53. Many white Northerners did not support the abolitionist cause because they
   a. wanted to have slaves themselves.
   b. believed in black inferiority.
   c. thought blacks should achieve abolition themselves.
   d. felt the emancipation would cost too much money.

54. The black abolitionist leaders of the 1840s and 1850s were
   a. rare.
   b. submissive to white leaders.
   c. not well known.
   d. frustrated by white abolitionists.

55. In the mid-nineteenth century, black Northerners confronted racial discrimination
   a. occasionally.
   b. only if they tried to vote.
   c. in every aspect of daily life.
   d. only if they traveled to the South.

56. Free blacks in the North quietly aided the abolitionists by
   a. donating money.
   b. purchasing and freeing slaves.
   c. boycotting public transportation.
   d. helping fugitive slaves.

57. According to historians, by the mid-nineteenth century _____ constituted about one-third of the American population.
   a. atheists
   b. church members
   c. active reformers
   d. Whigs

58. Transcendentalists, a group of _____, believed that individuals should not conform to the material world or abstract notions of religion.
   a. Southern slaveholders
   b. western farmers
   c. New England writers
   d. New York bankers

59. Utopian communities like those of the Fourierists aimed to become _____ to point the way to a better life.
   a. retreats from the world
   b. models of perfection
   c. extremely poor
   d. centers of intellectual activity

60. John Humphrey Noyes's Oneida community scandalized its neighbors by organizing a system of _____.
   a. sexual abstinence
   b. complex marriage
   c. phalanxes
   d. female social domination

61. Women _____ reform activities in the mid-nineteenth century.
   a. were barred from
   b. occupied leadership positions in
   c. avoided
   d. gained confidence and skills from

62. In 1848, female reformers issued the _____ Declaration, listing the ways in which women had suffered discrimination at the hands of men.
   a. Mott
   b. Stanton
   c. New York
   d. Seneca Falls

63. Close to two dozen _____ before 1860 called for women's suffrage.
   a. state legislatures
   b. newspapers
   c. prominent reformers
   d. women's rights conventions

64. _____ like Frederick Douglass, Henry Bibb, and Sojourner Truth lectured Northern audiences about slavery.
   a. White abolitionists
   b. Evangelical preachers
   c. Former slaves
   d. Northern blacks

65. In 1843 the black abolitionist _____ called for a slave insurrection.
   a. Sarah Grimké
   b. William Wells
   c. Henry Highland Garnet
   d. Lydia Maria Child

66. During the 1840s and 1850s, only four states permitted black men to _____.
   a. own property
   b. attend school
   c. vote
   d. marry

67. The phrase *manifest destiny* referred to Americans'
   a. sense of religious fervor.
   b. support for the Democratic Party.
   c. self-declared right to rule in the West.
   d. desire for more immigration.

68. Most Americans moved west because they
   a. were missionaries bent on conversion.
   b. were interested in travel.
   c. were involved in the fur trade.
   d. wanted land.

69. "Oregon fever" broke out because
   a. Methodist missionaries wanted to convert Indians.
   b. Americans were unhappy with the "joint occupation."
   c. Oregon was easy to get to from the East.
   d. Oregon was already full of British settlers.

70. The majority of the Plains Indians were
   a. friendly toward whites.
   b. agricultural peoples.
   c. nomadic and nonagricultural peoples.
   d. Catholic.

71. A critical component of the lives of the Plains Indians was
   a. corn.
   b. warfare.
   c. tobacco.
   d. Christianity.

72. Which one of the following actions by whites did not negative affect the Plains Indians?
   a. Whites settled on the Plains.
   b. Whites brought alcohol.
   c. Whites killed buffalo.
   d. Whites introduced new diseases.

73. When westward-bound migrants asked the federal government for protection against the Plains Indians, it responded by
   a. giving the migrants weapons.
   b. ignoring the migrants' pleas.
   c. jailing the Plains Indians.
   d. taking back the "permanent frontier" granted to the Indians.

74. The major threat to settlers moving west came from
   a. Indians.
   b. other settlers.
   c. the nature of life on the trail.
   d. the Mexican army.

75. Women found life in the Oregon Country
   a. friendly and sociable.
   b. lonely and primitive.
   c. good for farming.
   d. relatively easy.

76. Mormons established an efficient irrigation system in the Utah desert by
   a. cooperative labor.
   b. advanced technology.
   c. individualist enterprise.
   d. luck.

77. The Mexican government allowed Americans to settle in Texas because it
   a. wanted to populate and develop the area.
   b. hoped to encourage trade.
   c. needed the money from land sales.
   d. wanted to establish a slave system.

78. The Bear Flag Revolt referred to
   a. the American revolt in Texas.
   b. the American revolt in California.
   c. the grabbing of Franciscan missions' land.
   d. an Indian revolt in California.

79. Until the 1840s, the overwhelming majority of Americans lived east of the _____ River.
   a. Hudson
   b. Mississippi
   c. Charles
   d. Ohio

80. In the summer of 1845, New York _____ John O'Sullivan coined the term *manifest destiny*.
   a. journalist
   b. politician
   c. explorer
   d. minister

81. In 1818 the Americans and the _____ began a joint occupation of the Oregon Territory.
   a. British
   b. Mexicans
   c. Russians
   d. Spanish

82. The federal government responded to Oregon migrants' calls for protection by _____.
   a. ignoring them
   b. building forts along the trail and forcing Indians into specific areas
   c. providing army guides
   d. going to war with Great Britain

83. Mormons began migrating to Utah in 1847, after their leader, Joseph Smith, was _____ Nauvoo, Illinois.
   a. converted to Catholicism in
   b. driven out of
   c. killed by a mob in
   d. thrown out of the church hierarchy in

84. By 1835, the _____ population of Texas was less than 8,000.
   a. American
   b. Indian
   c. Tejano
   d. slave

85. After the defeat of General Santa Anna at _____, Texans succeeded in establishing the Lone Star Republic.
   a. the Alamo
   b. San Jacinto
   c. Goliad
   d. Mexico City

86. Spain originally moved into California to block _____ from moving south along the Pacific coastline.
   a. British merchants
   b. French trappers
   c. American missionaries
   d. Russian fur traders

87. Americans living in California in the 1840s saw themselves as _____ their Mexican neighbors.
   a. very similar to
   b. more wealthy than
   c. inferior to
   d. superior to

88. In 1846, Americans living in the Sacramento Valley raised _____ called the Bear Flag Revolt.
   a. a militia
   b. an independence movement
   c. a new government
   d. an Indian liberation movement

89. John Tyler's presidency was undermined by
   a. his devotion to principle.
   b. questions about the extent of his authority.
   c. salacious stories about his personal life.
   d. Andrew Jackson's opposition to him.

90. President Tyler was a Whig because he
   a. agreed with their political platform.
   b. was a protégé of Henry Clay.
   c. was in favor of abolition.
   d. had fallen out with Andrew Jackson.

91. President Tyler forfeited his claims to Whig leadership after he
   a. vetoed the repeal of the Independent Treasury.
   b. vetoed a bill for a new national bank.
   c. refused to give Henry Clay a cabinet position.
   d. put only Democrats in his cabinet.

92. After most of President Tyler's cabinet resigned, Daniel Webster remained to negotiate a treaty to settle
   a. the annexation of Texas.
   b. British trading concerns.
   c. Indian territorial disputes on the Great Plains.
   d. the boundary between Canada and the United States.

93. Annexing Texas was a dangerous political move because it
   a. was unpopular with almost all Americans.
   b. would be financially expensive.
   c. would make the nation too large.
   d. risked precipitating war with Mexico.

94. The British wanted Texas to
   a. reunite with Mexico.
   b. become part of the United States.
   c. become part of the British empire.
   d. remain independent.

95. John C. Calhoun doomed the first Texas annexation treaty by
   a. pointing out the cost of annexation.
   b. linking it to the defense of slavery.
   c. commenting that it would lead to war.
   d. making his own ambivalence obvious.

96. Henry Clay hoped to wage the 1844 presidential campaign on the basis of
   a. his personal popularity.
   b. Whig economic principles.
   c. the annexation of Oregon.
   d. the annexation of Texas.

97. Martin Van Buren's 1844 Democratic candidacy collapsed after he
   a. supported Clay's American system.
   b. promised to reinstate the independent treasury system.
   c. threatened to go to war with Mexico.
   d. announced his opposition to Texas annexation.

98. In the 1844 election, Democrats succeeded in championing Texas annexation without splitting their party or the nation along sectional lines by
   a. having a Northern vice presidential candidate.
   b. yoking Texas to Oregon.
   c. downplaying Texas.
   d. attacking Clay's economic program.

99. In 1844, Henry Clay destroyed his chances at the presidency by
   a. waffling on the issue of Texas annexation.
   b. making personal attacks on Polk.
   c. choosing a Democrat as his running mate.
   d. refusing to discuss Texas.

100. In 1846, President Polk settled the Oregon dispute by
   a. dividing the territory with Great Britain along the forty-ninth parallel.
   b. grabbing the territory all the way up to Alaska.
   c. starting a war.
   d. giving up the whole territory.

101. In the 1840s the issue of westward expansion become hopelessly entangled with questions about _____.
   a. slavery
   b. partisan politics
   c. national finances
   d. military competence

102. John Tyler was a Whig only because he had fallen out with Andrew Jackson over the _____.
   a. nullification crisis
   b. Removal Act
   c. bank wars
   d. Specie Circular

103. After Tyler moved into the White House, Whigs assumed that he would bow to _____, the party's leader.
   a. John Quincy Adams
   b. Daniel Webster
   c. Henry Clay
   d. Martin Van Buren

104. In 1844, President Tyler raised the issue of _____ in hopes of gaining the Democratic Party's presidential nomination.
   a. the Oregon Territory
   b. Texas's annexation
   c. Indian reservations
   d. a national bank

105. American officials in 1844 were afraid that Texas would be _____.
   a. added to the British empire
   b. invaded by Mexico
   c. convinced to emancipate its slaves
   d. more successful outside of the Union

106. Many _____ were appalled by the first Texas annexation treaty.
   a. northerners
   b. westerners
   c. southerners
   d. foreigners

107. The Whig Party initially attempted to _____ Texas annexation in the 1844 presidential race.
   a. remain silent on
   b. champion
   c. dismiss
   d. weakly endorse

108. In the 1844 presidential election, the Democrats ran on a platform embracing _____.
   a. high tariffs
   b. states' rights
   c. manifest destiny
   d. industrialization

109. In 1844, President Tyler used _____ to get congressional approval of the admission of Texas to the Union.
   a. bribes
   b. the outbreak of war with Mexico
   c. the Democratic victory
   d. popular petitions

110. President Polk _____ Great Britain over the issue of dividing the Oregon Country.
   a. went to war with
   b. compromised with
   c. offered cash payments to
   d. made no progress with

111. War with Mexico was made certain by President Polk's insistence on
   a. annexing Texas.
   b. annexing California.
   c. ignoring Mexican diplomats.
   d. having all of Mexico's northern provinces.

112. President Polk helped to spark the war with Mexico by ordering American troops to
   a. Mexico City.
   b. the Rio Grande.
   c. the Nueces River.
   d. Buena Vista.

113. The war with Mexico
   a. divided the nation.
   b. was deeply unpopular in all sections of the country.
   c. was popular in all sections of the country.
   d. ended quickly.

114. According to Abraham Lincoln, the war with Mexico was
   a. invigorating the nation's young men.
   b. worth the cost.
   c. not going to succeed.
   d. a deception against the American public.

115. In the war with Mexico, President Polk
   a. personally directed the war.
   b. planned for a quick war.
   c. had no military experience.
   d. all of the above.

116. President Polk's strategy in the war with Mexico
   a. seemed to work at first.
   b. did not work at all.
   c. led to Mexico suing for peace within a few months.
   d. was opposed by his generals.

117. The leading cause of casualties for American soldiers in the war with Mexico was
   a. accidents.
   b. bullets and shells.
   c. untended wounds.
   d. disease.

118. The American attack on Veracruz was intended to
   a. end the war immediately.
   b. destroy the Mexican army.
   c. provide a jumping-off point for the American army to march to Mexico City.
   d. show off the strategic abilities of the army and navy.

119. General Winfield Scott's march toward Mexico City was temporarily halted by
   a. the Mexican army.
   b. Mexican peasants.
   c. a lack of troops.
   d. the weather.

120. The most brutal fighting of the Mexican War occurred at
   a. Cerro Gordo.
   b. Buena Vista.
   c. Mexico City.
   d. Santa Fe.

121. The Mexican War ended in 1848 with the signing of the Treaty of Guadalupe Hidalgo, which required
   a. Mexico to pay $3.25 million in American claims against the government.
   b. Mexico to pay the United States $15 million.
   c. the United States to put the boundary of Texas at the Nueces River.
   d. Mexico to give up all claims to Texas, New Mexico, and California.

122. In the wake of the Mexican War, which one of the following was not true?
   a. The West became an Anglo American enclave.
   b. The United States stretched from the Atlantic to the Pacific.
   c. Mexico did not profit from the discovery of gold in California.
   d. Americans and Mexicans viewed each other relatively kindly.

123. President Polk initially hoped to _____ California and New Mexico from Mexico.
   a. steal
   b. purchase
   c. militarily wrest
   d. alienate

124. President Polk encouraged the outbreak of a war with Mexico by having _____ march his army to the Rio Grande.
   a. George G. Meade
   b. Zachary Taylor
   c. Winfield Scott
   d. Sam Houston

125. _____ news of the battle at the Rio Grande arrived in Washington, President Polk had obtained his cabinet's approval of a war declaration.
   a. Immediately after
   b. Before
   c. As soon as
   d. Weeks after

126. In the war with Mexico, the American army was composed largely of _____.
   a. volunteers
   b. regular soldiers
   c. state militia
   d. mercenaries

127. President Polk believed that the Mexican government would quickly _____ after the United States declared war.
   a. sue for peace
   b. offer to sell California
   c. collapse
   d. try to invade the United States

128. In the American campaign to occupy Mexico's northern provinces, the second prong centered on _____ and California.
   a. New Mexico
   b. Mexico City
   c. South America
   d. Texas

129. Superior American _____ and musket fire allowed the American army to win the Battle of Buena Vista.
   a. leadership
   b. artillery
   c. soldiers
   d. strategy

130. _____ was the major killer of American soldiers in the war with Mexico.
   a. Disease
   b. Dehydration
   c. Gunshot wounds
   d. Knife wounds

131. At the castle of Chapultepec, the Mexicans took four thousand _____, and the Americans one thousand, in a single day.
   a. prisoners of war
   b. casualties
   c. hostages
   d. new recruits

132. For Mexico, the terrible defeat in the war with the United States generated a sense of _____ for the first time.
   a. inferiority
   b. superiority
   c. nationalism
   d. pessimism

***Short Answer*** Write a paragraph response to each question.

1. What factors contributed to the increase in American agricultural productivity in the 1840s and 1850s?
2. Why did American manufacturers turn to mechanization in the mid-nineteenth century? What new system did they develop?
3. How did the expansion of the rail system affect other industries?
4. What did the free-labor ideal propose? What was it popular in Northern society?
5. How well did the free-labor ideal translate into reality? What effect did it have on American society?
6. Why did Irish immigrants have difficulty climbing up the free-labor ladder?
7. How did the philosophy of transcendentalism differ from that of the utopian movements of the 1840s and 1850s?
8. What role did women play in reform activities in the 1840s? How did that role contribute to the women's rights movement?
9. How did black and white abolitionists differ in their approach to ending the problem of slavery in the nineteenth century?
10. What was manifest destiny? What was its underlying agenda?
11. How did the Indians of the Great Plains live in the nineteenth century? Why were they so frightening to white migrants?
12. What policy did Mexico adopt toward Texas and California in the 1820s? How did it backfire?

13. What caused tension between President John Tyler and the Whig Party?
14. How did the Democrats handle the issue of Texas annexation in the 1844 election? Was their strategy successful?
15. How did the war between the United States and Mexico start?
16. What was President Polk's forced to do when his original strategy for fighting the war with Mexico misfired? Was his second plan successful?

***Building Historical Skills*** Historians use a variety of sources to think and talk about the past, including maps, illustrations, and written records. Maps provide a variety of different kinds of comparative information in a condensed visual format; reading them requires learning how to sort through this information. To deepen our understanding of the past by supplementing written records, historians frequently interpret material culture, such as a vase or a painting, with techniques borrowed from art history, archaeology, or anthropology. Written records, though familiar as sources, raise their own problems of interpretation. Every document reflects someone's particular perspective or assumptions. It is the historian's task to study and compare each document to other records with other perspectives. The following exercises introduce you to using maps, illustrations, and written documents as sources of information. Use these sources as well as the material in the chapter to think about different themes and topics discussed in the text.

***Map Activity*** Locate the following places on Map 11.5: Territorial Expansion by 1860 on page 399 in *The American Promise,* Second Edition.

1. Mexican cession
2. Oregon Country
3. Mexico
4. Texas annexation
5. British North America (Canada)
6. Louisiana Purchase
7. Florida

Answer the following questions in a paragraph based on Map 11.5: Territorial Expansion by 1860.

**READING THE MAP** List the countries from which the United States gained land. Which nation lost the most land because of U.S. expansion?

**CONNECTIONS** Who coined the phrase *manifest destiny*? When? What does it mean? What areas targeted for expansion were debated during the presidential campaign of 1844?

**WEB LINKS** To explore the topics discussed in the exercise above, visit the Web links noted below.

"Manifest Destiny"
http://odur.let.rug.nl/~usa/E/manifest/manif1.htm

"John Tyler and the Pursuit of National Destiny" by Edward P. Crapol
http://www.mtholyoke.edu/acad/intrel/crapol.htm

"The Webster-Ashburton Treaty of 1842"
http://www.yale.edu/lawweb/avalon/diplomacy/br1842m.htm

***Visual Activity*** George Catlin's portrait of Wi-Jun-Jon before and after his assimilation into white culture shows the dangers of rushing headlong into new cultural norms. In the portrait on the left, Wi-Jun-Jon has just arrived in Washington—the Capitol is depicted in the background on the left—and looks quite dignified. He is wearing traditional dress, a decorated tunic and pants that were probably made out of buffalo leather, carrying a long cape and a pipe, and wearing an impressive headdress made of feathers. He is looking into the distance; the overall effect is one of quiet authority. In the second portrait, he has returned to his village, symbolized by the teepees to the right, looking like a fop. He is dressed in a military uniform with gold braid and trim, he has an umbrella and a strangely dangling ceremonial sword, smoking a very American cigarette, and carrying alcohol in the back pockets of his coat. He gazes not into the impenetrable distance but at a flowered fan he carries. His expression has changed from grave to self-satisfied. And his assimilation is imperfect: his hair is too long, he has retained his earring, and his hat is adorned with a single red father. He is neither fully Indian nor entirely American.

Answer the following questions in a paragraph based on "Wi-Jun-Jon, An Assiniboin Chief," on page 386 in *The American Promise,* Second Edition.

**READING THE IMAGE** What kind of commentary is Catlin making about assimilation?

**CONNECTIONS** How typical was the experience of Wi-Jun-Jon? Did Plains Indians usually assimilate to white culture, or did they resist it?

**WEB LINKS** To explore the topics discussed in the exercise above, visit the Web links noted below.

"Assiniboin Indians"
http://www.pbs.org/lewisandclark/native/ass.htm

"Medicine Painter: George Catlin on the Upper Missouri, 1832"
http://www.archives.uc.edu/exhibits/catlin/catweb_page1.html

***Analyzing Sources Activity*** Answer the following questions in a paragraph based on "Historical Question: Who Rushed for California Gold?" on page 400 of *The American Promise,* Second Edition.

1. How did Chinese migrants to California see themselves? How were they treated by whites?
2. What was the American attitude toward the California gold fields? Who did they feel deserved to profit from them? Who did they feel did not deserve to profit, and how did Americans keep them from doing so?
3. What effect did the gold rush have on the *Californios* and Native Americans who already lived in California?
4. How did gold mining change over time in California? Did American men share equally in the wealth that was created?

**WEB LINKS** To explore the topics discussed in the exercise above, visit the Web links noted below.

"The Gold Rush"
http://www.isu.edu/~trinmich/home.html
Choose "All about the Gold Rush."

"The Museum of the City of San Francisco"
http://www.sfmuseum.org/
Choose "1849 California Gold Rush."

"The Great American Gold Rush"
http://www.acusd.edu/~jross/goldrush.html

# Answer Key

## Chapter 11: The Free North and West, 1840–1860

### *Chapter Overview*

#### *Chronology*

1. b
2. c
3. d
4. d
5. c
6. a
7. b
8. c
9. c
10. d

#### *Defining Terms*

1. singing plow
2. cradle
3. squatting
4. American system
5. telegraph
6. free labor
7. free-labor ideal
8. potato blight
9. coffin ships
10. transcendentalists
11. Fourierists
12. John Humphrey Noyes
13. Seneca Falls Declaration of Sentiments
14. underground railroad
15. manifest destiny
16. joint occupation
17. Fort Laramie, Wyoming
18. Deseret
19. *ranchos*
20. John Tyler
21. Webster-Ashburton Treaty
22. James G. Birney
23. "Fifty-four Forty or Fight"
24. Nueces River
25. "Mr. Polk's War"
26. Buena Vista
27. Veracruz
28. Treaty of Guadalupe Hidalgo

### *Chapter Review*

#### *Multiple-Choice*

1. c
2. d
3. a
5. d
5. c
6. c
7. c
8. a
9. c
10. b
11. a
12. c
13. b
14. a
15. c
16. c
17. d
18. a
19. b
20. b
21. c
22. d
23. b
24. a
25. a
26. a
27. d
28. d
29. d
30. a
31. c
32. d
33. d
34. d
35. b
36. a
37. b
38. a
39. b
40. c
41. a
42. c
43. c
44. a
45. b
46. b
47. a
48. a
49. d
50. d
51. c
52. a
53. b
54. d
55. c
56. d
57. b
58. c
59. b
60. b
61. d
62. d
63. d
64. c
65. c
66. c
67. c
68. d
69. a
70. c
71. b
72. a
73. d
74. c
75. b
76. a
77. a
78. b
79. b
80. a
81. a
82. b
83. c
84. c
85. b
86. d
87. d
88. b

| | |
|---|---|
| 89. b | 106. a |
| 90. d | 107. a |
| 91. b | 108. c |
| 92. d | 109. a |
| 93. d | 110. b |
| 94. d | 111. d |
| 95. b | 112. b |
| 96. b | 113. a |
| 97. d | 114. d |
| 98. b | 115. d |
| 99. a | 116. a |
| 100. a | 117. d |
| 101. a | 118. c |
| 102. a | 119. c |
| 103. c | 120. c |
| 104. b | 121. d |
| 105. a | 122. d |

### *Short Answer*

1. Increased agricultural productivity was largely the result of farmers' ability to bring more land under cultivation, not the improvement of yield per acre. The federal government made land available to farmers, and the opening of midwestern prairie lands, which had few trees and thus demanded less labor to prepare, had a significant impact on agricultural productivity. Labor-saving implements contributed as well. John Deere's steel "singing plow," which could slice cleanly through tough prairie soil, scythes with cradles that more than doubled the amount of wheat that could be harvested in a day, and, eventually, mechanical reapers all gave farmers the ability to plow, plant, and harvest more land.
2. The United States was land-rich and labor-poor; agricultural opportunities meant that there was not an enormous pool of factory laborers to keep wages low. Because of the shortage of workers, manufacturers were constantly looking for ways to save labor. One of the most important innovations was the "American system," which was the practice of manufacturing and assembling interchangeable parts. The system spread from gunmaking to other industries, including clocks, sewing machines, and axes. Eventually even machine-making was mechanized.
3. Railroads fostered the growth of other industries. In the decades before 1860, the demand for iron for rails, wheel, axles, locomotives, and iron bridges caused iron production to increase five times faster than overall population. Coal production more than doubled in the 1850s because of the need for fuel for iron furnaces and locomotive boilers. The telegraph industry was stimulated by railroads as well. The lines ran along railroad tracks, and railroad managers quickly realized that telegraphs could be used to schedule trains and avoid head-on collisions.
4. Free-labor spokesmen argued that the economy of the North and West allowed all men equal opportunity to succeed, regardless of their initial wealth and status. With hard work and careful planning, hired workers could save their earnings and open their own businesses or purchase land and become independent farmers. Every person possessed the same potential to succeed: some did and some did not because of individual discipline. The ideal was popular in the industrialized North because it explained the social disparities that continued to exist—the fact that some people benefited more than others from the changes that the economy was undergoing—without questioning the inherent fairness of the existing system.
5. The free-labor ideal claimed that all men could become independent producers, but while the United States had about 40 millionaires in 1860, most men did not achieve that kind of success. The average wealth of white men in the North was about $2,000; nearly half had no wealth, and nearly 60 percent did not own land. Even those who did achieve a measure of independence were in a precarious position, with bad debts, crop failure, sickness, or death posing a constant threat. According to free-labor spokesmen, inequality was the result of some individuals being more able, more determined, and luckier than others. Because Americans felt that their success or failure was self-generated, many were extremely anxious about the future: they moved about in search of opportunity, weakening community ties to neighbors and friends and resulting in isolation in difficult times.
6. Irish immigrants arrived in the United States with a disadvantage: most of them were profoundly poor. The bulk of Irish immigrants migrated because of the potato famine; they crossed the ocean half-starved and seldom had the resources to set themselves up in business when they landed. They faced prejudice in the hiring market as well. Native-born Americans disliked their Catholicism and saw them as only barely civilized. The Irish found themselves limited to unskilled work as laborers and domestic servants.
7. Transcendentalists were interested in a very limited kind of reform the restructuring of the self. They believed that the key to happiness lay in the rejection of conformity to outside influences and the adoption of extreme individualism and self-reliance. Utopians, by way of contrast,

wanted to reform the world by providing examples of better ways to live. For example, the Fourierists wanted to replace competition with cooperation based on communal ownership of property. John Humphrey Noyes, the founder of the Oneida community, tried to rid his followers of greed and selfishness by discarding the institutions of marriage and private property.

8. Women were very active in the reform activities that grew out of evangelical churches, where they outnumbered men two to one. They supported abolition, temperance, moral reform, and all kinds of other causes. They were, however, limited to support roles; the assumption of male superiority was sufficiently strong that women were seldom allowed to undertake the leadership of an organization. At the same time, their involvement increased women's political abilities and their self-confidence. These skills and attitudes helped spur the women's rights movement, which got its official start in 1848 at a convention in Seneca Falls, New York, organized by two female reformers, Elizabeth Cady Stanton and Lucretia Mott.

9. White abolitionists relied on moral suasion; that is, they appealed to whites' consciences to try to convince them that slavery was wrong. Black leaders were impatient with this approach. While they continued to work with white abolitionists, they increasingly called for a more uncompromising stance on slavery. Black abolitionists were also much more aware of and committed to eradicating discrimination in the free states. Regardless of their education or social status, blacks suffered discrimination at work, in politics, in school, at church, and in public places of all sorts. Black abolitionists organized campaigns against the pervasive segregation they suffered, but in most places white supremacy continued unabated.

10. Manifest destiny was a term coined in 1845 by the New York journalist John L. O'Sullivan, who argued that white Americans had both the right and the responsibility to claim the entire North American continent for their own use. This was, he claimed, for the benefit of Americans and also the foreigners who already occupied that territory, since they would be given a chance to thrive under democratic American institutions. While O'Sullivan made the project sound like a selfless undertaking, it had economic gain at its core. Westward-moving Americans wanted land above and beyond all else. Politicians saw the chance to expand American trade with the Far East, if they could gain control of the ports of the Pacific Coast.

11. While there was a great deal of diversity between the Indian tribes of the Great Plains, the majority of them were horse-mounted nomads who spurned agriculture in favor of buffalo hunting. They had become nomads after the Spanish introduced horses to the continent in the sixteenth century, and their constant migration meant that different tribes came into frequent contact with one another. As a result, competition and warfare were a common and accepted part of life on the Great Plains. Young men trained in the arts of war from an early age. Their riding skills and fierceness caused whites crossing the Great Plains on their way to Oregon a great deal of anxiety, even though the pioneers suffered far more from the hostile environment than from Indian attacks.

12. After winning independence from Spain in 1821, Mexico sought to encourage settlement and economic growth in its northern territories by inviting Americans to settle in the area. In the 1820s the Mexican government gave the American Stephen F. Austin an immense tract of land along the Brazos River in Texas, and with land selling for only ten cents an acre Southerners funneled into the area in ever-increasing numbers, bringing their cotton and slaves with them. In 1824, Mexico granted settlers in California *ranchos*, large cattle-raising estates with semi-enslaved Indian laborers. The problem was that American settlers did not attempt to assimilate: they were not Roman Catholic, they did not speak Spanish, and they wanted local government of the sort to which they were accustomed. By the time the Mexican government realized its mistake, Americans outnumbered Mexican citizens by a considerable margin. Both Texas and California eventually rebelled against Mexican rule.

13. John Tyler was nominally a Whig. However, he had been a Democrat until he fell out with Andrew Jackson over the issue of nullification. He was a states' rights supporter and strict constitutionalist who had opposed all the measures of Henry Clay's American System. His vice presidential candidacy had been designed to appeal to Southerners, but nobody expected him to become president. When he did, he refused to follow the lead of Henry Clay, the leading congressional Whig. Instead, he vetoed key measures of Clay's economic program, leading the Whigs to formally expel him from the party.

14. By the time of the 1844 presidential election, it was clear that the annexation of Texas was a divisive issue, with Southerners supporting it and Northerners opposed. Instead of simply picking one side or the other, the Democratic platform endorsed expansion in general, supporting the annexation of both Texas and Oregon. This would, Democrats contended, allow the nation to expand without favoring a single

section. The strategy was a successful one, allowing the Democrats to straddle the issue and James K. Polk to win the election. The Whigs, on the other hand, first opposed Texan annexation and then changed course and supported it, undermining their support in both the South and the North.

15. President Polk had hoped to purchase the Mexican territory of California and New Mexico, but Mexico was not interested in selling. Concluding that he would have to take the areas by force, he ordered General Zachary Taylor to lead 4,000 soldiers from the Nueces River to the Rio Grande. This inflammatory gesture seemed to the Mexicans to constitute an invasion because Mexico claimed that the Nueces River was the southernmost boundary of Texas, whereas the Americans put the dividing line at the Rio Grande. The Mexican cavalry attacked, killing or wounding sixteen Americans and capturing the rest. Before news of the battle had arrived in Washington, Polk had gotten his cabinet's approval of a war message, and the declaration of war passed Congress easily.
16. Polk expected that the American army would move into the territory he had hoped to purchase and quickly defeat the Mexican forces. Mexico, he expected, would sue for peace and the United States would keep the land it had occupied. But despite repeated losses, the Mexican government refused to back down. Once this became obvious, Polk decided to carry the war into central Mexico, tapping General Winfield Scott to land his army on the Gulf Coast and lead it 250 miles inland to Mexico City. Scott eventually was successful, and after the capitol fell, the Mexican government agreed to negotiate a treaty.

### *Map Activity*

Reading the Map: The United States gained land by means of purchase, cession, and war from nearly every country with an interest in the continent. Great Britain lost the original thirteen colonies and then ceded Oregon country, part of North Dakota and Minnesota, and a piece of Maine. France sold the immense Louisiana Territory to the United States, while Spain ceded the United States Florida and a bit of Louisiana, and the United States annexed territory in between the two states that constituted the southern borders of Mississippi and Alabama. Mexico, however, which had declared its independence from Spain in 1821, lost the most land the least voluntarily. With the Treaty of Guadalupe Hidalgo, Mexico gave up nearly a third of its territory, with land encompassing the modern states of California, Nevada, Utah, Arizona, New Mexico, Texas, and part of Colorado.

Connections: A journalist named John L. O'Sullivan came up with the phrase *manifest destiny* in 1845. He was referring to his vision of western expansion as something more than a selfish desire for more land and resources: in his view, it was only right that Americans, with their superior civilization and political system, should take over the entire continent, thus spreading the benefits of freedom and democracy. The issue became a major one in the presidential campaign of 1844. While Henry Clay and the Whig Party attempted to ignore territorial expansion, the Democrats seized on the issue. To avoid the sectional divide that had arisen when the annexation of Texas was proposed, they demanded that both Texas and the Oregon Country become part of the United States' territory.

### *Visual Activity*

Reading the Image: Catlin's image makes it clear that in his opinion, assimilation creates a person who is neither white nor Indian but instead an unhappy combination of the two. In his double portrait, Wi-Jun-Jon begins as a "traditional" Indian in paint, leather, and feathers: he clearly is not "civilized" by white standards, but he has a dignity of his own. In the second image, he is neither civilized nor dignified: he has been corrupted by white ways without being civilized by them. He is wearing westernized clothing, but he still does not look entirely white because of his long hair and his jewelry. Moreover, he has taken to drink, and his sword hangs between his legs in a manner reminiscent of the tail of a submissive dog. To Catlin, assimilation seems to be a futile goal, one that undermines what is good in Indian culture and replaces it with what is bad about white society.

Connections: In some respects, Wi-Jun-Jon is typical of the Plains Indians' experience with the American government; in other respects, he is unusual. Certainly, many Plains Indians succumbed to the lure of alcohol, which was introduced by migrants on their way to the Pacific Coast. Very few could avoid the influence of the army and the government, which dictated where they could and could not live and hunt. However, Wi-Jun-Jon's wholehearted assimilation was far from the norm. Plains Indians resisted American incursions for years, fighting until the end of the nineteenth century to keep their tribal lands. The fact that Wi-Jun-Jon himself was killed by a warrior from a nearby tribe is indicative of the distrust that Plains tribes held for those who were too closely associated with the American government

### *Analyzing Sources*

1. The Chinese constituted one of the largest groups of new arrivals to California, with 45,000 arriving

between 1848 and 1854. Almost no Chinese women immigrated, and most of the male migrants considered themselves temporary residents, there to work, save money, and return home. Whites, however, saw them as a threat. Culturally, they believed that the Chinese were devious and unassimilable; economically, they were afraid of the competition that Chinese workers presented. The Chinese were segregated, made ineligible for citizenship, denied public education and the right to testify in court, and were occasionally driven out of California towns by outbursts of mob violence.

2. White Americans believed that the fact that the discovery of gold coincided with the Treaty of Guadalupe Hidalgo was not an accident. Many contended that God had a personal interest in allowing white Americans to mine and develop California. Thus, they argued, no "foreigner" had the right to benefit from the bounty. The California legislature attempted to make it impossible for such a thing to happen by passing the Foreign Miners Tax Law, which levied high taxes on non-American miners to keep them out of the gold fields in any capacity except that of a paid laborer. Foreigners who insisted on remaining were sometimes lynched.
3. Most white Americans counted *Californios* and Native Americans as being among the foreigners who did not deserve to reap any profit from the discovery of gold. Prior to the American takeover, *Californios* could be found in every class, from ranchers to professionals to laborers; after it, prejudice and legal discrimination pushed most of them into the ranks of unskilled labor. Americans took their land and drove them from the gold fields. White miners were even more offended by the existence of Native Americans, who they wished to exterminate entirely. Starvation, disease, a falling birthrate, and wholesale murder caused the Indian population to fall from 150,000 in 1848 to 25,000 in 1856. Those Indians who survived were forced to move to the remote areas of California and avoid contact with whites.
4. The gold rush began with an explosion of individual miners from all over the globe heading to California, claiming land and panning for gold. But that era ended rapidly and was replaced by industrialized corporate deep-shaft mining. The first wave of miners created an enormous amount of wealth, amounting to eighty-one million ounces of gold in the four years between 1848 and 1852. However, not everybody shared in it equally. A handful of prospectors struck it rich, and the rest either took up farming or became wage laborers with the large companies that had pushed them out in the first place.

CHAPTER

# THE SLAVE SOUTH, 1820–1860 12

## Chapter Overview

### *Chapter Summary*

***Introduction*** This chapter begins with the plotting of a slave revolt by Nat Turner, a black slave living in Virginia. In 1831 he and his coconspirators killed fifty-seven whites before they were caught and either killed or arrested. Slave revolts constituted white Southerners' greatest nightmare, challenging the popular interpretation of southern slavery as benign and mild. In important ways, southern values and culture were increasingly diverging from those of the North in the nineteenth century. Slavery was the single most important factor in shaping the South and its inhabitants, although the region encompassed diverse peoples who did not always agree with one another. This chapter explores the complicated ways in which white and black Southerners, slaveholders and yeoman farm families lived and interacted in the South.

***The Southern Difference, pp. 411–421*** Despite many national, ethnic, and religious similarities, Southerners and Northerners were different. It was principally slavery that distinguished the two regions.

**COTTON KINGDOM, SLAVE EMPIRE** In the mid-nineteenth century, Southerners moved into the Southwest. The migration reflected the growing dominance of cotton, which adapted easily to a variety of climates and soils. Slaves cultivated 75 percent of cotton, and as the crop expanded, so did the slave population, which reached approximately four million by 1860. This extraordinary growth was the result of natural reproduction. By 1860, the South had the largest slave society in the New World.

**THE SOUTH IN BLACK AND WHITE** The presence of large numbers of African Americans generated deep-seated fears among whites, who in some parts of the South found themselves in the minority. Consequently, southern whites were dedicated to white supremacy and to maintaining a racial hierarchy supported by harsh slave codes. As northern abolitionist attacks mounted during the 1830s, southern apologists constructed a proslavery argument that claimed the institution was a "positive good" compared to the tyranny of northern capitalist "wage slavery." Not just planters and legislators promoted white supremacy; all white classes and professions had a stake in the system. Thus, to a certain extent, black slavery helped whites bridge differences in class, wealth, education, and culture, as both slaveless whites and slave masters stood opposed to black freedom and equality.

**THE PLANTATION ECONOMY** Most southern whites worked small farms, and only about 25 percent of white families owned slaves, most with fewer than five. Despite their minority status, planters dominated the southern economy, which in turn remained emphatically agricultural in character. The main staples of southern agriculture were tobacco, sugar, rice, and cotton. Tobacco was the oldest plantation crop in North America. Sugarcane plantations were reputed to demand the hardest physical labor and required a great deal of money to fund. Rice was also expensive to cultivate and required large number of slaves. Cotton was the dominant cash crop because it was relatively easy to grow and took little capital to get started. Although nearly every southern farmer grew cotton, large planters produced three-quarters of the region's cotton and got the majority of the income from it. The plantation economy was very profitable for planters, and it benefited the national economy as well. Northerners served as intermediaries between planters and British textile mills, warehoused cotton, shipped it, and sold their manufactured goods in the southern market. Unfortunately for the South, nonagricultural forms of economic activity, especially manufacturing, developed slowly, if at all. What diversification existed was principally in the processing of raw materials, and industry remained an insignificant force in comparison with the agricultural economy. Southerners were afraid that an industrial economy would upset the slave system. The South had no real urban centers equal to those in the North and very few immigrants. While the North developed a diversified economy—agriculture, commerce, and manufacturing—the majority of white Southerners remained devoted to agriculture.

***Masters, Mistresses, and the Big House, pp. 421–428*** Though they varied in style, size, and other features, southern plantations shared one key characteristic. Plantation masters dominated slaves and everyone else, including wives and children: they too were property.

**PLANTATION MASTERS** Most plantation masters conceived of their relationship with slaves as one that historians call "paternalistic"—one where, in exchange for labor and obedience, slaves were given care and guidance. Though in most instances, planters provided food, clothing, and shelter sufficient to sustain slaves, slaveholders' concern was rooted not in moral considerations but in the fact that slaves were valuable property. Moreover, after the transatlantic slave trade was banned in 1808, masters realized the expansion of the slave labor force could come only from natural reproduction by healthy slaves. White southern men tended to be obsessed with their reputation for honor, which contributed to the prominence of dueling as a part of southern culture. They were also expected to be proper patriarchs; within the big house, wives and children were expected to adhere to much of the same social hierarchy that governed the master-slave relationship. Masters' overwhelming power meant that southern laws against miscegenation were frequently broken. Despite the individualism planters displayed, duty to family was very important: slaveholders were bound together by marriage, ideology, and economic interest.

**PLANTATION MISTRESSES** In some respects, affluent southern white women occupied roles similar to those of their northern counterparts. Their lives generally centered on the home, where (according to the South's social ideal) they served as companions and hostesses for their husbands and as nurturing mothers for their children. However, the obsession among the white male elite with chivalry meant that southern white women were kept subordinate in southern culture. Southern white women had other burdens as well. Most faced the impossible task of reconciling the ideal of the refined southern lady with the daily hard work of helping to manage the plantation. A few southern white women rebelled against their roles and against their region's prevailing assumptions and even spoke out against slavery, as the Grimké sisters did. Another problem was miscegenation, with the children that slaveholders had with their female slaves serving as a constant reminder to white women of their husbands' infidelity. Most, however, expressed no open discontent because the mistress's world, like that of white children and slaves, was controlled by the plantation master.

***Slaves and the Quarters, pp. 428–435*** By the mid-nineteenth century, one in eight slaves could be found in virtually every skilled and unskilled occupation throughout the South, working in nonagricultural positions as domestics, sailors, bakers, barbers, fishermen, railroad workers, and more. Still, the majority of the South's slaves spent their lives working on plantations as field hands and house servants.

**WORK** Above all, slave owners wanted work from their slaves. Indeed, the desire for exploitable labor was the chief reason for slavery's origin in the New World as well as for its existence into the nineteenth century. The majority of slaves in 1860 were field hands. Slaves worked hard, performing light tasks as children and then working in the fields at the age of eleven or twelve. The few slaves who became household servants had a somewhat easier life physically than field hands had but were constantly at the master's or mistress's beck and call. Rarer than house servants were slaves who worked as skilled artisans for example, as blacksmiths, carpenters, millers, or shoemakers. They took pride in their skill and often showed what white owners felt was a disturbing independence of mind. A very small number of slaves served as drivers, overseeing the labor of other slaves in the fields.

**FAMILY, RELIGION, AND COMMUNITY** In their limited free time away from exhausting labor, slaves made the most of their families, religion, and communities. Although slave marriages were not legally binding, some slave owners encouraged unions to promote stability as well as slaves' reproduction. However, the breakup of marriages and families by sale occurred all too frequently. Slave husbands and fathers did not have the same powers as free men, but they did what they could to protect and provide for their families. Religion provided another bulwark against the oppressiveness of slavery, although masters hoped that it would foster obedience. Often meeting secretly, slaves created a distinctive variant of evangelical Protestantism, which incorporated elements of African religion and stressed those portions of the Bible that spoke to the aspirations of an enslaved people thirsting for freedom. Slave sermons and religious songs spoke directly to the plight of a people held in bondage and implicitly asserted their right to be free.

**RESISTANCE AND REBELLION** Black response to bondage was a combination of adaptation and resistance. Resistance sometimes took the form of simple defiant acts: sabotaging work by losing or breaking tools or performing tasks slowly or improperly. Thousands of slaves showed their discontent and desire for freedom by running away, a fraction making it to freedom in the North or Canada. For the majority, however, flight was not a real option because they lived too deep in the South to reach free soil. Open rebellion was the most dramatic and clear-cut form of slave resistance, but it was rarely successful. A handful of conspiracies and attempted revolts in the antebellum period, the most notorious being Nat Turner's uprising in 1831, showed slaves' willingness to risk their lives in a desperate bid for liberation.

***Black and Free: On the Middle Ground, pp. 435–437*** Of the 4.1 million blacks living in the South in 1860, approximately 6 percent—some 260,000—were free. Whether they were in the North or the South, free blacks stood on dangerous middle ground and were often denied legal and political equality with whites.

**FREE BLACKS AND THE WHITE RESPONSE** In the South after the Revolution, there was a brief flurry of manumissions that made free blacks the fastest-growing element of the population in 1810. The cotton boom ended the trend, however, and free blacks were subjected to humiliating rules that confined their activities, limiting many to a life of poverty and dependence as unskilled agricultural laborers or domestic servants. They were often forced to pay special taxes, to register annually with the state, and to carry papers proving their free status; in some states, they had to gain official permission to travel from one county to another. Most southern whites abhorred free African Americans, whose presence they believed undermined the racial hierarchy that was the essence of slavery.

**ACHIEVEMENT DESPITE RESTRICTIONS** Despite laws restricting them, free blacks had some advantages over enslaved ones. They could own property, choose occupations, marry, and pass on their heritage of freedom to their children. Free blacks varied in status. Most lived in poverty, but in a few cities, a small elite of usually light-skinned free blacks prospered. These men generally worked in skilled trades as tailors, mechanics, carpenters, and such and were patronized by prominent whites who appreciated their skilled services. Thus, most free blacks, especially those who were "succeeding" in a hostile white world, found it necessary to appear loyal to the planter regime. Some successful free blacks even owned slaves. On the whole, free blacks tried to keep a middle course, neither owning slaves nor inciting insurrection as Denmark Vesey did but just seeking to preserve their own freedom.

***The Plain Folk, pp. 437–441*** The typical white Southerner was not a wealthy planter and slaveholder but a modest yeoman farmer who owned his own land and did not have slaves. In the antebellum South, there were two yeoman societies, separated roughly along geographic lines.

**PLANTATION-BELT YEOMEN** Yeomen in the black-belt and delta regions lived in the midst of the plantation system and were linked to it in important ways. These small farmers, who grew mostly cotton, depended on the local plantation aristocracy, which allowed them access to plantation gins and baling machines, helped them ship and sell their cotton, and extended a helping hand in all kinds of ways to poorer neighbors. In many areas, kinship networks also connected yeoman farmers with wealthy planters. These many links ensured that poorer farmers shared the planters' commitment to white supremacy, thus considerably lessening the potential for class conflict.

**UPCOUNTRY YEOMEN** The majority of the yeoman farmers located in the western parts of Virginia, North and South Carolina, northern Georgia, Alabama, and eastern Tennessee and Kentucky had a different economy and society from that in the plantation belt—an economy and society not dominated by slavery or large plantations. The hilly geography and lack of transportation limited the prosperity of upcountry yeomen. Yeomen worked in family units. They devoted their efforts to growing subsistence crops as well as a little cotton or tobacco, but production of these was limited by their geographic isolation. Formal education was a low priority for most upcountry yeomen, who preferred the revival tent to the schoolroom. Indeed, evangelical revivalism found its most receptive and largest audiences in the South among upcountry yeomen. Although they did not benefit directly from slavery, most yeomen and nonslaveholders supported or at least tolerated the institution.

**POOR WHITES** There were other white Southerners who did not benefit at all from the plantation economy: members of the denigrated class of poor whites. Northerners argued that the slave system had shoved these whites so far down the social and economic ladder that they did not have the ambition to rise. Usually landless tenant farmers or day laborers, they lived in squalor. Their degradation resulted partly from dietary deficiencies and disease. Although impoverished, poor whites were not degenerate. Instead, many were ambitious people, scrambling to work their way up to become "respectable" yeoman farmers.

***The Politics of Slavery, pp. 441–444*** Southern politics, like much of southern society, reflected the impact of slavery. Throughout the antebellum period, political power rested securely in the hands of the slaveholding planter elite. Although white yeoman farmers made up a vastly larger portion of the population, the planter elite was able to wield power far in excess of its actual numbers because most southern whites believed that the slave system benefited them.

**THE DEMOCRATIZATION OF THE POLITICAL ARENA** The political reforms of the Jacksonian era had a considerable impact on the South. By the early 1850s, every southern state had established universal white male suffrage, and high voter turnout would become one of the hallmarks of southern politics. Thanks to democratization, southern politics also became increasingly partisan as candidates vied for attention and votes. Whigs and Democrats competed fairly equally in the South, and both presented themselves as champions of the plain folk. However, Whigs tended to favor government intervention in the economy, while Democrats believed that government intervention was a threat to individual liberty and risked concentrating economic power in a few hands.

**PLANTER POWER** Whether Whig or Democrat, the majority of southern officeholders were slave owners. The dominance of southern politics by the planter elite reflected the persistence of a culture that valued tradition and stability and deferred to the upper classes in political matters. But tradition was not enough to ensure planter rule. Slaveholders had to convince the majority of plain folk that slavery and plantation agriculture benefited all southern whites, and they worked hard to cultivate the favor and votes of the common people. The massive representation of slaveholders meant that legislatures preserved slavery in a variety of ways. Slaves were taxed at a lower rate than land, and public support of railroads was beneficial primarily to large planters. Beginning in the 1830s, slaveholders ceased to tolerate criticism and worked to suppress any arguments against slavery. Critics were censored, ostracized, even threatened. This could have a definite impact on poorer Southerners' awareness of attacks on slavery; southern politicians banned Hinton R. Helper's *The Impending Crisis of the South*, which argued that poor whites were hurt by the slave system, at a time when poor whites were beginning to experience economic stagnation. In the antebellum South, democratization was able to occur simultaneously with growing political elitism.

***Conclusion: A Slave Society*** Southerners and Northerners regarded the South as fundamentally different from the rest of the nation. Nearly a third of the region's population was enslaved, although the weight of bondage did not destroy black Americans. The South was overwhelmingly rural and agrarian, and its white population largely agreed that slavery was necessary and just, creating a pariah class of blacks that allowed whites to exist in a state of relative equality. During the 1850s, a dangerous division was emerging between the "slave" and "free" states.

***Chronology Activity*** Read the annotated chronology, and answer the multiple-choice questions.

1808 External slave trade outlawed. The closing of the external slave trade forced southern masters to provide their slaves with a certain minimum level of physical welfare because it meant that the expansion of the slave labor force could come only from natural reproduction. Slaves in the antebellum South continued to have a mediocre diet, poor housing, and insufficient clothing, and masters still used whipping as their primary means of coercion. However, slaves were given rest periods, and most masters ceased the eighteenth-century practice of punishing slaves by physical mutilation.

1810s–1850s Suffrage gradually extended throughout South to white males over twenty-one years of age. The democratization of southern politics was accompanied by extremely high rates of voter turnout and vigorous, partisan electoral competition. Whigs and Democrats fought for voters, with each party casting itself as the party of the people and the other as antidemocratic elitists. In reality, most politicians were wealthy planters, and the legislation they passed favored slaveholding Southerners rather than the nonslaveholding majority.

1820s–1830s Southern legislatures enact slave codes to strengthen slavery. Attacks on slavery, by means of both internal slave rebellions and external antislavery agitation, worried white Southerners, who moved to protect the slave system by passing new laws. State legislatures constructed slave codes that upheld white supremacy by requiring slaves to submit entirely to their masters and white society in general. Under the slave codes, any white person could correct slaves who did not show the proper deference.

Southern legislatures enact laws to restrict growth of free black population and to hem in freedom of free blacks. White Southerners disliked free blacks, who did not fit neatly into the South's idealized social order, in which blacks were supposed to be enslaved and free people were supposed to be white. Thus, after a brief burst of manumissions in the Upper South, state legislatures acted to halt the growth of the free black population. Laws made it impossible for masters to free their slaves and subjected free blacks to many of the same laws as slaves. This forced free blacks into lives of poverty and underscored the white supremacist belief that all blacks, whether free or enslaved, were inferior to whites.

Southern intellectuals begin to fashion systematic defense of slavery. Prior to the 1830s, most Southerners described slavery as a "necessary evil," but starting in the 1830s intellectuals begin to construct elaborate defenses of the institution as a "positive good." According to intellectuals, slavery had historical and biblical sanction. Moreover, they argued that it was more humane than the northern free-labor system, in which capitalists brutally exploited their work force; according to intellectual apologists, slave owners were engaged in a mass civilizing effort that would eventually lift blacks out of barbarism and savagery.

1820–1860 Cotton production soars from about 300,000 bales to nearly 5 million bales. Because 75 percent of all southern cotton was grown by slaves, the increase in cotton production was accompanied by the spread of slavery. As cotton agriculture expanded, more than 300,000 slaves moved west, some of them accompanying masters and others sold in the domestic slave trade. By 1860, the South contained more slaves than all other slave societies in the New World combined.

1822 Denmark Vesey executed for conspiring to lead a slave rebellion in South Carolina. Denmark Vesey, a free carpenter in Charleston, plotted to storm Charleston's arsenal, capture its weapons, kill any whites who resisted, and set fire to the city. He was betrayed by slaves and other free blacks before he had a chance to act on the plan. However, his arrest shook southern whites, who lived in fear of slave rebellions despite their insistence that their black population was content. Officials tracked down all of the accused, banished thirty-seven blacks from the state, and executed another thirty-five.

1831 Nat Turner's slave rebellion occurs in Virginia. Nat Turner believed that God had made him an instrument of divine vengeance to punish the sin of slaveholding. When a solar eclipse and green-tinted sun confirmed his status, he joined together with six trusted friends, killed his master, and then attacked neighboring farms. The insurgents killed fifty-seven whites before they were caught; white Virginians eventually killed a hundred or more blacks in a frenzied counterattack. Revolts like Vesey's demonstrated that white Southerners' claims that their slave system was benign and their slaves happy were less than accurate; however, whites responded to uprisings like Vesey's by blaming them on outside agitators, particularly abolitionists, and moved to strengthen the slave system by means of stronger slave codes and restrictions on free blacks.

1860 The slave population of the South approaches 4 million, an increase of 600 percent in seven decades. In 1790, the southern slave population stood at fewer than 700,000; as recently as 1830, there had been 2 million slaves in the South. The expansion of the slave system was due almost entirely to natural increase, making the slaves of the South not strictly African but African American.

## *Chronology Questions* Choose the letter of the best answer.

1. In 1808, the external slave trade was
   a. expanded.
   b. in a depression.
   c. outlawed.
   d. controlled by American traders.

2. Southern legislatures began to enact slave codes to strengthen slavery in
   a. 1800.
   b. the 1820s and 1830s.
   c. the 1840s and 1850s.
   d. 1860.

3. What is the correct order for the following events?
   1. Denmark Vesey plans a slave rebellion in South Carolina.
   2. The slave population of the South approaches 4 million.
   3. Cotton production begins to soar.
   4. Nat Turner's slave rebellion occurs in Virginia.
   a. 1, 4, 2, 3
   b. 4, 2, 1, 3
   c. 3, 1, 4, 2
   d. 4, 3, 1, 2

4. Between the 1810s and the 1850s
   a. the external slave trade was outlawed.
   b. the number of slaves began to rise from natural increase alone.
   c. the slave population of the South approached 4 million.
   d. suffrage was gradually extended throughout the South to white adult males.

5. Demark Vesey was executed for conspiring to lead a slave rebellion in South Carolina in
   a. 1808.
   b. 1822.
   c. 1840.
   d. 1857.

6. From 1820 to 1860, cotton production in the South
   a. increased from 300,000 bales to nearly 5 million bales.
   b. decreased from 5 million bales to 300,000 bales.
   c. remained static.
   d. was mostly undertaken by poor white families.

7. Between the 1820s and the 1830s,
   a. cotton production soared to nearly 5 million bales.
   b. Southern legislatures enacted laws to restrict the freedom of free blacks.
   c. suffrage was extended to white adult males throughout the South.
   d. the external slave trade was outlawed.

8. What is the correct order for the following events?
   1. Slave rebellion leads to stronger slave codes.
   2. Cotton production begins to soar.
   3. The slave population of the South reaches 4 million.
   4. Suffrage begins to be extended throughout the South to white males over twenty-one years of age.
   
   a. 2, 4, 1, 3
   b. 3, 2, 1, 4
   c. 1, 4, 3, 2
   d. 4, 2, 1, 3

9. Nat Turner's rebellion occurred in Virginia in
   a. 1803.
   b. 1817.
   c. 1831.
   d. 1850.

10. Southern legislatures began to restrict the growth of the free black population
    a. in 1808.
    b. in the 1820s and 1830s.
    c. from 1820 to 1860.
    d. in 1860.

***Defining Terms*** Match each term with the correct definition.

| | |
|---|---|
| ✓positive good | ✓poor whites |
| ✓cotton kingdom | ✓plain folk |
| ✓paternalism | ✓house servants |
| ✓drivers | ✓revivals |
| ✓George Fitzhugh | ✓chivalry |
| ✓upcountry | ✓Hinton Rowan Helper |
| ✓field hands | ✓"servant of the people" |
| ✓freedom papers | ✓planters |
| ✓miscegenation | ✓master |
| ✓William Ellison | ✓cotton curtain |
| ✓Mason-Dixon line | ✓Denmark Vesey |
| ✓white male suffrage | ✓slave codes |
| ✓free blacks | ✓plantation belt |
| ✓family | ✓overseers |

1. The surveyor's line drawn in 1763 that divided the northern and southern parts of the United States. Although the inhabitants of the two sections shared a common language and commitment to the Revolution and the national government created by the Constitution, the institution of slavery became more and more important as a dividing factor in the nineteenth century.
   Mason-Dixon line

2. The name given to the South in the nineteenth century. After the invention of the cotton gin, cotton fields spread out from southern Virginia to central Texas, and by 1860 the South produced three-fourths of the world's supply of cotton. The spread of cotton agriculture contributed to the growth of the slave system because slaves grew 75 percent of the crops. Cotton Kingdom

3. Laws passed by southern legislatures in the 1820s and 1830s requiring the total submission of slaves to their masters and white society. White Southerners were increasingly worried about slave rebellions and the criticism of northern abolitionists and hoped that strict laws would force slave to be obedient. Slave codes

4. An argument made in the 1820s and 1830s that slavery was not merely a necessary evil but was in fact beneficial to whites and blacks alike. According to defenders of slavery, whites got necessary labor out of black slaves, and blacks received the advantage of living among more "civilized" people. Positive good

5. A Virginian writer who argued that the northern free-labor system was heartless and exploitative. He contrasted the vicious relations between northern employers and workers with what he characterized as the humane relationship between masters and slaves. George Fitzhugh

6. The white husband, father, and slave owner who stood at the top of the plantation hierarchy. Masters had almost full control over their wives, children, and slaves, who were designated by the state as dependents under his rule and protection. master

7. Hired workers, usually either ambitious young white men or professionals, who made a career out of supervising slaves. By hiring overseers, wealthy planters could free themselves to concentrate on marketing, finance, and general plantation affairs. overseers

8. The idea that slavery was a set of reciprocal obligations between masters and slaves, with slaves providing labor and obedience and masters providing basic care and necessary guidance. The concept of paternalism denied that the slave system was brutal and exploitative. Paternalism did give slaves some protection against brutal treatment, but it did not guarantee comfortable living conditions or freedom from physical punishment. Paternalism

9. The sexual mixing of the races. Although southern laws forbade interracial sex, masters' almost unlimited power over their female slaves meant that liaisons inevitably occurred. miscegenation

10. The romantic southern ideal of male-female relationships, in which women were envisioned as weak, delicate, and in need of protection. The ideal glorified southern women but also subordinated them with its underlying assumptions about women's need for men's protective authority. chivalry

11. The occupation of the majority of slaves. Planters assigned men and women to separate gangs to perform difficult, monotonous, year-round tasks involved in raising various crops. field hands

12. The occupation of a minority of slaves and limited mostly to women. House servants cooked, cleaned, took care of children, washed clothes, and did dozens of other domestic tasks. While the working conditions were slightly better than those of the field hands, house servants were constantly on call and were less protected from the frustrations of their owners. house servants

13. The rare slaves, exclusively male, who worked overseeing other slaves. Probably no more than one slave in a hundred worked as a driver. drivers

14. One of the most important consequences of slaves' limited autonomy. While abolitionists and slave owners often claimed that slaves had lost their sense of family, slaves in fact joined together in long-term unions and formed loving, supportive families. Family

15. A free black carpenter who in 1822 planned to storm Charleston's arsenal, grab its weapons, kill any whites who stood in his way, and burn the city down. Although the plot was in its planning stages, white South Carolinians were badly shaken by it. His planned rebellion demonstrated that southern blacks were by no means as content as white Southerners like to believe. Denmark vesey

16. The unenslaved blacks who did not fit into the South's idealized social order, in which only whites were supposed to be free. They faced legal and social discrimination that left them precariously in between slavery and full freedom. Free blacks

17. The documents that free southern blacks had to carry to prove that they were not slaves. Freedom papers were part of the restrictions that southern legislatures placed on free blacks in the 1820s and the 1830s to reinforce their inferior status. Freedom Papers

18. A free South Carolina black (a former slave) who made enough money in the cotton gin business to purchase the home of a former state governor and become a big planter and slave owner in his own right. william Ellison

19. Southern whites who did not own slaves. Most were small country farmers, many of whom owned their own land. The plain folk constituted about three-fourths of the total southern population. Although the plain folk did not have slaves, they were committed to the institution of slavery and white supremacy. Plain folk

20. The southern flatlands that included the black-belt and delta regions. In the plantation belt, small landholdings outnumbered larger plantations, but they were not nearly as economically important. Generally, small landholders were linked to large planters by a network of personal relationships, and most of them hoped to gain access to the planter class themselves. Plantation belt

21. The hill and mountain regions of the South, where slavery was not as well established as in the plantation belt. The higher elevation, colder climate, rugged terrain, and poor transportation prevented commercial agriculture from making headway; as a result, the area was dominated by independent yeoman farmers who worked their land with family labor. upcountry

22. A popular form of evangelical Christianity among antebellum southern whites in rural areas. Revival religion involved large numbers of worshippers who gathered to hear a preacher speak, sometimes for days at a time. The message was usually one that emphasized free choice and individual worth. revivals

23. White Southerners without resources in cash or land. Northern critics claimed that the slave system pushed slaveless whites so far down the social and economic ladder that they did not have the initiative or the energy to try to get ahead. The term came to carry a moral implication, indicating that poor whites were ignorant, inbred, sick, and lazy. In fact, poor white Southerners were often struggling to survive in the face of dire poverty, lack of education, poor nutrition, and debilitating diseases. Poor whites

24. The extension of the vote to white males twenty-one years of age or older. By the early 1850s, all the southern states had removed property restrictions on political participation, which ushered in an era of high voter turnout and vigorous electoral competition. white male suffrage

25. The label claimed by both Southern Whigs and Southern Democrats. Each party cast itself as committed to republican equality and working to help ordinary white Southerners, while describing the opposition as rich, snobbish, and antidemocratic. "servant of the people"

26. Individuals who owned twenty or more slaves. By 1860, they were well represented in state legislatures; for instance, in North Carolina, 3 percent of the state's white families belonged to the planter class, but 36.6 percent of the members of the legislature were planters. Planters' dominance of southern politics demonstrated both the power of tradition and stability among southern voters and also the planters' success at convincing white voters that the slave system benefited all whites, even those without slaves. Planters

27. The social pressures that ended debate on the issue of slavery in the South starting in the 1830s. As the southern elite became more and more concerned about the growth of abolitionist sentiment in the North, southern critics of slavery were driven from public life, and sometimes fell victim to mob violence or vigilante action. Cotton curtain

28. The North Carolinian who moved to the North and published *The Impending Crisis of the South* in 1857. He contended that the slaveholding system hurt nonslaveholding whites by denying them the opportunities for advancement that were common in free-labor societies. Rather than confront the book's arguments, southern legislatures banned it, so it did not reach the struggling small farmers. Hinton Rowan Helper

## Chapter Review

***Multiple-Choice*** Choose the letter of the best answer.

1. Southerners moved west in the first half of the nineteenth century in search of
   a. more and better land for growing cotton.
   b. manufacturing jobs.
   c. opportunities to convert Indians to Christianity.
   d. a slave-free society.

2. The majority of cotton production in the antebellum period was done by
   a. white day laborers.
   b. free black laborers.
   c. slave labor.
   d. independent white farmers.

3. By 1860, the southern states had more slaves than
   a. South America.
   b. the Caribbean islands.
   c. Africa.
   d. all the other slave societies in the New World combined.

4. In the 1820s and 1830s, southern efforts to strengthen slavery often led to
   a. the punishment of owners who did not discipline their slaves.
   b. the requirement that all whites own slaves.
   c. demands for federal protection of slavery.
   d. the passage of elaborate slave codes.

5. Following the lead of southern academics, writers, and clergy, in the 1820s and 1830s white Southerners began to
   a. defend slavery aggressively as a positive good.
   b. defend slavery half-heartedly as a necessary evil.
   c. actively encourage the spread of slavery to the northern states.
   d. question the morality of the slave system.

6. Southerners claimed that slaves differed from northern laborers of the mid-nineteenth century because they
   a. had humane relations with their masters.
   b. were resentful of their masters.
   c. received a good education.
   d. were well-paid for their work.

7. The institution of black slavery in the nineteenth-century South encouraged whites to
   a. refuse to do their own manual labor.
   b. unify around race, not divide by class.
   c. divide along the lines of slaveholders and nonslaveholders.
   d. compete ruthlessly for the control of slaves.

8. By 1860, the southern economy was dominated by
   a. northern industrialists.
   b. nonslaveholding farmers.
   c. small slaveholding planters.
   d. large slaveholding planters.

9. Throughout the antebellum years, the slave-based economy of the South
   a. was a drag on the national economy.
   b. benefited only the southern economy.
   c. benefited the national economy.
   d. was stagnant.

10. Most nineteenth-century southern slave-holders saw economic diversification as
    a. a threat to plantation slavery.
    b. a desirable goal if the South was to remain economically viable.
    c. an unnecessary waste of capital.
    d. good for the yeomen

11. By 1860, the lack of economic diversification had made the South
    a. the most urban region in the country.
    b. the least urban region in the country.
    c. an area dominated by small towns.
    d. similar to the North in its urban growth.

12. The shortage of industrial jobs in the antebellum South meant that the area
    a. was incredibly poor.
    b. did not attract many European immigrants.
    c. attracted a lot of European immigrants.
    d. attracted a lot of immigrants from the North and the West.

13. The Mason-Dixon line was _____ dividing North and South.
    a. the surveyor's mark on a map
    b. along a river
    c. along the Appalachian mountains
    d. a long fence

14. By the middle of the nineteenth century, the South covered nearly a million square miles, much of it planted in _____.
    a. tobacco
    b. rice
    c. cotton
    d. sugarcane

15. In the antebellum South, _____ grew 75 percent of all cotton crops on plantations.
    a. families
    b. day laborers
    c. Indian slaves
    d. black slaves

16. By 1860, blacks were _____ the population in the Lower South states of Mississippi and South Carolina.
    a. the majority of
    b. a small minority of
    c. a little less than half of
    d. 90 percent of

17. The Virginian writer George Fitzhugh argued that the northern labor system rested on the _____ of workers.
    a. heartless exploitation
    b. humane treatment
    c. personal initiative
    d. physical punishment

18. The majority of antebellum southern whites worked _____.
    a. on small family farms
    b. on large plantations
    c. in textile mills
    d. as tradesmen and artisans

19. In the antebellum South, the work on _____ had the reputation of being the hardest.
    a. sugarcane plantations
    b. tobacco farms
    c. cotton plantations
    d. small, isolated farms

20. Although nearly all antebellum southern farmers grew cotton, _____ received a disproportionate share of the profits.
    a. northern middlemen
    b. yeoman farmers
    c. planters
    d. southern merchants

21. Nineteenth-century southern planters did not diversify the economy because they were _____.
    a. not aware of the opportunities that existed in the North
    b. short on money to invest
    c. earning healthy profits already
    d. afraid of losing their money

22. In nine of the fifteen slave states, only 2 percent or fewer of the residents were _____.
    a. slaves
    b. foreign-born
    c. native-born
    d. free blacks

23. Relationships on nineteenth-century southern plantations were
    a. governed by rigid, hierarchical roles.
    b. relatively equal among whites.
    c. dictated by state law.
    d. based on the prescripts of evangelical religion.

24. Nineteenth-century planters were able to concentrate on marketing, finance, and plantation affairs because they
    a. turned the supervision of field slaves over to their wives.
    b. trusted their slaves to work without supervision.
    c. knew little about agriculture.
    d. hired professional overseers.

25. Nineteenth-century planters characterized the master-slave relationship in terms of paternalism, which
    a. meant that planters legally adopted their slaves.
    b. meant that planters fathered most of their slaves.
    c. defined slavery as a set of reciprocal obligations between masters and slaves.
    d. defined slavery as giving masters complete control over their slaves.

26. The antebellum southern slave system differed from other New World slave systems in that southern planters
    a. gave their slaves excellent food and housing.
    b. lived where their slaves worked year-round.
    c. did not live where their slaves worked.
    d. never imposed physical punishment on their slaves.

27. Most southern masters in the antebellum period provided at least minimal care for their slaves because they
    a. were concerned about their reputation with their neighbors.
    b. were kindly people.
    c. were compelled to do so by law.
    d. knew that it made economic sense to do so.

28. The nineteenth-century southern concept of honor rested on
    a. prickly individualism and aggressive independence.
    b. the ownership of large number of slaves.
    c. the ownership of land.
    d. a good education.

29. In the antebellum South, slavery upheld the power of
    a. women.
    b. men.
    c. the young.
    d. the old.

30. Although individualism was a common characteristic of antebellum southern culture, planters were linked by
    a. a common proslavery ideology.
    b. economic interests.
    c. ties of blood and kinship.
    d. all of the above.

31. The defenders of the nineteenth-century southern slave system were often in favor of
    a. women's subordination to men.
    b. women's equality with men.
    c. interracial liaisons.
    d. lenient divorce laws.

32. The daily life of the nineteenth-century plantation mistress involved
    a. long hours of work.
    b. a great deal of leisure time.
    c. primarily socializing with family members.
    d. hours devoted to educational improvement.

33. For antebellum plantation mistresses, plantation life was
    a. a springboard into public affairs.
    b. extremely circumscribed by the plantation.
    c. never isolated.
    d. exciting.

34. For plantation mistresses, the most painful aspect of plantation life was
    a. boredom.
    b. subordination to their husbands.
    c. denial of church services.
    d. miscegenation.

35. On nineteenth-century southern plantations, _____ governed the relationships between masters, mistresses, children, and slaves.
    a. personal inclination
    b. local law
    c. a rigid hierarchy of roles
    d. religious precepts

36. On small plantations, _____ supervised the field labor of slaves.
    a. overseers
    b. the planters personally
    c. mistresses
    d. volunteer slave patrols

37. According to the doctrine of paternalism, the southern slave system was _____.
    a. a simple business relationship
    b. similar to the northern free-labor system
    c. brutal and exploitative
    d. a set of reciprocal obligations between masters and slaves

38. After 1808, southern slave owners realized that the slave labor force could expand only through _____.
    a. the illegal importation of African slaves
    b. natural reproduction
    c. the illegal importation of Caribbean slaves
    d. the enslavement of the area's remaining Indians

39. During the nineteenth century, most slave owners decided that was economically sensible to provide _____ care for their human property.
    a. at least minimal
    b. the least possible
    c. absolutely no
    d. really excellent

40. Nineteenth-century planters relied on _____ to coerce their slaves into obedience.
    a. rational arguments
    b. physical mutilation
    c. whipping
    d. slaves' loyalty

41. Laws prohibiting miscegenation did not always stop masters from _____ their female slaves.
    a. verbally abusing
    b. taking sexual advantage of
    c. selling
    d. freeing

42. Antebellum southern men characterized the perfect southern lady as _____.
    a. a capable housewife
    b. an independent thinker
    c. a delicate "ornament"
    d. an idiot

43. The southern notion of chivalry assumed that women were _____ men.
    a. weak and subordinate to
    b. the equals of
    c. smarter than
    d. of no interest to

44. Antebellum mistresses were expected to _____.
   a. enjoy a high degree of personal freedom
   b. take pleasure in the company of their slaves
   c. serve the family
   d. serve the community as a whole

45. By 1850, 52 percent of southern slaves worked
   a. on plantations.
   b. in factories.
   c. as artisans.
   d. as deckhands.

46. Antebellum masters were most interested in getting their slaves to
   a. respect them.
   b. work for them.
   c. convert to Christianity.
   d. bear children.

47. When slave boys and girls in the antebellum South reached the age of eleven or twelve, most
   a. chose future marriage partners.
   b. were sent to the fields to learn farm work.
   c. were removed from their families and sold to other plantations.
   d. received a basic education.

48. For nineteenth-century southern slaves, working in the big house
   a. was seen as a privilege.
   b. had serious drawbacks.
   c. provided a lot of spare time.
   d. was more physically demanding than field work.

49. In the antebellum period, no more than one southern slave in twenty
   a. learned to read.
   b. ran away.
   c. worked in the fields.
   d. worked as a skilled artisan.

50. The limited autonomy allowed to nineteenth-century southern slaves contributed to
   a. contentment of the slave labor force.
   b. the outbreak of a frequent slave rebellions.
   c. the preservation and persistence of slave families.
   d. the spread of Christianity among slaves.

51. The two most frequent events that ended slave marriages were
   a. the death or running away of one of the spouses.
   b. the death of both of the spouses.
   c. mutual unhappiness or infidelity.
   d. the sale or death of one of the spouses.

52. Most slave fathers in the antebellum South
   a. did not live near their children.
   b. were present in their children's lives.
   c. were able to fulfill the traditional roles of provider and protector.
   d. were held in contempt by slave society.

53. The Christianity adopted by slaves in the nineteenth century
   a. entirely drove out African beliefs.
   b. encouraged obedience to masters.
   c. emphasized justice.
   d. was encouraged by state governments.

54. Most slaves who ran away
   a. were killed when they were caught.
   b. made it to freedom in the North or in Canada.
   c. stayed close to the plantation.
   d. were turned in to their masters by other slaves.

55. The scarcity of large-scale slave revolts in the antebellum South demonstrates that
   a. slaves were inherently peaceful and nonviolent.
   b. southern slaves were contented.
   c. existing conditions made success unlikely.
   d. passive resistance alone was successful in improving their conditions

56. Southern whites were badly shaken when, in 1822, a free black carpenter named Denmark Vesey planned to
   a. open a seminary to train black ministers.
   b. storm Charleston's arsenal, capture its weapons, kill whites who resisted, and set fire to the city.
   c. help large numbers of slaves escape to the North.
   d. create secret schools to teach slaves how to read.

57. On most southern plantations, _____ were separated by only a few hundred yards.
   a. white neighbors
   b. the big house and the closest road
   c. the big house and the slave quarters
   d. the slave quarters and the houses of poor whites

58. By 1850, one in eight slaves worked _____.
   a. in agriculture
   b. in a nonagricultural job
   c. as a factory hand
   d. on the railroad

59. In 1860, the overwhelming majority of slaves worked _____.
   a. as carpenters
   b. as field hands
   c. tending livestock
   d. as house servants

60. Approximately nine out of ten of all house servants were _____.
   a. very young
   b. physically attractive
   c. male
   d. female

61. Slaves who worked as skilled artisans _____.
   a. learned their skills at segregated schools
   b. were as common as house servants by 1860
   c. were unusually independent
   d. usually won their freedom eventually

62. According to one scholar's estimate, between 1820 and 1860 _____ destroyed approximately 300,000 slave marriages.
   a. death
   b. desertion
   c. emotional stress
   d. sale

63. Planters promoted Christianity because they believed that it would make their slaves _____.
   a. happier
   b. more moral
   c. more obedient
   d. more family-oriented

64. Slaves interpreted Christianity as _____ the racist messages of white society.
   a. sympathetic to
   b. an antidote to
   c. reflective of
   d. completely separate from

65. For many slaves, _____ provided perhaps the mildest form of protest against the slave system.
   a. telling pointed stories
   b. breaking tools
   c. feigning illness
   d. running away

66. When slaves refused to accede to their masters' will, they established _____.
   a. limits beyond which owners and overseers did not wish to go
   b. the groundwork for later slave rebellions
   c. the limits to their own self-determination
   d. the pointlessness of resistance

67. The surprising thing about free black Southerners in the antebellum period was that
   a. they existed at all.
   b. there were so few of them.
   c. there were so many of them.
   d. they were economically prosperous.

68. In the years after the Revolution, slavery was challenged by
   a. southern intellectuals.
   b. the growth of American industry.
   c. the new national government.
   d. natural rights philosophy and evangelical Protestantism.

69. In the post-Revolutionary era, there was a brief flurry of manumissions
    a. in the cotton producing areas of the Lower South.
    b. among Southern politicians.
    c. in the rice-growing regions of the Carolinas.
    d. in the tobacco-growing regions of the Upper South.

70. By 1810, free blacks were growing more numerous and were
    a. becoming prosperous.
    b. demanding equal rights.
    c. becoming a source of worry to white Southerners.
    d. beginning to migrate to the northern states.

71. In the 1820s and 1830s, state legislatures in the South began to
    a. halt the growth of the free black population and curtail the liberty of free blacks.
    b. halt the growth of the free black population but protect the status of free blacks.
    c. encourage the growth of the free black population.
    d. protect the status of free blacks.

72. During the 1820s and 1830s, free blacks in the South were
    a. granted full civil rights.
    b. given limited civil rights.
    c. forced to migrate to other states.
    d. subjected to many of the same laws as slaves.

73. Most free blacks living in the antebellum South were
    a. able to ignore discriminatory southern laws.
    b. independent farmers.
    c. urban, uneducated day laborers.
    d. rural, uneducated, unskilled agricultural laborers and domestic servants.

74. In the nineteenth century, which one of the following privilege could free southern blacks not enjoy?
    a. They could marry.
    b. Their children were free.
    c. They had a lot of opportunity.
    d. They could choose occupations.

75. Unlike whites, the majority of the free blacks in the nineteenth-century South
    a. lived in cities.
    b. did not own property.
    c. gained basic literacy.
    d. farmed their own land.

76. During the nineteenth century, the cities of Charleston, Mobile, and New Orleans all had
    a. enormous slave rebellions.
    b. a small elite of free blacks.
    c. public schools for black children.
    d. strictly segregated neighborhoods.

77. Despite all the restrictions whites placed on free blacks in the antebellum period, whites did not limit their
    a. ability to vote.
    b. access to education.
    c. freedom of movement.
    d. right to own property, including slaves.

78. Most free blacks in the antebellum South wanted to
    a. escape to Canada.
    b. become slaveholders themselves.
    c. raise a major slave rebellion.
    d. preserve their freedom.

79. In 1860, about 260,000 (about 6 percent) of the South's 4.1 million blacks were _____.
    a. involved in educating other slaves
    b. field hands
    c. economically comfortable
    d. free

80. In the years immediately following the Revolution, _____ experienced a brief flurry of emancipation.
    a. the states west of the Appalachians
    b. small southern planters
    c. the Lower South
    d. the Upper South

81. By 1810, free blacks constituted the _____ of the southern population.
    a. most mobile part
    b. majority
    c. slowest-growing element
    d. fastest-growing element

82. The _____ meant that more and more southern whites were concerned about the growth of the free black population.
    a. outbreak of slave rebellions
    b. increase in miscegenation
    c. cotton boom
    d. tobacco depression

83. In the 1820s and 1830s, free blacks in the South were increasingly subject to the same laws as _____.
    a. upcountry whites
    b. slaves
    c. northern blacks
    d. immigrants

84. By the mid-nineteenth century, opportunities for _____ for free blacks were slim.
    a. work
    b. education
    c. community
    d. all of the above

85. Free blacks of the antebellum period were able to _____ and so could protect their families from arbitrary disruption by whites.
    a. testify in court
    b. legally marry
    c. physically defend themselves
    d. participate in the political process

86. The majority of free blacks in the nineteenth-century South owned _____ property.
    a. no
    b. a modest amount of
    c. agricultural
    d. a lot of

87. In nineteenth-century southern cities, the free black elite lived _____.
    a. in segregated ghettos
    b. in white neighborhoods
    c. on the outskirts of urban development
    d. very modestly

88. William Ellison, a free black South Carolinian, earned a fortune making cotton gins, and then became a _____.
    a. well-known philanthropist
    b. supporter of black civil rights
    c. big planter and slave owner
    d. politician

89. Most of the antebellum South's "plain folk" were
    a. well educated.
    b. skilled tradesmen.
    c. small farmers.
    d. slaveholders.

90. In the nineteenth-century plantation belt, small farmers' cotton crops
    a. tied them to large planters.
    b. made them economically independent.
    c. replaced food crops entirely.
    d. made them wealthy.

91. The slave patrols of the antebellum South served to
    a. increase poor whites' resentment of wealthy planters.
    b. undermine respect for the slave system.
    c. raise taxes to unbearable levels.
    d. reinforce yeomen and planters' commitment to white supremacy.

92. The typical plantation-belt yeoman of the nineteenth century
    a. tried to escape cotton agriculture.
    b. wanted to move to a city.
    c. hoped to become a large planter.
    d. believed that he was doomed to a life of poverty.

93. In the antebellum southern upcountry, most farms were worked by
    a. small numbers of slaves.
    b. large number of slaves.
    c. hired agricultural workers.
    d. family members.

94. In the antebellum southern upcountry, the female domestic sphere was
    a. considered subordinate to the patriarch of the family.
    b. considered more important than the male public sphere.
    c. seen as unnecessary to the success of a farm.
    d. nonexistent.

95. The typical crop of the upcountry yeomen of the antebellum South was
   a. cotton and tobacco for the national market.
   b. food crops for the national market.
   c. cotton and tobacco for home consumption.
   d. food crops exclusively.

96. Nonslaveholding white yeomen in the antebellum upcountry South reacted to the slave system by
   a. defending slavery and white supremacy.
   b. becoming abolitionists.
   c. resenting wealthy slaveholders in the lowland regions.
   d. giving wealthy upcountry slaveholders direct social and economic power.

97. Many nineteenth-century plain folk followed a religion that
   a. emphasized free choice and individual worth.
   b. taught poor whites to be obedient to their social betters.
   c. was critical of the slave system.
   d. emphasized intensive Bible study.

98. According to many nineteenth-century Northerners, the majority of the South's whites
   a. constituted an independent yeomanry.
   b. were energetic and ambitious.
   c. were better-educated than most Northerners.
   d. were shiftless, landless, and poor.

99. Many landless farm families in the antebellum South
   a. lived in cities and worked in factories.
   b. moved to the North.
   c. agitated against slavery.
   d. lived as tenants or worked as day laborers.

100. By the late 1850s, it was rare for poor white southern families to
   a. remain poor.
   b. experience upward mobility.
   c. suffer from hookworm, pellagra, and other debilitating diseases.
   d. attend religious revivals.

101. Most of the antebellum southern "plain folk" were _____, or yeomen.
   a. tenant farmers
   b. subsistence farmers
   c. small farmers who owned their own land
   d. wage laborers

102. In the nineteenth-century South, small farmers relied on _____ to help them process and market their cotton crops.
   a. northern middlemen
   b. local merchants
   c. wealthy planters
   d. bank loans

103. Antebellum small farmers viewed the planter regime as _____.
   a. something to which to aspire
   b. inimical to their interests
   c. an evil institution because of its enslavement of blacks
   d. a good way to keep blacks from competing with them for jobs

104. The _____ of the South had very few slaves or plantations.
   a. coastal regions
   b. hills and mountains
   c. western edges
   d. delta regions

105. The wives and daughters in most upcountry yeoman families worked _____.
   a. in and around their houses
   b. in the fields
   c. in nearby villages
   d. as domestic servants and nursemaids

106. Upcountry yeoman grew some cash crops like tobacco or cotton to use as _____.
   a. a source of ready cash
   b. barter with local merchants
   c. a way of getting economically ahead
   d. a hedge against future economic insecurity

107. Most upcountry people who owned slaves possessed _____.
   a. two or three
   b. ten
   c. twenty
   d. fifty or more

108. Many antebellum rural whites adhered to _____ faith.
   a. a deistic
   b. the Roman Catholic
   c. an evangelical Christian
   d. no religious

109. Antebellum southern farmers could be characterized by the fact that _____.
   a. one out of four was landless
   b. most of the men were illiterate
   c. half of them were black
   d. most of them owned no land

110. During the 1850s, the price of _____ went up, harming the opportunities of poor whites in the South.
   a. food
   b. health care
   c. education
   d. land

111. Political power in the antebellum South was
   a. divorced from class considerations.
   b. concentrated among upcountry yeomen.
   c. unevenly distributed.
   d. evenly distributed.

112. Most antebellum white Southerners accepted the planters' argument that
   a. the slave system gave every white man membership in the South's ruling class.
   b. they should leave the task of government to their social betters.
   c. taxes should be raised to support a more interventionist government.
   d. the age for suffrage should be raised.

113. By the early 1850s, in response to the political reforms that had swept the nation, every southern state had extended suffrage to
   a. white women.
   b. free blacks who were at least twenty-one years old.
   c. all white males who were at least twenty-one years old.
   d. all whites who were at least eighteen years old.

114. Whether they were Whigs or Democrats, all nineteenth-century southern political candidates
   a. refused to mix with ordinary voters.
   b. emphasized their wealth and refinement.
   c. emphasized their superior education.
   d. presented themselves as protectors of republican equality.

115. Antebellum Southern Democrats differed from Whigs in that they
   a. saw government intervention in the economy as a threat to individual liberty.
   b. backed state support of banks, railroads, and corporations.
   c. opposed the slave system.
   d. drew their support from urban areas.

116. The democratization of politics in the antebellum South
   a. overturned traditional patterns of class deference.
   b. did not prevent the political dominance of wealthy slaveholders.
   c. increased the number of yeomen and artisans in state governments.
   d. encouraged the spread of public schooling.

117. Slaveholders in the nineteenth-century South maintained their political power by
   a. encouraging voter apathy.
   b. persuading the white majority that their interests were the same.
   c. threatening voters.
   d. electoral fraud.

118. In antebellum plantation districts, most nineteenth-century politicians learned that electoral success depended on
   a. flexing their economic muscle.
   b. pretending to be poor.
   c. public acts of charity.
   d. winning the trust and respect of ordinary voters.

119. Southern legislatures demonstrated their commitment to slavery by
   a. establishing favorable tax policies.
   b. publicly financing railroads.
   c. censoring critics.
   d. all of the above.

120. In Georgia in the 1850s, planters in the state legislature protected themselves financially by
   a. getting rid of taxes entirely.
   b. taxing land at a lower rate than slaves.
   c. taxing slaves at a lower rate than land.
   d. granting special tax breaks for investment in industry.

121. In the 1830s, slaveholders responded to the growth of abolitionism in the North by
   a. encouraging debate on the slavery question.
   b. ending free speech on the slavery question.
   c. freeing their slaves.
   d. driving free blacks out of the South.

122. Slaveholders banned Hinton Rowan Helper's *The Impending Crisis of the South* because it argued that
   a. industrialization might improve the southern economy.
   b. a depression was going to destroy the southern economy.
   c. slavery denied nonslaveholding whites economic opportunities.
   d. a major slave rebellion was being organized.

123. _____ dominated the party politics of antebellum southern states.
   a. Slaveholders
   b. Democrats
   c. Whigs
   d. Yeomen

124. Since the eighteenth century, most southern whites had _____ large planters' contention that the slave system benefited all Southerners.
   a. been suspicious of
   b. rejected outright
   c. been unwilling to commit to
   d. accepted

125. By the early 1850s, most southern states had abandoned the _____ requirement for holding state offices and voting.
   a. property
   b. minimum age
   c. racial
   d. gender

126. Antebellum southern Whigs and Democrats both claimed to be _____.
   a. wishy-washy on the issue of republican equality
   b. serving the interests of planters
   c. better than the people
   d. the servant of the people

127. Antebellum southern Democrats argued that _____ threatened individual liberty.
   a. the institution of slavery
   b. too much education
   c. a lack of government intervention in the economy
   d. government intervention in the economy

128. In 1860, the percentage of _____ in southern legislatures ranged from 5.3 in Missouri to 55.4 percent in South Carolina.
   a. yeomen
   b. large planters
   c. artisans
   d. free blacks

129. In the antebellum South, planter status was _____ to political advancement.
   a. a detriment to
   b. the surest ticket to
   c. irrelevant
   d. not as important as money

130. John A. Quitman appealed to yeomen when he demonstrated his fitness for a seat in the Mississippi legislature by _____.
   a. engaging in learned debates with his opponent
   b. displaying his mastery of jumping, boxing, wrestling, sprinting, and marksmanship
   c. recounting his past political experience
   d. referring to his vast personal wealth

131. The largest public spending in antebellum Georgia, for _____, benefited planters far more than other social groups.
   a. financing railroads
   b. constructing a system of sewers
   c. building public grammar schools
   d. establishing public universities

132. In the antebellum South, the political rise of the common man _____ the planter class.
   a. diminished the power of
   b. existed alongside the growing power of
   c. displaced
   d. destroyed

***Short Answer*** Write a paragraph response to each question.

1. What factors allowed the South to become a cotton kingdom? Why did slavery spread with cotton?
2. What measures did white Southerners take to defend and strengthen slavery in the 1820s and 1830s?
3. What did southern state governments do to encourage diversification of the South's economy? Were their efforts successful? Why or why not?
4. How did nineteenth-century southern planters characterize the master-slave relationship? How accurate was their assessment?
5. What was the southern ideal of the plantation mistress? How did elite women's reality conform to that ideal?
6. What were the advantages and disadvantages of field work and house work for slaves?
7. What kinds of families did antebellum southern slaves form? What factors weakened their bonds?
8. How did slaves resist the demands of the slave system? What factors limited their options?
9. What caused the number of free blacks in the South to swell after the Revolution? How did white Southerners respond?
10. Did any free blacks in the antebellum South prosper? What circumstances made success possible?
11. How were planters and yeomen tied together in the plantation belt of the antebellum South? How did yeomen feel about their better-off neighbors?
12. What kind of labor force was typical of the upcountry regions of the antebellum South? How did the labor system affect upcountry yeomen's attitude toward slavery?
13. How did nineteenth-century Northerners describe southern poor whites? What did they think that the existence of poor southern whites demonstrated about the slave system? Was their opinion fair?
14. In what sense did southern politics become more democratic in the nineteenth century? How did democratization change the electoral process?
15. How did elite southern politicians use state government to protect slavery?

***Building Historical Skills*** Historians use a variety of sources to think and talk about the past, including maps, illustrations, and written records. Maps provide a variety of different kinds of comparative information in a condensed visual format; reading them requires learning how to sort through this information. To deepen our understanding of the past by supplementing written records, historians frequently interpret material culture, such as a vase or a painting, with techniques borrowed from art history, archaeology, or anthropology. Written records, though familiar as sources, raise their own problems of interpretation. Every document reflects someone's particular perspective or assumptions. It is the historian's task to study and compare each document to other records with other perspectives. The following exercises introduce you to using maps, illustrations, and written documents as sources of information. Use these sources as well as the material in the chapter to think about different themes and topics discussed in the text.

***Map Activity*** Locate the following places on Map 12.1: Cotton Kingom, Slave Empire: 1820 and 1860 on page 412 of *The American Promise,* Second Edition.

1. Mobile, Alabama
2. Charleston, South Carolina
3. Virginia
4. New Orleans, Louisiana
5. North Carolina
6. Tennessee
7. Kentucky
8. Texas
9. Georgia
10. Missouri

Answer the following questions in a paragraph based on Map 12.1: Cotton Kingdom, Slave Empire: 1820 and 1860 on page 412.

**READING THE MAP** Where was slavery most prevalent in 1820? In 1860? How did the spread of slavery compare with the spread of cotton?

**CONNECTIONS** How much of the world's cotton was produced in the American South in 1860s? While most slaves worked in agriculture, how else were slaves employed?

**WEB LINKS** To explore the topics discussed in the exercise above, visit the Web links noted below.

"Antebellum Louisiana: Agrarian Life"
http://lsm.crt.state.la.us/cabildo/cab9.htm

"The Antebellum Period" by Carole E. Scott
http://www.westga.edu/~cscott/history/antebell.html

***Visual Activity*** This image shows a steamboat, the *Henry Frank*, being loaded with bales of cotton at New Orleans. The sheer amount of the crop is staggering: the bales line the sides of the boat to such an extent that, except for the smokestacks, the ship itself is almost obliterated. This is not surprising; a bale of cotton weighed about four hundred pounds, and the banner on the ship's flagstaff says that it is carrying 9,226 bales, or nearly 1,850 tons of the crop. In a time when cotton was widely declared to be king, the bales are lined up in tiers like the Egyptian pyramids, with men resting on the upper levels. In fact, the gangplank leads into the cotton rather than over it, forcing the people getting on the boat to scurry over the bales to make it onto the deck. The cotton is clearly a source of fascination to the residents of New Orleans, and it dominates them: the crowd observing the loading is large, but the still cotton towers over them and overwhelms them visually.

Answer the following questions in a paragraph based on "Cotton Bales Loaded on the Steamboat Henry Frank" on page 417 of *The American Promise,* Second Edition.

**READING THE IMAGE** How does the image of the *Henry Frank* demonstrate the centrality of cotton to southern agriculture and southern people?

**CONNECTIONS** Where did most of the cotton on the *Henry Frank* likely come from?

**WEB LINKS** To explore the topics discussed in the exercise above, visit the Web links noted below.

"The Fabric of History: The Cotton Industry in New Orleans, 1835–1885"
http://www.hnoc.org/fabric.htm

"Economic Differences between Augusta, Virginia and Franklin, Pennsylvania in the Antebellum Period" by Daniel S. Schwartz
http://instruct1.cit.cornell.edu/courses/hist100.06/schwartz/page1.htm

***Analyzing Sources Activity*** Answer the following questions in a paragraph based on "The Promise of Technology: The Cotton Gin: 'Engine of the South'" on page 418.

1. Why wasn't there a market for southern cotton prior to the invention of the cotton gin?
2. Why did Eli Whitney fail to profit from the invention of the cotton gin?
3. What impact did the invention of the cotton gin have on the antebellum slave system and the American economy?

**WEB LINKS** To explore the topics discussed in the exercise above, visit the Web links noted below.

"Eli Whitney's Patent for the Cotton Gin"
http://www.nara.gov/education/cc/whitney.html

"Eli Whitney Museum"
http://www.eliwhitney.org/main.htm
Choose "Eli Whitney."

# Answer Key

## Chapter 12: The Slave South, 1820–1860

### *Chapter Overview*

#### *Chronology*

1. c
2. b
3. c
4. d
5. b
6. a
7. b
8. d
9. c
10. b

#### *Defining Terms*

1. Mason-Dixon line
2. cotton kingdom
3. slave codes
4. positive good
5. George Fitzhugh
6. master
7. overseers
8. paternalism
9. miscegenation
10. chivalry
11. field hands
12. house servants
13. drivers
14. family
15. Denmark Vesey
16. free blacks
17. freedom papers
18. William Ellison
19. plain folk
20. plantation belt
21. upcountry
22. revivals
23. poor whites
24. white male suffrage
25. "servant of the people"
26. planters
27. cotton curtain
28. Hinton Rowan Helper

### *Chapter Review*

#### *Multiple-Choice*

1. a
2. c
3. d
4. d
5. a
6. a
7. b
8. d
9. c
10. a
11. b
12. b
13. a
14. c
15. d
16. a
17. a
18. a
19. a
20. c
21. c
22. b
23. a
24. d
25. c
26. b
27. d
28. a
29. b
30. d
31. a
32. a
33. b
34. d
35. c
36. b
37. d
38. b
39. a
40. c
41. b
42. c
43. a
44. c
45. a
46. b
47. b
48. b
49. d
50. c
51. d
52. b
53. c
54. c
55. c
56. b
57. c
58. b
59. b
60. d
61. c
62. d
63. c
64. b
65. a
66. a
67. a
68. d
69. d
70. c
71. a
72. d
73. d
74. c
75. b
76. b
77. d
78. d
79. d
80. d
81. d
82. c
83. b
84. d
85. b
86. a
87. b
88. c

89. c
90. a
91. d
92. c
93. d
94. a
95. c
96. a
97. a
98. d
99. d
100. b
101. c
102. c
103. a
104. b
105. a
106. b
107. a
108. c
109. a
110. d
111. c
112. a
113. c
114. d
115. a
116. b
117. b
118. d
119. d
120. c
121. b
122. c
123. a
124. d
125. a
126. d
127. d
128. b
129. b
130. b
131. a
132. b

### *Short Answer*

1. Cotton became the most important southern crop because the region's climate and geography were well suited for its cultivation. Although the South encompassed over a million square miles of differing terrain, soil, and weather, the cotton Southern farmers grew was very adaptable, and most areas had the two hundred frost-free days, plentiful spring, and light fall rains that were necessary for cotton to flourish. Slavery was an essential component of the Southern cotton kingdom because the crop demanded a great deal of labor to cultivate. Slaves of African descent grew 75 percent of the crop on plantations, and as cotton agriculture expanded to the west, masters took their slaves with them or purchased new slaves through the domestic slave trade business.
2. Attacks on slavery from both blacks within the system and abolitionists spurred white Southerners in the 1820s and 1830s to defend slavery with intellectual arguments and to strengthen the system with practical legal and political measures. Spurred by intellectuals, Southerners developed the "positive good" argument, which maintained that slavery was not an unfortunate development but instead a beneficial system that was good for masters and slaves alike and was more humane than the northern free-labor ideal. State legislatures constructed elaborate slave codes to force slaves into total submission to both their masters and the general white society. Not only were slaves were required to give their masters unconditional and absolute obedience, but laws gave all whites authority over all slaves, whether the slaves belonged to them or not. Any white could stop a slave on a road and demand to see his or her written permission to be away from home, and any white could "correct" a slave who did not display the proper deference.
3. In the antebellum period, some southern state governments recognized the potential weaknesses of the region's undiversified economy and took measures to try to reverse that trend. State governments helped to create banking systems to provide credit for industrial and agricultural projects, and they joined with private investors to build an extensive railroad network. However, they did not create some of the essential services that would allow a modern economy to develop; for instance, no southern legislature funded a public school system, which left the illiteracy rate for whites at over 20 percent in the mid-nineteenth century. Moreover, the industries that legislatures encouraged mainly supported the production of staple crops. The rail lines that states built connected not connect towns and cities, as they did in the North, but port cities and farming areas. They did not exist to exchange manufactured goods and agricultural products but to speed the export of cash crops.
4. In the nineteenth century, southern planters described their relationship with their slaves in terms of what historians call "paternalism." They denied that the slavery they practiced was brutal and exploitative and instead characterized it as a set of reciprocal obligations between masters and slaves. According to planters, slaves supplied labor and obedience to masters, who provided care and guidance in exchange. In fact, the closing of the external slave trade in 1808 did make it economically sensible for masters to provide their slaves with a minimum level of physical care, and conditions for slaves did improve somewhat in the nineteenth century. Many planters gave their slaves rest periods, and most of them stopped the eighteenth-century custom of punishing slaves by physically mutilating them. Nonetheless, slaves continued to eat substandard diets, live in miserably poor housing, and suffer whippings.
5. The elite women of the antebellum South—"southern ladies"—were expected to epitomize the domestic sphere of piety, purity, chastity, and obedience. The southern husband was the patriarch; his ideal wife was cultured and charming but weak and dependent on his chival-

rous protection. Yet the reality of plantation mistresses' lives made it impossible for them to conform to the ideal set out for them. They spent long hours supervising the labor of their servants, without the help of an overseer or other intermediary. They were often responsible for taking care of hen houses, dairies, and slave hospitals, nurseries, and quarters; moreover, they bore the burdens of childbearing and child rearing at a time when families might include as many as ten or eleven children

6. Work was the major responsibility of slaves, and the vast majority of them worked in the fields cultivating various staple crops, including cotton, rice, indigo, and sugar. Field work was hard and tedious, involving year-round labor and monotonous routines. Many fewer slaves, perhaps one in ten, performed domestic work as house servants. House work was less physically demanding than field work, the food was better, and the quarters were more comfortable. However, domestic servants worked under the constant and often critical supervision of whites and were constantly on call.

7. Abolitionists and planters often claimed that black slaves did not have any family life, either because the slave system made it impossible or because they did not have any sense of family obligation. In fact, slaves put a great deal of effort into the maintenance of family life; young slaves married, set up housekeeping in their own cabins, and had children. Yet slave marriages were not recognized as legal, and masters had no obligations to honor slaves' bonds. This meant that it was easy for masters to sell one spouse and not another, making sale the second most frequent cause (after death) of the ending of slave marriages. According to one estimate, between 1820 and 1860 300,000 slave marriages were destroyed by sale.

8. One of the mildest forms of resistance was the oral tradition of folk tales, in which weak characters got the better of strong ones and gave listeners a vicarious sense of victory over their masters. Slaves also used different strategies to resist masters' demands for their labor; they would work slowly, pretend to be too stupid to understand simple instructions, break their tools, feign illness, or load rocks in their cotton bags before they were weighed. Although few slaves ran away permanently, "lying out" was not uncommon and deprived masters of their slaves' labor for as long as a few weeks. Occasionally slaves turned to outright rebellion, but this practice was quite rare because existing conditions made success virtually impossible. Communication between plantations was difficult, and there was not much wilderness in the South into which rebels could retreat.

9. After the Revolution, the natural rights philosophy of the Declaration of Independence and the egalitarian message of evangelical Protestantism joined to challenge slavery; this ideological assault was concurrent with a depression in tobacco prices in the Upper South. The combination of ideology and practical finances led to a burst of emancipations in the region, and by 1810 free blacks were the fastest-growing element of the southern population. The increasing numbers of free blacks worried whites, particularly after the cotton boom made the need for laborers more pressing. In the 1820s and 1830s, state legislatures worked to make it more difficult or even impossible for masters to free their slaves. They also worked to limit the rights of blacks who were already free by forcing them to pay special taxes, requiring them to register with the state or choose a white guardian, denying them basic civil and political rights, and subjecting them to many of the same laws as slaves.

10. There were a handful of free blacks in the antebellum South who managed to break out of the poverty and degradation that whites attempted to impose on them. Most of them were residents of urban areas like Charleston, Mobile, and New Orleans, where many of the restrictive laws that limited free blacks were not consistently enforced. The free black elite tended to be light-skinned, and they were almost all artisans who worked at skilled trades like tailoring or carpentry; their customers were elite whites who appreciated their skills and respectful service.

11. In the plantation belt, planters and yeomen were connected to each other in a variety of ways. Small farmers grew food crops, but they also devoted a portion of their land to cash crops, especially cotton. Because they could not afford expensive machinery and did not have links to merchants in port cities, yeomen relied on larger planters to help them process their cotton and get it to market. Planters encouraged friendly relationships with their poorer neighbors by helping them in times of need, occasionally providing the use of slaves for at peak times or hiring overseers from among the sons of local families. Small farmers generally did not resent the planter regime but instead hoped to join it through careful planning and hard work.

12. The upcountry regions of the South were not geographically or climatically suited for staple crop production for the market. Rather than plantations, the area was dominated by independent farms on which entire families performed labor. There were very few slaves in

the upcountry, and slave owners did not tend to have the large slave labor forces that were typical of the plantation belt. Despite the relative absence of slavery, the fiercely independent upcountry yeomen favored both slavery and white supremacy with the same enthusiasm as other Southerners.

13. Nineteenth-century Northerners claimed that poor white Southerners illustrated the perils of the slave system. They argued that slavery had deprived poor whites of opportunity and thus degraded them socially and economically to the point that they had no ambition or energy to pull themselves out of poverty. Poor whites were not just poor in material terms: they lacked education, breeding, and culture. In reality, poor whites tended to be as ambitious as other Americans, but they suffered from poor nutrition and debilitating diseases that often made it difficult for them to get ahead. This was especially true beginning in the 1850s, when a cotton boom drove land prices beyond the reach of poor families, cutting off their major avenue toward greater wealth.

14. For white men, southern politics became quite democratic in the first half of the nineteenth century. By the 1850s and usually much earlier, every southern state had abandoned property or wealth requirements for voting, and most of them had removed the property requirements for holding state office as well. Also, more officials, including justices of the peace, judges, and militia officers, were selected by voters. The spread of suffrage led to strong electoral competition and extremely high rates of voter turnout. For example, in 1810, South Carolina still had suffrage restrictions, and voter turnout was around 43 percent; by 1824, in the absence of restrictions, voter turnout had risen to 76 percent.

15. Planters in southern legislatures used the state government to protect slavery both by giving themselves economic privileges and also by suppressing criticism of the system. In Georgia in 1850, for instance, planters kept the tax rate on slaves at about a fifth of that levied on land; because land taxes were still fairly low, they were able to pay less relative to other whites without inspiring resentment from nonslaveholders. Planters benefited more than other groups from the limited public spending undertaken by states: state financing of railroads, the most expensive public projects of the antebellum South, tended to help larger farmers by carrying their crops to market. Southern legislatures also determined that slavery was too important to debate only and made it virtually impossible for Southerners to publicly advocate its abolition or even learn about arguments against the system.

### *Map Activity*

Reading the Map: In 1820, slavery was the most common in the seaboard states of Virginia, South Carolina, and Georgia and along the lower Mississippi River, with a significant cluster in Kentucky as well. By 1860, slavery remained prevalent in those areas but had increased substantially all over the inland South and had become especially common in central Tennessee, in Alabama, and along the Mississippi River in Missouri. Slavery had also spread into coastal Florida and Texas, the latter of which had not even been an American possession in 1820. While cotton was not necessary to the existence of slavery (for instance, in 1820 and 1860 Virginia, Kentucky, and Missouri had very little in the way of cotton but many slaves), it often encouraged the system's spread. For example, Alabama and the area around Macon, Georgia, experienced simultaneous booms in cotton production and the slave population.

Connections: About three-fourths of the world's cotton was produced in the South, particularly the Lower South, by 1860. Given that 75 percent of the American total was grown by slaves working on plantations, it is unsurprising that the vast majority of slaves were employed as field hands, performing hard and monotonous labor year-round. However, some slaves were employed in other capacities. Ten to twenty out of every hundred slaves—nearly all women—were domestic workers, responsible for the domestic labor of the plantation home. Perhaps five out of every hundred slaves—nearly all men—were skilled artisans. Rarest of all, maybe one in a hundred slaves was a driver, overseeing the work of other slaves in the fields.

### *Visual Activity*

Reading the Image: In a time when many forms of transit carried a variety of goods back and forth, it is clear that the *Henry Frank* was a one-commodity vessel, and that commodity was cotton. Cotton dominates the picture and even the steamboat itself: it looks more like a mound of cotton floating mysteriously along a dock than an actual ship. Not only is cotton the only thing the steamboat is carrying, but it has drawn the interest of a very large and heterogeneous crowd of city dwellers. The observers represent a cross-section of southern society—men and women, well-off and poor, and black and white—and all clearly interested in the proceedings.

Connections: The banner floating from the flagstaff of the *Henry Frank* claims that the steamboat is carrying 9,226 bales of cotton. Small southern farmers in the plantation belt customarily produced only a couple of bales each year, and yeomen in the upcountry regions grew even less for market. The quarter of the white southern population that owned slaves produced the majority of the cotton crop. More than 75 percent of the total southern cotton production was performed by slaves on plantations.

### *Analyzing Sources*

1. By the late eighteenth century, Great Britain's textile industry could not purchase enough raw cotton to produce cotton cloth. The American South, with its land resources, favorable climate, and large slave labor force, was in an excellent position to provide cotton, except that the green-seed cotton that flourished there was extremely difficult to clean. As long as the cotton stuck to the seeds, neither the English textile industry nor any other manufacturer could use it.
2. Whitney's basic design for the cotton gin was simple: the device was made of wire teeth set in a wooden cylinder that, when rotated, went through narrow slats, pulled cotton away from the seeds, and was cleaned by a brush that swept the fibers off of the teeth. The machine was thus easy to copy, and the demand for it was considerable; planters recognized immediately that the cotton gin would break the bottleneck in the commercial production of cotton. Whitney held a patent on the cotton gin. However, the Patent Act of 1793 placed the proof of both invention and infringement on the inventor. It was difficult and expensive to gain proof, and Whitney found that the revenue from his own gin factory could barely keep up with the cost of legal proceedings.
3. The invention of the cotton gin made cotton the major southern crop, quickly replacing indigo and tobacco in the upcountry. The commercial production of cotton contributed to the expansion of the slave system and pushed it westward. It also changed the economy of the North, as textile mills sprung up in New England. Moreover, the cotton gin made cotton fabric cheap and accessible; it displaced wool and flax as common textiles for clothing.

CHAPTER

# THE HOUSE DIVIDED, 1846–1861 13

## Chapter Overview

### *Chapter Summary*

***Introduction*** The chapter opens with an account of John Brown's violent commitment to abolishing the slave system in the United States. Brown had been responsible for the murder of proslavery settlers in Pottawatomie, Kansas, in 1856; in 1859, he and twenty-one other men attempted to incite a slave rebellion at Harpers Ferry, Virginia. The attempt was a failure, and most Northerners repudiated Brown's actions. However, in the context of sectional tensions that had been heightened by the territorial acquisitions of the Mexican War, white Southerners interpreted the raid as evidence of the North's desire to destroy their way of life.

***Fruits of War, pp. 450–456*** As it became clear that war with Mexico would result in new U.S. territories, politicians in 1846 began floating a variety of plans for resolving the issue of whether those states would be slave or free. This territorial issue seriously divided the Whig and Democratic Parties. In 1850, Congress put together a compromise settlement that most Americans hoped would end debate over the issue.

**THE WILMOT PROVISO AND THE EXPANSION OF SLAVERY** In August 1846, while the Mexican War was still in progress, antislavery Democrat David Wilmot proposed that Congress prohibit slavery in any territory acquired from Mexico. Many northern politicians and voters backed Wilmot's proviso because they opposed slavery as an institution, they did not want southern political power to increase, or they wanted to reserve western land for white settlers. Southerners universally denounced the proviso, arguing that Congress had no right to exclude slavery from a territory. Other congressional leaders supported a plan proposed by Senator Lewis Cass that became known as popular sovereignty, which would allow the people of each territory to decide the status of slavery there. Popular sovereignty had the advantage of being ambiguous: Northerners argued that the decision on slavery could be made when the first territorial legislature assembled, while Southerners declared that the status of slavery could be determined only when the territory drew up a constitution and applied for statehood.

**THE ELECTION OF 1848** The 1848 presidential campaign revealed sectional tensions in both parties, although both Democrats and Whigs tried to avoid the slavery question. When Polk declined to run again, the Democrats nominated Lewis Cass and adopted a vague platform. The Whigs nominated General Zachary Taylor, a slave owner from Louisiana and hero of the Mexican War and adopted no platform at all. Antislavery Whigs and Democrats, dissatisfied with the choice of candidates, formed the Free-Soil Party and nominated former president Martin Van Buren. The Free-Soil Party did not win a single state, although they did make slavery the primary issue of the election. Taylor won the electoral vote by 163 to 127, but the election showed that both parties had been shaken by the issue of slavery in the territories.

**DEBATE AND COMPROMISE** Once in office, Taylor surprised everyone by urging the immediate admission of California and New Mexico (whose largely antislavery settlers had begun writing free-state constitutions) to the Union as free states. The plan aroused intense opposition in the South because of the prospect that only free states would continue to emerge in the territories. To resolve the impasse, Henry Clay offered a series of resolutions involving compromise on all sides to restore sectional harmony, but the plan was vehemently opposed by John C. Calhoun, who declared that the plan favored the North over the South. Clay wanted the measures to pass as a single "Omnibus Bill," but the measure failed. Senator Stephen A. Douglas of Illinois stepped in and was able to fashion a compromise in the form of a series of measures that could be voted on separately. By mid-September 1850, Congress had enacted and the president had signed all the components of the Compromise of 1850: California entered the Union as a free state; New Mexico and Utah became territories where the question of slavery would be decided by popular sovereignty; Congress passed a more stringent fugitive slave law but ended the slave trade in the capital; and Texas had its preannexation debts assumed in exchange for relinquishing its New Mexico claims. The Compromise of 1850 passed because its key measures were supported by moderates who could be allied with larger sectional blocks. The compromise was more an example of Douglas's parliamentary skill than an indication of conciliation on the issue of slavery by the dissenting parties. The compromise was a temporary cease-fire that did not resolve the larger issues.

***The Sectional Balance Undone, pp. 456–464*** The Compromise of 1850 began to come apart almost as soon as it was passed. Southerners had accepted the package but demanded that Northerners strictly adhere to its components and especially to the fugitive slave law. This issue, very problematic in the North, contributed to reopening the controversy over slavery. Northerners also responded to Harriet Beecher Stowe's antislavery novel *Uncle Tom's Cabin*; but ultimately, politicians were the ones who brought slavery back to the forefront of national politics.

**THE FUGITIVE SLAVE ACT** Northerners did not like fugitive slave laws; they had responded to a 1793 federal law by passing "personal liberty laws" to give fugitives some protection. The Fugitive Slave Act, which required all citizens to assist in the apprehension of runaway slaves, provoked northern outrage because it demanded that citizens assist officials in capturing fugitives. Southerners regarded northern obstruction as a betrayal not only of the Compromise of 1850 but of the Constitution as well. Meanwhile, the enforcement of this unpopular law served to radicalize many Northerners against slavery, especially in New England.

***UNCLE TOM'S CABIN*** In 1851, Harriet Beecher Stowe's novel *Uncle Tom's Cabin* was published. Stowe's account was the single most powerful attack on slavery ever written. With 300,000 copies sold in its first year, it became America's first literary blockbuster and exerted an extraordinary influence on public opinion. In her book, Stowe succeeded in personalizing the abstract horrors of slavery with characters like Eliza, the slave mother fighting to keep her son from being sold away, and Simon Legree, the wicked overseer. The novel awakened millions of Northerners to the evils of slavery, while Southerners denounced the book as being full of gross distortions and fabrications. Perhaps more important, the book confirmed for increasing numbers of Southerners their suspicion that they had few northern supporters.

**THE ELECTION OF 1852** In 1852, the Democrats chose Franklin Pierce, a New Hampshire politician with southern sympathies, as their presidential candidate, while the Whigs turned to General Winfield Scott, military hero of the Mexican War. Still, the sectional question inevitably intruded on the election, and Whig divisions over slavery helped produce a Democratic landslide. Pierce sought to divert attention from the slavery issue by concentrating on foreign expansion, but his efforts to extend the nation's domain by purchasing Cuba inevitably became entangled with the sectional crisis. Although Pierce's Cuba initiative failed, he was successful in purchasing from Mexico 45,000 square miles of territory in present-day Arizona and New Mexico, a transaction known as the Gadsden Purchase. The purchase was the result of the American desire to build a Pacific railroad, an issue that became entangled with slavery.

**THE KANSAS-NEBRASKA ACT** As a senator from Illinois and a booster of western economic development, Stephen Douglas naturally wanted the transcontinental railroad for his city and region. He thus introduced a bill in 1854 to organize a new territory, known as Nebraska, west of Iowa and Missouri. To win southern votes, Douglas inserted a provision that the status of slavery would be determined by "popular sovereignty" and the repeal of the antislavery provision of the Missouri Compromise. In its final form, the measure was known as the Kansas-Nebraska Act, and after much debate it became law in May 1854, with the unanimous support of southern Whigs and Democrats. About half of all Northern Democrats refused to support it, however.

***Realignment of the Party System, pp. 464–469*** The Kansas-Nebraska Act had the fateful effect of realigning the nation's political parties along geographic lines. The new party system that emerged in the 1850s would mirror the divisions between the North and South.

**THE OLD PARTIES: WHIGS AND DEMOCRATS** The Whigs' weak showing in the election of 1852 made clear that they were no longer a strong national party. Their decline and collapse left the Democrats as the country's only national party. Since most of the northern Democrats who supported Douglas's Kansas-Nebraska bill were not reelected the following year, after 1854, the Democrats became by default a southern-dominated party. The collapse of the Whigs and the alienation of northern Democrats from their party meant that many Americans remained politically adrift. It was unclear who would attract these drifters.

**THE NEW PARTIES: KNOW-NOTHINGS AND REPUBLICANS** In the vacuum left by the collapse of the Whigs, a number of different parties emerged. One of the most powerful and successful was the American Party (also called the Know-Nothings), which was viciously opposed to immigrants and Catholics. The Know-Nothings enjoyed a series of successes in 1854 and 1855, particularly in Massachusetts. Of greater future significance was the rise of the Republican Party, which attracted a variety of disaffected elements across the political spectrum, all opposed to the extension of slavery in the territories. The Republicans also became the political voice of the free-labor ideology, arguing that the slave power of the South degraded work and whites alike and was driving to extend its oppressive system by undermining the Constitution.

**THE ELECTION OF 1856** The Republican Party platform revealed the strictly sectional nature of the new organization, as it called for congressional prohibition of slavery in all territories. Their nominee was John C. Frémont; the Democrats nominated James Buchanan; and the Know-Nothings turned to former President Millard Fillmore as their standard-bearer. During the campaign, Buchanan touted popular sovereignty as the key to the slavery issue and labeled the Republicans as antislavery extremists. The rhetoric worked, and Buchanan won a narrow victory, beating Frémont in the electoral college by 174 to 114. Despite losing, the Republican Party demonstrated that sectionalism had created a new party system, one that could prove dangerous for the Republic.

***Freedom under Siege, pp. 469–479*** The Republicans were a sectional party, with no need to compromise with a southern wing. The new party was boosted by a series of events in the mid- to late 1850s, including events in Kansas, an attack on a respected northern senator, and a controversial Supreme Court decision.

**"BLEEDING KANSAS"** When Kansas was organized in the fall of 1854, a bitter contest began for control of its territorial government. In the first territorial elections, proslavery settlers combined with thousands of illegal Missouri voters to give the proslavery forces victory. However, free-soilers, who were the majority of the actual territorial residents, established a rival government under a constitution outlawing slavery. A small-scale civil war erupted, culminating in May 1856 when proslavery forces attacked the antislavery town of Lawrence. A bloody reprisal was carried out by the antislavery fanatic John Brown and his followers at Pottawatomie Creek. For Republicans, "Bleeding Kansas" became a potent symbol of the existence of an aggressive slave power. Another symbol soon appeared in the U.S. Senate, where the hardcore antislavery Massachusetts Senator Charles Sumner was beaten unconscious by the South Carolinian Preston Brooks for having insulted in a speech Brooks's relative, Senator Andrew P. Butler.

**THE *DRED SCOTT* DECISION** Many hoped to see the troubling territorial issue resolved once and for all by a Supreme Court ruling. That opportunity came with the *Dred Scott* case. After his master's death, slave Dred Scott sued for his freedom on the basis that he had lived for many years in an area (the Wisconsin Territory) where slavery had been outlawed by the Missouri Compromise. The majority ruled against Scott, with Chief Justice Roger Taney proclaiming that because Scott was not a citizen he could not sue. Taney further argued that no African American, slave or free, could be a citizen. But the most significant part of the ruling was the court's declaration that Congress had no power to prohibit slavery in any territory. The decision made popular sovereignty an untenable solution to the territorial issue and undermined the Democrats while giving a boost to Republican claims of a slaveholder conspiracy.

**PRAIRIE REPUBLICAN: ABRAHAM LINCOLN** By the time of the *Dred Scott* decision, Abraham Lincoln had become a successful railroad lawyer in Illinois, but politics was his real passion. His idol was Henry Clay, and like Clay, Lincoln practiced a politics of moderation and pragmatism, especially on the issues of Union, slavery, and race. He opposed the Kansas-Nebraska Act because it effectively destroyed the Missouri Compromise, yet Lincoln accepted slavery where it existed. Still, he was convinced that slaveholders formed an aggressive and dangerous conspiracy to nationalize slavery. By 1858, Lincoln had so impressed Illinois Republicans that they decided to pit him against Stephen Douglas, the North's premier Democrat, in that year's Senate race.

**THE LINCOLN-DOUGLAS DEBATES** The 1858 Lincoln-Douglas debates attracted enormous crowds and received wide attention. By the time they ended, Lincoln's eloquent and passionate attacks on slavery had made him nationally prominent. At the heart of the debates was the issue of slavery. Lincoln argued that slavery was wrong, but he was no abolitionist and shared many northern whites' belief in white supremacy and in the Constitution's protection of slavery where it existed. However, he made it clear he opposed the institution's spread. Douglas maintained in the Freeport Doctrine that settlers could still keep slavery out of the territories by refusing to pass protective laws and accused the Republicans of promoting sectional conflict, of wishing to interfere with slavery in the South, and of advocating social equality of the races. Though Douglas ultimately won reelection, Lincoln emerged from the contest with a growing following both in and beyond the state.

***The Union Collapses, pp. 480–486*** By the late 1850s, many Southerners had begun to fear that they could not protect slavery and their way of life if they remained Americans. Events in late 1859 and early 1860 heightened southern anxiety about northern attitudes and policies, and threats of secession became increasingly common among slaveholders.

**THE AFTERMATH OF JOHN BROWN'S RAID** John Brown was tried in a Virginia court for treason, found guilty, and hanged on December 2, 1859. He died with dignity, causing some northern abolitionists to praise both him and his tactics. Although most Northerners repudiated Brown, Southerners became convinced that such fanaticism was supported by the Republican Party and that the North would resort to fomenting similar slave uprisings to put an end to the institution.

**REPUBLICAN VICTORY IN 1860** Between John Brown's execution and the presidential election of 1860, a number of events increased sectional tension. A convention of southern businessmen demanded the reopening of the African slave trade; Chief Justice Taney declared northern personal liberty laws unconstitutional; the business of electing a Speaker of the House almost became violent; and Jefferson Davis demanded a federal slave code for the territories. The Democratic Party was torn apart by the conflict over slavery. When the party convention endorsed popular sovereignty, delegates from eight Lower South states walked out, and the remaining delegates later nominated Stephen Douglas. In the meantime, Lower South Democrats met and nominated Kentuckian John C. Breckenridge. Still another group, made up of conservatives, formed the Constitutional Union party, nominating Tennesseean John Bell as their standard-bearer. This hastily thrown-together party endorsed the Union but remained silent on slavery. Smelling victory, the Republicans worked to broaden their party base with a platform that endorsed protective tariffs, internal improvements, a homestead bill, and a Pacific railroad to be built with federal financial assistance. It supported the right of existing slave states to maintain the system. The Republican convention nominated Abraham Lincoln as the party's presidential candidate, and he won the presidency with a majority of the electoral votes and 39 percent of the fragmented popular vote. Most Southerners viewed the election as a catastrophe.

**SECESSION WINTER** Almost as soon as the news of Lincoln's election reached the South, the region's militants—the "fire-eaters"—demanded an end to the Union. Within weeks, the secession process had begun. Unionists argued that the South should wait and see what Lincoln did in office, but secessionists emphasized the urgency of the moment and the dangers of delay. The South's minority status made it impossible for Southerners to defend slavery within the Union. South Carolina seceded first, on December 20, 1860. By February 1861, six other Deep South states had withdrawn from the Union and sent representatives to Montgomery, Alabama, to form a new nation—the Confederate States of America. Eight southern states remained undecided. Congressional efforts at forging a compromise failed. When President-elect Lincoln arrived in Washington for his inauguration, nothing had been resolved. Despite Lincoln's conciliatory statements about respecting slavery in the South, he made it clear that secession would not be tolerated.

***Conclusion: The Failure of Compromise*** Though the North and the South had divided over issues since the colonial era, compromises and solutions had always been found to preserve the union. But the extended crisis from 1846 to 1861 over the expansion of slavery brought the nation to a critical juncture. By secession winter, many doubted that the nation could survive "permanently half slave and half free," as Lincoln put it. But if the rupture of the union was inevitable, it remained to be seen whether this would mean war.

***Chronology Activity*** Read the annotated chronology, and answer the multiple-choice questions.

1846 Wilmot Proviso proposes barring slavery from all lands acquired in Mexican War. The Wilmot Proviso provoked a barrage of controversy. Many Northerners supported it: some because of abolitionist beliefs, but others because they wanted to restrain the political influence of the South or wished to preserve the territories for whites only. Southerners interpreted the Wilmot Proviso as an insult and a threat to the South's ability to protect the slave system from the growing power of the Northern states.

1847 John C. Calhoun challenges Wilmot Proviso on constitutional grounds, stating that Congress has no power to exclude slavery from territories. Calhoun contended that the territories were the joint property of all of the states. Therefore, Congress could not deprive any state of equal rights on the territories, including the right to migrate with property, human or otherwise.

Senator Lewis Cass offers compromise of "popular sovereignty," allowing people of territories to determine fate of slavery. Cass believed that popular sovereignty was congruent with the American tradition of democracy and local self-government and also removed the issue of slavery from the national government to distant territorial legislatures. The most attractive feature of the plan, however, was that it did not state precisely when slavery would be voted on. Northerners claimed that the decision would be made by the first territorial government, and Southerners stated that it would occur at the time the first state constitution was drafted. The ambiguity meant that both sections could support popular sovereignty.

1848 Opponents of expansion of slavery found Free-Soil Party. The 1848 presidential election demonstrated that both political parties were divided over the issue of territorial slavery. While the Democrats and Whigs attempted to avoid discussing slavery, antislavery members of both parties bolted and formed the Free-Soil Party to challenge the major parties. They lost the election but made slavery impossible to ignore.

Whig General Zachary Taylor elected president of United States, defeating Democrat Lewis Cass and Free-Soil candidate Martin Van Buren. Zachary Taylor had no platform at all when he ran for president; Lewis Cass ran on a platform that avoided giving a firm position on slavery. Taylor's victory showed that northern voters were not ready for the Free-Soil Party but that the major parties had been shaken by the issue of territorial slavery.

1850s Vigilance committees in North challenge and sometimes thwart Fugitive Slave Act. Since the 1790s, Northerners had interpreted fugitive slave laws as a license to kidnap free blacks; in the 1830s, northern states instituted "personal liberty laws" to provide runaways with some protection. Northerners were outraged by the strong Fugitive Slave Act that passed Congress in 1850, giving a slave owner the ability to reclaim his property by the simple means of swearing in front of a court commissioner that a runaway slave was his. It also stipulated that all citizens had to assist officials in apprehending runaways. Outraged, some Northerners refused to obey the law, and a few actively protected accused runaways.

1850 July 9. President Zachary Taylor dies; Vice President Millard Fillmore succeeds. Taylor's untimely death meant that Millard Fillmore signed the Compromise of 1850 into law, declaring it the "final settlement" of the slavery question.

Senator Henry Clay proposes Omnibus Bill to avert territorial crisis over slavery; bill ultimately defeated. Clay believed that his proposals would avert a political crisis and also that they offered enough to both sides that they could pass as a single measure. He wanted California to enter the Union as a free state, New Mexico and Utah to become territories where the issue of slavery would be decided by popular sovereignty, Texas to accept its boundary with New Mexico in exchange for having its preannexation debts assumed by the federal government, and Congress to end the slave trade in Washington, D.C., but enact a more stringent fugitive slave law. The strategy backfired when Free-Soilers, Conscience Whigs, and proslavery Southerners refused to support the measures in their entirety.

Senator Stephen Douglas's compromise bills (Compromise of 1850) pass Congress, signed into law by President Fillmore. The Compromise of 1850 split Clay's proposed Omnibus bill into its component parts, allowing Douglas to gain different majorities to pass each one.

1852 Harriet Beecher Stowe's *Uncle Tom's Cabin* published. For Northerners, Stowe's novel brought to life the injustices of the slave system—despite the fact that she had never been on a plantation. The novel was the nation's first literary blockbuster, selling 300,000 copies within a year; it crystallized the northern antislavery sentiment and reinforced Southerners' belief that they had no support in the northern states.

Democrat Franklin Pierce elected president of the United States, defeating Whig Winfield Scott. Franklin was a "doughface," or Northerner with southern sympathies. His victory demonstrated the collapse of the Whig Party: hopelessly divided between Cotton and Conscience factions, the Whigs won only four of the thirty-one states.

1853 Gadsden Purchase adds 45,000 square miles of territory in present-day Arizona and New Mexico. The purchase was the result of the American desire to bind the nation together by means of a transcontinental railroad to California. However, plans for the railroad ignited sectional rivalry as northern and southern cities maneuvered to become the eastern terminus of the railroad.

1854 American Party (Know-Nothings) emerges, advocating nativist positions. The Know-Nothing Party was one of the main contenders for national political power after the Whig Party disintegrated. The Know-Nothings were convinced that native-born Protestants were going to be subsumed by the immigration of Irish and German Roman Catholics. Members swore never to vote for foreign-born or Roman Catholic candidates and to refuse to reveal information about the organization. They had a series of dramatic victories at the state level in 1854 and 1855 but fell apart in 1856 when party leaders insisted that their platform include an endorsement of the Kansas-Nebraska Act.

Kansas-Nebraska Act opens the Kansas and Nebraska Territories to popular sovereignty. The Kansas-Nebraska Act was extremely controversial because it reopened the issue of slavery in land that had been declared off-limits by the Missouri Compromise. Stephen Douglas of Illinois had agreed to explicitly repeal the Missouri Compromise in exchange for southern support for the organization of the territory, which he hoped would contribute to making Chicago the eastern terminus of the Pacific railroad. The measure passed, but many of the northern Democrats who supported it lost their seats the following year, and it reopened the issues that the Compromise of 1850 was supposed to have settled.

Republican Party emerges on platform opposing extension of slavery in territories. The Republicans attempted to unite all of the dissidents and political orphans who opposed the extension of slavery into the territories. The party tapped into northern values, arguing that the slave system oppressed whites by degrading labor and thus removing opportunities for financial advancement. They believed that slave power—the planter aristocrats—was becoming more aggressive and hoped to expand slavery, subvert liberty, and undermine the Constitution by working through the Democratic Party.

1856 Armed conflict between proslavery and antislavery forces erupts in Kansas. The system of popular sovereignty fell apart in Kansas after proslavery Missourians invaded the territory to vote illegally in its first elections. The first territorial legislature was strongly proslavery; although President Pierce endorsed it, the antislavery majority elected a second government, wrote a constitution banning slaves and free blacks from the state, and applied for statehood. Fighting broke out when a mob of proslavery men attacked Lawrence, the center of free-state settlement; John Brown then retaliated by massacring five proslavery settlers along the Pottawatomie Creek. The events in Kansas gave credence to Republican claims of an aggressive slave power.

Preston Brooks of South Carolina brutally assaults Charles Sumner of Massachusetts on Senate floor. Sumner had given a speech attacking the events in Kansas, in which he insulted an elderly Senator from South Carolina. The senator's nephew, a representative, beat Sumner unconscious. He resigned his seat but was promptly reelected. The event provided the Republicans with a symbol of the violent nature of the South's "civilization."

Democrat James Buchanan elected president of United States, defeating Republican John C. Frémont. Although the Democrats won the election by running another "doughface" and portraying Republicans as extremists who would force the South to secede, the Republicans claimed a "glorious defeat." The party was almost brand-new in 1856, was entirely sectional, and ran a political novice. Nonetheless, it won 114 electoral votes and all but five of the northern states. The party's strength showed the sectional nature of the new party system.

1857 *Dred Scott* decision declares that African Americans have no constitutional rights, that Congress cannot exclude slavery in the territories, and that the Missouri Compromise is unconstitutional. The *Dred Scott* decision involved a slave who sued for his freedom on the grounds that he had lived in the free territory of Wisconsin. The Supreme Court, headed by the ultraconservative Chief Justice Roger B. Taney, used the case to settle the issue of slavery in the territories. However, the ruling inflamed northern public opinion by overturning popular sovereignty and making it virtually impossible to ban slavery in the territories. It also damaged the Democrats, who could no longer use the doctrine's ambiguity to hold their northern and southern wings together.

Nation experiences economic downturn, panic of 1857. Northeastern businesses and industries suffered disproportionately in the downturn, and many Northerners blamed the southern-dominated Congress for the economic difficulties the nation faced. In particular, they pointed to tariff duties, which had been reduced to their lowest levels in the nineteenth century a few months earlier. They saw this as an invitation for foreign competition to ravage the northern economy, while Southerners escaped hardship due to high cotton prices.

1858 In Illinois senatorial campaign, Abraham Lincoln and Stephen A. Douglas debate slavery; Douglas defeats Lincoln for Senate seat. The Lincoln-Douglas debates revolved around the central issue facing the nation: slavery and freedom. Lincoln challenged Douglas's support of popular sovereignty, particularly in light of the *Dred Scott* decision; Douglas argued that settlers could still exclude slavery by not protecting it and termed Lincoln an abolitionist. Douglas won the election because the Illinois legislature chose the state's senators and Democrats had a slight majority in that body. The debates thrust Lincoln and the Republicans into the national spotlight.

1859 October 16. John Brown's attempt to foment slave uprising in Harpers Ferry, Virginia, further alienates South and moves nation toward war. While John Brown's life was something of a failure, he died with dignity and a show of principle that aroused respect and admiration among a minority of Northerners. This was enough to convince Southerners that all Northerners who opposed slavery were bloodthirsty, despite the fact that most publicly denounced Brown's use of violence. The incident increased Southern fears of a Republican victory in the 1860 presidential election.

1860 Republican Abraham Lincoln elected president in four-way race that divides electorate along sectional lines. Southern Democrats from the Lower South walked out of the presidential nominating convention when it voted in favor of a platform that did not include a federal slave code. They met separately and nominated their own candidate, John C. Breckinridge of Tennessee; the northern Democrats nominated Stephen Douglas; pro-Union southern Democrats nominated John Bell of Tennessee; and the Republicans nominated Abraham Lincoln. The election broke into two two-way contests: Lincoln's name was not even on the ballot in ten of the fifteen slave states. Lincoln won with 39 percent of the popular vote and 180 electoral votes, and his election convinced Southerners that they no longer had the political clout to protect themselves within the Union.

December 20. South Carolina secedes from Union. South Carolina was the first state to secede and the only one to vote for secession overwhelmingly. In most Southern states, the vote was close; the eight states of the Upper South, which had a smaller stake in slavery, did not secede until after Lincoln's inauguration.

Representatives of seven southern states, meeting in Montgomery, Alabama, form Confederate States of America. The Confederate States of America elected Jefferson Davis as president and Alexander Stephens, who was not a supporter of secession, as vice president. James Buchanan, who was still the president, stated that secession was illegal, but that he could not stop it. Congressional attempts at compromise failed as well; they were not supported by Republicans or Southerners, who no longer focused on the territorial issue.

## *Chronology Questions* Choose the letter of the best answer.

1. What is the correct order for the following events?
   1. Senator Henry Clay proposes the Omnibus Bill to avert a national crisis over slavery.
   2. The Wilmot Proviso proposes barring slavery from all lands acquired from Mexico.
   3. Opponents of the expansion of slavery found the Free-Soil Party.
   4. Senator Lewis Cass proposes the doctrine of popular sovereignty.

   a. 4, 2, 1, 3
   b. 2, 4, 3, 1
   c. 3, 1, 4, 2
   d. 4, 1, 3, 2

2. In 1852
   a. John C. Calhoun challenged the Wilmot Proviso.
   b. the American Party emerged.
   c. Harriet Beecher Stowe's antislavery novel *Uncle Tom's Cabin* was published.
   d. the nation experienced a severe economic downturn.

3. The *Dred Scott* decision declaring that African Americans had no constitutional rights was made in
   a. 1846.
   b. 1850.
   c. 1857.
   d. 1861.

4. The Lincoln-Douglas debates that pushed Abraham Lincoln and the Republican Party into the national spotlight took place in
   a. 1848.
   b. 1852.
   c. 1858.
   d. 1860.

5. In 1848, the opponents of the expansion of slavery founded the
   a. Free-Soil Party.
   b. Republican Party.
   c. Know-Nothing Party.
   d. Conscience Whigs.

6. What is the correct order for the following events?
   1. Whig Zachary Taylor is elected president, defeating Democrat Lewis Cass and Free-Soiler Martin Van Buren.
   2. Republican Abraham Lincoln is elected president in a four-way race that divides the country along sectional lines.
   3. Democrat Franklin Pierce is elected president, defeating Whig Winfield Scott.
   4. Democrat James Buchanan is elected president, defeating Republican John C. Frémont.

   a. 3, 1, 2, 4
   b. 1, 3, 4, 2
   c. 4, 1, 2, 3
   d. 1, 2, 4, 3

7. Representatives from seven southern states met in Montgomery, Alabama, and formed the Confederate States of America in
   a. 1847.
   b. 1853.
   c. 1859.
   d. 1861.

8. Which one of the following did not occur in 1856?
   a. South Carolina Representative Preston Brooks assaulted Massachusetts Senator Charles Sumner.
   b. Armed violence broke out between proslavery and antislavery forces in Kansas.
   c. John Brown attempted to foment a slave uprising in Harpers Ferry, Virginia.
   d. Democrat James Buchanan was elected president of the United States.

9. What is the correct order for the following events?
   1. Armed conflict between proslavery and antislavery settlers erupts in Kansas.
   2. The Kansas-Nebraska Act opens the Kansas and Nebraska territories to popular sovereignty.
   3. The Gadsden Purchase adds 45,000 square miles of territory to the United States.
   4. The Compromise of 1850 passes Congress and is signed into law.

   a. 3, 4, 2, 1
   b. 4, 2, 1, 3
   c. 1, 4, 2, 3
   d. 2, 1, 3, 4

10. South Carolina became the first state to secede from the Union in December
    a. 1846.
    b. 1852.
    c. 1856.
    d. 1860.

***Defining Terms*** Match each term with the correct definition.

Cotton Whigs
New England Emigrant Aid Company
Conscience Whigs
federal slave code
Wilmot Proviso
Bleeding Kansas
Gadsden Purchase
Omnibus Bill
John C. Frémont
Freeport Doctrine
Free-Soil Party
Know-Nothings
Fugitive Slave Act

secession winter
Republican Party
Shadrach
Kansas-Nebraska Act
"glorious defeat"
Alexander Stephens
Sack of Lawrence
Constitutional Union Party
John Brown
popular sovereignty
*Uncle Tom's Cabim*
*Dred Scott* decision

1. Proposed legislation that would make slavery illegal in all lands acquired from the Mexican War. Proposed by a Democratic representative from Pennsylvania, the proposal was popular among Northerners for a variety of reasons, including principled opposition to slavery, the desire to reduce southern political power, and the hope of keeping the territories free of all black residents. It inspired outrage among Southerners, who saw it as an insult. Wilmot Proviso

2. The idea that people who actually settled in a territory should determine whether slavery would be allowed. This proposal was made by Democratic Senator Lewis Cass, who placed it in the tradition of local self-government. In reality, its ambiguity provided its national appeal: Northerners believed that the issue of slavery would be determined with the first territorial legislature, while Southerners thought that it would not be settled until a territory applied for statehood. Popular sovereignty

3. Conservative northern Whigs—many of them textile mill owners—who sought to hold the Whig Party together by compromising with Southerners on the issue of territorial slavery in the election of 1848. Cotton Whigs

4. The party created in 1848 by antislavery Democrats and antislavery Whigs. The group nominated Democrat Martin Van Buren for president and Whig Charles Francis Adams for vice president and ran on the slogan "Free soil, free speech, free labor, and free men." The party did not carry a single state but did bring the issue of slavery to the forefront of the election, despite the attempts of the established parties to avoid it. Free-Soil party

5. Kentucky Senator Henry Clay's attempt to settle the issue of slavery in the territories by offering a number of measures that he felt made concessions to both the North and the South. He proposed letting California into the Union as a free state but settling the issue of slavery in Utah and New Mexico by means of popular sovereignty; requiring Texas to maintain its current boundary with New Mexico but having the federal government resume its preannexation debt; and abolishing the slave trade in Washington, D.C., but passing a more effective fugitive slave law. The strategy of bundling the measures together failed because Free-Soilers, Conscience Whigs, and proslavery Southerners refused to vote for the measures they did not like. In the end, the legislation passed only when it was separated into its component parts by Stephen A. Douglas of Illinois. Omnibus Bill

6. The 1850 act that made it easier for slaveholders to seize alleged runaways. By the stipulations of the new law, a slave owner or his representative had only to swear in front of a court-appointed commissioner that a slave was in fact his; the commissioner earned ten dollars for every returned slave and five for each black who was set free. To Northerners, the most irritating part of the law was that it forced all citizens to assist officials in apprehending runaways, a role that many did not like. The law radicalized Northerners, especially in New England. Fugitive slave act

7. A runaway slave who in 1851 was seized from federal marshals by an angry Boston crowd and whisked away to Montreal, Canada. Rescues like this were rare but demonstrated the hostility of Northerners toward the 1850 Fugitive Slave Act. Shadrach

8. Harriet Beecher Stowe's 1852 antislavery novel. The book had a galvanizing effect on northern public opinion; it brought the human suffering imposed by slavery to life and became a blockbuster, selling 300,000 copies in its first year of publication. Southerners interpreted the novel's popularity as evidence of the North's lack of sympathy for the slave system. Uncle Tom's cabin

9. Part of President Pierce's attempt to shift national attention away from slavery and toward territorial expansion. In 1853, he sent James Gadsden to negotiate a $15 million purchase of 45,000 square miles of land south of the Gila River in Arizona and New Mexico, which was to be used as the route for a possible transcontinental railroad. The purchase was successful, but it reopened the issue of slavery as northern and southern cities fought to be named as the eastern terminus of the line. Gadsden purchase

10. Stephen Douglas's 1854 legislation for organizing the Nebraska territory. The bill raised controversy because, to win Southern support, Douglas revoked the Missouri Compromise and threw the territory, which was north of the 36° 30′ line, open to popular sovereignty. Kansas-Nebraska Act

11. Antislavery Whigs who saw slavery as a moral blight on the nation. By 1852, they had gained a majority in the Whig Party, a development that made it impossible for the Whigs to maintain their national standing. Conscience Whigs

12. A nativist political party that developed in the mid-1850s in response to the immigration of Roman Catholics from Germany and Ireland. Most immigrants entered the Democratic Party, which was seen as being more tolerant of newcomers than the Whigs. Recruits to the party swore never to vote for foreign-born or Roman Catholic candidates and to reveal no information about the party—hence the name. They enjoyed a string of electoral success in 1854 and 1855 and then collapsed when leaders demanded the endorsement of the Kansas-Nebraska Act in 1856. Know-nothings

13. A political party formed by political dissidents who opposed the Kansas-Nebraska Act and the extension of slavery into the territories. They drew on northern values and beliefs, arguing that the slave system degraded white workers by associating work with servility and blacks and maintaining that slaveholders were aggressively spreading the system throughout the nation. They became the primary challengers to the Democratic Party. Republican Party

14. The first Republican presidential candidate, running in 1856 against Democrat James Buchanan and Know-Nothing Millard Fillmore. He was a soldier and adventurer and politically inexperienced; he relied on his wife Jessie's considerable political savvy. John C. Fremont

15. The Republican loss of the presidential campaign of 1856. They interpreted it as a victory because despite being a new party and running a politically inexperienced candidate, they carried all but five of the northern states and won 114 electoral votes. "glorious defeat"

16. A New England antislavery group that sponsored 1,240 free-soil settlers in Kansas in 1854 and 1855. The application of popular sovereignty to the territory left its status as a free or slave state in doubt; both proslavery and antislavery groups tried to shape the territory by seeding it with sympathetic settlers. New England Emigrant Aid company

17. The name given to Kansas after corrupt territorial elections led to the creation of two competing governments, one of them proslavery and one of them antislavery. The violence that erupted in the territory in 1856 gave Republicans evidence that an aggressive slave power was indeed trying to spread the slave system throughout the territories. Bleeding Kansas

18. The first real fighting in Kansas, which broke out on May 21, 1856, when proslavery men entered the free-soil town of Lawrence. Only one man died—a proslavery raider who was killed when a burning wall collapsed—but the event flamed northern opinion and inspired John Brown to retaliate by killing proslavery settlers along the Pottawatomie Creek. It inaugurated a wave of guerrilla warfare that engulfed the territory. Sack of Lawrence

19. The 1857 Supreme Court decision that ruled that African Americans were not citizens and had no constitutional rights; it also declared that Congress could not prohibit slavery in the territories and that the Missouri Compromise was unconstitutional. The decision cut the ground from beneath the Republican Party by making its program of federal exclusion of slavery from the territories unconstitutional and undermined popular sovereignty by making it impossible to ban slavery in a territory until it wrote a constitution and applied for statehood. Dred Scott decision

20. Stephen A. Douglas's contention, made in Freeport, Illinois, during his 1858 debates with Abraham Lincoln, that popular sovereignty could still work; he maintained that settlers could keep slavery out of a territory by refusing to pass the laws that would protect it. Southerners condemned the doctrine, which they saw as a repudiation of the victory they had won with the *Dred Scott* decision. Freeport doctrine

21. A radical abolitionist who attempted to start a slave rebellion by raiding a federal arsenal at Harpers Ferry, Virginia, in 1859. While his plan failed, he died with dignity when he was hanged and made a ringing statement of principle that excited admiration among a minority of Northerners. Southerners increasingly conflated his admirers with all antislavery Northerners, even though the vast majority did not approve of the raid. This inability to distinguish between radical and moderate antislavery Northerners contributed to the southern fear of a Republican presidential victory. John Brown

22. A demand made by Mississippi senator Jefferson Davis, who argued that Congress could not only not prohibit slavery but had to offer it special protection. The Democratic nominating convention of 1860 fell apart when delegates voted against a platform containing a federal slave code. Federal slave code

23. A party formed in 1860 by John J. Crittenden of Kentucky and other southern moderates after breakaway Southern Democrats chose to run their presidential candidate on a radical southern rights platform. The moderates wanted to provide southern voters with a Union choice; they adopted a platform that made a vague commitment to the Union, the Constitution, and the enforcement of the law. Constitutional Union Party

24. A former Congressman from Georgia who argued against secession in the winter of 1860 to 1861. He believed that the South should not secede just because a Republican had been elected president and felt that the disruptions that would occur in the case of war would be more damaging to slavery than a Republican administration. Alexander Stephens

25. The period between Lincoln's election and inauguration, during which seven Lower South states seceded from the Union. Secession was not an automatic decision in most states: only South Carolina supported it overwhelmingly. Moreover, the states of the Upper South, which had less invested in slavery, were much more cautious about leaving the Union. Secession winter

## Chapter Review

### *Multiple-Choice* Choose the letter of the best answer.

1. When the war with Mexico ended in 1848, Congress had
   a. voted to prohibit slavery in the territories the United States gained.
   b. voted to allow slavery in the territories the United States gained.
   c. extended the Missouri Compromise line.
   d. not resolved the status of slavery in the territories the United States gained.

2. In the 1840s and 1850s, most Americans were concerned that slavery was
   a. immoral.
   b. becoming more widespread in the South.
   c. resulting in slave rebellions.
   d. expanding into areas where it did not exist.

3. Some Democratic politicians in the northern states opposed the extension of slavery into the land gained from the war with Mexico because they
   a. felt sympathy for the plight of slaves.
   b. feared that the issue would allow Whigs to pick up votes.
   c. did not have a strong southern wing.
   d. thought that slavery was harmful to ordinary white Americans.

4. Many northern voters in the 1840s and 1850s did not want slavery to expand due to their
   a. strong Protestant beliefs.
   b. belief that the slave system discouraged industrialization.
   c. desire to destroy the existing political parties.
   d. fear of increased southern political power.

5. In the debate over the Wilmot Proviso, John C. Calhoun contended that Congress did not have the authority to ban slavery in the territories because
   a. such a move would be unfair to the South.
   b. the Constitution specifically made such a measure illegal.
   c. southern congressmen would block the motion.
   d. Congress could not deprive any state of equal rights in the nation's territories.

6. The most attractive feature of Lewis Cass's doctrine of popular sovereignty was that it
   a. relied on a national vote to determine the issue of slavery in the territories.
   b. was ambiguous about the moment at which slavery's fate would be decided.
   c. had no support among northern voters.
   d. was opposed by southern congressmen.

7. The 1848 congressional territorial debate made it obvious that
   a. both the Whigs and the Democrats had antislavery factions.
   b. both the Whigs and the Democrats had become entirely sectionalized.
   c. the Whigs were united against slavery.
   d. the Democrats were united behind slavery.

8. The Free-Soil Party's 1848 presidential platform called for
   a. no slavery in the western territories.
   b. land to be given to settlers at no charge.
   c. a policy of popular sovereignty in the territories.
   d. the conquest of more western land.

9. The issue of slavery in the territories erupted in Congress in 1849 after President Taylor
   a. publicly supported the Wilmot Proviso.
   b. manumitted all of his slaves.
   c. switched to the Free-Soil party.
   d. encouraged California and New Mexico to apply for admission to the Union.

10. Which one of the following was not part of Henry Clay's Omnibus Bill?
    a. Admitting California as a free state and organizing the rest of the Southwest without restrictions on slavery
    b. Forbidding Congress to interfere with the interstate slave trade and resuming the international trade
    c. Requiring Texas to abandon its claims to parts of New Mexico but assuming its preannexation debt
    d. Ablishing the slave trade in Washington, D.C., but confirming slavery's existence there

11. Senator Stephen A. Douglas of Illinois managed to pass the Compromise of 1850 by
    a. breaking Henry Clay's Omnibus Bill into its various parts.
    b. browbeating Democrats into voting for Henry Clay's Omnibus Bill.
    c. bribing congressmen to vote for Henry Clay's Omnibus Bill.
    d. appealing to national unity.

12. The Compromise of 1850 was
    a. passed in the spirit of conciliation.
    b. able to resolve a lot of the conflict over slavery.
    c. not a true compromise at all.
    d. a complete failure.

13. In the years before the Civil War, most Americans maintained that the Constitution had left the issue of slavery to _____ to decide.
    a. the Supreme Court
    b. the president
    c. individual voters
    d. the individual states

14.. The debate over slavery in the 1840s and 1850s revolved around how much authority _____ had over western territories.
    a. Congress
    b. territorial governments
    c. settlers
    d. state governments

15. David Wilmot of Pennsylvania modeled the Wilmot Proviso after the _____, which banned slavery in American territory north of the Ohio River.
    a. Missouri Compromise
    b. Louisiana Purchase
    c. Constitution
    d. Northwest Ordinance of 1787

16. The Wilmot Proviso was also called the _____ Proviso.
    a. Black Man's
    b. White Man's
    c. Slave's
    d. Southerner's

17. Southern leaders opposed the Wilmot Proviso because they felt that they needed _____ to protect their region's interests.
    a. special economic treatment
    b. to spread slavery to the North
    c. political parity with the North
    d. lower tariffs

18. As a compromise solution in the debate over the Wilmot Proviso, Senator Lewis Cass proposed the doctrine of _____.
    a. popular sovereignty
    b. extending the Missouri Compromise line
    c. free soil
    d. equality of power

19. In the presidential election of 1848, the Whigs dealt with the issue of slavery by _____.
    a. ejecting the Conscience Whigs
    b. championing popular sovereignty
    c. nominating an abolitionist
    d. refusing to adopt a party platform

20. In 1848, _____ joined together to found the Free-Soil Party.
    a. economic radicals
    b. Southerners and Northerners
    c. proslavery Whigs and Democrats
    d. antislavery Whigs and Democrats

21. Henry Clay believed that his Omnibus Bill would pass because most congressmen wanted to _____.
    a. compromise on the issue of slavery.
    b. guarantee the existence of slavery in the West.
    c. debate issues other than slavery.
    d. protect his reputation as a legislator.

22. The Compromise of 1850 passed because Stephen A. Douglas allied _____ to gain a majority for each measure.
    a. extremists from both sides
    b. large blocks of Northerners and Southerners
    c. compromisers with larger blocks of Northerners and Southerners
    d. southern Whigs and southern Democrats

23. The issue that undermined the Compromise of 1850s was
    a. California statehood.
    b. runaway slaves in New England.
    c. the assumption of Texan debts.
    d. the ending of the slave trade in Washington, D.C.

24. Starting in the 1830s, northern states had started to provide fugitive slaves with protection from their owners by means of
    a. personal liberty laws.
    b. private bodyguards.
    c. publicly funded transit to Canada.
    d. laws preventing slaveholders from entering free states.

25. The Fugitive Slave Act of 1850 allowed the seizure of alleged slaves after a slaveholder or his agent
    a. and other witnesses identified the slave as his.
    b. paid a substantial fee to the court.
    c. provided physical evidence of ownership.
    d. appeared before an appointed commissioner and swore the slave was his.

26. To Northerners, the most appalling aspect of the Fugitive Slave Act of 1850 was that it
    a. fined communities that would not enforce the legislation.
    b. stipulated that all citizens had to help officials catch runaways.
    c. had passed with northern support.
    d. benefited wealthy slaveholders.

27. Moderate northern and southern politicians worried that if the Fugitive Slave Law were not enforced,
    a. more southern slaves would run away.
    b. the slave system would crumble.
    c. white Southerners would become more radical in their defense of slavery.
    d. white Northerners would make greater demands for total abolition.

28. A significant number of Northerners were turned against slavery in the 1850s by
    a. their religious scruples.
    b. new information about the domestic slave trade.
    c. a popular novel.
    d. slave narratives.

29. Responses to Harriet Beecher Stowe's *Uncle Tom's Cabin* varied according to
    a. sex: it was much more popular with women than men.
    b. age: older people liked it better than younger ones.
    c. religion: Catholics were not as fond of the book as evangelical Protestants.
    d. geography: Southerners hated it, while Northerners loved it.

30. Franklin Pierce, the Democratic presidential candidate in 1852, was nominated largely because he
    a. had a stellar congressional record.
    b. was sympathetic to Southerners' views on public issues.
    c. was a well-known military hero.
    d. was extremely popular with northern voters.

31. President Pierce's attempts to purchase Cuba in the early 1850s had the effect of
    a. galvanizing the opposition of antislavery Northerners.
    b. causing Southerners to bankroll a private invasion of the island.
    c. making Cuba into an American protectorate.
    d. inspiring fresh enthusiasm for Manifest Destiny.

32. The 1853 Gadsden Purchase, which involved buying 45,000 square miles of territory from Mexico, stemmed from the desire to
    a. subject all of Mexico to American rule.
    b. convert the area's Indians to evangelical Protestantism.
    c. build a transcontinental railroad to California.
    d. spread slavery further into the Southwest.

33. Stephen A. Douglas's Kansas-Nebraska Act was controversial because it required
    a. the new territories to allow slavery.
    b. the new territories not to allow slavery.
    c. land that was "permanently" granted to Indians to be given to whites.
    d. the Missouri Compromise line to be repealed.

34. Stephen A. Douglas's 1854 bill to organize the Nebraska territory passed after
    a. receiving overwhelming support from both northern and southern congressmen.
    b. the Whigs decided that it was a reasonable measure.
    c. receiving support from most southern congressmen and half of the Democratic northern congressmen.
    d. the Democratic Party closed its sectional rifts and rallied behind it.

35. Northerners were most offended by the _____ in the Compromise of 1850.
    a. adoption of popular sovereignty in Utah and New Mexico
    b. assumption of Texas's debts
    c. confirmation of slavery in Washington, D.C.
    d. Fugitive Slave Act

36. Every year a few hundred slaves _____ through the "underground railroad," a series of secret hideouts.
    a. forged freedom papers
    b. received an education
    c. met and conspired to rebel
    d. escaped to Canada

37. In February 1851, angry Bostonians protected a runaway slave named Shadrach by _____.
    a. barring his owner from entering the city
    b. refusing to convict him in a jury trial
    c. threatening federal marshals with legal action
    d. seizing him from a courtroom and helping him escape

38. The enforcement of the Fugitive Slave Act _____ Northerners.
    a. made radical abolitionists out of
    b. thoroughly demoralized
    c. had no effect on
    d. had a radicalizing effect on

39. Harriet Beecher Stowe's novel *Uncle Tom's Cabin* was _____.
    a. a narrative written by slaves
    b. America's first literary blockbuster
    c. a realistic depiction of slave life
    d. popular in the South

40. Harriet Beecher Stowe used her novel *Uncle Tom's Cabin* to _____ for tolerating slavery.
    a. congratulate Southerners
    b. blame Southerners alone
    c. congratulate all Americans
    d. condemn all Americans

41. Franklin Pierce, the Democratic presidential candidate in 1852, was a _____.
    a. Southerner with northern sympathies
    b. Northerner with southern sympathies
    c. radical abolitionist
    d. fire-eating southern radical

42. President Pierce attempted to leave sectional controversy behind by focusing on _____ instead.
    a. economic policy
    b. foreign expansion
    c. European conflicts
    d. electoral reform

43. Southerners initially refused to support Stephen A. Douglas's bill for the organization of the Nebraska Territory because the territory was _____.
    a. owned by Indians
    b. closed to slavery
    c. not suited to cotton cultivation
    d. dominated by abolitionists

44. Stephen A. Douglas's bill for the organization of the Nebraska Territory raised a storm of controversy by _____.
    a. revoking the Missouri Compromise
    b. revoking the principle of popular sovereignty
    c. gaining the support of both Democrats and Whigs
    d. guaranteeing slavery in the territory

45. The most crucial result of the 1854 Kansas-Nebraska Act was that it
    a. boosted the strength of the Whig Party.
    b. helped the popularity of the Democratic Party in the North.
    c. made Kansas into a slave state.
    d. realigned the nation's two major political parties.

46. The political system that developed in the mid-1850s was dominated by
    a. two big national parties.
    b. numerous splinter parties with limited appeal.
    c. two big sectional parties.
    d. southern Democrats.

47. The new political party system of the 1850s
    a. was split between Easterners and Westerners.
    b. muffled moral issues like slavery.
    c. made political compromise difficult.
    d. encouraged political compromise.

48. The Whig Party's showing in the presidential election of 1852 demonstrated that it
    a. did not need southern support to win elections.
    b. was placating its southern wing at the expense of its northern wing.
    c. needed to find better candidates.
    d. no longer had strong national support.

49. In the 1850s, the Democrats remained relatively united by
    a. ejecting antislavery party members.
    b. refusing to discuss the issue of slavery.
    c. supporting popular sovereignty.
    d. championing a free-soil west.

50. Democrats remained the dominant party throughout the 1850s because they
    a. gained support in the South.
    b. gained support in the North.
    c. had no competition.
    d. took popular stands on most major political issues.

51. The Know-Nothing Party that emerged in the 1850s was organized around the split between
    a. the educated and the uneducated.
    b. Roman Catholic immigrants and native Protestants.
    c. slaveholding Southerners and nonslaveholding Northerners.
    d. landowners and urban dwellers.

52. The Republican Party developed in the 1850s around the issue of
    a. civil rights for free blacks.
    b. religious freedom.
    c. tax policies that favored the South.
    d. slavery in the territories.

53. According to Republicans, slavery was a problem because it
    a. discriminated against blacks.
    b. benefited only a small number of white Southerners.
    c. degraded white labor by associating work with blacks and servility.
    d. gave Southerners extra political clout.

54. The only real issue in the presidential election of 1856 was the
    a. extension of slavery into the territories.
    b. abolition of slavery in the South.
    c. transcontinental railroad.
    d. immigration of Roman Catholics.

55. In the presidential election of 1856, Democrats portrayed Republicans as
    a. extremists who risked pushing the South out of the Union.
    b. supporters of the Kansas-Nebraska Act.
    c. supporters of popular sovereignty.
    d. Whigs under another name.

56. The presidential election of 1856 made it obvious that
    a. sectionalism had created a new party system.
    b. nativism was still a potent national issue.
    c. the Democrats were strongly united.
    d. the Whigs still had some national influence.

57. Prior to the 1850s, the party system forced Whigs and Democrats to_____ to achieve national strength.
    a. ignore controversial issues
    b. cater to one section or the other
    c. compromise between their northern and southern wings
    d. succumb to strict party discipline

58. While the Whigs began to experience internal problems as early as the Mexican War, the Party's disintegration began in 1849 and 1850 when Whig president Zachary Taylor sponsored a plan to _____.
    a. revive the Wilmot Proviso
    b. revoke the Kansas-Nebraska Act
    c. admit California to the Union under popular sovereignty
    d. admit California to the Union as a free state

59. The Kansas-Nebraska Act _____ in the free states.
    a. bolstered the fortunes of the Whigs
    b. created sympathy for the South
    c. destroyed the dominance of the Democratic Party
    d. increased the dominance of the Democratic Party

60. Throughout the 1850s, the Democrats remained in national power by _____.
    a. blacklisting extremists
    b. avoiding the issue of the expansion of slavery
    c. directly confronting the problem of slavery
    d. blatantly lying to voters

61. The Know-Nothing Party was organized by _____ in the early 1850s.
    a. abolitionists
    b. nativists
    c. temperance activists
    d. Democrats

62. The Know-Nothings experienced their greatest success in _____, a favorite destination of Irish immigrants, in the mid-1850s.
    a. New York
    b. Massachusetts
    c. Delaware
    d. Pennsylvania

63. In the mid-1850s, Republicans contended that slave owners planned to _____ through the Democratic Party.
    a. expand the slave system
    b. enslave whites
    c. destroy the northern economy
    d. make immigration illegal

64. In 1856, the _____ came apart after party leaders insisted on a platform endorsing the Kansas-Nebraska Act.
    a. Whig Party
    b. Know-Nothing Party
    c. Democratic Party
    d. Republican Party

65. In the 1856 presidential election, Republicans adopted a platform that focused on _____.
    a. expanding the primary education system
    b. industrializing the northern states
    c. keeping slavery out of the territories
    d. promoting equal rights for blacks

66. Despite the fact that the Republicans were a _____ party, they made an excellent showing in the 1856 presidential election.
    a. largely southern
    b. nativist
    c. disorganized
    d. brand-new and sectional

67. Unlike in New Mexico and Utah, popular sovereignty in Kansas was controversial because
    a. Kansas was a wealthy region.
    b. Kansas was so far to the north.
    c. people believed Kansas could go either way.
    d. there were already a lot of slaves in Kansas.

68. In 1855, popular sovereignty in Kansas led to
    a. a vindication of Stephen A. Douglas's strategy.
    b. a free-soil electoral victory.
    c. orderly elections that guaranteed the status of slavery.
    d. the formation of two governments.

69. South Carolina representative Preston Brooks's attack on Massachusetts senator Charles Sumner had the effect of
    a. cooling northern denunciations of slavery.
    b. ruining Sumner's political career.
    c. ruining Brooks's political career.
    d. giving the Republican Party a symbol of Southern villainy.

70. Dred Scott based his claim to freedom on
    a. the immorality of the slave system.
    b. his travels and residences in free areas.
    c. the fact that he had purchased his freedom.
    d. his master's intention of freeing him.

71. Chief Justice Roger B. Taney's 1857 decision in the *Dred Scott* case ruled that
    a. blacks were not citizens of the United States.
    b. travel in free territories did not make slaves free.
    c. Congress could not prohibit slavery in the territories.
    d. all of the above.

72. Northern Democrats found the *Dred Scott* decision disturbing because it
    a. undermined popular sovereignty.
    b. discriminated against blacks.
    c. included no dissenting opinions from the Court.
    d. was unopposed by the Democratic president.

73. For Republicans, the *Dred Scott* decision had the effect of
    a. jeopardizing the party's survival.
    b. weakening the party.
    c. strengthening the party.
    d. strengthening the party's radical wing.

74. Abraham Lincoln believed that the Constitution
    a. made slavery illegal everywhere in the United States.
    b. sanctioned slavery where it existed already but intended to contain its spread.
    c. sanctioned the spread of slavery to all parts of the United States.
    d. was silent on the subject of slavery.

75. Like the majority of Republicans, Abraham Lincoln held that slavery was
    a. immoral but that black equality was impractical.
    b. immoral and that black equality was desirable.
    c. not immoral but that it was financially backward.
    d. not immoral but that it undermined white prosperity.

76. Abraham Lincoln convinced Northerners to fight for free soil by appealing to their
    a. humanitarian concern for blacks.
    b. sectional pride.
    c. economic self-interest.
    d. political loyalty.

77. In 1857, Stephen A. Douglas came out against the proslavery Lecompton constitution for Kansas because he
   a. had decided that slavery was wrong.
   b. disliked the southern domination of his party.
   c. wanted to reinstate the Missouri Compromise.
   d. felt it violated the democratic aspect of popular sovereignty.

78. Stephen A. Douglas's Freeport Doctrine took the position that territorial settlers could bar slavery by
   a. passing laws against it.
   b. harassing slave owners.
   c. refusing to protect it.
   d. preventing blacks from entering the territories.

79. Kansas's first territorial government was a proslavery body elected by means of _____.
   a. massive electoral fraud
   b. true popular sovereignty
   c. congressional decree
   d. presidential decree

80. The events in "Bleeding Kansas" provided the Republican Party with evidence that _____.
   a. territorial representatives were all violent men.
   b. slavery and free labor could not coexist
   c. a dangerous, aggressive slave power existed
   d. Stephen A. Douglas was corrupt

81. The 1857 *Dred Scott* decision ruled that blacks could not be _____ the United States.
   a. residents of the free states of
   b. physically punished in
   c. enslaved in
   d. citizens of

82. Justice Benjamin R. Curtis's rebuttal to the *Dred Scott* decision argued that Congress had the ability to _____.
   a. legislate for the territories
   b. end slavery in the South
   c. overturn Supreme Court decisions
   d. ignore the Constitution in the name of "higher law"

83. The *Dred Scott* decision undermined the position of the _____ in the North by taking the ambiguity out of popular sovereignty.
   a. abolitionists
   b. Supreme Court
   c. federal government
   d. Democratic Party

84. Like many former Whigs, in the mid-1850s Abraham Lincoln was not able to _____.
   a. find a political party he liked
   b. get elected to office
   c. support nativists
   d. support the free-soil position

85. Abraham Lincoln believed that free blacks should _____ because whites would not give them full civil and political rights.
   a. get the full protection of the federal government
   b. be forced to leave the country
   c. try to educate white voters
   d. start a race war

86. Northeastern businessmen blamed the panic of 1857 on _____, which they attributed to southern congressmen.
   a. national foreign policy decisions
   b. a reduction in tariff duties
   c. a drop in the international price of cotton
   d. new western land policies

87. Stephen A. Douglas's Freeport Doctrine claimed that settlers in the territories could effectively ban slavery by _____.
   a. refusing to include it in the state constitution
   b. driving out proslavery settlers
   c. not passing laws to protect it
   d. petitioning Congress

88. In his 1858 debates with Stephen A. Douglas, Abraham Lincoln reiterated his belief that slavery was _____ and reaffirmed his faith in white rule.
   a. subject to being ended by Congress
   b. unfair because blacks and whites were equal
   c. a practical solution for cotton and sugarcane production
   d. constitutionally protected where it existed

89. Before the 1850s, Southerners used threats of secession to
   a. reinforce southern nationalism.
   b. reinforce northern opposition.
   c. destroy the Union.
   d. gain concessions within the Union.

90. Most Northerners believed that John Brown's 1859 raid on Harpers Ferry, Virginia, was
   a. undertaken in the name of a bad cause.
   b. a good idea but poorly executed.
   c. a lawless act of unwarranted violence.
   d. a justifiable attack on the slave system.

91. Shortly before the 1860 presidential election, a southern business convention meeting in Nashville, Tennessee, shocked Northerners and many Southerners by calling for
   a. the reopening of the African slave trade.
   b. the abolition of slavery.
   c. the secession of Tennessee from the Union.
   d. high federal tariffs.

92. In 1860, Jefferson Davis of Mississippi presented Congress with an extremely proslavery demand for
   a. a federal slave code in the territories.
   b. the admission of Kansas to the Union as a slave state.
   c. the election of a southern Speaker of the House.
   d. federal protection of the domestic slave trade.

93. The Democratic Party split in 1860 after the nominating convention voted in favor of a platform endorsing
   a. federal noninterference in the territories.
   b. a federal slave code.
   c. popular sovereignty in the territories.
   d. John Brown's raid on Harpers Ferry, Virginia.

94. The southern moderates who formed the Constitutional Union Party in 1860 wanted to provide voters with
   a. a Unionist choice.
   b. an alternative to the Republicans.
   c. a secessionist choice.
   d. an antislavery choice.

95. The Republicans' 1860 presidential platform
   a. supported full civil rights for free blacks.
   b. was built solely around opposition to the spread of slavery.
   c. demanded the abolition of the entire slave system.
   d. defined a broad social and economic agenda that appealed to Northerners.

96. The presidential election of 1860 was unusual in that it
   a. was a four-way contest.
   b. took place after southern states began to secede.
   c. broke along sectional lines into two two-way contests.
   d. was thrown into the House of Representatives.

97. Alexander Stephens of Georgia and other southern moderates opposed secession on the grounds that
   a. it was unconstitutional.
   b. ordinary Southerners opposed it.
   c. slavery was more protected in the Union than outside of it.
   d. the Republicans had the South's interests at heart.

98. Radical Southerners called for secession because they believed that
   a. their minority status meant that they could not defend themselves politically.
   b. Republicans would immediately abolish slavery.
   c. Republicans would legalize slave rebellions.
   d. Republicans would force them to educate their slaves.

99. In most of the states that seceded between December 1860 and February 1861, the vote for separation from the Union was
a. fraudulent.
b. overwhelmingly favorable.
c. close.
d. based on the support of upcountry yeomen.

100. As Deep South states seceded throughout the winter of 1860 to 1861, Congress attempted to reunite the nation by
a. reviving the Missouri Compromise.
b. passing a federal slave code.
c. overturning Lincoln's election.
d. reinterpreting popular sovereignty.

101. By the late 1850s, many Southerners questioned how _____ could hope to maintain control in a democratic government.
a. an economically deprived region
b. a minority section
c. an ill-educated population
d. an unrepublican slaveholding elite

102. When the Republican Party won the presidential election of 1860, many Southerners concluded that _____, so they could not remain within the Union.
a. their slaves would rebel when they heard the news
b. slavery would be abolished immediately
c. the balance of national power had shifted permanently
d. their taxes would rise precipitously

103. Most Northerners _____ John Brown's raid on Harpers Ferry, Virginia.
a. were apathetic about
b. celebrated
c. did not condone
d. did not know about

104. Among the many events that heightened sectional hostility in 1860 was _____.
a. an attack on Senator Charles Sumter
b. the *Dred Scott* case
c. the inability of Congress to choose a Speaker of the House
d. the Lecompton constitution

105. Missisippian Jefferson Davis contributed to the sectional tension of 1860 when he demanded _____, a longstanding goal of proslavery Southerners.
a. the reopening of the African slave trade
b. a federal slave code for the territories
c. the extension of slavery into the North
d. federal subsidies for slave owners

106. In the presidential election of 1860, Republicans _____ to win more northern votes.
a. tried to reconcile with Southerners
b. renounced their antislavery stance
c. broadened their platform
d. demanded a war with the South

107. In the presidential election of 1860, Abraham Lincoln _____ the free states except for New Jersey.
a. swept all of
b. barely won all of the
c. won none of
d. split the votes of all of

108. After Abraham Lincoln's election, Southern Unionists argued that _____ had created the current crisis.
a. Northerners singlehandedly
b. Southerners singlehandedly
c. Democratic incompetence
d. extremists in both the North and the South

109. In the winter of 1860 to 1861, _____ voted overwhelmingly in favor of secession.
a. most Deep South states
b. most Upper South states
c. only South Carolina
d. all of the southern states

110. Abraham Lincoln's inaugural address included a challenge to Southerners on the topic of _____.
a. appointing Northerners to federal posts in the South
b. interfering with slavery where it existed
c. the need to invade the South
d. the inviolability of the Union

***Short Answer*** Write a paragraph response to each question.

1. Why did Northerners support the Wilmot Proviso? What was the source of its appeal?
2. What happened in the presidential election of 1848? How was it influenced by the debate over slavery in the territories?
3. What was the Compromise of 1850? To what extent was it really a compromise?
4. What were the stipulations of the Fugitive Slave Act of 1850? What effect did it have on Northerners?
5. In the presidential election of 1852, how did the parties attempt to overcome the sectional tensions that had hurt them in 1848? How successful were they?
6. What was the Kansas-Nebraska Act? Why was it such a controversial measure?
7. How did popular sovereignty both help and hurt the Democratic Party in the 1840s and 1850s?
8. What was the basic Republican creed when it was organized in the 1850s? What was the early Republican platform, and why was it successful?
9. Why was the presidential election of 1856 called a "glorious defeat" for the Republican Party?
10. Why didn't popular sovereignty work in Kansas in 1856? What occurred as a result of the failure?
11. What were the basic issues in the *Dred Scott* case of 1857? How did the Supreme Court's decision in the case undermine the Democratic Party?
12. What was Stephen A. Douglas's Freeport Doctrine? How did it attempt to address the issues raised by the *Dred Scott* decision? How did Southerners respond to the doctrine?
13. How did Northerners feel about John Brown's 1859 raid on Harpers Ferry, Virginia? How did Southerners feel about it?
14. Why did the Democratic Party collapse in 1860? How did Democrats respond?
15. How did the southern states respond to Lincoln's election in 1860? Was the drive for secession unanimous or immediate?

***Building Historical Skills*** Historians use a variety of sources to think and talk about the past, including maps, illustrations, and written records. Maps provide a variety of different kinds of comparative information in a condensed visual format; reading them requires learning how to sort through this information. To deepen our understanding of the past by supplementing written records, historians frequently interpret material culture, such as a vase or a painting, with techniques borrowed from art history, archaeology, or anthropology. Written records, though familiar as sources, raise their own problems of interpretation. Every document reflects someone's particular perspective or assumptions. It is the historian's task to study and compare each document to other records with other perspectives. The following exercises introduce you to using maps, illustrations, and written documents as sources of information. Use these sources as well as the material in the chapter to think about different themes and topics discussed in the text.

***Map Activity*** Locate the following places on Map 13.3: The Kansas-Nebraska Act, 1854 on page 465 of *The American Promise,* Second Edition.

1. Indian Territory
2. Kansas and Nebraska Territories
3. California
4. Missouri
5. Utah and New Mexico Territories
6. South Carolina

Answer the following questions in a paragraph based on Map 13.3: The Kansas-Nebraska Act, 1854.

**READING THE MAP** How many slave states and how many free states does the map show? Estimate the percentage of territory likely to be settled by slaveholders.

**CONNECTIONS** Who would be more likely to support changes in government legislation to discontinue the Missouri Compromise, slaveholders or free-soil advocates? Why?

**WEB LINKS** To explore the topics discussed in the exercise above, visit the Web links noted below.

"An Act to Organize the Territories of Nebraska and Kansas"
http://www.yale.edu/lawweb/avalon/kanneb.htm

"The Reopening of Slavery Agitation—The Territory of Nebraska"
http://www.furman.edu/~benson/docs/nytkn1.htm

***Visual Activity*** "Fraudulent Voting in Kansas" is a clear indictment of the corruption that marred Kansas's first territorial election. The polling booth itself takes a partisan stance: it is graced with a sign reading "Down with the Abolitionists," which presumably would discourage abolitionists from voting. The men in line are rough, with long hair and scruffy beards, and some are carrying knives and pistols; many of them are in their shirtsleeves, a sign of low status in the mid-nineteenth century. The covered wagon in the background of the picture carries the implication that the men are not even real settlers to the area. They have simply come in from Missouri to undermine the implementation of popular sovereignty. They are receiving their payment in the form of whiskey. The booth is situated such that the whiskey line wraps around into the voting line, implying that voters are being bribed with alcohol and adding to the disreputable nature of the election.

Answer the following questions in a paragraph based on "Fraudulent Voting in Kansas" on page 473 of *The American Promise,* Second Edition.

**READING THE IMAGE** Based on "Fraudulent Voting in Kansas," what kind of people determined the outcome of Kansas's first territorial election?

**CONNECTIONS** Is this image of Kansas's territorial elections an accurate one?

**WEB LINKS** To explore the topics discussed in the exercise above, visit the Web links noted below.

"Bleeding Kansas"
http://www.pbs.org/wgbh/aia/part4/4p2952.html

"Bleeding Kansas Gallery"
http://raven.cc.ukans.edu/carrie/kancoll/galbks.htm

"Kansas Territory: Crucible of American Experience"
http://xroads.virginia.edu/~HYPER/CONTEXTS/Kansas/kansas.html

***Analyzing Sources Activity*** Answer the following questions in a paragraph based on "Documenting the American Promise: Women's Politics" on page 470.

1. Jessie Frémont did not interpret the Republican defeat in Pennsylvania in 1856 as a "glorious defeat." Can you suggest possible reasons why she did not?
2. What legal disabilities for women was the marriage contract of Henry Blackwell and Lucy Stone designed to overcome?
3. On what grounds, according to Harriot Hunt, should women be accorded the vote? Do you agree with her argument? Why or why not?
4. Does Elizabeth Cady Stanton's early version of "dressing for success" make sense? Why or why not?

**WEB LINKS** To explore the topics discussed in the exercise above, visit the Web links noted below.

"Elizabeth Cady Stanton"
http://www.nps.gov/wori/ecs.htm

"Not for Ourselves Alone: The Story of Elizabeth Cady Stanton and Susan B. Anthony"
http://www.pbs.org/stantonanthony/index.html
Choose "Resources."

"Lucy Stone (1818–1893)"
http://www.ccc.oberlin.edu/~EOG/OYTT-images/LucyStone.html

# Answer Key

## Chapter 13: The House Divided, 1846–1861

### *Chapter Overview*

#### *Chronology*

1. b
2. c
3. c
4. c
5. a
6. b
7. d
8. c
9. a
10. d

#### *Defining Terms*

1. Wilmot Proviso
2. popular sovereignty
3. Cotton Whigs
4. Free-Soil Party
5. Omnibus Bill
6. Fugitive Slave Act
7. Shadrach
8. *Uncle Tom's Cabin*
9. Gadsden Purchase
10. Kansas-Nebraska Act
11. Conscience Whigs
12. Know-Nothings
13. Republican Party
14. John C. Frémont
15. "glorious defeat"
16. New England Emigrant Aid Company
17. Bleeding Kansas
18. Sack of Lawrence
19. *Dred Scott* decision
20. Freeport Doctrine
21. John Brown
22. federal slave code
23. Constitutional Union Party
24. Alexander Stephens
25. secession winter

### *Chapter Review*

#### *Multiple-Choice*

1. d
2. d
3. b
4. d
5. d
6. b
7. a
8. a
9. d
10. b
11. a
12. c
13. d
14. a
15. d
16. b
17. c
18. a
19. d
20. d
21. a
22. c
23. b
24. a
25. d
26. b
27. c
28. c
29. d
30. b
31. a
32. c
33. d
34. c
35. d
36. d
37. d
38. d
39. b
40. d
41. b
42. b
43. b
44. a
45. d
46. c
47. c
48. d
49. c
50. a
51. b
52. d
53. c
54. a
55. a
56. a
57. c
58. d
59. c
60. b
61. b
62. b
63. a
64. b
65. c
66. d

67. c
68. d
69. d
70. b
71. d
72. a
73. c
74. b
75. a
76. c
77. d
78. c
79. a
80. c
81. d
82. a
83. d
84. a
85. b
86. b
87. c
88. d
89. d
90. c
91. a
92. a
93. c
94. a
95. d
96. c
97. c
98. a
99. c
100. a
101. b
102. c
103. c
104. c
105. b
106. c
107. a
108. d
109. c
110. d

### *Short Answer*

1. Northerners supported the Wilmot Proviso because many of them, regardless of party affiliation, wanted to keep slavery from spreading outside of the states where it already existed; however, they had many different reasons for wishing to stop slavery's growth. Abolitionists supported the "free-soil" stance because they saw slavery as a sin and wanted to get rid of the institution entirely. Other Northerners were in favor of the Wilmot Proviso because they did not like blacks, whether free or enslaved, and wanted to keep the territories segregated. Northern politicians who disliked southern economic policies hoped to prevent the South from gaining more political power through the addition of new slave states. Northern Democrats saw the measure as a way to support territorial expansion without upsetting their antislavery constituents.
2. In 1848, both parties attempted to elide the contentious topic of slavery. Democrats elected Lewis Cass of Michigan and avoided adopting a platform with a firm position on slavery; Whigs nominated General Zachary Taylor and refused to present a party platform at all. Antislavery elements from both parties rebelled, however, and in the summer of 1848 the two groups joined together in the Free-Soil Party, which nominated dissident Democrat Martin Van Buren for president and antislavery Whig Charles Francis Adams as his running mate. Taylor won the election. Although the Free-Soilers were solidly defeated, their existence demonstrated that the struggle over territorial slavery had the ability to undermine both the Whigs and the Democrats.
3. In 1849, a sectional rift broke out in Congress over President Zachary Taylor's demand that California and New Mexico be admitted to the Union, even as free states, a move that Southerners objected to vociferously. Senator Henry Clay attempted to end the rancor by proposing a series of measures that would balance the interests of the free and slave states. He wanted to admit California as a free state but organize the rest of the southwestern territory without restrictions on slavery; require Texas to give up its claims to parts of New Mexico but have the federal government assume Texas's preannexation debt; and abolish the slave trade in Washington, D.C., but confirm slavery in the capital; reinforce Congress's inability to regulate the interstate slave trade and enact a stronger fugitive slave law. The measures all passed but only because Senator Stephen A. Douglas broke them into their component parts and put together a different majority for each one. Because there had not been real agreement or compromise on the measures, the question of slavery in the territories had only been avoided, not solved.
4. Northerners had already shown their disapproval of fugitive slave laws; they had been appalled by the 1793 fugitive slave law and responded by passing "personal liberty laws" in the 1830s, giving fugitives some legal protection. The 1850 Fugitive Slave Act was stronger than the older version, allowing a slaveholder or his agent to remove an alleged runaway from the North by going before a court-appointed commissioner and swearing that the slave was his. The commissioner had a financial incentive to believe the slaveholder because commissioners received ten dollars for every black returned to slavery but only five dollars for those who were set free. Moreover, every citizen was expected to assist officials in apprehending runaway slaves, and while Northerners were often antiblack, they did not like to be forced into acting as slave catchers. The law had a radicalizing effect on Northerners and increased sectional tensions.
5. In 1852, the Democratic Party came together for Franklin Pierce, a "doughface," or Northern politicians with a sympathetic attitude toward the South. Whigs had more difficulty; deeply divided between Conscience and Cotton factions, they agreed not to renominate the sitting Whig president, Millard Fillmore, but disagreed on fifty-two ballots before they chose General

Winfield Scott of Virginia, a hero of the Mexican War. The Democrats won the election with little difficulty, in large part because the Whigs were so divided. However, as president, Pierce reignited sectional controversy by attempting to acquire Cuba, a move that galvanized antislavery Northerners.

6. The Kansas-Nebraska Act was Senator Stephen A. Douglas's 1854 bill to organize the Nebraska territory, which he hoped would lead to the construction of a Pacific railroad with its eastern terminus in Chicago, in his home state of Illinois. However, Nebraska lay north of the Missouri Compromise line and was thus closed to slavery by the terms of the 1820 Missouri Compromise. To pass the bill, Douglas had to win the support of southern congressmen, many of whom had no interest in helping a northern city win the railroad and did not want to help in the creation of another free state. To gain Southern support, Douglas agreed to repeal the Missouri Compromise and organize the Nebraska territory according to the doctrine of popular sovereignty. This meant that slavery would have a chance to develop in the area, and it reopened the issue of the expansion of slavery, which caused an uproar in the North.

7. While the Whig Party collapsed because it could not find a way to hold its southern and northern wings together, the Democrats were able to use popular sovereignty—the ideal that settlers in a territory should decide on the issue of slavery—to maintain their status as a national party. Yet popular sovereignty did not always work to unify the Democrats. When Stephen A. Douglas applied it to Nebraska, a part of the Louisiana Purchase where slavery had already been barred, northern Democrats were divided. Those who had voted in favor of the Kansas-Nebraska bill largely failed to be reelected the following year. Northern Democratic representation in the House of Representatives declined, and by the mid-1850s the Democrats had become a southern-dominated party.

8. The Republican Party was formed in the mid-1850s in response to the Kansas-Nebraska Act; it brought together people from all different political parties who opposed the extension of slavery into any territory of the United States. Northerners responded favorably to the Republicans because they drew on the basic beliefs and values of the northern public. Republicans contended that the slave labor and free labor were essentially incompatible systems and that the former degraded the latter by associating work with servility. Maintaining that the slave system was oppressive to whites as well as blacks, Republicans pointed to evidence that an aggressive slave power was actively attempting to expand slavery and thus undermine free labor. The Republican argument was very persuasive to a wide range of Northerners.

9. Despite losing the presidential election of 1856, the Republicans won 114 electoral votes and carried all but five northern states. This showing was impressive for several reasons. For one thing, the party was quite new. Also, Republicans had made no move toward incorporating southerners into the party: their platform focused almost exclusively on keeping slavery out of the territories. Moreover, they nominated explorer John C. Frémont, who had virtually no political credentials of his own, although his wife Jessie was the daughter of a Missouri senator and quite politically savvy.

10. Popular sovereignty rested on orderly elections, in which settlers would cast their ballots for or against pro- and antislavery candidates for the territorial legislature. In Kansas, the elections were tainted by the interference of proslavery Missourians who, with the encouragement of a Missouri senator, voted illegally in the territorial elections and instituted a radically proslavery government endorsed by President Pierce. Unhappy with the results of the election, free-state Kansans elected their own legislature. In May of 1856 fighting broke out, and guerrilla warfare engulfed the territory.

11. Dred Scott was a slave who sued for his own and his family's freedom on the grounds that his master had taken them to live first in a free state and then in a free territory. The Supreme Court's majority decision ruled that Scott could not claim that his constitutional rights had been violated by his enslavement because no black person, whether free or enslaved, was a citizen. The ruling also held that the laws of Scott's home state of Missouri determined his status, that Congress could not prohibit slavery in the territories, and that the Missouri Compromise was unconstitutional. The decision harmed the Democrats by casting doubts on the effectiveness of popular sovereignty, the idea that had held the northern and southern factions in the party together; if Congress could not ban slavery, neither could a territorial government, which was essentially a creation of Congress. Slavery could not be excluded until a state constitution had been drafted, by which time the system could already have taken root.

12. Stephen A. Douglas formulated the Freeport Doctrine at a debate with Abraham Lincoln in 1858. Lincoln attempted to force Douglas to admit that the *Dred Scott* decision had made his solution to slavery in the territories—popular sovereignty—untenable. Douglas responded

with the argument that while settlers could not pass legislation barring slavery, they could keep it out of a territory by refusing to enact protective laws. Southerners were appalled by the Freeport Doctrine, which they saw as Douglas's attempt to deny them the victory they had gained with the *Dred Scott* decision by allowing settlers to ban slavery from a territory.

13. The majority of Northerners were opposed to the spread of slavery, but they did not approve of John Brown's attempt to incite a violent southern slave rebellion. However, Brown went to his execution with dignity, and a handful of writers and abolitionists, including Ralph Waldo Emerson, Henry David Thoreau, and William Lloyd Garrison, celebrated him as a model of principle and humanity. Southerners almost universally saw Brown as a bloodthirsty murderer, and they increasingly conflated moderate antislavery Northerners with those who supported Brown and his cause. This inability to distinguish between the two heightened sectional animosity and estrangement and contributed to Southern paranoia at the possibility of a Republican president.
14. In 1860, the Democratic convention to nominate a presidential candidate fell apart when southern fire-eaters demanded a platform that included a federal slave code to protect slavery in the territories. Northern Democrats were well aware that their constituents would not accept the measure. When two platforms, one with a slave code and one with popular sovereignty, were voted on, the latter won, causing southern Democrats to walk out of the convention. The southern Democrats met separately and nominated a proslavery Southerner and adopted a platform with a federal slave code. However, southern moderates nominated a Unionist candidate, while Northerners nominated Stephan A. Douglas and a platform advocating congressional noninterference in the territories.
15. Most southern whites were united about the need to defend the slave system and protect their ability to take slaves into the territories, but they did not agree about whether the presence of a Republican in the White House was an immediate threat to their security. The only state to vote overwhelmingly in favor of secession was South Carolina, which left the Union on December 20, 1860. The vote in the other Deep South states was close, with a great deal of opposition from upcountry farmers. The Upper South was even more cautious; its residents had a smaller stake in slavery, and they did not secede until after Abraham Lincoln's inauguration.

### *Map Activity*

Reading the Map: In 1854, there were sixteen free states and fifteen slave states. There were also five open territories; the Washington, Oregon, and Minnesota territories were free and the Nebraska and Kansas and Utah and New Mexico territories were open to slavery. Under the terms of the Missouri Compromise, perhaps a quarter of the United States's territories could have turned into slave states, based on the restrictions of the Missouri Compromise that banned slavery above the southern border of Missouri and so would leave only half of the Utah and New Mexico territories as potential slave territory. However, even with the revocation of the Missouri Compromise line, most Americans did not expect that Utah or New Mexico would be useful for plantation agriculture. Instead, slaveholders set their sights on the Kansas and Nebraska territories, which constituted about half of the remaining territorial land.

Connections: Slaveholders had more reasons to want to discontinue the Missouri Compromise than Free-Soil advocates. With the admission of California to the Union as a free state, the amount of land available to turn into slave states was diminished to perhaps a quarter of the remaining territory. As long as the Missouri Compromise remained in effect, slave states were virtually guaranteed to lose their numerical parity with the free states and thus their ability to wield influence in the national government. With the withdrawal of the Missouri Compromise, however, slave states could conceivably spread into northern areas from which they had previously been barred.

### *Visual Activity*

Reading the Image: The cartoonist who drew "Fraudulent Voting in Kansas" believed that Kansas's elections had been determined by ruffians. The men are coarse and informal, and they are not treating the elections as a solemn affair. Instead, they line up at the whiskey stand to drink before they vote, and they wave their hats around in a celebratory manner when they are done. Moreover, they are potentially violent. Many of them are carrying knives and guns, and their eagerness to get at the whiskey indicates that they have little self-control.

Connections: The illustrator who drew this cartoon was obviously opposed to the proslavery government in Kansas and believed that it was instituted under corrupt circumstances. Certainly Missouri politicians encouraged ruffians from their state to invade Kansas and throw the election to proslavery forces. Moreover, many expressed their willingness to use violence to stop antislavery settlers from expressing their opinions at the polls. The one thing that the cartoon does not depict is abolitionists' attempts to sway the election in their direction. While less corrupt, New Englanders in particular financed groups of antislavery settlers into the Kansas territory in an analogous, if less violent, attempt to manipulate the territorial election.

### *Analyzing Sources*

1. Jessie Frémont believed that the Republican's failure to win Pennsylvania's electoral votes had thrown the Republican Party into a state of disorganization that would make later successes more difficult, while she felt that the Democrats' success had given them a decisive advantage. She clearly took the defeat personally, writing that her husband would have been the right person to "administer the bitter dose of subjection to the South" by supporting antislavery forces in Kansas. It is possible that her unhappiness was compounded by her realization that her husband was unlikely to get another shot at the presidency. She was the daughter of a powerful Missouri senator and doubtless aware that men who lost elections the first time around were unlikely to win in the future.
2. Henry Blackwell and Lucy Stone objected to the laws that gave husbands "an injurious and unnatural superiority" by giving them legal control over their wives' bodies and property. In their contract, they refused to acknowledge that Stone had given up her legal existence and thus maintained that she, unlike most married women, could still choose her residence, make a will, sue or be sued on her own name, and inherit property. They objected to the laws that allowed men full custody of the children they had with their wives, as well as ownership of a woman's property and income. In Blackwell and Stone's view, marriage ought to be an "equal and permanent partnership," a condition that was impossible given the current state of the laws applying to marriage.
3. Harriot Hunt based her argument in favor of women's voting rights on a comparison between women and the men who were given the franchise. According to Hunt, it was unjust that women had to pay taxes to the city when they had no voice in its governance. She then analyzes the arguments used to prevent certain classes of men who are taxed but cannot vote. Minors, she points out, do not have the "understanding" to vote, an objection that could hardly apply to women; immigrants supposedly lack interest in American institutions, although even they can vote after naturalization, even if they are illiterate. Her argument is compelling, although it is arguably somewhat elitist: she is appalled that "drunkards, felons, and lunatics," along with rough immigrants, can vote, while "respectable" women cannot.
4. Elizabeth Cady Stanton essentially argued that women would be much more successful if they got themselves up in drag. Merely dressing like men, she points out, would give women an enormous variety of privileges, including the freedom to travel without a chaperone and the ability receive higher wages for all kinds of work. She believes that dress helps accentuate the differences between men and women by artificially emphasizing them. To some extent, her argument makes sense; women were treated differently simply on account of sex, as opposed to talent, and to hide one's sex would open up an enormous range of possibilities. However, her contention that people would lead purer lives if sex was not so immediately evident seems farfetched.

# THE CRUCIBLE OF WAR, 1861–1865 14

## Chapter Overview

### *Chapter Summary*

***Introduction*** An account of former slave and abolitionist Frederick Douglass opens this chapter. When news arrived that the Confederacy had fired on Fort Sumter, Douglass cheered the outbreak of the fighting and Lincoln's vow to maintain the Union. Douglass recognized that the Union was fighting solely to uphold the Constitution and preserve the nation, not to end slavery; but he also understood, much earlier than most, that a war to save the Union would inevitably become a war to end slavery.

***"And the War Came", pp. 494–497*** President Lincoln was determined to stop the spread of secession and to take no action that would push the still undecided Upper South into seceding. He sought to reassure the Deep South of the safety of slavery, giving Unionists there the possibility of reasserting themselves and overturning the secession decision, but at the same time he made it clear that he was determined to uphold the Union. His Confederate counterpart, Jefferson Davis, was equally resolved to see an independent Confederate States of America. While neither man sought war, both knew that one side would provoke it sooner or later and that the war would come.

**ATTACK ON FORT SUMTER** Fort Sumter, a federally manned fort at the entrance to Charleston harbor, was a hateful symbol to the Confederacy of the nation it had abandoned. Union forces at the fort were running short of supplies and, unless they were reprovisioned, would have to evacuate. Lincoln knew that to surrender Sumter would be to abandon his commitment to preserving the Union, so he sent a relief expedition but no soldiers. Confederate officials debated whether to become the aggressors; the decision was made on April 12. When Fort Sumter's Union commander refused the southern order to surrender, Confederate forces began shelling the fort, which surrendered on April 14, 1861. The Civil War had begun. Northerners responded enthusiastically to Lincoln's call for 75,000 militia troops to put down the rebellion.

**THE UPPER SOUTH CHOOSES SIDES** Lincoln's call for troops forced the undecided slave states to choose sides. Robert E. Lee was typical of many Southerners who opposed secession but refused to fight the Confederacy. Within weeks of the attack on Fort Sumter, Virginia, Arkansas, Tennessee, and North Carolina seceded. The Confederacy now contained eleven of the fifteen slave states. In the border slave states of Kentucky, Delaware, Maryland, and Missouri, secession was thwarted by a combination of local Unionism and federal intervention, including the use of martial law to suppress Confederate sympathizers. The conflict in the border states was truly a "brother's war," and Confederate guerrilla bands roamed through Kentucky and Missouri for the duration of the war.

***The Combatants, pp. 497–502*** The outbreak of fighting at Fort Sumter had ended indecision, now that Yankee "aggression" and Confederate "insurrection" were no longer just theoretical possibilities. In the spring and summer of 1861, both sides took stock of their resources for fighting, began mobilizing their forces, and came up with their respective military and diplomatic strategies.

**WHAT THEY FOUGHT FOR** Confederate leaders wanted to protect slavery, but they defined their cause as a defense of states' rights, self-determination, and liberty. They appealed to the fervid patriotism of most white Southerners from planters to yeomen to artisans who, united in their belief in slavery and in the inherent inferiority of blacks, viewed Yankee domination as a form of tyranny similar to that faced by American patriots in 1776. For their part, Northerners viewed secession as an attack on the best government on earth, one that they believed best protected their property and interests, and they were determined to defend and preserve it.

**HOW THEY EXPECTED TO WIN** The balance sheet of war was overwhelmingly in favor of the North, whose population, industrial capacity, and transportation networks far exceeded those of the South. Initially, however, the North's material advantages were not as decisive as they eventually became. The southern armies, for the most part, fought a defensive war on familiar terrain. In addition, Southerners believed their fighters, though fewer in number, were far superior to the North's. The North would have to conquer a massive region, and this factor emboldened southern leaders, who alluded to the War for Independence, when the British, with superior resources, had failed to conquer the colonies. Southerners also reasoned that dependence on southern cotton would incline foreign leaders to favor and perhaps even come to the aid of the Confederacy. Most Americans underestimated the length and cost of the war, expecting it to be relatively painless, as the Mexican War had been.

**LINCOLN AND DAVIS MOBILIZE** Both the southern and northern political leaders ended up defying expectations. The aristocratic Jefferson Davis, unanimously elected to head the Confederacy, had superb qualifications but proved an ineffective administrator and an opinionated but uninspirational leader. Lincoln, while he lacked the demeanor of a cultured gentleman and impressive credentials, soon proved an able and inspirational leader in the North's drive for victory. Guided by their respective presidents, the North and South began mobilizing their armies. The South's lack of infrastructure meant it had to build much of its war machine from scratch, while Northerners had to convert their superior numbers and industrial resources into war readiness. To meet the challenge of financing the war, both sides resorted to selling bonds, printing large quantities of paper money that ultimately caused inflation to soar, and finally raising taxes. The North proved far more able than the South to adapt its public finances to meet the extraordinary demands of a wartime economy.

***The Battlefields, 1861–1862, pp. 502–507*** During the first year and a half of the war, the armies fought a dramatic campaign in Virginia and Maryland in the East and a decisive one in Tennessee and Kentucky in the West. All the while, the numbers of casualties rose at an alarming rate.

**STALEMATE IN THE EASTERN THEATER** The Union and the Confederacy fought their first major battle of the war in northern Virginia on July 21, 1861, at Bull Run, or Manassas junction. The battle was a severe defeat for the Union as well as a severe blow to Union morale. Lincoln replaced his first general, Irvin McDowell, with George B. McClellan, who took the dispirited Army of the Potomac and molded it into a powerful, well-trained force. However, McClellan was not very interested in using the army to fight battles, to Lincoln's frustration. In the spring of 1862, McClellan launched an offensive on the Confederate capital of Richmond but was stopped by Confederate forces under the excellent leadership of General Robert E. Lee. Lincoln replaced McClellan and then reinstated him. The two armies met again at Antietam Creek and fought the bloodiest battle of the war on September 17, 1862, a Union victory. Lincoln continued to shift commanders; one, Ambrose Burnside, oversaw the December 1862 Battle of Fredericksburg, one of the worst Union defeats of the war. By the end of 1862, military struggle in the East had settled into a long and frustrating stalemate.

**UNION VICTORIES IN THE WESTERN THEATER** The first decisive operations in 1862 occurred in the western theater of war, where the Union forces were attempting to capture the West's rivers to divide the Confederacy and give the North easy access to the southern heartland. Led by General Ulysses S. Grant, Union forces captured Forts Henry and Donelson on the Tennessee and Cumberland Rivers. Grant then pushed on to meet Confederate forces at the battle of Shiloh Church in Tennessee. Beaten on the first day of battle, Grant called for reinforcements and drove the Confederates from the field on the second day. By the end of 1862, most but not all of the Mississippi Valley lay in Union hands.

**WAR AND DIPLOMACY IN THE ATLANTIC THEATER** The Union had an overwhelming advantage in naval power, and its blockade against the southern coast grew tighter every month, shutting the Confederacy off from supplies and weakening its military strength. The Confederates made bold attempts to break the blockade, including using new ironclad warships, but the Union government was soon building ironclads of its own. Southern attempts to draw cotton-starved European nations into the war as allies failed for several reasons. English manufacturers had surplus cotton on hand in 1861 and could withstand a temporary loss of access to American cotton, especially since they had begun importing cotton from India and Egypt. Moreover, a thriving trade between the Union and Britain encouraged Britain to remain neutral. Last but not least, in the fall of 1862, Lincoln announced a new policy that made an alliance with the Confederacy an alliance with slavery.

***Union* and *Freedom*, *pp. 507–511*** In spite of Lincoln's assertions, the war to preserve the Union ultimately became a war for African American freedom. In the field among soldiers and commanders, in Congress, and in the White House, the truth gradually became clear: Since the Confederate war machine depended heavily on the labor of slaves, to win the war against the South, the North would have to destroy slavery.

**FROM SLAVES TO CONTRABAND** At the beginning of the war, Congress refused to declare it a crusade against slavery, stating that the war was for the preservation of the Union and not to change the domestic institutions of any state. However, in March 1862, Congress authorized the government to confiscate runaway slaves, who came to be called "contraband," and a year earlier it had passed the first Confiscation Act, allowing the seizure of any slave employed in the Confederate military. Still, Lincoln consistently refused to allow his commanders to free slaves in the areas occupied by Union forces. He also knew that one of the main obstacles to emancipation was northern white racism and was pessimistic about prospects for black equality in the United States. He thus coupled moderate proposals with a plea for government subsidies to support "colonization" of freed blacks outside the United States—an idea few African Americans embraced, especially after such an attempt in the Caribbean failed miserably.

**FROM CONTRABAND TO FREE PEOPLE** Despite the president's cautious views about emancipation, momentum began to gather behind it, especially in Congress. In 1862, Congress pushed through the second Confiscation Act, which declared free the slaves of persons supporting the insurrection. On September 22, 1862, after the Union victory at Antietam, Lincoln announced his intention to issue an executive order freeing all the slaves in the Confederacy. Despite criticism from Democrats who did not want to make ending slavery a war goal, on New Year's Day 1863, Lincoln issued the final Emancipation Proclamation, forever freeing all the slaves in the Confederacy. The edict did not apply to the border slave states, which had never seceded from the Union. The order also committed the federal government to the fullest use of African Americans to defeat the Confederates.

**WAR OF BLACK LIBERATION** Blacks tried to enlist for the armed services from the time the war broke out but were often rejected for armed duty and put into labor positions only. However, the Emancipation Proclamation eroded white resistance to black soldiers. With the Militia Act of July 1862, Congress authorized enrolling blacks in the armed forces. Approximately 180,000 African Americans, many of them newly freed slaves, eventually served in the Union armed services and made a vital contribution to the North's victory. Although they were enrolled in segregated units under white officers, were initially paid less than white soldiers, and were used disproportionately for garrison duty or heavy labor behind the lines, black soldiers fought heroically in several major engagements during the last two years of the war and served in disproportionately high numbers. Their experiences in the army helped prepare them for the civil rights struggle that emerged after the war.

***The South at War, pp. 511–515*** Though white Southerners were initially strongly united in their war against the Union, efforts to centralize power to prosecute war more effectively convinced many that the Confederacy had proven false to them and to the South's cause. In addition, severe economic privation, whose effects were felt more by some Southerners than by others, hurt solidarity among whites, and slaves themselves began to contribute to the destruction of the whole slave system.

**REVOLUTION FROM ABOVE** The Southern government had to build the military from scratch, supply it from its meager manufacturing resources, and pay for the whole thing out of a nonexistent treasury. As the Union blockade became more effective, the Confederacy had to build its own munitions plants and other industrial enterprises. Despite its determination, the Richmond government failed to transform the slave-labor, staple-producing agricultural economy into an industrial one. As Confederate armies became more desperate for materiel and food, the Davis administration resorted to impressment, which allowed officials to take from private citizens whatever they deemed essential for the war effort. The Confederate government also nationalized railroads and shipping. Though such centralizing policies were necessary to prosecute the war, many Southerners felt that their government, more than the Yankees, had become their main oppressor.

**HARDSHIP BELOW** Ironically, the greatest dividing force in the Confederacy came to be the foundation of southern political philosophy—the principle of states' rights, for which the South had seceded. A continual struggle between Richmond and the states for control of money, supplies, and soldiers obstructed the government's war efforts at many points. The war's principal social effect on the South was widespread suffering and privation. Once the full effects of the blockade were felt, the South experienced shortages of almost everything. As the war continued, the many hardships contributed to the increasing volatility of southern society. There were major food riots in many cities, and resistance to conscription, impressment, and taxation was widespread, as increasing numbers of Southerners became aware that the privations of war were not equally shared by people of different classes.

**THE DISINTEGRATION OF SLAVERY** In countless ways, the war disrupted the entire matrix of bondage. Almost immediately, traditional male authority on the plantation dissolved, as masters were called away to war, leaving white women to assume managerial roles. Many slaves were impressed into war service by Confederate officials, thus severing master-slave relationships. Slaves' running away to Union lines became endemic. In short, the war caused the balance of power between master and slave to shift in the slave's favor. Perhaps surprisingly, few slaves took revenge on whites for two centuries of bondage; instead, they undermined white mastery by taking greater control of their own lives.

***The North at War, pp. 515–522*** Northern farms, factories, and cities remained untouched by the fighting because battles generally remained within Confederate borders. Still, the northern home front was profoundly affected by the war, experiencing great social and economic changes.

**THE GOVERNMENT AND THE ECONOMY** With southern Democrats out of Congress, the Republican Party had free rein to enact an aggressive program to promote economic development. Examples of this program included the 1862 Homestead Act to aid western development; the Pacific Railroad Act, which provided massive federal aid to build a line from Omaha to San Francisco; the National Banking Act of 1863, which created a new national banking system; and the Legal Tender Act of 1862, which created a national paper currency. Congress also created the Department of Agriculture and passed the Land-Grant College Act (or Morrill Act), setting aside public lands to support universities that focused on agriculture.

**WOMEN AND WORK ON THE HOME FRONT** As fathers and sons joined the army, women assumed the management of farms or moved to the cities and took jobs in factories producing war goods. They protested their low pay, but they felt proud of their contributions to the war effort. Thousands of women became nurses, fighting to save lives in hospitals that too often were centers of filth and death. Women like Dorothea Dix, superintendent of Union army nurses, and Clara Barton, who later founded the Red Cross, put up with enormous personal privation to comfort those in pain. For many women, the war was a crucial moment in the redefinition of female roles and in the awakening of a sense of independence and new possibilities.

**POLITICS AND DISSENT** The party system survived the war and even helped to strengthen the government by providing clear channels for dissent. Democrats were, however, very unhappy with Lincoln's willingness to interpret the Constitution loosely. In 1862, to stifle popular opposition to the war, Lincoln proclaimed all persons who discouraged enlistments or engaged in disloyal practices to be subject to martial law, and many were arrested or imprisoned, albeit for relatively short periods. One former congressman, Clement L. Vallandigham of Ohio, was arrested; in 1866, the Supreme Court declared that it was unconstitutional to subject civilians to military trials when civilian courts were operational. Another problem for the government was a provision in the 1863 Conscription Act that allowed those who could afford it to avoid service by hiring someone to go in their place or by paying the government a fee of $300. Opposition to the measure was widespread, especially among laborers and immigrants, and occasionally violence erupted, as in the 1863 New York City draft riots during which demonstrators went on a rampage and killed African Americans, whom they blamed for the war. These were among the bloodiest riots in American history, with 105 people killed.

***Grinding out Victory, 1863–1865, pp. 522–531*** Though the Union's prospects looked dim in the early months of 1863, the balance was tipped in the Union's favor after General Ulysses S. Grant took supreme command. The North slowly ground out victory, but if the Confederacy was beaten, Southerners did not know it.

**VICKSBURG AND GETTYSBURG** In the spring of 1863, Ulysses S. Grant attacked the Confederate stronghold at Vicksburg, Mississippi, whose residents finally surrendered after a prolonged siege, giving the Union complete control of the length of the Mississippi River. At the same time that Grant was taking Vicksburg, the most decisive and bloody battle of the war was being fought in Gettysburg, Pennsylvania, on July 1–3, 1863. A series of Confederate attacks failed to dislodge Union General George Meade's troops from the high ground they occupied. The following day, Lee launched a final, desperate assault, with disastrous results. Gettysburg cost Lee 28,000 casualties, more than one-third of his army. The defeats at Vicksburg and Gettysburg would prove to be the turning point of the war, although this was not obvious at the time: the Confederacy still controlled the South's heartland, Lee's army was still capable of doing damage, and it was fully possible that the North would tire of the war before it was won.

**GRANT TAKES COMMAND** In the fall of 1863, Grant routed the Confederate army at Chattanooga, Tennessee, opening the door to Georgia and saving General William Rosecrans's army. By the beginning of 1864, Grant had become general in chief of all Union armies. Grant was not a subtle general; he simply believed in using the North's superior numbers of men and materiel to overwhelm the South. He accepted large numbers of casualties as long as he was inflicting similar or greater suffering on his enemy. After taking command, Grant ordered a multipronged offensive to finish off the Confederacy, the main movements of which were a march on Richmond and a thrust by the western armies, now led by General William T. Sherman, to Atlanta and the heart of Georgia. In May and June, Grant and Lee fought a series of bloody battles in northern Virginia, in which twice as many Yankees as rebels died—but the since the Confederates had only half the troops, the damage was considerable. While Grant harassed Lee, Sherman took Atlanta and undertook a scorched-earth campaign through Georgia, arriving in Savannah in the third week of December.

**THE ELECTION OF 1864** In 1864 the Democrats seemed to be in a good position to capitalize on Republican divisions and to capture the White House. Their platform appealed to war weariness by calling for a cease-fire, but they ran a war candidate, General George B. McClellan. Union successes, however, boosted Lincoln's popularity, and he won with 212 electoral votes and 55 percent of the popular vote. The victory was a mandate to continue the war until slavery was gone and the South surrendered.

**THE CONFEDERACY COLLAPSES** The concluding military operations revealed the futility of further southern resistance. More and more Southerners gave up on the war, not because they believed that their cause was not worthy but because they had been battered into submission. Jefferson Davis was so committed to the war effort that he proposed arming slaves and allowing them to fight in return for their freedom, an idea that the Confederate congress approved but slave owners resisted. Grant forced the Confederates to abandon Petersburg and Richmond on April 2, 1865, pursuing them westward for a hundred miles. Recognizing the hopelessness of further resistance, Lee surrendered his army in the village of Appomattox Courthouse on April 9, ending the war. But the North's joy at victory soon turned to sorrow and anger when John Wilkes Booth assassinated Abraham Lincoln at Ford's Theater on April 14. The man who had led the nation through the war would not lead it in its postwar search for peace.

***Conclusion: The Second American Revolution*** The Civil War had a profound impact on Americans. It devastated the South; while it led to massive casualties in the North, it also revitalized the region's economy. It set the nation on a new course, transforming antebellum America from a relatively decentralized political and economic entity to a nation dominated by industrial capitalism and headed by a strong federal government. Perhaps most important, slavery was abolished and free labor triumphant. But the real meaning of emancipation was still unclear in 1865, and the nation faced the daunting task of determining the status of four million freed slaves during Reconstruction.

***Chronology Activity*** Read the annotated chronology, and answer the multiple-choice questions.

1861 April 12–13. Confederate forces attack Fort Sumter, South Carolina, beginning Civil War. After his inauguration, President Lincoln faced the problem of how to resupply Fort Sumter, a federal installation at the entrance to the Charleston harbor. He knew that Confederates saw the fort as a symbol of the nation they had left and wanted the federal troops out. However, he also knew that withdrawing federal forces would be an unpopular move in the North and would give the Confederacy more legitimacy with other nations. His decision to reprovision the fort but not to provide military reinforcements left the decision of whether to fight to Jefferson Davis, the Confederate president. Davis's decision to attack the fort started the Civil War.

April. Dorothea Dix named superintendent of female nurses. Prior to the Civil War, most Americans felt that nursing was not a feminine occupation. However, women on both sides of the conflict showed their patriotism by volunteering to serve as nurses, working in the midst of horrible carnage but gaining satisfaction at a job well done and redefining traditional notions of femininity. In the North, some volunteer nurses became paid military nurses. Dorothea Dix, known for her insane asylum reforms, became the official superintendent, overseeing about three thousand women over the course of the conflict.

April–May. Four Upper South states secede and join Confederacy. After the Confederate attack on Fort Sumter, President Lincoln called for 75,000 militia to serve for ninety days to put down the rebellion. This put the residents of the remaining slave states in a bind: many of them opposed Southern independence but were unwilling to fire on Southerners and had believed that Lincoln would achieve reconciliation by allowing Unionists in the Confederate states to reassert themselves. In the end, Virginia, Arkansas, North Carolina, and Tennessee chose to secede as well; the other four slave states — Missouri, Maryland, Kentucky, and Delaware — voted to remain in the Union, although mostly by very slim margins.

July. Union forces routed at Manassas, Virginia, in first major clash of war. The Battle of Manassas pitted two raw, green armies against each other at a railroad junction in Virginia. At first, the Union army held its ground, but southern reinforcements blunted their attack and then counterattacked; Union soldiers responded by stampeding in a panic back toward Washington, D.C. The battle reinforced the southern belief that southern troops were superior to the northern forces. It demonstrated to Northerners that the war was going to be much longer and harder than they expected; within four days of the rout, Lincoln signed bills authorizing the enlistment of one million men for three years.

August. Congress approves First Confiscation Act, which allows seizure of any slave employed by Confederate military. In the early years of the war, Lincoln refused to move toward the emancipation of southern slaves, believing that such an action would alienate the loyal border states and defy northern public opinion. Congress, however, was influenced by Radical Republicans who felt that the Union could not be restored with slavery intact without mocking the sacrifices of Union soldiers. Its passage of the Confiscation Act over the objections of Democrats and border-state representatives showed its stiffening of attitude toward the issue of slavery policy.

1862 February. Legal Tender Act creates first national currency, called "greenbacks." The act was part of the Republicans' drive to use the federal government to encourage economic growth. With Democrats' power halved by the secession of eleven southern states, the Republicans had little difficulty translating their economic philosophy into law.

February. Union forces in West under General Ulysses S. Grant capture Fort Henry and Fort Donelson and drive Confederates from Kentucky and most of Tennessee. The victories in the western theater were of immense strategic importance to the Union. The Confederates claimed Kentucky but did not control it; and Tennessee was the source of vital resources for the Confederates, including food, mules, and iron.

April. Battle of Shiloh in Tennessee results in huge casualties and ends Confederate bid to control Mississippi Valley. There were 20,000 casualties at Shiloh, including General Albert Sidney Johnston, the commander of the Confederate forces. Winning the battle allowed the Union to take charge of the Western theater; after Shiloh, the Union grabbed Corinth, Mississippi, Memphis, and also New Orleans, controlling almost all of the Mississippi Valley by the end of the year. The high number of casualties also reinforced Grant's belief that the Union could be saved only by a program of complete conquest of the South.

April. Confederate Congress passes first draft law in American history. The Confederate war effort had the ironic effect of forcing the southern government to intrude in unprecedented ways on the private lives of its citizens. The draft law required all able-bodied white men between the ages of eighteen and thirty-five, and later seventeen and fifty, to make themselves available to serve in the army for three years. The law also convinced many southern yeomen that the conflict was "a rich man's war and a poor man's fight" because it permitted men with sufficient financial resources to hire substitutes to take their places in the army. Measures like the draft law convinced many Southerners that the government had betrayed the causes for which it was supposedly fighting—states' rights and unfettered individualism.

May. Homestead Act offers western land to those who would live and labor on it. The provision of free land to western settlers was one of the planks in the 1864 Republican platform; it was designed to encourage the distribution of western land. In time, the Homestead Act resulted in more than a million new western farms.

May–July. General George McClellan's Union forces defeated during peninsula campaign in Virginia. For months McClellan had resisted Lincoln's attempts to get him to fight the Confederate army. When he finally started his campaign, he took two and a half months to advance sixty-five miles from Washington, D.C., toward Richmond, Virginia. Six miles outside of Richmond, the Confederate general Joseph Johnston attacked, was wounded, and was replaced by General Robert E. Lee. McClellan retreated down the peninsula with 30,000 casualties in the process—a defeat typical—and the loss contributed to the continuing demoralization of the northern public.

July. Congress approves second Confiscation Act, freeing all slaves of rebel masters. The second act showed Congress moving more steadily toward emancipation of the southern slaves. This act freed most of the slaves in the Confederacy, since slaveholders had spearheaded secession and formed the backbone of the rebellion.

July. Congress passes Militia Act, authorizing enrollment of blacks in Union military. When the war first broke out, blacks who volunteered to fight were either limited mostly to noncombatant roles working as manual laborers or were rejected by the War Department, whose officials feared that blacks could not fight and that whites would not be willing to serve alongside them. As the Union experienced manpower shortages, however, Northerners turned to the black population, allowing blacks to fill any role in the military for which they were suited. Resistance to black enlistments declined after the Emancipation Proclamation made it clear that all Union soldiers were fighting and dying for black freedom. Over the course of the war, blacks served in disproportionately high numbers and showed bravery and courage in battle.

September 17. Battle of Antietam stops Lee's advance into Maryland, but Confederate forces escape back to Virginia. At Antietam, the Union army had a distinct advantage: a Union soldier had found a copy of Lee's orders to his army. The Union army under McClellan was able to do a great deal of damage to Lee's forces; the battle was the bloodiest day of the war, with 6,000 dead and 17,000 wounded. However, McClellan's slowness meant that he missed an opportunity to destroy Lee's army.

September 22. Lincoln announces preliminary emancipation proclamation. Lincoln was well aware that northern public opinion was opposed to emancipation as a war aim. At the same time, he was under pressure from abolitionists and realized that slaves represented an important source of labor that allowed the Confederates to continue fighting. He made his preliminary emancipation proclamation as a "military necessity," hoping to avoid criticism. Nonetheless, Democrats responded with anger, accusing Lincoln of succumbing to the "abolitionist faction."

1863 January 1. Emancipation Proclamation becomes law, freeing slaves in areas still in rebellion. The Emancipation Proclamation applied only to slaveholders in the rebellious states and excepted those in the loyal border states or areas under the control of the Union army. In a sense, Lincoln freed slaves where he had no power and left them enslaved where he did. Yet Lincoln did not have the ability to single-handedly free slaves in the loyal states, and the Proclamation gave the Union army the clear authority to free slaves in the Confederacy as they advanced.

February. National Banking Act creates system of national banks. This act was another Republican economic goal eased by the absence of Democratic dissenters in Congress. It created a system of national banks to replace the old system of decentralized state banks.

March. Congress authorizes draft. High casualties and battlefield losses halted the flow of volunteers for the Union army; the draft act aimed to fill the army by requiring that all men between the ages of twenty and forty-five make themselves available for a lottery that would then decide who went to war. Poor men were appalled by provisions that allowed a draftee to hire a substitute or pay a $300 fee to avoid service. When Democrats accused Republicans of using an unconstitutional draft to force men to fight for the unconstitutional goal of emancipation, antidraft, antiblack mobs went on rampages in northern cities. New York City had one of the worst riots, resulting in 105 deaths.

July. Vicksburg falls to Union forces under Grant, effectively cutting Confederacy in two along Mississippi River. Grant's success at Vicksburg gave the Union control of the important Mississippi River and was one of the decisive events in the war, making it virtually impossible for the South to win.

July. Battle of Gettysburg results in Confederate defeat and Lee's last offensive into North. Lee decided to undertake a northern offensive to relieve Virginia of the burden of the fighting and to defeat the Union on its own ground. On July 3, hoping to gain a decisive victory, he ordered a direct assault on entrenched Union soldiers. His forces were decimated: he lost more than a third of his entire army to casualties. Combined with Vicksburg, Gettysburg was a turning point in the war; Lee could not replace the soldiers that he lost, and he was unable to go on the offensive in the North again.

1864 March. Grant appointed general in chief of all Union forces. Grant's successes in the West convinced Lincoln to appoint him the commander of all Union forces. Grant proceeded to implement his strategy of war by annihilation, fighting the Confederates until they no longer had the manpower or the will to continue the war. He undertook two major campaigns: one under his own command against the Confederates in Virginia and the other under the command of General William T. Sherman against Georgia.

May–June. Grant's forces engage Confederates in Virginia in bloodiest fighting of war, from Wilderness campaign to beginnings of siege of Petersburg. Grant lost enormous numbers of soldiers in this fighting. However, although Lee lost only half the number of soldiers Grant did, the Confederates had half the soldiers to begin with and so lost proportionally as many men. Grant realized that the South could not replace its losses and so saw the campaign as a success.
September. Atlanta falls to Union forces under General William T. Sherman. Sherman moved 100,000 men through the mountains of northern Georgia and to Atlanta, a victory that helped Lincoln in his bid for reelection.

November. Lincoln reelected president. In the fall of 1864, Northerners were frustrated with the war effort, which had temporarily bogged down outside Petersburg, Virginia, and Atlanta Georgia, and also with inflation, the draft, the attack on civil liberties, and emancipation; thus, the Republicans were not sure they wanted to renominate Lincoln. However, the Democrats were divided into peace and war camps, and Republicans were afraid that the peace Democrats might overwhelm them if they switched candidates. In the end, the Republicans took on a new name—the Union Party—to make themselves more attractive to war Democrats, and a new vice president, Andrew Johnson of Tennessee, who was the only Southerner to remain in Congress after the secession winter of 1860 to 1861. Lincoln won by a margin of 212 electoral votes to opponent McClellan's 21.

December. Sherman occupies Savannah after scorched-earth campaign in Georgia. After Atlanta, Sherman moved his soldiers toward Savannah in a scorched-earth campaign designed to destroy the will of the southern people by destroying everything they could use to support the war effort.

April 9. Lee surrenders to Grant in the village of Appomattox Courthouse, Virginia, essentially ending Confederate resistance. By the beginning of 1865, the Confederate government was still committed to the war, but many southern soldiers had decided that the war was unwinnable and had begun to desert. In February, Lee abandoned Petersburg, forcing the Confederate government to flee Richmond. He surrendered on April 9; Grant offered him a generous peace that allowed his men to return home and take their horses to help them with their planting.

April 14. Lincoln shot by John Wilkes Booth at Ford's Theatre in Washington. He dies on April 15, succeeded by Vice President Andrew Johnson. Lincoln had been relieved by the end of the war, although he feared that the difficulties of reuniting the nation would be as onerous as those presented by the war. However, his untimely death meant that he was not able to participate in the postwar search for a just peace.

## *Chronology Questions* Choose the letter of the best answer.

1. The Battle of Gettysburg, a major Confederate defeat and turning point of the war, occurred in
   a. August 1861.
   b. February 1862.
   c. July 1863.
   d. September 1864.

2. Of the following events, which was the last to occur?
   a. The First Confiscation Act was passed.
   b. The Confederate Congress authorized a draft.
   c. The Homestead Act was passed.
   d. The northern Congress authorized a draft.

3. What is the correct order for the following events?
   1. Union forces under Grant capture Fort Henry and Fort Donelson.
   2. Union forces are routed at Manassas.
   3. McClellan's peninsula campaign fails.
   4. The Battle of Shiloh ends the Confederate bid to control the Mississippi Valley.

   a. 3, 2, 4, 1
   b. 2, 4, 1, 3
   c. 1, 4, 3, 2
   d. 2, 1, 4, 3

4. In April and May of 1861,
   a. Grant's forces engaged the Confederates in the bloodiest fighting of the war.
   b. four Upper South states seceded and joined the Confederacy.
   c. Congress approved the first and second Confiscation Acts.
   d. Sherman undertook a scorched-earth campaign in Georgia.

5. What is the correct order for the following events?
   1. Grant is appointed general in chief of all Union forces.
   2. Lincoln is reelected president.
   3. Vicksburg falls to Union forces under Grant.
   4. Atlanta falls to Union forces under William T. Sherman.

   a. 3, 1, 4, 2
   b. 2, 4, 1, 3
   c. 3, 2, 1, 4
   d. 4, 3, 1, 2

6. The Confederate forces inaugurated the Civil War by attacking Fort Sumter, South Carolina, on
   a. April 12–13, 1861.
   b. May–July 1862.
   c. September 22, 1862.
   d. March 1863.

7. The 1862 engagement that stopped General Lee's advance into Maryland was the
   a. peninsula campaign.
   b. siege of Petersburg.
   c. Battle of Antietam.
   d. Battle of Shiloh.

8. What is the correct order for the following events?
   1. Congress passes the first Confiscation Act.
   2. The Emancipation Proclamation becomes law.
   3. The Union Congress authorizes a draft.
   4. Congress passes the Militia Act, allowing blacks to enroll in the military.

   a. 1, 2, 4, 3
   b. 2, 4, 1, 3
   c. 1, 4, 2, 3
   d. 4, 3, 2, 1

9. The Legal Tender Act, which created the first national currency, was passed in
   a. July 1861.
   b. February 1862.
   c. March 1864.
   d. April 1865.

10. What is the correct order for the following events?
    1. The Battle of Shiloh ends the Confederate bid to control the Mississippi Valley.
    2. Lincoln announces a preliminary emancipation proclamation.
    3. Vicksburg falls to Union forces.
    4. Sherman occupies Savannah.

    a. 1, 2, 3, 4
    b. 4, 1, 3, 2
    c. 4, 2, 1, 3
    d. 1, 2, 4, 3

***Defining Terms*** Match each term with the correct definition.

Confederate Ordnance Bureau
Kentucky
offensive-defensive strategy
Confederate States of America
King Cotton diplomacy
ironclad warship
Battle of Manassas or Bull Run
Robert E. Lee
Appomattox Courthouse
Confiscation Act
colonization
National Banking Act
General Ulysses S. Grant
Militia Act
western theater
Fort Sumter
"people's contest"
contraband of war
conscription law of 1862
Homestead Act
Battle of Gettysburg
Emancipation Proclamation
"reign of terror"
tax-in-kind
Jefferson Davis
Copperheads
impressment policy
Confederate inflation
scorched-earth campaign
U.S. Sanitary Commission
Vicksburg
twenty-Negro law
West Virginia
General George McClellan
*Ex parte Milligan*

1. The independent republic formed by the southern states that seceded. To make the republic successful, it was necessary for its political leaders to sustain the population's commitment to independence and to gain as many slave states as possible. Confederate states of America

2. A federal fort located on a tiny island at the entrance to the Charleston harbor. Southerners saw the fort as a hateful sign of the Union; Northerners considered it a symbol of the continuation of federal sovereignty over the seceded states. President Lincoln's decision to resupply the fort with food but not soldiers precipitated Confederate military action. The taking of this Fort on April 14, 1861, marked the official beginning of the Civil War. Fort Sumter

3. A career military officer and descendent of one of Virginia's oldest families, his response to secession was typical of many other citizens of the Upper South. He denounced secession, but when Virginia voted to secede, he resigned his commission in the United States military forces and declared his loyalty to his home state. Robert E. Lee

4. A vitally important border state that stayed (just barely) in the Union during the Civil War. The state contained valuable resources, population, and wealth, and controlled major rivers and railroads, and Lincoln saw it as vital to holding on to Maryland and Missouri as well. Kentucky

5. The state voted into existence in 1863 by Unionists. All of the seceding states of the Upper South contained significant pockets of Unionists; in the western counties of Virginia that sentiment was so strong that residents created a whole new state that was loyal to the Union. West virginia

6. Lincoln's encapsulation of the Civil War, which he argued was intended to preserve the United States's republican government and give all Americans access to the opportunity to succeed. "People's Contest"

7. The southern assumption that when Great Britain and perhaps France were denied southern cotton, they would intervene in the war on behalf of the Confederacy. The strategy did not work; Europeans found new sources of cotton in India and Egypt, and none of the European nations ever recognized the Confederate states or came to their defense. King cotton diplomacy

8. Jefferson Davis's description of the Confederate strategy for prosecuting the war. Southerners intended to capitalize on the fact that a Union victory demanded that the North defeat and subjugate the South, while a Confederate victory demanded only that the South not lose. Thus, the southern armies would stay in the South, repel invasions, avoid all-out battles, and outlast the Northern will to fight, striking at the invaders only when the opportunity presented itself. offensive-defensive strategy.

9. The first and only president of the Confederate States of America. He was an aristocrat from a planter family, and with his extensive military and political experience, he appeared to be an ideal president. However, he faced the nearly impossible task of conducting a war while organizing a new nation, and his sharp tongue and tendency to meddle in military affairs undermined his effectiveness. Jefferson Davis

10. One of the few bright spots in the Confederate mobilization effort. At the outbreak of the Civil War, the South had virtually no facilities for manufacturing war materiel; by 1864, its head, Josiah Gorgas, proudly explained that the South was producing enough gunpowder, cannons, and rifles to supply its own armies. Confederate ordnance Bureau

11. The first major engagement of the Civil War, which took place in July 1861. The Union army attacked the Confederates at a railroad junction in Virginia. The battle started well for the Union, but when southern reinforcements counterattacked, Union soldiers panicked and ran. The battle convinced Southerners that they were going to win the war; it caused Northerners to realize that the war was going to be long and difficult. Battle of Manassas or Bull Run.

12. The military commander responsible for training and reorganizing the Army of the Potomac into shape after the disaster at Manassas at the beginning of the Civil War. He was a superb administrator and organizer. Unfortunately for Lincoln, he liked to train more than he liked to fight, and in the field he was indecisive and timid. His attempt to take the Confederate capital of Richmond, Virginia, in the spring of 1862, ended in failure, and he was replaced. General George McClellan

13. The Civil War fighting that took place between the Appalachian Mountains and the Ozarks, centering largely on gaining control of the Mississippi, Tennessee, and Cumberland Rivers. While the eastern theater received more attention, the western theater was more strategically important. Control of the rivers could either give the Confederacy access to the Union border states of Missouri and Kentucky or allow the North to split the Confederacy and take the resource-rich state of Tennessee. western theater

14. The key northern figure on the Civil War's western battlefields. A West Point graduate who was working as a dry-goods clerk when the war broke out, he was a pugnacious fighter whose military strategy drew on the North's strength, superior manpower, and his philosophy of war as annihilation. In 1863 he became general in chief of all Union armies; he was instrumental in the Union victory. General Ulysses S. Grant.

15. A radical new maritime design introduced by the Confederates in 1862. Wooden-hulled frigates were layered with two-inch thick armor plates. They were effectively against ships in the federal blockade for a single day; the following morning, the Union introduced ironclad ships of its own. ironclad warship.

16. Legislation passed by Congress in August 1861 that allowed the seizure of any slave who was employed directly by the Confederate military, prohibited slavery in the territories, and abolished the institution in Washington, D.C. It represented Congress's increasing firmness on the issue of establishing a policy toward slavery. Confiscation Act.

17. General Benjamin F. Butler's term for runaway slaves, indicating that they were confiscated property, not fugitives that had to be turned over to their masters under the terms of the Fugitive Slave Act. His attitude reflected the growing Union awareness that slave labor helped the Confederate war effort. Although this new status did not free slaves, and they were often put to work in the Union army, it did show a slight shift toward emancipation. Contraband of war

18. President Lincoln's offer to deport blacks from the United States to Haiti, Panama, or elsewhere. He defended the policy as a means of defusing the white racism that he felt constituted the major obstacle to emancipation. Black leaders, however, rejected it, and Congress was unwilling to provide adequate funding, especially after a failed attempt at colonization on a small island near Haiti. Colonization

19. President Lincoln's declaration freeing all slaves in the seceding states on January 1, 1863. Lincoln presented the measure as a military necessity and exempted slaves in the loyal border states and areas already occupied by the Union army. He hoped that he would blunt criticism by linking emancipation to the southern ability to prosecute the war, but Democrats were furious. Emancipation Proclamation

20. The July 1862 congressional measure designed to ease Union manpower shortages by authorizing the enrollment blacks in any branch of the armed service, including combat units. Prior to 1862, blacks who tried to enlist in the army were placed in labor battalions rather than combat units, when they were accepted at all. But after the Emancipation Proclamation, whites were fighting and dying for black freedom, and few were willing to insist that blacks remain behind the lines. Blacks responded enthusiastically, making up 10 percent of the total servicemen in the Union army. Militia Act

21. The Confederacy's legislation making all able-bodied white males between the ages of eighteen and thirty-five liable to being drafted into the Confederate army for three years. It was the first draft law in American history and was one of the many ways that the Confederate government intruded into the private lives of its citizens. Conscription law of 1862

22. The Confederate government's decision to allow officials to confiscate necessary supplies like food, horses, and wagons from private citizens and pay for the goods at below-market rates; after 1863, they were allowed to impress slaves to use as government military laborers as well. Many southern states were appalled by what they saw as the Richmond administration's usurpation of their rights. impressment policy

23. In the South, a flood of paper money to finance the Civil War caused inflation to rise by over 9,000 percent (as compared to 80 percent in the North). Inflation caused severe hardships for the poor, who found that basic food items like salt and flour were no longer affordable. The sufferings produced by inflation contributed to poorer whites' disenchantment with the war. Confederate inflation

24. A 10 percent tax levied by the Confederate government on agricultural harvests, which were often grown by wives whose husbands were serving in the army. The tax contributed greatly to the hardships poorer Confederate families suffered during the course of the Civil War. tax-in-kind

25. A piece of Confederate legislation that exempted from the draft one white man on every plantation with twenty or more slaves. It was intended to protect white women and ensure that slaves tended to the crops, but it inspired great resentment among yeomen farmers who saw it as a way for planters to avoid military service while their own wives had to tend to crops by themselves. twenty-negro law

26. An 1862 congressional act offering 160 acres of public land to settlers who would live and labor on it. The act contributed to the Republican Party's broad financial plan to encourage economic growth and ultimately resulted in the creation of more than a million new farms in the West. Homestead Act

27. An 1863 congressional act creating a system of national banks that within a decade largely replaced the antebellum system of decentralized state banks. The Republicans were able to wild enormous economic power through this revolution in American banking, coupled with sweeping changes in the monetary and tax structures. National Banking Act

28. A northern civilian organization that bought and distributed food, clothing, and medicine and recruited doctors and nurses during the Civil War. Many women defied notions of female delicacy and were drawn into nursing through this organization, which gave women a chance to express their patriotism in a nontraditional way and discover the satisfaction of displaying competence and serving well. U.S. Sanitary commission

29. The Democratic Party's label for President Lincoln's willingness to interpret the Constitution loosely to stifle opposition to the Civil War. They were particularly enraged by Lincoln's practice of placing under martial law civilians who discouraged enlistments, resisted the draft, or engaged in disloyal practices. In fact, most of the fourteen thousand people imprisoned under this measure were Confederate citizens, blockade runners, and foreign nationals, not Democratic politicians, but the tactics did suppress free speech. "reign of terror"

30. The Supreme Court's 1866 decision declaring that it was unconstitutional to order military trials of civilians where civil courts were still able to function. The decision stemmed from President Lincoln's decision to sanction the military arrest of a former Congressman named Clement L. Vallandigham for treason on account of his denunciations of the Civil War. Ex parte Milligan

31. The Mississippi city standing between the Union army and its control over the entire Mississippi River. The city fell in July 1863 after a lengthy siege by General Grant. The Union occupation effectively divided the Confederacy and contributed to turning the Civil War against the Confederates. Vicksburg

32. The Civil War battle that halted General Lee's 1863 invasion of Pennsylvania. After a major victory at Chancellorsville in May 1863, Lee decided to move the fighting out of Virginia and try to deliver a morale-crushing defeat on Union ground. Instead, his army was decimated when he attempted a direct assault against the Union center on Cemetery Ridge. It was Lee's last attempt to launch an offensive against the North. Battle of Gettysburg.

33. General William T. Sherman's march through Georgia in late 1864. His 62,000 troops marched in a column from 25 to 60 miles wide, destroying everything that might contribute to the southern Civil War effort, including food, cotton, machinery, and railroads, in the hopes of crushing the southern population's will to resist. Scorched-earth campaign

34. The Republican label for the Democratic Party's 1864 peace plank, demanding an immediate armistice with the Confederates. Copperheads were deadly, easily concealed snakes; Republicans argued that the peace plank would sell out the Union. Copperheads

35. The village in which General Lee surrendered to General Grant on April 9, 1865, marking the effective end of the Civil War. Grant offered a generous peace to the Confederate army, allowing Lee's men to return home with their horses. Appomattox Courthouse.

## Chapter Review

### *Multiple-Choice* Choose the letter of the best answer.

1. Abraham Lincoln's first goal when he took office as president was to
   a. declare war on the Confederate States of America.
   b. abolish slavery in the slave states that had not seceded.
   c. stop secession from spreading to other southern states.
   d. continue President Buchanan's tactic of ignoring secession.

2. When President Lincoln took office, he believed that he could convince states in the Deep South that slavery was safe there and thus
   a. give Unionists an opportunity to overturn the decision to secede.
   b. make fire-eaters renounce secession.
   c. fool them into returning to the Union.
   d. allow the Union time to build up its supply of armaments.

3. To establish the Confederate States of America as an independent republic, President Jefferson Davis knew that he had to
   a. modernize the slave system.
   b. convince Northerners that secession was a good idea.
   c. start a war with the United States.
   d. convince states from the Upper South to secede.

4. For South Carolinians, the presence of federal troops at Fort Sumter was hateful because the troops
   a. were firing on the city.
   b. were a symbol of the nation Southerners had abandoned.
   c. prevented cotton ships from leaving the Charleston harbor.
   d. enforced a boycott against the Confederacy.

5. President Lincoln decided not to abandon Fort Sumter because he
   a. did not think that the Confederacy would really attack it.
   b. wanted to force the Upper South to commit to the Union.
   c. realized that it was strategically vital.
   d. knew that abandoning it would divide the North.

6. By authorizing an expedition to take food but not military reinforcements to Fort Sumter, President Lincoln
   a. encouraged the remaining slave states to secede.
   b. divided public opinion in the North.
   c. showed that he had no intention of protecting federal property.
   d. forced President Davis to decide for or against peace.

7. After the Confederates bombarded Fort Sumter in April 1861, the free states responded by
   a. overwhelmingly supporting war.
   b. discouraging any further fighting.
   c. formally chastising the Confederacy.
   d. expelling the remaining slave states from the Union.

8. When President Lincoln called for troops in April 1861, the states of Arkansas, North Carolina, Tennessee, and Virginia
   a. joined the Confederacy.
   b. condemned South Carolina's attack on the federal property.
   c. erupted in guerrilla warfare.
   d. decided to stay in the Union.

9. After the Confederate attack on Fort Sumter, the border states of Delaware, Maryland, Kentucky, and Missouri chose to
   a. abolish slavery.
   b. remain loyal to the Union.
   c. be neutral in the war.
   d. form a breakaway country.

10. President Lincoln convinced Maryland to remain in the Union by
    a. suspending the writ of habeas corpus and marching troops into Baltimore.
    b. offering it tax incentives and bribes.
    c. threatening to shoot its residents.
    d. starting a guerrilla war.

11. In the western states of Kentucky and Missouri, the struggle over whether to secede or remain in the Union was
    a. decided overwhelmingly in favor of Unionism.
    b. very violent.
    c. marred by electoral fraud.
    d. not much of an issue because the war was fought in other places.

12. President Lincoln was especially interested in holding Kentucky in the Union because it
    a. had indispensable resources.
    b. had symbolic significance.
    c. was his home state.
    d. was badly wanted by the South.

13. When Abraham Lincoln was inaugurated president in March 1861, eight of the fifteen slave states had _____.
    a. remained in the Union.
    b. seceded.
    c. split over the issue of secession.
    d. supported his candidacy.

14. President Lincoln hoped that _____ would bring the Deep South back into the Union.
    a. military force
    b. southern Unionists
    c. economic catastrophe
    d. internal squabbling

15. President Jefferson Davis intended the Confederate States of America to be _____.
    a. an independent republic
    b. a temporary political entity
    c. a favored part of the United States
    d. limited to seven states.

16. According to the Confederates, Fort Sumter was _____ property, so the soldiers stationed there should leave.
    a. Union
    b. Confederate
    c. private
    d. public

17. President Lincoln realized that evacuating Fort Sumter would _____ the Upper South.
    a. divide public opinion in
    b. alienate
    c. lead to war with
    d. be popular with

18. On April 14, 1861, the Union troops at Fort Sumter _____.
    a. fought off the Confederate forces.
    b. escaped by sea.
    c. died during the Confederate attack.
    d. surrendered to the Confederates.

19. Many Southerners who opposed secession before Fort Sumter _____ after the attack.
    a. were even more loyal to the Union
    b. were appalled by southern behavior
    c. changed their minds and joined with the Confederacy
    d. were unable to make up their minds

20. Delaware, which had _____, was the only border state that decided easily in favor of the Union.
    a. been threatened by the Union army
    b. huge industrial concerns
    c. no plantation agriculture
    d. a tiny slave population

21. Missouri remained in the Union throughout the war but suffered from _____ that harmed both soldiers and civilians.
    a. food shortages
    b. epidemics
    c. fugitive slaves
    d. guerrilla bands

22. In the western counties of Virginia, Unionism was so strong that in 1863 the citizens _____.
    a. sabotaged Confederate military operations.
    b. forced the whole state back into the Union.
    c. voted to create a separate Unionist state.
    d. voluntarily freed their slaves.

23. Slaveholders had the greatest economic stake in protecting slavery during the Civil War, and
    a. they were nearly the only volunteers for the Confederate army.
    b. they forced an unwilling southern population to defend the institution.
    c. yet almost all white Southerners were united in defense of it.
    d. most of the nonslaveholding southern population was divided about the topic.

24. Most Southerners who backed the Confederate cause reasoned that they were
    a. engaging in treason.
    b. defending the slave system from the free-labor threat.
    c. saving southern civilization from subjugation.
    d. correcting a flawed presidential election.

25. To most white Northerners, southern secession constituted
    a. an attack on a valid republican government.
    b. a hasty but understandable response to provocation.
    c. an ill-considered decision.
    d. a legitimate if extreme way of challenging governmental decisions.

26. When the Civil War broke out in 1861,
    a. the South had many more resources than the North.
    b. the North had many more resources than the South.
    c. both the North and the South had about the same number of resources.
    d. neither the North nor the South had any resources.

27. In 1861, Southerners believed that they would win the Civil War because
    a. they had vast personal wealth.
    b. they were personally superior to Northerners.
    c. the North would tire of fighting within a matter of weeks.
    d. slaves would support the southern military effort.

28. Southerners expected that England and perhaps France would ally with the Confederacy to avoid having their
    a. sailors impressed.
    b. supply of cotton interrupted.
    c. source of tobacco cut off.
    d. bank loans defaulted on.

29. Europeans initially picked the South to win the Civil War because of its
    a. vast expanse of land.
    b. superior fighting skills.
    c. immense food supplies.
    d. lofty cause and ideals.

30. The Confederacy devised the offensive-defensive military strategy, which demanded that the South
    a. annihilate the Union army.
    b. blunt invasions, protect its army, and outlast the North.
    c. frequently invade Northern territory.
    d. rely on foreign mercenaries.

31. On April 19, 1861, President Lincoln sought to weaken the South by issuing a proclamation
    a. declaring a naval blockade of the Confederacy.
    b. freeing all Southern slaves.
    c. declaring all Confederate soldiers traitors.
    d. encouraging Northerners to persecute Southern sympathizers.

32. Jefferson Davis had the appearance of the perfect wartime leader; in reality, he was
    a. not able to live up to the image he projected.
    b. personally corrupt.
    c. extremely popular among Confederate politicians.
    d. not a good military or political leader.

33. From the beginning of the Civil War, the South's ability to provide its soldiers with supplies and transportation was
a. limited.
b. unquestioned.
c. dependent on region.
d. marred by political corruption.

34. The South suffered from a much higher rate of inflation than the North during the Civil War because it financed the war primarily by
a. printing paper money.
b. issuing war bonds.
c. raising taxes.
d. taking out enormous bank loans.

35. Although nonslaveholding whites in the South had _____ the slave system, they united in its defense.
a. some sympathy for blacks in
b. suffered as a result of
c. no real interest in
d. no direct economic stake in

36. In 1861, Southerners argued that they were fighting to _____ a tyrannical central government.
a. defend their economic interests from
b. maintain white supremacy in the face of
c. preserve slavery in the face of
d. protect their liberty from

37. To Northerners, the southern rebellion in 1861 was a challenge to _____.
a. their numerical authority.
b. their honor.
c. their financial well-being.
d. the idea that people could rule themselves.

38. When the Civil War began, about 40 percent of the southern population consisted of _____.
a. slaves
b. women
c. people under the age of eighteen
d. Unionists

39. In 1861, many Southerners argued that Northerners' dependence on _____ would allow the Confederates to win the war.
a. European approval
b. republican decision-making
c. southern markets
d. southern cotton

40. The Confederates believed that they could win independence by _____, as the American colonists had in 1776.
a. not losing the war
b. political maneuvering
c. all-out invasions
d. their economic might

41. In 1861, most Americans thought that the war would be like the _____, which had been a relatively small-scale conflict.
a. War of 1812
b. Mexican War
c. Revolutionary War
d. rebellion in Texas

42. President Lincoln showed his political shrewdness by appointing _____ to his cabinet.
a. southern moderates
b. only supporters
c. his rivals
d. very wealthy men

43. One-third of all Union army officers _____ when the Civil War broke out in 1861.
a. resigned their commissions and went south
b. volunteered to fight the Confederacy
c. vied to head the Union war effort
d. fled to Europe

44. Over the course of the Civil War, inflation in the North rose about 80 percent; in the South, it was over _____ percent.
a. 150
b. 1,000
c. 3,000
d. 9,000

45. In the summer of 1861, President Lincoln ordered General Irvin McDowell to
    a. train the raw recruits gathering outside of Washington.
    b. focus on winning the war in the West.
    c. attack the Confederate army at Manassas.
    d. stage guerrilla attacks on the Virginia countryside.

46. The significance of the Battle of Manassas was
    a. the incredibly high number of casualties both sides suffered.
    b. its strategic importance.
    c. the decision of European nations to intervene after it.
    d. the lessons both sides drew from it.

47. General George McClellan's weakness as commander of the Army of the Potomac was that he was
    a. from a nonmilitary background.
    b. a poor military trainer.
    c. unpopular with his troops.
    d. indecisive and slow.

48. General George McClellan's 1862 attempt to take the Confederate capital at Richmond ended
    a. in a draw.
    b. with the Confederates invading Washington, D.C., instead.
    c. in a retreat down the peninsula.
    d. very low southern casualties.

49. Although the Battle of Antietam in September 1862 was a victory for the Army of the Potomac,
    a. it did little to revive northern morale.
    b. it did little to dent southern morale.
    c. General McClellan missed an opportunity to destroy the Army of Virginia.
    d. it did nothing to alter the outcome of the war.

50. At the Battle of Fredericksburg in Virginia, General Ambrose Burnside's decision to order a frontal assault led to
    a. massive Union casualties.
    b. massive Confederate casualties.
    c. a major Union victory.
    d. a stalemate.

51. By the end of 1862, the military struggle in the East had
    a. demonstrated that McClellan was right to avoid battles.
    b. reached a stalemate.
    c. proved the overwhelming superiority of the Army of Virginia.
    d. proved the overwhelming superiority of the Army of the Potomac.

52. The decisive early encounters of the Civil War revolved around
    a. diplomatic efforts in Europe.
    b. the two opposing capitals.
    c. western rivers.
    d. the Deep South states.

53. The Battle of Shiloh was important because it
    a. was an easy Union victory.
    b. destroyed the Confederacy's chance to control the West.
    c. allowed General Grant to annihilate General Albert Sidney Johnston's army.
    d. showed that battles could be won with relatively low casualties.

54. The U.S. navy was able to enforce its blockade of the southern coastline in the Civil War by
    a. commissioning a new blockader almost weekly.
    b. making strategic use of ironclads.
    c. destroying southern ports.
    d. threatening Caribbean islands that traded with the Confederates.

55. Throughout the duration of the Civil War, European nations refused to
    a. grant the Confederacy "belligerent" status.
    b. recognize Confederate nationhood.
    c. purchase cotton from nonsouthern sources.
    d. sell the South goods and ships.

56. The Confederates' King Cotton diplomacy failed because
    a. the British had surplus cotton that lasted throughout 1862.
    b. the British and the Union developed a strong trade relationship.
    c. European manufacturers found new sources of cotton in Egypt and India.
    d. all of the above.

57. During the first two years of the Civil War, the battles _____ were the most decisive.
    a. in the East
    b. in the West
    c. around Washington, D.C., and Richmond, Virginia,
    d. at sea

58. The Battle of Manassas in July 1861 ended in _____ for the Union forces.
    a. a victory
    b. an orderly retreat
    c. a panicky stampede
    d. a stalemate

59. On the battlefield, General Robert E. Lee became _____.
    a. cautious and indecisive
    b. dependent on his subordinate officers
    c. conceited
    d. audacious and even reckless

60. The Battle of Antietam was the _____ of the Civil War.
    a. single bloodiest day of
    b. most decisive Union victory
    c. greatest Union defeat of
    d. only attack on northern soil

61. The North knew that if it could take the _____ River, it would split Arkansas, Louisiana, and Texas from the Confederacy.
    a. Tennessee
    b. Mississippi
    c. Ohio
    d. Cumberland

62. General Grant's philosophy of war as annihilation played to the North's strength, its _____.
    a. geographic advantages
    b. superior manpower
    c. excellent military leadership
    d. diplomatic strength

63. After the Battle of _____, the Confederacy lost its ability to control the western theater.
    a. Antietam
    b. Fort Donelson
    c. Fredericksburg
    d. Shiloh

64. The most important success of the Union's Civil War naval blockade was that it _____.
    a. allowed the U.S. navy to capture a large number of ships
    b. boosted northern morale
    c. convinced Europeans not to intervene in the war
    d. prevented many southern ships from sailing for fear of capture

65. Europeans helped the Confederacy by _____, enabling it to buy goods and build ships overseas.
    a. granting it "belligerent" status
    b. recognizing it as a nation
    c. intervening in the Union blockade
    d. providing it with financial help

66. By the end of 1862, Union _____ convinced Britain and France not to make formal alliances with the Confederacy.
    a. threats of violence
    b. bribes
    c. military successes in the East
    d. successes on the western rivers

67. As the Civil War dragged on, President Lincoln decided that emancipation was necessary because
    a. Democratic politicians demanded it.
    b. white Northerners were in favor of it.
    c. slaves supported the Confederate war machine.
    d. it would undermine Confederate morale.

68. In 1861, President Lincoln believed that emancipation would
    a. give congressional Republicans greater power.
    b. push the loyal border states into the Confederacy.
    c. be popular with most Northern voters.
    d. destroy Southern resistance.

69. Throughout 1861, abolitionists argued that President Lincoln could emancipate southern slaves because
    a. abolitionists were a strong political force in the North.
    b. in seceding, Southerners had forfeited their right to constitutional protection.
    c. the North was stronger than the South.
    d. the Republicans could survive without Democratic support.

70. Slaves helped place slavery on the northern wartime agenda by
    a. running away to Union lines.
    b. sabotaging the Confederate war effort.
    c. petitioning Congress.
    d. all of the above.

71. In March 1862, Congress established a national policy on fugitive slaves, which
    a. made runaways the property of border state slave owners.
    b. returned runaways to their masters.
    c. declared all runaways free.
    d. forbade the return of runaways to their masters.

72. To make emancipation more acceptable to white Northerners, President Lincoln initially
    a. tried to educate the northern public about racism.
    b. offered to deport African Americans out of the country.
    c. hoped to confine it to rebel slaveholders only.
    d. wanted to settle freed slaves in the western states.

73. In August 1862, Lincoln made a radical departure from his old position on emancipation when he
    a. refused to say that the institution of slavery was safe.
    b. issued the Emancipation Proclamation.
    c. threatened to court martial Union commanders who set slavery policy from the field.
    d. freed slaves in the border states.

74. President Lincoln finally decided to promulgate an Emancipation Proclamation on January 1, 1863, in response to
    a. pressure from abolitionists.
    b. his own conscience.
    c. the duration and difficulty of the war.
    d. congressional demands.

75. The Emancipation Proclamation that went into effect on January 1, 1863, liberated
    a. all of the nation's slaves.
    b. only slaves in the unconquered parts of the Confederacy.
    c. only slaves in the border states.
    d. only slaves owned by Confederate officers.

76. From the beginning of the Civil War, northern blacks had volunteered to fight; until 1862, the armed forces
    a. rejected them for all positions.
    b. accepted them for all positions.
    c. refused to make them soldiers.
    d. would not allow them to be officers.

77. Once they were accepted in the military in 1862, black soldiers discovered that
    a. the northern military was racist.
    b. they had a lot in common with white soldiers.
    c. the military was remarkably colorblind.
    d. their new status gained them respect among whites.

78. From the beginning of the Civil War, most blacks viewed the conflict as
    a. a fight to save the Union.
    b. a struggle for black liberation.
    c. mostly the concern of whites.
    d. a waste of money.

79. For a year and a half after the Civil War broke out, President Lincoln contended that _____ was not a goal of the war.
a. saving the Union
(b.) emancipation
c. upholding law and order
d. destroying the South's infrastructure

80. In 1861 and 1862, most white Northerners _____ emancipation.
(a.) supported
b. objected to
c. were neutral about
d. saw the necessity of

81. The 1861 Confiscation Act allowed the seizure of _____, as well as prohibiting slavery in the territories and Washington, D.C.
a. all slaves in the Confederate states
(b.) slaves employed directly by the Confederate military
c. all Confederate farms
d. Confederate property, food, and other supplies

82. As the Civil War progressed, the most insistent force for emancipation became _____.
a. radical Republicans
b. free northern blacks
c. northern Democrats
(d.) runaway slaves

83. During the Civil War, General Benjamin F. Butler provided runaway slaves with the status of _____.
a. government dependents
b. freedmen
(c.) contraband of war
d. fugitives

84. Most African Americans _____ President Lincoln's proposal of government-sponsored colonization for free blacks.
(a.) were appalled by
b. were neutral toward
c. supported
d. saw the logic behind

85. The _____ played a key role in ending President Lincoln's noninterference with slavery in the Confederate states.
a. large numbers of runaway slaves
b. influence of evangelical leaders
c. agitation of abolitionists
(d.) length and difficulty of the war

86. After President Lincoln proposed the Emancipation Proclamation, Democrats _____.
(a.) gained thirty-four congressional seats
b. won a large majority in Congress
c. lost public support
d. bolted for the Confederate states

87. When the Union began to _____, Northerners started allowing blacks into combat roles in the Civil War.
a. understand the importance of winning the war
b. experience exceptionally high casualty rates
c. fear a racial uprising
(d.) suffer from shortages of manpower

88. More than 38,000 black soldiers died in the Civil War; this was a mortality rate _____ that of white soldiers.
(a.) higher than
b. significantly lower than
c. a little bit lower than
d. the same as

89. The easiest task Jefferson Davis and the Confederate government faced was
a. working with the states.
(b.) building the armed forces.
c. financing the war.
d. creating an industrial sector to supply war materiel

90. The Union blockade of the Confederate states made it necessary for the Confederate government to
(a.) build its own industrial sector.
b. support a fleet of blockade runners.
c. socialize private industries.
d. smuggle manufactured goods in from the North.

91. It was difficult for the Confederate government to finance the Civil War because
    a. it controlled no wealth.
    b. its officials did not understand economics.
    c. Southerners had invested in land and slaves.
    d. all the banks were in the North.

92. Ultimately, the Confederate government's financial measures
    a. failed to transform the South's agricultural economy into an industrial one.
    b. successfully transformed the South's agricultural economy into an industrial one.
    c. at least produced the supplies the South needed.
    d. made no headway at all in industrial production.

93. Which one of the following did not result from the Confederate government's attempts to prosecute the Civil War?
    a. The passage of the first draft law in American history
    b. The increased popularity of Jefferson Davis and his administration
    c. The adoption of a policy of confiscating supplies from private citizens
    d. Richmond's taking control of southern railroads and shipping

94. During the Civil War, the Southern war effort created hardships that fell most heavily on
    a. small slaveholders.
    b. the poor.
    c. large planters.
    d. urban dwellers.

95. In the South, the severe deprivation brought on by the Civil War had the effect of
    a. solidifying the bonds between slaveholders and nonslaveholders.
    b. encouraging rich individuals to share their wealth.
    c. undermining white Southerners' support.
    d. encouraging the Confederate government to start a large social welfare program.

96. Many southern yeomen believed that the Civil War's burdens were
    a. not terribly heavy.
    b. being carried by slaveholders.
    c. spread out equally among the population.
    d. being shouldered disproportionately by themselves.

97. The Confederate government at Richmond hoped that Civil War would mold the South into a nation; its attempts
    a. were moderately successful.
    b. managed to create a united slave republic.
    c. simply made things worse.
    d. did not decrease tension between yeomen and planters or win over Unionists.

98. The practical destruction of the southern slave system was accomplished
    a. through a constitutional amendment.
    b. by means of congressional legislation
    c. through presidential proclamation.
    d. by the Civil War itself.

99. Slave owners who attempted to resist the freeing of their slaves by fleeing the Union army found that
    a. flight gave their slaves additional opportunities to resist bondage.
    b. relocating their slaves reinstated plantation discipline.
    c. travel under wartime conditions was virtually impossible.
    d. there was no place for them to go.

100. When slaves began to resist their masters' demands as the Civil War progressed, white Southerners were
    a. shocked by the betrayal.
    b. saddened, but not surprised.
    c. almost always willing to respond with violence.
    d. prone to blaming the Union army.

101. When the Confederate administration in Richmond attempted to _____, it convinced many Southerners that their government had betrayed them.
   a. draft free blacks
   b. end slavery
   c. centralize power
   d. negotiate with the Union

102. By 1863, the flood of paper money printed by the Confederate government had led to _____.
   a. a shocking deflation
   b. greater confidence in the government
   c. debilitating inflation
   d. economic stability

103. The Confederate government adopted a policy of impressment, allowing officials to _____ private citizens.
   a. confiscate food, horses, and other supplies from
   b. take money from
   c. demand war service of
   d. arbitrarily imprison

104. The Confederate war effort was damaged by fighting between _____ for control of money, supplies, and soldiers.
   a. southern counties
   b. southern states
   c. Richmond and the states
   d. different branches of the military

105. In the spring of 1863, _____ broke out in cities and villages throughout the South.
   a. bread riots
   b. antiwar demonstrations
   c. slave rebellions
   d. political violence

106. According to some estimates, when the Civil War ended in 1865 about a third of the Confederate soldiers had _____ as a consequence of severe deprivation.
   a. suffered from severe malnutrition
   b. defected to the Union army
   c. died of disease
   d. already gone home

107. The Confederate government's "twenty-Negro law" _____ and added to class tensions.
   a. allowed the army to confiscate twenty slaves from each large plantation
   b. exempted one white man from plantations with twenty or more slaves
   c. redistributed slaves to areas that were short on labor
   d. provided military guards for large plantations

108. The Confederate government's attempts to build consensus and unity _____ Unionists in the South.
   a. alienated
   b. amused
   c. did not win over
   d. won over

109. When white women assumed managerial control over plantations, they discovered that they _____.
   a. liked to be in charge
   b. felt sorry for their slaves
   c. had no interest in supporting the war effort
   d. could not maintain discipline

110. As the institution of slavery disintegrated, slaves increasingly _____.
   a. rebelled violently against their masters
   b. undermined white mastery
   c. showed their loyalty to their masters
   d. refused to work under any conditions

111. When the Republicans took office in 1861, they inherited from the Democrats a financial and economic structure that
   a. had helped to develop economic resources.
   b. reflected their own economic philosophy.
   c. was already strong.
   d. restricted the government's role in the economy.

112. During the Civil War, the Republicans were able to
   a. prevent the federal government from interfering in the economy.
   b. enact their platform of federal programs to encourage economic growth.
   c. pass very little of the legislation they supported.
   d. pass laws to undermine the Democratic Party.

113. When Congress passed the National Banking Act in February 1863, it created
   a. a national currency.
   b. the Bureau of Internal Revenue.
   c. a new system of state banks.
   d. a new system of national banks.

114. Legislation passed by the Republicans during the Civil War
   a. helped the northern war effort.
   b. permanently changed the nation.
   c. neither of the above.
   d. both of the above.

115. When northern farmers took up arms in the Civil War, their tasks were taken over by
   a. runaway slaves.
   b. women.
   c. paid agricultural laborers.
   d. government employees.

116. During the Civil War, when the northern industrial boom caused unemployment to decline and wages to rise,
   a. workers' standard of living fell due to inflation and taxes.
   b. owners found that their profits were decreasing.
   c. the trend toward specialization and mechanization was halted.
   d. rural people refused to remain on farms.

117. When women entered the manufacturing workforce during the Civil War,
   a. they became disillusioned with the war effort.
   b. employers cut wages.
   c. employers raised their wages to the same levels as men's.
   d. men refused to work with them.

118. Thousands of women on both sides of the Civil War expressed their patriotism in an untraditional way by
   a. becoming nurses.
   b. selling homemade goods at fairs to raise money.
   c. volunteering as soldiers.
   d. performing unpaid labor to support the war effort.

119. In the Union, the continued existence of a two-party system during the Civil War
   a. helped to structure political debate.
   b. made it impossible for President Lincoln to effectively prosecute the war.
   c. had little effect on the political scene.
   d. led to fruitless bickering.

120. The case of Democratic dissenter Clement L. Vallandigham raised the issue of
   a. how valid the Constitution was.
   b. whether Democrats should be allowed to remain in Congress.
   c. whether criticism of the war was free speech or treason.
   d. the extent to which Southerners were committing treason.

121. Poor northern men objected to the Union's 1863 draft law because it
   a. was unconstitutional.
   b. allowed a draftee to hire a substitute or pay a $300 fee to avoid service.
   c. forced recruits to pay a fee to the government.
   d. specifically exempted wealthy men.

122. During the Civil War, black leaders in the North
   a. championed emigration to Africa.
   b. made no progress on black civil rights.
   c. won a few victories for black civil rights.
   d. won overwhelming victories for black civil rights.

123. In the early 1860s, the Republican Party advocated an economic program that _____.
   a. called for the minimum amount of government intrusion
   b. advocated government ownership of most businesses
   c. divorced the government from the economy entirely
   d. rested on government support to develop economic resources

124. The _____ halved Democratic representation in Congress in 1861.
   a. secession of eleven slave states
   b. unwillingness of the party to support the war
   c. Lincoln administration's harassment
   d. poor handling of secession winter

125. The Homestead Act, which _____, was passed by Congress in May 1862.
   a. prevented speculators from purchasing government land
   b. provided settlers with land that railroads did not want
   c. gave settlers land at half the old price
   d. offered free land to settlers who would live on and work it

126. In the rural North, _____ resulted in prosperity during the Civil War.
   a. higher wages for day laborers
   b. the availability of factory jobs
   c. high prices and increased production
   d. massive government subsidies

127. The northern industrial boom of the Civil War years benefited _____ more than any other group.
   a. the workers
   b. white workers
   c. factory owners
   d. the federal government

128. During the Civil War urban factory workers _____ to try to improve their salaries.
   a. pleaded with owners
   b. petitioned the government
   c. went on strike
   d. sabotaged war production

129. Many northern women experienced a _____ from becoming nurses during the Civil War.
   a. lasting revulsion for war
   b. raise in their pay
   c. taste of action as combatants
   d. sense of profound satisfaction

130. President Lincoln's 1862 decision to _____ caused Democrats to label the administration a "reign of terror."
   a. place civilians who engaged in disloyal practices under martial law
   b. suppress the Democratic Party entirely
   c. execute political opponents
   d. use the army to intimidate voters

131. In 1866, the Supreme Court decision in *Ex parte Milligan* found that it was unconstitutional to _____.
   a. criticize the government during wartime
   b. subject civilians to military trial as long as civilian courts were in operation
   c. have a two-party system during wartime
   d. stifle all political debate during wartime.

132. In response to the 1863 draft act, mobs rioted against _____ in northern cities.
   a. the wealthy
   b. the federal government
   c. blacks
   d. southern sympathizers

133. General Grant took the Confederate stronghold of Vicksburg, Mississippi, by means of
   a. a direct assault.
   b. a complicated naval operation.
   c. delicate negotiations.
   d. a lengthy siege.

134. In 1863, General Lee decided to attack the Union army at Gettysburg, Pennsylvania, in the hope of
   a. convincing European nations that the South could still win the war.
   b. moving the fighting out of Virginia and defeating the Union army on its own turf.
   c. cementing his own reputation as a brilliant strategist.
   d. totally destroying the Union's ability to keep fighting.

135. General Lee's mistake at the Battle of Gettysburg was to
   a. retreat too quickly.
   b. allow his battle plan to fall into the hands of the Union army.
   c. rely too much on his junior officers.
   d. order a direct assault on dug-in Union soldiers.

136. After the loss of Vicksburg and the Battle of Gettysburg, the Confederates
   a. demoted General Lee.
   b. realized that they were going to lose.
   c. decided to launch another major offensive in the North.
   d. still believed that they could win the war.

137. General Grant's September 1863 victory over the Confederates at Chattanooga, Tennessee, was important because it
   a. was the first Union military success of the year.
   b. showed the renewed discipline of the Union forces.
   c. had immense strategic value.
   d. demonstrated the northern commitment to careful strategizing.

138. After General Grant became the general in chief of the Union armies in March 1864, he made two important decisions—to send the western armies into
   a. Georgia and take Lee on directly.
   b. South Carolina and avoid fighting Lee.
   c. Georgia and avoid fighting Lee.
   d. South Carolina and take Lee on directly.

139. Despite suffering heavy losses in his 1864 Virginia campaign, General Grant did not believe that he was defeated because he
   a. had easily taken the important railroad junction of Petersburg, Virginia.
   b. knew that the Confederates lost even more soldiers than the Union did.
   c. was able to take the capital of Richmond.
   d. knew that the Confederates were losing proportionally as many men.

140. General William T. Sherman's 1864 invasion of Georgia was intended to
   a. give the North control over Georgia's important natural resources.
   b. destroy the will of the southern people to fight.
   c. hunt down Confederate government leaders.
   d. force General Lee to abandon Virginia and protect the Deep South instead.

141. President Lincoln insisted on holding presidential elections in 1864 because he believed that
   a. he would easily win reelection.
   b. to fail to do so would be to concede a moral victory to the South.
   c. elections would give the Republicans a strong majority in Congress.
   d. the nation was ready for a change in administration.

142. When President Lincoln won reelection in 1864, he received a mandate to
   a. give northern blacks equal civil rights.
   b. crack down on the Democratic Party.
   c. negotiate peace with the South.
   d. continue fighting the war.

143. By the beginning of 1865, more and more southern whites lost the will to fight the Union because they
   a. had been battered into submission.
   b. had lost faith in the cause of southern independence.
   c. realized that they had been swindled by slaveholders.
   d. recognized that the North's free-labor system was superior.

144. In March 1865, Jefferson Davis made one last attempt to reinvigorate the Confederate commitment to the Civil War by proposing
a. higher pay for soldiers.
b. the arming of slaves.
c. the lowering of the age for enlistment.
d. a redistribution of slaves.

145. By the middle of 1863, the efforts of General _____ meant that the Confederates began to suffer a series of devastating military reversals.
a. George G. Meade
b. William Rosecrans
c. Ulysses S. Grant
d. George McClellan

146. The city of Vicksburg, Mississippi, was strategically important in the Civil War because it was the _____.
a. birthplace of Jefferson Davis.
b. major agricultural centerof the South.
c. producer of most of the South's military supplies.
d. only thing preventing the Union from controlling the Mississippi River.

147. The Confederate military disasters at _____ in 1863 were, in hindsight, the turning points of the Civil War.
a. Gettysburg and Fort Henry
b. Gettysburg and Fort Donelson
c. Vicksburg and Fort Henry
d. Vicksburg and Gettysburg

148. In the 1864 Battle of the Wilderness, _____ helped General Lee offset the Union army's numerical superiority.
a. improved artillery
b. scrub oaks and small pines
c. brilliant strategy
d. bad weather

149. In the 1864 fighting in Virginia, General Lee lost _____ General Grant.
a. proportionally as many troops as
b. more troops than
c. only a quarter of the troops lost by
d. a significant number of deserters to

150. General William T. Sherman used a _____ in Georgia in hopes of destroying southern resistance.
a. series of sieges
b. large number of black soldiers
c. campaign of kindness
d. scorched-earth campaign

151. In the 1864 presidential campaign, the Democratic Party ran General George McClellan on _____ platform.
a. a war
b. a peace
c. an antiblack
d. a pro-civil liberties

152. By the start of 1865, the Union controlled _____ of the Confederacy.
a. only the port cities
b. just the western part
c. the interior
d. all

153. As the Civil War continued into 1865, many southern whites _____ the rebellion.
a. grew to loathe
b. no longer believed in the cause of
c. strongly supported
d. gave up on

154. On April 9, 1865, General Lee _____ near the village of Appomattox Courthouse, Virginia.
a. died in battle.
b. escaped from General Grant
c. surrendered to General Grant
d. renounced the Confederacy

***Short Answer*** Write a paragraph response to each question.

1. What factors influenced President Lincoln's decision to restock Fort Sumter in April 1861?
2. Why did half of the eight slave states of the Upper South choose to secede after Fort Sumter? Why did the other half remain in the Union?
3. How did white Southerners justify their decision to secede from the United States? What did they present as their rationale for fighting? Was that their real reason?
4. How did Southerners expect that they could win the Civil War, given the North's overwhelming superiority in resources?
5. How did people perceive Jefferson Davis and Abraham Lincoln when they first took office? How well did each man actually perform?
6. What occurred at the Battle of Manassas? What lessons did Northerners and Southerners draw from it?
7. Why was the western theater so important to the Civil War effort?
8. What was King Cotton diplomacy, and why did it fail with Great Britain?
9. What forced the Union to confront the issue of emancipation?
10. What were the terms of the Emancipation Proclamation? How did Democrats respond to it?
11. How did military service in the Civil War affect black soldiers when their terms of enlistment were over?
12. Why did the South find it difficult to develop its economy during the Civil War? What measures did the Confederate government take to modernize the southern economy, and how successful were these measures?
13. What Southerners suffered most from wartime deprivation? What social effects did deprivation produce?
14. How did the Civil War transform the institution of slavery?
15. What financial measures did the new Republican administration pass during the Civil War years?
16. How did northern women contribute to the Civil War effort?
17. What argument did the Democrats use to protest the 1863 draft law? How did northern whites respond to the new law? What about it did they find objectionable?
18. What occurred at Vicksburg and Gettysburg? Why did those battles prove to be decisive to the outcome of the Civil War?
19. What differences of opinion split the Democrats during the 1864 presidential election?
20. What was Jefferson Davis's last proposal to keep the Civil War going? How was his suggestion received?

***Building Historical Skills*** Historians use a variety of sources to think and talk about the past, including maps, illustrations, and written records. Maps provide a variety of different kinds of comparative information in a condensed visual format; reading them requires learning how to sort through this information. To deepen our understanding of the past by supplementing written records, historians frequently interpret material culture, such as a vase or a painting, with techniques borrowed from art history, archaeology, or anthropology. Written records, though familiar as sources, raise their own problems of interpretation. Every document reflects someone's particular perspective or assumptions. It is the historian's task to carefully study and compare each document to other records with other perspectives. The following exercises introduce you to using maps, illustrations, and written documents as sources of information. Use these sources as well as the material in the chapter to think about different themes and topics discussed in the text.

**Map Activity** Locate the following places on Map 14.3: The Civil War, 1863–1865 on page 523 in *The American Promise,* Second Edition.

1. Richmond, Virginia
2. Cumberland River
3. Atlanta, Georgia
4. Vicksburg, Mississippi
5. Tennessee River
6. Appomattox Courthouse
7. Gettysburg, Pennsylvania
8. Savannah, Georgia
9. Chattanooga, Tennessee

Answer the following questions in four to six sentences based on Map 14.3: The Civil War. 1863–1865.

**READING THE MAP** Describe the difference between Union and Confederate naval strength. Were the battles shown fought primarily in Union-controlled or Confederate-controlled territory?

**CONNECTIONS** Did former slaves serve in the Civil War? If so, on which side(s)? Describe their efforts.

**WEB LINKS** To explore the topics discussed in the exercise above, visit the Web links noted below.

"Civil War Sites Advisory Commission Battle Summaries"
http://www2.cr.nps.gov/abpp/battles/tvii.htm
Choose "Battles by Campaign."

"Confederate States of America's Plan to Put Slaves in the Trenches"
http://www.coax.net/people/lwf/csa_ampt.htm

"Civil War Soldiers and Sailors System"
http://www.itd.nps.gov/cwss/

***Visual Activity*** Answer the following questions in a paragraph based on "Union Ordnance, Yorktown, Virginia" on page 519 in *The American Promise*, Second Edition.

**READING THE IMAGE** What does this image indicate about northern military might in the Civil War? "Ordnance" is a term that refers to all of the weapons and ammunition that are used in warfare, and the photograph of the Union's stockpile of it at Yorktown, Virginia, demonstrates that the North had a great deal of it. In the foreground of the picture is an orderly stack of cannonballs piled several layers deep. The middle of the photo is dominated by rows and rows of cannons. In the back, there are numerous sailing ships as well. The soldiers guarding the ordnance look as if they are doing well by the supply system too. They are all wearing full uniforms; they are dusty, but their clothes are not ripped or worn. The overall effect is one of plenty: the Union soldiers have adequate clothing and plenty of weapons to continue fighting the war.

**CONNECTIONS** What role did the North's industrial power play in the Union victory in the Civil War?

**WEB LINKS** To explore the topics discussed in the exercise above, visit the Web links noted below.

"Civil War Images of Northern Virginia"
http://www.gmu.edu/library/specialcollections/vaprints.html

"On the Road to Appomattox—Grant and Lee from War to Peace" by Professor John Y. Simon
http://www.tsa.si.edu/cw/simon/segments.htm

***Analyzing Sources Activity*** Answer the following questions in a paragraph based on "Documenting the American Promise: Home and Country" on page 516.

1. For Marion and Mary Epperly, what explains the suffering of the South in the Civil War? How do they see the matter differently?
2. How does Marion contrast life in the Union with life in the Confederacy?
3. In what ways does the Epperlys' perspective on the Confederacy reflect their social position as plain folk in Virginia society?
4. Marion makes it clear why he had such affection for his home; he is much less clear about why he fought for the Confederacy. What might some of his reasons have been?

**WEB LINKS** To explore the topics discussed in the exercise above, visit the Web links noted below.

"Journal of Colonel Allen L. Fahnestock, 86th Illinois Volunteer Infantry"
http://www.rsa.lib.il.us/~ilalive/files/pe/htm1/pe000001.html

"Civil War Correspondence of Lt. Sumner Paine"
http://www.people.virginia.edu/~mmd5f/paineletters.htm

"The Southern Homefront, 1861–1865" by William L. Barney
http://docsouth.unc.edu/imls/politintro.html

# Answer Key

## Chapter 14: The Crucible of War, 1861–1865

### *Chapter Overview*

#### *Chronology*

1. c
2. d
3. d
4. b
5. a
6. a
7. c
8. c
9. b
10. a

#### *Defining Terms*

1. Confederate States of America
2. Fort Sumter
3. Robert E. Lee
4. Kentucky
5. West Virginia
6. "people's contest"
7. King Cotton diplomacy
8. offensive-defensive strategy
9. Jefferson Davis
10. Confederate Ordnance Bureau
11. Battle of Manassas or Bull Run
12. General George McClellan
13. western theater
14. General Ulysses S. Grant
15. ironclad warship
16. Confiscation Act
17. contraband of war
18. colonization
19. Emancipation Proclamation
20. Militia Act
21. conscription law of 1862
22. impressment policy
23. Confederate inflation
24. tax-in-kind
25. twenty-Negro law
26. Homestead Act
27. National Banking Act
28. U.S. Sanitary Commission
29. "reign of terror"
30. *Ex parte Milligan*
31. Vicksburg
32. Battle of Gettysburg
33. scorched-earth campaign
34. Copperheads
35. Appomattox Courthouse

### *Chapter Review*

#### *Multiple-Choice*

1. c
2. a
3. d
4. b
5. d
6. d
7. a
8. a
9. b
10. a
11. b
12. a
13. a
14. b
15. a
16. b
17. d
18. d
19. c
20. d
21. d
22. c
23. c
24. c
25. a
26. b
27. b
28. b
29. a
30. b
31. a
32. d
33. a
34. a
35. d
36. d
37. a
38. d
39. d
40. a
41. b
42. c
43. a
44. d
45. c
46. d
47. d
48. c
49. c
50. a
51. b
52. c
53. b
54. a
55. b
56. d
57. b
58. c
59. d
60. a
61. b
62. b
63. d
64. d
65. a
66. d
67. c
68. b
69. b
70. a
71. d
72. b

73. a
74. c
75. b
76. c
77. a
78. b
79. b
80. b
81. b
82. d
83. c
84. a
85. d
86. a
87. d
88. a
89. b
90. a
91. c
92. a
93. b
94. b
95. c
96. d
97. d
98. d
99. a
100. a
101. c
102. c
103. a
104. c
105. a
106. d
107. b
108. c
109. d
110. b
111. d
112. b
113. d
114. c
115. b
116. a
117. b
118. a
119. a
120. c
121. b
122. c
123. d
124. a
125. d
126. c
127. c
128. c
129. d
130. a
131. b
132. c
133. d
134. b
135. d
136. d
137. c
138. a
139. d
140. b
141. d
142. d
143. a
144. b
145. c
146. d
147. d
148. b
149. a
150. d
151. b
152. c
153. d
154. c

### *Short Answer*

1. In April 1861, Fort Sumter, a federal fort located on a small island at the entrance of the Charleston harbor, needed supplies, a fact that confronted newly inaugurated President Lincoln with a difficult decision. If he evacuated the fort, he would gain the support of the Upper South, which was still threatening to secede if Lincoln used military force against the Confederacy. However, that decision would have numerous negative ramifications in the North, implying that President Lincoln accepted secession, dividing the northern public, and harming the new Republican administration. In the end, he chose what he hoped would be a middle course: he authorized an expedition to bring to the fort supplies but not military reinforcements. This honored his inaugural promise to protect federal property and avoid using military force unless attacked and shifted the decision of war to Jefferson Davis.
2. When President Lincoln called for troops after the Confederate attack on Fort Sumter, residents of the Upper South were forced to decide whether they preferred to fight Southerners or the Union. Many who opposed southern independence were still not willing to go to war against other Southerners, and so Virginia, Arkansas, North Carolina, and Tennessee seceded. However, the states of Delaware, Maryland, Kentucky, and Missouri stayed in the Union. Delaware had a tiny slave population; in Maryland, President Lincoln suspended civil rights to encourage the legislature to vote against secession. In Missouri and Kentucky, Union sentiment barely triumphed.
3. Southerners argued that, like the patriots of 1776, they were merely a minority group fighting to preserve their liberty against a tyrannical central government that wished to force its values and ways on them. They used language that focused on states' rights, self-determination, and the need to protect their special southern civilization from northern encroachments. In reality, however, slavery played a large part in the decision to secede and go to war. Yeomen and slaveholders alike benefited from the institution, which elevated the status of all whites; and slavery constituted a large part of what made the South distinctive.
4. The northern states controlled much more of the resources to make war than the South: they had more people, more railroads, and more manufacturing concerns. Yet Southerners believed that they had a number of significant advantages. They argued that their rural population would make better soldiers than the urban dwellers of the North. Many maintained that northern and European dependence on cotton would give the South an economic edge. Finally, Southerners pointed to the vast expanse of territory that the North would have to conquer, as well as the rugged terrain and bad roads that would complicate any such attempt.

5. When the war broke out in 1861, Jefferson Davis struck many observers as better presidential material than Abraham Lincoln. He had a long record of military and political service, while Lincoln had one term in the house and a brief stint in the Illinois militia. However, in office Davis turned out to be a clumsy politician, with a sharp tongue that won him enemies and an inability to stop intervening in military affairs. Lincoln, on the other hand, was an excellent leader who did not allow his personal feelings to cloud his judgment, and he had a superb understanding of military strategy.
6. At the Battle of Manassas, the first engagement of the Civil War, raw Union soldiers attacked the southern forces but were routed in a panicky stampede. Southerners concluded that the battle confirmed the superiority of their soldiers and their inevitable victory over the Union. For Northerners, the defeat demonstrated that the war was going to be much longer and more difficult than they had expected. Lincoln had initially 75,000 soldiers to serve for ninety days; after Manassas, he authorized the enlistment of one million men for three years.
7. In the early days of the war, most of the public's attention was focused on the eastern theater, but the decisive battles took place in the west because the control of western rivers—the Mississippi, the Tennessee, and the Cumberland—was important to both the North and the South. Taking the rivers would give the South access to Missouri and Kentucky, which the Confederacy claimed but did not control. Northerners realized that if they could grab the Mississippi River, they would split Arkansas, Louisiana, and Texas from the Confederacy. Moreover, control of the Tennessee and the Cumberland Rivers would allow Union forces to cut the South off from Tennessee, which was the South's major source of vitally important food, mules, and iron.
8. When the war began, Southerners assumed that Great Britain would intervene to protect its supply of southern cotton. Yet while Great Britain granted the Confederacy "belligerent" status, it did not recognize Confederate statehood and did not enter the war. The British had plenty of cotton throughout 1861 because of a bumper cotton crop in 1860, and when that ran out, they turned to Egypt and India. A brisk trade in war materiel, grain, and flour developed between Great Britain and the Union, giving it a strong financial reason to avoid becoming involved. Finally, in 1862 Union military successes in the West and President Lincoln's new policy that made an alliance with the Confederacy an alliance with slavery meant that Great Britain was unwilling to link its fate to that of the Confederacy.
9. The problem of what to do with runaway slaves was the single most insistent force behind the North's acceptance of emancipation as part of the wartime agenda. Tens of thousands of slaves ran away and took refuge behind Union lines, compelling federal commanders to determine whether the fugitives were free or slaves who had to be returned to their masters. At first many commanders sent slaves back, but others recognized that the army needed more laborers and put them to work instead. In Virginia, General Benjamin F. Butler gave the runaways a new status, "contraband of war," which meant that they were confiscated property. In March 1862, Congress officially forbade the practice of returning slave to their masters, although it did not free them either.
10. The Emancipation Proclamation that President Lincoln promulgated in January 1863 declared that all slaves in the seceding states were free. He hoped to maintain the loyalty of border states by maintaining slavery there, and he also exempted Confederate territory under Union control. By presenting emancipation as a military necessity that would deprive the South of an important source of labor and thus shorten the war, he thought that he could quell criticism. Instead, there was an outpouring of rage from the Democratic Party, which claimed that he had given into abolitionist demands and shifted the war from a fight to save the Union to one to protect blacks.
11. From its inception, blacks viewed the Civil War as a struggle for black equality, and they lobbied hard to be allowed to serve in combatant roles in the armed forces. Although black soldiers faced intense discrimination in the army and navy, they gained confidence, pride, and self-esteem from their service. The very process of forcing the military to accept black recruits gave blacks valuable political skills that they were able to use after their service was over.
12. Prior to the war, the South had almost no industrial sector; Southerners had invested heavily in land and slaves, which were not easy to use in support of the war effort. Because of these conditions coupled with the Union blockade, the Richmond administration had to modernize the economy by creating factories to produce war materiel from scratch. Yet despite radical measures like taking control of the South's railroads and shipping, the Confederacy was not able to produce all of the goods that it needed. The gap between southern and northern production widened steadily. In addition, the flood of paper money printed to finance the war effort caused runaway inflation.
13. Debilitating inflation was one of the greatest hardships produced by the war, and it hit poor

Southerners the hardest; in particular, rising food prices threatened the poor with starvation. As yeomen went to war, their wives and children were left to raise food crops on their own, without the aid of slaves, creating more suffering. The deprivation caused many poor white Southerners to abandon the war effort entirely. About a third of the Confederate armies had already returned home, oftentimes to help their families, before the war officially ended in 1865. The extreme suffering of the poor compared with the relative well-being of planters fueled class animosity, and friction between yeomen and planters increased.

14. By disrupting the routine, organization, and discipline of the slave system, the war contributed to the loosening and then the destruction of slavery. As slave masters went to war, they left plantations under the control of their wives, who could not maintain the same level of discipline. The war depressed the production of cotton, which had been slaves' principal work, and military action caused many slave owners to flee, giving slaves more opportunities to resist the terms of their bondage. As the war ground on, many slaves simply refused to follow plantation discipline, arriving in the fields late and leaving early. Many slave owners found that they had to bribe their slaves to perform any work at all.

15. The Republicans advocated government support to help develop economic resources, and the halving of Democratic strength in Congress allowed them to pass an aggressive program of federal intervention. Congress passed the Homestead Act, which gave settlers free land in exchange for their willingness to live on and work their new farms, and the Pacific Railroad Act, which provided federal assistance to build a transcontinental railroad. Republicans raised the tariff to protect manufacturers against foreign competition, created a national currency, and sponsored the National Banking Act, establishing system of federal banks to replace the old decentralized state banks. Congressional Republicans also overhauled the tax system, instituting sweeping new tax laws and establishing the Bureau of Internal Revenue to collect the new income.

16. Women in the northern states contributed to the war effort by stepping into jobs that men had vacated; in rural areas they took over agricultural production, and in cities they worked in factories and in the government civil service. Many women made traditionally home-centered contributions, laboring in sewing circles, wrapping bandages, and selling homemade goods at fairs to raise money for soldiers. Others took the less conventional route of volunteering as nurses, an occupation that had been seen as inappropriate for delicate females. Some even became paid military nurses.

17. Democrats were upset by the Republicans' 1863 draft law, which, they maintained, was an unconstitutional measure designed to force northern men to fight for the unconstitutional emancipation of southern slaves. Many northern whites seemed agree with the Democrats' assessment. Poor whites were especially enraged by the fact that a draftee could hire a substitute or pay $300 to get out of his military obligation, leading poor Northerners to call the military action "a rich man's war and a poor man's fight." In the summer of 1863, mobs went on antiblack riots in northern cities; in New York, a four-day riot left 105 people, most of them black, dead.

18. Vicksburg, Mississippi, and Gettysburg, Pennsylvania, were the locations of two major Confederate defeats. The fall of Vicksburg in July 1863 after a long siege gave the Union control of the entire Mississippi River, and the Confederate decision to mount a major assault against entrenched Union lines at Gettysburg resulted in General Lee's loss of more than a third of his army. After those disastrous losses, the Confederacy was never able to entirely regain its momentum. The southern armies could not replace the 60,000 soldiers who were captured, wounded, or killed and never again attempted to invade the North.

19. President Lincoln fully expected to lose the election of 1864 because of widespread dissatisfaction with the stalled war effort, inflation, the draft, the restriction of civil liberties, and emancipation. Yet the Democrats were divided between a peace faction that wanted to end the war and war Democrats who supported the conflict but not the way that the Republicans were fighting it. They tried to bridge their differences by nominating General George McClellan, the former commander of the Army of the Potomac, and running him on a peace platform that demanded an immediate armistice with the Confederacy.

20. In early 1865, Jefferson Davis, well aware that poor Southerners were abandoning the war, proposed that slaves could be made Confederate soldiers. He wanted to arm slaves in return for a vague promise of freedom. General Lee approved, as did the Confederate Congress. However, rural slaveholders were overwhelmingly opposed to the idea, preferring to sacrifice southern independence than to lose the slave system.

### *Map Activity*

Reading the Map: The North's navy was the one branch of the Union military that was in fairly good shape when the war broke out in 1861: there were three dozen ships in service, and most of the officers and men were Unionists. A major prong of the Union strategy rested on a naval blockade of southern ports, which would make it impossible for the Confederacy to ship its cotton overseas to pay for supplies, and by the end of the war the U.S. navy was commissioning a new blockader almost weekly. Southerners attempted to counter the vastly superior Union navy by experimenting with a new type of ship, the ironclad warship. However, the Union quickly produced its own, rendering the southern advantage temporary. By 1865, the Union blockade covered almost the entire southern coastline from Louisiana, around Florida, and all the way up to North Carolina. The blockade helped the Union maintain control of nearly half of the South's coastal areas.

Connections: About 100,000 former slaves fought as soldiers in the Union army over the course of the Civil War. Black Union soldiers proved to be ferocious fighters. They suffered a casualty rate proportionally higher than that of white troops, and they played a crucial role in the Union victory and the destruction of the slave system. Many thousands of runaways were employed less directly as well; Union commanders often defined fugitives as "contraband" and used them to perform various kinds of labor in army camps. By the end of the war, the Confederacy was so desperate for manpower that Jefferson Davis considered arming slaves and having them fight the Union in return for their freedom.

### *Visual Activity*

Reading the Image: The photograph of Union ordnance at Yorktown, Virginia, shows very clearly that the Union army was well stocked with basic military supplies. They literally possess stacks of cannonballs and rows of cannons. The sailing ships in the background indicate the Union's naval power. The picture also implies that the North was not running short of manpower either: the ordnance has plenty of protection in the form of well-dressed, well-armed soldiers.

Connections: Although the Confederates did better on the battlefield during the early days of the war, the North's industrial might stood as a counterweight to that advantage. The Union simply had more of everything—people, railroads, factories, and so on. The South was never able to produce enough to supply its armies, despite its efforts to become self-sufficient, and they were cut off from the rest of the world by the Union naval blockade. The cost of fighting the war caused the Confederate economy to plummet, and deprivation eventually contributed to ordinary citizens' disenchantment with the war. In the North, however, war production caused the economy to go into high gear, lessening popular discontent.

### *Analyzing Sources*

1. Marion believed that the South is suffering because it made the wrong political decisions: he wrote to Mary that "our own wickedness and disobedians has brought us to what we are." In a later letter, he commented that blame could also be laid on "the leading men," who were too interested in alcohol and "frolicking" to attend to the war as they should have. Mary was unhappy with the Confederate leadership as well; after the conscription law covered all males between the ages of seventeen and fifty she speculated that perhaps the government would draft women next. She felt that ordinary soldiers were contributing to the suffering as well, however, stating that she was "not afrade of the yankeys treating us any worse nor not half as bad as our own men dos," referring to the Confederate practice of impressment, in which officials had the authority to seize horses, personal property, and whatever they considered essential for the war effort.
2. Marion argued that life in the Union was a blissful time in which "we . . . was living happy and had all a man can wish for." He felt that life in the Confederacy had reduced Southerners to the status of slaves and that its leadership was drunk and dissolute. Having cut themselves off from the Union, Southerners had become "a ruend people." Marion hoped that returning to the Union would return the South to the prewar status quo.
3. The Epperlys clearly resented the Confederate leadership, which they believed was incompetent at best and morally corrupt at worst. Marion in particular complained that southern leaders were forcing soldiers to fight and suffer while they looked for "the Bottom of a Whiskey Barl." Mary showed outrage at things like high food prices, low pay for soldiers, and conscription, none of which were pressing issues for wealthy Southerners. They clearly did not feel any overwhelming loyalty for the Confederate government; both Marion and Mary expressed their sympathy for deserters, and Mary even hoped that desertions would force the government to stop fighting.
4. Marion's letters never explained why he chose to fight in the Confederate army. In fact, he seemed to have little but contempt for the Confederate

government and little attachment to the causes for which it was supposedly fighting. It is possible that he, like many other ordinary white Southerners, believed strongly in protecting the slave system to reinforce white supremacy. He does mention that the war "first started on a just course," but that it has lost its moral bearings, which could indicate that he believed in protecting the South against a tyrannical centralized government but felt that the Confederate government had not proved to be any more responsible than the old Union one had been.

CHAPTER

# RECONSTRUCTION, 1863–1877 15

## Chapter Overview

### *Chapter Summary*

***Introduction*** This chapter opens with an account of South Carolina slaveholder David Golightly Harris's response to emancipation, which he had a great deal of difficulty handling. In particular, he was not sure how he would get blacks to work if he were not allowed to force them to labor. General Carl Schurz's fact-finding mission to evaluate conditions in the formerly Confederate South showed that victory over the South might have destroyed slavery but it had not erased proslavery ideas. Over time, white Southerners would attempt to reconstitute as much as possible the antebellum social order, thus reducing emancipated African Americans to a level of economic subservience that virtually reenslaved them. Yet, at least temporarily, a program of radical reconstruction of the southern states would provide African Americans with the benefits and challenges of political and civil rights. The nation had embarked on a tumultuous and conflicted era—reconstruction.

***Wartime Reconstruction, pp. 538–545*** Lincoln's primary objective was to restore the Union through a program of speedy, forgiving political reconciliation. Many Republicans, however, opposed the president's agenda, fearing that such leniency would allow the southern antebellum elite to regain their power. Radicals wanted assurances of white loyalty and greater guarantees of black rights. Rival plans thus emerged during the war, but Lincoln and Congress managed to compromise on their respective courses.

**"TO BIND UP THE NATION'S WOUNDS"** In December 1863, even before the war ended, Lincoln formulated a Reconstruction plan—the "10 percent plan" that offered a general amnesty to all white Southerners, with the temporary exception of Confederate high civil and military officials. As soon as 10 percent of the number of 1860 voters in any state took a loyalty oath, they could set up a state government. At this juncture, Lincoln was interested primarily in restoring the Union as soon as possible and was willing to postpone questions about race relations. Concerned about the mildness of this program, in July 1864 Republicans pushed through Congress the stronger Wade-Davis Bill, which required the majority of voters in each conquered state to take the oath of allegiance before Reconstruction could begin and forbade former Confederates from participating in the drafting of new state constitutions. Lincoln refused to sign the bill. Lincoln did show some flexibility, declaring in his last public address in April 1865 that he endorsed the idea of limited suffrage for blacks. However, on the night of April 14, 1865, the president was shot; fatally wounded, he died the following day.

**LAND AND LABOR** As Yankee armies seized Confederate property and thousands of slaves became free workers, what to do with this land and how to organize labor on it became critical issues. A number of wartime labor experiments were attempted, but it was along the Mississippi Valley that a labor system developed that would most resemble postwar southern labor relations. Here, Union commanders enacted a labor code requiring planters to sign contracts with former slaves, to pay them wages, and to provide food, housing, and medical care. Though liberating slaves from formal bondage, the code forced black laborers to enter into contracts, work hard, and remain subservient to their white employers. In short, the army sought to restore plantation agriculture with wage labor, not to incite a social or economic revolution. Planters protested this new order, but so did many African Americans, who recognized it as merely a different manifestation of their previous bondage. A more promising development was the establishment of the Freedmen's Bureau in March 1865, which provided food and clothing to former slaves and was authorized to rent forty-acre plots of confiscated land to freedmen.

**THE AFRICAN AMERICAN QUEST FOR AUTONOMY** Emancipated slaves experimented with their newfound freedom in a variety of ways, from the symbolic act of simply leaving the plantation (though many at first chose to remain in or close to the familiar fields and kitchens) to a whole range of other experiences that had been off limits before emancipation. Among these were worshiping in their own churches, learning to read and write, and traveling in search of family members from whom they'd been separated under slavery. There were also more subtle though no less significant changes in demeanor and behavior, such as no longer acting deferential toward whites.

***Presidential Reconstruction, pp. 545–549*** The task of pursuing reconstruction fell to Lincoln's successor, Andrew Johnson of Tennessee. He was sworn into office while Congress was not in session and so was able to make critical decisions about reunification with the South without legislative oversight throughout the summer and the fall. When Congress reconvened, Johnson declared that reconstruction was over, but to congressional Republicans his modest demands made a mockery of the sacrifices of the war.

**JOHNSON'S PROGRAM OF RECONCILIATION** Johnson was born to a poor southern family and had made his political career championing the interests of the plain folk against wealthy planters. However, he was a staunch Democrat who had become vice president only because the Republicans wanted to broaden their appeal in the 1864 election, and he had no sympathy for freedmen. Johnson's reconstruction plan offered some form of amnesty to Southerners who would take an oath of allegiance, but wealthy rebels (those worth more than $20,000) would have to apply directly to the president for pardons. To win readmission to the Union, a former Confederate state's citizens had to revoke their secession ordinance, abolish slavery and ratify the Thirteenth Amendment, and repudiate Confederate war debts. Johnson envisioned a quick and easy reconciliation between North and South and demonstrated no concern for freedmen.

**SOUTHERN RESISTANCE AND BLACK CODES** Delegates to southern state constitutional conventions were reluctant to abolish slavery, renounce secession, and grant suffrage to freedmen. Many states even elected prominent former Confederates to represent them in Congress. Most egregious to many northern whites was the passing of laws in the South known as the black codes. These were designed to give whites almost complete control over former slaves. The codes authorized local white officials to apprehend unemployed blacks, fine them for vagrancy, and hire them out to private employers to satisfy the fine. The codes also taxed blacks who took any jobs other than as plantation workers or domestic servants. The black codes represented a return to slavery in all but name. Johnson won useful allies by supporting the new southern governments, and southern voters returned large numbers of former Confederates to Congress in the 1865 elections.

**EXPANSION OF BLACK RIGHTS AND FEDERAL AUTHORITY** Northerners were angered by the black codes, which they saw as a sign that the South had not accepted its defeat in the war. Opposition to Johnson's reconstruction unified the moderate and radical wings of the Republican Party, and in 1866 Congress responded to the black codes by passing an act extending the life of the Freedmen's Bureau. Johnson vetoed the bill. In April 1866, Congress passed the first Civil Rights Act, declaring blacks citizens of the United States and granting the federal government the power to intervene in state affairs to protect the rights of citizens. Johnson vetoed both measures, but Congress resubmitted them and overrode the next round of vetoes.

***Congressional Reconstruction, pp. 549–555*** In the summer of 1866, the stage was set for a serious showdown between President Andrew Johnson and Congress. Johnson's refusal to compromise on constitutional questions and reconstruction policy had alienated even the most moderate congressional Republicans and persuaded them that more federal intervention in the South was necessary.

**THE FOURTEENTH AMENDMENT AND ESCALATING VIOLENCE** In April 1866, Congress proposed the Fourteenth Amendment, which made anyone born in the United States (or naturalized) automatically a citizen entitled to all the "privileges and immunities" guaranteed by the Constitution, including equal protection of the laws by both state and national governments. The amendment penalized states by reducing their representation in Congress if they denied suffrage to any adult male inhabitants. This meant that northern Republicans could not lose: if the South did not allow blacks to vote, it would lose significant representation in Congress and bolster the power of Republicans; if it did, blacks would certainly vote Republican and give the party a base in the South. Moreover, there were so few blacks in the North that if northern states did not enfranchise them, their representation would barely be affected. Tennessee approved the Fourteenth Amendment, but Johnson encouraged other southern states to resist. In the meantime, violence engulfed southern cities, with freedmen as the principal victims, convincing white Northerners that harsher reconstruction measures might be necessary. In the 1866 congressional elections Johnson opposed the Fourteenth Amendment, but northern voters returned Republican majorities to both houses of Congress.

**RADICAL RECONSTRUCTION AND MILITARY RULE** Despite the clear signs of anger on the part of the northern public, Southerners continued to defy reconstruction measures. This boosted the radicals' standing in the Republican Party, and in 1867 moderates and radicals joined together to pass a series of measures nullifying the president's governments and reorganizing the South on a new basis. The Military Reconstruction Act, passed in March 1867, divided the South into five military districts and placed the region under army rule. Military rule was to last until the southern states framed and ratified constitutions providing for black suffrage. Former Confederates were disqualified from voting for constitutional convention delegates and from voting in the elections to ratify the new charters, but freedmen were allowed to participate in this process. The confiscation of land for redistribution among freedmen, however, was not implemented, disappointing both radicals like Thaddeus Stevens and black Southerners. With the passage of the 1867 Reconstruction Acts, congressional reconstruction was virtually complete. The measures had left whites in possession of most of the South's land, but blacks had been given the ballot.

**IMPEACHING A PRESIDENT** Johnson's continuing efforts to block implementation of congressional reconstruction in the South convinced Radicals that the only way effectively to stop the president's interference was to impeach him. Under the Constitution, Congress could only impeach a president for "high crimes and misdemeanors." Johnson's dismissal of Secretary of War Edwin M. Stanton, who supported congressional policies, was in violation of the Tenure of Office Act, which forbade the president from removing civil officials, including cabinet members, without the consent of the Senate. With this dismissal as a pretext, the Radicals were able to begin impeachment proceedings. In May 1868, however, after almost two months of testimony, Johnson was acquitted. Though the Radicals had to drop the impeachment campaign, Johnson called a truce and, for the remainder of his term, reconstruction proceeded unimpaired by presidential interference.

**THE FIFTEENTH AMENDMENT AND WOMEN'S DEMANDS** The Republican effort to make equal rights for blacks the law of the land culminated in the Fifteenth Amendment, ratified in 1870. The amendment prohibited any state from denying citizens the right to vote because of race, color, or previous condition of servitude. A secondary aim of the amendment's sponsors was to enfranchise African Americans in those northern states that still denied them voting rights. Some who supported women's rights were bitterly disappointed that the amendment did not extend women the vote. Suffragists Elizabeth Cady Stanton and Susan B. Anthony, angered by the amendment's gender discrimination, campaigned against its ratification. However, Republicans did not want to endorse anything that might harm black gains, while more moderate suffragists argued that women could afford to wait for the vote. It was, as Frederick Douglass put it, "the Negro's hour."

***The Struggle in the South, pp. 555–562*** Implementing the Reconstruction Acts and constitutional amendments in the South constituted a formidable challenge. Traditional southern politics might have been destroyed, but many southern whites still had strong opinions about the social and economic disposition of the postwar South. The young Republican governments and the blacks within them who sought to exercise their lately won legal and political rights had their work cut out for them.

**FREEDMEN, YANKEES, AND YEOMEN** The most numerous southern Republicans were the freedmen, most of whom had no previous political experience and tried, therefore, to build institutions through which they could learn to exercise their power. The Republicans also attracted white Northerners who had relocated to the South. Conservative Southerners called these Northerners "carpetbaggers," implying that they could fit their possessions into a suitcase and that they would soon be leaving the region with their ill-gotten gains, but most of them were ambitious and educated young men, many of them Union army veterans, who looked to the South as a new frontier of opportunity, more promising than the West. Native-born white Southerners were the third element in the southern Republican Party: conservatives called them "scalawags," a term for runty horses or rascals. Many of the "scalawags" were poor yeoman farmers living in remote areas who had never owned slaves; they had never felt comfortable in the Democratic Party and hoped the Republicans' program of internal improvements would help end their economic isolation. It was upon this three-part coalition of freedmen, Yankees, and yeomen that the Republican Party based its hope to become the majority party in the South. However, being a Republican in the South demanded courage. Democrats argued that the federal government had instituted an illegitimate political process and felt justified in combating it through vigilante violence.

**REPUBLICAN RULE** The reconstruction constitutions produced major changes in southern life, including universal male suffrage and expanded state responsibility for the general welfare.

Southern Democrats viewed the Republican program with horror and complained of "Negro domination" brought on by reconstruction, even though these claims had no basis in fact. In the South as a whole, the percentage of black officeholders was negligible when compared with the percentage of blacks in the population. The new Republican state governments confronted the daunting task of rebuilding the postwar South with activity in three main areas. They focused on building public education, attacking racial discrimination and protecting civil rights, and promoting economic development, especially through chartering banks and companies and extensive railroad building. While its ambitious agenda produced mixed results, the Republican Party had made progress in its early efforts to rid the South of aristocratic privilege and racist oppression.

**WHITE LANDLORDS, BLACK SHARECROPPERS** The postwar system of agriculture grew out of the military's wartime labor program. The Freedmen's Bureau tried to continue those policies after the war, requiring blacks to enter into labor contracts with whites and not forcing whites to make many concessions to emancipation. Freedmen wanted land of their own, which would help end planters' involvement in their personal lives and prevent whites from forcing them to work in labor gangs under white supervision. In particular, black women wanted to work in their homes, and many black families wanted their children to go to school. Very few freedmen achieved the dream of owning their own land. Instead, they resisted slavelike conditions by renting land from large landowners and paying with a share of the season's crop. The system introduced the country merchant into the agricultural equation. Merchants provided these sharecroppers with food and clothing on credit, taking out a lien against the crop as assurance of payment. Because they charged exorbitant interest rates, sharecroppers could end the year more in debt than they had begun.

***Reconstruction Collapses, pp. 562–569*** After dealing with issues of war and reconstruction for a decade, Northerners by 1870 wanted to return to other pressing affairs. As northern commitment to reconstruction declined, southern opposition to the changes that reconstruction had wrought escalated. One by one, the Republican state governments were toppled.

**THE GRANT REGIME: CRONIES, CORRUPTION, AND ECONOMIC COLLAPSE** Voters in 1868 hoped that General Ulysses S. Grant, war hero and revered national idol, would be a good choice to lead them through the tumultuous reconstruction years. Grant's tenure was troubled, however, marked by scandal, corruption, and ineptitude. He relied heavily on friends and was loyal to corrupt advisors, although he was not corrupt himself. By the end of Grant's first term, Republicans displeased with his administration left to form a third party, the Liberal Republicans, and agitated for a nonpartisan civil service system and the removal of federal troops from the South. Democrats were sufficiently impressed with the party's agenda that they endorsed Horace Greeley, the Liberal candidate, for president. Grant's popularity was such that, despite the problems of his first term, he was reelected. The Grant administration achieved its greatest successes in foreign affairs. The secretary of state, Hamilton Fish, proved an effective diplomat in his handling of negotiations with England over wartime damages caused by British-built Confederate ships. Grant's attempt to acquire Santo Domingo ended in failure, even though Lincoln and Johnson's secretary of state, William H. Seward, was responsible for the purchase of Alaska from Russia and for thwarting French efforts to set up a puppet regime in Mexico. Compounding Grant's and the nation's problems during his second term was the financial crisis known as the panic of 1873, precipitated by the failure of Jay Cooke's investment banking firm. There had been panics before, but this was the worst one yet, plunging the nation into a depression that would last several years.

**NORTHERN RESOLVE WITHERS** Though the Ku Klux Klan Act of 1871 and the Civil Rights Act of 1875 helped stem Klan violence and outlawed discrimination, several factors hastened the retreat from reconstruction that had begun during the Grant administration. A shifting political climate, economic hard times, increasing preoccupation with other issues, and deep-rooted racism contributed to the northern retreat from Reconstruction. In addition, Thaddeus Stevens and other prominent Radical Republicans died. Finally, two significant Supreme Court decisions hindered the federal government's capacity to protect black Southerners' rights. The Slaughterhouse cases (1873) distinguished between national and state citizenship and ruled that the Fourteenth Amendment applied only to rights stemming from the federal government; the *United States v. Cruikshank* ruling (1876) determined that Congress could legislate against discrimination by states but not by individuals. In 1874, the Democrats gained control of the House of Representatives for the first time in eighteen years.

**WHITE SUPREMACY TRIUMPHS** The northern retreat from reconstruction enabled southern Democrats to take full advantage of white hostility toward Republican governments. Southern Democratic "Redeemers," as they styled themselves, determined to unseat reconstruction regimes, championed "home rule," and proclaimed their mission to save southern civilization from African "barbarism" and "negro rule." By polarizing the Republican Party along racial lines and terrorizing Republican voters, black and white, the Democrats managed to regain eight of the former Confederate states by 1875. Only South Carolina, Louisiana, and Florida had Republican state governments by 1876.

**AN ELECTION AND A COMPROMISE** The 1876 presidential election between Republican Rutherford B. Hayes and Democrat Samuel J. Tilden was one of the most bitterly contested in U.S. history. While the election produced an apparent Democratic victory, disputed electoral returns from Louisiana, South Carolina, and Florida threw the outcome into doubt. Tilden had undisputed claim to 184 electoral votes, only one short of the majority, but Hayes could still win if he managed to receive all 20 disputed votes. To resolve the impasse, in January of 1877 Congress created a special electoral commission with equal numbers of Democrats and Republicans to make a decision about the disputed votes. The last-minute replacement of a Democratic commissioner with a Republican meant that the vote went in favor of Hayes. Democrats accepted the decision but only after an informal understanding among party leaders, known as the Compromise of 1877, in which Hayes promised not to use federal troops to uphold the few remaining Republican governments in the South. The South was also promised substantial federal subsidies for internal improvements. The Compromise of 1877 marked a return to the antebellum tradition of sectional compromise. As in the past, whites found a way to resolve their differences and maintain the peace, while blacks paid the price. When reconstruction ended, black Southerners were not yet completely subordinated to whites, but their status in the New South looked grim.

## *Conclusion: "A Revolution but Half-Accomplished"*

The Civil War remained only a "half-accomplished" revolution, as General Schurz put it. The nation had failed to fulfill most of the promises held out to former slaves. Still, given the odds confronting them, African Americans had reason for considerable pride in the gains they were able to make during Reconstruction. The Civil War changed racial relations in the South, and for the first time decisively confirmed the supremacy of the federal government over state governments. And future generations could be grateful for the crucial Fourteenth and Fifteenth Amendments which, although widely ignored at the time, would one day serve as the basis for a "second reconstruction"—one that would renew the drive to bring freedom to all Americans.

***Chronology Activity*** Read the annotated chronology, and answer the multiple-choice questions.

1863 December. Lincoln issues Proclamation of Amnesty and Reconstruction. Lincoln's amnesty proclamation reflected his commitment to treat former Confederates kindly; it offered a full pardon to rebels who renounced secession and accepted the abolition of slavery, and it excluded only a few groups of Southerners, like high-ranking civilian and military officers. A new state government could be formed when only 10 percent of the men who had been qualified to vote in 1860 had taken an oath of allegiance. The plan did not demand that freedmen be given social or political rights. It was a plan to restore the Union, not to reform the South.

1864 July. Congress offers more stringent plan for reconstruction, Wade-Davis bill. Congressional Republicans felt that Lincoln's "10 percent plan" was too lenient, and that Congress should control the terms of reconstruction. The Wade-Davis bill demanded that half of the voters in a conquered Confederate state take the oath of allegiance before reconstruction started, banned former Confederates from participating in the drafting of state constitutions, and guaranteed freedmen equality before the law. Lincoln refused to sign the bill, letting it die instead.

1865 January. General William T. Sherman sets aside land in South Carolina for black settlement. Sherman hoped to relieve himself of the burden of the thousands of impoverished freedmen who were following his army. This was one of the wartime developments that seemed to indicate that the federal government was going to offer land to slaves, linking black freedom with land ownership.

March 4. Lincoln sworn in for second term as president of United States. Lincoln's inaugural address laid out his feelings about reconstruction, in particular his belief that reconstruction had to be charitable toward the South.

March. Congress establishes Freedmen's Bureau. The Freedmen's Bureau was intended to help southern blacks make the transition from slavery to freedom. It distributed food, supervised labor contracts, and sponsored schools for blacks.

April 14. Lincoln shot, dies on April 15, succeeded by Vice President Andrew Johnson. Johnson was a southern Democrat who had been chosen as Lincoln's running mate in 1864 to broaden the Republicans' appeal. He proposed a version of reconstruction that was similar to Lincoln's in some ways. However, his unwillingness to enforce even the mild terms he laid out caused formerly Confederate states to believe that they could avoid making any changes in their race relations. Their intransigence pushed Congress into a much harsher reconstruction program.

Fall. Southern legislatures enact discriminatory black codes. The black codes were designed to reinstate the conditions of slavery by subjecting blacks to discrimination and forcing them to remain subordinate to whites. Black codes made it illegal for blacks to own guns, to make insulting gestures toward whites, or to serve on juries, and blacks were taxed for performing any job that was not agricultural or domestic. Northern anger at these measures caused moderate and radical Republicans to unite against both Johnson and the new state governments.

December. Thirteenth Amendment abolishing slavery becomes part of U.S. Constitution. Although passage of the Thirteenth Amendment was required as part of Johnson's reconstruction plan, many southern states resisted it. Mississippi, for example, rejected it outright, and Alabama rejected part of it, demonstrating the former Confederates' commitment to maintaining the prewar status quo.

1866 April. Congress approves Fourteenth Amendment making native-born blacks American citizens and guaranteeing all American citizens "equal protection of the laws." Amendment becomes part of Constitution in 1868. The Fourteenth Amendment was a complex piece of legislation, but its guarantee of the rights of citizens against abridgement by state governments was important in securing black rights. It also dealt with voting privileges by giving Congress the right to reduce the congressional representation of states that did not give suffrage to any part of its adult male population. This meant that if white Southerners did not enfranchise blacks, they would suffer reductions in representation, giving Republicans continued control of the national government: if they did enfranchise blacks, blacks would vote for Republicans, thus securing a Republican base in the South. Northern states could continue to refuse to allow blacks to vote, however, because their black populations were relatively low.

April. Congress passes Civil Rights Act over President Johnson's veto. Johnson had already vetoed a civil rights bill on the grounds that it violated states' rights. Had the veto stood, reconstruction would have been over on his terms. However, Republicans in Congress mounted a unified campaign against the president, pushed another bill through Congress, and passed it over the president's veto. The passage of the Civil Rights Act demonstrated that matters between the president and Congress were coming to a head.

May. Susan B. Anthony and Elizabeth Cady Stanton found Equal Rights Association to lobby for vote for women. Women's rights advocates had been disappointed by the inclusion of the word *male* in the Fourteenth Amendment and were furious when the Fifteenth Amendment ignored women. They believed that they had been betrayed by their abolitionist allies in the federal government, most of whom felt that black suffrage was a more pressing and urgent issue. Stanton and Anthony concluded that they could not trust men to help women achieve suffrage and formed their own organization.

July. Congress extends Freedmen's Bureau over President Johnson's veto. Johnson had already vetoed a Freedmen's Bureau bill on the grounds that it was an unconstitutional "system for the support of indigent persons." Energized by their opposition to the president, congressional Republicans were able to sustain another version of the bill.

Summer. Ku Klux Klan founded in Tennessee. The Ku Klux Klan began as a social club of Confederate veterans, but it quickly turned into a paramilitary organization that terrorized black and white Republicans throughout the South. Many white Southerners argued that reconstruction governments were illegitimate and so could be combated by any means necessary, including violence. The Klan undertook campaigns of whipping, hanging, shooting, burning, and throat-cutting to undermine reconstruction and restore white supremacy. Their methods were effective in keeping blacks and other Republicans away from the polls, since there were few federal troops in the South to offer protection to voters.

November. Republicans triumph over Johnson in congressional elections. Johnson believed that he could make the Fourteenth Amendment the overriding issue of the 1866 elections, and he felt that he could gather conservatives from the North into his new National Union Party. He went on a public-speaking campaign to convince white Northerners to oppose both the amendment and the Republicans who had sponsored it. However, his crude response to crowds did nothing to win converts to his cause. The Fourteenth Amendment was not radical enough to drive Republican voters to Johnson, and the war was still fresh enough in people's minds that they were suspicious of southern intransigence.

1867 March. Congress passes Military Reconstruction Act imposing military rule on South and requiring states to guarantee vote to black men. White resistance to presidential reconstruction boosted the standing of radical Republicans and encouraged moderates to join with them in demanding a more punitive form of reconstruction; the result was the Military Reconstruction Act (and three subsequent acts), which divided the formerly Confederate states into five districts, each headed by a general who was instructed to suppress violence and disorder. The military would undertake voter registration, which would include black men, and voters would select delegates to constitutional conventions. The constitutions had to guarantee black suffrage, and the first legislature had to ratify the Fourteenth Amendment. At that point, the state could apply to be readmitted into the Union. The measures were much harsher than those imposed by either Lincoln or Johnson and indicated Northerners' unhappiness with the South's lack of remorse.

1868 March–May. Senate impeachment trial of President Johnson results in acquittal. Johnson attempted to subvert congressional reconstruction by issuing pardons and replacing sympathetic government officials with conservative ones. Radicals wanted to impeach him, but conservatives argued that he had not done anything technically illegal. However, when he ignored the Tenure in Office Act to get rid of his secretary of war, Edwin M. Stanton, Congress decided to act, and every Republican in the House voted in favor of impeachment. In the end, Chief Justice Salmon P. Chase would not allow Johnson's opponents to raise the broad issue of misuse of power, causing the impeachment measure to fail in the Senate by a single vote. Although Johnson survived, he was not able to oppose reconstruction for the remainder of his time in office.

November. Ulysses S. Grant elected president of the United States. Grant was an obvious choice for the Republicans: his defeat of Lee made him one of the most popular public figures in the northern states. Moreover, he was acceptable to Republicans because he had supported congressional reconstruction, even if he did not have a deep commitment to black equality. Once in office, he proved to be a disappointment. He was not personally corrupt, but he tolerated and even defended corrupt friends and advisors.

1869 February. Congress approves Fifteenth Amendment prohibiting racial discrimination in voting rights; amendment becomes part of Constitution in 1870. By 1869, Republicans were growing worried about the increasing popularity of northern Democrats, who had made gains in the 1868 election. Black voters represented the balance of power in several northern states; enfranchising blacks contributed to Republicans' partisan advantage. However, the measure contained a major loophole: it did not guarantee the right to vote but rather prohibited exclusion on the grounds of race; over time, therefore, white Southerners would devise apparently nonracial means of keeping black voters away from the polls. Ironically, the Fifteenth Amendment convinced many Northerners that southern blacks had all the help they needed to achieve equality and that any failure to do so would be entirely their own fault.

1871 April. Congress enacts Ku Klux Klan Act in effort to end white terrorism in South. Republicans were concerned about the political terrorism surrounding southern elections; they were also anxious to resolve the problem and move on to new issues. The Ku Klux Klan Act made interfering with voting a felony and authorized the use of the army to enforce it. Federal marshals did come close to breaking the power of the Klan by arresting thousands of suspected members. Nonetheless, political violence continued.

1872 November. President Grant reelected. The corruption of the Grant regime inspired some Republicans to bolt and form the Liberal Republicans. The party condemned the Grant administration's vulgarity and dishonesty and proposed ending the spoils system. They also demanded the removal of troops from the South, a measure that caused the Democrats to support Horace Greeley, the Liberal Republican presidential candidate. Despite Grant's problems, the nation still felt enormous affection for him, and he was reelected with 56 percent of the popular vote, the most lopsided victory since the election of Andrew Jackson.

1873 Economic depression sets in for remainder of decade. The economy collapsed after a major Philadelphia bank, headed by Jay Cooke, poured money into railroads, became overextended with debt, and collapsed. Within two years more than 18,000 businesses had failed and more than a million workers lost their jobs. The misery and violence surrounding the economic hard times helped distract attention from the ongoing problems of reconstruction and fed northern apathy toward the whole subject.

1874 November. Elections return Democratic majority to House of Representatives. The Democratic success was partially a sign of voters' unhappiness with the ongoing depression, a calamity they blamed on the Grant administration. However, it also demonstrated that Northerners were tired of the never-ending problems associated with reconstruction and their disenchantment with Republicans who insisted on pursuing racial equality in the South.

1875 February. Civil Rights Act of 1875 outlaws racial discrimination, but federal authorities do little to enforce law. The Civil Rights Act outlawed racial discrimination in transportation, public accommodations, and juries. However, the measure was largely ignored by both white Southerners and the federal authorities. Segregation remained the rule throughout the formerly Confederate states.

1877 March. Special congressional committee awards disputed electoral votes to Republican Rutherford B. Hayes, making him president of United States; Hayes agrees to pull military out of South. The Compromise of 1877 that allowed Hayes to become president marked the end of reconstruction. His Democratic opponent, Samuel J. Tilden, was one electoral vote short of the majority he needed to win; but returns from three states were contested, and if Hayes received all of those votes, he would win. A partisan committee awarded the votes to Hayes, and outraged Democrats considered resistance to the decision; in the end, Democrats agreed not to block the inauguration in return for home rule in the South and federal subsidies. A few Republicans were angry, but most Northerners were simply relieved that the nation had averted a crisis. The decision was a return to the antebellum tradition of sectional compromise—in which the burden of the compromise fell on blacks.

***Chronology Questions*** Choose the letter of the best answer.

1. The 1875 legislation that outlawed racial discrimination was the
   a. Ku Klux Klan Act.
   b. Fourteenth Amendment.
   c. Civil Rights Act.
   d. Proclamation of Amnesty and Reconstruction.

2. A severe economic depression distracted northern attention from reconstruction beginning in
   a. 1863.
   b. 1867.
   c. 1873.
   d. 1877.

3. Which one of the following events did not occur in 1866?
   a. Elections return a Democratic majority to the House of Representatives.
   b. Susan B. Anthony and Elizabeth Cady Stanton found the Equal Rights Association.
   c. The Ku Klux Klan is founded in Tennessee.
   d. Congress approves the Fourteenth Amendment.

4. What is the correct order for the following events?
   1. Southern legislatures enact discriminatory black codes.
   2. A Senate impeachment trial of President Johnson results in acquittal.
   3. Congress extends the Freedmen's Bureau over President Johnson's veto.
   4. Congress passes the Civil Rights Act over President Johnson's veto.
   a. 1, 4, 3, 2
   b. 2, 4, 1, 3
   c. 1, 2, 4, 3
   d. 2, 1, 3, 4

5. Congress approved of the Fifteenth Amendment prohibiting racial discrimination in voting rights in
   a. 1863.
   b. 1865.
   c. 1869.
   d. 1875.

6. What is the correct order for the following events?
   1. Congress enacts the Ku Klux Klan Act in an effort to end southern terrorism.
   2. President Lincoln issues the Proclamation of Amnesty and Reconstruction.
   3. Congress offers the Wade-Davis Bill, its plan for reconstruction.
   4. Congress passes the Military Reconstruction Act imposing military rule on the South.
   a. 3, 1, 4, 2
   b. 2, 3, 4, 1
   c. 1, 4, 3, 2
   d. 3, 2, 1, 4

7. A special congressional committee awarded disputed electoral votes to Republican presidential candidate Rutherford B. Hayes in
   a. March 1867.
   b. November 1872.
   c. November 1874.
   d. March 1877.

8. In January 1865, General William T. Sherman attempted to deal with the problems presented by the impoverished freedmen who followed his army by
   a. encouraging the passage of the Civil Rights Act.
   b. settling them on land in South Carolina.
   c. establishing the Freedmen's Bureau.
   d. extending the life of the Freedmen's Bureau.

9. What is the correct order for the following events?
   1. Lincoln is shot and succeeded by Vice President Andrew Johnson.
   2. An economic depression sets in.
   3. Congress approves of the Fourteenth Amendment.
   4. Ulysses S. Grant is elected president of the United States.
   a. 1, 3, 4, 2
   b. 3, 1, 4, 2
   c. 2, 4, 1, 3
   d. 4, 1, 2, 3

10. The Thirteenth Amendment abolishing slavery became part of the U.S. Constitution in
   a. December 1865.
   b. February 1869.
   c. April 1871.
   d. February 1875.

***Defining Terms*** Match each term with the correct definition.

| | |
|---|---|
| Ku Klux Klan Act | *United States v. Cruikshank* |
| compulsory free labor | black codes |
| Civil Rights Act | Andrew Johnson |
| Slaughterhouse cases | scalawags |
| Proclamation of Amnesty and Reconstruction | Tenure of Office Act |
| Liberal Republicans | Ku Klux Klan |
| National Union Party | Military Reconstruction Act |
| carpetbaggers | Compromise of 1877 |
| Lincoln states | sharecropping |
| Freedmen's Bureau Bill | Sherman land |
| Fifteenth Amendment | Fourteenth Amendment |
| crop-lien | Wade-Davis Bill |
| "generation of vipers" | |

1. President Lincoln's plan for reconstruction, which he put forth in December 1863. The plan offered rebels a full pardon restoring property (except for slaves) and political rights in exchange for a renunciation of secession and slavery. When 10 percent of a state's registered voters in 1860 had taken an oath of allegiance, they could organize new state governments. The plan emphasized political reunification, but did nothing to change the position of freedmen. Proclamation of Amnesty and Reconstruction

2. Congress's plan for reconstruction, promulgated in July 1864. Congressman Henry Winter Davis of Maryland and Senator Benjamin Wade of Ohio jointly sponsored a bill that threw out Lincoln's "10 percent plan" and demanded that at least half of a state's voters take an oath of allegiance before forming a government. The bill also banned former Confederates from drafting new state constitutions and guaranteed freedmen equality before the law. The bill was not as mild as Lincoln's, although radicals objected to its neglect of black voting rights. Wade-Davis Bill

3. Louisiana, Arkansas, Tennessee, and Virginia, which met President Lincoln's reconstruction requirements. Congress, however, objected that the terms of reconstruction were too lenient and refused to seat the representatives from these states. Lincoln states

4. The labor system devised by the Union army as more and more southern land and freedmen came under federal control. The army's labor plan forced blacks to enter into contracts with planters. Employers would be forced to give them wages, food, housing, and medical care and would not be allowed to physically discipline their workers; however, blacks who would not work were subject to discipline from the army. The system was an attempt to supplant plantation labor with free labor, not to promote social or economic change. compulsory free labor

5. 400,000 acres of land on the coast of South Carolina south of Charleston, which General Sherman used as farms for the impoverished freedmen who were following his army. By June 1865, about 40,000 blacks had settled on the land, increasing freedmen's hopes that they would eventually be given land that had been confiscated from rebels. Sherman land

6. President Lincoln's successor to the presidency when he was killed in 1865. He was a poor southern white who had built his political career on opposition to elite planters. His hostility toward rich former Confederates convinced many people that he would deal harshly with the South, but in fact he was a lifelong Democrat with a commitment to states' rights. His dislike of blacks meant that he had no interest in using reconstruction to overturn traditional southern race relations. Andrew Johnson

7. A series of laws passed by southern states in the second half of the 1860s to keep blacks subordinate to whites by subjecting them to all kinds of discrimination. The laws made it impossible for blacks to own guns, use insulting gestures or language, or undertake nonagricultural or nondomestic work. Northerners were infuriated by the laws, which made a travesty of freedom and seemed to nullify the Union's wartime sacrifices, and President Johnson's refusal to act decisively against southern states helped spur the shift to a more radical reconstruction. black codes

8. The Republican view of former Confederates in 1865. Black codes and overwhelming support for former Confederates in the 1865 elections convinced even moderate Republicans that Southerners were unwilling to accept their loss in the war but were instead trying to reinstate slavery in all but name. Given their stubborn refusal to follow the terms of reconstruction, Republicans and many other Northerners saw the former rebels as untrustworthy and dangerous. "generation of vipers"

9. A bill passed by Congress in 1866 to prolong the life of the Freedmen's Bureau, which had been created by the previous Congress. The agency distributed food, supervised labor contracts, and sponsored schools for southern blacks; President Johnson vetoed it on the grounds that it represented an unconstitutional system for supporting "indigent persons." Congress initially failed to override the veto, but it was reintroduced and passed over a second veto in July 1866.
freedmen's bureau bill

10. A congressional measure designed to undermine southern black codes by affirming blacks' rights to enjoy the full and equal protection of the law. By requiring the end of legal discrimination in state laws, it represented an amazing expansion of both black rights and federal authority. President Johnson vetoed the act as "an unconstitutional invasion of states' rights," but it was submitted again and passed over a second veto in April 1866. Civil Rights Act

11. A complex amendment introduced in 1866 and designed to protect the rights of citizens against violation by their state governments by making all native-born or naturalized persons American citizens and prohibiting states from abridging their rights. The amendment also reduced the congressional representation of states that did not extend the vote to any portion of their adult male populations. The measure in essence forced Southerners to enfranchise blacks or suffer a loss of national representation without affecting the North, which had a very small number of blacks. Fourteenth Amendment

12. President Johnson's conservative political party, which he formed during the 1866 congressional elections to oppose the Fourteenth Amendment. He had hoped to attract conservative Republicans but instead gained most of his support from Democrats. His attempt to gain support by a public speaking tour was disastrous, and the Republicans won an overwhelming victory in the congressional elections of 1866. National Union Party

13. Congressional Republicans' version of reconstruction, this 1867 act divided the formerly Confederate states into five military districts, placed a Union general in charge of each district, and charged him with the task of imposing order and registering voters to elect delegates for constitutional conventions. Each new constitution had to guarantee black suffrage; when the constitution was accepted by the voters and the first legislature had ratified the Fourteenth Amendment, the state could apply for readmission to the Union. Unlike previous reconstruction formulas, this act demanded that blacks be allowed to vote and barred many former rebels from participating in the constitutional conventions, thus allowing for much greater social and political change. Military Reconstruction Act

14. An 1867 act that required the approval of the Senate for the removal of any government official who had been appointed with the Senate's consent. The legislation was designed to make it harder for President Johnson to remove government officials who supported congressional reconstruction; in particular, Congress hoped to protect Edwin M. Stanton, the secretary of war and only cabinet member who opposed Johnson. Johnson's decision to remove him despite his inability to gain the Senate's support led to his impeachment trial in the spring of 1868. Tenure of Office Act

15. The 1869 amendment that extended black suffrage to the entire United States by prohibiting states from denying citizens the right to vote on the basis of race, color, or previous servitude. Because it did not guarantee the right to vote but instead prohibited certain kinds of exclusions, southern states eventually found ways to deny black voters suffrage on the basis of literacy tests and other apparently nonracial measures. The amendment also roused the anger of women's rights supporters, who wanted women to receive the same voting rights as men and felt that they had been sold out by their abolitionist allies. Fifteenth Amendment

16. Northern migrants to the South after the Civil War who formed one part of the southern Republican Party. Southerners complained that northerners were poor men trying to capitalize in the South's misery. In fact, most of them were restless, relatively well-educated young men who looked on the South as a source of economic opportunity and saw the Republican Party as the source of programs that would encourage economic development along the lines of northern free labor. Carpetbaggers

17. A slang term for runty horses or good-for-nothing rascals that Southerners applied to native-born southern Republicans after the Civil War. Most southern Republicans were Unionists who were resentful of their treatment during the war or small farmers who disliked the political domination of large planters. They usually favored initiatives for public schools and expanding economic opportunities. Scalawags

18. A social club of Confederate veterans formed in 1866 that became a paramilitary organization that fought against Republicans. The Klan was part of the "white terror," or violence designed to reduce Republicans' political influence by discouraging black and white voters from joining the new party. The group worked to defeat reconstruction measures and restore white supremacy to the South. Ku Klux Klan

19. The land and labor system that emerged in 1865 from the Union army's wartime approach and soon dominated the South. Under the new system, landless farmers rented plots from large planters in exchange for a portion (usually half) of the year's crop. While they did not own their land, they were able to reduce planters' involvement in their personal lives by organizing their labor themselves. Sharecropping

20. The credit method that sharecroppers used to pay for goods like food and clothing at local country stores. Sharecroppers would purchase supplies in exchange for a lien, or claim, on their crops. Merchants took advantage of the system by charging extremely high rates of interest. Often farmers were more in debt at the end of the season than they had been at the start. Crop-lien

21. Anti-Grant Republicans who bolted and ran their own candidate, editor Horace Greeley, in the 1872 presidential election. The new party disliked the corruption of the Grant administration and proposed ending it by means of a professional, nonpartisan civil service; they also called for home rule in the South, a measure that gained them the support of Democrats. Liberal Republicans

22. A piece of legislation that was intended to stop white terrorism in the South. The 1871 act made interference with voting rights a felony and allowed the use of the army to enforce it. Thousands of suspected Klansmen were arrested as a result of the act and the Klan was nearly destroyed. Violence against blacks continued, however. Ku Klux Klan Act

23. A series of Supreme Court decisions promulgated in 1873 that distinguished between national and state citizenship and ruled that the Fourteenth Amendment protected only rights stemming from the national government. Since most rights originated with the state, this limited the federal government's ability to protect black citizens. The decision undermined the legal foundation of reconstruction. Slaughterhouse cases

24. The 1876 Supreme Court ruling that declared that the reconstruction amendments gave Congress the power to legislate against discrimination by states but not by individuals. Thus, dealing with crimes like assault—even politically motivated assault—was a state responsibility. The decision undermined the legal foundation of reconstruction. United States v. Cruikshank

25. An informal understanding between moderate southern Democrats and Republican presidential candidate Rutherford B. Hayes's lieutenants that settled the 1876 election in favor of Hayes. Democrats agreed to accept the decision of a partisan electoral commission that gave the electoral votes of three disputed states to Hayes, allowing him to win; in return, they demanded that federal soldiers be removed from the South and that the formerly Confederate states be given federal subsidies for internal improvements. The compromise marked the end of reconstruction. Compromise of 1877

## Chapter Review

### *Multiple-Choice* Choose the letter of the best answer.

1. An important political question that arose even before the Civil War had come to an end was that of
   a. what to do with Jefferson Davis.
   b. whether the South should be allowed back into the Union on equal terms.
   c. who had the authority to determine a plan of reconstruction.
   d. how to treat ordinary Confederate soldiers.

2. President Lincoln's reconstruction plan, the 1863 Proclamation of Amnesty and Reconstruction, offered
   a. full pardons to southern whites who had not owned slaves before the war.
   b. full pardons to rebels who would denounce secession and accept the abolition of slavery.
   c. partial pardons to rebels who had been enlisted men in the Confederate army.
   d. full pardons to Southerners who would turn in high-ranking Confederate officials.

3. By the terms of President Lincoln's reconstruction plans, former Confederate states would be allowed back into the Union when they
   a. extended social and political rights to former slaves.
   b. paid reparations for the cost of the war.
   c. had 10 percent of qualified voters in 1860 who would take the oath of allegiance.
   d. had a majority of the state's voters agree to renounce secession.

4. The Wade-Davis bill angered radical Republicans because it
   a. upheld Lincoln's reconstruction plan.
   b. did not ban former Confederates from contributing to new state constitutions.
   c. made no provisions for black suffrage.
   d. demanded that only half of the voters in a rebel state take the oath of allegiance.

5. When President Lincoln insisted on forming state governments under the terms of his "10 percent plan," Congress responded by
   a. supporting his wishes.
   b. snubbing the new representatives socially.
   c. refusing to seat the new representatives.
   d. taking the president to court.

6. As the Union forces freed increasing numbers of slaves during the Civil War, Republicans
   a. disagreed about what free labor would mean in the South.
   b. agreed that freedmen should be treated just like northern workers.
   c. unanimously felt that freedmen should be given their own property.
   d. wanted to greatly expand the political rights of freedmen.

7. The Union military solution to the employment of freedmen in the South was to
   a. force former slaves to continue working for their masters with no pay.
   b. confiscate plantations from Confederates and give them to freedmen.
   c. restore plantation labor with wage labor.
   d. force Confederates to work for their former slaves.

8. Large southern landowners complained that the army's solution to the transition from slave labor to free labor would not work because it
   a. would cost too much money.
   b. was in conflict with the free-labor ideal.
   c. threatened the status of poor whites.
   d. did not allow for the use of physical punishment.

9. Freedmen were very unhappy that the new labor regime imposed by the military during the Civil War
   a. declared that whites would not be allowed to perform field work.
   b. demanded that workers grow only cotton.
   c. did not provide them with their own land.
   d. made it impossible for black children to attend school.

10. On the whole, experiments in reconstruction during the Civil War showed that
    a. no important issues would be settled.
    b. the president would control reconstruction.
    c. Congress would control reconstruction.
    d. reconstruction would be relatively straightforward.

11. After emancipation, many southern blacks returned to their jobs in the fields and kitchens of whites because they
    a. were loyal to their masters and mistresses.
    b. did not enjoy the freedom of moving around.
    c. could not afford to do anything else.
    d. were forced to do so by the Union army.

12. In the aftermath of emancipation, southern blacks sought all of the following except
    a. racially integrated churches.
    b. economic independence.
    c. schooling for their children.
    d. legal recognition of their marriages.

13. When the Civil War ended, Congress wanted to control reconstruction policy, believing that President Lincoln's program would _____.
    a. lead to economic devastation
    b. oppress poor whites with rules and regulations
    c. restore the southern ruling class to power
    d. give blacks too many civil rights

14. President Lincoln and Congress inaccurately saw reconstruction almost entirely as a _____ problem.
    a. labor
    b. racial
    c. political
    d. southern

15. President Lincoln's plan for reconstruction allowed for the organization of new state governments when 10 percent of a state's _____ had taken an oath of allegiance.
    a. qualified voters in 1860
    b. total population
    c. ex-Confederate soldiers
    d. slave owners

16. In April 1865, after he had let the Wade-Davis Bill die, Lincoln publicly expressed his _____.
    a. qualified endorsement of black suffrage
    b. unwillingness to support black suffrage
    c. desire to see a more punitive reconstruction program
    d. interest in banning former Confederates from drafting new state constitutions

17. The Union army's labor code gave the occupying army in the South the right to _____ who refused to work.
    a. discipline planters
    b. discipline blacks
    c. draft any white
    d. arrest and deport blacks

18. In 1865, the Freedmen's Bureau was authorized by Congress to _____ to freedmen.
    a. offer civil service jobs
    b. rent confiscated land
    c. extend the vote
    d. extend the draft

19. By the end of the Civil War President Lincoln had organized several new state governments; Congress _____ into the Union.
    a. admitted all of them
    b. admitted only Virginia
    c. would not admit any of them
    d. admitted half of them

20. To former slaves, freedom meant _____.
    a. not having to work
    b. being able to run wild
    c. overturning the rules that governed slavery
    d. nothing: they continued in their old habits

21. Because the slave system had denied slaves secure family lives, after emancipation many slaves _____.
    a. worked to restore and legalize their families
    b. were uninterested in getting married
    c. did not know how to live in conventional family structures
    d. abandoned their old family bonds

22. After emancipation, many southern freedmen asserted their religious freedom by _____.
    a. adopting African beliefs
    b. becoming atheists
    c. leaving white churches
    d. joining the Catholic Church

23. In December 1865, Republican legislators argued that President Johnson's reconstruction program had
    a. been a complete success.
    b. not achieved political reunification.
    c. promoted black rights at the expense of political reunification.
    d. achieved political reunification but sacrificed black rights.

24. According to President Johnson, the South's yeomen had participated in secession because they had been
    a. led astray by slaveholders.
    b. inherently traitorous to the government.
    c. seduced by the benefits they felt they received from the slave system.
    d. too poorly educated to make a good choice.

25. During his time as a congressman and senator from Tennessee, President Johnson had
    a. supported Republican measures to expand the power of the federal government.
    b. been known as an abolitionist.
    c. argued against states' rights.
    d. supported traditional Democratic causes.

26. According to President Johnson, his reconstruction plan was
    a. considerably harsher than President Lincoln's.
    b. considerably harsher than Congress's.
    c. a continuation of President Lincoln's.
    d. going to protect the rights of southern blacks.

27. President Johnson shocked reformers when he instructed military and government officials to
    a. extend voting rights to pardoned former Confederates.
    b. return all confiscated and abandoned land to pardoned former Confederates.
    c. reimburse pardoned former Confederates for damage the Union army had done.
    d. protect freedmen's schools and businesses.

28. When Southern delegates met to draw up new state constitutions in 1865, they
    a. were relieved that President Johnson's requirements were so mild.
    b. conformed to President Johnson's requirements.
    c. refused to follow President Johnson's mild requirements.
    d. went beyond President Johnson's mild requirements.

29. Beginning in 1865 the southern states adopted a series of laws known as black codes, which were intended to
    a. overturn old discriminatory laws.
    b. provide blacks with schools.
    c. extend black civil rights.
    d. keep blacks subordinate to whites.

30. Many southern states used black codes to force blacks into
   a. leaving the South entirely.
   b. abandoning their children.
   c. returning to their prewar occupations.
   d. learning useful skills.

31. President Johnson found that by acquiescing to the southern refusal to follow his reconstruction plans, he
   a. became more popular in the North.
   b. won useful political allies.
   c. could talk former Confederates into supporting federal authority.
   d. did not suffer any political liabilities.

32. By 1865, the mainstream of the Republican Party wanted a reconstruction program that would
   a. establish racial equality.
   b. give assurance that slavery and secession were dead.
   c. give confiscated plantations to freedmen.
   d. guarantee black voting rights.

33. The 1866 Civil Rights Act was extraordinary in that it sought to
   a. restore the rights of former Confederates.
   b. expand the rights of Union veterans.
   c. deny former Confederates their civil rights.
   d. expand black rights and federal authority.

34. In April 1866, congressional Republicans achieved a historic first in American history when they
   a. overrode presidential vetoes of major legislation.
   b. disagreed with a sitting president of their own party.
   c. offered blacks the vote.
   d. voted with Democrats.

35. In the summer and fall of 1865, _____ was left to make critical decisions about the terms of reconstruction.
   a. Congress
   b. the Supreme Court
   c. President Johnson
   d. the northern public

36. By December 1865, when Congress reconvened in Washington, D.C., the president and the formerly Confederate states believed that reconstruction _____.
   a. was just getting started
   b. was finished
   c. would demand a lot of social changes
   d. was going to cost a lot of money

37. Throughout his political career, President Johnson had been _____ slavery.
   a. a defender of
   b. opposed to
   c. neutral on the subject of
   d. inconsistent about

38. President Johnson's 1865 reconstruction plan ignored President Lincoln's _____.
   a. acceptance of limited black voting rights
   b. state governments
   c. demand that states renounce the right of secession
   d. requirement that states renounce their war debts

39. In the summer of 1865, delegates to South Carolina and Georgia's constitutional conventions _____ their secession ordinances.
   a. merely repudiated
   b. declared null and void
   c. upheld
   d. refused to acknowledge the existence of

40. By the fall of 1865, many white Southerners had concluded that _____ would dictate the terms of reconstruction.
   a. the president
   b. freedmen
   c. the North
   d. they

41. Under the black codes, southern states attempted to _____ the old plantation economy and power structure.
   a. overturn
   b. restore
   c. make illegal
   d. subtly subvert

42. In the elections of 1865, the former Confederate states chose _____ to represent them in Congress.
    a. former Confederates
    b. southern Unionists
    c. Northerners
    d. southern Republicans

43. President Johnson's _____ helped inspire nearly unanimous Republican support for the 1866 Civil Rights Act.
    a. vocal defense of slavery
    b. acceptance of southern state governments
    c. veto of the Freedmen's Bureau bill
    d. commitment to black equality

44. In 1866 Congress responded to President Johnson's vetoes of major legislation by _____.
    a. beginning impeachment proceedings
    b. working to get a Democratic majority in the next election
    c. uniting in overriding the president's vetoes
    d. walking out

45. The Fourteenth Amendment nullified the 1857 *Dred Scott* decision by
    a. outlawing slavery in the territories.
    b. giving all black males the vote.
    c. reversing the court's decision that Scott had to remain a slave.
    d. making black persons citizens.

46. The Fourteenth Amendment's provisions for voting rights
    a. gave Congress the right to reduce the representation of states that withheld suffrage from part of their adult male population.
    b. explicitly granted the vote to blacks.
    c. implied that states that did not give blacks voting rights might be punished.
    d. gave the vote to all adults, regardless of sex or race.

47. President Johnson's response to the Fourteenth Amendment was to
    a. admit that Congress had outmaneuvered him.
    b. formally sever his ties with the Republican Party.
    c. advise Southerners to reject the amendment.
    d. call on the Supreme Court to declare in invalid.

48. The congressional elections of 1866 witnessed
    a. the birth of a new conservative party under President Johnson.
    b. a traditional contest between Democrats and Republicans.
    c. an outpouring of northern hostility toward the Fourteenth Amendment.
    d. enormous losses for the Republican Party.

49. White Southerners' rejection of the Fourteenth Amendment had the effect of
    a. increasing the influence of radical Republicans.
    b. increasing the influence of moderate Republicans.
    c. killing the measure entirely.
    d. boosting the fortunes of the Democratic Party in the North.

50. Congress's 1867 Military Reconstruction Act demanded the each reconstructed state
    a. write a constitution guaranteeing black suffrage.
    b. ratify the Fourteenth Amendment.
    c. both of the above.
    d. neither of the above.

51. In 1867, most Republicans believed that black voting would
    a. not be popular in the North.
    b. lead to anarchy in the South.
    c. cause the downfall of the federal government.
    d. bring about a permanent political revolution in the South.

52. The 1867 Military Reconstruction Act disappointed some radical Republicans because it did not
    a. confiscate and redistribute southern plantations.
    b. institute military rule in the South.
    c. protect black political rights.
    d. disenfranchise former Confederates.

53. President Johnson responded to radical reconstruction by
    a. grudgingly following its provisions.
    b. changing his opinion and supporting it wholeheartedly.
    c. sabotaging Congress's will.
    d. openly refusing to enforce it.

54. The House of Representatives voted for a resolution impeaching President Johnson after his August 1867 decision to
    a. ignore the Tenure of Office Act.
    b. pardon high-ranking former Confederates.
    c. remove sympathetic Freedmen's Bureau officers.
    d. appoint conservative Union generals to head military districts.

55. The Fifteenth Amendment, which guaranteed that suffrage rights could not be denied on account of race, was passed in large part because
    a. of the overwhelming support of the northern public.
    b. Republicans felt it would give them a partisan advantage.
    c. it was seen as important to support the rights of northern blacks.
    d. President Johnson disliked it.

56. In the long run, the passage of the Fifteenth Amendment meant that
    a. American blacks were guaranteed equal voting rights.
    b. Northerners became less racist.
    c. Southerners had accepted a certain level of racial equality.
    d. Republicans could ignore the issue of black equality.

57. The 1866 Fourteenth Amendment essentially protected the rights of American citizens against violation by _____.
    a. their own state governments
    b. the federal government
    c. former Confederates
    d. the Union army

58. In the 1866 congressional elections, President Johnson believed that he could use _____ to gather conservative whites into a new political party.
    a. the Fourteenth Amendment
    b. the Freedmen's Bureau
    c. mob violence against southern blacks
    d. radical Republicans

59. _____ followed President Johnson's advice to vote against the Fourteenth Amendment.
    a. Every southern state
    b. Half of the northern states
    c. Half of the states in the Union
    d. Every southern state except for Tennessee

60. By 1867 a small group of radical Republicans led by congressmen Charles Sumner and Thaddeus Stevens demanded that former slaves be given _____ the free-labor system.
    a. the same opportunities that whites had under
    b. special access to jobs and resources in
    c. the ability to work outside of
    d. fewer opportunities than whites had under

61. The Military Reconstruction Act of 1867 demanded that Union generals suppress disorder and _____ in their districts.
    a. begin political reform
    b. harass freedmen
    c. subject former Confederates to house arrest
    d. actively promote the Republican Party

62. When President Johnson vetoed the Military Reconstruction Act in 1867, Congress responded by _____.
    a. moving to impeach him
    b. drafting a new version
    c. accepting defeat
    d. overriding the veto the same day

63. In 1867, Congress passed the Tenure of Office Act in order to _____.
   a. undermine President Johnson's ability to subvert Congress's will
   b. limit presidential power
   c. keep the secretary of war, Edwin M. Stanton, from being dismissed
   d. all of the above

64. Chief Justice Salmon P. Chase refused to let President Johnson's opponents _____ in the 1868 impeachment trial, contributing to their defeat.
   a. focus narrowly on the president's flouting of the Tenure of Office Act
   b. raise broad issues of misuse of power
   c. make any arguments at all
   d. consider the issue of the President's flouting of the Tenure of Office Act

65. The Fifteenth Amendment _____.
   a. applied to the federal government only
   b. prohibited states from excluding voters on the grounds of race
   c. guaranteed the right to vote to all Americans
   d. demanded that voters be subject to literacy tests

66. The passage of the Fifteenth Amendment angered _____, who were upset that their voting rights had been ignored.
   a. immigrants
   b. women
   c. male youth
   d. black Democrats

67. The combination of black suffrage and large-scale rebel disenfranchisement meant that by the late 1860s congressional reconstruction had
   a. reestablished the Democratic Party in the North.
   b. destroyed the old system of southern politics.
   c. not done what it set out to do.
   d. permanently succeeded.

68. In the late 1860s, the majority of southern Republicans were
   a. Northerners who had relocated to the South.
   b. yeomen farmers.
   c. African Americans.
   d. former slaveholders.

69. Most Northern "carpetbaggers" who decided to move to the South after the Civil War were
   a. impoverished men with few skills.
   b. hoping to exploit the freedmen.
   c. interested in fomenting a complete social revolution.
   d. relatively well-educated young men looking for opportunities.

70. For the most part, native Southerners who joined the Republican Party after the Civil War supported
   a. equal rights for blacks.
   b. public schools and economic opportunity.
   c. the reestablishment of planter domination.
   d. the Fourteenth and Fifteenth Amendments.

71. Most whites in the reconstruction South believed that they could legitimately stamp out the Republican Party by means of
   a. promoting their own economic programs.
   b. convincing black voters to support Democrats.
   c. rational debate.
   d. vigilante violence.

72. Southern reconstruction constitutions introduced two major categories of changes into southern life—
   a. increased aristocratic privilege and expanded state responsibility for the general welfare.
   b. increased aristocratic privilege and lessened state responsibility for the general welfare.
   c. reduced aristocratic privilege and lessened state responsibility for the general welfare.
   d. reduced aristocratic privilege and expanded state responsibility for the general welfare.

73. Democrats' claims that the South was being subjected to "Negro domination" during reconstruction
   a. were accurate.
   b. had almost no basis in fact.
   c. stemmed from a handful of states.
   d. did not affect Republicans' standing in the former Confederate states.

74. Once southern Republicans were swept into power in the formerly Confederate states, they
   a. faced an enormous array of economic problems.
   b. were able to protect black voters.
   c. lowered taxes.
   d. broadened their appeal to whites.

75. The ambitious economic development programs of the Southern Republican administrations during reconstruction
   a. were supported by high spending on public schools.
   b. were so expensive that they were never implemented.
   c. did not solve the South's economic problems.
   d. solved the South's economic problems.

76. After the Civil War ended, the Freedmen's Bureau dealt with the shift from slave to free labor by
   a. giving freedmen their own land.
   b. selling freedmen land at reduced prices.
   c. renewing the army's campaign to force freedmen into wage contracts.
   d. inventing the practice of sharecropping.

77. When southern whites claimed that black women were "acting the lady," they meant that black women
   a. were acting like free wives and mothers.
   b. had adopted British speech patterns.
   c. were not doing any work.
   d. needed personal servants.

78. Sharecropping was different from the military system of wage contracts insofar as it
   a. gave blacks complete control over the crops they grew.
   b. increased wages for agricultural work.
   c. allowed blacks more freedom.
   d. gave blacks title to the land they farmed.

79. Nearly every eligible black man _____ after southern blacks won voting rights in 1867.
   a. registered to vote
   b. ran for office
   c. voted for the Democrats
   d. succumbed to electoral fraud

80. After the Civil War, the majority of white Republicans from the South were _____.
   a. former slaveholders from the plantation belt
   b. small farmers from the plantation belt
   c. yeomen farmers from the Piedmont
   d. urban dwellers

81. Many white Southerners argued that _____ was a reasonable response to reconstruction politics.
   a. open protest
   b. cooperation
   c. violence
   d. moving to the West

82. Because about 40 percent of the white electorate _____, three-quarters of the delegates to state constitutional conventions were Republican.
   a. were Republican supporters
   b. did not vote
   c. were unaware that elections were being held
   d. were unable to get to the polls

83. Former Confederates were _____ reconstruction state constitutions drafted beginning in 1867.
   a. disenfranchised in all of the
   b. not disenfranchised wholesale in any of the
   c. responsible for the writing of
   d. enthusiastic about

84. Republican spending meant that by 1875 half of Mississippi and South Carolina's eligible children, the majority of whom were black, _____.
    a. were forced into apprenticeships
    b. worked on railroad construction projects
    c. attended school
    d. were removed from their families

85. Laws against the separation of blacks and whites in public places were _____ in the postwar South.
    a. popular with whites
    b. not enforced
    c. strictly enforced
    d. prevented by state constitutions

86. Republican governments wanted the South to _____ economy in the postwar era.
    a. return to a plantation
    b. develop a diversified
    c. continue to have a depressed
    d. depend on a black market

87. After the Civil War, about a third of southern black women went to work full time _____.
    a. as schoolteachers
    b. in white households as maids
    c. as field workers
    d. in their own households

88. Postwar sharecroppers relied on _____ to provide them with food and clothing on credit until they could harvest their crops.
    a. family members
    b. their landlords
    c. the Freedmen's Bureau
    d. country merchants

89. General Grant was able to win the Republican nomination for president in 1868 because he
    a. had a deep moral commitment to black equality.
    b. had supported Lincoln and Johnson's reconstruction plans.
    c. supported congressional reconstruction.
    d. had had an outstanding political career.

90. Once he gained office, President Grant was notable for his
    a. clear, decisive leadership.
    b. naïve loyalty to corrupt advisors.
    c. personal corruption.
    d. intelligent appointments to government office.

91. In the 1872 presidential election, Democrats endorsed the anti-Grant Liberal Republicans because the Republicans
    a. had a candidate, Horace Greeley, who was a Democrat.
    b. supported the spoils system.
    c. had a policy of "home rule" for the South.
    d. condemned graft and materialism.

92. President Grant's greatest triumph during his eight years in office was his
    a. purchase of part of Mexico for $7 million.
    b. able handling of the 1873 economic crisis.
    c. annexation of Santo Domingo.
    d. settlement of the U.S. claim against Great Britain for damages caused by British-built Confederate warships.

93. In the early 1870s, Congress responded to the vigilante violence of the Ku Klux Klan by
    a. refusing to do anything.
    b. passing a series of laws.
    c. arming blacks against marauders.
    d. subjecting vigilantes to trial in federal courts.

94. The northern public's commitment to reconstruction was undermined by
    a. the program's high level of success.
    b. southern whites' suffering.
    c. vigilante violence.
    d. unyielding racial prejudice.

95. The Supreme Court's 1873 Slaughterhouse cases hurt blacks' civil rights by ruling that the Fourteenth Amendment
    a. protected only rights stemming from the federal government.
    b. protected only rights stemming from the state government.
    c. specified that blacks had state citizenship rather than federal citizenship.
    d. was unconstitutional.

96. Democrats in the South were able to harness white rage over reconstruction to politics after
    a. federal occupying troops repeatedly abused their power.
    b. the economic depression of 1873 struck.
    c. Republicans regimes had destroyed state economies.
    d. it became clear that Northerners were retreating from reconstruction.

97. In the reconstruction period, southern Democrats were able to gain white yeoman support by claiming that blacks
    a. enjoyed more political privileges than whites.
    b. were paid more than whites.
    c. held all the best government jobs.
    d. paid very little in taxes.

98. Which one of the following was not a reason for the Southern Democrats' victories in the Mississippi elections of 1876?
    a. They waged a fair, persuasive campaign.
    b. Their supporters went on a rampage of violence and intimidation.
    c. The federal government refused to intervene to stop electoral violence.
    d. They appealed to white supremacists.

99. The impasse in the 1876 presidential election was broken by the Compromise of 1877, in which Democrats agreed to support Rutherford B. Hayes's inauguration in exchange for the
    a. appointment of Samuel J. Tilden as the vice president.
    b. overturning of the Fourteenth and Fifteenth Amendments.
    c. Republicans' promise not to expose Democratic electoral violence.
    d. withdrawal of all federal troops in the South.

100. The Compromise of 1877 demonstrated that the United States had
    a. returned to the tradition of sectional compromise but at the expense of blacks.
    b. solved its racial problems.
    c. not resolved any of the political problems from the prewar period.
    d. become less politically conservative.

101. By 1870, the Republican Party was coming under the domination of _____.
    a. practical businessmen
    b. idealistic reformers
    c. young people
    d. the military

102. During the Grant administration, many white Northerners came to believe that _____ was a major cause of instability in the South.
    a. Democratic violence
    b. white intransigence
    c. recurrent federal intrusion
    d. northern callousness to freedmen

103. In 1873, overinvestment in _____ led directly to the bust that inaugurated a devastating depression.
    a. railroads
    b. the South
    c. Jay Cooke's Philadelphia bank
    d. western farmland

104. President Grant was uncomfortable with reconstruction because he feared that it _____.
a. was an overextension of federal power
b. did not do enough to protect black voters
c. was disrupting the southern economy
d. contributed to the economic depression of the 1870s

105. The 1876 Supreme Court decision in *United States v. Cruikshank* declared that Congress could legislate only against discrimination committed by _____.
a. states
b. individuals
c. the courts
d. the national government

106. By the early 1870s, southern Democrats had started to use _____ as their most potent weapon in their war against the Republican Party.
a. public information campaigns
b. outright bribery
c. Republicans' corruption
d. race

107. In the 1870s, Democrats in the South used yeoman farmers' _____ to bring them back into the Democratic fold.
a. party loyalty
b. sympathies with freedmen
c. racism and economic difficulties
d. all of the above

108. Samuel J. Tilden's failure to _____ cast the outcome of the 1876 presidential election into doubt.
a. win a majority of the popular vote
b. win a majority in the electoral college
c. manipulate the election returns in the southern states
d. support reform efforts

109. To determine which candidate would receive the 1876 electoral votes of South Carolina, Louisiana, and Florida, Congress _____.
a. voted as a body
b. created a special electoral commission
c. demanded a new round of elections
d. turned the issue over to the Supreme Court

110. On the whole, Americans were _____ the Compromise of 1877.
a. pleased by the peacefulness of
b. disgusted by the corruption of
c. neutral about
d. unaware of

***Short Answer*** Write a paragraph response to each question.

1. What terms did President Lincoln's "10 percent plan" propose for reconstructing the ex-Confederate states? Why did reformers object to the plan?
2. How did the army handle the transformation from slave to free labor during the Civil War? How did southern blacks and whites respond?
3. What did freedom mean to the southern blacks who were freed over the course of the Civil War?
4. What factors explained Andrew Johnson's Unionism during the Civil War? How did his sympathies affect his reconstruction plan?
5. What were black codes? How did President Johnson respond to them?
6. How did the Republican Party respond to the South's black codes in the later 1860s?

7. What were the voting provisions of the Fourteenth Amendment? In what way was it a no-lose policy for northern Republicans?
8. What were the provisions of the military reconstruction that started in 1867? Why did radical Republicans consider it flawed?
9. Why did Congress move to impeach President Johnson in 1868?
10. Which groups of people joined the Republican Party in the South after the Civil War?
11. What changes did reconstruction constitutions introduce into southern life? What reforms did they fail to achieve?
12. How did the sharecropping system structure southern labor after the Civil War? What did it offer blacks, and what were its shortcomings?
13. How did the Supreme Court contribute to the decline of reconstruction in the 1870s?
14. What strategy did southern Democrats adopt to overthrow Republican governments in the South in the 1870s?
15. What was the Compromise of 1877? How did Americans respond to it?

***Building Historical Skills*** Historians use a variety of sources to think and talk about the past, including maps, illustrations, and written records. Maps provide a variety of different kinds of comparative information in a condensed visual format; reading them requires learning how to sort through this information. To deepen our understanding of the past by supplementing written records, historians frequently interpret material culture, such as a vase or a painting, with techniques borrowed from art history, archaeology, or anthropology. Written records, though familiar as sources, raise their own problems of interpretation. Every document reflects someone's particular perspective or assumptions. It is the historian's task to carefully study and compare each document to other records with other perspectives. The following exercises introduce you to using maps, illustrations, and written documents as sources of information. Use these sources as well as the material in the chapter to think about different themes and topics discussed in the text.

***Map Activity*** Locate the following places on Map 15.2: Reconstruction of the South on page 567 in *The American Promise*, Second Edition.

1. Tennessee/1866
2. North Carolina/1868
3. Louisiana/1868
4. South Carolina/1868
5. Virginia/1870
6. Mississippi/1870
7. Georgia/1870

Answer the following questions in four to six sentences based on Map 15.2: The Reconstruction of the South.

**READING THE MAP** List in chronological order the readmission of former states to the Union. Which states quickly reestablished conservative governments?

**CONNECTIONS** What did the former Confederate states need to do to be readmitted to the Union? How did reestablished conservative governments react to reconstruction?

**WEB LINKS** To explore the topics discussed in the exercise above, visit the Web links noted below.

"Reconstruction," by Frederick Douglass
http://eserver.org/race/reconstruction.html

"Reconstruction: A State Divided"
http://lsm.crt.state.la.us/cabildo/cab11.htm

## *Visual Activity*

This cartoon was drawn by Thomas Nast, the best-known and most popular political cartoonist of the 1870s. It shows President Grant plunging headfirst into a barrel from which he is attempting to pull out the various scandals that plagued his administration. Grant is dressed in the striped pants usually shown on the "Uncle Sam" figure, demonstrating Nast's opinion that the Grant's problems taint the nation as a whole. The caption in the corner is an ironic comment on Grant's claim that he will ensure that these scandals would be thoroughly investigated. In Nast's view, Grant's probings did nothing but propel him further into the political mire. Nast implies that the underlying problem is Grant's association with different corrupt political interests by ringing the barrel with the names of special-interest groups who contributed to the scandals.

Answer the following questions in a paragraph based on "Grant and Scandal" on page 563 in *The American Promise*, Second Edition.

**READING THE IMAGE** How does Thomas Nast see President Grant's role in corruption? What does he feel has caused the problems?

**CONNECTIONS** How responsible was President Grant for the corruption that plagued his administration?

**WEB LINKS** To explore the topics discussed in the exercise above, visit the Web links noted below.

"The Presidency of Ulysses S. Grant: A Reconsideration"
http://saints.css.edu/mkelsey/presid.html

"The Gilded Age and the Politics of Corruption"
http://us.history.wisc.edu/hist102/lectures/lecture04.html

***Analyzing Sources Activity*** Answer the following questions in a paragraph based on Documenting the American Promise: The Meaning of Freedom on page 542 in *The American Promise,* Second Edition.

1. How does John Q. A. Dennis interpret his responsibility as a father?
2. Why do you think that former slaves wanted their marriages legalized?
3. Why, according to the Union Convention of Tennessee, do blacks deserve voting rights?
4. How would you characterize Henry Baker's attitude toward education?

**WEB LINKS** To explore the topics discussed in the exercise above, visit the Web links noted below.

"Reconstruction and Its Aftermath"
http://memory.loc.gov/ammem/aaohtml/exhibit/aopart5.html

"Reconstruction"
http://www.stanford.edu/~paherman/reconstruction.htm

# Answer Key

## Chapter 15: Reconstruction, 1863–1877

### *Chapter Overview*

#### *Chronology*

1. c
2. c
3. a
4. a
5. c
6. b
7. d
8. b
9. a
10. a

#### *Defining Terms*

1. Proclamation of Amnesty and Reconstruction
2. Wade-Davis Bill
3. Lincoln states
4. compulsory free labor
5. Sherman land
6. Andrew Johnson
7. black codes
8. "generation of vipers"
9. Freedmen's Bureau Bill
10. Civil Rights Act
11. Fourteenth Amendment
12. National Union Party
13. Military Reconstruction Act
14. Tenure of Office Act
15. Fifteenth Amendment
16. carpetbaggers
17. scalawags
18. Ku Klux Klan
19. sharecropping
20. crop-lien
21. Liberal Republicans
22. Ku Klux Klan Act
23. Slaughterhouse cases
24. *United States v. Cruikshank*
25. Compromise of 1877

### *Chapter Review*

#### *Multiple Choice*

1. c
2. b
3. c
4. c
5. c
6. a
7. c
8. d
9. c
10. a
11. c
12. a
13. c
14. c
15. a
16. a
17. b
18. b
19. c
20. c
21. a
22. c
23. d
24. a
25. d
26. c
27. b
28. c
29. d
30. c
31. b
32. b
33. d
34. a
35. c
36. b
37. a
38. a
39. a
40. d
41. b
42. a
43. c
44. c
45. d
46. a
47. c
48. a
49. a
50. c
51. d
52. a
53. c
54. a
55. b
56. d
57. a
58. a
59. d
60. a
61. a
62. d
63. d
64. b
65. b
66. b
67. b
68. c
69. d
70. b
71. d
72. d
73. b
74. a
75. c
76. c
77. a
78. c
79. a
80. c
81. c
82. b
83. b
84. c

85. b
86. b
87. d
88. d
89. c
90. b
91. c
92. d
93. b
94. d
95. a
96. d
97. d
98. a
99. d
100. a
101. a
102. c
103. a
104. a
105. a
106. d
107. c
108. b
109. b
110. a

### *Short Answer*

1. President Lincoln believed that the formerly Confederate states needed to be treated with kindness; therefore, his reconstruction plan offered a full pardon to Confederates who renounced secession and accepted emancipation. Under his terms, when 10 percent of the men who had been qualified voters in 1860 had taken an oath of allegiance, they could organize a new state government and apply for readmission into the Union. While the plan excluded several groups of Confederates, including high-ranking military and civilian officials, it did not require that Southerners extend civil rights to freedmen or that the federal government help freedmen economically. Reformers complained that by doing nothing to aid freedmen, President Lincoln's plan made blacks free in name only.
2. During the war, the military designed a new labor code to transform the slave plantation system into a free-labor system. The code forced planters to sign contracts with former slaves, pay them wages, and provide food, housing, and medical care to their workers. The code did not represent a true free-labor system, though, because freedmen were required to enter into these contracts, work hard, and remain subordinate. Moreover, while planters could not longer physically discipline their laborers, the army reserved the right to punish blacks who would not work. Blacks complained that the system was one of "compulsory free labor," while whites insisted that blacks would not work without the threat of physical coercion.
3. To most former slaves, freedom meant the ability to do all the things they were forbidden from doing under slavery. The ability to move about at will was an important aspect of freedom to people who had not been allowed to leave plantations without passes. Many freedmen refused to follow the elaborate racial etiquette that had forced them into subservient roles. Slaves had been kept illiterate, so freedmen were anxious to learn how to read and write. And because slaves' families had been subject to constant disruption by sale, many recently freed couples rushed to get legally married.
4. Andrew Johnson was from a poor family and had built his political career on defending the South's plain folk. He was the only senator from a Confederate state to remain loyal to the Union after the Civil War broke out, in large part because he believed that secession was the work of the slaveholders who exploited the poor. He was not at all sympathetic toward blacks and in fact had held slaves until the state of Tennessee confiscated them in retaliation for his Unionist leanings. His reconstruction plan reflected his resentment toward the wealthy and his dislike of blacks: he forced wealthy former rebels to apply to him directly for pardons, but he made no effort to help ease the transition of freedmen, and even instructed military and government officials to return confiscated land occupied by blacks to its former Confederate owners.
5. Blacks codes were laws that formerly Confederate states passed during reconstruction in an attempt to limit freedmen's rights and keep blacks subordinate to whites. For example, black codes in some states made it illegal for blacks to own guns and barred blacks from jury duty; the state of Mississippi declared insulting language or gestures a criminal offense. Black codes also focused on confining blacks to field work or domestic service by taxing them for performing other jobs or making them subject to fines or involuntary plantation labor of they could not produce proof of employment. President Johnson, a former Democrat and defender of states' rights, argued that he could not intervene because the citizens of a state had the right to construct their own laws and constitutions; also, he shared the views of most white Southerners in supporting white supremacy and black subordination.
6. Congressional Republicans were horrified by the black codes, which they interpreted as evidence that the South had not truly renounced secession and slavery. President Johnson's willingness to tolerate the South's intransigence caused moderate and radical Republicans to pull together and oppose the new southern state governments. The moderate majority and the radical minority refused to seat representatives who had met President Johnson's requirements. Moreover, they began to pass legislation designed to effect a revolution in the social relations of the South by guaranteeing blacks basic civil rights.

7. The Fourteenth Amendment did not ensure black suffrage. Instead, the measure gave Congress the right to reduce the congressional representation of states that did not allow parts of its adult male population to vote. This meant that if southern states gave their black populations the right to vote, Republicans would enjoy a new power base in the South and cement their national power. If southern states did not permit blacks to vote, their representation in Congress would decrease and Republicans could maintain their hold on national power. Northern states had such small black populations that they could easily continue to withhold suffrage from blacks without suffering a significant loss of representation.
8. The 1867 Military Reconstruction Act and three subsequent acts overturned President Johnson's state government and instituted military rule in the formerly Confederate states. The act divided the states into five districts, each headed by a general who was instructed to suppress violence and disorder and begin political reform. The military would register voters, including blacks, and the states would draw up new constitutions that had to guarantee black suffrage. When the constitutions were approved and the Fourteenth Amendment ratified, the state would be readmitted into the Union. While this was much more demanding than presidential reconstruction and did provide for black suffrage, radical Republicans were upset because it failed to provide freedmen with their own land, a measure that was seen as necessary to allow blacks real freedom from white control.
9. Throughout 1866 and 1867, congressional Republicans were incensed by President Johnson's willingness to subvert the work of reconstruction by issuing pardons and removing government officials sympathetic to freedmen. However, as long as he did not openly break any laws, moderates refused to impeach him. Then, in August 1867, President Johnson broke the Tenure of Office Act of 1867 (which demanded Senate approval for the removal of any government official appointed with Senate consent) when he forced secretary of war Edwin M. Stanton out of office. His open defiance of the law convinced moderates to vote for an impeachment resolution.
10. Most southern Republicans were freedmen who recognized that they needed political rights to protect themselves and turned to the party that had conferred suffrage on them. There were also Northerners, called carpetbaggers by Southerners, most of whom were enterprising young men hoping that the South would provide them with economic opportunities. Finally, some southern whites joined the Republicans, primarily yeomen farmers from the Piedmont who had sympathized with the Union during the war and hoped to end planters' political domination.
11. Reconstruction constitutions aimed to reduce the political power of wealthy Southerners and to expand state responsibility for the general welfare. Therefore, constitutions adopted universal male suffrage, got rid of property requirements for holding office, and reduced the number of appointive offices. They also adopted more social welfare programs, including prison reform, state orphanages, insane asylums, and homes for the deaf and mute. However, the constitutions did not confiscate and redistribute southern land, and none of them enacted a wholesale disenfranchisement of former Confederates.
12. Under the sharecropping system, planters divided their land into small plots that freedmen rented by giving up a share of each year's crop. This allowed blacks control over their working conditions: they could decide who worked where and when and they were free of physical coercion and white oversight. At the same time, it kept blacks dependent on white landlords, who could evict them at the end of the year. Also, black farmers were often indebted to country merchants, who advanced them credit at exorbitant interest rates in exchange for liens on their crops. The result was that often farmers' expenses were greater than their income, and they were quickly pulled into a cycle of debt.
13. In the 1870s, the Supreme Court promulgated a series of decisions that made it difficult for the federal government to protect blacks' civil and political rights under the Fourteenth and Fifteenth Amendments. The 1873 Slaughterhouse cases paved the way by distinguishing between national and state citizenship and ruling that the Fourteenth Amendment covered only those rights stemming from the federal government and that most rights were the prerogative of the states. In 1876, the *United States v. Cruikshank* ruling declared that Congress only had the power to legislate against discrimination by states, not individuals. Thus, ordinary crimes committed against blacks, including things like assault, were a state responsibility.
14. Democrats in the South used two methods of overthrowing Republican administrations. First, they sought to use race to encourage white voters to rejoin the Democrats. Sometimes this took the form of a direct appeal to white supremacy; in other cases, the Democrats used social ostracism of whites who were too friendly with blacks or blamed poor whites' financial problems on freedmen. Democrats also used political terrorism to drive black voters away from the polls.

Antiblack political violence rose to unprecedented levels, resulting in many deaths throughout the southern states.

15. The Compromise of 1877 involved an agreement on the part of Democrats to not block Republican Rutherford B. Hayes's inauguration as president and to deal fairly with freedmen in exchange for concessions from the new Republican administration. Hayes promised that he would not use the federal army to uphold the remaining southern Republican governments, and he also promised substantial federal subsidies for internal improvements. Most Americans saw the agreement as a sign that the nation could weather a severe political crisis, and, given the conservative mood of the nation as a whole, overall they were not unhappy about its provisions. A handful of radicals and also American blacks, however, saw the agreement as one that sold out southern blacks to their former oppressors.

## *Map Activity*

Reading the Map: Tennessee was the first Confederate state to be admitted back into the Union, reentering in 1866. Arkansas, Louisiana, Alabama, Florida, South Carolina, and North Carolina all rejoined in 1868, and Virginia, Georgia, Mississippi, and Texas were readmitted in 1870. Virginia had established a conservative government in 1869, a year before it reentered the Union; North Carolina, Georgia, Tennessee, and Texas all had conservative governments within a few years of their readmission. By 1877, every state had replaced their reconstruction governments with home rule.

Connections: The requirements for reconstruction changed a great deal between President Lincoln's initial proposal in 1863 and the advent of congressional reconstruction in 1867. Initially, a state had to renounce slavery and secession and get 10 percent of the qualified voters in 1860 to take an oath of allegiance and form a new government. Under Congress's military reconstruction, blacks were given the right to vote, former Confederates were barred from participating in constitutional conventions, and states had to ratify the Fourteenth Amendment, all changes that demanded a greater level of social and political reconstruction than either President Lincoln or President Johnson had envisioned. Conservative governments howled that they were being subjected to "Negro domination," even though blacks' representation in government was much lower than their proportion of the population. They encouraged campaigns of terror against Republicans; once they regained power, they dismantled reconstruction in fact, if not in name.

## *Visual Activity*

Reading the Image: Nast seems to feel that Grant was personally involved in administration scandals. He couples Grant's headlong fall into the barrel of corruption with the caption that indicates that he will get to the bottom of them—implying that he will get to the bottom of them by immersing himself in them. Nast clearly indicates that special-interest groups have caused the problems. He indicts the Tammany ring, the Democratic machine that controlled politics in New York City, but points also to state, county, town, and ward interests. He condemns the media and other groups that wanted to use the government to their own ends, including canal builders, Indian suppliers, and distillers, all of whom he lists on the bands keeping the barrel together.

Connections: Despite the difficulties he experienced, Grant was not personally corrupt. However, he exhibited a stubborn naivete when it came to choosing advisors and appointed officials. He surrounded himself with relatives and army friends and was unwilling to acknowledge their failings, sticking by them even when they had obviously betrayed his trust. During his time in office, his vice president, secretary of war, secretary of the navy, and private secretary were all tainted by or removed because of corruption charges.

## *Analyzing Sources*

1. John Q. A. Dennis clearly envisions his parental role as one that involves providing for and protecting his children. He mentions that he was separated from them and so "I Could Not do for them." It is obvious that his failure disturbs him because he also mentions that their owner did not feed or clothe them properly. Now that he is freed, he wants the Secretary of War to authorize him to retrieve his children from their owners, which indicates yet again his desire to help them and his sense of connection to them.
2. According to the report made by the Reverend A. B. Randall in February 1865, freedmen were anxious to legalize their marriages; he mentions that he legally wed twenty-five couples over the course of a month, most of them long-term partners with families. There were a number of reasons that freedmen wanted to marry. Randall comments that they saw marriage as part of the "road, to Responsibility; Competency; and an honorable Citizenship." Also, because slaves were not allowed the privilege of legal marriage, they had no marital rights that their owners had to respect. Owners could separate couples through sales, a common practice in the antebel-

lum South. The importance of marriage can be seen in the resistance of white Southerners: Randall notes that freedmen who were captured and reenslaved had their marriage certificates taken from them and destroyed.

3. The petitioners from the Union Convention of Tennessee make several different arguments for their voting rights. They point out that blacks support the Union war effort in a variety of ways, including working for it and fighting in it. They protest that they want to be good citizens and that only voting will allow them to fully discharge the duties of citizenship. Moreover, they point out that as a democracy the United States has an obligation to interest every resident in the welfare of the nation as a whole, something that is not likely to occur unless people feel that they have a political stake in the system. Finally, they note, it is unfair to treat any group of people who support the government as inferior. Even though they admit that suffrage may seem shocking, they remind their readers that black military service was also dismissed as impossible early in the war.

4. Henry Baker was interested in education: he tried to attend school several times during the course of reconstruction. He saw it as a means to self-improvement. Yet his attempts to receive an education were stymied by the demands of supporting himself and the interference of whites. He mentions that when his employer found out he was attending classes, he immediately found an excuse to put Baker back to work. Later, he comments that the demands of his farm made going to school impossible. In the end, he turned to religion to better himself.